DATE DUE			

THE JEWS:
THEIR HISTORY, CULTURE, AND RELIGION

The publication of this volume by The Jewish Publication Society of America was made possible by the Nehemiah Gitelson Fund, established in loving memory of Nehemiah Gitelson (1853-1932), scholar, rabbi, talmudic teacher, and merchant.

The present work is the fourth issued under this Fund. The first, *The House of Nasi—The Duke of Naxos,* the second, *Prince of the Ghetto,* and the third, *Pilgrims in a New Land,* were published in 1948.

THE JEWS

Their History,
Culture, and Religion

Edited by

LOUIS FINKELSTEIN

PRESIDENT
THE JEWISH THEOLOGICAL SEMINARY OF AMERICA

Volume II

Philadelphia

THE JEWISH PUBLICATION SOCIETY OF AMERICA

5710-1949

To

IRVING LEHMAN

(1876-1945)

Who in life and precept
integrated the ancient tradition
of the Hebrew prophets with the
spirit of American democracy

The preparation of this book was made possible
by funds generously made available by the
American Jewish Committee.

CONTENTS

THE JEWS: THEIR HISTORY, CULTURE, AND RELIGION

CHAPTER 17

HELLENISTIC JEWISH LITERATURE

By Ralph Marcus

1. INTRODUCTION

The name "Hellenistic" is given by students of classical civilization to the period of about three centuries following the conquests of Alexander the Great in the Near East. The Greek noun *hellenistes* commonly meant a non-Greek speaker of Greek or imitator of Greek fashion; "Hellenistic" is therefore an appropriate term for an age in which Jews, Egyptians, Syrians, Iranians and other Oriental peoples were united—so far, at least, as their wealthier urban classes were concerned—in a common pattern of Greek-Oriental culture with more or less important variations of local color.

Students of European history usually consider the lower limit of the Hellenistic period to be 30 B.C.E. because by that time the Roman Empire under Augustus had consolidated its control over the Greek-Oriental kingdoms of Egypt, Syria and Asia Minor. But the orientalist and the historian of Western culture are inclined to extend the lower limit another few centuries because the official and educated classes in the large cities of the Near East continued to be Greek rather than Roman in speech and culture long after the Hellenistic kingdoms had been incorporated as provinces of the Roman Empire. In the case of the Jews this is true even of the Diaspora communities in Italy and other parts of Europe.

While each age has, of course, its peculiar significance in the perspective of world history even for those who assume that historical development is continuous in most spheres of social activity, that significance may seem to later ages to be clearer in one form of culture than in others. Thus, the Hellenistic age is especially interesting to us because it saw the birth and early nurturing of a world-consciousness in philosophy, law, religion and politics. This cosmopolitanism, to use a term coined by the Stoic philosophers or possibly by the Jewish philosopher Philo under Stoic influence, was only partially realized in such forms as Jewish-Christian ethics, Roman law, Greek ethnography, pagan astrology and Gnosticism; but these forms of universalism or cosmopolitanism were sufficiently developed in the Hellenistic age to provide thought and impulse to action for many centuries afterwards.

2. The Septuagint

While the scribes of the Second Commonwealth were collecting and ordering the sacred books, many Jews both in Palestine and in the Diaspora were circulating didactic or historical or apocalyptic writings, some of them under the names of patriarchs or prophets, in order to obtain greater authority for their works. These books, even those written in Hebrew or Aramaic, were not admitted into the canon of Sacred Scripture by the Rabbinic scholars of the early talmudic period for one of two reasons: either the rabbis thought that they had been written after the close of the Persian period, when prophetic inspiration was supposed to have ceased, or else they regarded them as unorthodox in content. In a few cases, however, such postprophetic books were admitted into the canon; for example, the Book of Daniel, which represents itself as a work of the Babylonian period, and perhaps the Book of Ecclesiastes, ascribed to Solomon.

But the noncanonical Hebrew and Aramaic writings were translated into Greek and circulated among the Jews of the Diaspora. Some of these writings in their Greek version were included in manuscripts of the Greek Bible, and were preserved either as sacred or as edifying books by the Christian church. In a few cases the original Hebrew or Aramaic text, or one based on the original, has been preserved by Jewish scribes, for example, the Wisdom of Ben Sira and the Book of Tobit. But in the case of most of these so-called apocryphal or pseudepigraphic books, we have only the Greek version, handed down by Christian scribes.

Although this chapter does not discuss the apocryphal writings composed by Palestinian Jews in Hebrew or Aramaic, they have been mentioned because of their being preserved in Greek and included in manuscripts of the Greek Bible. We must now turn our attention to this translation, which is extremely important and interesting in its own right.[1a]

This great monument of Hellenistic Jewish literature is called the Septuagint, meaning "seventy" in Latin, because there was current among early Christian scholars of Western Europe the story, first told by a Hellenistic Jewish writer (see below on the Letter of Aristeas), that seventy-two elders were sent from Palestine to Alexandria in Egypt to translate the Law of Moses from Hebrew into Greek. In the course of time the title "Translation of the Seventy-two" was simplified into "the Seventy" and was extended to include the translation of the prophetic and hagiographic portions of the Hebrew Bible.

The Septuagint is of great importance for several reasons. In the first place, it is a valuable control of the traditional Hebrew text of the Bible, known as the Masora. The earliest complete Hebrew manuscript of the Bible dates from the tenth century c.e., whereas the principal manuscripts of the Greek Bible date from the fourth and fifth centuries c.e. (There are considerable papyrus fragments written still earlier but they agree very closely with the chief manuscript, *Codex Vaticanus.*) Moreover, the Greek translations of the various books of Scripture were made from unvocalized Hebrew texts. Thus they sometimes yield a reading of a form or the meaning of a root which makes better sense than that of the masoretic text.

In the second place, this early translation, having been made by competent scholars with some knowledge of early Palestinian exegesis, is of great aid in interpreting some obscure passages in the Hebrew. There is also a strong probability that in some passages the Hebrew text was altered by the Palestinian scholars for theological or legalistic reasons, and since the Greek version was made from an earlier text than that handed down to us by the Palestinian authorities, it sometimes enables us to recover the original meaning of the biblical passage.

In the third place, the Septuagint was the source of a number of secondary versions made for the early Christian churches in Europe and the Near East such as the Coptic, Ethiopic, Armenian, Slavonic, Gothic and Old Latin. (The Old Latin has not been entirely replaced by Jerome's translation, called the Vulgate, which became the official Bible of the Roman Catholic Church by decree of the Council of Trent in 1546.) Thus through the Septuagint the contents of the Hebrew Bible became known to the peoples of Europe and Western Asia and contributed greatly to the forming of their beliefs and institutions.

In the fourth place, the Greek Bible played a considerable part in the gradual transformation of Greek philosophy into the theology of the Church Fathers and into the influential body of thought known as Neo-platonism. These in turn exerted an immeasurably great influence on medieval Scholasticism, Christian, Jewish and Moslem. For example, it would be difficult to overrate the importance for following centuries of the synthesis effected between the Platonic theory of the creation of the world by a beneficent spirit, the Demiurge, as described in the *Timaeus,* and the account of the creation given in the first two chapters of the Greek Genesis. Such syntheses are presented by the Jewish philosopher Philo and by the Christian philosopher Chalcidius in his Commentary on Plato's *Timaeus.*

As we shall deal with Philo below, it may suffice to remark here that his great work of harmonizing Greek philosophy with Judaism, which deeply influenced Christian theologians, perhaps all the way down to Dante, would have been almost impossible if he had not had at his disposal an official Greek translation of the Hebrew Bible, which he regarded as no less inspired than the original text.

The most important fact about the Septuagint for those who are interested in the history of European civilization, as well as in Judaism, is that the existence of this version was indispensable to the rise of Christianity. The earliest Christian apostles to the Gentiles would probably have had much less success in converting Jews of the Diaspora and "God-fearing" Gentiles to Christianity if they had not had an authoritative Greek text of the Jewish Scriptures with which to support their claim that Jesus of Nazareth, whom they called the Lord Christ, was the Messiah whose coming had been predicted by the Hebrew prophets. The quotations from the Old Testament found in the writings of Paul and the Apostolic Fathers agree closely with the text of the Septuagint, although in some cases, of course, the Christian writers quote from memory or alter the wording to suit their apologetic purposes.

For the several reasons given above we may fairly say that the Greek translation of the Bible by the Jewish scholars of Alexandria was one of the most important translations ever made.

Before turning to the original Hellenistic Jewish writings, let us briefly consider some of the stylistic aspects of the Septuagint. Its vocabulary and inflections were not very different from those of contemporary pagan writings composed in the language used by the vast majority of people in the Hellenistic period, the so-called "common" Greek dialect or *Koiné*. But because the Septuagint was a translation from Hebrew and dealt with concepts and ways of living and speaking peculiar to Jewish Palestine, its Hebraic style and special usages of many terms must have made it seem a strange and un-Greek book to such Gentiles as may have chanced to read it or hear it quoted. Many Hebrew idioms, to be sure, were adapted to Greek usage, but most of them were taken over literally, with curious results to the Greek style. The various books of the Bible differ in this respect. Some of the narratives in the Greek versions of Samuel and Kings, for example, read fairly smoothly, while the Greek Book of Ecclesiastes is so literal as to be almost unintelligible to one ignorant of the Hebrew original.

On the whole, the Greek Bible is a poor specimen of literary Greek, not because of the linguistic incompetence of the translators but because their primary concern was to produce a faithful rendering of the Hebrew for Greek-speaking Jews. There are occasional surface Hellenizations, such as allusions to well-known mythological figures and the use of Greek metrical forms in parts of the Book of Proverbs. But beneath these superficial adaptations there is a thoroughly Jewish, even Hebraic, spirit in the Septuagint. Those Jews in the Diaspora whose reading was confined to the Greek Bible were in no danger of being seduced by the charm of Greek literature.

3. HISTORICAL LITERATURE

When we turn to the historical literature of the Jews originally written in Greek, we must not expect to find anything like the relatively scientific spirit of inquiry and concern for factual accuracy that we admire in such Greek historians as Thucydides and Polybius. Rather we shall find that most of the historical writing preserved to us is heavily weighted with self-conscious pride in Jewish cultural achievements and might more justly be called apologetic or hortatory than historical. Some of it is merely historical fiction.

1. *Demetrius, Eupolemus and Artapanus*

Let us begin by briefly discussing three (probably) Alexandrian writers of whose works we have only fragments preserved in the ninth book of the Evangelical Preparation of the Church Father Eusebius, written about 300 C.E. Eusebius took these excerpts from a *Universal History* compiled by Alexander Polyhistor, a Greek encyclopedist of the first century B.C.E.

Some time near the end of the third century B.C.E. a Jew named Demetrius wrote a history of Israel in brief chronological form. The extant fragments deal with some of the events in the lives of Jacob and Moses and with the number of years that elapsed between the Israelite deportation to Assyria and the writer's own date, the reign of Ptolemy IV. Although Josephus held Demetrius to be a Gentile, the author's painstaking attempt to fix the exact dates of Jewish history makes it more likely that he was a Jew. Neither the style nor the content of the remaining fragments is of exceptional interest.

More promising are the fragments of Eupolemus, who wrote a *History of the Jews* about the middle of the second century B.C.E. Whether he lived in Egypt or Palestine is not known. Some scholars identify him with the Eupolemus mentioned in I Macc. 8:17 as an envoy sent to Rome by Judas Maccabeus; they do so partly on the ground that Eupolemus the historian seems to have used a Hebrew as well as a Greek text of Scripture. But there is no reason why an Alexandrian Jew should not have known Hebrew in addition to Greek. On the whole, it is more probable that Eupolemus wrote in Egypt than in Palestine.

Like most of the Hellenistic Jewish historians known to us Eupolemus embellished his work with legendary material showing the Jews in the most favorable light. He tells us, among other things, that Moses was the first Sage and the first to introduce writing among the Jews; the Phoenicians took it from the Jews and the Greeks took it from the Phoenicians. The most extensive fragment preserved by Eusebius tells of the building of Solomon's Temple and includes the imaginary correspondence between

Solomon and Vaphres (biblical Hophra). We may cite from this the reply made by the Egyptian king to Solomon's request for assistance, which was obviously designed to impress Gentile readers with the greatness of the Hebrew king.

King Vaphres to the great king, Solomon, greeting. I have read your letter with great pleasure, and I and all my court regard as memorable the day of your accession to the throne, for you are a worthy man and one favored by a very great god. In accordance with your request I have sent you eighty thousand men from the following districts, etc.

Eupolemus, as we can see from this brief excerpt, was not an impartial historian of the Jews. But his partiality was moderate in comparison with that of his near-contemporary Artapanus.

On internal evidence it is clear that Artapanus wrote in Alexandria, but when he lived is more difficult to determine further than that he was active before the first century B.C.E., since he was known to Alexander Polyhistor, who flourished about 100 B.C.E.

Artapanus bettered the example of rationalistic Greek historians who taught that the popular gods were only deified men who had made useful discoveries in art and science. He went so far as to assert that Moses was none other than the Greek Museus and the Egyptian Hermes (Thoth). Not only were the Jews a distinguished people of Syrian origin, and not the descendants of plague-carrying outcasts from Egypt, as their enemies charged, but Moses had even given the Egyptians the elements of their culture. It seems strange to us that a Jewish writer should have attributed the origin of Egyptian idolatry to Moses, but perhaps, as some scholars have suggested, Artapanus meant to pass off his work as that of an Egyptian priest (some of whom, like Artapanus himself, bore Persian names after the conquest of Egypt by Cambyses). It is probable that Josephus in his narrative of Moses in the *Antiquities* used the writings of Artapanus, thinking him to be a pagan author.

A translation of part of the longest extant fragment of Artapanus may serve to show his inventive powers.

After the death of Abraham [a slip for "Jacob"] and his son and also Mempsasthenoth, the king of Egypt, the latter's son Palmenoth succeeded to the throne, but he proved to be unfriendly to the Jews. He first built Kessan and erected a temple there, and then built a temple in Heliopolis. He had a daughter named Merris, whom he married to a certain Khenephres, king of the region above Memphis; at that time there were several kings in Egypt. Merris, being childless, secretly adopted a Hebrew child whom she called Moses. By the Greeks he was called Museus. This Moses was the teacher of Orpheus. When he reached manhood he devised many things useful to mankind; he invented boats and stone-laying machines and Egyptian weapons and instruments for irrigation and war. He was also the founder of philosophy.

Moreover, he divided the country into thirty-six nomes, and to each of these he assigned the worship of a particular god. To the priests he gave the sacred writing [hieroglyphs]. Now these gods were cats and dogs and ibises. He also assigned to the priests separate estates. All these things he did in order to make Khenephres's rule more secure, for before that time the unruly populace had expelled some of their kings and installed others in their places or reinstalled the dethroned ones. Because of all these achievements Moses was loved by the common people and was granted divine honors by the priests under the name of Hermes ["interpreter"] because he had interpreted the sacred writings.

2. II Maccabees

The Second Book of Maccabees is no mere variant of the First Book of Maccabees even though their contents are in part the same. The differences between them are more interesting and significant than the similarities. I Maccabees was originally written in Hebrew; II Maccabees is a Greek epitome of an original Greek work in five books composed by an otherwise unknown Jason of Cyrene (in North Africa). I Maccabees covers a period of forty years, 175-135 B.C.E., from the persecution of Antiochus Epiphanes to the death of Simon and the winning of Judea's political independence; II Maccabees covers a period of only fifteen years, 175-161 B.C.E., from the persecution of Antiochus Epiphanes (or a little earlier) to the victory of Judas Maccabeus over Nicanor. I Maccabees is a rather matter-of-fact account of the military achievements of the Hasmonean family; II Maccabees is a partly legendary account of the Jewish heroes and martyrs whose noble deeds were achieved with the miraculous help of God. It is largely because of the exalted tone and picturesque marvels of II Maccabees that it has won a more favored place in biblical literature than the more sober and historical I Maccabees. The heroic loyalty to ancestral tradition of the old man Eleazar and the mother with seven sons, in spite of the tortures inflicted on them by the Syrian king, became a classical example of martyrdom that was imitated in the vast literature of persecution of both Jews and Christians.

To the historian of Judaism and Christianity the book is especially important because in addition to various statements about the observance of the Sabbath and other practices that may be said to reveal a Pharisaic point of view, it contains what are probably the earliest explicit references to the resurrection of the body. This particular belief became one of the few cardinal dogmas of Pharisaism. It is stated in several passages of the book. In 7:9 one of the martyred youths says to the king before dying under torture:

You braggart, you release us from this present life, but the King of the world will resurrect us to an eternal new life because we have died for His laws.

Again in 12:43-44 we are told that Judas made a sin-offering in Jerusalem because of his belief in resurrection.

For if he had not expected that those who had fallen would rise again, it would have been superfluous and foolish to pray for the dead.

Incidentally, this last passage is one of several which have made II Maccabees one of the biblical writings most esteemed by Roman Catholic theologians.

As a characteristic example of the author's (or perhaps epitomator's) love of the marvelous and his rhetorical inventions we may select the following passage, 3:24-28, concerning the Divine punishment visited on the Syrian official Heliodorus for attempting to rob the treasury of the Temple in Jerusalem.

But no sooner had he and his guards arrived before the treasury than the Lord of our fathers and Master of all authority gave a great manifestation, so that all those who had come with him in their recklessness were smitten by the power of God and paralyzed and routed in terror. For there appeared to them a horse bearing a terrible rider and adorned with most handsome trappings, which rushed swiftly on Heliodorus and struck him with its forefeet. And its rider appeared in golden armor. And two youths also appeared to him, remarkably strong and most handsome in form and splendid in dress. These stood on either side of him and flogged him continually, showering many blows upon him. Suddenly he fell to the ground and was overwhelmed by great darkness, and so his men seized him and placed him on a litter—the same man indeed who had just entered the treasury we mentioned before, with such pomp and so great a retinue they now carried off because he was unable to help himself. Thus did they clearly recognize the sovereign power of God.

The author's ability to use simpler but more effective rhetoric is illustrated by his account of the death of the aged martyr Eleazar, 6:30-31:

As he was about to die under the blows, he said with a groan, "The Lord with His holy knowledge knows that though I might have escaped death, I endure dreadful pains in my body, being flogged, but in my soul I am glad to suffer this through fear of Him." And so he died, leaving in his death an example of nobility and a memorial of virtue not only to the young but also to the greatest part of his nation.

3. III Maccabees

The Third Book of Maccabees is found in most manuscripts of the Septuagint and in the Greek editions of the Apocrypha but it is not included in the Vulgate version or in the King James version, and is therefore less known to English readers than are I and II Maccabees. The word "Maccabees" in its title is misleading since the book is concerned with the Jews of Egypt and has nothing to do with the Hasmoneans; still there is a certain appropriateness in connecting this book with the two books of the Maccabees since it bears an obvious resemblance to II Maccabees in conception and style and also to some extent in the incidents related.

III Maccabees supposedly dates from the reign of the Macedonian king of Egypt, Ptolemy IV Philopator, 221-203 B.C.E. It relates that Ptolemy, after defeating the Seleucid king Antiochus III at Raphia on the Egyptian-Palestine border in 217 B.C.E., attempted to enter the Temple of Jerusalem and was miraculously kept therefrom (like Heliodorus in II Maccabees). On his return to Egypt the wrathful king decreed that his Jewish subjects were to suffer the loss of some of their religious and political privileges unless they should register as worshipers of the Ptolemies' patron god Dionysius. On seeing that the vast majority of Jews remained loyal to their religion, he had Jews brought from the country to Alexandria and imprisoned in the Hippodrome to be trampled to death by intoxicated elephants. Through Divine intervention the elephants turned against the persecutors of the Jews, and King Ptolemy, being convinced that the Jews enjoyed Divine protection, repented of his hostility and allowed them to return home safely and to take vengeance, not on Greek or Egyptian persecutors, be it noted, but on Jewish apostates. The story and atmosphere of the book remind one strongly of II Maccabees, the Letter of Aristeas and the Book of Esther.

When the book was actually written and to what incident in Jewish history it refers is difficult to determine. The incident of the exposure to trampling by drunken elephants is practically the same as that described by Josephus in his *Against Apion* as having taken place in the reign of Ptolemy VII Physcon, almost a century after the time of Ptolemy IV Philopator; moreover, the political troubles of the Jews hinted at in the book seem to belong to the time of Ptolemy Physcon rather than to that of Ptolemy Philopator. On the other hand, the description of the battle of Raphia and other details of the official acts of Ptolemy Philopator indicate that the author had a good knowledge of the events of his reign. The various problems of date and composition are best solved by assuming that an Egyptian Jewish writer of the first century B.C.E. has combined events of the reigns of two different kings and has added picturesque details suggested by the Book of Esther and II Maccabees to make up a well-knit piece of historical fiction. Several scholars have argued that III Maccabees was written in the Roman period and really alludes to the persecution of the Jews in Alexandria (and Palestine) by the Roman emperor Caligula, but, for reasons which cannot be given here, the present writer believes that the book was written in the first century B.C.E. to encourage the Jews of Palestine and Egypt to hope for Divine intervention in the face of an invasion of Palestine by the Ptolemaic sovereigns Cleopatra and Ptolemy VIII Lathyrus during the reign of Alexander Janneus.

The book is written in quite respectable and sometimes rather polished

Greek. As a story it is continuously interesting and even exciting. Not the least skillful device of the author is the succession of pointed references to God's power to save the Jews from their enemies. As a whole the work has less of the miraculous than II Maccabees but is no less orthodox in doctrine. The following brief passage illustrates its style and theology:

6:16-21. And just as Eleazar was ending his prayer, the king came to the Hippodrome with the beasts and his whole insolent force. And when the Jews beheld this, they cried out to heaven so that the adjacent hollows re-echoed their cry and caused an uncontrollable wailing among all the host. Then the greatly glorious, almighty and true God manifested His holy countenance and opened the gates of heaven, from which two glorious angels of terrible aspect descended, being visible to all except the Jews. And these stood over against them and filled the army of their adversaries with confusion and fear and bound them with immovable fetters. And a trembling fell upon the king's body, and forgetfulness of his heavy-handed arrogance came upon him. And the beasts turned round against the forces that followed them and began trampling on them and destroying them.

4. Josephus

The late Henry St. John Thackeray began his discussion of Josephus in his admirable Stroock Lectures on the historian by reminding his audience that there was a time in his country (England) when almost every house possessed two books, a Bible and a Josephus in the old eighteenth-century version of William Whiston. The same thing might be said of Presbyterian Scotland and Puritan New England and of other Protestant countries of Europe with their various vernacular translations of Josephus. But translations and paraphrases of Josephus were popular long before Whiston's English translation was made. Great numbers of Jews from the early Middle Ages down to recent times have eagerly read the Hebrew *Yosippon*, which is to a large extent a paraphrase of Josephus's *Jewish War*, while the Latin paraphrase ascribed to Hegesippus found great favor among Christian Latinists. Few pagan historians of classical antiquity have been more widely read or quoted than Flavius Josephus, the Palestinian Jew, whose Greek works on the history of his people and their war with Rome and eloquent apology for Judaism have done much to atone for his adherence to the Roman cause when his country was conquered by Vespasian and Titus.

Joseph, son of Matthias, later called Flavius Josephus, claims, in his *Life*, to have been of priestly and Hasmonean descent. He was born in 37 or 38 C.E. in the year when Caligula became emperor. He tells us that he was so precocious a student of the Jewish law that learned Rabbis consulted him when he was only fourteen. He studied the doctrines of the various Jewish schools and even retired to the wilderness for three years of ascetic training with a certain Bannus.

At the age of nineteen Josephus became a member of the Pharisaic party. In 64 c.e. he sailed to Rome and succeeded, with the help of a Jewish actor and the Empress Poppea, in liberating some priests who had been sent to Nero for trial. Josephus's visit to Rome impressed him with the hopelessness of a Jewish revolt against Rome which the extremists were planning. However, during the interval between the defeat of the Twelfth Legion under Cestius in the autumn of 66 and Vespasian's arrival in Palestine in the spring of 67 Josephus became an important figure in the revolt.

What his private attitude was toward the Romans and the exact nature of the commission entrusted to him by the authorities in Jerusalem are matters of doubt. In his earliest work, the *Jewish War*, Josephus states that the responsible leaders appointed him commander of the Jewish forces in Galilee.[2a] In the *Life*, written some thirty years later, he writes that he and two other priests were chosen to induce the rebels in Galilee to lay down their arms and to leave the decision of war to the authorities in Jerusalem; only afterwards was he made supreme commander of the forces in Galilee. Those scholars are probably right who prefer the later account and hold that in the *Jewish War* Josephus has exaggerated the importance of his appointment in order to impress Roman readers. At any rate, it appears from both works that he fought without conviction though he may have shown resourcefulness and military skill.

After the fall of the town of Jotapata, which had held out against the Romans for more than a month, Josephus with a few companions escaped to a cave, and persuaded them not to kill him to prevent his capture or surrender but to draw lots to determine the order of their mutual self-destruction. "He, however—" the evasive writer tells us, "should one say by fortune or by the providence of God?—was left alone with one other, and anxious neither to be condemned by lot nor, should he be left to the last, to stain his hand with his countryman's blood, he persuaded this man also under a pledge to remain alive." Brought before Vespasian, Josephus predicted that the Roman general would become emperor (as the Roman historian Suetonius also attests) and thanks to this prediction was liberated from bonds when Vespasian was acclaimed emperor by his troops in July, 69 c.e. During the last two years of the war Josephus served as interpreter and mediator. At the end of the war he was given a piece of land outside Jerusalem and some sacred books; he also obtained the liberation of several of his friends.

The last thirty years or so of his life the Jewish careerist spent in Rome, enjoying for about a third of this time the patronage of the imperial family. But life was not wholly pleasant for him during his residence in Rome, for he was constantly subject to the criticism of his coreligionists as a deserter or as a falsifier of his part in the war. Whatever the justice of these charges, we must be sincerely grateful to Josephus for having left us the four works which have so greatly enriched our knowledge of Jewish and Greco-Roman history.

The earliest extant work, the *Jewish War* or *Capture* (of Jerusalem) as Josephus himself probably meant it to be called, was clearly written soon after 70 C.E. at the suggestion of the Roman government in order to discourage further opposition by the Jews and other peoples living in Parthian territory. Our Greek text is apparently a second edition of the book, the first presumably being closer to the original draft, now lost, written in Aramaic. Parenthetically I may say that it is a very doubtful assumption that the Slavonic version is a translation of the original Aramaic text rather than a secondary translation of the Greek. Various references to Christianity or Jewish prophecies of the Roman period, which are found in the Slavonic version, are probably additions made by Byzantine scribes.

The *Jewish War* has a rapid survey of Jewish history in the Hellenistic-Roman period in the first book, largely based on the *Life of Herod* by Nicholas of Damascus, and in the remaining six books dramatically narrates the course of the Jewish war against Rome and its aftermath. Josephus not only drew on his personal experience but also used the military journals of the Roman commanders Titus and Vespasian and other official Roman documents. For these reasons the work has the greatest value as a historical source. At the same time, like most ancient histories, it contains a number of rhetorical embellishments, especially in the speeches attributed to the leading actors, and various echoes of Greek writers, notably the tragic poet Sophocles. Also it naturally reflects the prejudices and private interests of Josephus himself. With the help of a well-trained Greek collaborator the Jewish historian was able to produce a work of considerable literary skill both in construction and in style. We may safely conjecture that educated Romans found considerable pleasure in reading it.

Of even greater interest to students of Judaism and Christianity is Josephus's second great work, the *Jewish Antiquities*, divided into twenty books like its partial prototype, the *Roman Antiquities* of Dionysius of Halicarnassus. The *Jewish Antiquities*, written during the reign of Domitian after Josephus had lost his royal patrons, was put out with a different motive from that which prompted him to publish the *Jewish War*. The later work was designed not to celebrate the achievements of the Romans but to acquaint them with the history of the conquered Jewish people and to show that the Jews had a glorious past worthy of the respect of their Roman conquerors.

The first ten books of the *Jewish Antiquities*, covering the history of the Jews from the patriarchal period to the Babylonian Exile are in the main a paraphrase of the Greek version of the biblical narratives from Genesis to Daniel. Josephus's paraphrase of the Septuagint is no mere stylistic variation of the biblical text. He has incorporated numerous legendary and homiletic additions, most of them from Alexandrian writers (including Philo) and Palestinian tradition. Recent studies have shown that in addition to the Greek Bible Josephus used the Hebrew original and an Aramaic version closely resembling the extant Targums of Onkelos and Jonathan. The *Jewish Antiquities* is, of course, a valuable check on the Septuagint text, but more than that, it is of great importance as one of the earliest specimens of Jewish biblical exegesis.

The second half of the *Jewish Antiquities* covers the period from the return of the exiles to Judea in the reign of Cyrus to the term of the last procurator before the outbreak of the war against Rome. For the history of the Persian period and the Hellenistic period down to the reign of Hyrcanus, Josephus has used as his chief sources the Books of Ezra and Nehemiah, Esther, the Letter of Aristeas and I Maccabees, supplemented by handbooks of Greek history written by Gentile historians. For the Hasmonean, Herodian and procuratorial periods he is chiefly dependent on Jewish tradition and on the works of the Greek historians Nicholas of Damascus and Strabo and some unknown Roman historians. His quotations and paraphrases of Nicholas and Strabo make up a considerable part of the fragments preserved of their lost works.

The *Jewish Antiquities* is not only our chief and in part our only source for the history of the Jews in Palestine and in the Diaspora during the Hellenistic and Roman periods but it is also a valuable source for some otherwise poorly documented episodes of Seleucid and Roman history; for example, it gives us the most detailed account we possess of the assassination of the Emperor Caligula and the accession of Claudius. Where the *Jewish War* and the *Jewish Antiquities* overlap, as in the reign of Herod the Great, a comparison of the two accounts reveals significant differences of arrangement and political attitude, and thus throws light on Josephus's methods and motives. Not the least interesting portions of the parallel passages in the *Jewish War* and the *Jewish Antiquities* are those dealing with the Jewish schools or parties, Pharisees, Sadducees and Essenes.[3a] Although Josephus, following the example of Nicholas of Damascus, who wrote for Gentile readers, has converted social and theological differences among the Jewish parties into matters of philosophy, his discussion of their doctrines and controversies must be recognized as one of our principal sources for the history of Judaism in the early talmudic period.

There is another reason why the *Jewish Antiquities* was studied and prized by Christian scholars after the time of Eusebius; in Book XVIII there occurs a brief passage about the life and death of Jesus, the so-called *Testimonium Flavianum*, which is the only extant explicit mention of the founder of Christianity, outside the New Testament of course, dating from the first century of the Common Era. A vast literature exists dealing with the problem of the genuineness of this passage. Almost no modern scholar regards the testimony to Jesus's miraculous powers and resurrection as genuine in its present form; a few scholars believe that it is a Christian revision of an original reference to Jesus that was quite neutral in tone; most scholars believe, with greater justice, that the entire passage is a Christian interpolation.

We have already mentioned the *Life*, published as an appendix to the second edition of the *Jewish Antiquities*. It was probably written to answer the criticisms of the *Jewish War* made by a rival Jewish historian, Justus of Tiberias. Besides being valuable as an account of Josephus's activities as commander of the Jewish forces in Galilee (see above), it provides us with our only though sketchy account of Josephus's entire career.

The latest work of Josephus, *Against Apion,* in two books, has a greater scope than the title indicates, since Apion was only one of several Greek writers whose calumnies against the Jews Josephus undertakes to refute. This little treatise is not only a persuasive and eloquent refutation of the various charges, some of them patently absurd, some more insidious, which were brought against the Jews by Egyptian and Greek anti-Semites and sometimes by more impartial Gentile historians, but it is also an inspired defense of the Mosaic Law and a triumphant vindication of Jewish morality and culture. Few champions of Judaism have more successfully presented their case; and so, this earliest reply to literary anti-Semitism must be regarded as ample atonement for any sins Josephus may have committed against his people as a military leader.

There are far too many quotable passages in Josephus's four works to make it easy to choose any single one in this brief sketch, but I cannot resist quoting part of the conclusion of the *Against Apion* in Thackeray's translation:

I would therefore boldly maintain that we have introduced to the rest of the world a very large number of very beautiful ideas. What greater beauty than inviolable piety? What higher justice than obedience to the laws? What more beneficial than to be in harmony with one another, to be a prey neither to disunion in adversity nor to arrogance and faction in prosperity; in war to despise death, in peace to devote oneself to crafts or agriculture, and to be convinced that everything in the whole universe is under the eye and direction of God? Had these precepts been either committed to writing or more consistently observed by others before us, we should have owed them a debt of gratitude as their disciples. If, however, it is seen that no one observes them better than ourselves, and if we have shown that we were the first to discover them, then the Apions and Molons and all who delight in lies and abuse may be left to their own confusion.

4. JEWISH PROPAGANDA IN GENTILE GUISE

The basic instincts and broad patterns of social behavior were not very different, whether among Jews or Gentiles, in the Hellenistic age from those of present-day peoples, but some of their conventions were dissimilar enough from our own to evoke surprise in a modern person when first he learns of them. The ancient attitude toward plagiarism and literary borrowing, for example, was much less proprietary than it is today. The same is true of their attitude toward the practice of foisting one's own work on the great names of classical tradition. Bearing this in mind, we should not be too greatly scandalized by the fact that some Jewish apologists composed works in prose or verse designed to show Jews in a favorable light, and published them as the writings of real or imaginary Gentile authors, just as Christian writers of the fourth or fifth century forged a correspondence between the Roman philosopher Seneca and the Apostle Paul. The present section deals with the best known works or fragments of this kind which have come down to us. In all probability they are only a small part of the entire body of this literature.

1. *Pseudo-Hecateus*

Among the Gentile historians of the time of Alexander the Great and his immediate successors whose works have been preserved only in excerpts by later writers of antiquity was a certain Hecateus who wrote, among other things, a *History of Egypt* including passages on the Jews. Some portions of this book have been preserved by the Greek historian Diodorus Siculus, who flourished under Augustus. There is no reason to doubt the genuineness of these passages. But there are other passages cited by Josephus and early Christian writers, supposedly from Hecateus's book *On the Jews* or *On Abraham*, which are generally regarded as extracts from a Jewish work passed off as Hecateus's and therefore known today as excerpts from Pseudo-Hecateus. Recently, however, some scholars have convincingly argued that the suspected passages in Josephus's *Against Apion* are really from the genuine Hecateus, and it is likely that as our knowledge increases through the discovery of new evidence, the extent of the assumed pseudepigraphic material will have to be considerably reduced. But the strong probability remains that other fragments from "Hecateus," for example, in Clement of Alexandria and Eusebius, are from Pseudo-Hecateus, the Jewish apologist, whose real name and date are unknown to us. That even in antiquity there was some suspicion of the supposititious character of passages quoted from Hecateus's book *On the Jews* is indicated by a statement in Origen that the author is so attached to this nation because of its wisdom that Herennius Philo [a Hellenized Phoenician, who flourished about 100 c.e.] in his work *On the Jews* in the first place expresses doubt whether the work is by the historian, and in the second place says, if it really is his work, that he has been ravished by Jewish persuasiveness and won over by their doctrines.

It is perhaps Pseudo-Hecateus, not the genuine Hecateus, who is quoted in the Letter of Aristeas (§5) as saying that pagan writers have refrained from discussing Jewish history because of the great sacredness attaching to it.

2. *The Letter of Aristeas*

Although the Letter of Aristeas was highly esteemed and used by such early Jewish writers as Philo and Josephus (and, of course, by Christian theologians), it was not until the sixteenth century that the liberal Italian Jewish scholar Azariah de Rossi rescued it from the neglect into which, because it was written in Greek, it had fallen among his coreligionists. De Rossi's Hebrew translation and discussion of the Letter of Aristeas are included in his critical history of Jewish tradition, called *Meor Eynayim*.

The Letter of Aristeas purports to be a letter written to a certain Philocrates by his brother, a court official of Ptolemy II Philadelphus (285-247 B.C.E.). It narrates the events leading up to the translation of the Hebrew Pentateuch into Greek made by the Palestinian scholars whom the king invited to Alexandria at the suggestion of the royal librarian, Demetrius of Phalerum. The account of the translators' methods takes up only the last twelfth of the book; the preceding sections describe the emancipation of Jewish captives in Egypt by royal command, the invitation to Eleazar, the High Priest in Jerusalem, to send scholars to Alexandria for the work of translation, the presents sent to the Temple in Jerusalem by Ptolemy, the impressions made on Aristeas by the Temple and the city, and the splendid reception given to the Palestinian scholars on their arrival in Alexandria; then comes a long philosophical discussion, in the form of question and answer, between the king and the Jewish Sages on matters of politics and morality.

Even a casual reading of this fascinating book reveals that the author was not, as he pretends, a Ptolemaic official narrating a series of historical events but a Hellenistic Jew writing a sort of historical novel (or novelette) about the translation of the Law and embellishing it with apologetic passages skillfully employing the devices of Greek philosophical literature.

The problem of the date has long exercised the ingenuity of scholars but the weight of learned opinion today favors a date not long after 200 B.C.E. Such a date would account for some slight errors about the history and court etiquette of Ptolemy II's reign made by the generally well-informed author as well as for his use of certain forms and phrases known to be current in Egypt in the early part of the second century B.C.E. It may be conjectured, though it would be difficult to prove, that in addition to giving a laudatory description of Jewish customs for the edification of Gentiles, the author had the more specific purpose of alleviating any suspicions entertained by the Ptolemaic ruler of his time that the friendly relations between the Jewish communities of Alexandria and Jerusalem might trouble the political situation in Egypt.

To the Jewish and Christian historians of antiquity the most important part of the Letter of Aristeas was that which told how the Law was translated into Greek. Josephus was content to paraphrase this account but other ancient writers, like the Christian Fathers, Ireneus, Clement and Epiphanius, repeat the picturesque invention of Pseudo-Justin that the seventy-two translators mentioned by Aristeas were placed in thirty-six cells and by Divine inspiration separately produced versions that were found to be in absolute agreement. The original account (§§301-309) reads in part as follows.

Three days later Demetrius [the royal librarian] took the men and passing along the sea wall of seven stadia to the island, crossed the bridge and went to the northern part. Here he called them together in session in a house built on the seashore; it was very splendid and located in a quiet place. He then encouraged them to carry out the work of translation, for everything had been well provided that was needed for this purpose. So they began their task, making their results agree by comparing them, and what was agreed upon was duly written down with the approval of Demetrius. The session lasted until the ninth hour [3:00 P.M.] After this they were dismissed to attend to their bodily needs, and everything they wanted was freely supplied to them. In addition they were given the same daily provisions as the king; Demetrius attended to this, having been ordered by the king so to do. Early every day they appeared at court and paid their respects to the king, after which they went back to their own place. And, as is the custom among the Jews, they washed their hands in the sea in order to pray to God and then began to read and translate the passages given to each. . . . And it so happened that the work of translation was completed in seventy-two days, as though this had been arranged of set purpose. When the work had been completed, Demetrius called the Jewish populace to the place where the translation had been made, and read it to all in the presence of the translators, who received a great ovation from the populace on the strength of the great benefits for which they had been responsible.

To a modern reader there are other equally interesting passages that deserve quotation, but lack of space forbids giving more than a part of the section (§§ 128-171) that contains the earliest moral allegory of some of the ritual prescriptions of Mosaic Law, such as was later richly developed by Philo.

For though in general all things are alike in their physical principles, being governed by the same power, in every case there is a deep reason why we abstain from the use of some things and enjoy the use of others. This I will summarily explain by one or two examples. For you must not get the degrading notion that it was out of respect for mice and weasels and such creatures that Moses showed such care in his legislation. Rather did he draw up all these solemn prescriptions for the sake of righteousness and to aid in attaining holiness and the perfecting of character. For all the birds we use [for food] are tame and distinguished by their cleanliness and feed on grain and pulse, such as pigeons. turtledoves, moorfowls, partridges, geese and other such birds. But the birds that are forbidden you will find to be wild and carnivorous and to dominate others by their strength and wrongfully prey on the tame birds mentioned above. . . . He therefore used them as examples, calling them "unclean," to show that those for whom the Law was ordained should practice righteousness in their souls and not dominate anyone in reliance upon their own strength nor deprive others of anything, but steer their lives by what is right, just as the tame birds mentioned above consume various kinds of pulse growing in the earth, and do not dominate their kindred species in order to destroy them.

3. *Pseudo-Phocylides*

Among the Greek moralistic poets of whose works only a few fragments have come down to us was a certain Phocylides of Miletus who lived in the sixth century B.C.E. Evidently he was a writer of considerable authority in later times, for a Jew of the Hellenistic period chose Phocylides as the pagan poet on whom to foist his own composition consisting of 230 hexametric verses in classical Greek style and with a content chiefly based on the moral prescriptions of Mosaic Law.

This crypto-Jewish work in Greek form is the more interesting for its failure to denounce pagan idolatry or to praise specific Jewish customs, as did outspoken Jewish Hellenists like Philo and the author of III Maccabees. Pseudo-Phocylides is so careful to conceal his Jewish origin that he presents only the most universalistic features of biblical morality and piety. This concealment, it is safe to say, is due to his technique of propaganda and not to expediency or timidity. Of course, there is a bare possibility that the author was not a Jew but a pagan admirer of the Greek Bible, or even a crypto-Christian. But in view of the assured Jewish character of similar works, it is far more probable that the author was Jewish. A few specimen lines (8-11, 84-85) are here translated in rough approximation of the Greek style and dactylic meter:

First honor God, and next after Him honor those who begot thee.
Deal out justice to all men, and twist not judgment to favor.
Turn not away the poor without right, and respect not men's persons.
Be not a wicked judge lest God in turn someday condemn thee.

Flee from false witness, and justice alone be what thou desirest.
Let no one take from the nest all the birds that are sheltered within it,
But set the mother bird free, and some other day thou'lt have her fledglings.

4. *The Wise Menander*

Most famous of the writers of the comedy of manners in the Hellenistic world was the Attic poet Menander, who flourished in the generation after Alexander the Great. His numerous plays were not only imitated and adapted by the two great Roman comedy writers Plautus and Terence but continued to influence Roman satirists of the imperial age, and like the plays of Shakespeare, became a part of the general culture of the Western world after their author had died. Echoes of Menander's informal philosophy are found even in the New Testament, for example, "evil communications corrupt good manners" in I Cor. 15:33. Moreover, wise and witty sayings were culled from the numerous works of Menander (of which, unfortunately, only fragments have survived) and included in anthologies of maxims from the Greek poets and philosophers.

It was probably the Attic Menander who was in the mind of the author or editor of a collection of gnomic sayings, probably in the iambic meter of six feet used for this purpose in Greek literature, of which a Syriac translation was found in a seventh century manuscript of the British Museum, bearing the title *The Wise Menander Said*. Thirty years after its publication by J. Land in 1862, another scholar, Frankenberg, showed that these verses, about a hundred and fifty in number, closely resembled sayings in biblical Wisdom literature, and thus, he argued, they represent the work of a Jewish writer of the Roman period. But since the collection contains a number of genuine sayings of Menander and other pagan writers, it is probable that the Greek original of this Syriac translation was a Jewish pseudepigraph, designed to convey Jewish ideas in a form that would appeal to Greek readers, particularly because of the prestige that was attached to the name of Menander. The following few verses are given in a translation that attempts to suggest the meter probably used in the lost Greek original of the Syriac text.

> Fear God, and honor too thy father and thy mother.
> Mock not old age, for thou thyself wilt come to it.
> If from his youth thy son emerge both meek and wise,
> Teach him the scribal art and wisdom; these two things
> Are good to learn and bring clear eyes and flowing tongue.
> What's hateful to thee, unto friends seek not to do.

In the expression "scribal art and wisdom" the reader will immediately recognize an allusion to Dan. 1:17.

5. *The Sibylline Oracles*

Among the ancient legendary givers of oracles and prophecies the mysterious women called Sibyls enjoyed great prestige in the Hellenistic-Roman period. Most high school boys of past generations were familiar with the story, told by Virgil in the sixth book of the *Aeneid*, of Aeneas's visit to the Cumean sibyl who foretold to him the future trials and triumphs of the Roman people and prepared him for his descent into the nether world. But the Cumean sibyl was only one of several whose prophecies, recorded in Greek hexameters, were widely circulated in the early days of the Roman Empire. Besides the Greco-Roman sibyls of Cumae in Italy, of Erythrae in Asia Minor, of Libya, of Delphi in Greece, there were also Oriental sibyls, Hebrew, Persian and Chaldean. Sometimes they were considered separate figures, sometimes the Persian and Chaldean sibyls were identified with the Jewish sibyl, Sabbe or Sambathe, the daughter of Berossus (Berossus actually having been a Babylonian historian of the third century B.C.E. who translated cuneiform records into Greek).

The extant manuscripts of Sibylline Oracles represent a collection made in the fifth or sixth century C.E., which contains several thousand verses, divided into fourteen or fifteen books. They are ostensibly pagan prophecies of the dire calamities about to overtake the Gentile world, but actually they are in large part Jewish and Christian compositions in pagan disguise, meant to warn their readers to repent of their sins and to recognize the truth of Jewish or Christian teaching. Some of the Jewish oracles probably date from the second century B.C.E. It is hardly necessary to state that they were not genuine predictions of things to come but, like many apocalyptic writings, were prophecies after the event.

It is not always easy to distinguish the Jewish from the Christian portions because the original Jewish prophecies were imitated or revised by Christian writers. However, there is general agreement that we have basically Jewish material in most of Books III, IV and V and in parts of later books. Many events of Jewish history in the Hellenistic-Roman period are alluded to in these supposed prophecies, but the language is often so poetically obscure and the symbolism so vague that it is not always possible for modern scholars to be certain of the exact incidents described. From the less ambiguous passages we can be fairly sure that the Jewish author or authors included a rapid survey of Jewish history from the reign of Antiochus Epiphanes to the decades following the destruction of the Temple of Jerusalem by the Romans in 70 C.E. Clearly Jewish is the tone of those passages in which the sibyl denounces pagan idolatry and immorality, announces the coming of a Messianic age and the punishment of the godless, and consoles the righteous with promise of Divine help.

Unfortunately there is not sufficient material to enable us to estimate how deep an impression was made upon pagan readers by these crypto-Jewish Sibylline Oracles, but it is safe to say that Virgil was influenced by them in writing his *Fourth Eclogue*, which describes the coming golden age of Roman imperialism. Occasional echoes of Messianic imagery in later Greek and Latin literature suggest that these Jewish verses in Greek form had considerable effect in forming certain types of pagan literature during the early centuries of the Roman Empire. Whether they had a more practical effect in winning pagan converts to Judaism can only be conjectured.

Of the large number of verses of undoubted Jewish origin, the following few are selected as representative; they are given in metrical translation suggesting the form of the Greek meter employed (Book III, 36-39, 46-52).

> O generation delighting in blood, crafty, evil and godless,
> Men who lie and are double-tongued and evil of nature,
> Stealing other men's wives, idolators, craftily plotting;
> Evil lurks in your breasts, like a maddening gadfly pursues you.
> But that day will come when Rome will rule over Egypt,
> Though it be still delayed, and then the almighty kingdom
> Of the eternal King will appear to mankind in glory.
> Then will the holy prince come and on earth bear the scepter
> Throughout all aeons forever, as time hurries onward.
> Then shall the wrath inexorably descend on the Latins,
> And by a pitiful fate Three will bring Rome into ruin.

5. EPIC AND DRAMA

Until quite recent times it was generally thought that the Jews of the Greek-speaking Diaspora were almost completely unaffected by the artistic impulses of their Greek neighbors. However, the excavations of synagogues decorated with mosaic and painted representations of human, animal and floral figures have caused us to revise our opinions concerning the lack of pictorial art among the Jews of the Hellenistic-Roman period. By contrast, philologists have long been aware that among Greek-speaking Jews there were persons of literary talent who showed skill in adapting the language and style of Greek epic and dramatic poetry to biblical themes. Unfortunately the works of all but three of such writers have been completely lost, and of the three whose poetry has escaped oblivion only scant fragments have survived in the ninth book of the *Evangelical Preparation* of Eusebius, the same writer who has preserved fragments of the Hellenistic Jewish prose writers mentioned above. For this reason it may be something of a surprise to the general reader that in the Hellenistic age there were Jews who wrote epics and dramas in Greek about the sacred history of Israel.

1. *Philo the Elder* (*Philo Epicus*)

The Jewish epic poet Philo was not, of course, the philosopher Philo of Alexandria (on whom see below) but was probably the same person whom Josephus, in his *Against Apion*, refers to as Philo the Elder and couples with the Hellenistic Jewish historians Demetrius and Eupolemus. Since Josephus and Eusebius depend for their information about Philo the Elder upon Alexander Polyhistor, who flourished about 100 B.C.E., it is clear that the poet must have written as early as the second century B.C.E.

According to Eusebius, Philo wrote an epic called *On Jerusalem*, but the learned Church Father has seen fit to quote only three fragments amounting in all to twenty-four lines. It is also unfortunate that the few extant verses are written in the recondite and labored style of Alexandrian epic poets and are somewhat difficult to understand. The following is a verse-translation of a five-line fragment on Joseph, quoted by Eusebius from the fourth book (we must amend ms. "fourteenth" to "fourth"). From the position of this fragment and the statement of Clement of Alexandria that Philo wrote about the kings of Israel, we may conjecture that the epic covered twenty-four books, like the *Iliad* and the *Odyssey*.

> For them a blessed abode did the great world leader establish,
> He, the Most High, of old for the children of Abram and Isaac
> And of the child-blessed Jacob. Thence came Joseph the dreamer,
> Prophet of God, who wielded the scepter over all Egypt,
> And revolved in his mind the secrets of time in the floodtide of fortune.

2. *Theodotus*

About Theodotus, the author of an epic *On the Jews*, we know as little as about his contemporary Philo Epicus. The forty-seven hexameter verses cited by Eusebius in the ninth book of his *Evangelical Preparation* from Alexander Polyhistor are concerned with the Israelites' conquest of Shechem and the revenge taken by Simeon and Levi for the seduction of Dinah. From the fact that the extant fragments narrate only this episode and that Shechem is called a "holy city" some scholars have inferred that Theodotus was a Samaritan rather than a Jew. But "holy city" is a stock epithet in Greek epic poetry, and there is no trace of anti-Jewish feeling in the poem, such as one would expect in a Samaritan work; moreover, the poem stresses the impiety of the Shechemites. We shall therefore probably be right in considering Theodotus a Jewish writer.

Theodotus writes in a simpler and more Homeric style than Philo Epicus, who, as we saw, preferred the artificial manner of contemporary

Alexandrian poets. In respect of the Hellenistic elements in this Jewish work it is interesting that Eusebius reports the author as saying that the city got its name from "Shechem son of Hermes." But in spite of Theodotus's use of the language of Greek mythology we must, I think, agree with the German editor Ludwich in regarding "Hermes" as a corruption of *Hamor* (Greek *Emor*), since Shechem is so designated in the poem itself as in the Greek version of Genesis, on which the extant fragments are based (ch. 34).

The following few lines from the passage describing Jacob's coming from Mesopotamia to Palestine (here called Syria) may suffice to give an idea of the style:

> Then Jacob made his way to the kine-bearing land of Syria,
> Leaving behind the stream of the wide, onrushing Euphrates,
> For he had come from there, leaving the bitter reproaches
> Made by his very own kin, though gladly had Laban received him
> Into his home, who was cousin to him, and sole ruler
> Over all Syria . . .

3. *Ezekiel the Tragic Poet*

Epic poetry was not the only field of Greek literature cultivated by the Jewish writers of Alexandria. Centuries before Christian monks and clerics produced dramas based on biblical themes, a Jewish poet named Ezekiel wrote tragedies on these subjects. Considerable fragments, amounting to over two hundred lines, from one of his dramas on the Exodus have been preserved by Eusebius in that precious ninth book of his *Evangelical Preparation*, again from the lost compilation of Alexander Polyhistor.

Ezekiel has taken the story of Moses and the Israelites' flight from Egypt from the Greek version of the Book of Exodus, and has given it dramatic form on the lines of classical Greek tragedy, especially under the influence of Euripides. There are, however, some deviations from the pattern of Attic drama, such as more frequent changes of scene and the omission of choral passages. Unity of action is obtained by making Moses the central figure in all the scenes. The meter used in the extant fragments is the iambic trimeter, regularly employed in the dialogue of Attic plays.

Modern scholars disagree on the question whether Ezekiel's *Exodus* was meant to be presented in an Alexandrian theater or merely to be read as a closet drama. The latter is more likely, not merely because of the technical problems presented by frequent changes of scene but also because it is difficult to believe that Jews would have attended a theatrical performance of a sacred legend in which God himself was one of the actors. Nor is it much more likely that there would have been a Gentile audience for such a play. But it would be foolish to speak dogmatically on this subject in the present state of our knowledge about the everyday life of Jews in the Hellenistic Diaspora.

It is also probable that Ezekiel wrote this drama about Moses and the Exodus not merely for the instruction or encouragement of Jews who had a Greek secular education but also for Gentiles whom he might hope to impress with the power of Israel's God to save His people from persecution. For translation I have selected part of the dialogue between God and Moses concerning the miracles which God wishes Moses to perform with his staff (based on Ex. 4:2-7). The language here is simple, rapid and almost prosaic:

GOD: What is this thing in thy two hands? Speak quickly now.
MOSES: It is a staff with which to strike both beasts and men.
GOD: Cast it upon the ground and quickly move away.
        For 'twill become a serpent dreadful to behold.
MOSES: See, I have thrown it down. O Lord, be gracious now.
        How dreadful! What a monster! Do Thou pity me!
        I shudder at the sight and tremble in every limb.
GOD: Fear naught, but stretch thy hand and take its tail,
        And once more it will be a staff just as before.
        Now thrust thy hand into thy bosom and draw it out.
MOSES: Thy bidding I have done. My hand is white as snow.
GOD: Now thrust it back again. 'Twill be just as before.

6. WISDOM LITERATURE AND PHILOSOPHY

Like the other nations of the ancient Near East the Israelites treasured the admonitions and counsels of their wise men concerning right behavior toward God and fellow man. These sayings, though written in language more prosaic, more reflective and less emotional than that used by the prophets, were no less religious in content, if we give to the word "religion" the more inclusive meaning that it had in antiquity. Sometime during the early part of the period of the Second Commonwealth, a collection of such wise sayings was published under the title the Proverbs of Solomon, though in fact a large part of the collection dates from a period after Solomon, and a few of the thirty-one chapters are actually a translation of Egyptian Wisdom literature written long before Solomon's time.

This Book of Proverbs became the model for Palestinian writers of the Hellenistic period, like the authors of the Book of Ecclesiastes and the Wisdom of Ben Sira,[4a] who further developed the ancient theme that "the beginning of wisdom is the reverence of God." In their choice of subjects to moralize about and their concern to identify *Hokmah* (Wisdom)[5a] with Torah (Revealed Law), they closely followed traditional lines of moral and religious speculation.

Among the Jewish thinkers of the Greek Diaspora, however, the contact with Greek philosophy and theology, however superficial it may have been in some cases, led them to give a more logical or systematic or metaphysical form to their expositions of Judaism. This is not to imply that the talmudists of Palestine were less acute in argument or less rational in ethics than the Greek philosophers or Hellenistic Jewish theologians. It is only to state the innocuous truism that the formal aspects of our Western intellectual traditions go back to the Greeks, and that it was the Greek philosophers, particularly those of the Hellenistic period, who created the terminology and methodology of our scientific thinking.

1. *The Wisdom of Solomon*

Of the three Hellenistic Jewish philosophical works that have survived in addition to the extensive remains of Philo, only the Wisdom of Solomon (which is also, of course, apologetic and eschatological in content) adheres to the pattern of Wisdom literature established by the Book of Proverbs. What distinguishes it most conspicuously from this and other Hebrew books of like nature, such as Ecclesiastes and Ben Sira, is its occasional use of Greek philosophical terms and forms of argument and its partial adoption of Greek notions of the pre-existence and immortality of the soul and of the Divine powers. In some passages, as in the catalogues of virtues and sins, its rhetoric reminds one of that of the Stoic diatribe, a kind of street-corner sermon.

On the other hand, it is clear from the frequent use made of biblical doctrines, imagery and phrases that the author must have been familiar with the Scriptures, probably with the Hebrew text as well as with the Greek translation. In this connection we are reminded that the book was well known to the apostle Paul whose own teaching was an even more subtle blend of Jewish and Hellenistic ideas and turns of expression. Perhaps it was Paul's admiration for the Wisdom of Solomon that caused the early Christian church to regard it as one of the most important books in the Apocrypha.

While there is an undeniable unity of tone and vocabulary throughout the nineteen chapters of the book, the subject matter is rather obviously divisible into three parts. Chapters 1-5 deal with future rewards and punishments for good and evil conduct and briefly allude to the part played by Wisdom in promoting righteousness. Chapters 6-10 form an eloquent dissertation on Wisdom which, as an effluence of God's power, has preserved the righteous throughout Israel's history. This section takes as its point of departure the famous passage in the Book of Kings in which Solomon prays for wisdom rather than riches and power, at least according to later tradition. In this part of the book Wisdom corresponds fairly closely to the Rabbinic personification of Torah as well as to the Stoic *Pronoia*, or Providence. Chapters 11-19 sketch Israel's earlier history and in Rabbinic fashion demonstrate how Israel's enemies have been punished on the principle of "measure for measure"; for example, the various plagues that afflicted the Egyptians were appropriate to the injuries they had done the Israelites. These chapters also present a well-reasoned argument against idolatry, having especially the Egyptians in mind, and give a quasi-anthropological account of the origins of this practice, which though more tolerant is not less effective than the prophetic denunciations of idol worship.

With the technical problems of the date, composition, authorship and original language of the Wisdom of Solomon we have not space to deal at length. It must suffice to say that the weight of evidence supports those scholars who believe that most if not all the book was composed in Greek by an Alexandrian Jew who probably spoke or at least read Hebrew as well as Greek. Though several distinct subjects are treated, perhaps based on different sources, the writer has combined them in such a way as to give the work the stamp of single authorship. The date of composition or final editing cannot be fixed exactly but was probably near the beginning of the Common Era. Some scholars of an earlier period conjectured that the philosopher Philo was the author of this apocryphal book, but this conjecture is no longer taken seriously.

With many interesting and eloquent passages to serve as quotations from a book which has had so great an influence on Christian thought, it is an ungrateful task to select a very few as illustrative of its doctrine and style. It is hoped that the following three passages are sufficiently representative.

In 3:1-5 we have, in answer to the age-old query of why "the good die young," a testament of faith that the righteous do not die but pass on to eternal life. This belief is found also in Philo and Rabbinic literature but there it is perhaps less poetically expressed.

> The souls of the righteous are in the hand of God,
> And no torment will touch them.
> In the eyes of the thoughtless they seem to have died,
> And their departure is reckoned as an evil,
> And their going hence as a disaster.
> But they are at peace.
> For if in the sight of men they have been punished,
> Their hope is full of immortality.
> Being chastised a little, greatly will they be rewarded.
> For God has tested them and found them worthy of Him.

When, in 6:17-20, the author commends to earthly rulers the study and practice of Wisdom, he attempts to show that Wisdom alone leads to kingship by using the *sorites*, or chain argument, favored by the Stoics. Thus he combines Stoic logic with the spirit of Judaism to make the point, central in the teachings of Plato and later Greek political thinkers, that kings should be philosophers.

> For her [Wisdom's] beginning is the most sincere desire for instruction,
> And the concern for instruction is love.
> Love is the keeping of her laws,
> And observance of the laws is assurance of incorruption.
> Incorruption brings men close to God.
> Thus does the desire for Wisdom lead men to kingship.

The last passage for which there is room here is part of a breathless catalogue, in 7:22-23, of the various beneficent aspects of versatile Wisdom. In this catalogue some commentators have found a striking similarity to a list of the attributes of wisdom or virtue made by the Stoic philosopher Cleanthes.

> For in her there is a spirit intellectual and holy,
> Only-begotten, of many parts, subtle,
> Mobile, delicate, undefiled,
> Clear, harmless, loving good, keen,
> Undeterred, beneficent, humane,
> Firm, sure, without care,
> All-powerful, all-seeing,
> Pervading all spirits
> That are intellectual, pure and subtle.

This spirit of Wisdom, the chapter continues, is a breath of God's power and a reflection of eternal light, which has passed into the holy souls of all generations and made them friends of God and prophets. Nowhere in Jewish literature except in Philo, who is more elaborate and sophisticated, does one find so appealing a fusion of Greek and Jewish teaching concerning the part played by Wisdom in human affairs.

2. *Aristobulus*

We have seen, in the brief discussion of the Letter of Aristeas, that that book contains some passages of a philosophical nature, but as they are merely incidental to the book's apologetic purpose, the author is hardly to be classed as a professional philosopher. Among the Alexandrian philosophers who preceded Philo, however, there is one writer of whose work extensive enough fragments have been preserved to enable us to form some notion of the more strictly philosophical literature produced by Philo's coreligionists.

This writer was Aristobulus who was, according to the Church Father Clement of Alexandria, a contemporary of Ptolemy VI Philometor who reigned 181-145 B.C.E. Some scholars place Aristobulus in the Roman period and some hold him to have been a Christian, but so far no convincing evidence has been offered to refute the traditional date. More doubtful is the accuracy of Clement's statement, echoed by Eusebius, that Aristobulus belonged to the Peripatetic, or Aristotelian, school of philosophy. What is clear from the extant fragments is that he attempted to harmonize the Law of Moses with the teachings of Greek philosophy in a work which bore the title *Interpretation of the Law of Moses*, or *Interpretation of the Sacred Laws*.

This harmonization Aristobulus sought to achieve partly through an allegorical explanation of the anthropomorphic allusions to God in the Pentateuch (that is, allusions to the eyes, arms, countenance, walking, etc., of God); partly by quoting Greek verses falsely attributed to Homer, Hesiod and other real and mythical poets who supposedly supported the statements of Scripture; and partly by attempting to show that Pythagoras, Plato and other Greek thinkers drew their theological doctrines from Moses. From these passages it appears, on the plausible assumption that Christian tradition correctly placed Aristobulus in the second century B.C.E., that he was a forerunner of Philo with respect to harmonizing Greek philosophy with Judaism. Whether he was Philo's equal in learning, subtlety and literary skill it would not be fair to decide, in view of the little we have from his pen compared with the extensive Philonic literature that has come down to us. From the few fragments that we have, however, it does seem that he was inferior to Philo in all three respects.

The following selections from the excerpts found in the ninth and thirteenth books of Eusebius's *Evangelical Preparation* may give some idea of the peculiar combination of ingenious interpretation and elusive phrasing that seems to characterize Aristobulus's writing.

For often what our lawgiver Moses wishes to convey when he is using language proper to other matters, by which I mean their appearances, he expresses by physical qualities and the forms of great things[?]. Now those who are able to think clearly admire the wisdom and divine inspiration for which the prophet is celebrated. To their number belong the philosophers we have mentioned and many others, especially poets who have taken notable arguments from him, for which they are admired. But to those who do not share his power and understanding and attend only to what is literally set down, he does not seem to be interpreting anything of great import. I will begin by taking each of the passages in question and explaining it so far as I am able. And if I do not find the truth or convince you, do not attribute the lack of sense to the lawgiver, but to me who am unable to make clear exactly what was in his mind. Now the arms are something that is clearly and commonly understood by us. And when you as king send out your forces with the intention of achieving something, we say that the king has a "great arm," for the word used is referred to the force which you possess. This is the very thing alluded to in our law by Moses when he says, "God brought you out of Egypt with a mighty arm."

The second fragment explains the passage in Genesis that describes how God rested on the seventh day after creating the world.

It is consistent with this that God created the whole world and, because daily life is a difficult experience for all, gave us the seventh day as a day of rest. Thus it may physically [*i.e.*, philosophically] be called the genesis of light, since by this all things are perceived. The same metaphor may be applied to Wisdom, for all light comes from her. And some of the Peripatetic school have said that she fills the part of a lantern, for those who steadily follow her will remain unconfused throughout the whole of life. But still more clearly and beautifully did one of our ancestors, Solomon, say that she existed before heaven and earth. And this is in harmony with what has been said before. For the interpretation of the statement in the Law that God rested on this day is not, as some have understood it, that God no longer continued to create but that He made an end of ordering things so that they were ordered as they were for all time. For [Scripture] indicates that in six days He made heaven and earth and all things in them that He might reveal what the various times were and foretell the order of their precedence. For once having ordered them, He preserves them and does not alter their positions. This He has made clear to us in the Law in order that we may have the principle of the number seven before us, and through this have knowledge of things human and divine. For the whole world of things that are born and grow revolves through periods of seven. And this seventh day is called the Sabbath which translated means "rest." Both Homer and Hesiod, who used our [sacred] writings as a source, have indicated that it is holy.

At this point Aristobulus introduces a number of spurious verses from Homer, Hesiod and the mythical Linos to show that the ancient Greeks also held the seventh day to be holy.

3. IV Maccabees

It was probably sometime near the beginning of the Common Era that an Alexandrian Jew with an intimate knowledge of Greek philosophy, especially that of the Stoic Posidonius (early part of the first century B.C.E.), and a formidable Greek vocabulary composed a sort of sermon or lecture on the theme: reason can control passion. This argument is illustrated by examples taken from Jewish history, especially of the Maccabean period.

Though this book, commonly known as IV Maccabees, is included in three of the oldest and most important manuscripts of the Greek Bible, it was (mistakenly) regarded by Eusebius, Jerome and other early Church Fathers as the work of Flavius Josephus; for this reason it is not found in the Latin Bible and consequently is not counted among the apocryphal books of the English and other modern versions of the Bible. IV Maccabees seems to have been entirely unknown to the Jews until modern times but it is not impossible that it was used, perhaps at second hand by the author of the medieval Hebrew work *Yosippon*. Christian writers, on the other hand, greatly admired the book, and the famous Erasmus made a free translation of the Latin version.

Like Aristobulus and Philo, the author of IV Maccabees is chiefly concerned to show that the great virtues of the Platonic-Stoic tradition are to be attained by observing the Law of Moses. The larger part of the book, chapters 4-18, is a glorification of the triumph of reason over passion achieved by the martyrs of the Maccabean period, Eleazar, and the mother and her seven sons, whose defiance of Antiochus Epiphanes had earlier been told in II Maccabees.

Chapter 1 is a philosophical introduction that reminds one forcefully of the treatises on reason and passion that are found in the writings of Cicero and Seneca, who, like the writer of IV Maccabees, were greatly influenced by Posidonius. The theme of the book is admirably announced in verses 13-17 of this chapter.

We are inquiring, then, whether reason is sovereign master ["autocrat" in Greek] of the passions. But let us define what reason is and what passion is, and how many forms of passion there are, and whether reason has power over all of these. Reason, then, is thought [or "mind"] based on correct principles, which chooses above all else a life of wisdom. Wisdom, moreover, is the knowledge of things human and divine and their causes. And this is education [or "culture"] acquired from the Law, through which we religiously learn things divine, and for our profit learn things human.

As historical examples of self-control in the face of great provocation or desire the author, in chapters 2 and 3, cites the cases of Moses when angered by Dathan and Abiram, of Jacob when incensed with Simeon and Levi at their cruel treatment of the Shechemites, and of David when his soldiers risked their lives to bring him water after an all-day battle with the Philistines (here our book considerably alters the account given in II Samuel and I Chronicles). In this last instance it gives a vivid impression of David's thirst and of the bravery of the soldiers who sought to bring him water.

But he [David], although burning with thirst, considered that the drink, being equivalent to blood, was a great danger to his soul. He therefore opposed his reason to his desire and poured the drink as a libation to God. For the temperate mind is able to conquer the constraint of passion and to quench the fires of goading desire and to wrestle victoriously with the pains of the body, however overpowering they may be, and by the excellence of reason to spurn the bid for power made by the passions. But now the opportune moment calls us to narrate the story of temperate reason.

With this introduction the narrator launches into the story of the persecution of the Jews by Seleucus IV and his brother (here called son)

Antiochus Epiphanes. In general the narrative follows the contents and order of II Maccabees, but there are many variations in detail and a more extended and philosophical treatment of the martyr episodes. In II Maccabees, for example, the aged Eleazar nobly meets death under torture with a comparatively few defiant words; in IV Maccabees, however, he makes a longer and more didactic speech. Though here the details of the torture and his suffering are realistically and horrifyingly described, the author does not hesitate to represent the aged martyr as taking time to make a philosophical defense of the Mosaic Laws. With a quotation of part of his eloquent address (5:33-38) this brief account of IV Maccabees may fittingly be concluded.

I will not belie thee, O Law, that wast my teacher, nor will I abjure thee, dear Continence, nor will I bring shame upon thee, O wisdom loving Reason, nor deny thee, honored Priesthood and knowledge of the Law. Neither shalt thou, O mouth, defile my revered old age or the years I have spent in living according to the Law. Pure shall my fathers receive me, nor do I fear thy [Antiochus's] torments even unto death. For over impious men thou mayest tyrannize, but neither by words nor by deeds shalt thou be master over my pious reason.

4. *Philo*

Of the Hellenistic Jewish writers whose works have come down to us in part or whole none is so intrinsically worthy of study or, with the possible exception of Josephus, so important in the Western tradition of learning as Philo of Alexandria. Throughout the whole period of scholarship since the Renaissance there has been a continuous and intensive study of his writings by theologians and exegetes. But it has been only during the past few decades that Philo has begun to achieve recognition as a creative or at least historically productive philosopher,[6a] and there has been an ever-increasing number of books and monographs devoted to this aspect of his work. Some indication of the attitude that prevailed half a century ago among historians of ideas is given by the fact that the great German historian of Greek philosophy, Eduard Zeller, in the fourth edition of his magisterial *Philosophie der Griechen* (1903) gives only half as much space to Philo as to Plotinus, and treats Philo as a theologian rather than as a philosopher. By the time this chapter has been published there will have appeared two substantial volumes from the pen of Professor Harry A. Wolfson of Harvard University which will seek to rehabilitate Philo as an original philosophical thinker and to give him his rightful place in the history of that discipline.

We are not concerned here, however, with the problem of whether Philo was primarily a theologian or a philosopher, since the distinction between theology and philosophy had far less, if any, meaning for the intellectuals of Philo's time than for us. What is of greater importance in this connection is the fact that his writings have a threefold value in the study of philosophy. In the first place, they furnish us with a body of thought with which to compare the theology and ethics of Paul and of the Rabbis of Palestine and thus enable us to arrive at a more just estimate of the intellectual climate in which Christianity arose. Second, on closer scrutiny they are revealed as the source of a great part of the synthesis of Hellenism and Judeo-Christian tradition that was effected by the Greek Church Fathers (many of whom liberally quoted or paraphrased Philo's interpretations of Scripture). Third, it was Philo more than any single predecessor of Plotinus who, as Zeller admits (iii. 2.89), gave the first powerful impetus to that fusion of Greek and Oriental thought known as Neoplatonism, which in turn became the inspiration of one of the chief currents of medieval Scholasticism and even of some modern idealistic philosophies.

Apart from the philosophical aspects of Philo's works one must notice the gratifying fact that among religious historians of today there has arisen a new appreciation of the poetry and mystical insights of Philo, which are so pervasive an element in his writings that some scholars have gone so far as to argue that he was primarily a mystic who used Judaism merely as an outer form in which to clothe an esoteric personal religion. Such a view, however, is a distortion of his whole manner of thought and expression and does not correspond to what we know of his practical activity. It is far more reasonable to regard Philo as the most gifted and versatile of those pious Hellenistic Jews who sought to find the highest truths of Greek philosophy, science and religion in the laws of Moses. Like Aristobulus, Pseudo-Aristeas and others, Philo tried to show that a life lived in accordance with the Jewish tradition was not incompatible with the attainment of Greek culture but that Judaism was as full and rich a doctrine as Platonism or Stoicism or Orphism or any combination of pagan beliefs. He further tried to prove that even the rigorous discipline and ceremonial requirements of the Mosaic Law might lead to a devout and unworldly inner life of piety and contemplation.

The little we know of Philo's life is based on a brief paragraph in Josephus and occasional personal remarks in his own writings. He was a resident of Alexandria and must have been born about 20 B.C.E., since he speaks of himself as "an elderly man" at the time of his mission to Rome in 40 C.E. The wealth and prestige of his family are indicated by the facts that his brother Alexander was an important tax official of the Roman government and that one of his nephews, a son of Alexander, was married to a daughter of King Agrippa I, while another nephew, named Tiberius Julius Alexander, was at one time Roman procurator of Judea and later a Roman prefect of Egypt and one of the leading Roman generals who took part in the siege of Jerusalem. Whether Philo quarreled with his brother's son because of his completely anti-Jewish attitude we do not know. Neither do we know whether Philo was throughout his life as active a political figure in the Alexandrian Jewish community as was his apostate nephew in the Roman government. We do know, however, that Philo was head of the Jewish legation sent from Alexandria to Rome in 40 c.e. to protest to the mad Emperor Caligula against the pogrom instigated by Egyptian and Greek anti-Semites and abetted by Roman officials. Incidentally, there is no trustworthy evidence to support the Christian story that while in Rome Philo met the Apostle Peter.

From incidental statements in his writings we learn that, though Philo scrupulously observed Jewish ritual, he attended the Greek theater, athletic contests and chariot races. Moreover, in addition to his firsthand knowledge of the more external aspects of Greek culture, Philo had a wide and deep knowledge, which would have been remarkable even in a Gentile scholar, of Greek poetry and philosophy.

Though we no longer possess the whole of Philo's work, to judge from the catalogue of his writings given by Eusebius we do have a large part of it, amounting to some thirty complete treatises and a large number of fragments. His writings have been variously classified by modern scholars on the bases of chronology, content and motivation (whether addressed primarily to Jews or to Gentiles). The following classification closely follows that made by Leopold Cohn, one of the greatest Philonic scholars of modern times.

I. Writings of Purely Philosophical Content.
These include four treatises: *On the Eternity of the World; That Every Good Man is Free; On Providence* (preserved partly in Greek, wholly in Armenian); *Alexander*, or *That Animals Have Reason* (preserved only in Armenian).

II. Interpretation of the Pentateuch (chiefly Genesis and Exodus).
This body of work is subdivided into three classes.

A. The Allegorical Commentary on Genesis. This is a running commentary on Gen. 2-41, consisting of sixteen treatises, concerned chiefly with the first half of the biblical book.

B. Questions and Answers on Genesis and Exodus. This is a briefer running commentary, preserved only fragmentarily in Greek and much more fully in Armenian. The Armenian version has preserved four of the original six books on Genesis and two of the original five on Exodus.

C. A Historical-Exegetical Commentary on the Mosaic Law. This is not a running commentary, except on the biblical narrative of the Creation, but a systematic treatment of the ethics of the Pentateuch, partly arranged under types of morality symbolized by the Patriarchs and Moses. This systematic work contains the following treatises: *On the Creation of the*

World; On Abraham; On Joseph or *The Statesman; On the Special Laws* (of the Decalogue) in four books with various subtitles.

III. Historical-Apologetic Writings. These include: *On the Life of Moses* in three (originally two) books; *Hypothetica* (preserved only in fragments); *Apology for the Jews* (preserved only in fragments); *On the Contemplative Life* (of the Therapeuts); *Against Flaccus* (the anti-Jewish governor of Egypt); *The Legation to Gaius*. The last two treatises once formed part of a larger work in five books dealing with the Divine punishments visited upon the persecutors of the Jews.

It would be foolish to try to give in the limited space at our disposal even an outline of Philo's metaphysical and ethical and theological doctrines, to say nothing of his views on education and politics. It must suffice to state summarily that Philo, like some of his Alexandrian Jewish predecessors, used whatever Greek philosophical theories were convenient for adaptation to his allegorical interpretation of the Bible, of which the Greek text was regarded by him as no less inspired than the Hebrew original. Thus, to give a few obvious examples, he makes consistent use of the Platonic doctrine that the immaterial ideas are superior to sense-perceived matter, that the world was created as a perfect thing by a benevolent God, and that the ills of human life arise from the victory of sense and passion over reason. From Plato and the Stoics he borrowed the formulation of the idea (though not the idea itself) that reason must control the senses and that through reason, which is a spark of the Divine in man, we can come closer to God. Philo was the first philosopher known to us who achieved any degree of success in harmonizing the idea of an eternal immaterial God with the God of Jewish history, and in showing how a transcendent God came into contact with a material world subject to the changes of time and with the human personality. Philo solves these problems, to his satisfaction and that of many of his Neoplatonic and Christian readers, by assuming that there were intermediaries between God and the world, these being hypostatized physical and moral powers emanating from God Himself. The first intermediary power was the *Logos*, which Philo poetically describes as the eldest son of God (but not in the sense that the Gospel of John has in making the pre-existent Word of God identical with Jesus). The *Logos* in turn produced from itself other powers of God, the royal power and the beneficent power, which remind us of the two *Middot* or attributes of God in Rabbinic theology, the attribute of mercy and the attribute of justice. Like the Rabbis, Philo connects one power with the name "Lord" and the other with the name "God," but differs from them in connecting mercy with "God" and royalty with "Lord" instead of the reverse. The history of the idea of a *Logos*, or immaterial principle, pervading the material world is too complex to be more than mentioned here. But it may be of interest to note that the

Logos plays somewhat the same role in Philo's theology that Torah does in Rabbinic theology.

What is probably of more interest to a casual reader is the ingenuity of Philo's allegorical interpretation of Scripture and his amazingly consistent use of biblical symbols to describe the unresting pilgrimage of the soul to the eternal truth of a God beyond space and time. His great allegory of the patriarchal history and the Mosaic Law is a kind of *Divine Comedy*. Though it is written in prose and without formal literary unity, it has the architectonic quality of Dante's great poetic synthesis of medieval theology and history.

Not only do the more obvious "properties," to borrow a theatrical term, such as the Patriarchs and the sacred cult objects serve Philo as symbols of moral and religious ideas, but even the most neutral and common things mentioned in the Pentateuch, such as rivers, mountains, plants and animals, are all made to play a meaningful part in this dramatic composition. His ability to create a consistent theological pattern out of bits of natural lore, folklore, Pythagorean number-mysticism and a vast assortment of materials constantly astonishes and sometimes wearies the faithful reader of his works.

Just as there is something Dantesque in the sustained dramatic intention of his allegory, so there is something Proustian in the psychological acuteness of his observation of human actions and in the overrich complexity of his discourses on morality and history. Some fifty years ago Claude Montefiore published in the *Jewish Quarterly Review* a delightful anthology of choice passages from Philo that deserves reprinting in more convenient form. The reader who has access to the files of that periodical is urged to read the whole of Montefiore's *Florilegium Philonis*. The following few passages, chosen independently by the present writer, are given not with a view to making a miniature anthology of the most appealing passages in Philo but merely to illustrate some of his characteristics.

The first selection is from Philo's later and briefer commentary on Genesis and Exodus, called *Questions and Answers* (preserved only in Armenian except for a few score incomplete paragraphs). This particular passage, from Book II:42, takes the biblical verse, Genesis 8:11, part of the story of the flood, and draws from it, as a magician might from a plain hat, a variety of colorful interpretations. The verse reads, "And the dove returned again to him at eventide; holding an olive-leaf, a dry branch" ("dry branch" is Philo's interpretation of the "plucked branch" of Scripture). Let us see how Philo skilfully transforms each of these simple words into complex symbols.

All these are chosen symbols and tests: The "returning again," the "at evening," the "bearing an olive-leaf," the "dry branch," the "oil" and the "in its mouth." But the several symbols must be studied in detail. Now the return is distinguished from the earlier flight. For the latter brought the report of a nature altogether corrupt and rebellious and one destroyed by the flood, that is, by great ignorance and lack of education. But the other repents of its beginning. And to find repentence is not easy but a very difficult and laborious task. For these reasons it comes at evening, having passed the whole day from early morning until evening in inspection, in word by passing through various places, but in actuality by looking over and inspecting the parts of its nature and in seeing these clearly from beginning to end. And the third symbol is "bearing a leaf." The leaf is a small part of a plant. However, it does not come into being without the plant. And similar to this it is to begin to repent. For the beginning of improvement gives a slight indication, as if it were a leaf, that it is to be guarded and can also be shaken off. But there is great hope that it will attain correction of its ways. The fourth symbol is that the leaf was of no other tree than the olive. And oil is the material of light. For evil, as I have said, is profound darkness, but virtue is a most radiant splendor. And repentance is the beginning of light. But do not think that the beginning of repentance is already in blossoming and growing things, but only while they are still dry and arid do they have a seminal principle. Wherefore the fifth symbol is that when it [the dove] came, it bore a "dry branch." And the sixth symbol is that the dry branch was "in its mouth," since six is the first perfect number. For virtue bears in its mouth, that is, in its speech, the seeds of wisdom and justice and altogether goodness of soul. And not only does it bear these gifts but it also gives a share in them to outsiders, offering water to their souls, and watering with repentance their desire for sin.

An aspect of Philo's thought which has no parallel in extant Hellenistic Jewish literature is his frequent use of the terms and ideas used in the pagan mystery-cults which professed to enable the initiate to be reborn and by divesting himself of earthly encumbrances to come into ecstatic union with a savior-god such as Dionysius or Osiris or Mithra. Philo's conception of mystical union with the Divine was less physical and emotionally primitive than that found in even the most spiritualized pagan mysteries, partly because Philo's God was less personal and more transcendent than Greek-Oriental gods, and partly because his healthy Jewish instinct or training kept him from too exalted or irrational a flight into unreality. The dangers of substituting pure symbolism for a life of active and traditional piety enriched by symbolism are pointed out in one of the more frequently quoted passages from Philo, *On the Migration of Abraham* (89 ff.), which reads in part:

There are some who take the literal laws as symbols of intellectual matters, and while they are overscrupulous about the latter, they carelessly neglect the former. Such men I for my part would blame for their offhandedness. They ought to give attention to both things . . . We should have to neglect the holy service of the temple and a thousand other things if we gave thought only to the things revealed in their deeper sense. Rather should we look on these [outward] things as resembling the body, and the other [inner] things as resembling the soul. Now just as we have to take thought for the body as the dwelling-place of the soul, so we have to pay attention to the letter of the laws, for if we keep them we shall have a clearer notion of the things which they symbolize, and at the same time we shall escape the blame and reproach of the multitude.

What seems to a modern reader most salutary in his writing is his adherence to a doctrine that while the senses are not to be completely suppressed they are to be constantly controlled by reason and that through this same reason the soul can be possessed by a mystical rapture. It is no mere use of picturesque quotation but sober truth to say that long before Spinoza the unique beauty of "the intellectual love of God" was celebrated by Philo. The following passage, from the *Sacred Allegories* (i. 39 ff.), illustrates Philo's belief that the soul achieves mystical rapture not by intoxication or other disturbances of normal behavior, as in the pagan mysteries, but by submerging the senses in a flood of reason, a flood that wells up from the hidden sources of the Mosaic Law rightly understood and practiced. The passage is a commentary on Gen. 2:7, "And God formed man by taking clay from the earth and breathed into his face the breath of life; and the man became a living soul."

Philo comments as follows:

There are two kinds of men, one the heavenly man, the other earthly . . . We must account the man made of earth to be mind in the process of being mixed with body but not already mixed. This earthly mind is in reality corruptible except that God breathes into it a power of true life . . . God projects the power that comes from Him through the mediating breath [or wind] till it reaches the subject. And for what other purpose is this than that we may obtain a conception of Him, for how could the soul have conceived of God if He had not breathed into it and seized it through His power? . . . For the mind imparts to the irrational part of the soul a share of that which it has received from God, so that the mind is besouled by God while the irrational part is besouled by the mind. For the mind is, as it were, the God of the irrational part, just as Scripture does not hesitate to speak of Moses as "a God to Pharaoh."

Of Philo's poetic metaphysics we have a good example in the treatise *On Creation* (20 ff.), where he compares the creation of the world through the instrumentality of the *Logos* with the planning of a city by an architect using charts which set down the ideal city he has in mind and from which he proceeds to build the actual city. The same idea of the divine architect is found in Plato's *Timaeus* and in the Rabbinic work *Bereshit Rabbah*, but Philo's metaphor is more sustained and more vivid. A part of the passage in Philo reads as follows:

Similarly one must think about God, that when He was minded to found the great city [*i.e.*, the world], He first conceived of the types of its parts, and from these He wrought an intelligible [*i.e.*, ideal] world, which He used as a model for the sensible [*i.e.*, visible] world. And just as the city formed within [the mind of] the architect has no place outside him but has been engraved in his soul as by a seal, so also the world of ideas would have had no other place than the Divine *Logos* which made this ordered world.

It is a great pity that lack of space makes it impossible to comment on many other aspects of Philo's work and to illustrate these by quotations. Perhaps this brief study can best be concluded with a quotation from the treatise *On the Change of Names* (39 ff.), which shows that this mystical thinker was not concerned solely with his own salvation but was also constantly mindful of his fellow man.

These men are possessed by a divine madness and live a wild and solitary life. But there are others who are familiars of a gentle and tame wisdom. They practice piety eminently and do not despise human things. This is attested by the oracle in which it is said to Abraham out of the mouth of God (Gen. 17:1), "Be well-pleasing before Me." "This means 'not to Me only but to My works also [*i.e.*, other human beings], while I as judge watch and oversee thee'" . . . And so Moses in his exhortations gives this charge (Deut. 12:28), "Thou shalt do what is well-pleasing before the Lord thy God," which means that you should do such things as shall be worthy to appear before God and which he will see and approve; such deeds are likely to be well-pleasing to our fellows as well.

NOTES

[1a Cf. above Elias J. Bickerman, "The Historical Foundations of Post-biblical Judaism," pp. 97-101.]
[2a Cf. above Judah Goldin, "The Talmudic Period," p. 143.]
[3a Cf. *ibid.* pp. 116-117.]
[4a Cf. Bickerman, *op. cit.*, pp. 95-96, 97-99.]
[5a Cf. above Robert Gordis, "The Bible as a Cultural Monument," pp. 482-487.]
[6a Cf. above Alexander Altmann, "Judaism and World Philosophy," pp. 625 ff.]

BIBLIOGRAPHICAL NOTE

A

The English reader will find the books here discussed most conveniently edited and translated in the following works:

The apocryphal and pseudepigraphic books are well translated and provided with instructive introductions and notes by various scholars in R. H.

Charles (ed.), *The Apocrypha and Pseudepigrapha of the Old Testament*. 2 vols. Oxford, 1913.

The best English translation of Josephus is that in the Loeb Classical Library, London, of which seven volumes have appeared to the present time: Vols. 1-4 were translated by the late Henry St. John Thackeray. Vols. 5-7 by Ralph Marcus.

The best English translation of Philo is also that in the Loeb Classical Library, of which nine volumes have appeared: Vols. 1-5 were translated by F. H. Colson and G. H. Whitaker, Vols. 6-9 by F. H. Colson.

The fragments of the Hellenistic Jewish writers will be found in the work of Wallace N. Stearns, *Fragments from Graeco-Jewish Writers*. Chicago, 1908.

B

The following books will be of interest to those wishing to have more detailed discussions of some of the writers here treated.

NORMAN BENTWICH, *Philo Judaeus of Alexandria*. Philadelphia, 1910. Though now antiquated in some respects, this book is still useful because of its abundance of information and its excellent judgment. Moreover, it is written in attractive style.

ERWIN R. GOODENOUGH, *Introduction to Philo Judaeus*. New Haven, 1940. The author, a well-known Philonist of Yale University, always writes in a stimulating and illuminating way though not all of his views are to be accepted.

CLAUDE G. MONTEFIORE, "Florilegium Philonis," in *Jewish Quarterly Review*, VII, 481 545. London, 1894-1895. The excellence of this anthology has already been mentioned.

ROBERT H. PFEIFFER, *Introduction to the Old Testament*. New York, 1941. A comprehensive and authoritative, though somewhat technical, study of Old Testament literature with valuable chapters on versions of the Bible and excellent bibliographies, including apocryphal literature.

HARRY A. WOLFSON, *Philo: Foundations of Religious Philosophy, Judaism, Christianity and Islam*. 2 vols. Cambridge, 1947.

Since this bibliography was prepared in 1946, Professor Harry A. Wolfson's monumental work on Philo has appeared. It should therefore be added to this original list.

CHAPTER 18

JUDEO-ARABIC LITERATURE

By Abraham S. Halkin

Judeo-Arabic literature comprises works composed in Arabic, almost always in Hebrew script, by Jewish authors who lived in lands where Arabic was the dominant language. More specifically the title is applied to the output of authors from, roughly, the ninth to the thirteenth century. But if one were to write a comprehensive history of Judeo-Arabic literature, one would extend the limits at both ends, to the sixth century and to our own time, respectively.

The most striking aspect of this literary activity is its variety of subject matter and its novel approach. Jewish creativity, which for centuries had confined itself to religious themes, so that even purely literary material was clothed in a religious garb, developed a catholicity of expression which included medicine, mathematics and other sciences, philosophy, history. Under the same impetus, secular poetry and belles-lettres appeared in Hebrew. Even within the field of religion new disciplines were introduced. Investigation of Hebrew grammar was pursued far more seriously than at any time in the past, commentaries were written to explain the Bible text and systematic codification of the law occupied the minds of great talmudists.

Before we undertake to account for this efflorescence it is important to know something of the environment within which the literature developed, to appreciate the economic, political and cultural conditions under which the Jews labored. They lived in a world which was predominantly Moslem in religion and Arabic in vernacular. Judged by any standard and, particularly, by the conditions prevailing in non-Moslem regions, this world was quite comfortable.[1a] Upon the payment of a special tax, collected from all *Dhimmis* (non-Moslems who were permitted to live by their faith), they were not harassed on religious grounds, nor did they, save for isolated occasions, suffer from any serious disability. They were privileged to engage in all economic activities, including services in the administration. They were not segregated and thus came in contact with the non-Jewish population. Moreover, politically they benefited from the characteristic concept of the state in medieval times, especially in Moslem lands. The Islamic state was a theocracy, and its head a representative or successor (caliph) of the prophet. The Koran, which is the revealed Book of the followers of Mohammed, was the source of all Islamic law. Like Judaism, it did not distinguish between a civil and an ecclesiastical law, different from each other in origin. Both were derived from the same religious sources. To be a member of the Moslem body politic was a privilege which only adherents of that faith could enjoy. Non-Moslems lived under the protection of the dominant group as a result of a special agreement between the sovereign church-state and them. The state was organized along religious lines. The dominant group possessed the right to administer the state and to regulate its affairs. But the tolerated religious minorities, in addition to the guarantee of the right of domicile, of earning a livelihood, and of the safeguarding of life and limb, were also granted internal autonomy. All matters in which the state had no direct interest would be regulated within these units by their duly authorized administrators, in conformity with the laws of the particular group. As a result, it was possible for a non-Moslem individual not only to share in the rights and privileges that belong inherently to a human being, but also to identify himself with his own group and participate in its life and functions.

Undoubtedly, the political theory of the Islamic state, or even its application, did not eliminate difficulties or friction among the several sections of the population. We know of a considerable amount of animosity, of literary polemics, of religious persecutions, and of occasional outbreaks of violence. In Jewish writings we read complaints of the state of exile, and yearnings for the restoration of Zion and the realization of Messianic hopes. While such themes were to some extent conventional, they certainly indicate some dissatisfaction with conditions as they were. The pathetic terms in which the highly placed and wealthy Jewish public official, Hasdai ben Shaprut, expresses his readiness to come and kneel before the distant Jewish king of the Khazars, or the pitiful plaints of oppression by Christians and Moslems which resound so loudly in the writings of the Jewish poets of Spain, certainly reveal an awareness of being alien and the existence of difficulty and trouble. Yet, in general, life under Moslem rule was as comfortable a one as the Jews have ever had under foreign domination, and the average individual probably found little to complain of on religious grounds.

The Arab-speaking world within which the Jews lived was the most cultured center of medieval times. Having absorbed through conquest the civilized centers of Christianity and Zoroastrianism—within which Greek culture, in modified form, no doubt, had previously continued its existence after the classical period—the Arabs became disciples, and set about learning what the two civilizations of East and West had to offer. A wave of translations marks the ninth and tenth centuries, in the course of which scientific and philosophic writings of the ancients were rendered into

Arabic. Thanks to the interest of enlightened caliphs, the efforts of zealous translators, and the gratitude of a substantial body of readers and students, the Arabic-reading public fell heir to the scientific and philosophic thought of the Greeks, the Syrians, the Persians and the Hindus. The new cultural possessions served as the groundwork for a ramified and intensive pursuit of study and enlightenment among the Moslems. In the wake of the translated texts, original works in Arabic followed in the same fields, and thus the Greek cultural tradition, with all its modifications, found its redeemer and heir in the lively activity in which the Moslems were now engaged. In all this literary productivity neither ethnic nor religious boundaries interfered. Although literary polemics abounded along both national and religious lines, the efforts of the numerous men of letters, of diverse national and religious origin, all contributed to the enhancement and enrichment of Arabic literature. As a result, during the centuries when Western, and even Eastern, Christendom passed through the so-called Dark Ages, the vast Moslem empire, particularly after its decentralization into several states, housed learning and enlightenment. Indeed, the eventual awakening of Christian Europe, the age of Scholasticism, and the subsequent Renaissance are indebted to the impetus given by Islam.

The Jewish communities in the Moslem countries had, of course, a long cultural history behind them. In Mesopotamia, Palestine, Egypt, North Africa and Spain, all now dominated by rulers who professed Islam, the Jews possessed, to a greater or lesser degree, the Rabbinic literature produced over the many centuries from the beginning of the Common Era or earlier to the rise of Islam. With all allowance made for external influences in the centers where this literature was created, it cannot be denied that it bears a native Jewish stamp. It is Jewish in spirit, in emphasis, in form. The successive additions to the cultural treasures, visible as the effect of foreign ideas and environments may be, are all—with the possible exception of the esoteric literature of that period—genuinely Jewish, natural and logical outgrowths of the earlier strata to which they are added.

As time passed, these Jewish communities found themselves increasingly within a milieu which, religiously, was akin to their own and, culturally, challenged their self-sufficiency. As no hard and fast social, economic or political boundary lines separated them from their Moslem countrymen, they responded to the lure and challenge of the larger world within which they were continuing their Jewish existence. They gradually abandoned Aramaic, which had been their vernacular, and became speakers of Arabic; they studied works in Arabic; nor did they limit themselves to translations from other languages into it. They also read and learned original writings in poetry, history and grammar. They even studied the Koran. In a word, they went through a profound process of adaptation to the environments.

As a result, the cultural history of the Jews in Moslem countries necessarily followed new paths. New interests and problems engaged the intellectuals, and they found expression in a multitude of works written in Arabic and Hebrew. The Moslem world is not the only instance in Jewish history where the Jewish way of life encountered another which it regarded with interest and was impelled to emulate. Both before and after there were occasions when Jews came in contact with a civilization which had much to offer and from which they gladly took. There have been environmental conditions other than the Moslem where Jews looked to the environment with respect and felt themselves called upon to defend and justify their adherence and loyalty to their way of life before themselves and the larger world. Yet, if we exclude modern Hebrew and Yiddish literatures, which have their own causes and explanations,[2a] and cannot therefore figure in this generalization, the Arabic period is the only one where this contact resulted in a lasting and positive contribution to the Jewish cultural heritage, and produced works which have been recognized and revered by Jews of other days and other lands.

For an explanation of this phenomenon it is necessary to dwell briefly on the character of the civilization that developed within Islam. It has already been stated that Greek culture came into this world from the outside. Its presence confronted the adherents of Islam with the problem of adjustment. Greek ideas of God, of man, of the world, and of their relation to one another, were not at all like the basic conceptions in the Koran or the subsequent literature that elaborated upon it. And while the majority of Moslems knew little about the imported ideas and cared less, and, on the other hand, some individuals may have been so completely captivated by them as to divorce themselves entirely from the traditional faith, a large number of intelligent and honest people found themselves in the throes of an inner conflict. The situation paralleled to an extent that which existed for Hellenistic Jewry.[3a] This section in Islam was driven by the philosophic discussions and doctrines of Greek origin not only to ponder and analyze religious dogmas and problems which were either nonexistent in the native Moslem world or definitely stated and put beyond question but also to agree with a good deal of what was taught by the ancient philosophers. But when this happened, a reconciliation was made necessary between what was rationally acceptable to them and what they received on faith. The result was a theology which made some concessions to philosophic method and discipline, and a philosophy which nominally paid homage to religion, but essentially adhered to the truths it inherited from the classical environment. It cannot be truthfully said that the compromise was a success, when objectively studied; it may even be doubted whether a compromise is possible. But it worked for a time, and in one form or another it won adherents.

The experiences of the Moslems were an inestimable boon to the Jewish communities in that world. The issues they later had to face were almost identical with those confronting the dominant group of that time. The problem that both groups were called upon to solve was to establish peace and harmony between two truths: the truth of religion and the truth of philosophy. The product of the peace was not a real synthesis in which the two components were integrated. Whether religion was the core and philosophy the veneer, or *vice versa*, it was not difficult to discern the dichotomy, the dualism that remained, although the two were seemingly poured into one mold. Moreover, the compromise was not one which was adopted by all adherents of Islam. Many remained the same simple believers their forefathers had been, hostile to the encroachment of philosophy on their precious holdings. But some saw clearly the logical conclusions to which philosophic speculation led, and remained faithful to them, even if they were ready to pay lip service to the accepted tenets of the faith, and appreciated the benefits it bestowed on the uninitiated. All this facilitated the problem of the Jews. The dominant civilization remained a religious one. This naturally made the Jewish religion secure among its followers. There was no group with which one could have identified oneself without involving one's religion. There was no trend away from the religious outlook to a secular point of view which left religion, or the lack of it, to the conscience of the individual. As for that section of Jewry which, like its counterpart in Islam, was faced by a problem of reconciliation, it, too, profited by the discernible dichotomy in the Moslem compromise. All that it was necessary to do was to replace the Moslem component in the theology with the Jewish one. For better or worse, whatever fate the Moslem achievement would enjoy within its domain would be shared by the Jewish one within its realm. In this way a guarantee of survival and vitality was provided for the Jewish way of life by the experiences of the Moslem way of life.

Thus it happened that the encounter of Judaism within the world of Islam with the Greek tradition was a positive beneficial influence. It acted as a leaven, stimulating activity in fields not hitherto cultivated and suggesting new directions and points of view in previously pursued activities. It opened the eyes of Jewish students to secular subjects: to medicine, to mathematics, to history. It aroused Jewish interest in secular poetry and in literary prose. It fostered a rational approach to religious prescriptions, whether of creed or of deed. It instilled a love of style and form, of systematization and organization. It added much, very much that was new to Jewish culture, but it did not shake the foundations of Judaism. Jewish civilization became much more variegated, much more diverse, but it remained Jewish. Not only were the authors and creators of that culture thoroughly Jewish in their background and in their knowledge of

Jewish literature, or in their profession of their Jewish faith and in their observance of its commandments, but they also exhibited their Jewishness in their writings. Even in books which were totally devoid of Jewish content, such as books on medicine or on some other science, an introduction was included in which the gratitude to God and other items testified to the author's group and religious affiliation. In addition, an occasional reference to a biblical or talmudic matter indicated the religion of the author.

The adaptation, beneficial as it was, also produced some negative effects. Of necessity it failed to discriminate between emulation and imitation. The positive gains also showed an obverse side which was not so commendable. The new vistas that opened before them through the acquisition of Arabic led to an attitude toward Hebrew which was not quite wholesome. One writer actually seeks to justify the composition by Saadia Gaon of a work in Hebrew. Another keeps harping on the relative poverty of Hebrew as compared with Arabic. The admiration of Moslem achievements or, perhaps more correctly, the trend of assimilation, led to some surprising and distasteful manifestations. The Koran was transcribed in Hebrew characters, evidently for people who could not read Arabic script. A fortune book exists in Hebrew which lists Mohammed as one of the Prophets. Other strange facts indicate similarly the relaxation of the Jewish way of life, sometimes all the way to "the dogmatic barrier between Judaism and Islam," and occasionally even beyond that.

The tensions and strains within Islam in its process of adjustment, the rationalism that penetrated from without and was so disturbing yet so persuasive, the individual investigations and interpretations of religion that, in this realm, are very significant, marking as they do the assertion of the individual in the face of sacred tradition, even if nominally it is within the framework of that tradition—all these found their parallels within Judaism in thought and in literature as well as in deed. The condition generated a sectarianism which produced little and insignificant schisms, and also a large and threatening party like the Karaites. It gave rise to many questionings, doubts and perplexities to which the works of medieval Jewish philosophers bear witness, and an intellectualism which at least in some cases was tantamount to a rejection of the cardinal principles of Judaism. At any rate, this intellectualism is potentially at least always a threat to the wholehearted, sincere and unquestioning faith of the simple believers. It may even be that the behavior of the Jews of Spain some centuries later, in the catastrophes of 1391 and subsequently,[4a] so strikingly different from the martyrdom of the Franco-German Jews in 1096 or 1348, has its explanation in this "liberalism." These and other alarming signs and effects are true enough; but they do not alter the fact of the rich and ramified productivity that is the subject of this chapter.

In their writings, the Jewish authors who lived in Islamic lands em-

ployed two languages. Poetry and a small part of their prose were composed in Hebrew. But the bulk of the prose and a little of the poetry were
written in Arabic. The quality of the language is generally colloquial. It
becomes apparent, from a study of the work, that the authors paid but little
attention to the artistic aspect of their composition, and did not strive to
imitate models in style and eloquence, as did their Moslem contemporaries.
Their language is clearly akin to the speech of the environment, except
for the peculiarly Jewish expressions and the Hebrew words and phrases
that found their way into Arabic as they have into every other language
spoken by Jews. By the use of the vernacular even in tracts on law or commentaries on the Bible the Jews in Moslem countries distinguish themselves from their contemporaries in Christian lands who did not employ
their daily language for writing, and resemble Jews in modern times in
Western countries who likewise utilize the language of the land for
specifically Jewish works. (It may be said in passing that the similarity
between the two civilizations manifests itself in other aspects as well, as
any comparison will show.) This unhesitating readiness to write in a
language other than Hebrew demonstrates of course an identification with
environment which was not reached in other lands, and a rather remarkable
lack of consciousness of the importance of the medium of expression. That
the problem presented itself to them is evident from the regrets and
protests over the neglect of Hebrew voiced by individuals who themselves
composed works in Arabic. They were also undoubtedly familiar with a
Rabbinic word of praise for the Jews in ancient Egypt who were redeemed
because they had not abandoned their language. Yet they continued to use
Arabic. Reasons have of course been advanced, such as, for example, the
desire of the author to reach the widest audience possible. This may be
true in one instance or another, but we ought not to exaggerate its
applicability. There is no reason to assume that the masses in Islamic
countries were more interested in matters intellectual than in other
centers at other times, or that the authors were so democratically minded
or so unaware of the cultural gradations as to strive to reach everyone.
Maimonides specifically declares in the introduction to his *Guide* that he
does not desire to have his work on philosophy fall into the hands of the
masses, or even of the whole intellectual group within them. Moreover,
one may venture the assertion that the readers who were mature and
sufficiently interested to read and study these books could read Hebrew
with the same fluency as Arabic. Another reason which has been offered
may again be partly true though it is not cogent. The inadequacy of
Hebrew for expressing what they had to, allegedly prompted authors to
fall back on Arabic. But this argument, too, is not strong. Had the desire
existed, the way would have been found. It was found by translators into
Arabic who had to adapt their language to the logic and the syntax of

Greek and had to coin a new vocabulary. It was found by later translators from Arabic into Hebrew who succeeded in developing a terminology and a style to meet the exigencies of the undertaking, and it could have been found by the authors themselves. Again Maimonides may be cited, who, in the first part of his major Hebrew work on Jewish law, gives an eloquent example of his facility in Hebrew, a facility which is unquestionably superior to that of his subsequent translators. The most probable explanation is that they did it because it was the most natural and the most effortless thing to do. Furthermore, they probably did not feel that in compositions on science the language selected preserved an ideological importance as in the case of artistic creations.

The almost consistent use of Hebrew in poetry also is an interesting problem. The naturalness of which we spoke should certainly have asserted itself in their poetic writings, in which the individuality of the writer comes to the fore. It is hardly correct, however, to suggest, as has been done, that the lyric character of poetry made the use of Hebrew imperative because the poet was compelled to sing in the language with which he felt himself most intimate. It simply goes against the facts to assume that Arabic, which they spoke from birth and used in all situations, was less their most intimate vehicle than Hebrew, which was an externally acquired medium. The explanation is to be sought more plausibly in the character of their poetry. It was considered by the people of the time as an art which approached perfection in proportion to its excellence in externals: rhythm, rhyme, language and various skills in the handling of the language. Technique, in other words, was the most important endowment of the artist, and his poetic talent an additional gift. It is to be remembered that, unlike their prose, the poetry of the Jews was grounded in an old tradition, much older than the impact of Islam. The origins of medieval poetry[5a] are to be sought in the liturgical compositions of earlier days. Since those were all written in Hebrew, a precedent was established which was maintained in later days not only in sacred but also in secular compositions. Furthermore, Moslem poetry, more perhaps than any other genre of their literature, was regarded by Moslems as a national expression, a genuinely Arab creation. It was the preferred vehicle for showing off the glory of Arabic and singing the praises of the Arabs. Jews very likely reacted by displaying a pride in their language, in its glories, its antiquity and its tradition. There may also have been involved a religious issue. The Koran was accepted by Moslems as a literary masterpiece, and although the models were pre-Islamic poets, the holy book was nevertheless respected as an ideal. One of the dogmas of orthodox Islam is that the Koran is a miracle, both because of its revelation and because of its inimitable style. It provoked among the Jews a natural desire to lean on their greatest literary masterpiece, to draw on the Hebrew Bible, and to benefit from its perfection.

Among the basic productions in Judeo-Arabic literature we must undoubtedly include the translation of the Bible. Apart from its significance as a barometer of the conquest of Arabic, to the loss of Hebrew and Aramaic, comparable to a similar phenomenon in other countries— Hellenistic Egypt or the English-speaking communities—it is further important as evidence of the interest in the Bible which led to a large output of studies connected with it and the Hebrew language. The written translations were probably an outgrowth of oral traditions with their local variations. Hence the similarity in terminology among several translations which otherwise show some divergences. The best known version is that of the great and many-sided scholar Saadia ben Joseph al-Fayyumi (882-942),[6a] who, though actively participating in Jewish affairs of his day and even assuming leadership, nevertheless wrote on many subjects. He seems to have rendered almost all, if not all, of the Bible into Arabic, even if to date a comparatively small portion of his work is known. While he may have been prompted by certain apologetic motives, such as the desire to display proudly before the non-Jewish world the grandeur of Jewish Scriptures—achieved by the apparent employment of Arabic script in his version—or the wish to make the Bible palatable to intellectuals who might have objected to some rationally unacceptable items in the Sacred Text, his primary goal seems to have been to render this necessary service to a public which had no access to the Bible other than through Arabic. In his work he strove consistently to present a smooth-reading, logically arranged text. With this in mind, he took certain liberties with the original, inserting words and phrases, eliminating repetitions, and occasionally offering somewhat free renderings. He was particularly aware of the need of modifying all references to God which might hurt the sensibilities of a rationally minded person, such as himself, who conceived of God in a highly philosophic and abstract manner. And while he believed that the chief duty of a translator or a commentator was to adhere to the literal text, he asserted unequivocally that a free translation or interpretation was required whenever the literal text appeared contrary to sensual experience or to reason, to another specific statement in the Bible or to authoritative tradition. Besides Saadia's we possess remnants or complete versions by other translators, both Rabbanite and Karaite, but there is little point in either listing or characterizing them.

However, a bare translation provides only a meager understanding of biblical literature. Apart from the need for an interpretation of difficult passages, which should be fuller and longer than a translation, there were other factors which made commentary writing on the Bible a necessity.

The Bible, which was accepted by Judaism as its guide in life, was, as is known, interpreted and thus expanded by the Rabbis in order to yield that vast harvest which is termed the Oral Law. While no commentator could venture to include in his commentary all the Oral Law that he believed to be implicit in the Bible, he undoubtedly regarded it as his duty to interpret biblical passages in the spirit of Rabbinic Judaism, particularly where the failure to do so might lead to a wrong conclusion. Care also had to be exerted to take note of and refute unorthodox explanations that were circulated in large quantity by the Karaite sect, which was virile and aggressive in the ninth and tenth centuries.[7a] One may cite in illustration a discussion between Saadia and a Karaite regarding the meaning of "an eye for an eye." Saadia not only renders it "the value of an eye for an eye," as expected—since this is Rabbinic—but seeks to demonstrate that it is the only rationally tenable interpretation. The Karaite, on the contrary, disputes his rendering. The celebrated medieval polygraph, Abraham ibn Ezra, who reports this debate, realizing that no rational proof is possible, concludes with this comment: "We are unable to explain the laws of the Torah correctly unless we depend on the words of the Sages. For in the same way that we have received the Written Law from the ancients we have also received the Oral Law. There is no difference between them." This point of view necessitated a reinterpretation of the Bible in at least its prescriptive portions. The need of commentaries was felt on still another ground. The Bible, which is central in Jewish life, and regarded as the last word in truth, was not unnaturally viewed by each age as the repository of whatever it accepted as valid. In other words, as the scientific and philosophic truths developed and changed from age to age, the adherents of these evolving truths were always intent on finding them in the Bible. Since the period during which Judeo-Arabic literature was written was strongly under the influence of Greek thought in its medieval garb, it strove to read its beliefs and doctrines into the Bible. This, too, made commentary writing a basic need.

The outstanding commentator who wrote in Arabic is the previously mentioned Saadia. He composed either complete commentaries or selected notes probably on the whole Bible. These products, to the extent to which they are known to us, are masterpieces in their field. It is evident that Saadia's chief aim was to clarify. With this in mind he appended introductions to the various books, in which, from a philosophic point of view, he undertook to elucidate the purpose of the book, its method, its teachings and its plan. In his commentaries on the first half of the Five Books of Moses (it was completed by Samuel ben Hofni, see below) he is much more prolix than in the other books. The reason for it lies in the central position of the Torah in Jewish life and the consequent need for elaboration. In addition to the obvious task of explaining what is not clear, he also supplied grammatical notes whenever a knotty language problem arose, he sought to rationalize incidents and events which taxed men's credulity, and endeavored to raise the level of what sounds mythical to a philosophic plane. He is particularly ardent, in his Pentateuch commentary, in his defense of Rabbinic tradition, and in its counterpart, the attack on the Karaites, the opponents and critics of that tradition. In his commentaries on the other books he is noticeably briefer and sparser so that his explanations are in the form of occasional notes and not of a full commentary.

Another important commentator who lived in the Orient is Samuel ben Hofni, head of the Sura Academy (d. 1013).[8a] He prepared an Arabic translation of the Pentateuch, generally more literal than Saadia's, completed Saadia's commentary on the Pentateuch and wrote a commentary on it, and perhaps also on other books of the Bible. He was lengthy in his explanations, giving little attention to linguistic matters, but elaborating on various topics related to the verse or subject under discussion. He was an exponent of rationalism in his exegesis, but he accepted the halakic interpretation of the Bible and believed, contrary to Saadia's view, that all laws could be arrived at rationally. Unlike his critical attitude to the wonders related in the Talmud, he conceded the literal truth of the biblical miracles. But his rationalism forced him to approach certain biblical matters in a manner which aroused opposition. He rejected astrology and necromancy, and hence considered the success of the Witch of Endor a clever trick, and the performance of Joseph's cup the result of some mechanism with which it was equipped. He explained all dreams naturally, even those which were prophetic in character. By the same sober reasoning, however, he also shunned the discovery of the philosophy of his day in the words of the Bible.

Moslem Spain from the eleventh century on overshadows the Orient as a center of Jewish activities, and the Bible commentators of that period were almost all residents of Spain. Judah ibn Balam (c. 1080) wrote commentaries on most if not all of the Bible. An interesting light is shed on his conception of the function of a commentator by this statement of his: "I acceded to his request [i.e., of the man who asked him for an explanation of the ambiguous and difficult words which occur in the Bible], knowing that this undertaking involves three requisites: (1) that I render each word by the most approximate equivalent which Arabic furnishes; (2) that I cite in evidence other texts in the Bible where the same root is employed or, if such are not available, support from the ancients or from Aramaic or Arabic; (3) that I explain the inflection and syntax of the word. . . . As an additional favor to him I shall mention, besides, some interpretations which belong there and which come to mind, whether they are taken from others or derived from my own reasoning." While he does not display much originality in his explanations, his commentaries are valuable because of their eclectic character. We find numerous grammatical notes as well as exegetic comments. He had a faculty for conciseness and organization of his material. He was critical of Saadia, whom he accuses of violence to the Arabic in his translations. He was rather free in condemnation of others, and was not restrained in his remarks. He sometimes attacked his master, Jonah ibn Janah to whom he is indebted for a great deal, much of it without due acknowledgment. His chief target was his contemporary Moses ibn Chiquitilla, whom he criticized for his excessive rationalism. But it is his merit that he did not hesitate to admit his inability to give an adequate explanation of a word or phrase when such was the case.

Moses Ha-Cohan ibn Chiquitilla is unfortunately represented to modern scholarship by relatively few remnants culled from others who cited his explanations. He seems to have written commentaries on the bulk of the Bible, but unlike those of his younger contemporary, ibn Balam, whose works have survived in large part, ibn Chiquitilla's seem to have perished. From the little that remains it is possible to draw certain conclusions regarding his method. He attempted to apply all prophetic predictions to the immediate time of the Prophet rather than to a distant Messianic future. Accordingly, not only general prophecies but apparently Messianic sayings were related to the time of the Prophet who spoke them. The oracles of Isaiah, for example, in which he looks forward to an age of universal peace, refer, according to ibn Chiquitilla, to the time of King Hezekiah. He also made every effort to explain miracles rationally. In an apparently oral dialogue between himself and ibn Balam he denied that at Joshua's bidding the sun and moon ceased their revolutions, "for it is impossible for perpetual motion ever to be interrupted," and explained that the miracle consisted in the continued reflection of the sun even after its setting. By virtue of his enlightened approach to his work he did not hesitate to assign to sections of the Bible dates which run contrary to tradition. He believed that the chapters in Isaiah from 40 on form a separate section. While it may not be warranted to credit him with the recognition of a "Second Isaiah," he sensed the difference between the two portions of the book. He recognized a number of psalms to be of exilic date. In short, it may be stated that ibn Chiquitilla is a clear example of the rational, enlightened spirit of the Jewish-Arabic age as it manifested itself in exegesis.

But the rationalism that characterizes the commentaries of Saadia or ibn Chiquitilla was carried much further by a school of exegetes which adopted the views of Aristotelian philosophy. The beginnings of this extreme intellectualism were made by men who wrote in Arabic. Indeed, the Nestor of this school was the great Maimonides, who, without devoting much of his time and energy to the field of exegesis, indicated the lines it was to follow. The method employed by this school is that known as allegory, *i.e.*, the presumption that the Bible stated abstract truths and concepts in the form of stories, of personalities or of other figures of speech. Its tradition is old and venerable, going back to Rabbinic times, but its consistent application and, perhaps, the assumption that it is the real purport of the Bible, is the contribution of the disciples of Maimonides. The master himself is wrongly credited with an interpretation of Psalm 45, originally apparently a wedding song, which converts the entire chapter into a philosophic discourse. A few remarks by him on some verses in the Song of Songs make it clear that this booklet was conceived by him as a highly philosophic allegory of the Soul and the Active Intellect. The latter interpretation was executed in detail in the lengthy Arabic commentary on the book by Maimonides's contemporary, Joseph ibn Aknin. However, the full results of this method of exegesis became evident in a series of commentaries written in Hebrew by admirers of Maimonides who lived in Provence or in Italy.

The Orient likewise produced a commentator who was an ardent disciple of Maimonides, but his exegesis was by no means one-sidedly allegorical. Tanhum ben Joseph of Jerusalem (d. after 1260) wrote a commentary probably on the entire Bible, and his work is still extant, in whole or in part, or is at least attested for all the books except Ezra and Nehemiah. Besides the expected aid that it offers toward an understanding of the text, his exegesis is rich in discussions of realia, medicine and physics, geography, chronology and philosophy. He displays independence of mind remarkable for his age. In chronological matters he occasionally disagrees with the calculations of the universally accepted Seder Olam and suggests that the Bible sometimes gives round numbers rather than the exact extent. He recognizes copyists' errors in the transmission of names or numbers, and introduces emendations, although not explicitly. He treats the Aggada[9a] more critically than most of his colleagues. The attention he pays to the aesthetic beauty of the biblical rhetoric and to its stylistic traits is a marked feature of his approach. In this he was probably influenced by Moses ben Ezra (see below). Notwithstanding his rationalism, he nevertheless indulges in allegorical interpretation to a considerable degree. His commentary was preceded by a comprehensive introduction, with a separate title, in which he discoursed on grammar, and on other matters such as the relation of the Aggada to the literal meaning, the attitude toward Midrash[10a] and philosophical and ethical problems.

The desire to understand the Bible led to a necessary interest in Hebrew grammar, and its study resulted in notable advances. Its importance was appreciated by those who undertook to elucidate the Scriptures, as is illustrated by the large quantity of grammatical discussion and analysis in the works of the commentators, and also by those who, noting the increasing employment of Hebrew in liturgical and secular poetry, were ardent in their desire to see the language used correctly.

Like the study of the Bible, the investigation of grammar commenced in the Orient. Saadia made his contribution to this as to other fields. There were many who wrote on it, Karaites as well as Rabbanites, mostly in Arabic and some in Hebrew, but in this necessarily sketchy analysis we shall confine ourselves to three men, each of whom made a distinguished and specific contribution. Judah ibn Kuraish of North Africa, who apparently flourished during the first half of the tenth century, addressed an Epistle to the community of Fez in which he reprimanded them for neglecting to read the Aramaic version of the Pentateuch and the Prophets. He relates that when he pointed out to them how many obscure words and passages in the biblical text could be elucidated through Aramaic, and how closely related the two were, they realized the importance of the study of Targum. This experience impelled ibn Kuraish to compose his Epistle in which he would give a list of the numerous biblical and mishnaic words that have Arabic and Aramaic cognates. Of the latter about one-half has survived, but the comparisons with Arabic are lost. He attempted to account for the similarity by the physical proximity of the speakers of these languages and the common ancestry of the people who spoke them. We thus have in his Epistle the first recognition of the importance of comparative study in language, a fundamental of philological research in our day. It is noteworthy that, although the Jewish interest in Hebrew received an impetus from Arabic, the emphasis on comparative linguistics is original with them. Unlike the Arabs whose needs were adequately filled by their one language, the Jews utilized all the three and eventually came to realize their interrelation.

The man who laid the foundation of Hebrew grammar as we know it today, a veritable genius in philology, is Judah ben David Hayyuj of Fez. He was born about the middle of the tenth century and came to Spain early in life, spending the rest of it in Cordova, where he passed away early in the eleventh century. In two basic works on verbs containing weak and double letters, he established the principle that *all* Hebrew verb roots are composed of three radicals, whether they appear in every inflected form of the root or not. Before him, scholars had been inclined to argue from forms in which only one or two of the root letters appeared that such roots consisted of only one or two radicals. Hayyuj discovered both the triliteral scheme and the morphological changes that govern the "irregular" verbs. In his introduction he relates that he was pained to discover wrong verbal forms in the works of poets. He realized that if this procedure were not checked it would lead to a complete breakdown of the linguistic structure of Hebrew. He undertook, therefore, through a systematic analysis of the classes of weak verbs, followed by an alphabetic arrangement of them according to their classes, to fix and regulate the proper treatment of each root both in the interpretation of the biblical text and in the creation of new forms in contemporary compositions.

After Hayyuj discovered the principles underlying the Hebrew verb and noun, his achievements were summarized and further developed by his outstanding disciple, Jonah ibn Janah, who flourished in the first half of the eleventh century. In a comprehensive work, called *al-Tankih*, which comprises a grammar and a lexicon, he covers the various questions pertinent to Hebrew grammar, and also lists most of the roots with their definitions and illustrations of their forms as they occur in the Bible. He explains that he resented the supercilious attitude to Hebrew and to its proper use, and was annoyed to find that, whereas the Arabs devoted so much energy to the study of their language, the Jews paid but little attention to theirs. His grammar, called *Sefer Ha-Rikmah* (*Florilegium*), reviews the principles of the organs of speech, the distinction between radicals, auxiliary letters and affixes, the laws of mutation of letters, inflection of nouns and verbs and numerous other topics. It also includes valuable material on the syntax of the language. Although Janah did not deal with the subjects discussed by Hayyuj, his grammar, together with two or three of his minor works, can well serve as textbooks even for the modern scholar. His work marks the pinnacle of grammatical achievement. His successors, whose writing was almost entirely in Hebrew, not only failed to surpass him but lost ground by comparison with him by introducing views which were wrong yet were adopted for centuries. His dictionary also is exceedingly helpful. Assuming a general knowledge on the part of his readers as well as an acquaintance with his earlier contributions, he did not compile as complete a lexicon as modern standards require. But it is valuable for the light it sheds on vague and doubtful points, and the attention it pays to shades of meaning.

Other Hebrew-Arabic dictionaries were compiled, both before and after Janah's time. Hai Gaon (see below) wrote *al-Hawi* (the Compendium), a dictionary of biblical and Rabbinic Hebrew. Only fragments of it have been recovered thus far. From these we learn that he discussed under one heading words made up of similar groups of letters even if the order of the letters differed. His definitions were brief, but he seems to have elaborated where he felt it necessary. An early lexicographer, his etymologies are often faulty. The Karaite David ben Abraham al-Fasi (tenth century) composed a biblical dictionary which is really a concordance. Following a strictly alphabetical order—vitiated, however, by his belief in the existence of one- or two-letter roots—he gives the meaning of the vocables, often adding explanatory comments of grammatical, philosophical or other nature. Three centuries later, the commentator Tanhum of Jerusalem issued his *Adequate Guide*, which was designed to serve as a convenient handbook in Arabic for the vocabulary of Maimonides's Hebrew code, *Mishne Torah*, and for that section of the mishnaic terminology which was not utilized by the codifier. He felt that notwithstanding the existence of the *Aruk*, an eleventh-century talmudical dictionary, his work was needed because the former was rare, too compendious and of defective arrangement, due to its faulty understanding of grammar. Although Tanhum did not carry out his program fully, his work is useful because of the Arabic translation of the words, and also because by applying the triliteral system it accomplished for mishnaic Hebrew what Hayyuj and Janah did for its biblical phase.

Unlike the fields of biblical exegesis and philology, which were comparatively recent developments and, directly or indirectly, owed their existence to the stimulus received from Islam, the study of Talmud does not seem to have been interrupted from the time when it was first initiated. When the talmudic text was compiled, edited and declared closed, its study continued, although little material is traceable to the years 500-750. At any rate, the earlier works in Halaka during the Moslem period—responsa and codifications—were written in the Aramaic dialect which we find in the Talmud. But Arabic encroached on this field as well and challenged the supremacy of the former, and actually almost superseded it. Both the language and the method of presentation eventually attest the influence of the environment. A greater interest in systemization, in summaries, introductions and lexicography characterizes many of the halakic works in Arabic.

Once again the first outstanding author is Saadia. He enjoyed an illustrious reputation throughout the Middle Ages when his works were better known. From his extant writings, from fragments and from quotations found in books by later authorities, it is clear that he was an absolute master in Rabbinics, which he conceived to be not something additional and posterior to the Bible but an integral part of the one great unity, of Judaism, which dates from the time of Moses. His output was voluminous. He compiled compendia on legal subjects such as ritual slaughter, incest, documents and inheritance. He may have written an Introduction to the Talmud, of which, if the conjecture is correct, we still have his discussion of the thirteen hermeneutic principles for the study and expansion of the biblical law. He is also credited with either a commentary on, or a translation of the Mishna, or both. He seems to have compiled a Book of Commandments which, to judge from a recently discovered fragment, was a comprehensive list and analysis of the precepts of Jewish law. He is also the author of Responsa on various subjects. All the surviving halakic writing, and doubtless also the lost material exhibit the same system, logical order and comprehensive treatment that characterize his output in other fields. It is indeed unfortunate that so little of his contributions to Halaka has been preserved, probably because it was not translated into Hebrew.

Another Oriental talmudist who wrote in Arabic was Hefes ben Yasliah.

He probably lived after Saadia, but like those of the latter, his works also suffered a sad fate. Only fragments have survived. He compiled a comprehensive compendium of Jewish law called *Book of Precepts*, which he organized according to some plan into at least thirty-six sections. His method was to state the biblical source of the law and follow it with development and ramification in Rabbinic literature. But, ambitious and comprehensive as this program was, he went beyond it. He wrote a lengthy introduction in which, among other things, he expounded his plan and criticized the method and arrangement used by predecessors. In the body of the book he often digressed into lexicographic, philosophic and other fields, all of which undoubtedly enhanced both the quantity and the quality of the book. The extant portion includes about fifty precepts of probably 613, if, as appears probable, he followed the traditional pattern of listing that number. His influence was widespread, his book having been utilized by philologists like ibn Janah, exegetes like ibn Balam and halakists and philosophers like Bahya ben Pakudah and Maimonides.

Samuel ben Hofni (d. 1013), the most important Gaon of the Sura Academy after Saadia, seems to have employed Arabic in all his halakic writings. His output was so voluminous that a mere list of his works occupied two notebooks. He composed an Introduction to the Talmud in 145 chapters of which considerable fragments have survived. It included the history of the Talmud as well as an analysis of its method and terminology. In addition to a Book of the Laws, which may have presented a philosophic treatment of rational and traditional law and their sources, he wrote a large number of tracts on legal subjects, such as contracts, partnership, agency, court procedure, marriage and others. He seems to have participated in the lively religious polemic of his time, contributing a work which apparently dealt with the disputed problem of whether the Mosaic dispensation could be abrogated, as the Moslems contended.

Samuel's son-in-law, Hai Gaon (d. 1038), who became head of the Academy of Pumbedita after his father, the equally renowned Sherira (d. 1006), author of the famous epistle on the history of the Oral Law, wrote a number of volumes in Arabic on subjects of Jewish law. Of these, which included discussions on oaths, judges, pledges, loans and others, only fragments, if anything, have remained, either in Arabic or in Hebrew translation. The only complete item extant—in a Hebrew recension—is on purchase and sale. He is further credited with commentaries in several talmudic tractates. He also corresponded extensively, as did his predecessors and successors, replying to inquiries in the Bible, Talmud, law, prayer and worship, faith and reason and other subjects. From his responsa it can be concluded that he sought to interpret the Aggada rationally, eliminating the anthropomorphisms, and characterizing some miraculous incidents as dreams or visions of the mind's eye. He emphasized that one cannot rely on Aggada alone. His comparative broad-mindedness is illustrated by his request of aid from a Christian patriarch in the explanation of some biblical words.

By the end of the tenth century the Orient, generally speaking, yielded to the Spanish-Jewish center and the Franco-German Jewish communities, and the stream of halakic compositions continued in the West. However, on our way from the older to the newer homes of Jewish culture, we must linger with the North African settlement of Kairouan where, since the tenth century, a prosperous and intellectually alert Jewish community was in existence. Home of scholars in various fields, such as medicine, astronomy, philosophy and philology, its renown rests on its great Talmudists. Outstanding among them was Nissim ben Jacob, who flourished in the eleventh century. One of his major works, written in Arabic, is *The Key to the Locks of the Talmud*. Covering the entire Talmud, its aim was to shed light on indefinite and unsupported statements in this vast compendium by quoting the support and proof from where it may be found and by citing the *locus classicus* of all the Halakas that are stated elsewhere in the Talmud as accepted truths. A considerable portion of this voluminous work is still extant. His other major work, *A Secret Scroll*, is a compilation in Hebrew and Arabic of discussions of halakic and aggadic matter in Rabbinic literature. This work enjoyed wide circulation. Nissim also left us an interesting work which plainly ascribes its origin to the influence of Arabic literature. Its probable title was *Stories of the Sages, Being a Worthy Compilation for Comfort*. In the Introduction we are told that it was written for his father-in-law when the latter lost a son. Its purpose was to provide a book of Jewish content in place of the writings of "heretics," that is, Moslems, which his father-in-law would have read. It belongs to a type of literature which is known in Arabic by the name of "Comfort After Distress," and was calculated to distract people in their hour of sorrow. It is the popular counterpart of a more serious class of consolation literature which was produced by Jews, Christians and Moslems alike in the Middle Ages.

In Spain, the versatile Samuel Ha-Nagid (d. 1056),[11a] son-in-law of the preceding, statesman, poet and philologist, also excelled in talmudic studies. He is the author of an Arabic *Introduction to the Talmud* of which a considerable fragment is available in a Hebrew version. In this section he defines various technical terms and their implications and also establishes principles to determine whose opinion is to be accepted in case of controversy. It is evident that the Introduction was marked by a systematic and scientific approach. He also compiled a Code, which he called *Major Laws*, as a token of gratitude to God for having delivered him from his hostile captor. Too little is known of the work to enable us to characterize it, but in his poem, in which he tells us of his resolve to undertake this labor, he declares that it is his purpose to confound the Karaites. He also states there that Hai Gaon's works will be his chief guide.

The outstanding eleventh-century scholar is Isaac ben Jacob al-Fasi (d. 1103), but his main work is in Hebrew and Aramaic. His legacy in Arabic consists of some responsa and elucidations. The same is true of Joseph ibn Migas, for, although he also achieved great fame, his Arabic writings consist only of some responsa.

However, all these men are overshadowed by the truly gigantic achievements in Halaka[12a] of Moses ben Maimon, or Maimonides (d. 1204). Possessed of a vast erudition and an extraordinarily logical mind, he made an inestimably great contribution to Halaka. His first major work, chronologically, is a commentary on the complete Mishna, which he compiled while still a young man. His method of explanation is by the use of paraphrase. In each small unit—or Mishna, as it is called—he defines the difficult words and then summarizes its contents. Sometimes the definitions are woven into the paraphrase. In addition to the lucidity of the interpretation, evident throughout, and particularly in the order of *Toharot* (Laws of Cleanliness), his work is remarkable for the introductions and digressions of which there are several. It begins with a lengthy preface on the place of the Mishna in the Oral Law and on the plan followed by Rabbi Judah, the compiler of the Mishna, in the arrangement of the material. Besides this relevant matter it contains a statement on the author's views regarding the objectives of the world's creation and his assumption that all creation was meant to serve the intellectually and morally superior. He has brief introductions to the various tractates, and occasional notes within the body of the tractate in which he strives to put the reader in a position to understand the discussion in the text, a very helpful device in view of the practice of the Mishna to plunge into a subject in the belief that the reader is equipped to follow. To the ethical tractate of *Abot,* Maimonides wrote a lengthier preface in which he stated his views of the soul, its aspects, and the ethical and psychological principles that ought to guide an individual's life. Sometimes, as in the case of the chapter in the tractate of Sanhedrin which lists those who are and those who are not deserving of a portion in the world to come, he also prefaced an introduction on the subject, and, in the course of it, stated the thirteen articles of faith that are incumbent on the Jew. These, despite vigorous opposition, became virtually the accepted creed of the Jewish people.

Maimonides's greatest work in Halaka is his *Mishne Torah,* a compendium of the entire body of Jewish Law, both the part that is always operative and applicable and the part that is pertinent only in a Jewish state, or in Palestine, or when the Temple is in existence. This work, however, was written in Hebrew, the only one of his major works in that language. But he prepared a kind of outline of it in Arabic, which is known by its Hebrew name of *Sefer Ha-Mizvot*. Its purpose is to list the 613 laws that are traditionally regarded as Sinai-given. Before listing them, he enters into a lengthy discussion of the correct method in selecting the laws that properly form part of the 613. He points out errors and inconsistencies in the lists of his predecessors, stressing particularly the need to discriminate between a Mosaic and a Rabbinic ordinance. The work is characterized by the same strict logic that is evident in all his writings.

From the sketch of Maimonides's halakic writings we turn to consider important epistles left by him and by his father. The latter is the author of a pious and warm *Letter of Comfort* to the many Jews in the Moslem world who, as a result of the grievous persecutions by the Almohades in the middle of the twelfth century, were troubled and almost despaired of redemption. In the epistle, Maimon emphasizes that the promise which God made, supported as it is by the Bible and, notably, by the prophecy of Moses, whom the author characterizes in the most glorifying and adulatory terms, will most certainly be fulfilled. In connection with his exhortation he offers an edifying interpretation of Psalm 90, and recommends it as reading for those who are in difficulty.

From Maimonides's pen we possess a letter addressed to the same circle of readers, but more practical in its purpose and significance. He was deeply angered by the verdict of a contemporary Rabbi who ruled that crypto-Jews were apostates from Judaism. He felt rightly that the psychological effect of this ruling on the victims of the persecution would be disastrous, and he undertook to refute it. In his tract he makes a fine distinction between genuine and apparent conversion, and between the outward acceptance of Christianity and that of Islam. He offers the Jews sound advice to do everything possible to rid themselves of the duplicity by leaving the country, but at the same time he is passionate in his encouragement to the Marranos and in his desire to allay their fears.

Another writing, known as the *Epistle to Yemen*, also deals with persecution, this time in Arabia Felix. The contention of a converted Jew that Islam superseded the Mosaic dispensation, and the claim of another individual that he was the Messiah confused the Yemenite Jews and made a difficult life more difficult. Again Maimonides stepped in to bolster up failing spirits, to restore reason to well-meaning enthusiasts, and to keep alive in every Jew's heart the faith that he was following the right road, and the hope that salvation was not far.

Family talent was not exhausted by Maimon and his illustrious son. Abraham, the son of Moses, wrote a commentary on the Pentateuch, and a compendious work on Judaism, its principles, character, requirements and rewards. David, the son of Abraham, compiled a very readable commentary on the *Ethics of the Fathers*.

At least passing notice should be taken of a prayer book arranged by the indefatigable Saadia Gaon. In his usual manner he converted even this task into an important contribution. It comprises the laws of prayer in general, the regulations for the special occasions of the year, the ordinary prayers for private and public recitation, and a considerable body of liturgical poetry by him and by others. All this adds up to a very impressive performance, which is enhanced by the independence of mind that Saadia displays here as elsewhere.

A unique representative in Jewish literature of a genre which is extremely common in Arabic is found in a work produced by the renowned poet Moses ibn Ezra. As its florid Arabic title is a little hard to render, we may identify it by the title given it in its recent Hebrew translation: *The Poetry of Israel*. In response to a request for information, the author discusses such topics as the natural propensity of the Arabs toward poetry, the reason for the superiority of Spanish-Jewish poetry to that of other Jews, and the history of Hebrew poetry. His longest chapter is devoted to a discussion of the art of Hebrew poetry. In it he lists the various devices for enhancing the aesthetic appeal of verse and illustrates them by example from the Bible and later works. In this manner, as indicated previously, ibn Ezra displays an appreciation of the literary beauty of the Bible, which was generally overlooked until modern times. The charm of the work lies in its rambling, informal and intimate style, which puts the reader at ease. Ibn Ezra does not hesitate to digress, whether for the length of a chapter, as in his essay on the credibility of dreams, or for shorter stretches. This style of writing, generally known as *Adab*, is a very prominent feature of Arabic literature.

It is in the field of philosophy or, more correctly, religious philosophy or theology that the spirit of Judeo-Arabic literature reveals itself most fully. For one thing, the concern with the problems that form the substance of theological speculation marks a new departure. There was, it is true, Philo in Alexandria who wrote on philosophy. There are, it is true, numerous questions touched on in Rabbinic literature which properly belong to the realm of theology. But Philo's work and conclusions were not directly absorbed into the stream of Jewish thinking even if its influence may be discovered in one Rabbinic statement or another. Philo's work was not sufficiently rooted in Jewish lore, for his knowledge of that lore was deficient, so that extrinsically, let alone intrinsically, it had the appearance of an alien product.[13a] And the Rabbinic manner of dealing with its problems, by finding its support in a biblical verse, or reconciling two seemingly contradictory verses, however definitely it may represent an earnest desire to understand a certain problem or to solve a certain difficulty, cannot be called formal theology. Nor can the mystical speculations that were influenced by Gnosticism be regarded as theology, even if they concerned themselves with the celestial sphere, God and His throne, or the angels. The theological literature that was produced in the period under consideration is the effect of factors which played a major role in that period, characterized by qualities inherent in it, and permeated by an attitude peculiar to it.

Basically the impact that brought about this theological activity came from Greek and Oriental philosophy. The Jews, however, became conscious of this influence in the Moslem milieu and in an Arabic version. Within this milieu they discovered not only some of the original writings of Plato and Aristotle with their Neoplatonic commentators, but also the clash and the consequent compromise evolved in the Christian church; the polemics between the Christians and the Moslems, or between Oriental religions and the Moslems; the questionings and the doubts within the Moslem world; the rational, antireligious challenge and attacks by various people; the anti-Jewish arguments from several quarters; and certain centrifugal, disruptive tendencies which had developed in the Jewish community under these several influences. As a result, the theological or philosophical inquiries and analyses that abound in Judeo-Arabic may be reasonably regarded not as a luxury but as a necessity. Of course, it may not have been a necessity for those who remained entirely unaffected by the lively discussions and disputations, but it was a necessity for those who felt the challenge, either in their own lives or in the lives of fellow Jews whom they wished to set aright.

For purpose of simplification it is best to classify the Jewish philosophic writings, like their Moslem parallels, into three categories. One of these is known as Kalam.[14a] Its underlying physical premise is that all existence is composed of atoms, which form the substance, characterized by certain properties, which are called accidents. The latter are constantly changing since their duration is only momentary. As no object can be conceived without its properties and these are constantly created, it follows that all existence must have been created, and in this way it establishes creation. It further argues that this created world must have been fashioned by an outside force, namely, God. Among the Jewish philosophers who employed the system of Kalam, not all adopt the atomic theory. The most notable among them, Saadia Gaon, does not incline to it, preferring a variety of the Aristotelian conception of matter and form. They all, however, share in common the view that God's existence is proved by establishing the fact of creation and thus necessitating a creator. The Jewish philosophers, following the Mutazilites, one of the two schools of Moslem Kalam, are inclined to deny that God possesses attributes which stand in the same relation to Him as do properties to substances. Again, like their Moslem models, they devote much attention and space to God's justice, discussing under this heading revelation and prophecy, reward and punishment, good and evil, freedom of the will, the problem of the suffering of the righteous, and so forth. The best known work of this type is the *Book of Beliefs and Doctrines* by Saadia Gaon. He accounts for his composition of the book by explaining that as a result of the philosophic currents, doubts and perplexities and criticism have been engendered in the minds of many Jews, which threaten their loyalty to the faith. He defines our sources of knowledge, counting, in addition to the three channels of perceptual, conceptual and rationally necessary, also historical, or information reported from others. This last means, by the aid of which, as is known, so much of our knowledge is attained, serves Saadia to confirm the other source of truth, revelation. For, although he is convinced of the divine character of the Bible, and also of the complete identity of true revelation and reason, he is scientist enough to seek to demonstrate the veracity of the tradition regarding revelation, so that it might not be challenged on the basis of method. Moreover, he is rationalist enough, despite his unshaken faith in the truth of the Bible, to concede that whenever the biblical text contradicts reason the text is to be interpreted so as to obviate that contradiction.

His method in elucidating the verities of the Jewish faith in the light of reason is on two levels. In the case of a large part of the Jewish creed, he works on the assumption that it is rationally demonstrable. In this manner he proves, for example, that reason compels the belief in creation, in the existence and unity of God, in revelation, in reward and punishment, and in freedom of the will. In the case of some specifically religious articles of faith, such as the purely traditional laws, the graphic description of the procedure in the world beyond, the resurrection, Messianic times and the like, he feels it his task to prove that they are not contrary to reason. It is interesting to note that Saadia succeeds in preserving the entire religious legacy, even to details which are really incidental, from the attack of rationalism.

There were other able Kalam theologians among both Rabbanites and Karaites, with more or less original contributions. But while among the latter Kalam remained the accepted system to the end of the philosophic writing activity, Rabbanite philosophers turned from it to other systems, to Neoplatonism and to Aristotelianism with Neoplatonic coloring.

In the view of Neoplatonic philosophy, the cardinal difficulty is that of reconciling the composite, corruptible world, in which evil and wickedness inhere, with its Creator, the perfect and unique God. Its basic principle, formulated in order to resolve that difficulty, is emanation, that is, the doctrine that the entire universe, including the sublunar world, stems from God not by an act of creation but by a series of evolutions. God, as it were, separated part of Himself from Himself, without however, diminishing Himself in any way, and this part, in turn, evolved another from itself, and the next as well, and the next, until the celestial, as well as the terrestrial, world came into being. Taken over by some Jewish phi-losophers, it confronted them with the task of integrating this conception with the Jewish doctrine. The work of Philo, the first-century Neopla-tonist, who, in his Greek writings, sought to identify the Jewish and the philosophic teachings, left little or no effect on Jewish thinking except, perhaps, through indirect channels. Medieval thinkers who favored this view were compelled to find their own solutions. The celebrated Jewish physician Isaac ben Solomon Israeli (d. *c.* 950), for example, made room for the belief in creation by apparently excluding the terrestrial world from the system of emanations and regarding it as an outcome of a *fiat* by God.

On the other hand, the most important and profound Jewish Neo-platonist, Solomon ben Judah ibn Gabirol (d. *c.* 1050),[15a] the renowned poet and ethical writer, whose philosophic work *The Fountain of Life,* originally written in Arabic, is extant only in a Latin translation, was evidently so firmly convinced of his view of the universe that he made almost no concession to Jewish beliefs, but chose rather to write philosophy pure and simple with no effort at reconciliation and no utilization of alleged proof from biblical or Rabbinic texts. Believing that matter, which he defined as that aspect of an object on which the form is impressed, underlies every existing thing, he assumed the existence of Universal Matter. Parallel to it, he postulated the existence of Universal Form, which is what distinguishes one object from another. This dualism which, in his view, extends from the lowest to the highest entities in the universe, could not be accounted for by the usual Neoplatonic explanation that as the emanations receded further from their source they became more composite, coarser, more material and corruptible. Since, in his opinion, matter is at least as noble as form, and is found in the celestial and in the intellectual worlds, he was obliged to trace both to God, their primary source. As he did not resort to creation, he endeavored to obviate the difficulty by assuming an intermediate force between God and the world. This force, which he calls the Will, he defines but vaguely (perhaps, as a statement in his *Fountain of Life* has been understood, because he discussed it separately in a no longer existing work), and students are perplexed as to its nature and to its capacity to serve as the source of both matter and form. However, notwithstanding some difficulties in his system he is acknowledged by modern scholars as an original and deep thinker. Although among Jewish philosophers his theories did not spread widely, owing to the domination of Aristotelianism among them, he exerted a far-reaching influence on Christian theologians such as William of Auvergne and Duns Scotus, who adhered to his views, and even on opponents like Albertus Magnus and Thomas Aquinas.

Ibn Gabirol is also the author of a popular and none too profound ethical work, *On the Improvement of the Qualities of the Soul*. Starting with the assumption that physically man is the most harmonious of all creatures, and intellectually he is on a par with the angels, he teaches that man, a microcosm, should strive to preserve in the exercise of his qualities the same harmony which is so evident in his counterpart, the macrocosm. In an original, if forced, distribution of ten cardinal virtues and ten cardinal faults among the five senses, four to each, he urges control and discipline of these, counseling the practice of the Aristotelian golden mean. The work abounds in biblical citations, as also in sayings of Greek philosophers. Of the latter, ibn Gabirol compiled a collection called *The Choice of Pearls*, which enjoyed much popularity.

Bahya ben Joseph ibn Pakudah (d. *c.* 1100), author of the *Duties of the Heart*, is correctly described as a religious thinker rather than as a philosopher. Philosophically, as evident from his proof of the existence of God, he stands on Kalam ground. In his ideals, however, and the means to attain them, he is firmly rooted in Jewish tradition, although he is also beholden to Neoplatonism and to Moslem asceticism, which is itself deeply colored by the latter. The ideal he urges is the attainment of the stage in which the individual experiences a love of God. It is reached when man has realized God's greatness and providence, on the one hand, and man's insignificance and helplessness, on the other. The means required to reach that are given in the chapters of the book and their contents can be surmised from the headings, which include God's unity, consideration of creation, trust in God, humility, penitence, love of God and others. Bahya's work in its Hebrew version has become one of the most popular Jewish books and was studied by Jews even in cultural centers where philosophy did not gain a foothold.

Although certain Neoplatonic influences may be discovered in his system of philosophy, the most beloved medieval Jewish poet, Judah Ha-Levi (d. *c.* 1140), is the most independent and original thinker of the Jewish-Arabic period.[16a] Like his older contemporary in the Moslem world, Abu Hamid al-Ghazali, he was aware of the inadequacy of metaphysical reasoning, and, in his book called *Al Khazar* with its subtitle, the "Arguments and Proofs in Behalf of the Disparaged Religion," he followed another road. Ha-Levi was far from being an antirationalist. On the contrary, to the extent to which he believed its reasoning valid, he utilized the method and conclusions of philosophy. Moreover, it was his purpose to make his own doctrine rationally demonstrable. But he objected to the position taken by philosophy on matters which, in his mind, were within the domain of religion and hence superrational. He did not feel that its evidence for the existence of God was adequate. He resented its conception of God as an inactive, disinterested force, and its indifference to religious works or to the relative validity of one religion as over against another. He disagreed entirely with the conceit of philosophers that by their efforts or methods they could attain the rank of prophecy, or the true knowledge of God, and the bliss which that elevated state bestows on man. The precious gifts that living with God brings to man are acquired not by man's intellect but by knowing and doing what God has taught. The basic capacity to lead such a life is bestowed by Him. It is "a Divine matter," as Ha-Levi calls it, a special talent or quality which God grants. Historically, Ha-Levi finds, following the story of the Bible, the "Divine matter" became the heritage of Israel. Moreover, Ha-Levi, alone among medieval Jewish philosophers, regards Palestine as an essential factor in the destiny of Israel. It is the only land where Israel, endowed with the Divine matter, can, in an almost biological sense, grow and prosper, in the same way as fruits and vegetables will grow only in the appropriate soil and climate. This special quality of the Jewish people is what gained for them the revelation of God and the rank of prophecy. The revelation on Mt. Sinai, an undoubted fact, as judged by medieval standards of historical knowledge, is at once the firmest proof of the existence of God, the most valid evidence of the election of Israel, and the clearest statement of the correct and only method of attaining the coveted degree of God's favor and love. Thus, in Ha-Levi's view, the Jewish religion as it was developed and practiced by the Rabbis, rather than any philosophy, is the proved way to follow, and the Jewish people, rather than any self-appointed group of elect individuals, are humanity's most privileged species. Their present sad state is due to their sins and, particularly, to their failure to return to the appropriate soil when the opportunity was afforded. It is significant that the Jewish spokesman (the book is in the form of a dialogue between a pagan king who is eventually converted to Judaism and a representative of the Jewish faith) concludes the discussion with the decision to settle in Palestine, so as to find for himself the proper place in which he can best live the fullest Jewish life. Because of its religious fervor and its passionate defense of Israel and its Law, the book enjoyed tremendous popularity among the Jews.

Medieval Aristotelianism and Neoplatonism were not so sharply divided as in ancient times. The latter, though it postulated the emanation of the entire universe from God, recognized a dualism of matter and form in the sublunar world and, in the philosophy of ibn Gabirol, this dualism is evident in the entire universe. Aristotle's teachings, on the contrary, were suffused with a strong Neoplatonic coloring because, through a bibliographic error, part of a work by the Neoplatonist Plotinus was accepted as a writing of Aristotle. As a result, medieval Aristotelianism also speaks of emanation, and the dualism that is so fundamental in the master's teachings is at first confined to the terrestrial world, and is no longer a universal principle. It also considers the bliss that comes from a union with God, rather than from a knowledge of God, as the goal of man.

Yet certain differences remained or became more emphasized. The dualism of matter and form, as the two extreme poles of existence, was much more prominent in Aristotelianism, and eventually matter was excluded from the process of emanation. Not only God, pure form, and the source of all form, is eternal and pre-existent, but also pure, formless matter. In Aristotelianism, one could talk with even less justice than in Neoplatonism of an act of creation, in view of the eternal coexistence of both matter and form. Aristotelianism further taught that God is Thought thinking Itself, creating the problem of what God knows of the world. The soul was regarded by it as the form of the body rather than an emanation of the Universal soul of Neoplatonism, and immortality became a more difficult problem. The theory of knowledge, too, although influenced by the Neoplatonist view of the action of the Active Intellect on a passive human mind, regained much of Aristotle's contention that it is dependent on perceptual knowledge and the abstraction of the latter, giving a new importance to logic and to natural philosophy.

Moreover, in the problem facing medieval Moslem and Jewish philosophers, the reconciliation of philosophy and religion, Aristotelianism proved to be a formidable system to bend and adapt. For despite the apparent similarity between reason and faith in their recognition of God, of purpose in the Universe, of a variety of immortality, of a discipline to which man must subject himself, the divergences nevertheless remained distinct. The God of Aristotle, even in his medieval definition, is most impersonal and inactive; the philosopher's purpose of the Universe is the result of a natural order which necessarily proceeds from certain eternally functioning laws, and is not subject to any direct control or voluntary regulation; its immortality a vague abstraction in place of the richly colored belief of religion; its discipline an intellectual rather than a moral system. It left little room for prophecy or revelation; it had no need of what were called traditional, or revealed, laws. In general, it was intellectual, rational, rigid and antagonistic to the irrational, romantic and intuitive, which religion brings with it.

Of the two outstanding Jewish Aristotelians, Abraham ibn Daud (d. *c.* 1180) did not achieve great importance because he was justly overshadowed by his superior successor Maimonides. Although he justified the composition of the book *The Noble Faith* as a solution to the issue of the freedom of the will, he does not treat the latter more prominently than other philosophic problems. He gives a lengthy exposition of the physical world in preparation for the proof of the existence of God, and of the psychological world as background for the proof of the belief in immortality. He adopts the Aristotelian argument in proof of the existence of the First Cause, but for him, as for Moslem Aristotelians, it is not only the first cause of motion, but also the first cause of existence, and God the Creator. The contradiction between this and the theory of universal emanation, superimposed upon Aristotelianism, he solves by rejecting the latter, because it does not fit his Judaism; yet he adopts some of the teachings of emanation, such as the development of the terrestrial world out of the superlunar. In his teachings regarding the soul, he argues, like his Moslem predecessor ibn Sina, that, although it may be regarded as the form of the human body, the postulate that the form perishes with the object does not apply to it. It is obviously an independent, immaterial force in the body, and as such, immortal even if the body is mortal. This immortality, however, is limited to the intellectual part of the soul, which receives its knowledge from the Active Intellect. Its highest degree is prophecy, but it is unique in that it receives knowledge concerning the future. He goes even further and sees in prophecy, contrary to its apparently natural origin, a mission from God by which He instructs the less gifted, and even limits this gift to Israel and to Palestine. He predicates complete freedom of the will for man, and obviates the difficulty of accepting this freedom in the light of God's omniscience by limiting God's foreknowledge just as His omnipotence is limited from including human actions. In his ethical teachings, he naturally identifies the doctrines of Plato and Aristotle, which were joined by medieval philosophers, with the teachings of the Torah. While, in Aristotelian fashion, the knowledge of the celestial world is the goal of man, his main ideal is to know God, and through knowledge to gain the love of God, which is the highest happiness of man.

By his comprehensive work in philosophy called *Guide for the Perplexed*, and by the dominant position he held in Jewish and in general philosophy for the three centuries following his, Maimonides came to be recognized as the outstanding medieval Jewish thinker.[17a] While he assumed as fully as his predecessor that philosophy and religion teach the same truth, he was far more conscious than ibn Daud of the disagreements of the two sources of truth, much more conscientious in threshing the difficulties out, and much more desirous of arriving at a valid synthesis. He opens his work, which is divided into three parts, with a penetrating analysis of words and phrases in the Bible which at first glance are anthropomorphic and anthropopathetic. He disposes of them by predicating that such expressions, when applied to God, have a different meaning, and that their purport is to indicate the effect of God's work or providence in the Universe. From this he proceeds to a keen study of the vexing question of God's attributes, and takes the position that whereas we have the right to describe God by adjectives which indicate our reactions to Him, such as merciful, sovereign and the like, we have no right to apply to God any term which will imply that a certain characteristic is inherent in Him. He is so singularly One, so uniquely Himself, that any statement regarding His essence impugns His Oneness. The best we can do is to speak of Him negatively or to understand that when we say anything positive of Him we merely mean to imply that He is not the opposite. When we say, for example, that He is existent, we assert that He is not nonexistent, not that His essence possesses the attribute of existence. What it really amounts to is that all of God's attributes are really He, and not distinguishable from Himself. The concept, however, is so difficult to understand that Maimonides justly admits that we have no way of knowing God except in a moment of illumination.

Only after the author has stated his views of God's attributes, and critically refuted the philosophy of Kalam, does he turn to the question of God's existence. His purpose is to make the proof of the existence of God independent of the problem of the world's creation, so that if the latter should prove to be nondemonstrable, the belief in the existence of God would not thereby be affected. With this in view, he utilizes the Aristotelian argument of the First Mover, Who is the cause of all motion in the Universe, and is God. He also employs an argument from Moslem Aristotelians, distinguishing between the universe which is possibly existent, that is, might or might not exist, and God, Who is necessarily existent, implying that God is not only the Prime Mover, but also the First Cause of the Universe. By these proofs Maimonides establishes God's existence, simplicity and eternity. After developing the system of emanations which came into Aristotelianism, he turns to the problem of creation versus eternity. After a lengthy and intricate examination of the pros and cons of both, he concludes that neither is demonstrably certain, and therefore decides in favor of creation by bringing the religious belief as an arbiter.

In his interpretation of prophecy, Maimonides shares with Aristotelian philosophy the view that it results from the close natural relation between the potential prophet and the Active Intellect. However, he recognizes that a naturally endowed prophet requires God's Will before he can prophesy, and that the figurative form in which prophecies are delivered is the result of the imaginative faculty of the soul in addition to the intellectual. The prophet, although he is necessarily a philosopher, is superior to the latter in that he succeeds in acquiring that knowledge of God which comes through illumination alone. Maimonides also makes an exception for Moses, declaring him to have been a prophet *sui generis*. In this way he makes Moses unique and similarly his revelation or the Torah. They are not higher degrees of certain types but single examples in their fields. The purpose of prophecy is to bring a certain amount of necessary information to the masses who are not equipped to acquire it by their own initiative.

Maimonides, as we have seen, diverges from strict Aristotelianism in the problems of creation and of prophecy. He also shows his independence in the assertion that the miracles related in the Bible are true and that they formed from eternity part of God's plan of the universe, and that God knows every human action. Maimonides at the same time preserves the freedom of the will by arguing that God's foreknowledge is essentially different from the human, and the apparent contradiction between freedom of the will and knowledge is not true of God. There are, however, important religious principles regarding which Maimonides follows the Aristotelian view more closely. He defines the rational soul as the part that acquires knowledge from the Active Intellect, and limits immortality to it alone. He relates providence to the same Active Intellect and man's share in providence in proportion to his share in the knowledge which can be acquired from it. Although he recognizes the importance of moral living, it is only a means to a higher end, the intellectual perfection toward which man should strive. This makes Torah and religious living not ends in themselves but means to a loftier goal. Maimonides makes a strong effort to find a rational explanation for the laws of the Torah, and endeavors to show that traditional laws whose reasons are not apparent are either pedagogical in aim, in that they strengthen certain moral qualities within us, or a reaction to the habits and practices of the times when the Torah was revealed, whether as a concession to them or a rejection of them. The highest perfection is that which can be reached by the philosopher. In a famous example of Maimonides in which he likens the Object of human striving, as he conceives it, to a king within a palace, and the several classes of people to groups who seek to stand before the king, the talmudists are not successful in entering the palace. It is the philosopher who comes closest to Him. It should be noted that this highest bliss is not a union with God in any mystical sense but a supreme state of knowledge and the love that results from it.

After the departure of Maimonides from Spain in 1148, as a result of the religious persecutions instituted by the fanatical Moslem sect, known as the al-Muwahhidun (Almohades), he lived in the Orient and produced his greatest works there. His son Abraham compiled an ethical work called by the translator of a part of it *The Highway to Perfection*, and his disciple Joseph ibn Aknin is similarly the author of an ethical treatise *The Hygiene of the Soul*. From his grandson's pen we have an interesting commentary on the *Ethics of the Fathers*. Since then, down to the present, Judeo-Arabic literature has continued in lands where Arabic has remained the spoken and written language, but its significance, save for some few exceptions, is minor, and its importance is local.

In Spain, Arabic writing practically ceased among the Jews after Maimonides. The period of intense religious zeal was finally succeeded by sweeping victories celebrated by the Spanish Christians, who were bent on freeing their land from Moslem hold. The thirteenth century saw the almost complete liberation of Spain. With the fall of Islam and the

domination of Latin and Spanish, Judeo-Arabic production virtually came
to an end. Subsequent creations were usually written in Hebrew. It may be
added in passing that Hebrew played a significant role at this stage in the
transmission of Moslem lore to the Western world. Many works were
rendered into Latin not from their original Arabic but from the Hebrew
version, either prepared for Jewish consumption and utilized by a Latin
translator, or deliberately made for retranslation by a man who did not
know Latin for a man who did not know Arabic.

But the gradual elimination of Arabic as the vernacular of the Jews in
Spain did not simultaneously result in the elimination of the written
monuments from Jewish life in Christian countries, not to speak of the
Moslem world. Even before that time came, an interest in Judeo-Arabic
literature was aroused among the Jews in neighboring Provence and
Italy. Already in the twelfth century we find Judah ibn Tibbon busily
engaged in Provence in translating grammatical and philosophical books
into Hebrew at the request of Jewish intellectuals. This activity was
maintained in succeeding generations by members of his family and others
in Spain, Provence and Italy, until a considerable portion of the Judeo-
Arabic legacy became available in Hebrew. Many works were unfortunately neglected, and of these some were preserved in libraries as silent
witnesses of an outlived era in Jewish life, and others irretrievably lost.
We should not, however, overlook the numerous Hebrew works written
by men who were still conversant with Arabic, in which more or less of
the lore of the ancients is preserved. Several of the translations, particularly in philosophy and ethics, made their way even into the German-
Polish center, which knew little of, and was interested even less in, the
diversified Jewish productivity that had flourished in the Moslem environment. Indeed, it is an irony of fate that some originally Arabic works
enjoyed a far better fortune than many, if not most, of the originally
Hebrew works which did not deal with Halaka or exegesis. The reaction
against secular literature that was especially prevalent in northern Europe
and Poland hit belles-lettres hardest, and it is remarkable to record that
poets and storytellers who deliberately preferred to write in Hebrew even
when the vogue was to employ Arabic were the men whose creations were
the least sought after, so that they became the easiest prey of the ravages
of time and bookworms.

The work pursued so actively in Moslem Spain was taken up in the
Hebrew language in Spain, Provence and Italy. In the first two centers
until the expulsion, and in Italy even after, individuals continued to write
poetry and literary prose and to study science and philosophy. This work
maintained the tradition so nobly begun under the Moslems, and although,
as was the case of the authors who functioned in Italy, the Renaissance that
was experienced by that land unquestionably left its mark on Jewish

creativity, the activity was the continuation of the literary life begun under Judeo-Arabic stimulation and, what is just as important, the subject-matter and even the artistic devices were clearly modeled after the products of that period. Above all, however, the noteworthy fact is that the interest in belles-lettres, in science, in philosophical and theological problems, and the general concern with the world beyond their own kept alive and furthered a stimulus begun in Spain and bequeathed to these lands. And just as in its day Jewish Spain was distinguished from other European Jewries by this diversity of culture,[18a] so Italian Jewry was alone in Europe in the cultivation and preservation of the secular studies. Northern and eastern Europe remained virtually as unaffected by either the legacy of Spain or its extension in Italy as it had been centuries before when southwestern Europe went through a rich development. Only when the European Enlightenment began to show its effects in central and eastern Europe, and Jews were stirred to ask more of life politically as well as culturally, did they develop an interest in secular literature.

On the threshold of this transformation stands the great eighteenth-century Italian-Jewish poet and mystic Moses Hayyim Luzzatto.[19a] Scholars are divided on whether to consider him the father of the new wave of cultural creativity, which was imminent in Germany, Austria and Russia, or the last of the era in Italy, whose beginnings go back to the twelfth century. This uncertainty regarding the individual carries a symbolic significance. One is hardly entitled to claim that modern Hebrew literature is indebted to Judeo-Arabic writings, but one can say with full justice that it is a link in the golden chain that was first forged in biblical times, and, after a long interruption, resumed in the Moslem world, whence it has continued steadily to our day. Indeed the contribution of the Judeo-Arabic period lies not alone in the rich legacy of works which exerted a profound influence on subsequent Jewish thought, but in that it kindled a light which, sometimes glowing brilliantly, sometimes merely flickering, continued to burn until it gained a new brilliance in modern Hebrew literature. Traveling by way of Provence, Italy and Holland, medieval literature found a fertile soil in eastern Europe, where Jewish life pulsated at its strongest in the nineteenth century, and there it once again began a rich and variegated activity which continues right to the present in several Jewish centers and, most notably, in Palestine.

NOTES

[1a Cf. above Judah Goldin, "The Period of the Talmud," pp. 181 ff.]
[2a Cf. above the chapter by Hillel Bavli, "The Modern Renaissance of Hebrew Literature," and the one below by Yudel Mark, "Yiddish Literature."]

[3a Cf. above Elias J. Bickerman, "The Historical Foundations of Post-biblical Judaism," pp. 93 ff.]

[4a Cf. above Cecil Roth, "The European Age in Jewish History (to 1648)," pp. 233 f.]

[5a Cf. above the chapter by Shalom Spiegel, "Medieval Hebrew Poetry."]

[6a Cf. Goldin, op. cit., pp. 197 f.]

[7a Cf. ibid., pp. 191 f.]

[8a On the Sura Academy, cf. ibid., pp. 177-178.]

[9a Cf. ibid., pp. 161 f.]

[10a Cf. ibid., pp. 148-149.]

[11a Cf. Spiegel, op. cit., pp. 549-550.]

[12a Cf. Goldin, op. cit., pp. 159-160.]

[13a Cf. above Alexander Altmann, "Judaism and World Philosophy," pp. 627 ff.; also Ralph Marcus, "Hellenistic Jewish Literature," pp. 775 ff.]

[14a Cf. Altmann, op. cit., pp. 638-639.]

[15a Cf. Spiegel, op. cit., pp. 550-551.]

[16a Cf. Altmann, op. cit., pp. 642-643; for his poetry see Spiegel, op. cit., pp. 551-553.]

[17a Cf. Altmann, op. cit., pp. 643 f.]

[18a Cf. Roth, op. cit., pp. 223-224, 234.]

[19a Cf. Spiegel, op. cit., pp. 557-558.]

BIBLIOGRAPHY

HALPER, BEN-ZION, "Jewish Literature in the Arabic Language," (Hebrew) in *Ha-Tekufah*, XXIII, 262-275. Warsaw, 1925. And XXIV, 359-388. Berlin, 1928.

KARPELES, GUSTAV, *Geschichte der juedischen Literatur* (3rd. ed.) Berlin, 1920-1921. Vol. I, 398-448.

STEINSCHNEIDER, MORITZ, *Die arabische Literatur der Juden*. Frankfort a.M., 1902.

———, *Jewish Literature from the Eighth to the Eighteenth Century*. London, 1857. Pp. 59-203.

WAXMAN, MEYER, *A History of Jewish Literature from the Close of the Bible to Our Own Days*. New York, 1930-1941. Vol. I, pp. 155-375.

ZINBERG, ISRAEL, *Geschichte fun der literature bei Yiden* (Yiddish) (History of Literature among the Jews). Wilna, 1929. Vol. I.

ARNOLD, SIR THOMAS, and GUILLAUME, ALFRED (eds.), *The Legacy of Islam*. Oxford, 1931.

FRIEDLAENDER, ISRAEL, "Jewish Arabic Studies," in *Jewish Quarterly Review*, new series, I, 183-215; II, 481-516; III, 235-300. Philadelphia, 1910-1912.

O'LEARY, DE LACY, *Arabic Thought and its Place in History*. London, 1922.

TRITTON, A. S., *The Caliphs and Their Non-Muslim Subjects*. London, 1930.

CHAPTER 19

ISRAEL IN IRAN
(A Survey of Judeo-Persian Literature)

By Walter J. Fischel

INTRODUCTION

The history of Persia from its very beginning until today, from Cyrus the Great to Riza Khan Pehlevi—a history covering twenty-five centuries equally divided by the Arab conquest of the year 642 into a pre-Islamic and an Islamic period—has seen an uninterrupted and continuous association between Iran and Israel. Israel has been living on Iran's soil from the dawn of the first Persian Empire on, as an inseparable part of Iran's national destiny and development. Jews were the eyewitnesses of all the historical events in Persia under every dynasty—the Achamenids, Parthians and Sassanids, the Omayyads and the Abbassids, the Seljuks, Mongols, Safavids and Kajars, under every ruler, Caliph, Sultan, Il-khan, Emir or Shah. Jews were the contemporaries of all the manifold religious movements and sects that were born on Persian soil, such as Zoroastrianism, Manicheism, Shi'a, Sufism, Bahaism; they were companions of the great classical poets, of a Firdusi, Hafiz, Sa'adi, Jami, and of all the other great Persian masters of art, literature and philosophy who made their everlasting contributions to world culture.

Did this twenty-five centuries old association of "Iran and Israel" produce any literary works of value on the part of the Persian Jews? What is the literary heritage of Persian Jews that has come down to us as a result of twenty-five hundred years of Iranian-Jewish association? Have Persian Jews left a cultural legacy, a literature which bears the distinct stamp of Israel in Iran and which could be regarded as a typical and specific contribution of their own in the sphere of Jewish and Persian culture and literature?

In other words, did this association of twenty-five hundred years between Israel and Iran produce any lasting values in the realm of culture and scholarship?

EARLY INTELLECTUAL CO-OPERATION BETWEEN MOSLEM AND JEWISH SCHOLARS

The first recorded appearance of Persian Jews in the cultural sphere after the Arab conquest took the form of sectarian and heterodox movements. More than any other group of Oriental Jewry it was the Persian Jews who had been affected by the intellectual commotion which the conquest of the Arabs and the collision of victorious Islam with older religious systems and movements on Persian soil had produced. It was, as has been recognized, in conjunction with and parallel to the sectarian movements in Persia and as their reflection that Persia became also the birthplace of Jewish sects, the home of pseudo-Messianic rebels and heretics. All the various manifestations of Jewish sectarianism in early Islam are geographically as well as spiritually, to a large degree, products of the Persian Shiite environment, and bear very clearly the marks of Shi'a Islam. As the names and the origin of their spokesmen already indicate, Abu 'Isa came from Isfahan, his disciple Yudghan from Hamadan, Mushki from Kum, Hivi from Balkh, Abu 'Isa ben Levi, the friend of Ibn ar-Ravendi, from Ahwaz.

Even the Karaite movement,[1a] though basically different from these sectarian groups, was led by personalities who sprang from Persian soil, such as Benjamin from Nehavend, and Daniel ben Moses from Qumis, and many of their adherents, according to Kirkisani, were to be found in Khorasan, in Jibal, Fars, Tustar and other parts of the Eastern Caliphate.

The leaders of these sectarian movements and their followers were mostly "a community of simple-minded, uneducated Jews, removed from the Babylonian center of talmudic learning," and therefore an easy prey to Messianic and heterodox ideas. They were described as "barbarian and ill-bred people, destitute of intellect and knowledge," and were condemned as "more ignorant than the rest of the Jews." In the light of statements of that kind, though they actually referred only to the sectarians, it was maintained that Persian Jews as a whole had ceased to be a cultural factor, that they had exhausted themselves and remained in a state of lethargy and intellectual stagnation. This assumption, however, can hardly be justified.

Despite their legal status as nonbelievers and hence separated from the Mohammedans, Persian Jews did not live in a spiritual vacuum. They were by no means mere eyewitnesses and observers. They may have lived physically in a Ghetto, but they shared the cultural and intellectual climate of their time and of all times, and were continuously affected by the cultural and religious conditions and conflicts in the world of their neighbors. The very rise of these sectarian movements, irrespective of

A PAGE FROM A JUDEO-PERSIAN MANUSCRIPT

From the Adeshir Book by the poet, Shahin, written in the 14th century in Hebrew in Persian characters. This manuscript was copied c. 1650.

In this illustration Shah Bahman (in the center) is being told of the disappearance of his son, Shero Bahman, according to Jewish tradition, especially by Shahin, was identified with Artaxerxes of the Book of Esther, and Shero was supposed to be the son of Vashti. (This information is given by Professor Walter J. Fischel.)

their merits, proves this interrelationship and interdependence of Iran and Israel.

This sectarianism was, however, but one manifestation of that inter-relationship. It can hardly be overlooked that Jewish scholars from Persia and Khorasan actively participated in the intellectual trends of the "Golden Age" in the ninth and tenth centuries. One has only to glance through the famous literary depository, the *Fihrist*, or other con-temporary Islamic sources, to realize how interwoven the intellectual activities of Jews and Moslems were and how numerous were the bonds that connected Israel and Iran.

Persian Jews could hardly have sunk as low as has been believed, when among them translators, scientists, poets, mathematicians and astronomers were found who served the rulers and their court, or who readily gave help and information whenever called upon. It is only because of the general anonymity of the process of cultural revival of Islamic civilization in the Middle Ages that more names of Jewish scholars from Persia and Khorasan have not been preserved.

It must also be noted that when the Old Testament and the history of Israel became the object of investigation by Persian scholars—as was already the case with Arab authors, such as Mas'udi—they called on Jewish scholars for authoritative advice and authentic information.

Largely responsible for this kind of intellectual co-operation, for the development of a sort of "Hebrew scholarship" among Persian scholars, was the so-called "*Shu'ubiyya*" movement. This movement, in the ninth and tenth centuries, was a literary reaction among Persian and other non-Arab Moslems against the claim of the Arabs concerning their racial, literary and linguistic superiority over non-Arab peoples. The leaders of this movement challenged this contention and tried to prove the equality of all Moslems or even the superiority of the non-Arab Moslems in the field of literary and linguistic accomplishments. It was this attitude that stimulated non-Arabs, composed of Syrians, Greeks, Copts, Persians and others, to stress the specific values of their own national and religious culture and to emphasize their own particular contribution in the fields of science and literature.

It is not without interest to mention that one of the most active pro-moters of these Shu'ubite, Iranophile tendencies was Abu Ubayda M'amar b. al-Muthanna (d. 825), a scholar whose grandfather was allegedly a Jew from Persia.

These endeavors, especially on the part of Moslem scholars of Persian origin, led to an interest in comparative studies of religion and culture. They satisfied their urge for knowledge of the culture of ancient peoples by getting into direct touch with the living representatives of ancient civilization. Stimulated by these Shu'ubiyya tendencies, some of the outstanding scholars, such as the historian Hamza al-Isfahani and the scientist, al-Biruni, consulted with Jewish scholars in order to understand the Jewish past.

This Hamza al-Isfahani (d. 963), by origin and education deeply rooted in Iranian civilization, devoted his energy to the acquiring of knowledge about the Bible and the Jewish past. Just as he derived his knowledge of other religions through personal contact with their respective representatives, he sought information concerning the Bible through the method of direct and personal contact with Jewish scholars. In his *Annals* he expressly mentions a book on Jewish chronology by an otherwise unknown Pinhas ibn Bata al'Ibraniya, which he had consulted with the help of a Jew. He refers also to the personal contact he had with a Jew by the name of Zidkiya, from whom he obtained a historical sketch of biblical chronology. Nor does he omit reference to another Jewish scholar, of whom he said, "I met in Bagdad in the year 921, one of the Jewish scholars who claims to know the books of the Torah by heart. I heard from one of his disciples that he could recite twelve books of the Prophets."

Al-Biruni (d. 1048), who might be regarded as the greatest of Moslem-Hebraists and who is justly considered the most original and profound thinker that Islam has produced in the realm of physical and mathematical science, derived his knowledge of Judaism by this very method of personal consultation with Jewish scholars. He drew his knowledge of Judaism not only from books of his predecessors, among whom that of al-Eranshahr must have figured prominently, but also, like Hamza al-Isfahani, from learned Jews whom he consulted during his travels through Persia, Khorasan and elsewhere. He recognized his indebtedness to Jewish scholars more than once and mentions the oral and written Jewish sources he had used. He pays tribute to a Jewish scholar by the name of Jacob ben Musa al-Nikrisi, of Jorjan, in the southeastern corner of the Caspian Sea, as one of his collaborators, and gives quotations also "in the name of a Jew who is considered a wise and learned man." He undoubtedly met with other Jewish scholars, Rabbanites or Karaites, who co-operated with him, and it was probably due to such co-operation that he also had access to such Hebrew written books as *Seder Olam* and *Megilat Taanit*. That his informants were Persian-speaking Jews is evident from the manner in which the many Hebrew terms and words which he mentions in his studies, notably in his *Chronology of Ancient Nations*, are vocalized and transliterated in his works.

Al-Biruni is, however, not the only one who offers proof of the cultural interchange between Israel and Iran. The study of the Bible and of Judaism, as well as other religions, was stimulated also by a movement, quite different from that of the *Shu'ubiyya*, namely, the *Isma'ili* movement.

The leaders of this branch of Shia Islam, in their attempt to propagate their ideas concerning the seventh Imam among all religions and creeds, and in their endeavor to bind together Arabs and Persians, Christians and Jews, and, indeed, all mankind, regarded as necessary the study of the holy books of other religions, including the Old Testament.

Nasir-i Khusraw (d. 1083), traveler, poet and scholar, one of the most colorful figures of eleventh-century Persia, was one of those Isma'ili missionaries who included in his studies the religion and history of other peoples. This keen observer of foreign lands and peoples put his impressions in his Persian-written *Safer-nama*, which is not only the first diary of a traveling philosopher known in the Persian language, but also the first and earliest Persian description of Palestine of the eleventh century. Nasir-i Khusraw noticed the flocking of the Jews to the Wailing Wall in Jerusalem and states: "From all the countries of the Greek, and from other lands, the Christians and the Jews come up to Jerusalem in order to make their visits to the Church of Resurrection and the Synagogue . . . that is there."

In Tiberias he noticed "a mountain upon which has been built in hewn stone, a castle, and there is an inscription in Hebrew characters, stating that at the time it was cut, the Pleiades stood at the head of the zodiacal sign of the Ram." This passage in his diary may allow the assumption that he was able to read the Hebrew script. Indeed, in his *Autobiography*, he mentions Hebrew among the various languages he had studied.

The interest of Isma'ili leaders in Hebrew and the Bible found an even clearer expression in the work of al-Kirmani (d. 1013), the chief missionary of the Isma'ili movement in Persia in the eleventh century. He inserted into his Arabic-written work on the *Imam*, Hebrew and Syriac Bible passages, which he quoted, not in translation, but in transliteration. We must assume in this, as in previous cases, that he derived his knowledge of Hebrew from a co-operation with Jewish scholars who, in view of the specific pronunciation and transliteration of the Hebrew words, were undoubtedly Persian Jews.

Kirmani does not stand alone in this usage of Hebrew quotations and transliterations. The interest in comparative religious studies led more than one Moslem scholar to acquaint himself with the Hebrew Bible and other aspects of Jewish life. Shahrasthani of Ghazna (d. 1153), one of the outstanding Moslem historians of religion in medieval Islam, had a forerunner in Abu Ma'ali Mohammed ibn 'Ubaidallah (d. 1092), a Sunna Moslem. His *Bayyan al Adyan* (Treatise on the Religions), written as a result of a theological disputation at the court of the sultan in Ghazna, is not only the most ancient treatise on comparative religion in the Neo-Persian language, but also the first which does not limit itself to Islam alone, and encompasses all religions of the world.

This Persian scholar dealt also with the various Jewish sects and beliefs, the institution of the Exilarchate,[2a] the Hebrew names of God in the Bible. Of particular interest in his account of the Jewish religion is his insertion of the first three words of the Pentateuch in their Hebrew form in Persian transliteration. As in the case of Kirmani and al-Biruni, these quotations undoubtedly presuppose direct contact and co-operation with Jewish scholars in Khorasan, though Abu Ma'ali does not reveal his source of information.

The existence of Jewish scholars among Isma'ili groups, such as the Assassins in medieval Persia, is well attested by the Jewish traveler, Benjamin of Tudela, who states: "There are learned men among the Jews of these lands."

This intellectual help which Persian Jews had rendered to Mohammedan scholars, this mutual borrowing, giving and taking through direct personal contact, must be regarded as an important factor, as a constructive and creative contribution of Persian Jews to the learning of their times. It undoubtedly serves as a barometer of the degree of their cultural assimilation and sheds light on one phase of the relationship between Israel and Iran.

The question, however, must still be asked, whether the century-long association of Israel and Iran has produced something more tangible and feasible than this intellectual co-operation indicates, and whether Jews have produced any literary works of their own in the language of the Persian Jews. In other words, was there developed a Judeo-Persian literature?

In the first centuries after the Islamic conquest a Persian literature of the Jews could hardly be expected. Just as there was no literary production in the Persian language by Persian Mohammedans, so in these first centuries there could be no literary production in the Persian language by Persian Jews. It may be recalled that the Arab conquest of Persia in 642 meant not only the end of the political and national independence of Persia for many centuries to come; the military conquest of Persia was at the same time accompanied by a religious transformation leading gradually to the triumph of Islam over Zoroastrianism, to the replacement of Ormuzd by Allah, of Zoroaster by Mohammed, of the Avesta by the Koran, of the Fire-Temple by the Mosque.

But this religious transformation of Persia led also to a linguistic conquest which brought about another fundamental change in the cultural structure of Persia. With the introduction of Islam, Aramaic—then the lingua franca of the East—was superseded by the Arabic language and Arabic alphabet. This linguistic conquest, more effective than the religious one, ultimately made Arabic, the language of the conqueror, the only instrument and vehicle of expression by any creative Persian mind for centuries to come.

The Jews within Persian territory were also fundamentally affected by the victorious march of the Arabic language. Their literary productivity, if any, would no longer be expressed exclusively in Hebrew or Aramaic, but in Arabic. For the Jews in the realm of the Caliphate Arabic indeed became the language of conversation and literary production.

If we define Judeo-Persian literature as works composed by Persian Jews in the Persian language and written in Hebrew characters, then this type of literature could be expected to come into existence only when the Persian language had penetrated so deeply into the daily life of Persian Jews that they could use it for literary expression: when they had attained such a degree of cultural assimilation to their surroundings that they could become productive and creative in this language.

Early Judeo-Persian Documents

No attempt is made here to describe the various stages in the penetration of the Persian language into the daily life of Persian Jews. Nevertheless, it is evident that after the conclusion of the Talmud an ever-increasing infiltration of Persian into Jewish circles took place. Indications of this process are the presence of Persian linguistic elements in the late responsa literature; the use of Persian by Jewish scholars, especially Hai Gaon, to explain difficult Hebrew, Aramaic or Arabic words; the frequent occurrence of Persian words in the works of Karaite scholars of Persian origin. Moreover, some early documents have come to light which reveal the actual use of Persian by Persian Jews.

The earliest document that attests to the use of modern Persian by Jews is a fragment of a Persian business letter, only recently found at Dandan-Uylik, near Khotan, in Chinese-Turkestan—comprising thirty-seven Persian written lines in Hebrew characters by a Jewish merchant, probably of the early eighth century. This letter represents the sole specimen of early Hebrew script and at the same time the earliest available document in modern Persian of any sort. Also extant are four signatures in Persian with Hebrew characters by Jewish witnesses on a copper plate referring to a grant for a Christian church on the coast of Malabar (early ninth century), as well as a letter in Judeo-Persian from Ahwaz in Khuzistan of the year 1020.

We may assume that as a result of the revival of Persian language and literature from the end of the tenth century on, Persian became even more definitely established as the language of the Jews within the orbit of Persian culture. The statement of Judah ibn Tibbon that "most of the Geonim in the Dispersion under the rule of Ishmael in Babylon, Palestine and Persia were speaking Arabic, and likewise all the Jewish communities in those lands were using the same tongue . . . and whatever commentary they wrote on the Bible, Mishna and Talmud, they wrote in Arabic"

was no longer applicable to Persian Jews of that time. This is confirmed
by the fact that the Jewish leaders in Bagdad in the twelfth century
found it necessary to use Persian in their correspondence with the Jewish
communities in Persia. The *Igrot* of Rabbi Samuel b. Ali, the Gaon of
Bagdad, which reveal so many details concerning the internal religious
and cultural life of Jews in Babylonia and Persia, include a letter written
by the Gaon Salomon of Bagdad in 1152 to a Jew in Hamadan by the
name of Safi. This letter contains not merely Persian words, but is written
almost entirely in the Persian language. It may well be that but for the
fragmentary character of the correspondence we would have much more
evidence for the ever-increasing assimilation of Persian Jews to the Persian
language and culture in the twelfth century.

But these documents and letters, indicative of the new trend as they may
be, can hardly be classified as literary products. In view of the absence
of any literary records in Judeo-Persian until the thirteenth century, it
seems that the Jews of Persia had not yet attained that degree of assimilation which would have enabled them to be creative in the Persian language.
It took, as we shall see, another century for the spiritual energies, accumulated by the Persian Jews over centuries, to be released, and for conditions
to be ripe for the birth and growth of a genuine Judeo-Persian literature.

The Genesis of Judeo-Persian Literature

It is significant that the first fruits of a genuine Judeo-Persian literature
became visible only at a time when Persia again had acquired the leading
place in the cultural life of the East, and when Persia as a whole was in a
position to make its most valuable contributions in the Persian language to
science, history and literature. This was not under the rule of the Caliphate
but under the Mongol Il-khan rule over Persia, from the middle of the
thirteenth century on.

For the understanding of the background out of which grew the
Judeo-Persian literature, it must be recalled that the Mongol conquest of
Persia brought about a decisive transformation in the life and culture of
Persia as well as in the position of the Jews in Persia. After the victorious
march of Hulagu and the fall of Bagdad in 1258, Islam lost its dominant
position in the eastern provinces of the Caliphate and became just one
religion among others. With this, the Islamic concept of the *Ahl adh-
dhimma*, the Protected People, was deprived of significance. The Mongols
regarded all men as belonging to one and the same stock and did not
differentiate between believers and nonbelievers, Christians, Jews, pagans.
This change in the religious attitude under Hulagu Khan and his immediate successors meant for the non-Moslems in Persia, for Jews and
Christians alike, a considerable improvement of their status, and afforded
them a few decades of the greatest political and religious freedom ever
experienced in Persia before or after.

At no time in the centuries-long association between Israel and Iran have Persian Jews been as prominent in public life as in the thirteenth and fourteenth centuries. They had by that time attained that degree of assimilation which enabled them to become court officials, court physicians, court astronomers and, above all, political leaders, viziers of the great Mongol Persian Empire.

It was particularly under the Il-khan ruler Arghun (1281-1289), a grandson of Hulagu, that Persian Jews appeared almost suddenly on the stage of history and began to participate actively in the political and cultural life of Persia. This awakening of Persian Jewry under the Mongols, the freeing of their intellectual energies, found its dramatic expression in two ways, politically and culturally.

The political rise of Persian Jewry in the thirteenth century is connected with the names of Sa'ad ad-Daula and Rashid ad-Daula.

The rise of Sa'ad ad-Daula, a Jew from Abhar in Persia, from the position of a physician to the Il-khan Arghun to the highest possible political office, that of vizier, prime minister, is one of the most spectacular chapters in Persian Jewish history. Though this appointment of a faithful Jew as vizier for a heathen ruler over a region predominantly Moslem was short-lived, and ended in a catastrophe for Sa'ad ad-Daula and the whole upper strata of Jewish officialdom in Babylonia and Persia, Sa'ad ad-Daula can be regarded, after the biblical heroes Esther and Mordecai, Ezra and Nehemiah, as the most important Jew ever to play a decisive role in the political life of Persia.

Rashid ad-Daula, too, attained the rank of vizier, serving in continuous succession three Il-khan rulers. He was a Jew from Hamadan, who, at the age of thirty, turned Moslem. His Jewish descent, long controversial, is now definitely established, not only by his familiarity with Jewish customs and his knowledge of the Hebrew language, but by his own confession shortly before his tragic end. Unlike Sa'ad ad-Daula, however, Rashid ad-Daula entered the annals of Persian history not only as a vizier but also as a famous scholar, as a writer on medical sciences, and above all as one of the greatest historians Persia ever produced. His great historical work *Jami-i Tawarikh*, is described as "unquestionably one of the most important historical works in the Persian language"; it opened a new epoch in Persian historiography.

It was in this very atmosphere, in which Persian Jews could play such a leading role in public life and make their contribution to the culture of their country, that signs became evident of an intensified interest in the Jewish past and of a Jewish cultural awakening. There arose Jewish scholars, rooted in Persian-Islamic culture, who not only began to apply their abilities to public services but who tried to cultivate their own Jewish heritage and to promote Jewish literary values in their own language, in Persian written in Hebrew characters. It was due to these circles that a genuine Judeo-Persian literature came into existence which found its expression mainly in three fields: in Bible translations and Bible research, in Hebrew transliteration of classical Persian poetry, and in composition of original Judeo-Persian poetry.

Judeo-Persian Bible Translation

This circle turned its attention first of all to the Bible text and attempted to produce a correct translation into Judeo-Persian. Despite the long association between Iran and Israel, no translation of the Bible into Persian by Jews had been known until then. The discussion in talmudic literature of the use in the synagogues of Bible copies in foreign characters, in transliteration or in translation—especially the question of the reading of the Book of Esther in Greek, Coptic, Elamite or Median—may allude to the existence of such transliterated or translated biblical books. The numerous biblical quotations in Pehlevi literature in the ninth century, especially in the polemic works called *Dinkard* and *Shikand* suggest an existing translation in Pehlevi. It is impossible to decide from which source these Bible quotations were taken. Possibly they were based on versions common among Jewish communities in the times of the Sassanids. It may be that the Mazdeans obtained their Bible knowledge through Christian writers or, perhaps, through the medium of Mohammedan scholars, for it was just in the time of the author of *Shikand* that the knowledge of the Old Testament became rather widely known among Mohammedans, because of the Mohammedan polemics against the *Ahl al-Kitab*, the People of the Book. The assertion of Theodoret, the Syrian bishop of the fifth century, that there existed an old Persian translation of the Bible, or the view of Maimonides that an old Persian translation was extant long before Islam, cannot be substantiated; in any event, no record of such a translation has come down to us.

The first Judeo-Persian Pentateuch translation that has become known outside Persia goes back to the sixteenth century. The publication of the Jewish Polyglot Bible, in 1546, by Eleazar b. Gerson Soncino in Constantinople, contained, side by side with the Hebrew original, the Targum and the Arabic version of Saadia Gaon, as well as a Judeo-Persian translation of the Pentateuch in Hebrew characters. The author of this Judeo-Persian translation was Jacob b. Joseph Tawus, a Jewish scholar from Persia, who apparently functioned as a teacher at the Jewish Academy in Constantinople, established by the Jewish physician of Sultan Sulaiman, Moses Hamon (1490-1576).

It is astonishing that this Judeo-Persian product, the first printed work in modern Persian of any sort, remained rather unnoticed and failed to attract the attention of the Jewish scholarly world of that time. Only when over a century later, in 1657, the Tawus version was transliterated from its Hebrew alphabet into Persian characters by Thomas Hyde, and incorporated into the famous London Polyglot Bible of Bishop Bryan Walton, was interest aroused in this new field of Persian and Jewish literature. It was long believed that this Judeo-Persian Pentateuch translation was not only the oldest but also the only literary achievement of its kind produced by Persian Jews until then. Yet this Tawus Pentateuch translation, though the first to become known and the first to be printed, was far from opening a new field in the literary achievement of Persian Jewry. According to our present state of knowledge it seems actually to stand at the end of a long chain of Bible translations, and represents only the culmination in Judeo-Persian Bible studies, which had been going on for several centuries.

The available manuscript material, housed in European libraries, establishes that the oldest Judeo-Persian Pentateuch version dates back to the year 1319; the manuscript, now in the collection of the British Museum, has as its translator or copyist a certain Joseph b. Moses. Also other manuscripts, which are now known—particularly that which the Italian traveler Giambattista Vechietti[3] brought back from Persia at the beginning of the seventeenth century, now in the Vatican; as well as other manuscripts in the collections of Paris, Petersburg and London—though they may have been copied in the seventeenth century, all go back to copies or originals which can be "not earlier than the thirteenth century, and not later than the fourteenth century," as Salomon Munk had already observed.

At what exact time Persian Jews started to occupy themselves with Bible translations cannot be established. The references in Ibn Ezra's Bible commentary to two Jewish scholars of Persia, Yahuda Ha-Parsi and Moses ben Amram Ha-Parsi, indicate only the interest of Persian Jews in biblical exegesis. It is also impossible to localize the particular communities where these activities were fostered, though Isfahan, Hamadan, Shiraz, Yezd and Lar figure prominently as places of origin of the Judeo-Persian Bible manuscripts. These questions can be answered only on the basis of a future comparative study of all available Judeo-Persian Bible manuscripts; though it can be assumed that in view of the uniformity of style, the general use of Aramaisms, and the choice of the same Persian equivalents, the version of Tawus and all the other manuscripts may belong, if not to the same translator, at least to one and the same school of translators, which must have flourished as early as the fourteenth century.

The activities that centered around the Bible led in the course of time to the translation of all the canonical books of the Bible, and even of some books of the Apocrypha, copies of which are preserved in various libraries.

The translations of the books of the Bible into Judeo-Persian were supplemented in the fourteenth and fifteenth centuries by Bible commentaries and lexicographical studies. Only a few fragments of this branch of Judeo-Persian literature (such as a Judeo-Persian commentary on Ezekiel and a commentary on Samuel, *Amukot Samuel*) have been preserved.

The study of the Bible by Persian Jews led also to the composition of lexicographical treatises for the understanding of the language of the Bible. Already in the earliest Judeo-Persian Pentateuch of 1319 reference is made to a certain Abu Sa'id. He is said to have composed a treatise concerning difficult words in the Bible and their meaning. Manuscripts such as *Biur Milot Ha-Torah*, *Perush Ha-Milot* and similar treatises indicate the interest Persian Jews always had taken in the lexicographical field. Two real Bible dictionaries composed by Persian Jews have come down to us which are of particular importance. The earlier of these, a vocabulary of the Bible, Talmud, Targum and Midrash with Persian translation, called *Sefer Ha-Melizah*, was finished in 1339 by Salomon b. Samuel, who hailed from the city of Urgenj in Transoxiana. It must have been quite popular, since it was copied by a Jew of Merv and from there came into the possession of a Jew of Samarkand.

The other Hebrew-Persian dictionary, *Agron* (fifteenth century), covering the vocabulary of the Bible in its Hebrew and Aramaic elements, originated in northern Persia. Its author was Moses b. Aron of Shirwan. Both these dictionaries attest to the spiritual interests of Jewish communities in the remote regions of central Asia as well as in the equally unknown settlements of northern Persia, and indicate that Jewish scholars, well acquainted with Rabbinical literature, occupied themselves with Bible studies of that kind.

Historical and Philological Importance

These early Judeo-Persian Bible translations, commentaries and lexicographical works are of interest in more than one important aspect. Historically they show that Jews in medieval times in Persia and even in the remote settlements in Transoxiana were far from being altogether as isolated from the rest of the Jewish world, as was hitherto believed. The authors of these works seemed to be well acquainted with the leading Rabbinical authorities of western Europe, and show to an astonishing degree the penetration of European Bible exegesis into their works. The Judeo-Persian Bible translations, from the very first available manuscript of 1319 on, indicate that the Persian Jewish scholars remained faithful to the Rabbinical traditional method of Bible exegesis and that they used as sources not only the Targum but also the works of Rashi, David Kimhi, ibn Ezra. It was to them that Persian Jews looked for guidance and advice in their search for the understanding of the Bible text. There can be no doubt that Rashi's commentary was well known to the Jewish scholars of Persia. In the dictionary of Salomon b. Samuel, Rashi is expressly referred to as "Salomon the Frenchman"; and how closely the anonymous author of *Amukot Samuel* followed in his Persian commentary that of Rashi is indicated by the fact that he incorporated into his work whole portions of Rashi's commentary, along with its French explanations. Rashi and, no less, David Kimhi were freely used by the school of translators of the Bible into Judeo-Persian and many of their interpretations have been incorporated into the Judeo-Persian translation of the Pentateuch and Prophets. How, and through what channels, the works of the Jewish scholars from Europe reached the Persian Diaspora, how they were transmitted and received, has still to be determined.

The philological and linguistic value of these old Judeo-Persian texts is of no less importance than the historical one. They enable us to establish the specific nature and structure of the dialect spoken by the Jews in Persia, with all its linguistic peculiarities. The archaic flavor of the vocabulary, the many ancient phonetic, lexical and grammatical forms, the retention and conservation of many old words and forms of the Persian language not to be found in the oldest Persian documents, the strange combination and amalgamation of Semitic and Indo-European linguistic elements, have made these Judeo-Persian literary productions a rich and important source for Iranian lexicography. The systematic utilization of these products will undoubtedly continue to yield important results for Persian philology, and will enrich Iranian lexicography. This has been recognized by Semitists and Iranists, foremost among them Paul de Lagarde, who stated: "From now on nobody can claim to know the Persian vocabulary who has not utilized from the very beginning to the very end these Judeo-Persian translations."

Classical Persian Poetry in Hebrew Transliteration

With all the devotion of the Jews of Persia to their own religious and cultural heritage, and despite their efforts to cultivate and translate into Judeo-Persian the literary values transmitted to them from the Bible down to the poetry of a Judah Ha-Levi,[4a] a Salomon ibn Gabirol,[5a] an Israel Najara and others, Persian-speaking Jews manifested (as we shall see) a special interest in the classical poetry of Persia. This Persian poetry must have made a lasting impression on them; for they share with their Mohammedan neighbors a deep admiration for the great masters of classical Persian poetry: for Firdusi, Nizami, Rumi, Sa'adi, Hafiz and others. The Jews probably knew by heart many verses by these poets and tried to familiarize themselves, as well as wider Jewish circles, with these literary products. However, there was one great obstacle to this objective: the Arabic alphabet used in writing the Persian language.

Although Jews in Islamic countries learned the language of their neighbors, whether Persian, Arabic or Turkish, they never completely surrendered to that language. Jews in the Islamic world would not adopt the alphabet of their neighbors. Whatever they wrote in Persian, private correspondence, poetry, or prose, they wrote exclusively in Hebrew characters. Thus, Persian Jews deliberately excluded themselves from Persian literature in general and maintained a graphic independence with their Hebrew script—however complete their assimilation to the language of their neighbors may otherwise have been. Jews regarded the Hebrew characters as so integral a part of their religious and national heritage that the use of a foreign alphabet and one of a religiously different group would have been considered as a sign of conversion, an act of betrayal, yes, as a breach of religious loyalty. It was probably this reason which made Judeo-Persian literature in all its manifestations a kind of literary Ghetto, removed from general Persian literature; and this accounts for the fact that in the annals of Persian literature Judeo-Persian productions remain unnoticed and unknown. It was probably because of the association of the Arabic alphabet with the religion of Islam that Christian Syrians also preferred to write their Arabic mother tongue in Syrian letters, just as the Armenians and Greeks used their respective characters for their writings in the Turkish language.

The refusal of Persian Jewry to employ the Arabic alphabet for their writings and literature did not, however, prevent them from attempting to popularize Persian poetry among their fellow Jews. To overcome the graphic problem the method adopted was to transliterate or transcribe the content from the Persian into the Hebrew script. Thus some of the most important works of Persian authors were put into Hebrew dress; they were transferred into Hebrew characters with strict and exact retainment of the language, rhyme and meter of Persian poetry.

To these remarkable efforts we owe a new branch of Persian literature, which led a kind of independent existence though parallel to the general body of Persian literature. That this task of bringing some of the literary products of Persia into the Hebrew camp was carried out is evidence, indeed, of a great love of Persian poetry by Persian Jews and of their liberal spirit. Through this process of transplanting, Persian-speaking Jews were enabled to participate in the cultural achievements of their surroundings.

The few manuscripts so far known bear testimony that all the various types of Persian classical poetry were selected to be put into Hebrew characters. In this form we have *Khosroe and Shirin* and *Haft Peikar* by Nizami (d. 1202), the exponent of romantic poetry; Jalal ad-Din Rumi (d. 1273), the most eminent Sufi poet Persia has produced, was represented by parts of his *Mathnawi*. Sa'adi (d. 1291), the exponent of didactical poetry, entered Judeo-Persian literature with some parts of his *Gulistan*. The *Diwan* of Hafiz (1390), the master of lyrical poetry, was entirely transliterated. So, too, the whole of *Yussuf and Zuleika* of Jami (d. 1414), the last great classical poet of Persia. Even part of the *Diwan* of Sᶜaib of Isfahan (d. 1670), the prominent court poet of the post-classical period, and many other minor poets, were made accessible in Hebrew transliteration. In this way also Persian prose became part of Judeo-Persian literature. Stories by Farid ad-Din Attᶜar from Nishapur (1157-1201) and stories by other, later Persian authors were translated or transliterated.

It is worth mentioning that the *Rubaiyat* of Omar Khayyam, so famous in Europe through FitzGerald's English translation, did not find a transliterator, as far as we know; but translation into modern Hebrew has repeatedly been made in recent years.

In connection with the Judeo-Persian manuscript of Saᶜadi's *Gulistan*, it is interesting to see that the refusal of Persian Jews to use anything but Hebrew characters continued well into the nineteenth century. In this manuscript one poem appears in Persian-Arabic script, but the Jewish owner or copyist, uneasy about the presence of these verses in Persian characters in an otherwise purely Hebrew transliteration, felt the need for an explanation or apology, for he adds that "a Moslem official of the governor, by the name of Jemjid of Ghilan, inserted this poem of Saᶜadi in the Persian script, in the year 1833."

The interest in Persian poetry in Hebrew transliteration seems to have been alive in some Jewish communities of Persia until recent times. Joseph Wolff, a visitor to Meshhed in 1831 was surprised to find there "a sort of Judaized Sufis with translations of Koran, Hafiz, Rumi into Hebrew . . . many of them had actually imbibed the mystery of the Persian Sufis. We heard them instead of singing the hymns of Zion reciting in plaintive strains the poetry of Hafiz and Firdusi and the writing of Masnavi . . ."; and it sounded like a great discovery when, in 1888, an English observer wrote that "the Jews of Persia have the 'Diwans' of Hafiz, Saᶜadi, the Khamsa of Nizami and the prose and metrical works of other popular Persian authors in their own character."

How this process of transliteration was carried out, if and to what degree an intellectual co-operation between Jewish and non-Jewish Persian scholars was established, in what particular communities and at what exact time and by whom this type of Judeo-Persian literature was produced, can hardly be established on the basis of the limited material available.

It would be illuminating if the criterion according to which the authors of these transliterations selected their material could be established. Was it no more than the individual translator's or copyist's taste and love of poetry? Was the "Jewish element" in the classical Persian poetry perhaps an attraction? This can hardly be assumed, since the Persian authors and poets—except for Saᶜadi—mention astonishingly little of the Jews and Judaism of their own time and place, and contain only allusions and hints to biblical heroes and symbols, to Moses, Sinai, Torah, synagogue and the like. It is much more likely that the special attraction of these works came from the philosophy behind the poetry, which was the philosophy of Sufism, the doctrine of equality of all religions, with its general human appeal, with the removal of confessional ties and its drifting from Islamic anchorage. It is a philosophy which found eloquent expression in verses such as

> Rites and Creeds count for little with God
> Who dwells neither in Mosque nor Church nor Temple
> But in the pure heart . . .

or in verses by Jalal ad-Din Rumi:

> I adore not the cross nor the crescent
> I am not giaour or a Jew
> East nor West, Land nor Sea is my home
> I have no kin nor with angel nor gnome
> I am wrought nor of fire nor of foam
> Soul and body transcending
> I live in the soul of my loved one anew.

Such a view could hardly fail, despite the deep-rooted attachment of Persian Jews to their own heritage, to make a strong impression on their minds. There is even documentary evidence from the Jews in the Arabic-speaking environment of Bagdad and Egypt which attests as early as the tenth century to the penetration of Sufic thoughts into Hebrew circles as evidenced from fragments of the *Genizah*. Hebrew transliterations from Sufic thoughts of Hallaj, the famous mystic of the tenth century, of Ghazali (d. 1111), the greatest of the Islamic theologians, and later material prove an early encroachment of Islamic Sufism and it is not unlikely that these Persian transliterations of Sufic thought into Hebrew constitute the result of the same tendency.

Judeo-Persian Miniatures

Persian Jews, combined with their admiration for Persian poetry, the love for the pictorial art and miniatures of their neighbors. It should therefore not be surprising to find that to these Hebrew transliterations of a Nizami, Sa'adi, Hafiz, Jami and to the Judeo-Persian poetry of a Shahin and Imrani, colored illuminations were added which in color, technique, representation of figures, are hardly distinguishable from those illuminations in pure Persian poetical works. These miniatures could well be regarded as typical Persian artistic products were it not for the explanations added in Hebrew characters. Of these miniatures in Judeo-Persian manuscripts twelve large illustrations in Nizami's *Khosroe and Shirin* and miniatures in his *Haft Peikar* are outstanding, as well as illuminations in

Jami's *Yussuf and Zuleika* and the thirty-one illuminations in a Shahin manuscript.

Again, many questions arise from these illuminations. We do not know whether this pictorial art was cultivated by Jewish artists or only the Hebrew explanations were the work of a Jew; whether there was a school of Jewish artists in existence specializing in this field; and if so, how far, if at all, co-operation went between Jewish and Persian scholars and artists. An interesting example of co-operation in this field between Jewish scholars and religious leaders of Persia is provided by a manuscript of Bible illustrations dating back to the time of Shah Abbas I and preserved now in the Morgan Library in New York. It was in 1607 that there arrived in Isfahan from Cracow an ambassador on behalf of Pope Clement VIII, who wished to solicit the tolerance of the Shah toward the Christians in Persia and also to ask for his aid in a war against the Turks. As a present from the Polish cardinal of Cracow, this ambassador submitted a manuscript of Bible illustrations containing eighty-six full-page miniatures of Old Testament illustrations. These illustrations, probably from the middle of the thirteenth century, had at the bottom an explanation in Latin made in Naples about 1300. Shah Abbas I, after receipt of this manuscript, gave orders "to take an expert mulla [clergyman] to the Christian missionary and to get from him the meaning of each picture and insert it below in the Persian tongue."

Owing to unknown circumstances, probably after the destruction of Isfahan in the Afghan-Persian wars in 1722, these illustrations came back via Cairo to London where they were for sale in 1833 and were later, in 1916, purchased by J. Pierpont Morgan of New York. It must have been quite surprising to find that these illustrations contained not only the explanatory text in the original Latin and the Persian translation as ordered by Shah Abbas, but also Hebrew transliterations of the Persian text at the margins of each miniature. Whether the Shah had ordered a Persian Jew to add explanations in Hebrew or a Jew who got possession of the illustrations added the Hebrew to the Persian and Latin of his own initiative can hardly be decided. The fact, however, sheds light on the existence of Jewish copyists and scribes in Isfahan, the residence of Abbas I, and may serve to indicate a close contact between Jewish and Persian scholars.

A clear proof of intellectual co-operation in Isfahan of the eighteenth century is furnished by a Persian source, namely, the famous "Memoirs" of Sheik Mohammed Ali Hazin (1692-1779), *Tadhkirat al Ahwal*. This Persian traveler and scholar was very eager to obtain reliable information from representatives of the various religions and established contact with a learned Jew in Isfahan. About this we read in his book: "Among the Jewish inhabitants in Isfahan, who, as they believe, have been dwellers in that town since the time of Moses, there was one named Shuaib, the most learned of his brethren. I gained his confidence and took him to my house. From him I learned the Bible and its interpretations which were written out for me, and informed myself of the truth of all that they maintain."

Judeo-Persian Poetry

These productions of Judeo-Persian literature in the field of Bible studies and the Hebrew transliterations of classical Persian poetry are, however, not the only expressions of the literary awakening of Persian Jewry which can be traced back to the times of the Mongol Il-khans' rule over Persia in the thirteenth and fourteenth centuries. The creative abilities and intellectual vitality of Persian Jews opened another field of Judeo-Persian cultural activity. Under the influence of classical Persian poetry, there arose Jewish poets who, closely following the patterns of Persian verse, began to compose poetry devoted to Jewish subjects.

The man who can be hailed as a pioneer of Judeo-Persian poetry, as the first Jewish poet in the Persian language so far known to us, first in time and in importance, was Maulana Shahin. Scanty as are the data concerning his life, we know that he was born at the end of the thirteenth century in Shiraz, the seat of a large Jewish community, and wrote during the rule of the Mongol Il-khan Abu Sa'id al-Behadur (1316-1356), to whom he dedicated his first work.

Inspired by a keen desire to promote a knowledge of the Jewish past among his fellow Jews, Shahin applied the form, meter, structure and language of Persian classical poetry, particularly of Firdusi and Nizami, to the biblical narrative. His lifework represents nothing less than a poetical commentary on the Bible, a poetical paraphrase of the Pentateuch, known as *Sefer Sharkh Shahin al Ha-Torah,* written in Persian with Hebrew characters, and divided into a "Book of Genesis," a "Moses Book," an "Ezra Book" and an "Ardeshir Book." It is an *Epos of the Jewish Past* in Persian, shaped after Firdusi's *Epos of the Iranian Past.* By selecting Jewish themes as the subject of his poetry and by celebrating the heroes of the Bible, particularly Moses, in a way typical of Persian classical poetry, Shahin has put the past of Israel in Iranian garb, and has thus produced the most typical literary expression of the association between Israel and Iran. He must have been conscious of the originality of his achievement, for he speaks of himself as having kindled a new lamp in composing this work to tell everyone of the greatness of Moses.

In making biblical themes and heroes the content of his poetry, Shahin combined Persian art and form with Israel's religion and history. He used three heterogeneous sources and combined them into one organic entity. Along with a thorough knowledge of the Bible and Rabbinic literature (Talmud, Midrashim) he, the Persian Jew of the fourteenth century, showed an amazing mastery also of the Koran and Islamic tradition, and an equally great knowledge of classical Persian poetry. His work testifies to his wide Jewish knowledge and consciousness, and reveals the degree of assimilation and absorption of the cultural values of his environment.

It seems that with his *Epos* Shahin satisfied the particular taste of his countrymen; it must have enjoyed great popularity. He lives on in the memory of Persian Jews as "our Master," "Maulana" Shahin, as the founder of Judeo-Persian poetry, as the Firdusi of the Jews. It is indicative of his popularity that manuscripts of his works were widely spread among many Jewish communities throughout the Persian-speaking Diaspora, to Shiraz, Teheran, Bukhara, Balkh, Samarkand and elsewhere, where they were read and studied in synagogues and at home. Yet Shahin's work might have fallen into oblivion and been entirely forgotten were it not for a Jewish scholar from Bukhara, Simon Chacham, who, at the beginning of the twentieth century rescued part of Shahin's literary heritage, the Genesis Book and the Moses Book, by publishing it in Jerusalem.

It was in the very birthplace of Shahin, in Shiraz, that two centuries later a successor in the person of the Jewish poet Imrani appeared. Inspired by Shahin's poetical paraphrase of the Pentateuch, Imrani made the post-Mosaic period of the Bible, the historical books from Joshua to Kings, until the time of Solomon, the object of his poetical presentation. Closely following the example set by Shahin, in method, form and language, combining also (though to a lesser degree) Islamic and Persian sources with the biblical narrative, Imrani in 1523 wrote his *Fath Nama* (The Book of the Conquest) which, due to its resemblance in style, was erroneously attributed to Shahin.

Imrani is also the author of *Ganj Nama* (The Book of Treasures), composed in 1536; it is a poetical paraphrase of the Mishna treatise *Pirke Abot*, which is used, however, only as a frame for themes of general meditation and religious contemplation.

Evidently that type of Judeo-Persian poetry initiated by Shahin and followed by Imrani was quite popular, for it was continued by another Jewish poet called Yahuda Lari; of his *Makhsan al-Pand* (The Treasure House of Exhortation) only a small part (151 verses) has come down to us.

It is not surprising that neither Shahin nor Imrani nor Lari, so typically Persian in their compositions, entered the annals of Persian literature. By using Hebrew characters for their poetry, they kept themselves from becoming known to their Persian Moslem neighbors.

Under the Safavid Dynasty (1502-1736)

The Safavids, the new dynasty which ruled for more than two centuries, put Persia on entirely new foundations, very different from those of the Il-khan rulers. By introducing Shi'a as the state religion, by establishing a powerful hierarchy of the clergy, and by regarding all nonbelievers as ritually unclean, the Safavid rulers effected a change in the political and cultural climate, and this change had far-reaching repercussions on all aspects of Jewish life.

To illustrate the changed atmosphere, it might suffice to mention the attitude of Shah Tahmasp (1524-1526) toward the famous English traveler and merchant, Anthony Jenkinson. Upon arrival in Kazvin, then the capital of the Safavids, with a letter from Queen Elizabeth of England, he was immediately ordered to depart: "Oh thou unbeliever," said the Shah, "we have no need for friendship with the unbelievers!" Or again, Shah Isma'il II (1576-1577) hesitated to mint new coins of silver or gold because he could not bear the idea that these coins, which had on their obverse the Mohammedan confession of faith, should be touched by and fall into the hands of nonbelievers. Another shah threw a golden ring into the sea when he heard that it had been made by a Christian goldsmith. Shah Sephi II (1667-1694), at the advice of his chief minister, changed his name into Sulaiman, "in order to prevent that the Jews, having practiced some sorcery upon his person . . . have any power over him."

A change for the better was effected only through Shah Abbas I (1587-1629), the outstanding Safavid ruler. He introduced extensive reforms to weaken the theocratic basis of the state which his predecessors had built up, to free Persia from the fetters of its all-too-powerful Shi'a clergy, and to put an end to the political, economic and cultural isolation of Persia. Shah Abbas, realizing that the most urgent requirement for Persia was increased population and economic ties with the outside world, fundamentally changed the policy of the state toward non-Moslems and foreigners. Far from being antagonistic toward Europeans and nonbelievers, as his predecessors had been, he encouraged the immigration of foreigners, merchants, settlers and artisans from neighboring countries such as Armenia, Georgia, Turkey, as well as from Europe. By granting freedom of religion and special privileges and facilities to all those who were ready to come to his territory, he was able to succeed in this purpose. It was his liberal and tolerant attitude that made Persia at that time the meeting place of European envoys, emissaries, diplomats, merchant-adventurers, missionaries —all eager to obtain commercial, political or religious concessions and privileges. Never before in the history of Persia's relationship with the outside world were the ties between Persia and Europe, economically and politically, closer.

This close relationship between Persia and Europe did not fail to have its effect on Judeo-Persian literature. It was because of this contact that the literary activities of Persian Jews became known for the first time to the outside world. Jewish history is particularly indebted to the Italian diplomat and traveler, Giambattista Vechietti (1552-1619), for having brought to Europe knowledge of Judeo-Persian literature (in the form of Judeo-Persian manuscripts). On behalf of Pope Gregory XIII, toward the end of the sixteenth century (1584), Vechietti went to the East entrusted with a double mission, to conciliate the Patriarch of Alexandria and to enlist the assistance of the Persians in the Pope's fight against the Turks. Unlike other envoys and diplomats of that time, Vechietti combined with his diplomatic pursuit a great interest in old manuscripts and versions of the Bible. It is of utmost significance that it was the city of Lar from which some of his material originated. It is expressly stated that in 1601 he commenced the revision of the Persian translation of the Psalms and other biblical books in Lar.

Lar was not only the home of a Jewish poet but must have been the seat of a school of scribes, translators and copyists who devoted themselves with great zeal to the cultivation of Jewish traditional values and to translating or copying books of the Holy Scripture into the Persian language, written, however, in Hebrew characters. Not a few of the Judeo-Persian manuscripts found today in European libraries and containing translations of the prophets Isaiah, Jeremiah and Ezekiel as well as of Joshua, Judges, Samuel, Kings, Ruth, Ezra and Nehemiah, Chronicles and the translations of apocryphal books such as Tobit, Judith, Bel and the Dragon, Megilat Antiochus and others, can be traced in their geographical origin to Lar, where in the first decade of the seventeenth century they were either translated or copied by a zealous group of Jewish scholars.

Under Shah Abbas II (1642-1666)

The second part of the seventeenth century was, for the Jews of Persia, a time of great suffering and persecution. The conception of the ritual uncleanliness of the Persian Jew, which led to the introduction of a special headgear for all Jews in Persia and to a crusade against secret, cabbalistic Hebrew books, culminated under Shah Abbas II in the forced conversion of all the Jews in Persia, a catastrophe which brought them to the very brink of destruction. This persecution, a tragic parallel to the Inquisition of Spain centuries earlier,[6a] regarded as "more cruel than that of the time of Ahasuerus and Haman, more terrible than that of the time of Hadrian," came as an unexpected blow. The Jews were thrown "into dreadful consternation when all of a sudden an edict from the king [Abbas II] was issued and published in every place in Persia, commanding them on pain of death to abjure the Jewish religion and profess thenceforth that of Mohammed."

The available sources describe in great detail how the Jews were compelled to abandon their religion, how the synagogues were closed, how they were forced to eat meat boiled in milk in order to emphasize their break with Jewish tradition, how they were now called *Yadid al-Islam* and were taken to the mosque and instructed in their new religion. The heroic resistance of the Jews led to the phenomenon of "Marranos," or Anusim, and for years they lived a dual religious life, in secret remaining Jews while confessing Islam officially. Only when it became evident, after almost seven years of forced conversion, that "whatever pretenses the Jews made to Mohammedanism, they still practiced Judaism, so that it was necessary to permit them again to become bad Jews because they could not make good Mussulmans," did the vizier and leaders of the Shi'a clergy allow them to return to their former religion.

In such an atmosphere of hatred and intolerance, when all the energies and efforts of Persian Jews had to be concentrated on physical survival, one could hardly expect any kind of literary activity on their part. The kind of Judeo-Persian literature that was nevertheless produced bears all the marks of the time and mirrors the grim and tragic reality of Jewish life.

It was in the city of Kashan that the torch of Jewish learning was rekindled in the seventeenth century and it was there that the martyrdom of Persian Jewry found its literary expression in a Judeo-Persian chronicle entitled *Kitab-i Anusi: The Book of the Events of the Forced Conversions of Persian Jewry to Islam;* its author was the Jewish poet Babai ibn Lutf from Kashan, himself not only an eyewitness, but a victim of the events. The poet began his work in the very midst of the persecutions under Shah Abbas II in the year 1656 and his chronicle covers the events from 1617 down to his own time. His account is one of the most important sources we possess for this or for any other period of the history of the Persian Jews. From no other source in Persian or in any other language do we obtain such an interesting glimpse into the inner life of the Jewish communities in Persia of the seventeenth century. His work is a mine of information in regard to their political persecution, their life as Marranos, their geographical distribution and economic structure, their religious customs, superstitions, places of pilgrimage and names.

It sheds a most interesting light on the relationship between the authorities, the shah, the vizier, the governors, the clergy and the Jews; at the same time it reveals the pettiness and jealousy, the lack of unity and leadership in the Ghettos of the Persian Diaspora, faults which in no small measure were responsible for the Jews' political sufferings.

The chronicle reflects also the personality of its author. He must have been a deeply religious Jew who interpreted the tragedy that had befallen his people as a punishment for their own sins, for the neglect of Torah and mitzvot, and for disunity among their leaders. "In the period of the Flood there was a Noah, in another period there arose an Ezra, in our time there is no leader," he exclaims; and adds, "We have neglected the five books of Moses, therefore God has delivered us for five years to Islam; we have abandoned the Torah, now we are forced to learn the Koran; we neglected the fast days, now we must fast the whole month of Ramadan, we did not visit the synagogue, so God caused us to go to the mosque."

In language and form, in the arrangement of facts, in the symbolism and in the metaphors, this chronicle, though written in Hebrew characters, is typically Persian. It bears witness to the great influence that Persian classical poetry, especially Hafiz and Sa'adi, no less than Shahin and Imrani, had exerted on this Jewish poet of the late seventeenth century.

Despite its unique historical importance and its reliability, by no means lessened through its poetical form, its place within the annals of Jewish historiography has hardly been given due recognition. Yet this Judeo-Persian chronicle could very adequately be called the *Emek Ha-Bakha* or the *Shebet Yehuda* of Persian Jewry, for it made Jewish life in an Islamic country, and particularly the Galut within the Shi'a Islamic world, its main theme.

Babai ibn Lutf, whose chronicle describes the events from 1617 to 1656, found a continuator in his grandson Babai ibn Farhad, also of Kashan. In language, form, meter, symbolism and in the presentation of facts, his chronicle closely follows the work of his grandfather, leads to the events that occurred sixty years after Babai ibn Lutf's report, and covers the sufferings and persecution of Persian Jewry during the troubled times of the Persian-Afghan wars up to 1725.

Among other literary productions of that time, mirroring the martyrdom of Persian Jews, mention should be made of a Judeo-Persian poet by the name of Mashiakh b. Raphael and also of Mulla Hiskijahu of Isfahan, whose elegies reveal the heroism, endurance and courage of the victims of the forced conversion.

Sabbatai Zevi

The sufferings of Persian Jewry at that time were intensified by the disappointment caused through the Sabbatai Zevi incident.[7a] As in Turkey, so in Persia Sabbatai Zevi aroused tremendous excitement, and Persian Jewry, always in an attitude of Messianic expectation and yearning for the deliverance from the yoke of the Galut, were then in a perfect mood to receive the message of the new Messiah with the utmost inner readiness. The only reference so far known to the reaction of Persian Jewry to Sabbatai Zevi illustrates this readiness. From the French traveler J. Chardin, an eyewitness of the events in 1666, we hear:

I remember, when I was in Hyrcania in 1666, just at the time when the Jews of Turkey made so much ado about a false Messiah by the name of Sabbatai Zevi—that also the Jews of Hyrcania believed like the others that the redeemer for whom they had so vainly waited so long, had arrived. They left their houses, went out in the fields, covered themselves with sack and ashes, fasting and praying for the appearance of the Messiah.

The governor of the province sent to them asking: "What are you doing, you poor devils, thus to abandon your work, instead of thinking of paying your taxes?" "The taxes, sir," they answered, "we shall not have to pay any more, our redeemer has arrived." They negotiated with the governor of the province to allow them to offer their prayers without interruption, for the time being—if within three months the redeemer would not appear with a strong hand in Persia, they would very promptly pay the taxes they owed.

Jewish Colony in China

At the beginning of the seventeenth century, in the time of the Safavids, another center of Jewish settlements appears on the horizon of Jewish history. This is the Jewish community in Kai feng Fu in China, of which nothing was known before then.

Its romantic discovery in 1607 by European missionaries, its history as revealed by stone inscriptions and the question of its origin—did the original immigrants penetrate into China along the sea route via India, or along the land route via Khorasan and Turkestan?—cannot be dealt with here. Mention of these Jews is justified, however, because their liturgy and literature show a distinct Judeo-Persian influence.

Persian touches in the writings of these Chinese Jews are very numerous. They divide the Pentateuch into fifty-three sections as do the Persian Jews and, like them, count twenty-seven letters of the Hebrew alphabet by treating the final letters as separate consonants. The instructions in their prayer books are given in Persian, they call their religious leader, their rabbi, with the Persian word *Ustadh*; a Hebrew inscription in their synagogue contains lines in the Persian language; to a Chinese manuscript of Genesis a colophon in Judeo-Persian is attached, and in their prayer books "the rubrics are all in Persian and most of the Pismonim therein also exist among the Persian Jews." The manuscript of their Pesah Haggada contains verses translated into Judeo-Persian.

All this indicates that this Chinese Jewish colony was liturgically and linguistically under the influence of the Jews of Persia.

Nadir Shah (1736-1747) and Judeo-Persian Literature

The dynastic struggles, the anarchy and revolts that fill the pages of the history of Persia in the eighteenth century, following the overthrow of the Safavids by the Afghan dynasty in 1722 under Mahmud, made the whole of Persia a vast battlefield. While Persia faced the Afghan invaders from the east it had to encounter the Turkish invaders from the west and the Russians from the north. This was hardly a time for cultural concentration and relaxation. "At a time when the Mohammedans fought against each other, how much less safe were the Jews?" exclaimed the Jewish chronicler, Babai ibn Farhad, of that period. These dynastic changes and struggles meant for the Jews only "that they fell into the hands of new oppressors."

From out of this chaos there arose a man who at least for a short while brought back to Persia order and stability; he also has a particular significance for the Jews and Judeo-Persian literature. The man was Nadir Shah. Not only was he one of the greatest military geniuses of the East (he restored Persia's military power and extended her frontiers far into India and Afghanistan) but he was at the same time a kind of religious reformer and thinker. With his ascent to power, he abolished Shi'a Islam as state religion, which it had been under his Safavid predecessors, and replaced it with Sunna Islam. Motivated by religious as well as political considerations, he not only aimed at a unification of Sunna and Shi'a but fostered the idea of a universal religion, comprising Islam, Christianity, Judaism and Zoroastrianism. It was with this purpose in mind that he arranged public religious disputations in which the various religious representatives participated and in which the Shah showed an amazing degree of tolerance. As his court physician he appointed the Jesuit Father Louis Bazin. Nadir Shah took a great interest in the holy books of all religions and it is reported that he ordered the translation of the New and the Old Testament into Persian. He sent a mulla to Isfahan to collect such Jews, Armenians and Franks as were considered necessary for this translation. The translation of the New Testament was started in May, 1740, with the help of Roman Catholic missionaries and Orthodox Armenian monks, while the translation of the Old Testament was entrusted to Jewish rabbis. Also the Koran was ordered to be translated into Persian. Of the Old Testament only the Pentateuch and the Psalms seem to have been completed, by a Jew from Isfahan, Baba ben Nuriel, copies of which are preserved.

Nadir Shah's importance for the Persian-speaking Jews manifested itself not only in his tolerant attitude but also in the establishment of a new Jewish settlement, out of which a center of Judeo-Persian culture emerged. This settlement was in Meshhed, his own residence.

Meshhed, the holy city of Shiites in Persia, seat of the mausoleum of Imam Riza, the most important place of pilgrimage for the Shi'a Moslems, was to become, under Nadir Shah, an important strategic point for the protection of the eastern borders of his empire. In order to increase its permanent population and not to have to rely on the fluctuating elements, the pilgrims, he transplanted groups of people from other corners of Persia to this city. Through this shifting of population, Meshhed became the seat of a Jewish community, which originated in Kazvin, in northern Persia. Prior to Nadir Shah there were no Jews in Meshhed, for its holy character excluded nonbelievers from this part of Persia. Neither the Safavid rulers nor the population with its religious fanaticism would have permitted their holy city to be "contaminated" even by the mere presence of Jews. Only Nadir Shah, a man with strong Sunna convictions, a foe of the Shi'a, and bent on religious reforms, could dare, despite the opposition of the Shi'a clergy, to establish a Jewish community in such a city.

Without going into the development of the community thus created, we have evidence that it prospered economically as well as culturally. The exponent of the literary activities carried on here was Siman Tob Melamed, a poet and philosopher, the spiritual leader through whom Meshhed entered the annals of Judeo-Persian literature. Melamed is the author of *Azharot*, a collection of liturgical poetry in Judeo-Persian, parts of which were written in Persian, as well as Aramaic and Hebrew. The poems often carry his name in acrostic. Though his songs became a great source of inspiration for the Jews of Meshhed and other communities in central Asia and exerted great influence on their liturgy, his fame lies in his philosophical-religious book, *Sefer Hayyat ar-ruh*, a kind of commentary to Maimonides's teachings, dealing with Israel's *Galut* existence and ultimate salvation. The work is strongly influenced by the ethical and Sufic ideas of Bahya ibn Pakudah's *Hobot Ha-Lebabot*. For more than a century kept as a manuscript, this *Sefer Hayyat ar-ruh* found a redeemer in an Afghan Jew, who printed it in Jerusalem in 1898.

The tradition of Siman Tob Melamed was carried on even after the forced conversion of the whole community in 1839, which led to the phenomenon of *Yadid al-Islam*, Marrano Jews in an Islamic version, still in existence today, as observed by the present writer during his stay in that city in 1936. Among the leading figures of this community, which secretly remained Jewish though officially Moslem, Mordecai ben Raphael Aklar, known as Mulla Murad, stands out prominently through his many contributions to Judeo-Persian literature. He translated into Judeo-Persian the prayer book for weekdays and Sabbath known as *Oneg Shabbat*. There is also incorporated a Hebrew poem by another Jew from Meshhed, Solomon ben Mashiakh. This poem describes the tragic events that led to the forced conversion of the community. Apart from his *Oneg Shabbat*, Mulla Murad translated into Judeo-Persian *Selihot*, *Piyyutim*, the *Haggada shel Pesah*. These were published in Jerusalem after he succeeded in settling there, and there he died a few years ago, having served two generations as the secret *Rav* of the community in Meshhed.

Bukhara

Towards the end of the seventeenth century the center of gravity in the field of Judeo-Persian activities shifted to an area which until then had remained a rather unknown spot on the map of the Jewish Diaspora in

Asia, namely, Bukhara. Bukhara, once an important center of Islamic culture in central Asia and a rallying point of Islamic scholars and scientists, must have had a Jewish community from early days. However, the origin of the community is shrouded in great obscurity. The Jewish traveler of the twelfth century, Benjamin of Tudela, refers only to Samarkand and to the leader of its Jewish community, Rabbi Obadya Ha-Nasi. The earliest authentic reference to Jews in Bukhara comes from an Arab chronicler of the thirteenth century, Ibn al-Fuwati, who reports that in 1240 a Mohammedan ordered the killing of all the Christians and Jews then living in Bukhara. It seems, however, that the Jews survived this threat, as also the vicissitudes which must have come upon them in consequence of the Mongolian invasion and the rule of Timur. Bukharian Jews entered the arena of Jewish history, however, only toward the end of the seventeenth century. They then gained prominence through their literary achievements in the field of Judeo-Persian literature which, discovered only in the nineteenth century, has shed an entirely new light on this least known group of the "Remnants of Israel" in Asia.

Remote from the dynastic quarrels and civil wars on Persian soil, spared also the afflictions and persecutions that swept over their brethren in Persia, the Jews of Bukhara could devote themselves with a greater degree of leisure to literary activities in their own language than their brethren across the border. Their literary heritage shows that they possessed Jewish scholars, poets and translators, who, with great scholarly and intellectual perfection, cultivated the field of Judeo-Persian poetry in their own particular dialect.

The outstanding contribution to Judeo-Persian literature by these Jewish scholars of Bukhara was made by the poet Maulana Yussuf Yahudi (1688-1755). An exponent of that branch of Persian poetry in Hebrew characters which goes back to Shahin and Imrani and which in previous centuries was deeply appreciated by Persian Jews, he became the author of a famous ode, *Mukhammas*, devoted to the praise and glory of Moses, and of *Haft Braderan* (The Seven Brothers), based on the Midrash of the martyrdom of the seven brothers and their mother. These works, together with his hymns in honor of biblical heroes such as Elijah, as well as other poems bearing his name in acrostic, some of which are bilingual and trilingual, form even today an integral part of the spiritual heritage of the Persian-speaking Jews of Bukhara. His *Tafsir* to *Megillat Antioch* deserves particular mention.

Yussuf Yahudi was not less fruitful as translator. Many of the *Zemirot* of Israel Najara, which are incorporated in the collection of the Judeo-Persian songbooks, such as *Yismah Yisrael*, were introduced into Judeo-Persian literature by Yussuf. He must have inspired many of his contemporaries, since in his time a "School of Jewish Poets" was established in Bukhara and they, following his example, composed Judeo-Persian poetry.

Among these Bukharian poets was Benjamin ben Mishal, known also as Amina, who not only published *Megillat Ester* in Judeo-Persian translation in metric form but also translated into Judeo-Persian some poems by Salomon ibn Gabirol, such as *Azharot* and *Yigdal*. It is quite likely that a Daniel Apocalypse, *Daniel Nama,* of a Khodja Bukhari (1705) goes back to this Amina.

Of the many other Jewish poets of that circle, whose names are preserved in acrostics, special mention should be made of Elisha ben Samuel, also known as Mulla Raghib, who translated into Judeo-Persian the romantic story of "Balaam and Joseph," after the Hebrew version of Abraham ben Chisdai, under the title *Shah-Zadeh and the Sufi* (The Prince and the Dervish).

One of the finest poetical products in the Bukharian Jewish dialect came from the Jewish poet ibn Abu-l-Kheir. In his famous *Khodaidad* he narrates the tragic story of a Jewish merchant by the name of Nathaniel (Khodaidad) who, refusing to become a Mohammedan despite all the promises and temptations of the Mohammedan ruler and his Mohammedan neighbors, died a martyr. In making this touching and moving event the object of his poem, the author gives an interesting picture of the religious and political conditions in which the Jews of Bukhara lived in the second part of the eighteenth century, under the rule of the Emir Masum (1788). At the same time this work furnished a most authentic contribution to the linguistic peculiarities of the Persian poetry of Bukharian Jews (publ. by Salemann 1897).

This Bukharian-Jewish school of poets seemed to have had a great share in the popularization also of Persian classical poetry, and cultivated that branch with particular eagerness.

Toward the end of the eighteenth century Bukharian Jews seem to have ceased their creative activity; at any rate we have little knowledge about them. However, their cultural development was decisively influenced by a *shaliah,* a messenger from Morocco, R. Joseph b. Maman al-Maghrebi, who is credited with a revival of religious and cultural life of the Bukharian Jews, which led them at the end of the nineteenth century to emigrate to Palestine, where, as we shall see, they again began to play a decisive and active role in the promotion of Judeo-Persian literature.

Afghanistan

The literary activities of the Jews in centers such as Meshhed and Bukhara seem to have inspired Jews in Afghanistan, about whom hitherto little was known. Though Afghanistan, as part of medieval Khorasan, entered Jewish history in the ninth century particularly through Hivi al-

Balkhi of the city of Balkh, and through Jews from Maimaneh, Merv, and Ghazna, Afghanistan Jewish life fell into oblivion until Judeo-Persian literary evidence in the nineteenth century shed, unexpectedly, new light on these long-forgotten Remnants of Israel.

The history of the Jews in Afghanistan in the nineteenth century is closely connected with that of the Jews of Persia, particularly of Meshhed. Here it can only be stated that no other event so considerably affected the map of the Jewish Diaspora in Asia and also in Afghanistan as the destruction of the community in Meshhed. As a result of the forced conversion, many of the Jews of Meshhed fled and found a haven of refuge not only in Bukhara and Samarkand, but also in the territory of Afghanistan, in Herat, Maimaneh, Kabul and Kandahar, where the more tolerant Sunna Islam allowed them to live as Jews. These fugitives created new Jewish settlements or increased already existing ones, bringing a new spirit to the stagnant cultural life of Afghanistan Jewry. The origin of Afghanistan Jewry of the nineteenth century, from Meshhed, is well attested by one of the leading rabbis of Herat, Mulla Matitjahu Garji: "Our forefathers used to live in Meshhed under Persian rule but in consequence of the persecutions which occurred against them my forefathers came to Herat to live under Afghan rule."

Without any contact with the outside world, Afghanistan Jews led a religious and cultural life of their own and produced liturgical and religious poetry in Judeo-Persian and in Hebrew which can be regarded as a valuable contribution to Judeo-Persian literature. It was in particular the Garji family, successively the leading rabbis of Herat, who wrote commentaries on the Bible and on the Psalms such as *Sefer Hanukkat Zion, Sefer Minhat Shmuel, Sefer Tehillim, Sefer Oneg Shabbat* and others.

These and other literary treasures would have remained unknown but for the migration of Afghanistan Jews to Jerusalem where, thanks to another Jewish family from Herat, the Shauloff brothers, much of the literature of the Afghan Jews was published. Through the initiative of the Shauloffs, deeply devoted to their own literature, the *Sefer Hayyat ar-ruh* by Siman Tob Melamed was published as well, thus symbolizing the close ties that bound Jews from Meshhed with Jews from Afghanistan.

Jerusalem: The Center of Judeo-Persian Activities

Judeo-Persian literature experienced an unforeseen development toward the end of the nineteenth century, not in Persia itself, however, but in Jerusalem. This was due to a wave of immigration of Persian-speaking Jews from Bukhara, Turkestan, Afghanistan and Persia into Palestine. Almost parallel with the *Hovevei Zion* movement from Russia, but probably without direct contact, a great number of Persian-speaking Jews, imbued with a passionate love for Zion, set out for Palestine and in a continuous stream poured into the Holy Land. They came from Teheran and Shiraz, from Hamadan, Yezd and Isfahan, from Kashan and Meshhed, from Herat and Kabul, from Bukhara and Samarkand and from many other centers of Jewish settlements in the Middle East. They settled in Tiberias and Safed, in Haifa and Jaffa (Tel-Aviv); but the bulk of these lovers of Zion went to Jerusalem and established there a colony of Persian-speaking Jews. It was particularly the Jews of Bukhara who went exclusively to Jerusalem; in 1889 they established a "Society of the Lovers of Zion" and built, in 1893, a *Shekuna*, also called *Rehovot*; the present Bukharian quarter of Jerusalem, which in the course of time became the focal point of the settlement of Persian-speaking Jews.

The establishment of this Jewish-Persian colony in Jerusalem not only opened a new chapter in the history of the urban colonization of that city, but inaugurated a new epoch in the history of Judeo-Persian literary activities. The leaders of the Persian-speaking colony in Jerusalem, though content with having attained the realization of their long hoped-for return to the Holy Land, were eager to help their brethren, in both a spiritual and a physical sense, who still remained in the lands of their origin. They intended to create stronger ties between "Zion and Iran," between Jerusalem and the Remnants of Israel in the remote Oriental Diaspora, by offering them religious education and inspiration. With this consideration in mind the leaders of that Persian-speaking colony embarked on a unique enterprise, with far-reaching results for the cultural level of each of the Persian-speaking groups. The enterprise was the establishment in Jerusalem of a publishing center, a printing press, for Judeo-Persian literature, intended to rescue the literary legacy that Persian Jews had brought with them in the form of manuscripts. These works were to be printed and distributed among all Persian-speaking Jews, in Palestine and abroad. Though the press was established partly as a token of gratitude for having reached the land of their hopes, partly to honor the memory of their forefathers, it was destined to bring about a decisive change in the history of Judeo-Persian literature, not yet recognized in its far-reaching effects. Though Jerusalem was not the first place of Judeo-Persian printing activities, and some Judeo-Persian books had been previously published by European scholars as well as by Bukharian Jews (particularly in Vienna and Vilna by the latter)—not to mention the first Judeo-Persian print of any time in Constantinople in 1546—Jerusalem became the exclusive center of Judeo-Persian printing activities. From then on all the liturgical and literary needs of Persian-speaking Jews were satisfied from Jerusalem and its Judeo-Persian press.

It can hardly be attempted nor is it intended here even to enumerate the results of these printing and publishing activities in Jerusalem during two decades; their extent and quantity would preclude such a survey. Almost everything that was thought fit to strengthen the religious and literary interests of Persian-speaking Jews was printed and published. Every field of Jewish literature, Bible, Bible commentaries, prayer books for every occasion, Rabbinical writings, Mishna and *Zohar*, religious philosophy, medieval Jewish poetry, *Piyyutim, Selihot, Pismonim*, Midrashim, historical narratives, anthologies of songs and stories—all this was translated into Judeo-Persian, printed and distributed. Even secular literature from other than Jewish sources, such as parts of the *Arabian Nights*, and a part of Shakespeare's *Comedy of Errors*, which appealed greatly to the imagination of the Oriental Jew, found its way to the translators and printers.

Thus for the first time the Jewish world at large began to realize the quantity and quality of a hitherto unknown branch of Jewish literature.

It is of great significance that these Judeo-Persian publishing activities represented a collective effort, a co-operative endeavor of all the various groups of Persian-speaking Jewry; Jews of Bukhara joined hands with the Jews of Persia and Afghanistan and participated in the greatest common cultural enterprise in the history of Oriental Jewry.

Among the many outstanding figures of the various Persian-speaking communities, although many of them would deserve special reference, only two, one from Samarkand and one from Bukhara, can be presented here.

Solomon Babajan b. Pinchasof of Samarkand, an editor, author, translator and publisher, entered the field of Judeo-Persian publications with his translation of Job, which was followed by Judeo-Persian translations of Judah Ha-Levi's *Mi Kamoha*, Solomon ibn Gabirol's *Keter Malkut* and other liturgical and religious poetry. However, his greatest service to Judeo-Persian literature was closely connected with the *Hibbat Zion* movement of Oriental Jews. A great part of the literary output in Jerusalem was clearly aimed at the furthering of the ideals of Zion and at promoting the knowledge of the Hebrew language among those Jews who remained in Central Asia. A typical expression of this tendency was the Judeo-Persian translation of *Ahabat Zion*, with all its romantic biblical background; so, too, the translation of the *Hatikvah* into Judeo-Persian was attached to many of the Judeo-Persian publications.

However, this tendency was manifested also in lexicographical and linguistic treatises intended to familiarize the Persian-speaking Jews with the Hebrew language and to enable them to attain a sound knowledge of Hebrew, if and when they began to immigrate into Palestine. This trend is evident in a Hebrew-Persian-Russian dictionary, *Sefer Kitzur Ha-Milim*, by David b. Jacob Chwailof, published in 1907 in Jerusalem; it contained about five thousand words in Persian, with their Russian and Hebrew equivalents in Hebrew transcription. The whole edition of this linguistic guide was sent to Bukhara for distribution among the Jews, many of whom, under the influence of Russia, were familiar with the Russian language.

A more interesting and even more curious document is the *Sefer Millim Shisha* by Solomon Babajan b. Pinchasof of Samarkand (Jerusalem, 1909), a dictionary in six languages (all in Hebrew characters) with which the author intended to provide a linguistic equipment for all those Jews of Central Asia who intended to come to Palestine. In the brief Hebrew preface to this little language guide the author says: "I have composed it for the use of our Jewish brethren who intend to go to Jerusalem, to enable them to learn all the languages necessary—without too much trouble and effort."

As such necessary languages in addition to Persian there appear Russian, French (later, in the second edition Ladino), Arabic, Turkish and Hebrew. That this "philological Baedeker" was in great demand and fulfilled its purpose is borne out by the fact that it went into two editions, the second of which appeared in 1912.

When the history of this *Hibbat Zion* movement among Oriental Jews comes to be written, it will be recognized how important a role Zion played in the thoughts and feelings of central Asiatic Jews, and how Jerusalem, thanks to these literary endeavors, has become in a very real sense a spiritual reservoir and cultural center for Persian-speaking Jews and for Oriental Jews in general.

Simon Chacham

Judeo-Persian publishing activities in Jerusalem are intimately connected with the name of a great Jew from Bukhara, Simon Chacham. Born in 1843 in Bukhara, to which his father, Eliahu, had emigrated from Bagdad, he received a thorough Jewish education and became deeply rooted in Jewish tradition. Simon Chacham then went in 1890 to Jerusalem, to join the rapidly increasing colony of Bukharian Jews. It was in Jerusalem that he began his manifold activities as author, translator, editor and publisher.

With the establishment of the Judeo-Persian printing center in Jerusalem, he brought to press for publication not only his own literary compositions and translations but also many of the manuscripts written by his Bukharian countrymen and by Persian authors.

The long, impressive list of Judeo-Persian publications which are due to the initiative of Simon Chacham, to his functions as editor, translator or author, contains almost everything which could meet the religious and liturgical needs of his fellow Jews. Without intending to give here a full bibliography of his works and a detailed description of his contribution, special mention should be made of his Judeo-Persian translation of the biblical novel *Ahabat Zion* by Abraham Mapu. It appeared in Jerusalem in 1908, and became immediately such a popular book among Oriental Jews that a second edition was printed in 1912. Simon Chacham was himself so enthusiastic about this novel that he concluded his translation with the following words: "Whoever reads this book only once, has certainly not yet comprehended it; he who reads it twice has only slightly understood its contents; only he who reads it thrice will fully grasp its meaning and penetrate into the depths of its ideas; but even he who reads it a hundred times until he knows it by heart will certainly wish to read it a hundred and one times."

A special service was rendered by Simon Chacham in publishing part of the *Epos of the Jewish Past* by Maulana Shahin of Shiraz of the fourteenth century; to this work he added his own poetical compositions. Of great service, too, was his publication of the Judeo-Persian translation of the *Shulhan Aruk*, under the title *Likutei Dinim*, prepared by his countryman Abraham Aminoff, the leading rabbi of the Bukharian colony of Jerusalem. These and many other publications were thus preserved and saved from oblivion through the literary efforts of Simon Chacham and his collaborators.

The crown and glory of his literary contributions, however, is his translation of the Hebrew Bible into the Judeo-Persian dialect of the Bukharian Jews. It was a custom among the Jews of Bukhara to have the Bible explained, in schools and especially in the synagogue, orally, by a *meturgeman*, or translator, on the basis of a commentary which had been orally transmitted. This oral method created in the course of centuries differences of text versions and explanations, departing from the traditionally accepted interpretation, and not always faithful to the text of the Bible. In order to eliminate further confusion in this respect, Simon Chacham wished to create "a fixed coin"—a written text of the *tafsir* (commentary) in the dialect of his fellow Jews.

He was motivated also by another factor; he saw in Jerusalem the Remnants of Israel from the four corners of the earth, each using the prayer book and the Bible in his own language and dialect. The Ashkenazim had their Yiddish, the Sephardim their Spaniolish, the Yemenites and Maghribim their Arabic; "Why do we Persian-speaking Jews of Bukhara not possess a translation in our own dialect as well?"

Proud of the culture and language of his country of origin, Simon Chacham desired to make the Bible again a popular work by creating a written standard, authorized Judeo-Persian translation. He knew, of course, of the existence of the Pentateuch translation of Jacob b. Joseph Tawus (1546), but this version could hardly be used for his educational purposes; no copies were available and the versions differed from the specific Bukharian dialect; nor could the Bible edition of the Christian missionaries be used—for obvious reasons. Translations of some parts of the Bible into Judeo-Persian, such as the Psalms (1883), Proverbs (1885), Job (1895), *Shir Ha-Shirim* (1896 and 1904), did exist, but a complete Bible translation for the daily use of Bukharian Jews was lacking, and it was this consideration which prompted Simon Chacham to embark on this great enterprise. His *tafsir*, started in 1906, appeared in successive volumes, along with the Hebrew text, Targum Onkelos and Rashi, and, but for his death in 1910, the whole translation would have been accomplished. He completed the Pentateuch, and the Prophets up to Isaiah 41:9, and it was for his collaborators to complete the translation of the whole Bible.

With this monumental achievement Simon Chacham entered the ranks of the great Jewish Bible translators. What Saadia Gaon did for the Arabic-speaking Jews,[8a] what Moses Mendelssohn did for the German-speaking Jews,[9a] Simon Chacham did for the Persian-speaking Jews of Bukhara. With all his merits as editor, author, translator and promoter, it is his Bible translation that made him pre-eminent in the history of Judeo-Persian literature.

Europe and Judeo-Persian Literature

1. Elkan N. Adler, the Great Collector of Judeo-Persian Manuscripts

In the same period when, through the collective efforts of Persian-speaking Jews, Jerusalem was made the center of Judeo-Persian literary activities, European scholars, Jewish and non-Jewish, began to turn their attention to this branch of literature. It was not only Jerusalem but also Europe that saved the literary heritage of the Jews of Persia. Because of the close contact between Europe and Persia in the nineteenth century, an ever-increasing number of Judeo-Persian manuscripts reached the leading libraries of Europe. Short descriptions of Judeo-Persian manuscripts began to be included in the printed catalogues of libraries, such as Parma, Vatican, Paris, Petersburg, London, Oxford, Berlin, apart from private collections.

To judge from these catalogues European libraries possessed approximately fifty-five Judeo-Persian manuscripts.

A real conception of the size of Judeo-Persian literature was, however, revealed to Europe only when almost parallel with the discovery by Solomon Schechter of the *Genizah* in Cairo, an unexpectedly large collection of Judeo-Persian manuscripts was brought to Europe. The man who, more than anyone else, has enriched our knowledge of the size of Judeo-Persian literature, was Elkan N. Adler. The travels of Elkan N. Adler to Persia and Bukhara, in the years 1896 and 1897, were revolutionary in the history of the collection of Judeo-Persian literature.

Seldom has a journey to the Middle East yielded such far-reaching results for Jewish literature and scholarship in general. While other Jewish travelers to Persia, in the nineteenth century, brought back impressions and observations on Jewish life and conditions, Adler was one of the few who, in addition to this, brought back the literary records of the peoples he visited in far-off lands. He returned from his travels with treasures hitherto unknown and hidden, with over one hundred Judeo-Persian manuscripts which changed fundamentally the prevailing conception as to quantity and quality of the literary productivity of the Persian-speaking Jews.

The collection that Adler brought from Persia and Bukhara to Europe corrected also our knowledge as to the character of Judeo-Persian productions. Most of the manuscripts in European libraries were translations of books of the Bible or of the Apocrypha, and the impression was created that their works were mostly of a religious character. The collection of Adler, however, revealed an all-embracing literature, not only translations, but also original works, not only religious literature, but literature of a secular character, poetry and prose, liturgy and philology; Adler's collection showed that no sphere of literary endeavor had been neglected by Persian Jews in their own language. Though European libraries have been continuously enriched since Elkan Adler with new Judeo-Persian manuscripts, Adler's collection has remained the outstanding single contribution to the field. With the acquisition of Elkan Adler's manuscript collection by The Jewish Theological Seminary of America, in 1923, this great treasure has found its home in New York and will enable scholars to utilize this greatest of all Judeo-Persian manuscript collections.

2. Wilhelm Bacher (1850-1913), the Great Investigator of Judeo-Persian Manuscripts

The efforts of bringing Judeo-Persian manuscripts from Persia and Bukhara to Europe, as manifested in Adler's collection, were supplemented by similar efforts in the field of the investigation and exploration of the Judeo-Persian texts, in the libraries of Europe. Already in the nineteenth century scholars, Semitists and Iranists, such as Salomon Munk, Hermann Zotenberg, Alexander Kohut, Ignazio Guidi, Paul de Lagarde, Theodor Noeldeke, Carl Salemann and Hermann Ethé, to mention but a few, had turned their attention to some of these Judeo-Persian manuscripts. A number of texts, ranging from small excerpts to complete versions, were published during that century, and language and contents have been made the object of these investigations.

Yet none of the scholars has made the study of Judeo-Persian literature so much his own and has so cultivated this new field of literary history of the Jews, as Wilhelm Bacher. While Simon Chacham could be regarded as the greatest *translator* and *publisher* of Judeo-Persian literature, and while Elkan Adler figures as the greatest *collector* of Judeo-Persian manuscripts, Wilhelm Bacher ranks undoubtedly highest among the *investigators* of Judeo-Persian literature.

Wilhelm Bacher, whose very first publication was a dissertation on the Persian poet Nizami (1871), was well equipped for the task of investigating the Judeo-Persian manuscripts. In 1895 he published his first contribution in that field in a Hebrew-Persian dictionary from the fifteenth century. With the availability of Elkan Adler's collection his interest was particularly stimulated and from then until his death in 1913 there passed no year in which he did not write numerous and valuable studies on the Judeo-Persian literature and language; there appeared in those years a continuous flow of publications that made him the undisputed authority in the field.

Elkan Adler's Judeo-Persian manuscript collection would hardly have received its proper evaluation had not Wilhelm Bacher made it one of his main tasks to utilize it exclusively.

There are undoubtedly still hidden treasures of Judeo-Persian literature in the countries of the East, in all the places in which Persian Jews settled (Jerusalem, Afghanistan, Bukhara, Turkestan, etc.); only after a systematic search for them and their description and publication, together with those in European and American libraries, will it be possible to appraise fully the literary production of Persian Jewry and to understand more fully the relationship between Israel and Iran.

Judeo-Persian Literature under the Kajar Dynasty (1796-1925)

In the nineteenth century, under the Kajar dynasty, the cultural life of Persian Jews reached its lowest level. The persecution and humiliation caused by the unchecked rule of fanatical masses, incited by a no less fanatical clergy, brought the Jews, deprived of any help or support, to the very edge of physical and moral dissolution.

In addition to the political pressure against them, there were other forces which threatened their existence as Jews, particularly the Christian missionary activities and the Bahai movement.

In the nineteenth century various Christian missionary societies in England and America embarked on a policy of spreading the gospel not only among the Nestorian Syrians in northern Persia, but also among the Jewish communities throughout Persia and Central Asia. Being fully aware of the deplorable political and social conditions of the Jews in Persia, who, as a result of centuries of persecution by the Shiite fanatics, were weakened in body and in spirit, the Christian missionaries expected to find a fertile soil in the Jewish Ghettos of Teheran, Hamadan, Isfahan and other communities.

That the Jews of Persia as a whole were by no means willing to forget their past and their religion and to follow the new message is borne out by a unique literary product which manifests very clearly the reactions of the Jews to these missionary efforts. The literary expression of the reaction is a *Toledot Yeshu* manuscript, the well-known medieval treatise on the life of Jesus; the Judeo-Persian translation was made in 1844. In translating that polemic treatise into Judeo-Persian, the author was no doubt motivated by the desire to combat the activities of the Christian missionaries of that time and to furnish a weapon of defense to the Persian Jews in their discussions with the Christian envoys. Apart from being the first literary instance that introduced the person of Jesus into Judeo-Persian literature in a polemic and apologetic way, it may even have appealed to the story-loving mind of the Persian Jew as a fantastic and interesting tale. This *Toledot Yeshu* manuscript indicates the kind of writing Persian Jews could produce in the nineteenth century, writing that bears the mark of apology and defense; indeed, Judeo-Persian literature became chiefly a weapon in the fight of Persian Jews for survival.

One of the main tasks of the Christian missionary activities was the distribution of pamphlets and stories with Christian tendencies, which, however, had to be rendered into Hebrew script in order to be read by Jews. For this they needed the help of Jewish converts to Christianity. Fully aware of the linguistic peculiarities of the Jewish population in Persian-speaking countries, the Christian missionaries started preparations as early as 1840 for the translation or transliteration of books of the New Testament into Persian with Hebrew characters. According to the British and Foreign Bible Society, "authority from Calcutta was given to issue an edition of Henry Martyn's translation of the New Testament with Hebrew characters for the use of the Jews in the northeast and southwest of Persia, whose language was Persian but who wrote it only in their traditional script." Thus, in 1847 the first Persian translation of the Gospels, transliterated into Hebrew characters, was printed in London to be distributed among the Jews of Persia.

The London Society also took steps to publish the Old Testament, particularly the Pentateuch, into Judeo-Persian. This task was entrusted to a Jewish convert, Mirza Nurallah of Teheran; he became one of the most active figures in the Protestant mission in Persia.

At the request of the British and Foreign Bible Society, Nurallah prepared, on the basis of the Persian version of the Pentateuch as published by Bruce, a transliteration of the Five Books of Moses into Hebrew characters. This was printed in London in 1895 and then distributed among the Jewish population in Persia.

Nurallah was supported in his efforts by another Jewish convert, Mirza Khodaidad, with whose help the entire Old Testament in Persian translation, transcribed in Hebrew characters, was completed in 1907. For lack of any other Judeo-Persian translation of the Bible in print, it was, curiously enough, this Bible translation which penetrated into the Jewish homes and helped to make the Jew acquainted again with his own Bible.

It is symptomatic of the cultural level of the Jews in that century that to a large degree they ceased to be the creators of a literature of their own, and that others, non-Jews or former Jews, took the lead in creating Judeo-Persian writings for specific propaganda purposes.

This state of affairs is furthermore illustrated by the activities of another religious movement, born on Persian soil, which turned its attention toward the Jews, namely, the Bahai movement. This movement, Babism or Bahaism, a reaction to Shi'a Islam, had no small appeal to certain strata of Persian Jews who were attracted by the fact that this movement had abolished the influence of the clergy and the conception of ritual uncleanliness and treated all the various religious groups on an equal footing. A special apostle was entrusted with the task of winning over the Jews of Persia to that movement. Most prominent as a Bahai apostle was Mirza Abu'l Fadl of Gulpaigan, whose book *Istidlaliyya* was translated and transliterated into Hebrew for propaganda purposes. Other pamphlets, written in Persian with Hebrew characters, as well as the correspondence in Judeo-Persian between a Bukharian Jew Azizullah and a Bahai leader, preserved in the library of Edward G. Browne, are literary manifestations of the effect of the Bahai movement on Persian-speaking Jewry.

The Revival in Teheran

That Persian Jewry did not succumb to the dangers that engulfed it in the nineteenth century became evident in the first quarter of the twentieth century. Thanks to the establishment of schools in the main cities of Persia by the *Alliance Israélite Universelle*, thanks to a more liberal spirit in public life as expressed by the first constitution given to Persia under Muzaffar ad-Din Shah (1909), thanks to a closer contact with the Persian-speaking colony in Jerusalem, and last, but not least, thanks to the renaissance of Jewish life in Palestine, as the result of the Balfour Declaration, a new awakening began also among the Jews in Persia.

This awakening had a particular bearing on Judeo-Persian literature: it led to the transfer of Judeo-Persian printing activities from Jerusalem to Teheran and for the first time in history, made a Persian city, Teheran, the center of a Hebrew printing press, and with it of Judeo-Persian literature.

The first expression of the cultural renaissance of the Jewish youth in Persia was the founding of a "Society for the Promotion of the Hebrew Language" in 1917. Motivated by the endeavor to halt the stagnation and decline of Jewish life, to combat assimilation, ignorance and indifference, this society in 1918 published as the first fruit of its activities a work entitled *Sefer Hisuk Sefat Eber*, a textbook for modern Hebrew. The author was Salomon ben Cohen Zedek of Teheran, a leader of the community and a Persian government official. In more than 170 pages the fundamentals of Hebrew grammar with reading and translation exercises from and into Persian are given. The work is the first attempt of its kind; and it is typical that it concludes with the Hebrew and Persian text of the *Hatikvah*.

This society published also the first *History of the Zionist Movement* in the Persian language in Hebrew characters (Teheran, 1920) by Aziz ben Yona Naim, giving a survey of the Zionist movement and the organizations and colonies in Palestine. The numerous biblical quotations from Isaiah and the Psalms in that history indicate the strong religious and Messianic character of Persian Jewry's conception of Zionism.

This Jewish circle published also a Jewish newspaper in the Persian language, *Ha-Geulah*, and later another paper called *Ha-Hayyim*, which became the mouthpiece of the Jewish renaissance movement in Persia. Some poems of the Hebrew poet Chayyim Nahman Bialik,[10a] were first translated into Persian in these periodicals by Aziz ben Yona Naim. The only other Judeo-Persian newspapers of which we have any knowledge were *Rushnai*, published in Samarkand, and *Rahamim*, published in Bukhara.

The leading figure in this group, which tried to revive Jewish consciousness among the Persian Jews, was Mulla Eliahu Chayyim More, the "most intelligent and cultured rabbi in the whole of Persia." He is the author of three important works on Jewish tradition, history and philosophy in Judeo-Persian, namely, *Sefer Derek Chayyim* (Teheran, 1927), *Sefer Gedulat Mordecai* (Teheran, 1924), *Sefer Yede Eliyahu* (Teheran, 1927), which have exerted a tremendous influence on his generation. Though blind from his early youth, this rabbi represented the most important factor in the efforts to lead Persian Jewry toward a Jewish revival. It is due to him that a new Jewish school, Koresh, was founded in Teheran in 1931, that modern Hebrew was incorporated into the curriculum and that new textbooks such as *Sefer Ha-Mathil* (Teheran, 1933-1934), modeled after Palestinian textbooks, and new prayer books for the Sabbath and holidays, were published to satisfy the religious needs of the Jewish youth.

In these activities a leading role was played also by the brothers Berukim in Teheran, who became the publishers of Hebrew-Persian and Hebrew books.

The political consequences of World War II for Persia have interrupted the process of regeneration and rejuvenation of the Jewish communities. The sound beginnings, aiming at a revival of Persian Jewish life, however, had already opened for the Jews in Persia as well as for all the communities in central Asia new perspectives of the revival of the cultural life of "Israel in Iran."

NOTES

[1a Cf. Judah Goldin, "The Period of the Talmud," pp. 190-194.]

[2a Cf. *ibid.*, p. 175.]

3 For further details on Vechietti, see below pp. 836 f. and also the *Enciclopedia Italiana.* Vol. XXXIV.

[4a Cf. above Shalom Spiegel, "Medieval Hebrew Poetry," pp. 551-553.]

[5a Cf. *ibid.*, pp. 550-551.]

[6a Cf. above Cecil Roth, "The European Age in Jewish History (to 1648)," pp. 237 ff.]

[7a Cf. above Roth, "The Jews of Western Europe (from 1648)," p. 260.]

[8a Cf. Goldin, *op. cit.*, pp. 197 ff.; cf. also above Abraham S. Halkin, "Judeo-Arabic Literature," pp. 792 ff.]

[9a Cf. Roth, *op. cit.*, pp. 261-262.]

[10a Cf. above Hillel Bavli, "The Modern Renaissance of Hebrew Literature," pp. 581 f.]

BIBLIOGRAPHY

With this study a first attempt is made to survey the main and typical literary productions in Judeo-Persian, to place them in their historical background and to interrelate them with the trends manifest in the general Persian cultural development.

A more detailed treatment of the subject with full documentation and annotations will be given in the author's forthcoming book, *The Jews in Persia, Their History and Literature.*

Therefore, a brief selected bibliography will suffice here. Technical reasons prevented a more consistent transliteration of the Arabic, Hebrew and Persian words.

ADLER, ELKAN N., *Ginze Paras u-Madai . . . The Persian Jews, their Books and Ritual.* London, 1899.

BACHER, WILHELM, "Les Juifs de Perse au XVII et au XVIII Siècles." Strassburg, 1907.

———, "Judaeo-Persian Literature," in *The Jewish Encyclopedia.* New York and London, 1905. Vol. VII, pp. 317-324.

———, *Zwei juedisch-persische Dichter, Schahin und Imrani.* Budapest, 1907-1908.

BARTHOLD, V. W., *Mussulman Culture.* Calcutta, 1934.

BLOCHET, EDGARD, "Catalogue des Manuscrits Persans de la Bibliothèque Nationale." Paris, 1905.

BROWNE, EDWARD G., *A Literary History of Persia*. Cambridge (Eng.), 1906 ff. Vols. I-IV.

CURZON, G. N., *Persia and the Persian Question*. 2 vols. London, 1892.

DARLOW, T. H., and MOULE, H. F., *Historical Catalogue of the Printed Editions of Holy Scriptures in the Library of the British and Foreign Bible Society*. London, 1911, Vol. IV, p. 1209.

ETHÉ, HERMANN, "Neupersische Litteratur," in *Grundriss der iranischen Philologie*, ed. Wilhelm Geiger. Strassburg, 1896-1904.

FISCHEL, WALTER J., "Judeo-Persian," in *Universal Jewish Encyclopedia*. New York, 1942. Vol. VI, p. 256.

———, "Literature, Judeo-Persian," in *Universal Jewish Encyclopedia*. New York, 1942. Vol. VII, pp. 96-98.

———, "Persia; from the twelfth to the twentieth century," in *Universal Jewish Encyclopedia*. New York, 1942. Vol. VIII, pp. 464-465.

———, *Jews in the Economic and Political Life of Medieval Islam* (Royal Asiatic Society Monographs). Vol. XXII. London, 1937.

———, "The Region of the Persian Gulf and its Jewish Settlements," in *Alexander Marx Jubilee Volume*. New York, 1949.

———, "Jews and Judaism at the Court of the Moghul Emperors in Medieval India," in *Proceedings of the American Academy of Jewish Research*. New York, 1949.

———, "Secret Jews of Persia: A Century-old Marrano Community in Asia," in *Commentary*. New York, January, 1949.

———, "The Jews under the Persian Kajar Dynasty (1795-1925)," in *Jewish Social Studies*. New York, 1949.

FRIEDBERG, BERNHARD, *Bet Eked Sefarim* . . . Antwerp, 1928-1931.

GRAY, LOUIS H., "The Jews in Pahlavi Literature," in *The Jewish Encyclopedia*. New York and London, 1905. Vol. IX, pp. 462-465.

GUIDI, IGNAZIO, "Di una versione persiana del Pentateuco," (Reale Accademia dei Lincei) Rendiconti. Rome, 1885.

KOHUT, ALEXANDER, *Kritische Beleuchtung der persischen Pentateuch-Uebersetzung des Jacob ben Joseph Tavus*. Leipzig, 1871.

LAGARDE, PAUL DE, "Persische Studien," in *Gesellschaft der Wissenschaften. Abhandlungen*. Goettingen, 1884.

LEVY, REUBEN, *Persian Literature; an introduction*. London, 1923.

LOCKHART, LAURENCE, *Nadir Shah; a critical study based mainly upon contemporary sources*. London, 1938.

MARGOLIOUTH, GEORGE, "Persian Hebrew Mss. in the British Museum," in *Jewish Quarterly Review*, VII, 119-120. London, 1894.

MENASCE, JEAN DE, *Skand-Gumanik Vicar, Une Apologétique Mazdéenne du IX Siècle*. Freiburg, 1945.

MINORSKY, VLADIMIR, "Early Hebrew Persian Documents," in *Journal of the Royal Asiatic Society*. London, 1942, pp. 181-194.

MUNK, SALOMON, "Notice sur Rabbi Saadia Gaon et sa Version Arabe." Paris, 1838.

NICHOLSON, R. A., (ed. and tr.), *Jalal al-Din Rumi: Selected Poems from the Divani Shamsi Tabriz*. Cambridge, 1898.

ROSENTHAL, FRANZ, "A Judaeo-Arabic Work under Sufic Influence," in *Hebrew Union College Annual*, XV, 434-484. Cincinnati, 1940.

SALEMANN, CARL, *Judaeo-Persica; 1. Chudaidat*. Petersburg, 1897.

——, *List of Oriental Mss. Presented to the Asiatic Museum*. Petersburg, 1898.

SELIGSOHN, MAX, "The Hebrew-Persian Mss. of the British Museum," in *Jewish Quarterly Review*, XV, 278-301. London, 1903.

YAARI, ABRAHAM, *Sifre Yehudei Bukhara*. Jerusalem, 1942.

ZOTENBERG, HERMANN, *Catalogue des Manuscrits Hébreux de la Bibliothèque Nationale*. Paris, 1866.

CHAPTER 20

YIDDISH LITERATURE

By Yudel Mark

The Five Periods in the History of Yiddish Literature

Language is one of the principal elements distinguishing the Ashkenazic Jews from the Sephardic. The language of the Ashkenazim is Yiddish, that of the Sephardim, Ladino. Prior to World War II more than ten million persons, about two-thirds of all the Jews in the world, spoke or at least understood Yiddish.

Yiddish evolved from the mixture of several German dialects, through the adaptation of the language of the immediate environment to a unique *modus vivendi* and earlier language patterns, and by the continuous influence of Hebrew, the language of piety and learning. Later, the Slavic tongues exerted an influence over the language. This process of language formation began almost a thousand years ago.

Yiddish literature is only slightly younger than the Yiddish language and accompanied Ashkenazic Jewry wherever it moved. When Ashkenazic Jews arrived in sixteenth-century Italy, it became, for a short time, a center of Yiddish literary work. When an Ashkenazic community flourished in seventeenth-century Amsterdam, it became a center for the printing of Jewish books; there theatrical art in Yiddish was developed and the first Yiddish newspaper founded. When the focus of Jewish life shifted to the Slavic countries, they in turn became nuclei of Yiddish literature. Yiddish literature came to the United States of America with the Eastern European immigrant masses, and the same is true in the Argentine, South Africa or Australia. Yiddish literature will be found on all the continents, wherever there are Ashkenazic, Yiddish-speaking Jews.

The history of Yiddish literature, which is almost eight hundred years old, may be divided conveniently into five periods:

I. The period of oral and manuscript literature—from the beginning to the close of the fifteenth century.

II. The folkbook period—the sixteenth and the first half of the seventeenth century.

III. The period of relative decline—the latter half of the seventeenth and first half of the eighteenth century.

IV. The later half of the eighteenth century to 1864 (the year Mendele Moicher Sforim began writing in Yiddish).

V. The past eighty years (1946).

The first three stages, up to the middle of the eighteenth century, represent the period of old Yiddish literature, reflecting as they do a life governed by tradition, stable, and relatively distinct from the surrounding Christian community, despite ever-present influence from the outside. Some scholars, *e.g.*, Nokhum Shtif, have also included the works of period IV in the older literature. The past eighty years (1946) may also be further subdivided into two periods: the first fifty years, to World War I, and the past thirty years.

1. THE PERIOD OF ORAL AND MANUSCRIPT LITERATURE

A. The Old Yiddish Literature

From the outset, Yiddish literature was limited to a modest role. It was not meant to serve as the vehicle for scholarship; that was the prerogative of Hebrew. Yiddish was to provide recreational, light reading matter for the people of all social strata. At the same time however, it became a means of instructing those who had no access to Hebrew literature— women and the barely literate men. For hundreds of years the title pages of Yiddish works often carried this note: "Beautiful and instructive for Women and Girls" (for it would not have done to advertise that it was for the untutored!). Women were thus the avowed readers of Yiddish literature. A serious and scholarly man was often ashamed to be discovered frittering away his time with a work meant only to entertain.

It would be a mistake to compare the relationship between the literature in Yiddish and Hebrew with that between the vernacular and Latin literatures of Europe. For among the Jews almost every man was literate and the number who understood Hebrew was always incomparably greater than the number of educated medieval Christians who knew Latin. There was another significant difference: all didactic literature in Yiddish was either a direct outgrowth of Hebrew literature or influenced by it. Until very recent times the bond between the two literatures was so strong that one may justifiably speak of one literature in two languages (this, incidentally, was the view of Mendele Moicher Sforim, Baal Machshovos, and currently of Samuel Niger).

Yiddish literature, like many another, stems from folklore, in this instance the folklore of an ancient and sorely tried people. This folklore is, on the one hand, didactic, full of tales of holy men, religious parables and scholarly aphorisms and, on the other, recreational, full of general human themes. The didactic literature is based on traditional elements; the recreational works drew on the German heroic epic, chivalric tales,

European folk songs and folk plays. For a short time there was a direct influence on Yiddish literature from Italian; indirectly there was influence even from Provençal.

While all the works based on general literature were often popular they were never held in high esteem by the people. Pious folk disparaged this literature, permitting its use only at celebrations, weddings, feasts. There were also periods when some rabbis expressly opposed the literature, because of its alien themes. This opposition stimulated the creation of devotional works which would be as absorbing as the secular adventure stories. As a result, the quality of the didactic literature improved.

B. The Scribes and the Singers

There are extant some one hundred manuscripts containing about 150 works. Most of the manuscripts were lost as a result of the many expulsions and persecutions, and therefore our picture of the first period of Yiddish literary history is necessarily incomplete. Either the earliest manuscripts are concerned with popular medicine or they are translations of prayers and parts of the Bible.

Since handwritten works were expensive, only wealthy women could afford them. They would order scribes to prepare little anthologies for specific occasions. These scribes were not always mere copyists; they were also translators, adaptors, and even authors of original material. The scribes—or "servants of pious wives," as they called themselves—were often supported by their patronesses. These anthologies were conglomerations of songs, stories, amusing sketches, translations or new renditions of biblical passages, important religious rules to be observed by women, and sundry helpful hints on proper conduct.

The principal disseminators of old Yiddish literature were the bards (singers) and jesters (fools), the comedians of their day. The bards sang ballads and selections from long metrical works or gave readings. Like the German *Spielmann*, or minstrel, they recounted sagas of heroism and of unusual events. The whole technique of the Yiddish bard—the tunes and stunts and terms—as well as a considerable portion of his repertoire, was adopted from the German minstrel. Almost all the better known works of the *Spielmann* reached the Jewish audiences, generally in some modified form. For example, passages referring to Christianity were either eliminated or replaced by Jewish allusions; the original work was abridged and thus made more compact; brutal scenes were somewhat humanized and made less offensive; chivalric details were omitted. Sometimes the changes were even more profound: Jewish motifs and details would be introduced and the elements of tragedy might be heightened the more effectively to arouse sympathy.

Much more interesting than the variations on foreign themes are the troubadour romances based on Jewish sources: generally, biblical stories adorned with midrashic and fanciful detail. The principal work of this genre is the *Samuel Book* (fourteenth or possibly fifteenth century), an adventure novel about David. It is a magnificent Davidiad containing details of chivalric combat, with scenes and episodes reminiscent of knighthood romances. Another such popular work was the eighty-stanza poem called *The Sacrifice of Isaac, or Jewish Descent*. With delicate lyricism and religious pathos it tells of Abraham's struggle with Satan as Isaac was being led to the sacrifice.

Not many lyrics have survived from this early period—and these only of the professional scribes and troubadours. Of the lyrics extant we find three types: (1) religious songs in praise of God and in honor of the Sabbath and the holidays; (2) didactic poems underscoring the Jewish view of life; (3) poems on general moral and folkloristic themes.

This lyric material is also closely connected with the beginnings of Jewish drama, the humorous skits and didactic monologues and dialogues performed for the most part in the homes of the wealthy on festive occasions and during the Purim or Hanukkah holidays. Such a work was the popular *Dance of Death*; it may date back to the Spanish-Jewish period. Apparently the *Purimspiel* was already developing during this period; those we know, however, have come down to us from a later period.

C. The Religious Popular Tales

In the period between the Crusades and the sixteenth century many new legends were developed. New tales were told of the lives of great personalities. There are whole cycles of legends on men like Rabbenu Gershom, Rashi and Rabbi Judah Chassid. Every community had its local tales. These folk stories reflect life under constant threat of expulsion, the blood libel, the pogrom and, withal, the faith that all these dangers will be surmounted. Irrespective of the language in which they were first recorded, all these stories were developed in Yiddish.

2. THE PERIOD OF THE FOLK BOOK

A. Literary Upswing in the Sixteenth and the First Half of the Seventeenth Century

1. Elijah Bochur and the Bouva Story (*Bova Bukh*)

The invention of printing gradually made the scribe superfluous and diminished the importance of the bard and the jester. Their tales could now be read and they had hundreds of thousands of readers. Unlike the previous period whose figures are anonymous, the great writers and folk teachers are distinct personalities. By far the most interesting figure of the first half of the sixteenth century is Elijah Bochur (1468?-1549).

Elijah Bochur's fame rests principally on his Hebrew scholarship; but he was interested in Yiddish too, and his poetic works were written exclusively in this language. His two great Yiddish novels are the *Bova Book* and *Paris and Vienna* (the latter never became popular). Both works are free adaptations of Italian romances and both are written in the Italian *ottava rima* stanza. The *Bova Book* is a parody of the *Spielmann* novel. The author is playful and ironic; his jumbling of elements of Jewish folkways with stories of knightly exploits is grotesque. In short, he makes merry with the old claptrap of the troubadour's art.

The popular, short fantastic tale gave rise to a rich repository of novella, legends and prose versions of the poetic works of the preceding period. The *packen treger* (book peddler) who bore his library upon his back was the special agent who disseminated this literature, trudging all the way into the twentieth century with his bag of diverting merchandise.

Typical of the sixteenth century is the brief prose tale or novella based, usually, upon folklore, Hebrew literature or foreign themes. Yet there were also some completely original works, the pearl among these being the anonymous *A Story in Song and Music*, a glorification of that abiding love which is stronger than death.

2. The Storybook and the Moralistic Tracts

The Storybook (*Masseh Bukh*) of the latter sixteenth century (the oldest printed edition extant is dated 1602) is a compilation of the earlier *belles-lettres* and the cradle of later folk tales. This *Storybook*, which exerted a powerful influence on the style and content of Yiddish prose tales up to the modern period, is a collection of talmudic legends and medieval folk tales embellished with new particulars. If the *Storybook*, blending naïveté and deep faith with color, fantasy and dramatic suspense, may be classified as didactic literature, it is the gem of that literary genre, displacing such frivolous works as the Cow Book (*Kuh Bukh*) and the earlier items in the bard's repertoire.

Although glossaries, like the *Chariot of the Viceroy*, by Reb Asher Anshil, and translations of the Pentateuch, intended as aids to the teacher (*melamed*), never became folk books, they did start a trend which led to the *Woman's Pentateuch*. The so-called morality books, which showed great development during this period, applied the ethical principles of Judaism to everyday life. Whereas its prototype, the Hebrew morality book, is briefly formulary, severe and dryly apropos, the Yiddish version is more picturesque in style and less moralizing in tone. Aimed at the twofold audience of the untutored man and the woman reader, it contains a parable at every step, illustrates the moral by an epigram and arouses interest by means of a story. Although the goal is to influence the conduct of the reader, the method is nevertheless to entertain him. The oldest Yiddish moralistic work handed down to us is the *Book of Manners*

(Izni, 1542). Some morality books were meant only for the female reader such as *The Fiery Looking Glass* (Basle, 1602). Later the most popular of these works was the *Good Heart,* by Reb Isaac (Prague, 1620), which was addressed to both men and women and is fervently religious.

3. The Woman's Pentateuch and the Special Prayers

Literal translations of the books of the Bible, removed as they were from the sphere of everyday life, failed to gain especial favor, and it was not until several efforts, such as the translation of the Pentateuch by Reb Isaac ben Samson, had been made that the most widely read and influential work of all Yiddish literature, the *Woman's Pentateuch* by the Polish Jew, Jacob ben Isaac Ashkenazi (1580?-1628), appeared. Ostensibly a translation of the Pentateuch, the Prophets and the Five Scrolls, it is actually a unique mosaic of commentary, legend, allegory, epigram and ethical observation. The author drew upon the entire popular literary heritage from the canonization of the Bible to his own day, choosing those stories which related to the passages of the Pentateuch he was paraphrasing. Directed to the feminine reader, the work became a kind of woman's Bible which has been the source of Jewish knowledge for generations of mothers, who, Sabbath after Sabbath, have absorbed its cabbala-flavored philosophy of life.

The *Woman's Pentateuch,* reflecting the triumph of individual interpretation over literal translation, the prominence of the woman's role in everyday Jewish life and the paramount influence of Polish ritual over the more worldly Germanic overshadowed all previous works in Yiddish and affected the life of the general population more deeply and more lastingly than any other.

Although Yiddish, like Aramaic before it, had become the language of the Jewish religion, the attempt (characteristic of the Reformation era), such as that of Joseph Bar Yakir (1544) to inaugurate a Yiddish prayer book, was not successful. However, the prayer of entreaty voluntarily added to the canonized Hebrew prayer did become popular. This supplementary prayer is concrete, speaks for a single individual and concerns a specific situation. Humbly pious and for the most part femininely delicate, many of these prayers were composed by women. The oldest collections we know are dated 1590 and 1599, while others were composed as late as the middle of the nineteenth century.

This special prayer, in reality a prose poem, expresses the religious lyricism so strongly developed in this period. A number of these Yiddish religious poems were incorporated into the Hebrew religious ceremonial. Of the numerous poets mention is made of "the pious Reb Jacob" of Teplitz and the poetesses Rebecca Tiktiner and Toibe Pan of Prague.

Some secular works were invested with a religious quality, such as the biting epigrams and doggerel of the misogynist Seligman Ulma (*The Tidy Woman's Mirror,* Hanau, 1610). Although less completely developed, "wine, women and song" poetry did make its appearance—the collection of Isaac, son of Moses Wallich of Worms (end of sixteenth century).

During the latter half of the sixteenth century Prague was the center of Yiddish poetry and the home of the most popular poet of the time, Solomon Zinger. He was famous for his wit and the few lyrics of his that are known today are distinguished for their humor and forcefulness.

The outstanding poetic form was the historical epic describing and commemorating some important occurrence in the life of the community such as a pogrom, a fire or an epidemic. The historic poem followed a set pattern, opening with a passage in praise of God, recounting the main events in considerable detail, and ending with a prayer for the speedy advent of the Messiah. An example of such a poem is the *Vints-Hans-Song* by Elchanan, son of Abraham Heln (Frankfort on the Main, 1616), describing the anti-Semitic attack organized by Vincent Fettmilch, the expulsion of the Jewish community and its return. This scroll of Vints was read every year in Frankfort during the observance of Purim.

The historical works in prose, of which the most popular was the *Yosifon* (Zurich, 1546) an adaptation of Josephus's *Antiquities*, followed the pattern of the earlier didactic morality books which did not separate fact from legend. Exile and proscription are the principal themes of these historical works, such as the Yiddish translation of the *Tribe of Judah*, which recounts the expulsions from Spain and Portugal.

Descriptions of journeys are similar to the storybooks. Most popular and most fantastic of these travelogues was *The Regions of Eretz Israel* (Israel, 1635), which was publicly burned by Jesuits in Warsaw. This book later was republished under the title *Path of Holiness*.

Although the stories and legends of the time were rich in dramatic detail, they did not become the bases for dramatic works. For this period we know only of Purim plays and of a rollicking comedy called *A Play About Deaf Yeklein, His Wife Kendlein and His Two Sons Fine* (end of sixteenth century).

3. The Latter Half of the Seventeenth and First Half of the Eighteenth Century

The Sabbatai Zevi movement[1a] gave a kind of ascetic and mystical overtone to Jewish life in eastern Europe, which also became increasingly conservative. While these tendencies are reflected in the literature, no new forms were evolved or great works written to supplant the old favorites. The only center of a freer life was Amsterdam.[2a] There attempts were made during the 1680's to turn from individual interpretation to the use of original biblical sources.

However, the focal work of the period was not the Bible but the *Zohar*, the holy book of the cabbala.[3a] Indicative of the interest in Jewish mysticism is *The Work of the Lord* (Frankfort on the Main, 1691), a collection of fifty stories about its heroes from the founder (?) Reb Simon ben Jochai to Reb Isaac Luria. The morality book *The Wealth of Israel* (Frankfort, 1711) by the Cracow cabbalist Zevi Hirsh Chotscz also became popular and was known as the "explained *Zohar.*" In the main the cabbalists addressed themselves to the male reader, appealing to the emotions of the ordinary man of the people, and in doing so took a strong stand against the intellectual aristocracy of the talmudic scholars. Zevi Hirsh Koidanover, in his *Righteous Path* (Frankfort, 1705) inspires pious fear in the hearts of his readers, threatening them with punishment for their sins in the hereafter. Closely akin to the spirit of this stern work are the translations from the Hebrew of the early morality books, of which one of the best known is the gentler and more mystical *Duties of the Heart* (1716). A work of this period, which foreshadowed the Hasidism of a later era, was Elchanan Kirchban's *Delights of the Soul* (Frankfort, 1707).

A. Poetic and Narrative Works of the Period

Laments over proscriptions and expulsions, usually entitled "new" (*e.g.,* *A New Lament upon the Destruction in Worms; A New Lament over the Expulsion from Tannhausen*) were the most important poetic works. Their titles are ironic, for their themes are as old as the Diaspora, the form set by tradition and the only changes, those of place, year and detail of horror.

The tradition of "Sacred Poems" continued, as exemplified by Aaron ben Samuel of Eggershausen's collection entitled *Gentle Prayer or Powerful Medicine for Body and Soul* (Fuerth, 1709). Containing poetic variations of the traditional prayers along with new and original songs of praise, the work was printed in square letters like those of the authorized prayer book, instead of in "woman's script" used for Yiddish translations of Hebrew books, and consequently was banned by the rabbis.

Folk songs were the source for much vibrant poetry, such as numerous lyrics of the "one kid" variety and paraphrases of the "Who Knows One?" verses. The most important piece of satiric expression of the times is the anonymous *Description of Ashkenaz and Pole* in which Polish, German and Czech (Prague) Jews are compared. Motifs of social protest also occur in some of the laments.

The narratives, such as the humorous story about the bigamist, *A Nice New Song About What Happened in Hamburg* (Amsterdam, 1675) still follow the verse form of the "singer" or "bard." However, the "storybook" pattern is used with increasing frequency, as in *The Story of Miracles,* a collection of twenty-five popular legends of Worms, by the sexton of the community, Jeptha Yuspa ben Naftoli. A curious work is the *Story of West India* in which the new and foreign literature of adventure is combined with the old fount of Jewish legend. Quite characteristically Jewish is the travel romance entitled *Amsterdam Story* which describes the experiences of a rabbi who set out to comb distant lands in search of the Ten Lost Tribes of Israel.

The best prose work of this period, however, remained in manuscript. The splendid memoirs of Glueckel of Hameln, written between 1691 and 1719, tell the life story of a prominent woman, well acquainted with old Yiddish literature. The work gives an account of the contemporary way of life, of family and economic affairs, of important historical events and of private joys and sorrows. In her entries Glueckel reveals a gift for accurately observing life and still greater facility for narration.

The great events of the period aroused an interest in history manifested by a Yiddish translation of *Deep Mire*, an account of the decrees of 1648-1649. Menachem ben Solomon Amekander's original historical work, *Remnants of Israel* (Amsterdam, 1741), an account of Jewish history from the destruction of the Second Temple to the author's own time, enjoyed great popularity.

Of the travelogues worthy of note is the early eighteenth-century work *A Description of the Travels of Abraham Levi*. Sabbatai Bass's geographical work, *Ways of the World*, contains, in addition to directions for reaching a number of large cities, prayers to be said en route. This period also witnessed the appearance of many popular medical works, account books and collections of model letters.

Amsterdam, center of Yiddish book production, was also the home of the first Yiddish newspaper, the *Tuesday and Friday Courant*, a biweekly publication which compared favorably with contemporary Dutch papers.

Despite the growth of religious feeling during this period and despite the Jews' seclusion from the rest of the world, the Yiddish theater was well liked both as a temporary stage for Purim players and Yeshiva students and as the theater of professional actors. A number of plays from the first half of the eighteenth century have come down to us, such as *The Betrayal of Joseph, The Sacrifice of Isaac, David and Goliath, The Exodus from Egypt, King Solomon's Verdict, Sodom and Gomorrah.*

4. THE SECOND HALF OF THE EIGHTEENTH AND THE FIRST HALF OF THE NINETEENTH CENTURY

A. The Decline of Yiddish Literature in Western Europe

Yiddish literature, like the Yiddish language, had its beginnings in Western Europe. For hundreds of years there had been a lively interchange of books and authors between West and East, when, at about the middle of the eighteenth century, a cleavage became apparent.

The period began with the abandonment of the spiritual Ghetto by the Yiddish intelligentsia of the West and its involvement in the capitalist system, which Jews helped to erect. In contradiction to its intended function, the Enlightenment movement became one of increasing assimilation, as evidenced by the use of the derogatory term "jargon" to describe the Yiddish language. For the first time Jewish scholars took pains to disparage their own language in the eyes of their people. Thus literary art in Yiddish declined rapidly; it was, however, preserved in Eastern Europe, where it later came to fruition.

In the West we find only epigonian works in the spirit and style of the foregoing period: historical poetry, chronicles, memoirs (such as the recollections of Aaron Isaacs, the first Jew in Sweden), translations of world literature (like that of *Robinson Crusoe* published in Metz in 1764). A unique work that attempted a compromise between tradition and Enlightenment, but which remained in manuscript, was *Love Letters* by Itsik Vetslar. We have only two plays of the Enlightenment school in Yiddish, both belonging to the late eighteenth century and both excellent literary creations in the style of the bourgeois drama—*Reb Hennach* or *What's to be Done with It* by Isaac Eichl and Aaron Wolfson's *Frivolity and False Piousness*. The final remnants of Western Yiddish literature in the nineteenth century are the dialect parodies of Joseph Herts and the lampoonery and playlets of Morits Gotlib Saffir.

Of the many periodical publications not one was long-lived. The *Privileged Newspaper of Duernfort*, a biweekly (1771-1772) was directed primarily to the Jews of Poland. In Amsterdam the new scholarly community of the Enlightenment and followers of the revolutionary movement published the periodical *Discourse* (1797-1798). Amsterdam, the most stable center of Yiddish literature in the West, was also the birthplace (1784-1802) of the Yiddish operatic theater of Jacob Dessoier, himself the author of various *Singspiele*. In Vienna the musical comedies of David Leib Biderman were produced during the 1830's and 1840's.

B. Hasidic Literature

Hasidism, which brought a stream of joyousness and exaltation into the life of the ordinary man, made greater use of Yiddish than had earlier religious movements. Famous Hasidic rabbis frequently prayed in Yiddish and gave expression to their teachings in that tongue, thus enriching and refining the language. The Hasidic movement also gave impetus to a renascence of popular creativity: stories, poetry, parable, apothegms and adages. The popular tale acquired a new hero, the Hasidic rabbi, while the former hero, the *Lamed Vov*, took on new importance. Thus inspired,

Jewish popular fancy expressed itself in a whole series of marvelous tales which became part of the "literature of praise" of the Hasidic rabbis, the most popular being *Praises of the Besht* (1815). In this manner a new holiday spirit entered the soul of the people and the heavens moved a little closer to earth.

The allegories and stories of the Baal Shem Tov [the Besht] himself gave the impetus to Hasidic literature. His skill in relating these tales raised them to the level of recited Torah. His students, in retelling these anecdotes, always added embellishments of their own, thus laying the foundation for a new and widespread oral tradition among the less educated and even wholly untutored Jews. Of these Hasidic rabbis, whose courts became centers of artistic creativeness in the fields of poetry, music and the dance, the Maggid of Mazaritscz, Reb Levi Yitschok Barditshever, was an outstanding allegorical poet. A great lyricist and musician, his works reveal the rather unusual union of exalted pantheism, a sense of intimacy with the Creator and a feeling of personal worth.

One of the greatest Jewish narrators of all time was the mystic dreamer Reb Nachman Brahtslever (1772-1840). A great-grandson of the Besht, rocked in the cradle of Hasidism, he lived more in a visionary realm than in his actual environment, against which he rebelled. While some of the elements of his fantasies are taken from the folk tale, and even from universal motifs, the essential construction, the winged scope, the delicate form and the ethical-mystical ideas are all completely original. His romanticism, so characteristic of the period, is deeper and more revealing than the vague longings of the *Weltschmerzler*, imbued as it is with the fervor for serving God.

One group of his stories is realistic, containing details of everyday life, while the majority of his tales are of the cloth of free fantasy interwoven with lyricism. After Reb Nachman's death, his colleague and pupil, Nathan Brahtslever, published the stories (which his disciples believed disclosed the secrets of the Torah and of life) in a collection entitled *Narrative Tales* (1815). The pupil recorded the sayings of his master verbatim, regarding every word as a holy utterance. Thus we have an accurate picture of the style of Reb Nachman, whose wonderful personality left so deep an impression upon his followers that they never acknowledged another leader—they remained the "dead Hasidim." Up until the outbreak of World War II, they made annual pilgrimages to his grave in Uman and always conducted themselves differently from all other Hasidim.

In the *Narrative Tales* we see a link in the chain of the centuries-old narrative tradition begun with the *Maaseh Book* and to be continued in the works of Isaac Leibush Peretz.

At the same time that the Western European Jew was beginning to assimilate and cease creating anything in Yiddish, Eastern European Jewry was being influenced by the Hasidic movement to delve deeper into itself, to amass new vitality and to bring to the fore new works of art in Yiddish letters, music and dance.

C. The Literature of the Enlightenment, to the Middle of the Nineteenth Century

The movement for enlightenment (*Haskala*) followed two roads from West to East: the principal one, through Galicia to southern Russia and Poland; the other, directly to Lithuania. The *Haskala*, embracing the intelligentsia and the merchant class, aimed to free the individual from the restraints of tradition by educating him and by remodeling Jewish life on a freer foundation so that he might deserve and achieve emancipation.[4a] But the *Haskala* also brought with it from Germany the desire to forget Yiddish and adopt the language of the land. However, the more realistic of the enlightened readily realized that they had to make use of Yiddish in order to spread their beliefs. Another point of difference, and a more fundamental one, was the clash (which continued throughout the nineteenth century) between the elements opposed to Yiddish and those cultured Eastern European Jews who loved the rejected masses and were devoted to their language.

The *Maskilim* (followers of *Haskala*) created two types of literature in Yiddish; one of instruction, to propagate their ideas, and the second, a polemic literature opposing the old way of life. In the first of these we have the modern continuation of the morality book, while the latter consists almost wholly of satirical works. The dramatic form was used by the Maskilim only as a means of faithfully recording daily events and for the purpose of debate. The narrative form is also rich in realistic detail but it is often exaggerated and interrupted by journalistic digressions.

Oddly enough it was a German Jew, Dr. Moses Markuse, a physician in the small towns of Poland and Lithuania where he was stranded, who wrote a most unusual book, *The Book of Remedies*, highlighting the differences between the *Haskala* of the East and that of the West. The work, a mixture of popular medicinal practice and Enlightenment ideology, reveals a great love for the common man. At the same time, Maskilim made new translations into Germanic Yiddish of works in other literatures, such as Kampe's *Discovery of America*, with a view toward contributing to the education of the public. This version by the Lithuanian Maskil, Mordecai Aaron Ginsburg, was not particularly successful but that of the Barditchev merchant, Chaim Chaikl Hurvits, *Tsofnas Paneach* (1817), was immensely popular. The language of this work, based as it was upon spoken Yiddish, represents a definite departure from the old literary language, which had become too archaic and Germanic.

The theoretician and chief protagonist of this new trend, which was making rapid headway, especially among the Maskilim of Galicia and Podolsk, who used it in revising earlier Yiddish works, was Mendl Leffin, or Mendl Satanover (1749-1826), as he was known, a dominant figure in the Enlightenment and a link between the Berlin *Haskala* and that of Galicia and southern Russia. He proposed to translate the Bible into the idiomatic Yiddish of his Ukrainian dialect, intending, as did Moses Mendelssohn,[5a] to turn the people toward the Bible. Satanover hoped to do this by relating the Scriptures to Yiddish in contradiction to the endeavors of Mendelssohn. Satanover's plan was not realized because of disputes which arose concerning it, and only the Book of Proverbs was published (1814), several other sections circulating in manuscript. The whole project was not completed until the twentieth century through the translation by Yehoash in the United States. However, the new Yiddish literary language was strengthened and at the same time the practice was established of using square characters for printed Yiddish instead of the cursive "woman's script."

At the beginning of the nineteenth century the new forms and ideas worked their way into the model-letter pamphlets which for generations had served as texts from which to learn Yiddish style as well as the writing of the language itself. Illustrative is Levin Lion D'Or's *New Artistic Letter Writer* (Vilna, 1825), which went through ten editions.

The Maskilim directed their sharpest satire against the Hasidim and the courts of their rabbis. In 1815 the rabbinical judges of Lemberg excommunicated the local Maskilim and by way of comment there appeared the excellent anonymous *The Duped World*, a Tartuffian comedy of much wit. Undoubtedly the author belonged to the circle of Mendl Satanover, as did Joseph Perl, wealthy merchant of Tarnopol, who authored the clever *Scroll of Secrets* and the satirical story, *The Greatness of Reb Wolf of Charni-Ostrow*. Consisting of more than 150 letters of twenty-six correspondents, this latter work is an imitation of the humanist *Epistolae Obscurorum Virorum*. The aping of the style of devout Hasidim was so successful that there arose many a dispute among them as to whether the little book was Hasidic or profane, arousing sharp opposition to the work.

The ill and poverty-stricken Isaac Baer Levinson, known as the "Philosopher of Kremenetz" and the "Mendelssohn of Russian Jewry," wrote a social satire attacking the injustice of the community to the poor masses. Entitled *Heedless World*, this work marks the beginning of the militant social writing of the nineteenth century. "Rib'l," as he was known, also wrote a satirical poem, *Purim Play*. The Polish Maskil, Efraim Fishlzon, composed a three-act comedy, *Theater of Hasidim*, an anti-Hasidic satire in the form of arguments. The anonymous derisive poem, *Troubles of the Teachers*, gives a sad picture of traditional education. The above-mentioned works are important for their social message rather than for their artistic merit.

In addition to the hindrances imposed by the Russian government, the fact that they were but scattered groups, prevented the Maskilim from developing a journalistic press. In 1823-1824 the weekly *Observer on the Vistula* was published in Warsaw; its language being quite Germanic, the publication did not long survive. It was not until the revolution of 1848 that a Yiddish weekly made its appearance, the *Newspaper of Lwow*, Galicia, whose publication was renewed in 1863 as the *Jewish Newspaper*.

D. Israel Oxenfeld and Solomon Ettinger

Almost all the *Haskala* writers mentioned thus far also wrote in Hebrew and regarded their Hebrew works as the more important. Now we turn to two writers of the first half of the nineteenth century who wrote exclusively in Yiddish.

Israel Oxenfeld (1787-1866), an Odessa lawyer, was the first great storyteller of the Enlightenment. Although as a youth he had been a Hasid, indeed a colleague of Reb Nathan Brahtslever, he devoted all his literary talents to combating "Baal-Shemism" and Hasidism. In the main, the naturalist in him triumphed over the satirist, and his characterizations, patterned as they were after actual persons, are vital if primitive. Yet he lacked the power for synthesis so necessary in a truly great realistic writer. The Maskilim read his many novels and stories in the manuscript form used in the days before the invention of printing. He was more fortunate in getting his dramatic works published and his play, *The First Jewish Recruit*, was performed with evident success on the Yiddish stage of the 1920's and 1930's. Oxenfeld's sketches of milieu are still interesting today as source materials and his influence upon Mendele Moicher Sforim (see below) was considerable.

Although Galicia and southern Russia produced most of the writers of this period, the most important talent came from Poland. Dr. Solomon Ettinger (1800-1865), who has been called "the great-grandfather of modern Yiddish literature," wrote in Yiddish not for the purpose of spreading cultural or social ideas but for art's own sake. He was the first to attempt to refine Yiddish, to create new words and polish his style. The first lyricist per se, he described nature and his own moods even though they were subjective and pointed no moral. His clever allegories and good-humored epigrams are lively and witty; the poetic descriptions of character types lack the sharpness of the *Haskala* satire. Ettinger pioneered in the kind of literature that focuses upon the individual and his feelings rather than upon the group and its problems, and widened the scope of Yiddish literature, linking it with that of Europe.

Ettinger's masterpiece is the dramatic comedy *Serkele (Little Sarah)*;

a story of character and environment in which the central figure is a capable woman who dominates her household and is unscrupulous in her drive for wealth and power. Although Ettinger did borrow a few secondary details from the militant comedies of David Eichl and Aaron Wolfson, his plot, technique and characters were his own and became the prototypes for later works, such as Jacob Gordin's *Mirrele Efros* (see below) and the plays of Abraham Goldfaden. Ettinger's works, censored by the czarist regime, did not appear until after his death.

E. The Fifties and Sixties of the Nineteenth Century

The first nineteenth-century Yiddish author to enjoy a reading public numbering in the tens of thousands, was the Vilna Maskil, Isaac Meir Dyk (1814-1893). His hundreds of realistic short stories and more romantic novels were especially popular in Lithuania and were always to be found in the itinerant peddler's pack. His intention was to enlighten and instruct the people, refine their ways and teach them German by using many German expressions in his writings, translating them into pure Yiddish. Dyk's style often reminds us of that of the morality book. He addresses himself to the "dear lady reader" and discourses with her about child education, the dangers of luxurious living, purity in family life, the value of living off the soil and of educating oneself. Isaac Meir Dyk is a combination of the maggid and the modern storyteller, embodying the old tradition and at the same time foreshadowing the realistic literature of a later period.

The theoretician among the conservatives of the *Haskala* was Eliezer Tsvi Tsveifl, whose aim it was to combine the positive elements of Orthodoxy and Hasidism with the newer teachings of the Enlightenment. He not only sought to interest his colleagues and disciples at the rabbinical school of Zhitomir in writing in Yiddish, but was the author of some good stories himself, such as *The Fortunate Maftir* and the half-literary, half-journalistic *Life's Punishments*. Influenced by Mendl Satanover, he in turn affected Mendele Moicher Sforim and was the first to give impetus to the Neo-Hasidism of the late nineteenth and the early twentieth century.

The radical wing of the *Haskala* was distinguished by the fighting spirit of Abraham Gotlober, who had led the difficult life of a wanderer. His comedy, *The Veil, or Two Weddings in One Night*, shows the influence of Ettinger's *Serkele*. Of principal importance to Yiddish literature are his poems, such as *The Poor Yisroilik*, which was exceedingly popular and topically characteristic of the Enlightenment. His humorous Yiddish version of Schiller's *Song of the Bell* became the *Song of the Sabbath Pudding*. Incidentally, Schiller was the German writer most popular with the Maskilim, and there are several curious versions in Yiddish of his aforementioned *Song of the Bell*, the most felicitous of which is Hirsh Reitman's *The White Prayer Mantle*.

Alongside the poetry of the more intelligent Maskilim there existed the folk lyrics in the old tradition of the bards. During the middle years of the nineteenth century we have two great poets of the people: the wandering, bohemian Berl Margolius, known as Berl Broder, and the more colorful but refined Wolf Ehrenkrants, who went by the name of Velvl Zbarazer.

In the city of Brody, the center of trade and of the *Haskala*, Berl Broder established a cabaret troupe for which he created the repertory. These "Singers of Brody" became very popular and made guest appearances all over Galicia, southern Russia, and Poland, spreading Broder's merry yet melancholy songs of the fate of the common man as well as his lyrical nature poems. The collection, entitled *Song Poems*, was published in 1860.

Velvl Zbarazer sang of wine and love, of the eternal yearning for peace and of the pettiness of life in the wine cellars of Rumania and Bessarabia, in Vienna and Constantinople. Motifs of the intellectual *Haskala*, the mundane details of everyday life, old lyric balladry and modern writing—all were interwoven in the works of these two poets, the last in the many generations of bardic singers.

With the exception of the little-theater performances by the Singers of Brody and by sporadic companies in Warsaw (1838-1839; 1866-1870), there had not developed a permanent professional Yiddish theater. However, this did not prevent the writing of a number of dramatic works, some of them rather effective, such as *The Town Community*, by Wolf Kamrash; Joel Berish Falkovitch's *Reb Chaim the Rich* and *Little Rachel, the Singer; Heaven-Made Match* by Hirsh Reitman; Isaiah Gutman's *The Three Cousins* and *The Scoundrel*. Such works were read aloud at small gatherings and performed by amateurs.

By the middle of the nineteenth century there was a large reading public thirsty for new books. The lack of a Yiddish press, barred by the Russian government, retarded the development of Yiddish literature. In 1862, however, the *Voice of the Messenger* appeared in Odessa, and from that time forward Yiddish journalism developed very rapidly. Many talented new writers appeared and the earlier authors became more strongly established as their works were reprinted.

At about this time important changes occurred in Jewish life with the emancipation of the Russian peasant in 1861, the migration from the small towns to the big cities, the development of commerce and trade in which the Jews took a more active part, and the rise of the working class, struggling for a freer and a better life—all related to the rapid advance of Yiddish literature.

5. The New Yiddish Literature

A. Mendele Moicher Sforim, His Contemporaries and Disciples

The central figure in Yiddish literature in the last three decades of the nineteenth century is Mendele Moicher Sforim. The major trend is his trend: the realistic. The major achievement is his, too: the establishment of form, style, technique and language. All the literati may be grouped about him: those who walked with him and those who followed, the ones who opposed him and the ones who wrote during his time but belonged to that of his predecessors. We begin with the last mentioned.

The most important in the line of Yiddish authors linking the folk song with individual poetry is the Vilna-born Michl Gordon (1823-1892), who criticized the traditional way of life in his works. In a rhythmic and lucid style he created ballads of milieu such as *The Divorce, The Beard, After the Wedding*. And in pained elegiacs he bemoaned his impoverished life (*My Years, My Lifetime, My Last Day*). His brother-in-law, the great Hebrew poet, Yehuda Leib Gordon, touched upon social themes of the Enlightenment in his Yiddish poems collected under the title *Commonplace Talk* (1886). The Vilna poet, S. Y. Katsenelenbogen (Rashik), treated of the most diverse topics with delicate lyricism which reveal the influence of Heine and the Russian poets, and paved the way for the poetry of Frug.

The most popular song writer was the last bard of Yiddish poetry, Eliokum Tsunzer (1835-1913). Didactic and moralizing, Tsunzer propagandized for the Enlightenment and later for Zionism. In his ballads, as in those of the bards, personification is common (*The Ferryboat*). Sung first at celebrations in well-to-do homes, his songs found their way to the masses and *The Plow, The Aristocrat, The Nineteenth Century* became extremely popular. More polished and more individual is the poetry of Abraham Goldfaden (1840-1908), author of romantically nationalistic poems and skilled in the art of versification. (On his operettas, see below.) There also belong in this line of writers Samuel Bernstein, poet and writer of comedies, and Ludwig Levinson, author of the very apt *Pin Money*.

We may now turn to the central figure, the grandfather of modern Yiddish literature. Sholem Jacob Abramovitch (1835-1917) was born in the small town of Kapulye in the province of Minsk. After several years of the hard life of a Yeshiva student, he became the companion of a wandering beggar. But in Kamenets Podolsk he met Abraham Gotlober, who influenced him to take up cultural pursuits. For a time he lived in Barditchev, but was obliged to leave because of his work *Die Takse* (The Meat Tax) in which he exposed the local clique of "do-gooders." He struggled in Zhitomir and finally settled in Odessa, where he became the director of a Talmud Torah. When he began writing in Yiddish (1864) he took the name Mendele Moicher Sforim, which is more than just a pseudonym: through his works there passes the figure of an elderly Jew who rides about with his wagonful of books providing the people with prayers of supplication and lament, all the time smiling good-naturedly as he observes life around him. This figure helped to narrow the distance between the author and his readers. Mendele Moicher Sforim, inspiring love and admiration, was the first to establish a really intimate relationship between the Yiddish writer and his public.

During the first twenty years of his creative life, Mendele was a fighting satirist. Becoming more tranquil with the passage of time, he turned from satire to humor, from social crusading to memorializing a bygone way of life. True to the teachings of Eliezer Tsvi Tsveifl, he did not oppose Hasidism and never wounded the religious feeling but directed his social satire against those in power who wrong the people (*The Little Man, Die Takse*), against economic injustice (*The Wishing Ring, Fishke the Lame*), against the helplessness of the small town and its ignorance of the world (*The Travels of Benjamin the Third*).

The motifs of the *Haskala* gain depth in his work, personified as they are by a gallery of realistic figures. Mendele is a perfectionist and does not hesitate to rewrite his works, improving and adding to them. In *Die Takse* (see above) he not only mentions the clique of exploiting benefactors, but also gives us the autobiographical figure of Shloime Wekker, forerunner of the revolutionary movement among the Jews of Russia.

In the symbolic *Old Mare* (1873) we have, ten years before its active acceptance, the manifestation of a national idea which did not become current until the eighties, as well as a penetrating economic critique of the *Haskala*. Thus the author also occupies an outstanding place in the history of Jewish social consciousness. This parallel development of literary art and social awareness is a fundamental characteristic of the years between 1864 and 1914, the period of the greatest advance in Yiddish literature.

In making Kabtsansk (*kabtsen*-Hebrew: poor man) his typical town and Gloops (*gloop*-Slavic: foolish) his typical city, Mendele is a synthesist. His broad canvases depict the most ordinary small-town happenings and present the house of study and the house of the poor, the home and the public bath, the weekday and the Sabbath, the philosophy of life and the merest grimace. It is curious, however, that this richly detailed picture of Jewish life has a definite limit in time. Anything later than the 1870's escapes Mendele's brush. In the main he relies upon his memory, so that it is not surprising that his autobiography, *Schloime, Son of Reb Chaim,* is also a splendid objective novel.

Since Mendele is extremely exacting in his realistic portrayals of a rather static life, his plot structure suffers. This careless attitude toward plot development became characteristic of the entire realistic school in Yiddish literature. (Is this perhaps due to the influence of the Russians?) But his masterful descriptions of exceptional types, specifically Jewish in flavor, and his wonderful pictures of nature have a beauty which has never been surpassed.

Mendele is primarily responsible for the standardization of modern literary Yiddish. Eschewing the use of his own dialect, he was the first to strive consciously toward a synthesis of the Lithuanian and Ukrainian dialects and to include words and usages from earlier works. Mendele is the hub of the whole nineteenth century: as a social satirist, as the creator of a plastic yet statically synthetic realism, as the molder of a new style, he embodies the sum total of the Enlightenment movement. His antecedents, Mendl Satanover and his circle, lived before the nineteenth century and his influence extends far beyond its close.

Appearing at the same time as Mendele's writings in the *Voice of the Messenger*, was *The Polish Boy* (in the second edition, *The Hasidic Boy*), a satirically biting autobiographical novel by Isaac Joel Linetski (1839-1916), whose indictment of Hasidic practices was the strongest ever written. The work created a great furor, but Linetski showed no further development and accomplished nothing with his anti-Mendele position.

Temporary success was enjoyed by *The Dark Young Fellow*, a sensational, melodramatic novel by Jacob Dinnezon (1856-1919). At first Dinnezon was opposed to Mendele in principle, claiming that the latter was too refined and too indifferent to the receptive capacity of the mass of Jewish readers. Although Dinnezon's themes are inclined to be those of primitive folklore, the triumph of Mendele's artistic approach is apparent. In *Hershele* and *Yossele*, which appeared in the nineties, Dinnezon did preserve his sentimentalism, but it is subtler, revealing the influence of Mendele.

The less educated reader, in particular the women of the lower social strata, could not enjoy the Mendele literature. To fill the need of this audience, there appeared during the seventies and eighties colorful and unrealistic novels of improbable romances between a Yeshiva student and a princess or a count and a servant maid, with detailed descriptions of their misfortunes before the inevitable happy ending, thus affording the reader a chance for a good cry.

Dozens of such novels were written by Shomer (pseudonym of Nokhem Meyer Sheikevitch), founder of a whole school of hack writers (Blohstein, Buchbinder, *et al.*). These Shomerians challenged, so to speak, the disciples of Mendele Moicher Sforim: There, let us see you create artistic works that will be intelligible as well as entertaining to all. Sholem Aleichem quite consciously took up the gauntlet and emerged the victor.

B. Pioneers in Poetry, Drama, Criticism

Before proceeding to Mendele's disciples, we pause for those who performed his task, that of laying the foundation for future development, in the fields of poetry and drama. Among the poets, there were Simeon Frug (1860-1916) in Russia and Morris Rosenfeld (1862-1923) in the United States.

Brought up on Russian poetry and himself a recognized Russian-Jewish poet, Simeon Frug achieved mastery in fashioning facile, rhythmic Yiddish verse despite his complaint about the crudity of the underdeveloped language. Raised in a Jewish colony in southern Russia, he was close to the land and his lyrical descriptions of nature have a directness and matter-of-factness quite foreign to Yiddish poetry. A Zionist, Frug lamented the bitterness of the Dispersal and dreamed in his poetry of the happy future when everyone would sit under his own fig tree. He made many paraphrases of the Bible and drew upon folklore in his ballads. Nor is social pathos foreign to him. He is many faceted but none of his faces is really distinct.

Immeasurably more profound and more effective is Morris Rosenfeld. He lifted social poetry to new heights. The socialist Morris Vintshefski (1856-1932), the anarchist David Edelstadt (1866-1892), Joseph Bovshover (1872-1915), and many other poets of lesser stature had depicted the difficult life of the workingman. But theirs was a poetry aimed at arousing its readers to the social struggle and only indirectly expressed deeply personal experiences. However, in Morris Rosenfeld's social poetry are the very sighs and pain of the worker.

Himself a sweatshop slave, Rosenfeld went through the many metamorphoses of the Jewish immigrant in England and the United States. He portrays the worker lashed to the sewing machine, spending his strength without any brighter prospects for the morrow, crying out his protest in anguish and despair. National motifs of Jewish homelessness and the dream of deliverance also are prominent in his rough-hewn, glowing verses. The breadth and depth of his poetic creativeness, the range and frequent unexpectedness of his imagery, more than compensate for certain roughnesses of diction. Rosenfeld was the first Yiddish poet to attract foreign readers and to have his works translated into many languages.

Both Frug and Rosenfeld, pioneers in Yiddish poetry, so different in expression, paved the way for later poets who drew upon the formal elements of the one and the sincerity of the other.

Abraham Goldfaden, the founder of the first modern professional Yiddish theater, was at the same time its manager, director, composer and playwright. He had evinced all these talents as early as 1876, in Jassy, where he laid the cornerstone for the rapid development of the theater.

His operettas, setting a pattern for the Yiddish theater, which aims primarily to entertain and only secondarily to educate its audience, were of two types: comedies which make sport of the negative elements in Jewish life (*e.g., The Two Simpletons, The Sorceress*) and nationalistic-romantic plays (*e.g., Shulamit, Bar Kokbah*).

The comedies contain grotesque and entertaining exaggerations and are in the tradition of the Purim play and the wine cellar art of the Singers of Brody, but also include themes of the Enlightenment and telling portrayals of mores. The dramas are melodramatically sentimental interpretations of Jewish history, combining elements of heroism and buffoonery. Tuneful melodies played no small part in making Goldfaden's operettas great favorites. The negation of Mendele's realistic approach and the catering to the popular taste, first evident in Goldfaden's works, opened the way to the banalization of his own method by such hacks as Joseph Lateiner, "Professor" Hurwitz, Shomer and others who, in the United States particularly, brought empty melodrama and quite vulgar operetta to the theater.

The early nineteenth-century Yiddish movement is linked with Mendl Satanover; but after the pogroms in Russia during the eighties, came the upheaval in social ideology and men turned from the Enlightenment to Zionism and nationalism. Part of the Jewish intelligentsia turned "homeward" and became more interested in the life of the masses, allying themselves more closely with those leaders of popular thought who had never strayed. At that time there were those, called the "Jargonists," who quite consciously wanted to strengthen the position of Yiddish. Thanks to this movement, such writers as I. L. Peretz, David Frishman, Simeon Frug, *et al.*, were attracted from the Hebrew and Russian literatures to the Yiddish. Simultaneously, interest in folklore increased, attempts were made to set up a uniform orthography and works of previous years were reprinted.

A number of new writers appeared on the scene: Moishe Aron Shatskes, with his excellent, mildly satirical *Before the Jewish Passover*; Paltiel Zamosciner, author of the short verses *Pictures of Life*; and "Yachnan," with his pleasant descriptions of small-town life. In almanacs such as the *Jewish People's Library* by Sholem Aleichem and Mordecai Spector's *Home Companion*, literary criticism first appeared. The young Sholem Aleichem wrote a very keen and witty critique of Shomer's novels; Joshua Honon Ravnitsky analyzed literary works instead of merely judging them; Joseph Judah Lerner introduced the positivist approach.

C. Sholem Aleichem and Isaac Leibush Peretz

Mordecai Spector (1858-1925) and Sholem Aleichem made their literary debuts at the same time and in the same weekly publication, the

Yiddish Folk Paper of 1883. Spector was faithful to Mendele's technique of detailed description, but his style is almost as colorless as the lives of his poor characters. His novels (*The Jewish Peasant, The Humble and the Needy, Reb Treitl*) and numerous stories are humorous and sentimental. With calm resignation and great insight he portrays the fate of the downtrodden. There is in Spector's work a deep sympathy for the poor man but no indication of any way out of his lot nor of any spiritual elation.

Sholem Rabinovitch (1859-1916), who took the pen name, Aleichem, was born in the warm and fertile Ukraine. A difficult adolescence followed his idyllic childhood and it was not until he became private tutor in the home of a Jewish landowner, whose daughter he later married, that things began to go well for him. For a short time after the death of his father-in-law he conducted a successful business but subsequently lost his fortune and began to live by his writing. Illness sent him to Switzerland and Italy. Whenever he came to a Jewish Ghetto city to give readings of his works, he received a great ovation, for he was the most popular of all Yiddish writers. The final years of his life were spent in New York City.

Sholem Aleichem began by writing realistic short stories and novels (*Stempeniu, Yossele Solovay*). In these early works he stood, so to speak, on the shoulders of Mendele, from whom he adopted many qualities of language and style. His originality came to the fore in *Little People with Little Ideas* where he first portrayed Kasrilevke, the composite town of poor but cheerful Jews with its happy-go-lucky Kasrillik. Later on in *Menachem Mendl*, his Kasrillik begins to wander, lands on the exchange and becomes a "speculator." Sholem Aleichem's vocabulary contains the wealth of idiom and the picturesqueness of expression found in spoken Yiddish, and his style ceases to be that of Mendele but becomes nervously dynamic. Instead of dwelling upon every detail, he sketches only a few particulars, usually the most humorous. At times he tends to become grotesque, but at his best he is a master of characterization.

Sholem Aleichem writes with especial tenderness of simple folk and of children. In the series of sketches, *Tevya the Dairyman*, we have the naïve yet deeply philosophical laborer who has intuitively absorbed the Jewish faith and its unshakable affirmation of life. In the children's stories, such as the *Song of Songs*, there is an additional individual lyricism which gives them much charm. In *Motl Paysie, the Cantor's Son*, a bright child gives an account of the life of a group of immigrants across the sea "in the golden land." The longer novels that first appeared as newspaper serials (*Wandering Stars, The Bloody Joke*) show only in part the excellence of his pen. And in the autobiographical novel *From the Fair* the writer abandons his favorite monologue form and speaks as the Nestor. Of his dramatic works, the most performed were *Scattered Far and Wide*, concerning the life of a Jewish family about the year 1905, and *The Great*

Winnings, where Shimmele Soroker, the main character, is a simplified Tevya the Dairyman.

Sholem Aleichem's genius has both breadth and depth. His characters are drawn from every class, although the background is always characteristically Jewish, whether it be Kasrilevke or the East Side of New York. While writing of spiritual and emotional experiences in a seemingly cursory fashion, he is in reality plumbing the depths of an inward struggle. Thus Sholem Aleichem is interesting not only to the folklorist or the ethnographer, but also to the psychologist. His writing gives pleasure to the simplest reader who relishes the aphorisms and the humorous situations, while the most discriminating will find a philosophical depth and a symbolism of character rare in the works of other writers.

Everyone who read Yiddish at the turn of the century read Sholem Aleichem and even those who could not read knew of him, as it was virtually customary to read his works aloud at celebrations and family gatherings. His unrivaled popularity is due largely to his humor, a humor which is many sided: fresh, carefree laughter, tearful smiles, subtle wit and grotesque exaggeration. Particularly characteristic of Sholem Aleichem is his treatment of sad and even tragic events with a kind of levity which springs from the faith that man can overcome any adversity. He gives us the comfort of a laughter which does not belittle the values of life but rather serves to emphasize them.

The genius for humor of the sorely tried Jewish people, formerly manifested in jest and epigram, shone in Sholem Aleichem's works through hundreds of characters four of which are outstanding: Kasrillik, Menachem Mendl, Tevya the Dairyman, and Motl, the Cantor's Son. These figures came to be regarded almost as members of the reader's own family. Indeed, the extent of the influence of Sholem Aleichem upon the daily life of the Eastern European Jew can hardly be exaggerated.

The third member of this trio of classicists, Isaac Leibush Peretz (1852-1915), affected his readers and society in quite another manner. Born in the Polish city of Zamosc, Peretz showed great intellectual ability as a youth. To earn his livelihood, he first practiced law and then worked for the Warsaw Jewish community. By his own efforts he became thoroughly versed in European literature. He was past middle age and had already written many Hebrew verses before his writings appeared in Yiddish.

At first there were succinct, realistic short stories and during the period of the *Holiday Folios,* he devoted himself to works of the Enlightenment and to the popularization of scientific material. His poetry is strongly influenced by that of Heine and Chamisso; his *Haskala* motifs are sarcastic and militant; his portrayal of the lot of women and children, sentimental and romantic.

However, it was not until the nineties, when he took up Hasidic themes, that Peretz reached the height of his career. His Hasidic stories in which he idealized the rabbis, painting them as the model men of the future, helped initiate a Neo-Hasidic trend in Yiddish and Hebrew literature. But Peretz did not seek the "Sabbath and the Holy-day" Jew only among the great. He wrote the series *Silent Souls* and other tales of the "thirty-six saintly Jews" where the hero—a woodcutter, a water carrier, or a confused youth—plumbs the profoundest depths of the soul. Thus Peretz went from the realistic to the romantic, from the romantic to the symbolic. His drama *The Golden Chain* embodies the basic principles of every religion and stresses the continuity of the age-old chain of Jewish culture. His last symbolic drama, *A Night at the Old Marketplace,* is a pessimistic summation of his own achievements, for Peretz was not satisfied to create a work of art for its own sake, but wanted to use his talents to refine the soul of his generation.

The conflict between the way of life of the Jewish radical and that of the towering personalities of the traditional past is revealed in Peretz's works. In feverishly sharp and impressionistic *feuilletons,* he champions true freedom of thought and at the same time stresses the traditional quest for God and the belief in the chosenness of the Jewish people—tenets which found new strength in the years bridging the nineteenth and twentieth centuries. While Peretz's literary technique is Western European, it also stems from the folk tale and there is a direct line from the stories of Nachman Brahtslever with their romantic symbolism to the works of Peretz.

During the last fifteen years of his life, Peretz was not only the dominant literary figure of the great center in Warsaw, but was also the leader of those who hoped to modernize Jewish life through the use of Yiddish and to effect a national cultural renaissance in all the lands of the Dispersion. He was one of the leaders at the language conference at Czernowitz (1908), where Yiddish was proclaimed a "national language." Near the end of his life he helped establish Jewish schools for refugee children and died while composing a poem for a children's home.

Almost all the young authors whose writings appeared in Peretz's publications or who made their debuts in the early years of the twentieth century were influenced by Peretz, whose attitude toward them was fatherly and encouraging. When the younger writers bestowed upon him the honorary title of "Father of Modern Yiddish Literature," they were expressing their esteem and affection for him.

The constellation of Mendele, Sholem Aleichem, and Peretz is a happy combination of mutually complementary temperaments. Mendele criticizes yet memorializes what is characteristic and typical of his age; Sholem Aleichem brings us the comical and the humorous with no apparent motive; Peretz evokes the exotic past as a model for the future. Mendele is static, the other two are dynamic. Sholem Aleichem definitely draws upon Mendele while Peretz is tangential. Mendele and Peretz demand concentration from the reader; Sholem Aleichem is universally familiar and satisfying. All three created a new centripetal force linking, through literature, the present and the past, the intellectual and the untutored, the Jew of one region and the Jew of another.

D. The Expansion of Yiddish Literature to 1914

Until 1914 the whole of Yiddish literature in Russia reflected the influence of Mendele, Sholem Aleichem, and Peretz.

In the United States other forces were at work: (1) The "green" immigrant needed to become organized and literature took on the character of propaganda; (2) the low cultural status of the newcomers led to semi-literate writing which impeded the development of the artistic; (3) a great, new power arose in the form of a free Yiddish press.

It is curious that Russian literature exercised a lesser influence upon Yiddish literature in Russia than it did upon Yiddish writing in America. Some of the more important American prose writers are: Z. Libin (pen name of Israel Kurwitz), who, with restrained warmth faithfully records the life of the Jewish worker; Leon Kobrin, who dwells upon the problems of the individual, particularly the sexual aspect; Bernard Gorin, who, for the most part, portrays the old country; Abraham Cahan, whose stories are dominated by socialist propaganda; Tashrack (Israel Joseph Zevin), who depicts the difficulties in the adjustments the immigrant has to make to his new environment.

In addition to this socially aware writing, such as that of Morris Rosenfeld (see above), we have the popularly oriented songs of Joseph Jaffe; the tender, idyllic poesy of Jacob Adler, et al. While the Yiddish theater had been banned in Russia in 1883, it developed rapidly in America. The Tolstoian Jacob Gordin raised the level of the theater, producing more than sixty plays, many of which were based on foreign themes, and others that were original plays of milieu which were extremely successful (Mirrele Efros, God, Man and the Devil).

In Europe the seventeen years from 1897 to 1914 are ones of remarkable social progress. The philosophies of Zionism, socialism and autonomism are hotly debated; parties are organized; new ideas are on the march. Yet the Jewish press in Russia is banned until 1903 when The Friend appeared in Petersburg, to be followed by Yiddish newspapers in Odessa, Warsaw and other provincial cities. Life was particularly stormy from 1904 to 1906. There was a temporary mood of despair immediately after the failure of the 1905 revolution, but hopes soon rose and the Yiddish movement was strengthened.

The most important literary publications were: *Literary Monthlies* (1908), edited by Samuel Niger, Shmarahu Gorelik and A. Veiter (pen name of Meyer Davenishsky); *The Book of Records: Yearbook of the History of the Yiddish Literature and Language, Folklore, Criticism and Bibliography* (1913); and the monthly magazine, *Jewish World,* also edited by Samuel Niger. Most of these publications appeared in Vilna, seat of the modern Kletskin Publishing House. The Warsaw publishing firms were modernized as well, and the output of books was great.

Again during this period a group of Hebrew writers were attracted to Yiddish literature: Chaim Nachman Bialik translates his *Poems of Grief and Wrath* into Yiddish and wrote directly in that language; Jacob Fichman composed delightful children's songs; Judah Steinberg painted idyllic pictures of Hasidic life; Miche Yosef Berdichevsky wrote of ordinary people. Zalman Itzkhok Onuchi, who created the character of the philosophizing Hasid in his *Reb Abbo,* was one of the many new writers.

Folklore was very popular and Sholem Aleichem discovered a Jewish Béranger in a Kiev lawyer, Mark Varshavski (1848-1907), whose *Genuine Folksongs* are so widely sung that many are amazed to learn that *Oif'n Pripetchok Brennt a Fierl* comes from his pen. The most prominent of the folklorists was Shloime Anski (1863-1920). His *Dybbuk* became popular in a later period and influenced both the Yiddish and Hebrew theaters. The work of Reb Mordechele (Chaim Tshmerinski, 1862-1917), with its diverting allegories and satirical poetry, is also based upon an unusual familiarity with the popular idiom.

The career of Abraham Reisen, who wrote both poetry and prose, illustrates the fact that the influence of the folk song is more lasting than that of the folk tale. His poetry shows the impact of the folk song while his short stories have a European and Peretz-like flavor. Reisen's poems are short, unaffected melodic revelations of mood with distant echoings of *Weltschmerz,* filled with great sympathy for the lonely and the oppressed. His lucid style found great favor and Reisen early became one of the most popular poets.

Abraham Liesin (1872-1938), who was a contemporary of Reisen, individualized social-revolutionary poetry. Yehoash (pen name of Jehoash Shloime Blumgarten) (1871-1927) began with romantic nationalistic ballads, fables and lyrics. Both these poets reached their peak in later years and we shall return to them.

The Lithuanian-born David Einhorn wrote with resignation of the decline of the small town in *Quiet Songs,* while his *Jewish Daughters* introduced idyllic love motifs. His work has unusual individuality of tone and pleasant rhythm. The work of the Galician Shmuel Yakov Imber is more turbulent, more erotic.

Although the development of poetry during this period was rapid, the principal advance took place in narrative prose. In this field we have a threesome to start: Abraham Reisen, Sholem Asch and Hersh David Nomberg. Reisen's short stories deal with daily problems and simple spiritual conflicts. They are often just barely humorous, often lyrical with compassion for Man who, after all, is not so highly developed as is sometimes believed.

The perennially enamored Sholem Asch is quite different; he began by singing the praises of the small town (Samuel Niger has called him the "Prophet of the Soil"). But he soon turned to the problems of the big city, to the life of the new immigrant in America and to the underworld, creating a series of interesting novels. We shall return to him.

Hersh David Nomberg (1876-1927) introduced psychological analysis in portraying the dissatisfied, introverted intellectual. The clarity of style and masterly construction of his stories give him a prominent place in Yiddish literature, although he wrote little and in a single vein.

The earthiness of the writings of Itshe Meyer Veisnberg (1881-1937) is in direct contrast to Sholem Asch's idyll of the small town. Veisnberg, himself a workingman, describes the worker's life with unrelenting realism, stressing the crude and the brutal. Jonah Rosenfeld, also a laborer, began with realistic stories but went on to psychological analysis. Lamed Shapiro painted impressionistic portraits of nature and his powerful stories of pogroms are impregnated with the spirit of vengeance. Itzkhok Doiv Berkowitz, son-in-law of Sholem Aleichem and his splendid translator into Hebrew, portrays ordinary people in extraordinary circumstances. Toward the end of the period appeared David Bergelson, delineating moods and highlighting the autumnal tragedy of the young woman in *After All*.

The drama developed much more slowly than *belles-lettres*. David Pinski, who began in the nineties with stories of the laboring classes, is the author of plays which demonstrate the conflicts arising out of the breakup of the patriarchal-religious family relationship. Sholem Asch created a sensation with his *God of Vengeance*. He also attempted historical drama and contemporary comedy. Peretz Hirshbein, himself the organizer of a dramatic troupe, first wrote realistic plays, turned to Maeterlinckian dramas of mood, and finally found himself among simple country folk and their rustic surroundings. There is less continuity in Yiddish drama than there is in poetry and prose. The thread Goldfaden had spun was broken, and a definite rift between the professional theater and the literary drama became apparent. The devotees of this more cultivated theater (including the semisymbolic plays of A. Veiter) are definitely characteristic of the Yiddish cultural life of this period.

Literary criticism was especially popular and was written not only by the editors of periodicals, but also by a considerable number of cultural workers. Yet there was no outstanding literary critic before Baal Machshovos (Isidor Eliashev, 1873-1924). With strict aesthetic standards he became the servant of Jewish letters, giving encouragement to almost every beginner. A follower, in principle, of the school of Hippolyte Taine, Machshovos nevertheless employed the environmental method, especially in the interpretation of realistic works. From Yiddish circles emerged Samuel Niger, who early proved a talented critic. His work is characterized by detailed analysis particularly of the relationship of the writer to his surroundings. (More of him later.)

After 1905 the stream of immigration brought to America many authors who had already won fame in the old country, as well as young writers who had taken their first steps in the literary field. In 1908 there evolved from among these the group known as "the Young," militant beginners dissatisfied with the status of literature on the Continent, and calling for its independence of social ideologies. They published collected *Writings* (edited by David Ignatoff) in which they followed the course and even anticipated the literary development in Eastern Europe. The principal works of these "Young" were not to appear until 1914.

In summary: The fifty years between 1864 and 1914 witnessed the development of a worldly, many-sided Yiddish literature; principally realistic yet with more than a tinge of romanticism, it showed tendencies toward modern symbolism as well. Although centered in Russian Jewry, there was a parallel development of Yiddish literature in America. With its unshakable affirmation of life and its intimate family spirit, this literature was an instrument of social progress and a mighty force for unifying the scattered Jewish people.

E. Yiddish Literature in America, 1916-1946

World War I rent asunder Russia's Jewish community of six millions. The settlements in the Soviet Union, in Poland and the small center of the Baltic countries and Rumania became completely distinct. The hegemony of Jewish life was transferred to the American center.

A kaleidoscope of literary groups, trends and forms, such as had never been known before, developed in New York, and to a lesser extent in other North American cities such as Montreal, Chicago and Los Angeles. While social motifs were characteristic of literary endeavors of the late nineteenth and the early twentieth century, national consciousness has marked the writings of the past thirty years (1916-1946). Negative traits, too, became apparent such as the rift between the reader and the ultra-modern author, the language assimilation of the younger generation, the halting of immigration, thus raising the average age of the reading public with little prospect of building for the future. All these factors could not help but influence the writer and his work.

Especially important was the development in the field of poetry with the appearance of a variety of temperaments, styles and themes. The two elder poets, Yehoash and Liesin, renewed their creative activities. The imagery of Yehoash became richer and more satisfying, Apollonian in its lyrical restraint. Abraham Liesin, the most nationalistic of Yiddish poets, is inspired by the *Kiddush Ha-Shem* motif and relives his youth in mystical songs of remembrance. Younger than these two are the ever-changing and very prolific Hayim Roisenblatt and the constant, introspective Joseph Rolnick.

Theoretically, Zisha Landau (1889-1937) is an antisocial aesthete but actually he celebrates the joys of everyday life in his delicate, mildly imagist songs. Mani Leib, influenced by the Russian poets, particularly Fett and Alexander Block, writes tender, romantic lyrics, as well as charming children's poems and ballads based on folk motifs. Israel Jacob Schwartz is equally fond of the European background of his pious rabbi father and the American environment of his children. He introduced American themes in his long poem *Kentucky*, as well as in a number of shorter works. He is also an untiring translator of both old and new Hebrew poetry.

Most impassioned of the modern Yiddish poets is Moishe Leib Halperin (1886-1932). Torn between an inborn romanticism and the cynicism of a chaotic world, he incorporates the disillusionment of the postwar generation and the spiritual "otherness" of the immigrant, who, to the very end, is unable to come to terms with his environment.

Faithful to the teachings of Peretz, that ethics is the goal and aesthetics but the means, is H. Leivick,[6a] who voices the sorrow and unrest of our generation. In his great symbolic dramas, *The Golem*, and *The Comedy of Redemption*, are unfolded the problems of world deliverance and the struggle for progress. During long years of serious illness his poems dealt with death and destruction, but his *Songs of Paradise* are touched with the joy of life. In these last years he expresses deep wrath and sorrow over the devastation of Europe.

Ten years after "the Young" came the group known as "the Introspectionists" (after their magazine *Within Oneself*). Urbane intellectuals, they espoused free verse, abstraction, allusion and metaphor. Aaron Leyeles (Aaron Glanz) and Jacob Glatshtein headed this group. The latter was a bold experimenter with language; of late his poetry has been less revolutionary in form and more profound in spirit.

The feeling of instability, the anxiety about the course of the development of Jewish life in America, Hitler's persecutions and devastation of Europe—all these factors had the effect of strengthening traditionalism. Poetic form acquired simplicity and purity and ever recurrent were themes from the Old World. This traditionalism is apparent in the works of almost all the Yiddish-American poets, one of the outstanding being

Menachem Boraisha, whose face is turned toward the past in his great work *The Pilgrim*. In Jacob Itzkhok Segal's lyrics we hear the maternal prayer; Ephraim Auerbach concludes that *The Old Spring Is Pure* and drinks from it. Benjamin Jacob Bialostotzki and Naftoli Gross also are part of this trend.

Quite distinct was the realistic "Proletpen" group, whose spiritual home was the Soviet Union. Only the capricious, bitterly sarcastic poems of Moishe Nadir (1885-1943) rose above the average monotony of their writings.

Many stories and novels were serialized in the Yiddish press. Undoubtedly the most popular narrative writer was Sholem Asch, whose particular strength lies in the scope of his canvas and in his vivid mass scenes. He is guided by a deep faith in man and by real affection for his characters. His trilogy *Three Cities: Petersburg, Warsaw, Moscow*, depicting scenes of Jewish life before, during and after World War I, enjoyed great success. His finest talents came to the fore in *Salvation*. Asch aroused some difference of opinion with *The Nazarene* and *The Apostle*.

Israel Joshua Zynger (1893-1944) limited his subject matter to life in Poland in the recent past. Like Balzac, he portrayed the bitterness of the "Human Comedy," but even more coldly and more naturalistically than did the French master. His principal novels are *Yoshe the Calf-like*, *The Brothers Ashkenazi*, *Comrade Nachman* and *The Karnovski Family*.

Zalmen Schneour, Hebrew poet and Yiddish author, became known largely by way of the New York newspaper *Forward*, and is therefore included among the American writers, although it is difficult to ascribe him to any one country. In his stories he delights in physical prowess and is prone to linger over erotic passages. Schneour's series *Jews of Shklov* was very popular and his favorite hero is the young butcher, Noah Pandre.

Master of the short story is Joseph Opatoshu, who has a special affinity for the psychological. In his trilogy (*In Polish Woods, 1863, Alone*), which treats of Jewish life in Poland in the mid-nineteenth century, there is an added romantic undertone. He turns easily from Old World themes to both Jewish and Christian life on the American continent. His diction is scrupulously refined. More the painter than the storyteller was Isaac Raboi (1882-1943), who introduced both the far West (*Mr. Goldenbarg*) and New England (*A Strip of the Sea*) to Yiddish literature; Samuel Niger described Raboi's novels as "masses of arrested lyricism."

David Ignatoff attempted to record the history of the American Jewish intelligentsia in his novels. Boruch Glossman dwells on the psychology of the lonely and 'he maladjusted; Shihe Miller depicts the disintegration of Jewish life in America and in the Soviet Union. B. Demblin is one of the few Yiddish writers who portrays Gentile types as well (*West Side*). Although the skeptical Moishe Nadir undertook to "de-create" the silly world and "disenchant" foolish man, an unexpected warmth is to be found in his stories. We end this review of prose works with mention of the narrator of charming children's stories, Leon Elbe, and Jacob Glatshtein, who combines creative writing and factual reporting in his *When Iash Went Away* and *When Iash Returned*.

In America as in Europe, the drama does not keep pace with poetry and prose. In this field, David Pinski tends to be symbolic and abstract; Peretz Hirshbein refined his idyllic folkplays (*Green Fields*); Hersh Sackler found his characters in the romantic popular tale, while H. Leivick's *Rags* presents the true drama of the immigrant. More recently he has dramatized the revolt of the Warsaw Ghetto (*The Miracle of the Ghetto*). Leon Kobrin portrayed dramas of everyday life in such plays as *The Country Fellow*.

In America, too, almost all poets and publicists engaged in literary criticism but none of them approximated the influence exerted by Samuel Niger, whose diligence and sincerity have made him the guardian as well as the judge of Yiddish literature. Of the multitude of critics, we mention Alexander Mukdoni, impressionistic and discerning; Borukh Rivkin, obscure and casuistical; Hillel Rogoff, a literal interpreter and Abraham Cahan, the very influential editor of *Forward*.

In the broad field of the essay, distinction has been won by Dr. Haim Zhitlovsky, leader of the nationalistic-socialist intelligentsia; Dr. Abraham Coralnik, sensitive aesthete; Haim Greenberg, editor of the *Yiddisher Kempfer*, and Abraham Liesin, for many years editor of the *Future*.

What makes Yiddish literature in America American? Much more fundamental than the subject matter is the influence of life in the New World upon the writer who began to see the old country in a different light, and to interpret the problems of the Jew in a way which stamps his work as peculiarly American.

F. Yiddish Literature in Poland between the two World Wars

The second most important center of Yiddish literature was Poland, whose three and a half million Jews had been rooted in Polish soil for some eight hundred years. Geographically close to Russia, Polish-Yiddish literature was separated as by a wall from that of the Soviet Union. Of the two, it was the Polish center that was in contact with America.

In Poland, Yiddish literature was closely connected with the diversified communal activities and the firmly patterned everyday life. Yet it also reflected the dissensions and the gnawing uncertainty about the future. World War I destroyed the established order; the older generation of writers died out; the younger men, who had come to Warsaw from the provinces and felt insecure in their new environment, were caught up in the crosscurrents of a belated *Haskala*, radicalism and nationalism. This milieu gave rise to an antiaesthetic and antisocial expressionism particularly among those poets of the magazine *Khalastre* (*The Bunch*). To this group belong the prose writers Ozer Varshavski, who, in his *Smugglers*, gave an angry picture of wantonness during the war period, and Avrom Moishe Fuchs, who skillfully portrayed shady characters from the dregs of humanity.

The leader of a group of poets from Lodz was Moishe Broderzon whose rhythmic poetry illustrated his primary interest in form; but underneath his playfulness there lurked a corroding pessimism. Two Lithuanian poets introduced a fresh, youthful romanticism: Leib Neidus (1890-1918), who was a master at versification, and Moishe Kulbak, who wrote impetuous, unaffected and somewhat modernistic poetry.

The strongest and most enduring poetic stream was fed by tradition, by a pessimistic sentimentalism, and by a universal yet specifically Jewish restlessness. Some sought solace in mysticism and a fancied traditionalism.

The traditional and the mystical are basic qualities of the creative works of Aaron Zeitlin, son of the God-seeking publicist, who was put to death by the Nazis. The mystic and moralist, Israel Shtern, always had a premonition of martyrdom and actually perished with those martyred by Hitler.

The well of folklore is mirrored in the lucid, prayerlike poems of Miriam Ulinover, who drew all *From Grandmother's Treasure,* as she called one of her poetry collections. An original combination of the grotesque and the romantic is found in the bohemian carelessness and the anguished sentimentality of the poems by Itsik Manger. The poetess Kadya Molodovski found herself in singing of the lives of the poor. Just before the war, Yechiel Lehrer, also one of the martyred, produced the long poem of day-to-day life, *My Home.* The "Young Vilna" group was very much under American influence. Outstanding among them are Chaim Grahde and A. Sutskever, who were able to save themselves only to lament the devastation of Vilna, but not of Vilna alone . . .

Mention has already been made of the narrative writers who left Poland for America. Among those remaining in Poland were: Zalman Segalovitch, who depicted either capricious female characters or himself in his popular novels; Joshua Perla, who had a great love for the land of the Vistula; Efraim Kaganovski, who portrayed the poverty-stricken and the underworld of Warsaw; the tragically fated Simeon Horontchik (1889-1939), whose long novels deal with the lives of working people. In the works of Isaac Bashevis (brother of Israel Joshua Zynger) are to be found purity of form and vividness of imagery. His *Satan of Gorei* depicts the aftermath of the Sabbatai Zevi movement. Just prior to World War II there appeared some powerful young writers of small-town life.

In general the drama (*Dybbuk* has already been mentioned) departed from gray reality. Jacob Pregger builds upon the folk tale (*The Tempta-*

tion, Simcho Plachte), as does Aaron Zeitlin; Alter Kacyzne uses the story of the "true proselyte" of Vilna in *The Duke*; Jekheskal Moishe Neiman gives us the idyll of *The Sabbath Fruit* while Fishel Bimko's *Thieves* dramatizes the exotic underworld.

Of the more than one hundred periodicals flourishing at that time, *Book World, Jewish World, Art and Life, Literary Leaves* and *Weekly* were among those devoted to literature. Some of the many critics and essayists were Nachman Maisil, editor of *Literary Leaves*; the philoso-phizing Yekhiel Yeshaye Troonk; the enthusiastic Zalmen Raizen, compiler of the four-volume *Lexicon of Yiddish Literature, Press and Philology*; the historian Isaac Shipper and the philologist Noah Prilutsky.

With the advent of Hitler, the deeply rooted Polish Jewish community faced extermination. Yet its spiritual strength was inexhaustible and in the Ghettos of Vilna and Warsaw, in the shadow of the concentration camps, Jews conducted literary meetings and celebrated the anniversaries of famous authors. Some writers fled to the Soviet Union, others came to the United States and a painfully large number perished with their readers.

G. Yiddish Literature in the Soviet Union

In 1915 the czarist regime forbade the use of the Yiddish alphabet in the printing of periodicals and books. Immediately following the March Revolution of 1917 and during the first years of the October Revolution (1917-1921) literary creation was relatively unhampered. Gradually the situation changed: one had to become "proletarian" or remain silent.

Yiddish literature in the Soviet Union became a "Soviet" literature and no longer regarded itself as part of world Yiddish literature. Quite deliberately the leaders of this controlled Jewish life did everything possible to separate the Jews of the Soviet Union from the Jews of the rest of the world. Even the orthography was changed radically and Yiddish writers avoided phrases and expressions which stemmed from the *heder* or were associated with religious Judaism. It was not until the Popular Front of the thirties that this isolationist policy began to weaken.

In addition to the geographical isolation there was a spiritual departure from the earlier literature. A writer who walked *In Step* (a typical name for a literary collection) received greater material compensation than did the average Yiddish writer elsewhere. He also had an audience, for the reading and discussion of literary works became a routine part of club activities. However, the writer always had to fulfill a "social assignment": to defend one point of view, to oppose another. Thus he felt that his writing filled a definite need. It is impossible to understand the fluctuations of Yiddish literature in the Soviet Union without taking into consideration the constant political changes.

Even more so than elsewhere, poetry in the Soviet Union is the most important form of expression. An example of the revolutionary romanticism of the civil war period is the work of Osher Shvartsman (1890-1919). The deeply nationalistic David Hofstein, influenced almost all Soviet-Yiddish poets with respect to poetic form. Peretz Markish, in his long, versified novels, depicted the struggle against the vestiges of the old order. Leib Kvitko is modest and refined. Somewhat younger than those mentioned are Itsik Feffer and Izzi Charik; the former, faithful to the Soviet regime, earned official recognition while the latter was a victim of the purges. Yet both sing with joy of the new life and glorify the fatherland.

Yiddish prose in the Soviet Union has developed much more slowly. The novels and stories dealing with the revolution are, to quote David Bergelson, "scarcely finished literary works with their roughness of style and characterization." In the twenties social progress was the principal theme; later it was praise of the champions of production and of the victory over saboteurs. In addition to following the "party line," Yiddish writers glorified the establishment of new Jewish colonies and the development of Biro-Bidjan.

David Bergelson stands head and shoulders above his Soviet colleagues. One of the finest stylists in Yiddish literature, his chief power lies in describing environment and mood. At first he saw the revolution as *A Measure of the Law* and later accepted it fully; his characters conform to the new order. In his great autobiographical novel *Beside the Dnieper* he gives a graphic account of his childhood and youth. The novelist "The Nestor" (Froyim Kahanovitch), who stood apart from the others, won renown with his recent book *The Mashber Family*. A return to classicism is found in the stories of Itsik Kipnis, whose idyllic *Months and Days* aroused much controversy. Moishe Kulbak paints a pleasantly humorous portrait of a lower-class family in his *Zelmenians*. The Yiddish theater is well developed in the Soviet Union, but not the art of the drama.

No field of letters was so completely under the influence of Soviet dogma as was that of literary criticism. Moishe Litvakov, editor of *Truth*, was the overseer of political *kashrut* (yet he died in prison). The excellent analyst, Nochum Oislender, is the freest and the most interesting of his colleagues. Dr. Israel Tsinberg spent many years on his ten-volume *History of Literature Among the Jews*, which was being printed in Poland but remained unfinished. The author is presumed to have died in a Soviet prison.

Western Russia with its dense Jewish population was the first to suffer Nazi attack. Most of the writers of Minsk and Kiev fled deep into Russia, thus avoiding the fate of their readers. At present the only center of Yiddish literature in the Soviet Union is Moscow. Commencing with the summer of 1941, such motifs as the defense of the fatherland, the horrors of the Nazi massacre of the Jews, topics from Jewish history and a revival of national Jewish sentiment characterized Yiddish writings appearing in the Soviet Union during the war period.

H. The Universality of Yiddish Literature.

Yiddish literature is not limited to the three great centers of America, Poland and the Soviet Union. Wherever there were Yiddish-speaking settlements there appeared literary works of all kinds to meet the great demand of the large reading public.

In Rumania between the two World Wars there was a Jewish population of about a million. Despite persecution which obstructed the development of the Yiddish press and the expansion of cultural societies, a number of vigorous talents appeared. Our best allegorist is Eliezer Steinbarg (1880-1932), who introduced social motifs into the fable giving them a witty, typically Jewish flavor.

Lithuania, with Kuanas as the principal center, teemed with young poets and authors. Outstanding was the poet Jacob Gotlieb. There were literary groups in Latvia too, and even in the small settlement of Estonia.

The Argentine, with its quarter of a million Jews, is the second largest Jewish community in the New World. With its great daily newspapers and a flourishing cultural life, it has distinguished itself in the short fifty years of its history by an unusual interest in *belles-lettres*. In his truly artistic memoirs, Mordecai Alperson has told of the hardships of thirty years of Jewish colonization. Moishe Pintshevski was the first to write Yiddish poetry in which the South American landscape is described. The energetic Jacob Botashanski is prominent in the field of the essay, memoir and literary criticism. The much younger Jewish community in Mexico has its literary circles, too, with the poet Jacob Glants in the vanguard.

In Palestine, where Hebrew is the official language, there was an energetic group of Yiddish poets and narrative writers who gave expression to the joys and sorrows of the pioneers. In 1937 the collection entitled *Writings of Eretz Israel*, appeared in Tel-Aviv.

The other continents, too, are represented in Yiddish literature. The community in South Africa has its publications and literati, among them the poet David Fram. Australia also has added new names to the field of Yiddish letters, as noted in the *Australian Yiddish Almanac* (Melbourne, 1937).

It has not always been easy to describe a roving writer as belonging to a particular country, and in the case of the following men it is impossible to do so: Leib Malach, who wrote a drama, *Mississippi*, a novel of South America, *Don Domingo's Crossroad*, and highly literary reports of his many travels; Melach Ravitch, wandering ambassador of Yiddish poetry, whose *Continents and Oceans* embraces most of the world and whose *Poems and Ballads* displays a great variety of subject matter; Daniel

Charney, of Berlin, Paris and, since 1940, New York, whose penetrating memoirs are distinguished by humor. These three prove that Yiddish literature transcends all boundaries.

Despite this geographical distribution, one sees a similarity of literary development linking one land to another and the present with the past. Although weakened by language assimilation, Yiddish literature has, nevertheless revealed in recent times a breadth of vision and a sense of responsibility for the course of development of the whole Jewish people, which is striving to clarify for itself and for the world its spiritual physiognomy.

NOTES

[1a Cf. above Cecil Roth, "The Jews of Western Europe (from 1648)," p. 260; cf. also above Walter J. Fischel, "Israel in Iran: A Survey of Judeo-Persian Literature," pp. 839-840.]

[2a Cf. Roth, op. cit., pp. 253-254.]

[3a Cf. above the chapter by Abraham J. Heschel, "The Mystical Element in Judaism."]

[4a Cf. above Hillel Bavli, "The Modern Renaissance of Hebrew Literature," pp. 567 f.]

[5a Cf. Roth, op. cit., pp. 261-262.]

[6a H. Leivick's first name was Leivick, and second name was Halper, but he has become known as H. Leivick.]

BIBLIOGRAPHY

BIRNBAUM, SALOMO, "Literature, Yiddish," (A & B, I, II) in *The Universal Jewish Encyclopedia*. New York, 1942, pp. 125-129.
A very brief account of the history of Yiddish literature to the end of the nineteenth century; since the discussion is merely of types of works, the development of the literature as a whole is lost sight of.

MARK, YUDEL, "Yiddish Literature," in *Encyclopedia of Literature*, J. Shipley, editor. New York, 1946. II, pp. 1026-1045.

MINKOFF, NOKHUM BORUKH, "Literature, Yiddish" (B, III), "The Twentieth Century," in *Ibid.*, pp. 129-135.
Too formalistically schematized into three schools: impressionism, expressionism, traditionalism. For this reason the distinctness of the three principal centers (America, Poland, Russia) is not recognizable.

NIGER, SAMUEL, "New Trends in Postwar Yiddish Literature." in *Jewish Social Studies*. I, No. 3. New York, July, 1939, pp. 337-358.
A very good review of trends in the modern literature.

PINÈS, M. *Histoire de la littérature judéo-allemande*. Paris, 1911.
This work is based mainly on that by L. Wiener.

ROBACK, ABRAHAM A., *The Story of Yiddish Literature*. New York, 1940.

> With a great deal of love for Yiddish literature and with a tendency to apologetics, this book gives a brief picture of ancient and later Yiddish literature and dwells principally on the contemporary; it presents many facts, not always free of inaccuracy but without a clear scheme. The bibliographical notes on pp. 403-420 are valuable.

WAXMAN, MEYER, *A History of Jewish Literature from the Close of the Bible to our Own Days*. 4 vols. New York, 1930-1941. II, pp. 613-615; IV, pp. 463-566, 996-1047.

> The author provides many facts, but the attitude is as to a foreign matter and not free of inaccuracies.

WIENER, LEO, *The History of the Yiddish Literature of the 19th Century*. New York, 1899.

> Written with love for Yiddish literature but without a thorough knowledge of its history to the middle of the nineteenth century, this book has interesting passages only concerning the middle and the second half of the century; unfortunately, there are a number of inaccuracies.

ERIK, MAX, *Die Geschichte fun der Yiddisher Literatur fun die Aeltste Zeiten bis Haskala-Tekufa*. Warsaw, 1928.

> A very valuable book for the older literature but with an exaggerated evaluation of the importance of the "bardic" period.

MINKOFF, N. B., and NIGER, S., "Literatur bei Yiden" in *Algemeine Enziklopedie*. New York, 1942. III, Columns 1-174.

RAIZEN, ZALMEN, *Fun Mendelssohn bis Mendele*. Warsaw, 1923.

> An anthology, with introductory articles, concerning a number of writers of the second half of the eighteenth and the first half of the nineteenth centuries.

————, *Lexicon fun Yiddisher Literatur, Presse un Philologie*. 4 vols. Vilna, 1926-1929.

> A very good, almost always trustworthy source of information; fairly long accounts of all the more important writers.

SHIPPER, ISAAC, *Geschichte fun Yiddishe-Kunst un Drama fun die Aeltste Zeiten bis 1750*. 2 vols. Warsaw, 1923-1925.

> A very valuable monograph.

SHTIF, NOKHUM, *Die Aeltere Yiddishe Literatur*. Kiev, 1929.

> An anthology with brief biographies and characterizations of the writers.

SHULMAN, ELIEZER, *Sefat Yehudit-ashkenazit vesifrata*. Riga, 1913.

> A brief and good review of the old and the *Haskala* literature without, of course, the related facts that have accrued during the past forty years.

TSINBERG, ISRAEL, *Die Geschichte fun Literatur bei Yiden*. Vilna, 1935-1937. VI and parts of VII and VIII.

> Very good articles concerning the ancient and later literature, with many details of the lives of the writers and of their times.

WEINREICH, MAX, *Bilder fun die Yiddishe Literatur-geschichte, fun die onhaben bis Mendele Moicher Sforim*. Vilna, 1928.

> Excellent detail studies of the older literature.

CHAPTER 21

THE ROLE OF EDUCATION IN JEWISH HISTORY

By Julius B. Maller

The survival of Jews and Judaism is in a large measure due to the continuous emphasis, throughout Jewish history, upon the transmission of
ideas and practices from old to young and from one generation to another.[1]
The educative process, an integral part of all varieties of religion and
culture, was at the very core of Judaism and the Jewish way of living
since biblical times.

The quest for an understanding of the meaning of life and the sustained
effort to pass that meaning on from generation to generation have eternally motivated Jewish endeavor. This searching for knowledge, which
in its practical aspect we call education, served as a central factor in Jewish
life. The chief preoccupation of the Jewish Sages of all time was learning
and teaching—Torah and Talmud.

During the First and Second Commonwealth, for approximately a
thousand years of Jewish self-government—with one brief interruption,
the Babylonian Exile—the process of developing the way of the good
life and teaching it to the people was the major responsibility of the
nation's judges, priests, and prophets. After the conquest of Palestine by
the Roman legions and the forced dispersal of the Jews, *The Book* became
the portable homeland. The loss of territorial unity strengthened the urge
to preserve spiritual continuity. Community of ideas took the place of the
physical community; indeed, the Jews became known as "the People of
the Book." The transmission of a complete system of ideas became the
bulwark against disintegration, and education moved to the head of the
Jewish table of values.

To be sure, the educational concepts did not develop in the Jewish
community isolated from the world. The ideas of Jews about education
were influenced by, and in turn exerted influence upon, the educational
theories of Egypt, Phoenicia, Babylonia, Persia, Greece and Rome. Because
of the relative inaccessibility of original Jewish sources, the Jewish contribution to the conceptual aspects of modern education is not generally
recognized in textbooks on the history of education. Classical Jewish
education is often described as a direct outgrowth of Greek education or

it is relegated to obscurity in discussions of education during early Christianity. What must be recognized is that education was so much a part of Jewish thought and way of living that it was taken for granted; Jewish Sages considered it hardly necessary to set down an articulated plan of its principles and practices. In a similar sense, the advanced conceptions of social ethics, abundant in Jewish classical writings, were not preserved as an organized system but rather as dynamic expressions on how to live.

The present chapter will be concerned primarily with the development of educational concepts as revealed in classical Jewish sources. The organizational aspects of the school, the curriculum and administration are discussed in another chapter.[1a]

Some Basic Educational Concepts

Certain fundamental concepts of education found in the records of earlier eras continued to be stressed through subsequent periods of Jewish history. Among the basic concepts that appear to have been accepted in Jewish lore, the following may be noted:

(1) An abiding faith in the efficacy of education, that human character is modifiable and improvable. (2) Learning and doing must be integrated; knowledge of ethics must be expressed in proper conduct. (3) Education is a continual process, to be carried on literally from the cradle to the grave. (4) Environment is an important factor in the educative process. (5) Education, to be most effective, must start with the very young. (6) Individual differences among pupils must be recognized; tests reveal differences in knowledge and convictions. (7) The process of education must be gradual from the known to the unknown from the simple to the complex, and from the immediate to the remote. (8) Responsibility for education rests with the parents and the community. (9) Training for work is regarded as both essential and honorable. (10) The teaching of history as illustrations of the continuity and meaning of Jewish experiences.

Jewish teaching emphasized above all else that study is essential and worth while and must be brought to the people for guidance in everyday affairs. The emphasis was definitely on the pragmatic aspects of education. The Greek concepts of contemplation or dialogue as forms of diversion and enjoyment were uncommon in Jewish lore.

The Biblical Period

The concept of one God, invisible, imageless, and ruler of human destinies, tolerated no compromise with the primitive tribal practices of paganism. The explicit concept of the unity of God and the implicit corollary of the unity of mankind were so ingrained in all Jewish thought that subsequent conceptions of life and education naturally sprang from it.

Religion, as introduced in the period of the Bible, was a synthesis of theological concepts and ethical precepts which man had to obey in order to live as a social being. Failure to fulfill Divine commandments was considered the cause of human misfortunes and national disasters. This is not to say that the lofty concepts of morals and monotheism were either fully understood or accepted by the Hebrew masses. The Hebrew leaders were constantly aware of the tendency to relapse into paganism and immorality and they spared no effort to counteract that tendency and to educate the people in the way of the good life. In every book of the Bible this concern for education and the application of ethical principles is emphasized. The people were repeatedly admonished not to forsake Divine laws, but to pass them on from one generation to another.

Thus education, which was at once religious and national, served to bind the people together and aided in their survival through centuries of invasion, servitude and oppression, under the Egyptians, the Babylonians, the Persians, the Macedonians, the Syrians and the Romans. "If ever," declares a Swiss educator, "a people has proved the power of national education, it is the Jewish people."[2]

The Scriptures are the primary source for many of the educational theories that recur throughout Jewish history, many of which are as acceptable now as they were in the days of the Jewish commonwealth.

Mankind as a group, born of the common flesh and blood, and subject to the universal desires, aspirations, temptations and weaknesses, is considered to be capable of improvement, therefore of learning. All men are exhorted to seek out wisdom, to know its blessings.

> Happy is the man that findeth wisdom,
> And the man that obtaineth understanding . . .
> Her ways are ways of pleasantness
> And all her paths are peace (Prov. 3:13, 18).
>
> Get wisdom, get understanding . . .
> Yea, with all thy getting get understanding . . .
> I have taught thee in the way of wisdom . . .
> Take fast hold of instruction, let her not go;
> Keep her, for she is thy life (Prov. 4:4, 13).

Knowledge of the Law and observance of it were held to be of equal importance. The bonds of the nation were strengthened through the educative principle, which demanded proper ethical behavior.

And Moses called unto all Israel and said unto them: "Hear, O Israel, the statutes and the ordinances which I speak in your ears this day that ye may learn them and observe to do them" (Deut. 5:1).

And thou shalt teach them the statutes and the laws and shalt show them the way wherein they must walk and the work that they must do (Ex. 18:20).

The concept that learning was a continuing process, functioning at all times and in all places, was stressed from the very beginning of the history of the nation.

And ye shall teach them your children, talking of them, when thou sittest in thy house, and when thou walkest by the way and when thou liest down and when thou risest up (Deut. 11:19).

This book of the law shall not depart out of thy mouth, but thou shalt meditate therein day and night (Josh. 1:8).

The early Hebrews recognized the importance of proper associations and of the home influence on the young person.

He that walketh with wise men shall be wise; but the companion of fools shall smart for it (Prov. 13:20).

My son, hear the instruction of thy father and forsake not the law of thy mother (Prov. 1:8).

They knew that the proper time to start education was when the child was very young.

Train up a child in the way he should go, And even when he is old, he will not depart from it (Prov. 22:6).

While accepting the fact that all human beings are capable of learning and improving, the scholars of the time also pointed out that individual differences in students must be taken into account.

There are the stories of Jacob and Esau, and Isaac and Ishmael, to illustrate different personality types.

Even a child maketh himself known by his doings whether his work be pure and whether it be right (Prov. 20:11).

The Prophets, who were closely concerned with the instruction of the people, understood the necessity for using gradual methods of imparting knowledge.

Whom shall one teach knowledge?
For it is precept by precept, precept by precept, line by line, line by line, here a little, there a little (Is. 28:10).

In the teachings of the Prophets the emphasis was upon behavior.

And what the Lord doth require of thee: only to do justly, and to love mercy and to walk humbly with thy God (Mic. 6:8).

The Concept of Testing

There are several biblical references to the concepts of testing devices.

For example, the ability to pronounce a Hebrew word properly was used as an identification test.

> When any of the fugitives of Ephraim said, "Let me go over," the men of Gilead said unto him, "Art thou an Ephraimite?" If he said, "Nay," then they said unto him, "Say now Shibboleth," and he said, "Sibboleth," for he could not frame to pronounce it right (Judg. 12:5-6).

(It is interesting to note that this word "shibboleth" found its way into other languages to signify a watchword or the test word of the party.)

Another example of the application of a performance test is found in the recorded manner by which the bravest three hundred soldiers were selected by Gideon from an army of 32,000 men (Judg. 7:5-6).

Tests of courage and of implicit faith are also mentioned abundantly. Abraham's willingness to sacrifice his son and the trials and tribulations of Job are striking illustrations.

The Postbiblical Period

The restoration of a Jewish community in Palestine after the Babylonian Exile brought a number of important changes in the educational concepts of the Hebrew people. Gradually the role of the prophet diminished; the priest and the Levite concerned themselves more and more with the religious functions of the Temple. Education was stressed as never before, and its function was entrusted to the scribe.

The scribes were scholars, without official designation or office, who steeped themselves in the study of Sacred Wisdom and imparted their knowledge to disciples. This institution—the teacher and his circle of students—became the characteristic mark of Jewish life for centuries. The power of the scribe was inherent not only in his learning but in his leadership in the community. ·

Teaching, no matter what the subject, was based on the continuity of tradition. Instruction meant conveying the dicta and interpretations of preceding scholars. There was room for originality and some Sages forged new paths in law and commentary; but no break with tradition was tolerated. Teachers and disciples approached their intellectual labors with avidity and devotedness. They were regarded as the elite of the nation, men who considered the learning of the Law as the very purpose of life. The great masters won general recognition and their opinions became authoritative.

A new system of schools gradually came into being. Young children studied the Scriptures in a lower school called the *Bet Ha-Sefer*; the youth, particularly those showing intellectual ability, studied at an institution of higher learning known as the *Bet Ha-Midrash*. And for the mass of the people there arose the *Bet Ha-Keneset*, a democratic institution where members of the community participated in discussions concerning interpretations of the Written and Oral Law. A *Bet Ha-Keneset* could be organized by any ten people. Gentiles were welcomed at such groups. At meetings every Sabbath a portion of the Scriptures was read and later discussed by the participants. Later still, prayers were introduced at the meetings, such as the *Hallel* after the reading of the Scripture portion. Eventually the *Bet Ha-Keneset* became a house of prayer and in its final metamorphosis was known as the synagogue, from the Greek term for *Bet Ha-Keneset* (House of Assembly).

A succession of teachers carried on the study and interpretation of the holy writings. The scribes interpreted the Bible in its application to daily life and evolved a system of traditions which later was expounded and codified in the Mishna.[3a]

This compilation of traditional lore, the Mishna, was the work of over a hundred scholars called *Tannaim*. They were succeeded by generations of *Amoraim*, commentators on the set tradition. The work of all these generations of scholars was eventually collected in one body of decisions and opinions that formed the Gemara. The Mishna and the Gemara were combined to form that collection of thought and law known as the Talmud.[4a]

The popularization of education fostered a high regard for learning and the learned man. The illiterate became an object of disrepute and was called *am ha-aretz*, a term used to designate a grossly ignorant person.

Early in the century (*c.* 65 B.C.E.), preceding the fall of the Jewish state, Simon ben Shatah, a president of the Sanhedrin, established schools of advanced studies for young men in every district of the country. Later in the same century Joshua ben Gamala[5a] instituted elementary schools for boys of six to seven years of age. Teachers were appointed for all the schools, which were supported by the communities. Thus, in a sense, free public education was introduced in the Jewish community.

It was toward the end of that century that a new development took place in Jewish cultural and spiritual life. For the first time in the history of the Jews, an intellectual center of Judaism was established outside Palestine, in Babylonia. This development was not without its drawbacks. The Palestinian schools were an integral part of the whole country, in close contact with the people's political, social and economic life, and were influenced and guided by their needs. In Babylonia the Jewish schools as well as the Jewish community were not completely integrated with the larger community. They lacked the vitalizing influence and leaned toward a rigid interpretation of the Law and tradition.

Throughout this period of Jewish history there is ample evidence that the educational concepts of earlier times were in practice and that new ones emerged and were accepted by the people.

The concept that all were capable of being educated and that education was necessary for all appears in the writings of the postbiblical period.

As water is free for all, so is the Torah free for all. As water is priceless, so is the Torah priceless. As water brings life to the world, so the Torah brings life to the world. As water brings a man out of his uncleanness, so the Torah brings a man from the evil way into the good way. As wine does not remain good in vessels of gold and silver, but only in cheap earthenware vessels, so the words of the Torah remain pure only with him who makes himself lowly. Like wine, the words of the Torah rejoice the heart. As wine grows better by keeping, so the words of the Law become better as a man grows older.[6]

Take care of the children of the poor, for it is they who advance learning.[7]

The precept that learning and doing must be closely associated is mentioned repeatedly.

An ignorant man cannot be saintly.[8]

He whose works exceed his wisdom, his wisdom endures; but he whose wisdom exceeds his works, his wisdom does not endure.[9]

For children, religious education was bound up with ritual practice:

At the Passover Seder the son asks the father the four questions and if the son lacks understanding his father teaches him.[10]

Which is greater, study or doing? Rabbi Akiba answered: Study. The majority agreed that study is greater, for study leads to doing.[11]

The value of educational continuity is expressed in several places.

Say not when I have leisure I will study; perchance thou wilt never have leisure.[12]

The Torah says: "If thou forsakest me for a single day I shall forsake thee for two days."[13]

The Sages saw the home environment and companions as important educational factors.

Let thy house be a meetinghouse for the Sages and sit amid the dust of their feet and drink in their words with thirst.[14]

The younger the child the more impressionable he is; starting education at an early age was accepted as necessary.

He that learns as a child, to what is he like? To ink written on new paper. He that learns as an old man, to what is he like? To ink written on paper that has been blotted out.[15]

The Sages of the Mishna classified students according to their differences in the following manner:

Some hear [perceive] with facility and lose with facility. Some hear with facility and lose with difficulty. Some hear with difficulty and lose with facility. Some hear with difficulty and lose with difficulty.[16]

The element of attrition in the educational process was well recognized:

It is the custom of the world that a thousand people go in to study the Bible, a hundred complete it satisfactorily; one hundred proceed to [the study of] Mishna, ten of them complete it satisfactorily; ten advance to the study of the Talmud, only one completes it successfully.[17]

As a rule, the rabbis of the Mishna advocated a system of gradation in education. They cautioned against introducing advanced studies at an early age.

At five years one is fit for the Scripture, at ten years for the Mishna, at thirteen for the fulfilling of the Commandments, at fifteen for the Talmud.[18]

Later scholars insisted on the same principle.

Just as water descends drop by drop until it becomes a stream, so it is with the words of the Torah—a man studies two laws today and two laws tomorrow until it becomes like a living spring[19]

Members of the Jewish community took cognizance of the common responsibility for education.

He who teaches his neighbor's son Torah, it is as if he had begotten him.[20]

Form groups for the purpose of study, for Torah can be acquired only in a group.[21]

Education for work was considered both honorable and necessary.

Just as a man is required to teach his son Torah, so is he required to teach him a trade.[22]

The Sages emphasized that correct pedagogical methods require respect for the personality of the pupil, guiding him to knowledge rather than forcing him. The attitude of the teacher to the pupil must be sympathetic and considerate.

An impatient man cannot teach.[23]

Let the honor of thy disciple be as dear to thee as thine own.[24]

If you see a student who finds his studies as difficult as iron it is because his teacher does not take the proper attitude toward him.[25]

As with perfume, any one who desires may be made fragrant by it, so the scholar should be willing to teach any one who desires to profit by his learning.[26]

Examples of Testing

In the Talmud we find references to a situational test used in determining the normality and concomitant responsibility of a young child. The subject was presented with the choice between nuts and pebbles. If he made the proper choice his sense of responsibility was established.[27]

An interesting test was used to determine the legibility of a written text of the Scriptures. (The law required that each word in the Scroll be of unmistakable legibility.) In case of doubtful legibility of a word it was shown to a child who was "neither wise nor foolish" (the concept of average). If he read the word correctly, it was declared legible.[28]

Period of the Geonim

The academies of Palestine and Babylonia, which were closed for a brief time in the sixth century, were reopened in 589 c.e. under the supervision of the Geonim (heads of the academy).[29a] The period has been described by Professor Louis Ginzberg as the "Middle Age of Jewish history or the dark age, dark in the sense of obscure. No period in the history of postexilic Israel is more momentous than this and none so obscure."

In this era the Talmud became a comprehensive guide of Jewish conduct in everyday life and the leadership of Babylonian Jewry became well established. Attempts at interpreting talmudic Judaism in the light of Greco-Arabic philosophy gained currency among Jews.

While knowledge of the period is scant, certain writings of the scholars of the time reveal a good deal about the spread of education, the standing of the teacher in the community and the general concern for education. It is evident that the educational principles prevailing during the talmudic period were also advanced under the leadership of the Geonim.

The form of academic conference known as the *Kalla*, established in talmudic time, continued throughout the Geonic period. The *Kalla* assembled twice a year, in the spring and the fall when farmers could leave their work, and were open to all who desired advanced education in Jewish lore. The meeting place was usually the *Yeshiva* and hundreds of students would gather to listen to the wisdom of the Sages, and to discuss a portion of the Talmud. In addition to serving as a free school of higher education, the *Kalla* was able to reach out to the various communities through the students who came to study from all sections of the country. It also helped to extend education to distant communities which were not represented at the *Kalla* through written responses prepared by the Soferim, signed by the Geonim and sent to those communities.

The parents' responsibility for education was made clear.

If thou shalt bear sons and daughters . . . purchase for them books according to the best of your ability, and arrange to provide a teacher for them at a tender age.[30]

The Middle Ages

The dissolution of the Roman Empire after the barbarian invasion spelled the beginning of the decline of that civilization. Learning virtually disappeared; the monastery became the sole place of study, the monk the only literate person. In eastern Christian states learning survived in some centers but was limited to theological disputations or historical and legal writings.

Historians point out that intellectually the Jews suffered no medieval relapse into ignorance, that they were more educated than those among whom they lived, and that even the ordinary Jew knew the Scriptures better than the churchman of that time. The Jews contributed in large measure to the rebirth of civilization in Europe, disseminating Greek culture as interpreted by the Arabs. Jews were prominent in the Spanish cultural revival and in the early renascence in Provence and in Sicily under Frederick II.[31a]

Jewish communities scattered along the Mediterranean shores and in northern Europe, by the medieval period, had developed an educational system which was an integral part of their everyday life. Education was closely allied with religious thought. A Jewish community without a school was as rare as one without a house of worship. The most respected man in the community was the scholar; there was no greater disgrace than to be an ignoramus. Families took pride in the education of their children and were honored to have scholars in their midst.

In small communities the rabbi was usually the most learned man of the group, respected not only because of the authority vested in him, but also because of his erudition. Study, to the medieval Jew, was as important as prayer. The synagogue was more than a refuge from persecution and misery; it was a place where the Jew engrossed in study envisioned a world of truth and justice.

In the progressive Arab countries, educational facilities were easier to organize; education made greater advances and developed a wider scope than in Christian Europe. Under the Arabian influence, in Syria and Palestine and, to a lesser extent, in Babylonia, philological studies of the Hebrew language were greatly in vogue. Two systems of punctuation to represent vowels were devised. The exegetical and homiletical intrepretations of the Bible were developed in Palestine; in Babylonia the rationalist interpretation continued to prevail. The great academies in Palestine and Babylonia functioned throughout the medieval period, existing in Babylonia until the beginning of the eleventh century.

In Arabic Spain and in the Jewish communities of Provence and Italy the curriculum of studies in Jewish homes and schools included, in addition to the Bible and the Talmud, secular subjects, such as philosophy, mathematics, geometry, astronomy, medicine, poetry and music. This varied curriculum contributed to the growth of Jewish poetry and philosophy in Spain during that period. Digests of the Talmud were prepared for use by the students. Grammar was taught with the aid of especially prepared books.

In northern France, Germany, and other central European countries, the Jews confined their studies to religious matters. Education was based exclusively on the Bible and the Talmud.

Scattered as the Jewish communities were among so many countries, no fixed pattern prevailed. In general, however, the training of children started in the home, continued in an elementary school, and from there the pupil was sent to a religious academy or college, over which a famous scholar presided. Practical training began with active participation in holiday services and ceremonies.

In Germany there were schools for advanced learning of almost monastic discipline. There were also "wandering students," young men who traveled from academy to academy so that they might study with all the great scholars of the time. The teacher's task was not only to educate but to inculcate in his students a respect for the traditions and their application to daily life.

Teachers were paid by the parents when they gave private instruction at home and by the communities when they taught at a community school. The talented children of parents who could not afford to contribute to their children's education were educated at community expense. Funds for schools were raised through a special school tax. Education was practically compulsory in every Jewish community and school attendance started with a solemn ceremony when the child was very young, at the age of four or five. School was conducted throughout the year, being closed only on the Sabbath and holidays. Eventually the old principle of volunteer instruction was discarded and teaching became a profession, remuneration for which varied in different communities.

An extensive literature on education was produced during the medieval period by Jewish scholars in many lands. Education being an accepted value, most of the writers concerned themselves with the enrichment of the prevailing standards. They discussed methods of arousing public interest in educational values and how to improve pedagogical techniques; they recommended subject matter for various age groups. There was general agreement on the principle that study was not to be undertaken merely for the enjoyment of knowledge. Professions and trades were recognized as necessary for maintaining a place in society, and professional or vocational training was encouraged. Learning was considered the basis of ethical conduct in everyday matters.

During the medieval period some deviation from the rationalist interpretation of the Bible and Talmud took place; a reaction which was in a sense brought about by the oppressive conditions of the time. Nevertheless, intellectual activity never ceased. Many of the outstanding medieval Jewish scholars lived through tragic events; many died, victims of persecution, but the continuity of education remained unbroken.

Rashi (1040-1105) lived through the Crusades and witnessed the destruction by fire and sword of the central European Jewish communities. His monumental commentary on the Bible and Talmud did much to facilitate the study of Jewish lore. Rabbi Meir of Rothenburg (1220-1293) died in jail as a hostage; he was the author of a stirring poem commemorating the burning of twenty carloads of invaluable Jewish books and manuscripts in Paris (1242): "They cast thee as one despised and burn the wealth of God Most High." Ibn Tibbon (1120-1190) and Moses Maimonides (1135-1204) fled the savage pogroms of the Almohades (1146). Joseph ibn Caspi suffered under the Pastoureaux pogroms (1320). Solomon Alami survived Fernando Martinez's cruel campaign to baptize or exterminate the Spanish Jews.

The didactic poem, *Mussar Haskel*, attributed to the last Gaon, Hai ben Sherira (d. 1038),[32a] outlined the principles of education conceived as a continuation of the tradition going back to biblical times. Study, according to ben Sherira, had no other purpose than the acquisition of knowledge and sound judgment. The course of study included virtually all the known sciences of the period: religion, Divine law, philosophy, mathematics, medicine, and calendar computation. A man of education was taught to be gentle, seeking to comprehend the unknown. He was expected to rise early in the morning, have a book in his hand at all times, and ask questions of those who were more learned than himself. He was to be guided by the learned man so that he, too, might become an educational leader.

Judah ibn Tibbon fled from the fanaticism of the Almohades to Lunel, France, where he practiced medicine.[33a] He was the founder of a family of scholars and translators who brought to Europe a knowledge of Arab civilization and Arab studies of the Greek philosophers. In his treatise, *Father's Admonition*, written in the form of a will to his twelve-year-old son, ibn Tibbon combined his ideas on education with rules for the good life. He advised his son to devote himself to science and religion. He agreed with al-Ghazzali that there were only two sciences, ethics and physics, and he urged his son to excel in both.

Ibn Tibbon was a lover of books and he advised his son on how to care for his library. His son was told to have two or three copies of some books so that he could lend them to friends who could not afford their own. He was also urged to make a systematic catalogue of the books and twice a year collect those he had lent to others. Ibn Tibbon wrote: "My son, make thy books thy companions, let thy cases and shelves be thy pleasure grounds and gardens. Bask in their paradise, gather their fruit, pluck their roses, take their spices and their myrrh. If thy soul be satiate and weary, change from garden to garden, from furrow to furrow, from scene to scene. Then will thy desire renew itself, and thy soul be filled with manifold delight!"

Moses Maimonides, a renowned physician, had great influence on the promotion of secular studies among Jews,[34a] but he had little interest in poetry and history. He advised young men to study languages, philosophy, and the sciences.

Jacob Anatoli (b. c. 1194) represented the early renaissance in southern France. A fervent admirer of Maimonides, he interpreted the Bible according to the master's method, rationally, philosophically and allegorically. He deplored the fact that the Rabbis of his time neglected the study of the Bible for talmudic dialectics. He insisted that scientific investigation was essential for comprehension of religion. He advocated the study of languages and secular sciences. He fought against fanaticism, whether Jewish or Christian, and urged his fellow Jews to accept truth from Jew and Gentile alike. He was perhaps the first scholar to define the differentiating characteristics of the Greek, the Roman and the Jewish cultural genius. The first is exemplified by the pursuit of wisdom; the second, the pursuit of power; the third, the pursuit of morality. In his book, *Malmad Ha-Talmidim*, he outlined methods of study.

Joseph ben Judah Aknin (1160-1226) was the foremost educator of his age. In his book, *Healing of the Soul*, he, like most of the contemporary writers on ethics, devoted a chapter to education. He set high standards for teacher requirements. A teacher had to know his subject so thoroughly that he could detect errors in fundamental premises. The teacher's attitude to his pupil was likened to that of a father to his child; a friendly and pleasant manner was considered an essential quality in a teacher. A teacher was required to conduct himself according to ethical principles and by precept and example to encourage his pupils to do the same. The elementary curriculum was to include reading, writing, and grammar. At the age of fifteen the pupil was to start the study of the Talmud, followed by the secular sciences. Poetry and music were to be taught, as were natural sciences, practical mechanics and medicine.

Judah ben Samuel Abbas, who lived in the thirteenth century, published a treatise on ethics and religion, the *Illumination of the Path*. One chapter treats the problems of pedagogy. Abbas advised starting the education of the child at the age of three, so that by the age of thirteen he would have mastered the Bible and the Hebrew and Aramaic languages. According to Abbas's schedule, when the pupil reached the age of eighteen he should have mastered the Mishna, the Talmud and the commentaries of Maimonides and Rashi. After that came the study of philosophy and secular sciences.

Shemtob ben Joseph Falaqera (1225-1290) wrote, among other works, a didactic treatise in the form of a dialogue on the importance of scientific study, contending that an understanding of religion actually required a knowledge of science.

Imanuel ben Solomon (1268-1330), who was a friend of Dante, advocated the study of secular subjects before religious subjects. His interpretation of the Bible was allegoric and mystical.

Joseph ibn Caspi (1297-1340), born in France, was an admirer of Maimonides, a traveler and a well-educated man. In keeping with the custom of the time, he wrote an ethical will and a guide for his son, *Book of Admonition, and Guide to Knowledge.* The guide outlined a program of study leading to the good life. He emphasized that good deeds were more important than acquisition of knowledge.

His schedule of study was arranged so that until the age of fourteen the pupil was to learn the Scriptures and the Talmud. After fourteen he was to add the study of mathematics and astronomy, and also the moralist writing contained in such books as *Proverbs*, the mishnaic *Fathers* and Aristotle's *Ethics*. At the age of eighteen there was to be a general review and then natural sciences were added to the curriculum. At twenty, the student could start on metaphysics.

Solomon Alami wrote his *Letter of Admonition* in 1415, interpreting the Fernando Martinez massacres in Spain as God's punishment for the moral and religious laxity of the Jewish community. He was bitterly opposed to the trend, then popular, of integrating Greek philosophy with interpretation of the Laws of Moses. He reproached the talmudists for indulging in hairsplitting arguments, the modernists for cloaking the Torah in Greek philosophy, and the wealthy for neglecting to observe religious tradition. Alami set up technical rules for writing manuscripts and for methods of study. He stressed the true purpose of study, acquisition of knowledge. He declared that man must use his wealth to acquire knowledge and not his knowledge to acquire wealth.

Throughout the Middle Ages, it was evident that Jewish thought was following a pattern of continuity from earlier times. Such basic concepts as the necessity for universal education and the ability of man to improve through it became rules for living. The method of imparting education was improved and the scholars devoted much time to the practical aspects of education.

There are many references to the principle of learning through participation. The Passover Seder is centered around participation by the young who ask the traditional four questions. Every element in the ritual is arranged to provoke such questions by the children. On other holidays, too, provision was made for children's activities.

On the festival of Sukkot the children would make decorations for the *sukkah* and at the end of the festival they would amuse themselves with the burning of the covering of the *sukkah*.[35]

On the days of Hanukkah and Purim they would make them happy with small gifts and they would also use them as messengers to give gifts to poor people in order to accustom them to the giving of charity and good deeds.[36]

The children were asked to carry the prayer books for their parents to the synagogues. There, small benches were set aside for them upon which they sat to listen to the prayers.[37]

On Friday after the afternoon prayers the parents would send their children from the synagogue to their mothers to let them know that it was time to kindle the Sabbath lights.[38]

Study of the Torah was recognized as a lifelong process which must never be halted.

How long is a person required to study Torah? Till the day of his death . . . Some of the greatest of the wise men of Israel were wood choppers, others water drawers. Some even blind, and nevertheless they engaged in the study of Torah day and night.[39]

Differences in ability were recognized both in teaching methods and in the planning of the curriculum.

He who teaches children and finds that one is sharper than his companions should not remain quiet [but rather] he should say to their parents, these require separate teachers (and these again require separate teachers) even though he will lose money if they are separated. If he sees that he succeeds in the study of the Bible but not in the study of the Talmud he should not force him to study Talmud. He should teach him that which is suited to his knowledge. As soon as a man sees that his son is not deemed worthy (or rather cannot grasp) Talmud, he should teach him important laws and Midrash and Bible.[40]

And the rabbi would proceed to ask questions and each would answer according to his ability and each student would proceed to derive deeper understanding through discussion with his neighbor.[41]

The medieval scholars adhered to the principle that the simple must precede the complex for the educational process to work.

First they would teach the children to recognize the letters, then to join them together. Afterwards to read the words and then the sentences and after that the portion.[42]

In order that he should understand the language of the Talmud it is necessary for him to study the Bible in its Aramaic translation. Then he ought to start reading the first prophets to help him understand the arrangement of their words and letters and subjects. Each sentence should be read first in Hebrew and then in his own language.[43]

Community responsibility for education was acknowledged by the Rabbis of the time.

The salaries of the teachers in the small villages which cannot be paid by individuals are to be paid by the community as a whole.[44]

We make a rule that in all cities and in all communities each one shall be required to provide for the study of Torah.[45]

In suggesting methods of study, the Sages cautioned the people to respect the dignity of the student; they urged the teacher to inspire and guide rather than coerce.

He should treat his students the way he treats his own children as it is written "thou shalt teach thy children." . . . He should teach them according to their ability to grasp the arrangements of the subject matter, until he teaches them to reach the stage of perfection.[46]

The Jewish Community in Eastern Europe

The migrations of Jews from western to eastern Europe occurred in the centuries following the Middle Ages. In Russia and Poland, and in neighboring countries, where the vast majority of Jews settled, education continued to be the consuming interest of the Jewish communities.

The educational institutions that grew up in east European countries were similar to those in other countries from which the Jews came. At the beginning of the sixteenth century there was a huge wave of immigration from Bohemia into Poland, and the Jews who came from Bohemia and Germany brought with them their language, which developed into Yiddish, as well as their culture and communal organizations.

In the autonomous Jewish community in Poland, education was practically compulsory for children from six to thirteen years of age, and under the supervision of the authorities. The *Kahal* prescribed the curriculum of the *heder*, at times in great detail, even mentioning the commentaries to be used in the teaching of the Bible and the number of pupils per teacher. Jewish authority also regulated the kind of teachers, decided upon the relationship between teachers, provided free education to orphans and vocational education to those children who became of age and did not show the required abilities to pursue studies in the Talmud and the Codes.

In 1639 we find a provision in the record book of the Council representing the chief communities in Lithuania in which the rabbis are enjoined to examine the young men in the community to see whether they are continuing their studies. The students are advised that even after they start to study Mishna and Talmud they must not drop the study of the Bible until they know it thoroughly. The teachers are also warned against proceeding to teach Mishna before the children know the Bible.

In Poland, Jewish autonomy produced remarkable results in education. As late as 1790 the great Polish masses were unschooled, while the Jewish masses had community-supervised schools and practically all Jewish children were exposed to some education. The educational requirements of the Jewish school were rather high, although few of the schools trained their students for the rabbinate. The ideal of the Polish Jewish mother was that her son should be a man of learning.

The educational institutions consisted of the *heder* and the *Yeshiva*. The curriculum of the *heder* included the Bible with its Hebrew commentaries, Hebrew prayers and other Hebrew books. The *Yeshiva* developed the lay scholar and the learned rabbi; it emphasized a knowledge of the sources of Jewish literature. To the extent that the Pentateuch, Mishna, and especially Talmud and the Codes were the means of regulating the life of the Jewish people, their study had functional value, preparing its students for life in the Jewish community.

The *Haskala*, the movement toward enlightenment,[47a] which started in Germany, was associated with hopes of emancipation and had some effect upon the curriculum of the *heder* and Talmud Torah, particularly in the revival of Hebrew language. The *Haskala* movement in Russia intensified the Jew's feeling of difference from the Russian culture and Jewish nationalism followed. It resulted in a modern educational institution as a counterpart to the government schools, the *heder Metukkan*, which did not attempt to adjust the Jewish child to the Russian culture but aimed rather at imbuing him with a love for his own national culture.

Examinations

In the *heder*, the examination given orally played an important role. It was usually given on Thursday of each week and covered the material studied during the week. It served as a strong motivation for study and only the most capable students were expected to answer the questions with proficiency.

In the home, too, it was customary for the father to examine his son every Friday night or Saturday afternoon.

Modern Times

The treatment of the Jewish contribution to educational theory in modern times is beyond the scope of the present article.

The intermingling of Jews and non-Jews and the universal acceptance —if not practice—of educational values make it difficult to differentiate between Jewish and general concepts of education.

Emancipation in western Europe saw the gates of education open to Jews. The Jews flocked to the university with a zeal and consuming devotion nurtured for ages. Moses Mendelssohn[18a] and his colleagues, who strove to make German culture palatable to Jews, were eminently successful because they appealed to the Jewish yearning for knowledge and passion for learning. The same applied to Jewish communities in other west and north European countries and, in more recent years, in the United States.

Throughout the history of the Jews, from biblical days to modern times, education was the key to survival and the very basis of adjustment.[49]

Notes

[1] Acknowledgment is made by the author of valuable assistance by Blanche Bernstein and Geraldine Rosenfeld of the staff of the Library of Jewish Information, American Jewish Committee, and many suggestions by Leo Shpall and Mark Solitenberg.

[1a Cf. below the chapter by Simon Greenberg, "Jewish Educational Institutions."]

[2] F. Dictes, *Geschichte der Erziehung und des Unterrichtes,* Leipzig, 1871.

[3a Cf. above Judah Goldin, "The Period of the Talmud," pp. 164-166.]

[4a On the Palestinian and Babylonian Talmuds, cf. *ibid.,* pp. 169, 172 and 179-181.]

[5a Cf. Greenberg, *op. cit.,* p. 923.]

[6] Sifre Deut. Ekeb 48.

[7] Nedarim 81a.

[8] Abot 2.6.

[9] Abot 3.10.

[10] Pesahim 10.4.

[11] Kiddushin 40b.

[12] Abot 2.5.

[13] Berakot, end.

[14] Abot 1.4.

[15] Abot 4.20.

[16] Abot 5.15.

[17] Lev. R.2.

[18] Abot 5.21.

[19] Shir Ha-Shirim Rabba 1.2.

[20] Sanhedrin 19b.

[21] Berakot 63b.

[22] Kiddushin 29a.

[23] Abot 4.12.

[24] *Ibid.*

[25] Taanit 8a.

[26] Erubin 54a.

[27] Gittin 64b.

[28] Menahot 29b.

[29a Cf. Goldin, *op. cit.,* pp. 186-189.]

[30] Ascribed to R. Hai, cited in Asaf, *Mekorot Letoldot Ha-Hinuk Be-Yisrael,* II, p. 8.

[31a Cf. above Cecil Roth, "The European Age in Jewish History (to 1648)," *passim.*]

[32a Cf. above Abraham S. Halkin, "Judeo-Arabic Literature," p. 800.]

[33a Cf. below Charles Singer, "Science and Judaism," p. 1055.]

[34a Cf. above Alexander Altmann, "Judaism and World Philosophy," pp. 643 ff.; cf. also Singer, *op. cit.,* pp. 1051-1055.]

[35] Maharil, *Minhagim* (Customs), (14th-15th century), sec Sukkoth.

[36] *Ibid.*

[37] *Responsa of Maharam* (Meir ben Gedalia of Lublin), (17th century).

[38] *Eben Ha-Ezer,* by Rabbi Eliezer b. Nathan of Mayence, (12th century), #342.

[39] *Mishneh Torah,* Hilkot Talmud Torah, (Laws of Teaching the Torah), Maimonides, (12th century).

[40] Judah ben Samuel Ha-Hasid, *Sefer Hasidim* (Book of the Pious), (13th century), ed. Wistinetzky, par. 823-825, p. 209.

[41] Elijah Capsali, *Chronicles,* (16th century), cited in Asaf, *op. cit.,* II, p. 104.

[42] Isaac ben Moses of Vienna, *Or Zarua,* (13th century).

[43] Judah ben Samuel, *Yair Natib* (Will Light the Path), (17th century), cited in Asaf, *op cit.,* II, p. 29.

[44] Mayer Ha-Levi Abulafia, in *Or Zaddikim* (Light of the Righteous) by Judah ben Manoah Said, (13th century), cited in Asaf, *op. cit.,* II, p. 52.

[45] Abraham Benevista, *Takkanah,* (15th century), cited in Asaf, *op. cit.,* II, p. 81.

[46] Joseph ben Judah ibn Aknin, *Tabb al-Nufus* (Healing of the Souls), (13th century), cited in Asaf, *op. cit.,* II, p. 37.

[47a Cf. above Hillel Bavli, "The Modern Renaissance of Hebrew Literature," pp. 567 ff.]

[48a Cf. above Roth, "The Jews of Western Europe (from 1648)," pp. 261-262.]

[49] The markedly positive attitude toward education among Jewish youth in the United States was revealed in a research study by the writer based on an attitude test given to several hundred Jewish college students. One part consisted of a series of words to which the students were to indicate positive or negative attitudes. The word "education" showed the highest incidence of

positive attitudes, with only one per cent of negative attitudes. See "The Personality of Jewish College Students" by Julius B. Maller, *Jewish Education,* III, No. 2. The author is preparing a larger work on patterns of adjustment in contemporary Jewish life with special reference to the State of Israel.

Bibliography

Abrahams, Israel (ed.), *Hebrew Ethical Wills.* Philadelphia, 1926.
  V. The Gate of Instruction attributed to Maimonides.
  VII. Guide to Knowledge by Joseph ibn Caspi.
  III. A Father's Admonition by Judah ibn Tibbon.
———, *Jewish Life in the Middle Ages.* London, 1896. Pp. 340-356.
Baron, Salo W., *The Jewish Community.* Philadelphia, 1942. Vol. II, Ch. XIII.
Bertholet, Alfred, *A History of Hebrew Civilization,* translated by A. K. Dallas. London, 1926.
Cohen, Abraham, *Everyman's Talmud.* London, 1937.
Drazin, Nathan, *History of Jewish Education from 515 B.C.E. to 220 C.E.* (with a Bibliography). Baltimore, 1940.
Funk, S., *Die Entstehung des Talmuds.* Leipzig, 1910.
Gamoran, Emmanuel, *Changing Conceptions in Jewish Education.* New York, 1924.
Gollancz, Sir Hermann, *Pedagogics of the Talmud.* Oxford, 1924.
Guedemann, M., *Das juedische Unterrichtswesen waehrend der spanisch-arabischen Periode.* 3 vols. Vienna, 1888.
———, *Quellenschriften zur Geschichte des Unterrichtswesens und der Erziehung bei den deutschen Juden.* Berlin, 1891.
Guignebert, Charles, *The Jewish World in the Time of Jesus,* translated by S. H. Hooke. London, 1938. "The Law," "The Scribes," "The Synagogue."
Leipziger, Henry M., *Education of the Jews.* New York, 1890.
Marcus, Samuel, *Die Paedagogik des israelitischen Volkes.* 2 vols. Vienna, 1877.
Morris, N., *The Jewish School.* London, 1937.
Neuman, Abraham A., *The Jews in Spain.* Philadelphia, 1942. Vol. II, Chs. XV-XVI.
Schuerer, Emil, *A History of the Jewish People.* Edinburgh, 1893. Vol. II, "The Scribes," "School and Synagogue."
Strack, Hermann L., *Introduction to the Talmud and Midrash.* Philadelphia, 1931.
Tscharno, Y., *Studies in Education in Israel (Letoldot Ha-Hinuk beyisrael).* Jerusalem, 1939. Parts I-II, the Biblical and Talmudic Periods.

CHAPTER 22

JEWISH EDUCATIONAL INSTITUTIONS

By Simon Greenberg

I. INTRODUCTION

Educational activity performs two functions. It broadens the range of man's knowledge and skills, and transmits this knowledge and these skills from one generation to another, or from one man to his fellow.

Educational activity is inherent in human societies on all levels of development. One society is distinguished from another, however, not merely by the quality of its intellectual inquisitiveness and the character of its accumulated knowledge and skills. Intellectual and spiritual progress are equally reflected by the institutions a society creates or adapts in order consciously to increase its knowledge and skills, consciously to transmit them to the groups as a whole.

Until comparatively recent times the educational institutions of all peoples of the world were each concerned almost exclusively with the transmission of the skills, the knowledge and the traditions of its own particular group. Educational institutions were not expected to be centers for the discovery of new knowledge or channels for the transmission of truth and beauty and wisdom, regardless of their source of origin.

In the following pages we shall attempt to sketch only in briefest outline the history of the main types of educational institutions created by the Jewish people from the earliest times to the present. Another chapter in the work is devoted to the educational philosophy underlying the work of these institutions, and to the pedagogic principles adopted to achieve their goal. While a certain amount of duplication is inevitable, because it is virtually impossible to discuss any aspect of an educational institution without some reference to its philosophy and curriculum, this chapter will seek to limit itself primarily to the external history of the institutions, to the occasions that brought them into being, and to the conditions that enabled them to function.[1a]

The recorded history of the Jewish people extends over a period exceeding three thousand years and is divided into rather well-defined eras. Moreover, Jewish life took on differing forms in the various countries in which it existed. We might, therefore, treat our theme either chronologically or geographically. However, since many of the educational institutions existed during more than one era and in more than one land, we chose to present chronologically the story of the individual institution as it developed and changed from one era to another and from country to country.

II. THE HOME

The home is mankind's universal educational agency. It was but natural that within the family fathers should transmit a knowledge of their occupations to the sons and mothers teach their daughters the skills required for homebuilding. Thus, while there are no specific references in the Bible to this particular matter, we have every reason to assume that Jewish sons learned from their fathers how to plow, plant, care for vineyards, tend sheep, the art of the potter and the warrior and the other arts in ancient Israel.

But the home was not used by all groups with equal awareness and effectiveness for transmitting the spiritual and ethical teachings and the treasured historic memories of the group. The biblical record clearly indicates that among the Jews the home was at a very early period *consciously* employed for such educational purposes. Responsibility for transmitting the group's spiritual heritage to one's children is specifically enjoined upon parents, particularly the father. Abraham is known "of the Lord" in order that "he may command his children and his household after him, that they may keep the way of the Lord, to do righteousness and justice" (Gen. 18:19). A well-defined body of instruction is to be transmitted. "And these words which I command thee shall be upon thine heart and thou shalt teach them diligently unto thy children." The family is commanded to practice prescribed ceremonies for the express purpose of perpetuating the knowledge of great historic events and for stimulating the inquisitive mind of the child. His questions provide a natural setting for the father to explain and emphasize some precious traditions of the group. "And it shall come to pass, when your children shall say unto you: What mean ye by this service? that ye shall say: It is the sacrifice of the Lord's passover, for that He passed over the houses of the children of Israel in Egypt, when He smote the Egyptians and delivered our houses" (Ex. 12:26-27). In the same spirit every Jewish family was commanded to dwell in booths for seven days "that your generations may know that I made the children of Israel to dwell in booths, when I brought them out of the land of Egypt" (Lev. 23:43). The festivals and ceremonies were not and are not merely means of worshiping the Lord. They were and are the re-enactments of great historic moments in the people's past, not only to stimulate appropriate religious sentiments but also to preserve and transmit precious group memories. While the parents are commanded consciously to teach their children, the children are urged to take to heart the instructions of their parents. They are not only to "honor thy father and thy mother" (Ex. 20:12) but also to obey the instruction of the father and not to reject or neglect the teaching of the mother (Pr. 1:8).

The records do not indicate the extent to which parents gave formal instruction at regular intervals to their children. But it seems fair to imply that in the case of intellectually and spiritually alert parents that type of instruction was not entirely lacking. Hannah's relation to her son Samuel, the careful training given to Samson by his parents, a mother's recorded instruction to her son (Pr. 31:1-9), the care with which Job is reported to have supervised the religious life of his children (Job 1:5)—these and other indications justify the assumption that there were parents in early Israel who performed their duties as teachers with a high degree of seriousness.

During the days of the Second Temple, when Judaism, under the leadership of the scribes and Sages, acquired the traditional forms associated with Rabbinic or normative Judaism, the home became a far more effective educational agency. From the moment the child learned how to speak the father recited the morning and evening prayers with him; and as the child developed the father trained him in the performance of the mitzvot. Even though elementary schools were plentiful, the Rabbis stressed the father's duty that he himself teach his son, for a "child's true father is he who teaches him Torah." In addition, it was incumbent upon the father to teach his son a trade or profession, even how to swim, for lack of a trade may lead him to a life of violence and inability to swim may endanger his life.

In observing how the mother conducted the household, children learned the detailed dietary laws and the manner of daily Jewish living. They saw her welcoming the Sabbath every week not only by numerous and arduous labors in the kitchen; they also saw her dressing her home, herself and her children with particular attention, and kindling the Sabbath lights. The father's *kiddush*, recited over a cup of wine or two loaves of bread to usher in the Sabbath or the festival meal, the washing of the hands before meals, the grace after meals, the celebrations of holidays, major and minor festivals, particularly the unique and remarkable Passover eve Seder service, the fast days of the Jewish year—these and a host of other religious observances inculcated piety and faith in the growing child's heart, and acquainted him with the noblest spiritual and historical experiences of his people.

If the Jewish girl until very recent days was most often not sent to receive formal instruction in a school, it was not merely because of a widespread attitude that a girl needed no formal education. It was due rather to the feeling that her mother and home training could provide her with all the instruction she needed to live a good and pious Jewish life. Until very recent times, the expectation was, by and large, fully realized. And because the Jewish home was so effective an educational institution, the Jewish school could devote itself exclusively to the formal teaching of the sacred texts, leaving instruction in personal religious matters to the home.

For two thousand years and more, the Jewish home continued to be the most effective institution for educating the Jewish child. The social and economic forces that, after the French Revolution, tended to minimize family and home influence among Western peoples, had even more disastrous effects upon Jewish life. In addition, the vast migrations of millions of East European Jews to the West severed Jewish family life from its moorings in a well-organized community with an established public opinion. Today in America and throughout the Western world, therefore, the home as a Jewish educational institution, though still important, does not approach in effectiveness the Jewish home of Eastern Europe before World War I, or of any part of Europe before the French Revolution.

The breakdown of the Jewish home as an effective, primary Jewish educational agency in the Western world has placed enormous responsibilities upon the other educational agencies of the Jewish community. All educators are agreed, however, that the best school cannot possibly substitute for the home. At present, particularly in America, the reconstitution of the Jewish home as an effective educational agency for rich religious life represents one of the greatest challenges to Jewish educators and religious leaders.

III. THE SYNAGOGUE

Next to the home the synagogue was and is the most democratic and universal Jewish educational institution affecting the lives of old and young, men and women.[2a] Our records give us no clear picture of the place, the age or the circumstances under which it came into being. But it is safe to say that the element of instruction played at least as great a part in the founding of the synagogue as did prayer. Many unique and specifically educational features were combined in the synagogue almost from its very inception; these have remained an integral part of it to our own day.

The first and probably the oldest of these is the reading from the Scriptures. The Bible relates that Moses, after having written the Torah, commanded the priests, the Levites and all the elders that "when all Israel is come to appear before the Lord thy God in the place which He shall choose, thou shalt read this law before all Israel in their hearing. Assemble the people, the men and the women and the little ones, and thy stranger that is within thy gates, that they may hear, and that they may learn, and fear the Lord your God" (Deut. 31:11-12). While this reading was to take place on Sukkot, it was apparently to be held in every community throughout the land and not only in Jerusalem, for the women, children and strangers were not commanded to make the pilgrimage to Jerusalem, but they were commanded to hear the reading. Such a reading of Scripture before a vast throng is recorded as having taken place on various occasions before the establishment of the Second Temple.

The revolution introduced by Ezra into the religious life of the post-exilic Jewish community made the Torah at once the core and the foundation of the community's spiritual life. Scripture readings gradually became a fixed feature of the gatherings on the Sabbath and on Monday and Thursday, the two market days when the peasants came into town. Reading Scripture in itself, however, could not serve the educational purpose adequately. Hence, there was added either a translation into the vernacular or a religious message based upon the passage that was read. In time, the Five Books of Moses were divided into sections, so that the whole Pentateuch might be read from beginning to end on the Sabbaths once in three years or once every year. To the readings from the Pentateuch, passages from the Prophets were later added. Today in every traditional synagogue the Pentateuch is completed once a year through weekly Sabbath readings. The portion read is no longer orally translated into the vernacular, for in most synagogues the congregation is provided with a printed text and translation. This scriptural reading is still the central feature of the traditional Sabbath synagogue service. Many have objected to it because of the time it requires and its noninspirational quality as read in many synagogues today. Nevertheless, it continues to hold its place in the vast majority of the synagogues of the world; and it continues to exercise, though far less effectively than it might, the educational function of instructing the congregation in the contents of the Pentateuch.

In addition to the Scripture reading the synagogue became the center where spiritual leaders of the people regularly delivered their message of inspiration or information. In biblical days the prophet addressed the people in the courtyard of the Temple. On various occasions the prophet would be visited at home by his followers in order to be blessed or instructed by him. In Babylonia Ezekiel's home was apparently the rendezvous for the pious who wanted to hear a Divine message. Ezekiel's complaint that many of his listeners came to be entertained rather than instructed, sounds very modern indeed.

When a knowledge of the Torah became the *sine qua non* for spiritual leadership among the Jews, it was but natural that the message of the leader should become associated with the Torah and more particularly with the portions read on any given occasion. Until modern times that message would most often be delivered in the synagogue on the Sabbath afternoon immediately preceding the afternoon service. In more recent times a message or sermon in the vernacular based on the weekly penta-teuchal portion has become a permanent feature of the Sabbath morning service in well-nigh all synagogues, particularly in America. This message is inspirational and informative and serves as a significant educational medium.

But the sermon and the Scripture readings are not the only direct educational features of the synagogue service. The traditional prayer book itself contains many educational features ordinarily not associated with a liturgy. In the first place, Judaism considers study as being superior even to prayer as a means of worshiping God. Hence passages of an ethical and historical nature from the Talmud are incorporated into the prayer book. The prayers are modified for various occasions of the year, so that the festival celebrated, or the historic occasion remembered, is given its meaning and interpretation. The synagogue liturgy does not stress merely the *individual's* relation to God, the *individual's* needs and hopes, and the *individual's* longing for Divine salvation. Equal emphasis is placed upon the *group's* relation to God, upon the *group's* needs and hopes, upon the *group's* yearning for collective salvation.

Moreover, the synagogue by its organization and form of worship has been a mighty force making for democracy within the Jewish community. Any ten male adults may conduct a regular service. Any-one among them may be their reader or preacher. There is a complete absence of anything like a clerical hierarchy. Knowledge and piety alone are the paths to leadership. Where a congregation diverges from these principles, it does so not because of the requirements of ritual or liturgy. On the contrary, it does so in violation of those requirements and merely as a concession to the human limitations of those who compose that particular congregation.

The synagogue's role as a Jewish educational agency is by no means exhausted by the above-mentioned activities. The synagogue building has always been a center of study for either children or adults. But that aspect of the synagogue's contribution to Jewish education we shall discuss later under the general subject of schools.

Thus, through its liturgy, scriptural reading, sermon and organiza-tion, the synagogue was, next to the home, the most significant educa-tional agency in the life of the Jewish people. Together with all other religious institutions throughout the world, the synagogue's influence as a house of prayer has perceptibly waned in modern times. Other

aspects of it have, however, taken on new vitality in our day. Moreover, among the Jews no other institution has as yet been created to
take its place, nor to approach it even in its present weakened condition,
as an influence for the moral, ethical and religious education of the
people.

IV. THE ELEMENTARY AND SECONDARY SCHOOL

A. IN BIBLE TIMES

The Bible contains no direct reference to the existence of schools
for either children or adults. But there can be little doubt that educational activity in biblical times was not limited exclusively to the home.
There undoubtedly were men who taught children other than their
own either as pupils or as apprentices. Bezalel and Oholeav, the artists
who built the Tabernacle and all its vessels, were endowed by the Lord
not only with the skill of their own hands, but also with the ability
"to teach" others. The children of the royal family most likely had
their own private teachers. The elders of Samaria seem to have trained
Ahab's seventy sons. Moreover, members of the court apparently studied
the dominant language of the age, as well as the Hebrew language. The
ability to write—no mean achievement in ancient times—was apparently
quite prevalent among Israelite children.

Priests and Levites are spoken of most frequently as the teachers of the
people. King Jehoash was instructed by the priest Johoiada. Jehoshaphat,
King of Judah, sent officers, together with priests and Levites, to teach
throughout the Land of Judah. The Bible refers to "teacher," "instructors"
and "wise men," who acted as teachers. These presumably had some fixed
place and time for teaching. That the priests and Levites received some
kind of systematic and formal instruction must be taken for granted. The
priest had to be thoroughly acquainted not only with an elaborate and
complicated sacrificial system but with the equally intricate laws of
Levitical purity and physical health. The Levites had to be proficient as
assistants to the priests and as members of the Temple choir. They could
not possibly enter upon their duties without thorough previous instruction.
The advanced age at which they started to perform their duties in the
Temple, the priest at thirty and the Levite at twenty-five, probably reflects
the extended period of training they had to undergo.

The early prophets appear also to have had schools or at least groups
within which they trained the novitiates and developed their own spiritual
powers.

However, the elementary school for the education of all Jewish children
did not come into its own until well toward the end of the Second
Commonwealth.

B. From the Second Commonwealth to Modern Times

The following short talmudic passage gives us the most significant information available regarding the establishment of Jewish elementary schools:

However, that man is to be remembered for good, and his name is Joshua ben Gemala [c. 64 c.e.]; for were it not for him Torah would have been forgotten in Israel. For at first he who had a father was taught Torah by him, and he who had no father did not study Torah. It was then decreed that teachers of children should be appointed in Jerusalem. However, he who had a father, the father would bring him to Jerusalem and have him taught, while he who had no father, would not come to Jerusalem to study. It was then decreed that teachers of the young should be appointed in every district throughout the land. But the boys would be entered in the school at the age of sixteen and seventeen and if the teacher would rebuke one of them, he would resent it and leave. Thus it was until Joshua ben Gemala decreed that teachers of children should be appointed in every district and every city and that boys of the age of six and seven should be entered.[3]

It is obvious from the above passage that the elementary school had a very long development behind it by the time Joshua ben Gemala instituted his reform. Simeon ben Shatah (first century b.c.e.)[3a] is credited with the decree requiring children to go to a *Bet Sefer*, a school, while another passage has it that Ezra was the one who sought to "set a scribe next to a scribe," that is, to multiply the number of schools in the community. The chief educational contribution of Jewish religious leaders of the Second Commonwealth was the principle that a basic elementary Jewish education must be provided by the community for every Jewish boy regardless of his social or economic status. The goal thus set was probably never fully attained, no more than any modern society with laws for universal compulsory elementary education has attained its goal. But it can be said without fear of serious contradiction that except for periods of communal disintegration or impoverishment following mass persecutions and plagues, or accompanying the pioneer efforts of recently established Jewish settlements, universal elementary education for boys was more fully attained among Jews up to the end of the eighteenth century than among any other contemporary group. The rabbis forbade a Jew to live in a community which had no elementary school teacher. Every community having at least ten Jewish families could be compelled by law to maintain a teacher in its midst although not all of the ten families may have had pupils for him. It was, moreover, a widespread practice during these centuries for a family living in isolation to invite a teacher to become a part of the household in order to teach the children. An authority of the fourth century suggests that only if a Jewish child were captured as an infant and raised among non-Jews could he grow up without an elementary

Jewish education. This is most likely an exaggeration, as are the traditions about the hundreds of elementary schools in Jerusalem before its destruction in 70 C.E.,[4a] and the thousands of elementary schools in Bethar before the failure of the revolt of Bar Kokbah (*c.* 135 C.E.).[5a] But none can gainsay the fact that the elementary Jewish school in which Jewish children learned how to read Hebrew and translate the Pentateuch has been the most widespread institution of the Jewish community for the past two thousand years.

1. THE BET HA-SEFER AND THE BET HA-KENESET

From the very beginning there was a very close relationship between the school and the synagogue. The synagogue premises were the meeting place of the school, and synagogue functionaries very often acted as teachers. The elementary school was referred to in talmudic times as a *Bet Ha-Sefer* (Aramaic—*Bet Sifra* or *Bet Mikra*), House of the Book, or *Bet Ha-Keneset* (Aramaic—*Be Kenishta*), the House of Gathering. The second name is most likely derived from the place where the school met. The first name may indicate the subject matter taught, namely, the Bible, or perhaps the fact that instead of meeting in the synagogue the school met in a special community building or in a private home, and was the private enterprise of the teacher.

2. THE BET TALMUD

Secondary education, which consisted in study of Rabbinic texts—particularly the Mishna—and in an introduction to the method by which the Oral Law was discussed and developed, was provided by the *Bet Talmud*, and Talmud school. The relationship between it and the *Bet Sefer* is indicated by the Rabbinic dictum that a boy should start to study Bible at five, Mishna at ten and Talmud at fifteen, and by the remark that out of every thousand pupils who started to study Bible only one hundred continued with the study of the Mishna.

3. THE HEDER AND THE TALMUD TORAH

The twofold aspect, private and communal, of the Jewish elementary school has characterized it throughout the centuries. The duty to educate the Jewish child never became the exclusive responsibility either of the community or of the father. Circumstances determined which of the two assumed the responsibility in any particular instance. The average Jewish parent made great sacrifices to pay for his child's education. Together with other parents he could make his own arrangements with a private teacher. But when a child had no parents or when the parents were too poor to pay, the community would step in and either pay all or part of the child's tuition to a private teacher or else, where the number of indigent children warranted it, a community school supported by voluntary contributions and self-taxation would be established.

Among the Jews of Eastern Europe the private elementary school for children was called a "heder" (a room). It took its name from the fact that it usually met in one of the rooms of the teacher's home. There a group of fifteen to twenty-five children of varying ages, usually below thirteen, would meet during the whole day. Within each heder there was a minimum of gradation. But there was gradation among the various hedarim serving a community. The most elementary heder catered to children who were beginning to read and write Hebrew and to translate sentences from the Pentateuch. Above that was the heder supervised by a rabbi who taught only those prepared to master the translation of the Pentateuch and selected passages from Rashi's Commentary. The highest Heder introduced the student to the Talmud and prepared him to go on to the *Yeshiva*.

The curriculum, the school year, the financial arrangements varied but little from community to community. They were governed by the prevailing cultural standards, by well-established traditions or by special communal enactments.

The communally supported school was called the Talmud Torah, a house for the study of the Torah. It offered the same opportunities to the children of the poor as the heder did to the others. In rare instances, as in the case of the Amsterdam Talmud Torah of the seventeenth century, it was by far superior to the private heder, having a comparatively rich, graded curriculum, a staff of well-equipped teachers, and catering to all children of the community, not merely to the poor. The Talmud Torah often occupied a structure of its own, though just as often it would meet on the synagogue premises.

Both of these educational institutions continued to flourish in Eastern European Jewish communities as late as the twentieth century. They disappeared in Russia only with the Russian Revolution and continued among the Jews of Poland until the 1939 debacle, which overwhelmed Polish Jewry.

4. MODERN JEWISH SCHOOLS AND THE RISE OF SECULAR EDUCATION AMONG JEWS

The heder and the Talmud Torah held undisputed sway in Jewish communities throughout the world until the end of the eighteenth century. These schools, though they taught some elementary arithmetic and the reading and writing of Judeo-German, were otherwise devoted exclusively to religious subject matter. Whatever secular education was attained by

Jewish individuals here and there was the result of private instruction or personal initiative and persistence. Moreover, all government schools were either closed to Jews or were boycotted by them. In the second half of the eighteenth century a perceptible change occurred. The activities of Moses Mendelssohn (1729-1786)[6a] and his colleagues resulted in the organization (1778) in Berlin of the first Jewish free school which included German and French, as well as Hebrew, in its curriculum. The Edict of Toleration issued by Emperor Joseph II of Austria in 1781 was enthusiastically greeted by German Jewish intellectuals, and elaborate programs for the reform of Jewish education were proposed by them. Modern Jewish schools, sponsored by the government and supported by special taxes levied upon the Jewish community, were established particularly among the Jews of Galicia. While Jewish intellectuals welcomed the schools, the Jewish masses rightly suspected that the schools intended not merely to impart information but also to wean Jewish children away from Judaism and the Jewish people. Though a Jew was appointed inspector, and though some hundred such schools were opened after 1790, resistance of the Jewish masses and other factors led to their close in 1806.

Somewhat the same situation was repeated in Russia, where in 1844 a special decree permitted Jews to open their own modern schools to be supported by special taxes upon the Jewish community. The Russification and proselytizing aspect of these schools was so pronounced, however, that after ten years of functioning only a little more than three thousand Jewish pupils were attracted by them. A change in the Russian government's attitude in 1857 eliminated the element of religious proselytization from these schools, and Jews flocked to them in large numbers. But such was the zeal for Russification, which inspired even the Jewish supervisors of the schools, that before long the distinctly Jewish subjects were practically excluded from the curriculum. By that time Jewish students and parents could discern little or no difference between these Jewish government schools and the general government schools. As a result, Jewish youth turned to the general school, which had been open to them since 1804 but had been almost unanimously boycotted by Jews heretofore. By 1873 it became apparent that, from the government's point of view, the special Jewish elementary and secondary schools were no longer necessary, and they, plus the two government-sponsored rabbinical seminaries, were closed. Jewish youth was coming in increasing numbers to the general Russian government schools; within twenty years, from 1853 to 1873, the percentage of Jews in the total student body rose from 1.25 to 13.2. By 1880 Russian educators started to advocate and apply a *numerus clausus*.

a. The "Heder Metukan" and Modern Jewish School Systems in Eastern Europe

Until the last quarter of the nineteenth century all efforts to bring secular education to the Jews, whether sponsored by Jews themselves or by Gentiles, were inspired primarily by the desire to assimilate the Jew into the general population. By about 1885 a change of attitude became discernible in the ranks of Jewish intellectuals. The high hopes entertained by Jews that complete civil and social emancipation would automatically follow the secularization and modernization of Jewish life, were rudely shattered by one unhappy event after another. At the same time, a renewed spirit of self-respect was awakened within the ranks of those Westernized or modernized Jews who were deeply and irrevocably attached to Judaism and to the Hebrew language and literature. Zionism and modern Hebrew literature made remarkable headway among all classes of the Jewish community. The Yiddish language and literature simultaneously experienced an unprecedented development. All this inner cultural revival was bound before long to be reflected in the community's educational activities. A new modern Jewish school appeared, the Heder Metukan, the modern progressive heder. The language of instruction was Hebrew. There was less emphasis on religious piety and on Rabbinic literature, but there was a positive attitude toward the Jewish religion and toward all the spiritual and cultural treasures of the Jewish people. The hope for a re-established Jewish state in Palestine was at the heart of this educational activity.

Though these new schools increased in number and flourished, they never replaced the heder and the Talmud Torah, which remained predominant within Eastern European Jewry until 1914.

5. ELEMENTARY AND SECONDARY JEWISH EDUCATION IN SOVIET RUSSIA

The Soviet government soon after it was firmly established effectively outlawed the heder, the Talmud Torah and every other Jewish educational institution devoted to the preservation of the Jewish religious heritage or of the Hebrew language and culture. In their place, regular government supported schools using the Yiddish language as a medium of instruction were established in neighborhoods with preponderantly Jewish populations. The curriculum in these schools followed the curriculum of all other government schools of similar grade, except that Yiddish literature and some elements of Jewish history were taught. Since Jewish children had the choice of attending either these schools or other government schools, the percentage of the Jewish children in the Ukraine and White Russia attending Jewish schools rose to the high point of sixty-four per cent in 1932 but declined steadily since then.

Moreover, Jewish citizens of the Soviet Union today may not and do not maintain supplementary schools in which their young children can legally and systematically achieve some knowledge of the tenets of Judaism, or of the grammar and literature of the Hebrew language. No official information is at present available regarding the number of Jewish children attending Yiddish-language schools, and consequently receiving some instruction in Jewish history and Yiddish literature. We do know, however, that, with the exception of a Yiddish daily which is reputedly appearing in Biro-Bidjan, no other Yiddish periodical is now being published in all of the Soviet Union. We know, too, that so basic and elementary a religious need as a Jewish calendar indicating the religious holy days and festivals, is not available to Jews in Soviet Russia at the present time.

6. ELEMENTARY AND SECONDARY JEWISH EDUCATION IN POLAND BETWEEN THE TWO WORLD WARS

Despite the depressed economic position of Polish Jewry between the two World Wars and the patent anti-Semitic policies of the government, elementary and secondary Jewish education achieved much during those hard years. The minority rights granted to Polish Jewry by the Treaty of Versailles included the power of self-taxation for educational purposes. Funds thus made available were in themselves not sufficient to maintain the schools. Tuition fees, voluntary contributions and help from abroad supplemented government funds. Unfortunately, Polish Jewry could not unite on any one educational program. Three main national groups competed for the child. These schools paralleled the regular Polish government school in hours of sessions and in general subject matter. However, they added distinctly Jewish subjects to their curricula. The largest unit consisted of the Jabne-Mizrachi religiously and Zionistically oriented schools, claiming some fifty-six thousand pupils in 1936. Next to them came the Tarbut schools, with Hebrew as their language of instruction and Zionism as their chief ideological orientation. In 1938 forty thousand pupils attended three hundred Tarbut schools. The smallest of the three groups consisted of the Yiddish-language schools with their antireligious and antinational, or anti-Zionist, approach. In 1934-1935, some sixteen thousand pupils were registered in their classes. Obviously, a very large percentage of the Jewish children of Poland's prewar 3,300,000 was not found in any of these school systems. Many of them preferred to attend the regular Polish government schools and get their Jewish education either in a heder or from a private teacher. Horeb, a non-Zionist fundamentalist religious group, claimed in 1934-1935 to have sixty-one thousand boys in the hedarim and Talmud Torahs affiliated with it, and twenty thousand Jewish girls in its Bet Jacob schools. In addition, there undoubtedly were many private hedarim and local Talmud Torahs independent of all nationally organized groups. The heder and Talmud Torah thus continued to play an important role in Polish Jewry up to 1939.

7. ELEMENTARY AND SECONDARY JEWISH EDUCATION IN THE UNITED STATES

a. The Heder in the United States

The heder and the Talmud Torah were brought to this country by Jewish immigrants from Eastern Europe. The heder, however, deteriorated rapidly in America. Without a well-formulated and clearly articulated public opinion to supervise it, the heder became the happy hunting ground of numerous ill-prepared, maladjusted individuals who brought it into disrepute despite many self-sacrificing and noble private teachers who established hedarim a generation ago in American Jewish communities. While some thirty years ago a majority of Jewish boys in America were still receiving their religious education in such private "rooms," the number attending them today is well-nigh negligible.

b. The Talmud Torah in the United States

The Talmud Torah followed a unique course of development in this country. Since, in the beginning, American Jewry almost unanimously gave wholehearted and enthusiastic support to the American public school system, Jewish education was conceived as being supplementary to it both in curriculum and in hours of instruction. Schools maintained by the Jewish community were to limit themselves exclusively to distinctly Jewish content and were to meet during hours other than those when the public school was in session. The Talmud Torah, therefore, started its sessions at four o'clock in the afternoon on weekdays and nine o'clock on Sunday mornings. The pupil was expected to attend five two-hour sessions. Moreover, influenced by the example of the American public school, builders of the American Jewish community of the first two decades of this century sought to make the Talmud Torah the communally supported Jewish elementary school for all Jewish children, boys as well as girls, rich as well as poor. Organizationally and physically it was to be completely dissociated from the synagogue. Many imposing Talmud Torah structures were built by Jewish communities throughout the land in the first quarter of the twentieth century. Graded courses of instruction were developed by well-trained modern pedagogues. Central bureaus of education attempted to guide and co-ordinate the activities of the schools and tens of thousands of Jewish children flocked to their classes.

But Jewish life in the United States was destined soon to take a course which halted the growth of the Talmud Torah along the lines originally anticipated. As the wealthier and more Americanized Jewish families moved out of the congested areas to new neighborhoods, they organized their Jewish communal life around the synagogue. The school in which their children were to receive a Jewish education was an integral part of the synagogue and the congregation. In addition, the conflict among the religious and social ideologies struggling for supremacy within the Jewish community resulted in the establishment of a variety of weekday afternoon school systems. Finally, the number of parents willing to subject their children to ten hours of weekly afternoon or evening instruction steadily diminished. The Talmud Torah, therefore, was not able to fulfill the role originally conceived for it by American Jewish educators. It is still an extremely important educational factor, but it no longer dominates the scene as it did a generation ago. The bureaus of Jewish education of the larger Jewish communities of the land no longer give their exclusive attention to it. The leaders of these bureaus strive incessantly to make the bureaus serve all Jewish schools regardless of their religious or social ideologies.

c. The Congregational Schools

1. The Sunday School

Jewish elementary education in the United States has in the past two decades shown a definite tendency to come under congregational auspices. It was thus at the beginning of American Jewish history.[7a] The first communal Jewish school was organized in America by Congregation Shearith Israel in New York (1731). Since no other schools were then available to Jewish children, the Shearith Israel school taught secular as well as Jewish religious subjects. The following century witnessed attempts by other congregations, individually or in co-operation with one another, to establish similar day schools. All these attempts came to an abrupt end with the rise of the American public school. At first these congregations made efforts to maintain weekday afternoon schools for Jewish instruction. But, following the dominant tendency of American Protestantism at the time, most of the congregations soon limited the religious instruction of their children to Sunday morning. Since not all Jewish families were affiliated with synagogues, communally sponsored Jewish Sunday schools were also organized for the children of the poor and the unaffiliated. The Philadelphia Sunday School Society organized by Rebecca Gratz in 1838 was the most effective and proved to be the most long-lived of such communally maintained Jewish Sunday schools. It celebrated the centenary of its existence in 1938 and is still functioning vigorously. The overwhelming number of Sunday schools today are, however, integral parts of well-established synagogues. Every synagogue organized by American-born or Americanized Jews considers an elementary school to be an indispensable part of its function. Most Reform congregations consider their responsibilities for the Jewish education of their children fulfilled by maintaining a Sunday school only. But even the Orthodox and Conservative congregations, which usually strive for a more intensive elementary Jewish education, maintain Sunday departments meeting from one and a half to two and a half hours each Sunday morning. These departments are intended for children who cannot or will not take more intensive instruction, or for boys and girls still too young to carry the more exacting curriculum.

2. The Congregational Weekday School

Many Reform Jewish congregations, all Conservative, and the comparatively small number of Orthodox congregations that sponsor elementary schools have found Sunday morning instruction completely inadequate for the transmission of the Jewish religious and cultural heritage. Many of the members of the present Conservative congregations were formerly the main supporters of the communal Talmud Torah. Hence, these congregations have organized weekday afternoon schools, and require their children to attend from four and a half to six and a half hours per week divided into three to five sessions including Sunday morning. The curriculum of these schools is very similar to that of the communal Talmud Torah, the chief emphasis being upon the study of Hebrew, primarily for the sake of understanding the prayers and the Pentateuch. Jewish history and the Jewish religious calendar are the other principal subjects of instruction.

Each of these congregational schools is in theory and can in fact be a law unto itself. However, national organizations with which the individual congregation is affiliated maintain commissions on education which publish textbooks and suggest curricula. The same is done by various local congregational organizations and city bureaus of Jewish education. It is but natural for the individual congregation to seek help and guidance from these central bodies. Some measure of uniformity in educational goals and procedures has thus been attained.

While many of the congregational schools are open only to children of members of the congregation, there is a tendency to depart from this unhappy procedure and to admit any child on the payment of a fixed tuition fee ranging from ten dollars per year up. Most congregations also admit at reduced rates or free of charge those children whose parents cannot afford to pay the regular rates.

3. Other Jewish Weekday Afternoon Schools

Religious, national and social ideologies have given rise to other types of Jewish weekday afternoon schools, which appeal to a comparatively small group within the Jewish community. Though these schools differ among themselves in ideological minutiae relating to attitudes on general social problems and Zionist aspirations, by and large they agree on two basic matters. The first has to do with the Yiddish language. All schools previously discussed adopt a neutral or negative attitude toward the preservation of the Yiddish language in America. These schools, on the other hand, have a positive attitude toward the Yiddish language and make it the chief subject of instruction. Some have a positive attitude toward the Hebrew language also. But most of them have a neutral and some a definitely negative attitude toward it. Secondly, the curricula of all these schools display a neutral or definitely negative attitude toward all religious instruction. Recently a marked change has become evident in the attitude toward the Jewish religion, and particularly toward Jewish customs, holidays and festivals. Ways are being sought to reintroduce these into the school curriculum as "folk ways" and Jewish cultural values rather than as religious observances. But some seek to go further than that and are rethinking their attitude toward religion itself.

4. The Jewish Day School in the United States

We noted above that the rise of the American public school found practically the whole of American Israel committed to it. In more recent years various factors have modified that unanimity. In the first place, the expectation that Sundays and weekday afternoons would offer ample opportunity for adequate instruction in Jewish religious and cultural subjects has by and large not been realized. These schools have not produced men and women thoroughly at home in the Hebrew language and familiar with even a considerable portion of the Hebrew Scriptures, of Rabbinic literature and of modern Hebrew literature. Though there are those who maintain that this failure is to be attributed to factors other than the hours of instruction, others consider the time element the root of the evil. Hence, they seek to create schools in which a greater number of hours during the morning and early afternoon can be devoted to Jewish studies. The proponents of the Jewish day school also find that the separation of church and state is not as complete in the public schools as it should be. Not only are Christian religious festivals such as Christmas and Easter celebrated with great impressiveness in most public schools, but attendance on Jewish religious holidays is very often definitely encouraged.

Moreover, among a group of progressively minded Jewish parents there is the desire to effect a more complete integration between the general and the Jewish education of their children than that which attendance at two separate schools makes possible. Thus there have come into being all-day Jewish elementary and secondary schools providing a rich curriculum of Jewish subjects in addition to the regular school curriculum. The distribution of the hours of study devoted to the various subjects differs from school to school.

The schools organized by the progressively minded parents, usually called academies, are maintained completely out of the tuition fees or special additional contributions made by the parents, though in all instances the meeting place of the school is provided free or for a minimum rental by a congregation. These schools also give the fewest number of hours weekly to Jewish subjects, though even this minimum is more than the maximum offered by the weekday congregational school. They have the further obvious advantage of preferred hours and highly trained teachers.

Most of the other all-day schools, usually referred to as *Yeshivot Ketanot,* junior *Yeshivot,* started with devoting the whole of the morning and most of the afternoon to Jewish religious studies. General studies were taught only after public school hours, so that the services of public school teachers might be obtained at a minimum expense. The law and the parents compelled most of the schools to shorten their teaching day and to distribute their time more judiciously among the various subjects. The average all-day school now meets practically during the same hours as the public school and divides its time about evenly between Hebrew and secular subjects. Financially, the schools are maintained only in part by tuition fees. The balance of the budget is met by special campaigns conducted by the individual schools and by one national campaign whose proceeds are shared by the co-operating schools in proportion to their efforts. Many of these schools have well-equipped dormitories to accommodate numerous out-of-town students. In 1945 there were approximately nine thousand Jewish children attending sixty-five all-day schools, concentrated mostly in New York City but found also in twenty-five other Jewish communities. But their number has been steadily increasing as the smaller Jewish communities throughout the country are being stirred to organize such day schools.

8. Jewish Elementary and Secondary Education in Palestine

a. Introduction

The Jewish population of Palestine assumed significant proportions numerically and spiritually soon after the expulsion of the Jews from Spain. It declined, however, in both respects during the eighteenth and the first half of the nineteenth century. The Damascus blood libel of 1840 and Sir Moses Montefiore's repeated visits to the Holy Land brought Palestine,[8a] as well as all of Oriental and Turkish-governed Balkan Jewry, into the orbit of general Jewish interest. The awakened concern of the emancipated Western European Jewries of France and England in their brethren of the Orient was reflected also in educational endeavors in their behalf. Heretofore, the heder and the Talmud Torah were alone in the field of Jewish educational activity throughout these regions. Nor were these institutions in too flourishing a state. In 1867 through the initiative of the *Alliance Israélite Universelle*, the first modern school for Jewish children in the Balkans was opened in Adrianople. In 1937 ninety-five schools with a reported pupil enrollment of 47,822 were maintained and subsidized by the *Alliance* in the Balkans, North Africa and the Near East. Of these, five were in Palestine, among them the outstanding agricultural school at Mikveh Israel, founded in 1870. English Jewry followed some time later with the organization of a few modern schools in Palestine and the Orient. At the beginning of the Twentieth century, German Jewry through the *Hilfsverein der Deutschen Juden* also entered the field and by 1914 had established or aided some fifty schools catering to about seven thousand pupils. Each one of these groups did worthy work.

b. Effects of the Zionist Movement

However, the remarkable revolutionary change in Jewish education in Palestine resulted wholly from the activities of the Zionist movement and its national and international agencies. Impressive beginnings were made even before World War I in establishing the Herzliah Gymnasium in Tel-Aviv, the Bet Sefer Reali, Hebrew Secondary School, in Haifa, and the schools in the small and struggling Jewish settlements of that era. By 1914 there was no longer any doubt that Hebrew was to be the language of the modern Jewish community of Palestine and of its school system. When after World War I the Palestinian Jewish community reorganized itself within the political framework of the Balfour Declaration and the League of Nations mandate, one of its first and chief concerns was the creation of a national system of Jewish education, which should reflect not the economic impoverishment and cultural backwardness characteristic of 1920 Palestine as a whole but the high cultural aspirations and the rich spiritual history of the Jewish pioneers who came to rebuild Jewish life in the land of their fathers. The Jewish community in Palestine resolved on complete autonomy in its educational work. The lure of larger government educational subsidies did not succeed in breaking this resolution. Since the resources of the Jews of Palestine were at the time extremely limited, and since the Palestine government appropriated only a small percentage of its meager budget for educational purposes and out of that gave a ludicrously small subsidy to Jewish education, the bulk of the educational budget of the modern Jewish schools in Palestine up to 1927 was met by the Zionist Organization. The Vaad Leumi, the nationally and democratically elected, politically recognized, representative body of Palestine Jewry then assumed sole responsibility for the educational budget of the schools affiliated with it. The government subsidy was gradually increased though never represented more than about twenty-two per cent of the total educational budget. Nor did the sum granted by the government to Jewish schools represent a percentage of the total educational budget of the government equal to the percentage paid in taxes by the Jews of Palestine or to the percentage of the Jewish school population within the total school population of the country. Furthermore, the authority of the Vaad Leumi was not complete, for Jews could choose to remain outside its authority and organize separate Jewish communities. Despite these legal and financial handicaps, the Education Department of the Vaad Leumi dominated elementary and secondary education in Palestine. The budget for the schools under its supervision was met out of the parents' tuition fees and special educational taxes wherever the community had the legal right to levy them, the government subsidy, and the general funds made available to the Vaad Leumi by the Zionist movement through the Jewish Agency for Palestine.

Three distinct educational systems were united under the Vaad Leumi's supervision. The largest of these was composed of the schools organized, directed and completely controlled by the Educational Department of the Vaad Leumi itself. These were usually referred to as the General Zionist Schools. They corresponded very closely to the American public schools in philosophy and curriculum. Religion as such was not formally taught in them. The Bible and Rabbinic literature formed part of the curriculum and Jewish national and religious holidays were observed and celebrated. In 1943 there were 181 such schools with a pupil population of 38,936.

The second group of schools were under the direct supervision of the Mizrachi, the Orthodox branch of the World Zionist Organization. The curriculum of these schools and the general atmosphere pervading their classrooms and administration represented the intense religious interests of their sponsors. Much more time was given to Rabbinic literature and to Bible study in their curriculum. In 1943 there were 84 such schools with an enrollment of 14,486.

The third group was composed of the schools organized and sponsored by the Palestine Labor and the left-wing Zionist groups. They were found chiefly in the communal or co-operative colonies founded in the last quarter of a century, and in urban centers occupied by members of these groups. While the Bible was taught and Jewish holidays were celebrated, Rabbinic legal literature was hardly touched. A neutral or negative attitude toward religion pervaded the ideology and the pedagogy of these schools. Their outstanding characteristic was an emphasis upon vocational training, upon the history of the labor movement throughout the world and upon the most progressive pedagogic methods. The 218 schools of this group taught 14,561 students in 1943.

The 65,983 pupils of the schools thus united in the Education Department of the Vaad Leumi represented approximately two-thirds of the total Palestine Jewish child population of school age. Of the remainder a goodly number of girls of the Oriental or older Jewish communities in the country received no formal education of any kind, some 24,000 attended either a heder, a modern private school, or a school sponsored by some other Jewish body, while some 1,200 were in the schools of the Christian missionaries. It is a strange fact that many a poor pious Jewish parent did not hesitate to send a daughter to acquire a general elementary education in a Christian missionary school, where no tuition fee was required and where occasionally some article of clothing or other assistance was given.

Judged by modern standards, the schools of the Vaad Leumi undoubtedly represented the best organized, most adequately financed and staffed, most efficiently supervised, best housed, pedagogically and educationally best planned elementary and secondary school system ever maintained by any Jewish community in all of Jewish history. The schools formerly under the supervision of the Vaad Leumi are now, 1949, part of the Education Department of the State of Israel. The rapid expansion, transformation, and modernization of the schools within Israel are keeping pace with the many other extraordinary events that have taken place there in so kaleidoscopic a manner since the State came into being on May 14, 1948.

c. Elementary and Secondary Schools for Vocational Training

The vocational and technical school was the last to appear within all modern school systems. Among the Jews agitation for such schools first appeared at the beginning of the nineteenth century. But no practical step was taken to create such schools until the late sixties and early seventies in Russia. Because of the government's attitude, these sporadic attempts soon petered out. In 1880 the ORT, an organization for advancing trades and agriculture among Jews, was established. Its chief aim was to support existing handicraft schools, establish additional ones, and subsidize those seeking vocational training in a school or as apprentices. But all ORT's efforts were impeded by government restrictions. Only in 1905 was a charter finally granted, after which its activities among the Jews of Russia rapidly advanced. Since then ORT has been functioning on a world-wide scale, helping the Russian Jews after the revolution to retrain themselves within the new economic framework of Soviet Russia, creating retraining opportunities for victims of the Nazi persecutions, whether in concentration camps or as refugees, and establishing schools in Poland, in the Near East and in other Jewish communities for vocational training of their youth.

In Palestine the vocational and technical school has been assuming increasing importance within the Jewish educational system. The Mikveh Israel Agricultural School, established in 1870, proved to be the most successful institution of its type. In 1943 there were seven well-established agricultural schools, in addition to a number of girls' training farms and the agricultural courses given to refugee youth in labor co-operative and collective settlements. Since 1932 there has been a marked increase in the attention given to industrial education. The report of the survey of the Vocational Training Committee of the Jewish Agency for 1943 listed ten such schools including a nautical school with a total enrollment of 1,105 pupils.

V. JEWISH INSTITUTIONS OF HIGHER LEARNING

A. Bible Times

Just as poetry preceded prose in the history of literature, so organized institutions for higher learning preceded elementary and secondary schools. This was true in Israel, as well as among other peoples. We noted above that, though the Bible makes no mention whatsoever of elementary schools, it does speak of "schools" of prophets. Moreover, the Bible's reference to the manner in which people came to listen to Solomon's wisdom, which surpassed that of all the other wise men of old, would indicate that these wise men had schools very much like those of the Greek philosophers of later generations. King Hezekiah's men who copied the proverbs of Solomon (Pr. 25:1) were most likely members of some kind of academy of the learned maintained by the royal house, in order to preserve the cultural treasures of the people. The scribes and secretaries of the government,[9a] the Levites and priests of the Temple, surely had to be trained somewhere for their work.

B. The Second Commonwealth

For a period of some 150 years, very little is known of the inner or outer life of the Jewish community that reestablished itself in Palestine after the activities of Ezra and Nehemiah.[10a] But when with Alexander's conquest of Palestine the Jewish community of the Holy Land reappears in the light of history, it seems to possess a well-established and well-organized authoritative religious body. This was the *Keneset Ha-Gedolah*, the Great Synagogue. Scholars differ on the exact nature of this body, its composition, its function, and its history. We do know, however, that one of its guiding principles was "to increase the number of students." The reference is obviously not only to children but also to adults. From what we know of the character of this body, it may be safe to assume that the *Keneset Ha-Gedolah* exercised the threefold functions of court, legislature and center of higher learning and research.

The *Keneset Ha-Gedolah* was superseded by the Sanhedrin. Considerable controversy and conjecture also surround every aspect of the history, the composition and the functioning of the Sanhedrin. But all agree that in one manner or another it, too, functioned as a legislative, judicial and educational institution. The various parties and schools of thought which multiplied in the Jewish community during the century immediately preceding the destruction of the Temple (70 c.e.) had their own centers of discussion and learning. But the conflicting viewpoints were all reflected in the seventy-one elders who composed the Sanhedrin.

C. THE ACADEMY AND THE BET MIDRASH

When the Temple was destroyed by the Romans, the authority formerly lodged in the Sanhedrin was transferred by the towering personality of Johanan ben Zakkai to the academy he founded at Jabneh.[11a] This academy, and the others which succeeded it in Palestine, continued to exercise the function of courts, legislatures and universities. They administered the law, they amended it when necessary, legislated when necessary, and continued ceaselessly to explore the hidden recesses of the Torah, in order to bring to light some previously unnoticed moral or legal implication. The Talmud records indicate that the question, "What new thought was expressed at the session of the academy today?" was frequently asked by members who had been absent. The intimate contact maintained by the academy, by virtue of its judicial and legislative functions, with the daily life of the members of the community kept its purely intellectual pursuits from departing too far into the realms of the impractical and theoretical.

The members of these academies most often supported themselves. But many were maintained out of the treasury of the patriarchate or through the generosity of individuals.

As the body of knowledge and tradition increased, various schools of interpretation and of methods of study inevitably appeared. It was but natural that similarly minded scholars should have a common meeting place for study and discussion. Moreover, outstanding teachers and scholars attracted younger men seeking knowledge of the Torah. The most natural place for such gatherings of scholars or of teachers and pupils was some room in the local synagogue, though a special structure for such purposes, usually near the synagogue, was undoubtedly frequently used. The place where these scholars, individually or in groups, pursued their studies was called a Bet Midrash, a house for studying and interpreting the Torah, to distinguish it from the Bet Tefilah, the room used primarily for prayer, or the *Bet Sefer,* the place used for instructing the young. One room could at various times of the day be used for any one of the three purposes. Apparently, however, in the early days of the Bet Ha-Midrash, scholars would not use it for prayer, but would leave off their studies and join the congregation in the synagogue. The stress laid upon study by the rabbis is perhaps best reflected in the law that a synagogue structure may be turned into a Bet Ha-Midrash but a Bet Ha-Midrash may not be sold for exclusive synagogue use, for one is permitted to elevate an object from a lower to a higher state of sanctity, but not to reduce it from a higher to a lower state.

The Bet Ha-Midrash required practically no financing. Its meeting place was supplied either by the synagogue or by voluntary contributions for the erection of a special structure. Its teacher was not a paid officer, its students were self-supporting adults, and its curriculum of studies was determined completely by the interests and desires of the participants.

The Bet Ha-Midrash remained an integral part of the synagogue throughout the ages. Practically every synagogue had a room, usually the basement, containing a library of Hebrew books including the Bible and its commentaries, the various Midrashim—homiletic interpretations of Sacred Scripture—and the Talmud and its commentaries. In the long-established communities of Eastern Europe this room would buzz with activity from early morning till late at night. Busy laymen would meet here daily in the morning or the afternoon to spend a fixed period in study either by themselves or with a companion, or with a larger group under the leadership of the rabbi or of one of their own more learned lay companions. The most advanced studied the Talmud, others studied the Mishna, while the less learned devoted themselves to the Midrashim or the Pentateuch with its commentators, especially Rashi.

American synagogues, by and large, still have a library of Hebrew books, but the men to study them are unfortunately no longer available, except in very rare instances. The modern Bible class, or study circle, meeting usually about fifteen to twenty times during the year under the leadership of the rabbi, is a very pale reflection of the intense advanced Jewish studies carried on in the Bet Ha-Midrash of some of the smallest Jewish communities of Eastern Europe up to 1939.

The discussions that took place in the academies and the Bate Midrashim until about the middle of the second century C.E. developed the vast storehouse of law and tradition that Judah the Nasi drew upon when in the second half of the second century he edited the Mishna. His compilation did not include everything that was said and taught. What he had omitted, others collected and edited. But his work, because of its intrinsic excellence and his own great personality, became almost immediately popular and authoritative, and formed the chief text for the studies in the academies of the following centuries. The Palestinian academies continued to exist and to exercise great influence throughout the Jewish world until about the fifth century. The discussions and decisions of the last two hundred years of their existence were included in the Palestinian Talmud.

D. The Babylonian Academies

With the beginning of the third century, Babylonian academies started to challenge the schools of Palestine in erudition, in creativity, and later even in authority.[12a] The greatest of the Babylonian academies was founded by Rav in Sura about the year 219. It continued to function with only brief occasional interruptions until approximately the thirteenth century. The second academy founded at about the same time by Samuel at Nahardea, was transferred by Judah ben Ezekiel in 260 to Pumbedita. There it also continued to flourish with some intermission for about eight hundred years. These two academies were the recognized leaders of Jewish religious and cultural life throughout the world from the fifth to the eleventh century. The discussions, opinions and reflections of the members and the leaders of these academies during the first three centuries of their existence form the contents of the vast treasure trove of law, history, morals, ethics and folklore, known as the Babylonian Talmud. The heads of each of these two academies from the end of the sixth century on bore the title of Gaon. Jewish communities throughout the world turned to successive Geonim for religious guidance and leadership and students came to them from great distances to study. In the beginning, the Babylonian Jewish community itself was in a position to maintain these academies through taxation and voluntary contributions. But with the deterioration of the Jewish position in the eastern Mohammedan world, the academies found it necessary to send messengers to Jewish communities throughout the Diaspora for additional support.

E. The Kalla

A unique feature of the activities of these academies was the *Kalla*. Twice a year during the month of Ellul, the month preceding Rosh Ha-Shanah and the High Holy Day season, and during the month of Adar, preceding the Passover festival, thousands of students and scholars would come to the academies from all parts of the Diaspora and spend the month in study and discussion. The talmudic tractate analyzed during the month's session of the *Kalla* was one which had been announced at the end of the previous *Kalla* gathering and had thus been studied by the participants during the preceding five months. During the *Kalla* sessions difficult passages in the tractate would be explained, the text corrected, the diligence of the students tested, important legal decisions rendered and the subject to be studied in preparation for the next session announced. Little imagination is required to recognize the tremendous influence such semi-annual gatherings of large numbers must have had in stimulating and directing scholarly pursuits and thus influencing the spiritual and intellectual life of Jews in the remotest communities.

F. THE TARBITZA

In connection with the *Kalla* sources frequently mention the *Tarbitza*. The exact nature of this institution has not been established. Some are of the opinion that the *Tarbitza* was for those who were not sufficiently well-prepared to attend the *Kalla* sessions. At the *Tarbitza* gathering each student studied whatever tractate he preferred.

G. THE YESHIVA

The most widespread institution for higher Jewish learning developed by the Jews on the European continent was the *Yeshiva*. It was a natural outgrowth of the Babylonian academy and the Bet Ha-Midrash. No European *Yeshiva* ever attained the stature of any of the Babylonian or Palestinian academies. The European *Yeshivot* did not prove to be intellectually as bold and as creative as their predecessors, nor did they enjoy the same authority either within the Jewish community or in relation to the non-Jewish authorities. However, their outstanding leaders and students equaled their predecessors in mental acumen, in depth and breadth of erudition, in piety, and in lives of exemplary holiness and singleness of devotion to the study of Torah.

The only requirement for entrance into a *Yeshiva* was talmudic knowledge and the ability to follow the more involved talmudic debates. Exceptionally brilliant youngsters of ten or twelve could, therefore, sit side by side with men twice and three times their age to listen to the lecture and participate in the debate that followed. The Talmud and all its commentaries constituted practically the exclusive subject of study, though in some *Yeshivot*, moral and ethical texts also were read and discussed for brief periods weekly or daily. Every sizable Jewish community sought to have a *Yeshiva* in its midst and every rabbi coveted the honor of having a *Yeshiva* under his guidance. A description of the Jewish community in Poland before the massacres of 1648 relates that there was not a Jewish community of fifty families or more which did not have at least one *Yeshiva* with some thirty students.

After the Chmielnicki massacre of 1648, a period of intellectual deterioration set in for almost a century. By the middle of the eighteenth century, Polish Jewry had recovered from the disastrous effects of the massacres. There was a great revival of higher learning, particularly in Lithuania. It reached its high-water mark in the personality of the Gaon, Elijah of Vilna (1720-1797), intellectually a giant and spiritually a saint. In 1803 his student, Hayim of Volozhin, organized the *Yeshiva* of Volozhin, which for over a century exercised considerable influence on Jewish life. Other outstanding *Yeshivot* arose in impressive numbers during the subsequent century and a half until 1939. These *Yeshivot* attracted thousands upon thousands of students. As long as the Jewish communities had the legal right to impose and collect taxes, *Yeshivot* received their support, at least in part, from such taxes and from the billeting of some of their students in local Jewish homes. For the past hundred and fifty years, they were maintained exclusively by self-imposed meat or slaughtering taxes and by additional voluntary contributions, not only of money but of meals and lodging for students.

The East European *Yeshiva* devoted itself exclusively to Jewish studies. Because of the weakening of the religious bonds evident among those Jews who had acquired a secular education, secular studies, even the reading of modern secular Hebrew literature, were excluded from and forbidden by the *Yeshiva*.

The *Yeshiva* consisted most often of little more than one or two large rooms with tables at which the students sat, or with individual lecterns at which the student stood while studying his text. Except for the hour or two each day when the headmaster or other teacher gave his lecture, examined the students or discussed the text with them, each student studied aloud by himself or with a companion. Because most students at a *Yeshiva* came from a distance and dormitories and dining rooms were provided by only a few of the larger and more adequately supported modern *Yeshivot*, sleeping quarters and food were frequently arranged for in the homes of local families. Poor students were often supported by meager grants from the treasury of the *Yeshiva* or the community. Householders, however, considered it a great deed of piety to offer one daily meal or more to a *Yeshiva* student or a bed in which he could spend the night. As a result, a student frequently ate his meals each day at a different home and had various sleeping quarters for his use, including the bench in the *Yeshiva* on which he sat and studied during the day. The privations under which the average *Yeshiva* student pursued his studies are thus easily imagined and have been frequently described. Nor did the *Yeshiva* grant a rabbinic title or degree to all its students. Comparatively few desired or attained this distinction. The primary aim of the *Yeshiva* was to produce *Talmide Hakamim*, Disciples of the Wise, learned Jews who would live their lives in accordance with the laws of the Torah and set aside daily periods for its study all the days of their lives. Such was the intensity of the thirst for knowledge and such the devotion to Torah that despite the hardships the *Yeshivot* never lacked students. They produced a veritable galaxy of exceptionally learned and saintly rabbis and of highly erudite laymen for the Jewish communities of Eastern Europe.

H. THE YESHIVA IN THE UNITED STATES

Until very recently the traditional *Yeshiva*, which proscribed all secular knowledge and concentrated all its attention on talmudic studies, was nonexistent in the United States. The American Jewish day school which called itself a *Yeshiva* and is now spoken of as a *Yeshiva Ktana*, a junior *Yeshiva* (because it caters to boys of elementary and high school age), of necessity included the American public school curriculum in its studies. It never directly or indirectly discouraged or prohibited its students from pursuing further studies at a college or a university. As a matter of fact, the Isaac Elchanan Yeshiva founded in 1896,[13a] one of the oldest and today the best known of the *Yeshivot* in America, was the first to add the regular high school to its curriculum (in 1919) and hoped from the very beginning to be able to grant the regular bachelor's degree to its qualified students. That hope became a reality when in 1928 the Yeshiva College was organized, and in 1948 it was granted university status, thus becoming the first *Yeshiva* in Jewish history to make the regular college and secular postgraduate studies an integral part of its program. Nor is there a ban on modern secular Hebrew literature. Indeed, in the Teachers' Institute which was incorporated into the over-all organizational structure of the Isaac Elchanan Yeshiva in 1921, Hebrew is the primary language of instruction and modern Hebrew literature one of the main subjects of study. While many American *Yeshivot* do not consider the college degree a prerequisite to the granting of a rabbinic degree and ordain men as rabbis only on the basis of their talmudic and general Jewish knowledge, the attitude toward secular studies reflected in the American *Yeshiva* is a far cry from what it was in the East European *Yeshiva*.

We noted above the increased number of Jewish all-day schools on the elementary and secondary level in America within the past two decades. The unparalleled catastrophes which in five years' time completely destroyed Polish Jewry and every one of its educational centers brought many of the deans, faculty members and students of the Polish *Yeshivot* to this country. They at once set about with their customary energy and self-sacrifice to organize *Yeshivot* here. Their labors have not been unproductive. The *Yeshivot* thus far established have had no lack of students. Moreover, there is little likelihood that the attitude of the *Yeshiva* leaders in America toward secular studies will be what it was in Eastern Europe a generation and more ago.

I. RABBINICAL SEMINARIES

Until the middle of the nineteenth century, the *Yeshivot* produced the men who were called to rabbinical leadership of Jewish communities. But Jews who had themselves acquired secular knowledge and who were culturally part of the Western world required differently trained men as their religious leaders. Hence, for the first time in Jewish history there were established schools whose express purpose was to prepare men for the modern rabbinate. The seminaries of necessity reflected the theological views of the groups who organized and maintained them. During the past hundred and fifty years Western Jewry divided itself religiously into three main groups, usually distinguished as the Orthodox, the Conservative, and the Reform. Seminaries to serve the needs of each of them were first founded in Germany. In 1854 the Conservative Jewish Theological Seminary of Breslau was founded by Zechariah Frankel. In 1872 two seminaries were opened in Berlin, the Reform *Hochschule fuer die Wissenschaft des Judentums* and the Orthodox Rabbinical Seminary in Berlin.

No seminary for the training of modern rabbis was opened by the Jews of Eastern Europe. Between 1844 and 1873 there were two rabbinical schools sponsored by the Russian government. Their graduates, known as "government rabbis," were never regarded by the Jews as religious leaders. Jews in Eastern Europe by and large either remained orthodox in their religious outlook or became agnostics or nonbelievers.

In the United States the first rabbinical school, the Hebrew Union College, was opened by Reform Jews in 1875 under the leadership of Isaac M. Wise.[14a] During its seventy-five years of existence, the school has graduated some five hundred rabbis. It maintains a large library, has a distinguished faculty, and has published many scholarly volumes. The well-equipped and spacious buildings include a dormitory for students. A bachelor's degree is a prerequisite for entering upon the rabbinic course. The college is maintained by income from an endowment fund, supplemented by contributions from individuals, Reform congregations and community chests.

In 1886 The Jewish Theological Seminary of America[15a] was founded in New York City by Sabato Morais, rabbi of Congregation Mikveh Israel of Philadelphia. In 1902, it was reorganized under the presidency of Solomon Schechter. Though the Seminary as such consistently refuses to identify itself as a school for the training of rabbis for any one group or party in Israel, nevertheless, because of the character of its faculty and its avowed traditional leanings, it is generally referred to as the school of the Conservative, or Historical, party. Since its reorganization the seminary has graduated some four hundred rabbis. A bachelor's degree is a prerequisite to its four-year rabbinical course. The seminary's scope of activities has steadily broadened. Its imposing buildings erected in 1930 in the Morningside Heights educational center, include the Jacob H. Schiff Library building housing the largest collection of Judaica ever gathered by Jews; the Unterberg building with quarters for the Teachers Institute of the Jewish Theological Seminary, organized in 1909, and the Seminary

College of Jewish Studies. In addition, the Brush Dormitory building, including a spacious lounge and dining hall, offers dormitory quarters for the students.

The Jewish Museum, housed in the former home of Mr. and Mrs. Felix M. Warburg, at Ninety-second Street and Fifth Avenue, is an integral part of the Seminary. So is the University of Judaism in Los Angeles, whose classes began in the autumn of 1947.[16a]

The Seminary's budget is met by income from endowments and by special annual contributions from individuals, Conservative congregations and community welfare chests.

The Isaac Elchanan Yeshiva described above is the best known institution preparing rabbis for modern American Orthodox congregations. It, too, is housed in a spacious building with dormitories and library and has a Teachers' College affiliated with it.

In 1922 the Hebrew Theological College of Chicago was founded. Its graduates are prepared to serve Orthodox communities. The other *Yeshivot* also qualify their graduates to lead this type of congregation.

In 1922 Dr. Stephen S. Wise founded the Jewish Institute of Religion in New York to train rabbis for any of the religious groups in Israel. The institute permits complete freedom to its faculty and student body in all theological and ideological matters. Its students and graduates choose whatever Jewish theology or ideology appeals most to them and seek to serve congregations most congenial to their point of view. The Institute also requires a bachelor's degree of those applying for matriculation. Its financial support comes from contributions of individuals and of community welfare funds and of congregations served by its graduates. In 1948, the Jewish Institute of Religion and the Hebrew Union College merged under the name of Hebrew Union College-Jewish Institute of Religion.

At the present time (1948) the United States is the only country with modern seminaries training rabbis for groups other than those who are orthodox in the traditional sense of that word.

Jewish teachers' training schools also first appeared in the nineteenth century in Germany. The Kassel community opened such a school in 1810, Muenster in 1827, Berlin and Hanover in 1859, and Wuerzburg in 1864. The last of these was the only one which continued after 1926.

In Russia the first teachers' school was opened in Grodno in 1907. Other similar schools were founded later, particularly in Poland, to serve the needs of the various school systems existing there between 1920 and 1939. The Soviet government also provided teachers' training schools to prepare teachers for its Yiddish-language schools.

The first modern teachers' training school was opened in Palestine in

Jerusalem by the Ezra Verein in 1905. Similar institutions were organized by the various groups affiliated with the Education Department of the Vaad Leumi. The development of teachers' training schools is one of the most pressing problems facing the Education Department of Israel.

In the United States the first teachers' training school, Gratz College, was opened in Philadelphia in 1895. Its establishment was made possible by a bequest of Simon Gratz. The school has been functioning uninterruptedly since it was opened. In 1909, the Teachers Institute of the Jewish Theological Seminary was organized and since 1931 has been permitted to grant the graduates of its regular department the degree of Bachelor of Jewish Pedagogy. By special arrangement, its students take some of their courses at Columbia's Teachers College. In 1921, the Teachers' College formerly maintained by the American Mizrachi organization became a part of the Yeshiva College. Other teachers' training colleges were founded in various communities, such as the Baltimore Jewish College, the Chicago School of Jewish Studies, the Boston Jewish College and others. Few of these schools limit themselves exclusively to the training of teachers for the Sunday or weekday schools. They have extension departments for the education of adults and some have high school departments to prepare students for the more advanced studies.

J. Dropsie College

Unique among Jewish institutions of higher learning is Dropsie College,[17a] founded in 1907 in Philadelphia with funds bequeathed by a Philadelphia lawyer, Moses Aaron Dropsie. Under the presidency of Cyrus Adler the college was organized as a postgraduate institution granting only the Ph.D. degree in the field of Hebrew and Cognate Studies. It occupies attractive quarters, has an excellent working and reference library and a distinguished faculty. In its student body and among its graduates, Jew and Christian, men and women, are represented. More recently the college has expanded its program to include a postgraduate department in Jewish Education and an Institute on the Near East.

K. The Hebrew Institute of Technology

In 1912 a Russian Zionist, Wolf Wissotzky, with the help of Jacob H. Schiff, the Jewish National Fund and the Hilfsverein established the Hebrew Institute of Technology in Haifa. It was at this school that the language question came to a head. Many of the school's supporters wanted German to be the language of the institution. After a long and bitter struggle, the pupils, teachers and the Palestine Jewish community succeeded in making Hebrew the official language of the school. After World War I the institution was taken over by the Zionist Organization and reopened with increased facilities in 1925. Today it is the most advanced school for the training of engineers of all types found in the whole Near East. In its field it occupies relatively the same position that the Hebrew University occupies in the field of the humanities, sciences and free professions.

L. The Hebrew University in Jerusalem

The most rapidly developing Jewish institution of higher learning of our day is perhaps the Hebrew University in Jerusalem. Its organization was suggested at the first Zionist World Congress in 1897. Its cornerstone was laid by Dr. Chaim Weizmann in the presence of Lord Allenby, conqueror of Jerusalem, in July, 1918, while the din of battle still clearly resounded on Judea's hills. In December, 1924, the first regular classes of the university's Institute of Jewish Studies began their sessions and on April 1, 1925, Sir Arthur James Balfour in the presence of Sir Herbert Samuel, the British High Commissioner of Palestine, Dr. Chaim Weizmann, and Dr. Judah Magnes, first president of the university, officially opened and dedicated this new center of Jewish and universal learning.

The university began as a research institution. The first undergraduate department was opened in 1928 with a four-year course given by the faculty of Humanities and leading to the degree of Master of Arts. Since then the faculty of Natural Sciences has been offering a four-year course leading to the degree of Master of Science. Courses qualifying graduates of the Hebrew University or other universities for the degree of Doctor of Philosophy have also been arranged.

Since its opening, the university has become the greatest modern institution of higher learning throughout the Near East. Some fifteen different departments and institutes now exist. The foundations have been laid for a first-rate modern medical center. During the war the various scientific laboratories maintained by the university made invaluable contributions to the welfare of the fighting forces of the United Nations stationed throughout the Near East.

The student body of the university now numbers over a thousand men and women of all creeds and races, and the faculty includes some of the best known names in all fields of study. Many of them, forced out of European universities by the Nazi regime, have found in the center of learning on Mt. Scopus an opportunity to continue their teaching and research.

Given an extended period of peaceful development, the Hebrew University is destined to exert tremendous influence upon the cultural life of the whole of the Near East as well as upon the cultural life of the Jews of Palestine and the Diaspora.

NOTES

[1a Cf. above the chapter by Julius B. Maller, "The Role of Education in Jewish History."]

[2a Cf. below Louis Finkelstein, "The Jewish Religion: Its Beliefs and Practices," pp. 1354 ff.]

3 Baba Batra 21a.

[3a Cf. above Judah Goldin, "The Period of the Talmud," pp. 120-121.]

[4a Cf. ibid., pp. 141 ff.]

[5a Cf. ibid., pp. 153-155.]

[6a Cf. above Cecil Roth, "The Jews of Western Europe (from 1648)," pp. 261-262.]

[7a Cf. above Moshe Davis, "Jewish Religious Life and Institutions in America," pp. 357 ff.]

[8a Cf. Roth, op. cit., pp. 271-272.]

[9a Cf. above Elias J. Bickerman, "The Historical Foundations of Post-biblical Judaism," pp. 97-99.]

[10aCf. above William Foxwell Albright, "The Biblical Period," pp. 50 ff. and Bickerman, op. cit., passim.]

[11a Cf. Goldin, op. cit., pp. 146-149.]

[12a Cf. ibid., pp. 175 ff.]

[13a Cf. Davis, op. cit., p. 390.]

[14a Cf. ibid., pp. 382-383, 398-399, and on Isaac M. Wise, pp. 366 f.]

[15a Cf. ibid., pp. 388-389, 400-403.]

[16a Cf. ibid., pp. 428-429.]

[17a Cf. ibid., pp. 411-412.]

BIBLIOGRAPHY

CHIPKIN, ISRAEL, Twenty-five years of Jewish Education in the United States. New York, 1937. Reprint from American Jewish Symposium of the Jewish Day School.

DRAZIN, NATHAN, History of Jewish Education from 515 B.C.E. to 220 C.E. Baltimore, 1940.

DUSHKIN, ALEXANDER, M., Jewish Education in New York City. New York, 1918.

GAMORAN, EMANUEL, Changing Conceptions in Jewish Education. New York, 1924.

GREENBERG, LOUIS, The Jews in Russia. New Haven and London, 1944. I, Chs. IV-VII.

KAPLAN, MORDECAI M., The Future of the American Jew. New York, 1948. Chapter XXVI.

MORRIS, NATHAN, The Jewish School—an Introduction to the History of Jewish Education. London, 1937.

Nardi, Noah, *Education in Palestine*. New York, 1945.

Scharfstein, Zevi, *The History of Jewish Education in Modern Times* (Hebrew) (*Toldot Hahinuch Beyisrael bedorot haachronim*). New York, 1945. I.

Sherrill, Lewis Joseph, *The Rise of Christian Education*. New York, 1944. Chs. I-IV.

Tscharno, Y., *Education Among the Jews*. (Hebrew) Jerusalem, 1939. (*Toldot Hahinuch Beyisrael*).

CHAPTER 23

THE JEWISH CONTRIBUTION TO MUSIC

By Eric Werner

Preface

Laudamus veteres, sed nostris utimur annis.

Any attempt to evaluate the Jewish contribution to the world of music will, at the very outset, be confronted by a number of controversial premises. These premises must first be clearly defined or at least circumscribed. Hence, we shall distinguish in the following pages between the musical contributions of Judaism, and those of individual Jews. In a few cases these accomplishments coincide, but certainly not always. Furthermore, it would be a misuse of an otherwise fruitful method to abstract certain elements of style from the works of composers like Mahler, Mendelssohn and Schoenberg—to name only a few—and then to pose these personal mannerisms as general criteria in a discussion of Judaism's musical accomplishments. Aside from the purely hypothetical character of all conclusions arrived at in this way, we must bear in mind two important, yet antithetic facts:

The musical contributions of Judaism lie chiefly in the realm of collective and anonymous *folk music*, the basis of its musical culture. On the other hand, individual composers of Jewish birth concerned themselves, naturally, with the *art music* of their time and environment. Considered together, it is obvious that the former aspect (folk music) far surpasses and outweighs the latter (individual works of art). Yet we must not disregard the efforts of individual composers and musicians, for they form a characteristic part of that involved mosaic known as the Jewish-Gentile symbiosis. It must be remembered that these composers speak for themselves rather than for the Jewish group.

This study endeavors to implement such general theses with essential and concrete details.

The Time of Royal Singers

Judaism originated in the Near East and migrated to the West. So simple a fact accounts for the unique position of Jewish culture, the gigantic bridge spanning the gulf between Orient and Occident. This bridge was to bear the traffic of Babylonian astronomy, as well as Greek philosophy, songs of the desert along with legalistic discussions of the academies.

Even in biblical times the Jewish people must have enjoyed an outstanding reputation as a musical nation. That is known from Jewish sources as well as from those of their hostile neighbors. An Assyrian document tells us that King Sennacherib demanded and received as tribute from King Hezekiah many Jewish musicians, male and female.[1] During the Exile, the Babylonians mockingly asked the Jewish captives to entertain them with music they brought out of Palestine. "Sing us one of the songs of Zion!" (Ps. 137). Musicians as tribute, and interest in a vanquished enemy's folk music, was unusual indeed.

Nor is it a coincidence that the idolized King David became the patron saint of Jewish music. Even if only a small fraction of the psalms attributed to him are in fact his, he would still tower above all ancient rhapsodists, except possibly Homer. David is the perfect embodiment of that unforgettable age of seers, poets and rhapsodists, which so many subsequent centuries ardently admired. Quite aside from the many legends that adorn his story in the Bible, the historical facts remain clearly to demonstrate his significance for the history of music. It was he who organized the cult music of the Levitical orders, as we learn from various biblical passages. If we understand I. Sam. 19:18-20 correctly, David combined in his person the gift of the professional prophet with that of the born poet and musician. We are entitled to assume that he was actually the author of Psalm 18, which is included *in toto* in II Sam. 22. Here is a psalm quite detached from the style of primitive folk song, as the Hebrew text will reveal. This would mean that with David artistic poetry and art music entered the history of Judaism. A great king, a brilliant soldier, and a highly gifted poet and musician! Small wonder that posterity saw in him the ideal of all pious men. Byzantine Christianity identified him with Jesus, the "faithful shepherd," and with Orpheus, the divine singer.

The biblical period, in general, created an abundance of musical forms and institutions which, later on, through Christianity, became the adored and incessantly imitated standards of Western civilization. The principal form, of course, was the psalm and the principal institution was the musical service of the Temple in Jerusalem.

A Sacred Ensemble

The literary parallelism so characteristic of the Psalms demands a corresponding musical rendition. Here is the origin of the manifold formal types we encounter in the Psalter. In the simple solo psalmody, one person alone sings its prayer (Ps. 3-5). In the response psalm, the congregation answers the chanting soloist with short and concise formulae (Ps. 48, 100, 118). The antiphon has two groups chanting alternately (Ps. 136, 148), while in the refrain psalm a refrain verse is sung by a group and interjected into the singing of the full text, as rendered by a soloist (Ps. 135: 1-3). The very acclamations "Hallelujah" and "Amen" and even the often misunderstood "Selah," have themselves become texts of thousands of compositions, following the call "Sing unto the Lord a new song!" We shall see later how, through constant use of the Psalter by Christians and Jews, the parallelism of the Psalms (which all translations retained) contributed greatly to the universality of certain musical forms.

Perhaps even more important than the psalm forms was the ideal of Temple music. It was here that a permanent example was set, and music became an integral and indispensable part of solemn worship. Up to this very day, the conception of cult music, as first represented in the Temple, has closely associated the art of music with the spirit of true religion. Musical services are described in the passages of II Chron. 15:16-24; 16: 4-7; 25:1-7, and the minute, meticulous organization of such services became the ideal of cult music for all Christianity. Many Popes—latterly Pius XI—in decrees and constitutions have praised the musical service of the Sanctuary as the model *par excellence* of all truly sacred song.

Two facts pertaining to the Psalms and the music of the Temple should not be forgotten, for they disclose the continuity of musical practice and rendition: the usage of the so-called *contrafact*, and the function of the organ.

A contrafact is the use of a familiar melody for a new text. Thus, the anthem, *America* (*My Country, 'tis of Thee*) is a contrafact of the older *God Save the King*; the hymn beginning "Rock of ages, let our song praise Thy saving power," is a perfect contrafact of the older *Maoz Tzur*. This practice is long established in the history of liturgy. Upon the idea of the contrafact the Roman Church built many of its greatest hymns and sequences. Martin Luther made quite a point of his policy "to take the songs from the streets and to use them [with sacred texts] in the church. Why should the devil have all the fine tunes?" The use of the contrafact is probably as old as mankind, yet the first records of its being employed are found in the Psalms. Some of them bear superscriptions which have nothing whatever to do with their contents, *e.g.*, Psalm 22, "To the chief musician upon the 'Hind of the Morning,' a psalm of David"; or Psalm 56, "To the chief musician upon 'Mute Dove far away' by David"; and so on. These odd superscriptions gave the first lines of folk songs, then familiar to the Psalmist. They indicated that the respective psalms were to be sung to particular tunes which, unhappily, have long since been lost.

The organ was used regularly in the Second Temple and is called *Magrepha* in talmudic literature. The tractate *Arachin* gives us a fairly good description of the *Magrepha*. We learn that it was an instrument somewhat between a siren and a primitive organ with ten pipes. It seems that its sound was powerful enough to be heard far outside of Jerusalem proper. Just how this organ worked is not quite clear. We know that it cannot have been operated by water power, for the Greek water organ, *hydraulis*, is mentioned in the Talmud, and its use in the Temple was expressly prohibited.

All these facts come to us from a time which rarely recorded the names of inventors, composers or organizers. Thus almost all Jewish musical contributions of this period are necessarily anonymous. However, they are not, for this reason, any less important. Quite the contrary! They must be considered the core of Jewish musical lore.

The Establishment of Musical Tradition

If, in a rather rough simplification, we call the biblical period one of naïve creativity, we must consider the following thousand years—(200 B.C.E. to 900 C.E.)—as the epoch of creative reflection. The external events that give meaning to these terminal dates are the beginning of Hellenism[1a] and the decline of the Gaonate (the Babylonian talmudic academies).[2a] These years encompass the period when Judaism lived in close relationship with the Greeks, the Romans, the Persians and the Arabs. The civilizations of these peoples were, at that time, not too distantly related to the Jewish orbit. Then, about 900 C.E., the great Jewish migrations from the Near East westward began. To the cultural history of Judaism this event is of even greater importance than the catastrophe of the Temple's destruction in the year 70 C.E. and the severance of Christianity from the mother religion at the Council of Nicea in 325 C.E. For as long as Israel lived and worked among kindred civilizations the perpetual problem of its culture, the problem of positive and negative assimilation, was not essentially acute. Jewish contributions to music during that period grew organically out of the germ cells firmly implanted in previous centuries. Especially noteworthy is the fact that cultic music flourished proudly, resisting the fate that had doomed the Sanctuary itself.

A direct remnant of that glorious Temple music was the melismatic element. This is the technical term for expanded coloratura singing. We know this technique to have been a distinctive feature of Temple worship and it has never since ceased to be characteristic of the Jewish chant. Melismatic practice was borrowed by the church; it became a principal attraction of its music in the famous Jubili or Alleluias, of which we shall hear more later. The idea to envelop, as it were, the priestly blessing in a rich array of musical ornaments was probably common to all Semitic peoples, but it was through Judaism that the practice became so characteristic of all devoutly exalted music. To this very day, certain parts of the Jewish prayers, especially the *Avoda* of the Day of Atonement, are adorned with these ancient forms of pious ecstasy.

We see in this illustration how some melisms are built up to quite impressive chain coloraturas. Such an effect can be achieved only when certain musical motifs are retained and varied. This principle of motif technique conquered the music of the church and thereby the music of the Occident. There is no doubt that the ancient Greeks, and probably the Egyptians too, knew the technique and made full use of it. But it so happened that it was through the Bible and the Judeo-Christian liturgy that this form structure became common property and was eventually systematized by musical theory.

How does a motif penetrate the memory and imagination of the listener? Obviously, it must bear certain characteristic features either in melody or in rhythm. (Harmony is excluded, since it came into being much later.) Apparently, the melodic element is by far the most effective "carrier," being easily variable, in contradistinction to rhythm, which soon loses its identity through variation. Frequent recurrence of the same motifs leads eventually to the establishment of so-called modes. The basic term "mode" is best explained as a melodic pattern which consists of two or three motifs and retains its identity through all kinds of variations.

Traditional music of the synagogue is based upon numerous modes, well known to every cantor. Most of old Jewish melodies are derived from these basic modes of the tradition. One example may illustrate this important point:

Magen - Abot - Mode

Vayekulu

The numbers indicate the "standing tones" of the mode.

Va-ye-ku-lu ha-sho... o-retz; vekol tze-vo-om, va-ye-kal..ha-shvi-i me-lach-to a-shero-so, va-yish-bos ba-yom hash vi-i mi-kol me-lach-to a-sher o-so.

Sephardic Tune for the Tal-prayer
after Idelsohn

Lech le-sha-lom ge-shem u-vo le-sha-lom tal ki rav le-ho-shi-a u-mo-rid ha tal a-shir shi-ra-ti ve-a-sim di-vra-ti v'ag-bi-ra se-fa-ti le-tzur ye-shu-a-ti.

Hatikvah

Spanish Cancion
("Virgen de la Cueva")
after Idelsohn

German Catholic Hymn
("Der Himmel jetzt frohlocken soll" 16th Century)

The first is the bare framework of the so-called *Magen Avot* mode, termed after the responsorial prayer on Friday evening; the following three tunes are melodies based upon that mode. First, is the *Vayekulu* of the Friday evening service, second the well-known *"Tal"* and *Hallel* of the Sephardic Jews, third, the familiar *Hatikvah* tune. It is easy to recognize the *Hatikvah* as just an extended version of the older *Hallel* and *Tal* tune. (Is any further evidence required to dismiss the widespread notion that the *Hatikvah* was borrowed from Smetana's *Moldau*? As a matter of fact, we have here one of the many "itinerant tunes" that permeate the folk music of several European and American nations.)

The principle of modality, common to the music of the entire Near East, is not a result of theoretical speculation but of the incessant reiteration or variation of living melodies, which, in the course of centuries, finally crystallized into a series of melodic skeletons. These skeletons were adorned with individual embellishments, melisms and other accessories. The finished (individual) product is a modal melody. Every musician knows some modes from his studies in counterpoint, where the so-called *church-tones* usually form his raw material. Both Jews and Greeks bequeathed their systems of modality to the incipient church, which combined them into magnificent musical synthesis.

Here the question arises: Who promoted this remarkable development? Fortunately, we can answer this question exactly and in detail, supported by many ancient sources. The institution of the cantor (*hazan*) is old and venerable. Although his functions changed somewhat in the course of centuries, it was the *hazan* who, from the sixth century to the end of the nineteenth, originated innovations of the liturgical music, and yet strove assiduously to preserve elements of the old tradition. It was definitely to the *hazan's* credit that in the period between 400 and 1000 the music of the synagogue attained an organic unity.

In the most critical part of this period—during the Babylonian Gaonate —it must have been a commanding personality, indeed, who with the full weight of his authority supported the *hazanim*. This man, according to various old sources, seems to have been R. Yehudai Gaon, a great Rabbi of the eighth century in Babylonia. It was he who officially introduced the "ternary" form (ABA) into the sphere of our religious music. He recommended that the opening eulogy (*berakah*) and the closing eulogy (*hatimah*) be chanted in the same mode, the prayer between them in a different, but "not too divergent" tune. We know also that he introduced the chanting of the *Kol Nidre* into the synagogue. Moreover, two ancient documents state that the "first *hazanim* received the authentic tradition from him." The ternary form, a part of that tradition, prevailed in European art music from the late Middle Ages down to Bach and Handel, thereby assuming an importance which cannot be overrated. In written form it occurs first in the *ballades* of the French *trouvères* (twelfth century). Its recommendation and sanction by Yehudai Gaon, three centuries earlier, should therefore be appreciated to a far greater extent than heretofore. Be it noted, Yehudai's endorsement of the ternary form was the first utterance (to my knowledge) of a rational and artistic sense of form in medieval music, and it was the music of the synagogue to which it was first applied.

Attempts at Musical Notation

At about the same time (eighth-ninth century) the problem of musical notation was at least temporarily solved by Jewish scholars and musicians. Art music was almost nonexistent and instrumental music had been forbidden since the fall of the Temple. What remained was a traditional chanting of the prayers and the cantillation of the scriptural lessons, according to certain ancient modes. The Rabbis felt the urgent need of a codified system, consisting of mnemonic signs which would facilitate the study and ensure the preservation of those modes. These symbols did not purport to give a precise code of musical notation; such was incompatible with other aims of these rhetoric signs. Actually, they had to serve grammatical, exegetic and musical purposes simultaneously. Consequently, the individual marks—the accents or the *teamim* of Scripture—do not indicate *single tones*, as does modern notation, but each sign stands for a *whole musical phrase*. These semimusical devices existed since the sixth century in rudimentary form; their perfection was accomplished around 900 by the masoretes.[3a] The modes of cantillation that these accents symbolize are, of course, much older, and some of them might go back to the time of Jesus and even earlier. It should be emphasized that this rather primitive kind of notation has little musical value without the indispensable support of oral tradition and personal teaching. Yet, through personal instruction, the system has worked very efficiently, as the following facts demonstrate. In 1518 the great Christian scholar Johannes Reuchlin, with some assistance by Jews, managed to transliterate the ancient Jewish signs into the musical notation of his time. Since that day this procedure has been emulated by a good many scholars whose musical transcriptions show but negligible differences from each other. Moreover, when we compare our contemporary practice of scriptural cantillation with Reuchlin's text, we find that in all essential points there has been little change in the more than four hundred years that have elapsed since Reuchlin.

Where did these mysterious signs or accents originate? A definite answer has, thus far, not been furnished, but all indications point to southern Syria, where early Christianity, Judaism and other sects faced the same problem, *viz.*, how to preserve the musical modes of the public recitation of the Scriptures. Hence it is not surprising that both the Eastern and the Western Church employed a system closely akin to the Jewish. Out of the system of the Roman Church evolved slowly, in the course of many centuries, our modern musical notation. Thus, while we may say that Judaism was one of the pacemakers of our notation, we must add that its own markings remained in a somewhat primitive state. The illustration on page 959 shows the similarity of the so-called ekphonetic signs of the Greek Church compared to Hebrew scriptural accents.

THE CHURCH SINGS HEBREW TUNES

The musical interrelation between synagogue and church, while not entirely unknown, is still frequently overlooked or disregarded. Yet, it was through the church that Judaism made its lasting, its strongest and its most characteristic musical contribution. As a matter of fact, it is no exaggeration to state that about sixty per cent of the Gregorian chant, the authentic music of the Catholic Church, is of Jewish origin. Considering the tremendous authority of the Roman Church in all musical matters up to the eighteenth century, it is not difficult to appreciate the indirect Jewish legacy to the music of the Western world. Nor is this a recent discovery or claim; the attitude of the church on this question is quite unequivocal. The principle covering all ecclesiastical activities has been expressed in these terms: The Christian church is the sole legitimate heir of the synagogue both *de jure* and *de facto*. This statement, repeated innumerable times by the Church Fathers, explains why the church has always made open claim that both its liturgy and its music are of Hebrew origin.

Aside from theology, the outstanding musicologists all agree upon the close connection between early Christian and ancient synagogue music. Most outspoken are two great authorities on the Gregorian chant, Peter Wagner and Father Dechevrens, both priests. The latter goes so far as to maintain that "the Gregorian chant is the music of the Hebrews, and there is for the totality of the Roman Catholic melodies but one modal system, not that of the Greeks, but that of the sacred nation of the Hebrews."

FORMS OF CHURCH MUSIC

The central elements of the Christian liturgy, *viz.*, the Psalms, the Doxology, the Thrice Holy and the Lord's Prayer, all originate in the Hebrew language. With the exception of the Lord's Prayer, they form the core of synagogue liturgy to the present day. However, they were not used to the same extent in the service of the Temple.

Early Christianity, a movement of the poor and the meek, was born in the rural sections of the country, and opposed the rigid service and the hierarchy of the metropolitan Temple in Jerusalem. This was an institution

THE JEWISH CONTRIBUTION TO MUSIC 959

8–9th century

EARLY MEDI-EVAL GREEK	EKPHONETIC NAME	LATIN NEUMES	HEBREW NEGINOT IN THE ('ת'מ'א–BOOKS)
⌒	ὀξεῖα	Acutus (Virga)	Tifha
\	βαρεῖα	Gravis	Legarmeh
⅀	ὑπόκρισις	Quilisma descendens	Darga or Shalshelet
⌣	καθίστη	Circumflexa	Zarqa
∧	κρημαστὴ ἀπ' ἔξω	Flexa	Atnach
∼	συρματική = περισπωμένη	Circumflexa	Zarqa-silluq

Later development
11th–12th Centuries

EARLY MEDIEVAL GREEK	BYZANTINE	LATIN NEUMES	HEBREW NEGINOT ('ת'מ'א)
⌒	ὀξεῖα	Virga	Tifha or Yetib
—	ὀλίγον (ἴσον)	Virga iacens	—
∧	κρημαστή ἀπ' ἔξω	Flexa or clivis	Atnach
⌣	κρημαστή ἀπ' ἔξω	Podatus	Shofar or baby-lonian Tifha
✝	τέλεια	Punctus	Sof Pasuq

The most frequent combinations of accents at the close of sentences are:

I. ⌒ + ✝ = ⌒

II. ∼ + ✝ = ∼ (∧)

of the priestly aristocracy, whereas Christianity concentrated upon the ideology of the Kingdom of Heaven and did not recognize the rule of priestly dynasties. It was the forms of synagogue worship that presented the pattern for the liturgy of the young church. Hence the Christian hostility to instrumental music through the first eight centuries. For the Temple employed a large priestly orchestra and a trained choir, while the provincial synagogue had available only a lay cantor and no accompaniment, except congregational response.

Five forms of musical liturgy, all born of the Hebrew genius, constituted the worship of the synagogue and later became integral parts of the ecclesiastical service: Simple Psalmody, Response, Antiphone, Litany and Lesson.

The *simple psalmody* was the usual chanting of the Psalms by one precentor; here the congregation did not participate actively. The *response* divides one or several verses in halves, of which the first part is rendered by the cantor, the second by the congregation; *e.g.*:

CANTOR: Blessed be the name of the Lord;
CONGREGATION: Forever and ever.

Or:

CANTOR: Praise ye the Lord, to whom all praise is due;
CONGREGATION: Praised be the Lord, to whom all praise is due forever and ever.

The *antiphon* divides not only the verses, but also the performers into two groups; *e.g.*:

1st GROUP: O give thanks unto the Lord, for He is good.
2nd GROUP: For His mercy endureth forever.
1st GROUP: So let Israel now say:
2nd GROUP: For His mercy endureth forever.

In this special example the second group reiterates the same verse, which is not necessarily the general practice; this refrain-antiphon is a type closely related to the *litany*, in which the cantor chants a short stanza, and the entire congregation responds with one or two refrain verses; *e.g.*:

CANTOR: Give us thy protection; deliver us from danger; grant us joy and honor as the closing hour draws nigh.
CONGREGATION: O Lord, we stand in awe before thy deeds (or:) Help us, O Lord.
CANTOR: All their sins forgiving, show favor to thy chosen as the closing hour draws nigh.
CONGREGATION: O Lord, we stand in awe before thy deeds (or:) Help us, O Lord.

All these are poetic forms, inviting music, and therefore all Christian churches made full use of such structures. The reasons for retaining the cantillating rendition of the lesson, as practiced frequently in the Roman and regularly in the Greek Church, are less of a practical and more of a traditionalist nature. Here emphasis is laid upon the continuity with the spirit and expression of the Near East, the cradle of every church. Usually the cantillation as practiced in the church is more primitive than that of the synagogue. But there is one remarkable exception: In the Lamentations, which are chanted during Holy Week, Catholicism has preserved what is probably its oldest stratum of Jewish origin. The numbers of the verses are sung in Hebrew to this day, and the body of the verse is cantillated in a tune which has many a parallel in synagogue tradition. This mixture of psalmody and cantillation is a form characteristic of the most ancient and venerable portions of Catholic liturgy. In the examples on page 962, a few analogous cantillations and melodies are given, together with the tune of the Lamentations.

THE WORDLESS HYMN

Most of the Church Fathers, especially St. Augustine, considered the Hallelujah and its solemn rendition the pinnacle of ecclesiastical music. From earliest Christianity, the Hallelujah displayed a propensity toward disembodiment, that is, to being sung without the actual word "Hallelujah," even without its consonants. Such obviously mystic, ecstatic practice led first to the omission of the consonants, and later the vowels A E U I A were replaced by those of the doxology: E U O U A E-seculorum amen. This "wordless hymn" was called Jubilus and praised as the kind of glorification most appropriate to the Divine Being.

There are many indications that triumphant laudation of this manner, too, is of Jewish origin. The Talmud speaks most eloquently about the glorious chanting of the Hallel, of which the Hallelujah is the very epitome. Numerous passages compel us to infer that the wordless hymn was an ancient Jewish custom. During the Middle Ages a number of Rabbis raised their voices against wordless chanting, a practice they deemed cabbalistic and devious. In the sphere of Hasidism,[4a] however, the form of the wordless hymn achieved new and vigorous life. Among the Hasidim it was called Niggun, and many of these ecstatic, wordless tunes have come down to us. They were frequently composed by the Hasidic Saddikim (Saints) as means to attain the highest transport, hitpashtut hagashmiut, disembodiment. Innumerable are the tales in which, through the Saddik's musical intercession, fallen souls were purified, sick ones healed, and frenzied men soothed and led back to sanity. The famous

The Mode of Lamentations in the Roman Church

Lamentations I, 1.

A

A – – – leph quo-mo-do se-det so-la ci-vi-tas ple-na po-pu-lo:

fac - ta - est qua-si vi-dua do-mi-na Gen-ti-um.

Some Catholic and Jewish Chants in Comparison

Lamentations — Yemenite Jews, after Idelsohn

(1) Na-ha-mu, na-ha-mu 'a-mi, yo-mar esh-kol ko-fer, le-na-hem nimtzo ko-tub ba-se-fer.

Lamentations III, 1. — Gregorian (Naples version)

(1a) E - go vir vi-dens, pau-per-ta-tem me-am, in vir-ga indignatio - nis e-ius.

Tonus Peregrinus Ps. 114. — Gregorian

(2) In exitu Israel ex E-gyp-to, Domus Jacob de po-pu-lo bar-ba-ro.

Sephardic — after Consolo and Aguilar

(2a) Ka-ra-ti shim-cha A - do - nai mi bor tach - ti - yot.

Ps. 81, 1. — Yemenite Jews, after Idelsohn

(3) cf. with A

La - me-na-tze-ach al ha-gi - ttit, mi - ze-mor l' - A - saph.

Ps. 45, 2. — Gregorian

(3a) Eruc - tavit cor meum ver-bum bo-num, di-co e-go: lin-gua mea...ca-la-mus scribae.

Priestly Blessing. — Yemenite Jews, after Idelsohn

(4) cf. with A

Ye - vo - re - che - cho A - do - nai etc.

Invitatorium Sixti Toni (Ps. 95, 1-2) — Gregorian

(4a) Ve - ni - te exsultamus Do - mi - no, prae-oc-cu pamus.. fa-ciem e-ius. etc.

Barchu of the High Holidays. — Ashkenazic Jews

(5) etc.

Hymnus: Iste confessor. — Gregorian

(5a) I ste con - fess - or, Do - mi - ni co - leu - tes. etc.

Saddik Shneour Zalman indicated clearly his preference for wordless tunes, stating: "The songs of the soul . . . consist of tones only, dismantled of words."

Such conceptions of the ethical power of music, whose roots are as old as mankind itself, display a striking affinity to the musical philosophy of the Church Fathers. In the latter milieu, the rich synthesis of Hebrew and classic spirit tended toward Neoplatonism. In the Hasidic realm, the infiltration of mystic lore into traditional Judaism likewise created an atmosphere of esoteric speculation. These two philosophies of religion, although separated by a millennium, ran parallel in many respects.

MUSICAL PHILOSOPHY IN JERUSALEM AND ATHENS

All too often we forget that man not merely experiences emotions but insists upon contemplating them as well. Music, acclaimed as the most expressive of the arts, was early to become a favorite subject of these reflections. Now, some ideas on music were to a certain degree common to all peoples of the Near East. When we probe into the earliest history of these notions, we find that they originated in a magical conception of music. The art supposedly possesses powers which surmount the ordinary faculties of man. Countless legends of the magic of music show clearly the primeval functions of music. Such ideas are met with all over the world, and they found their way even into the guarded enclosure of biblical lore, as may be seen in various narrations, *e.g.*, in the stories of the battle of Jericho, David and Saul, Elisha before the king, and so on.

Greek philosophy sublimated the magic ideology and explained the powers of music in a more rational way. According to the Greek theories, each musical mode, each tune even, is endowed with a particular *ethos* of its own, expressing its character and, conversely, attuning the listener to its individual spirit. When this principle merged with certain Oriental ideas on the harmony of the spheres and the basically cosmic order of music, a grandiose, universal concept was established which influenced the entire theory of music up to the eighteenth century.

Some of the Church Fathers championed this Greek philosophy of music and added biblical, that is, Jewish elements to it. With Clement of Alexandria, of the late second century, this *ethos doctrine* assumed a very practical character. He ordered the devout and faithful Christians not to emulate, in their chants, the sensuous tunes of the voluptuous and decadent Greeks. Christians should praise God in a classical mode of ancient Greece which was, according to him, identical with the Hebrew mode of certain psalms. This *Tropos Spondeiakos*, for which Clement found most eloquent words of praise, has come down through the writings of Greek music theorists. Being identical with ancient Jewish tunes, it is almost the only concrete source from which we may draw reliable information on Jewish music in the time of Jesus and shortly afterward. Indeed, while investigating this mode, the writer found certain old Jewish parallels to the originally Greek melody. In the illustration on page 965, the mode, as we know it from Greek sources, is compared with some Hebrew chants. The similarity is obvious. Moreover, we can perceive how this mode made its way into the traditional and authentic music of the Roman and the Greek Catholic Church.

TRANSFUSION OF TUNES

In what way were Hebrew melodies carried over into the Christian cult? All sources tell us that the road over which the liturgical music traveled westward was paved by Judeo-Christians, the Apostles and their disciples. The bearers of the Jewish musical tradition in the Diaspora were the lay ministers and cantors of the great communities in Asia Minor and Greece. These men sympathized openly or secretly with the new Messianism of Christianity and, when they joined the new church, brought with them as gifts their old "hymns, psalms and spiritual songs," as St. Paul called them. In Palestine, the situation was somewhat different. There the Christian community consisted almost exclusively of Jews, and the transition from the old to the new ritual was a slow, gradual, organic process—going on for centuries—as we learn from the Acts of the Apostles, and Eusebius's *History of the Church*. Although the entire problem bristles with difficulties, it is possible to state that for the liturgical texts created before the eighth century more than half the corresponding tunes are of Jewish origin. The church borrowed from the synagogue up to the ninth century. Then the relationship gradually reversed itself and, at the time of the Renaissance and later, Jewry was heavily indebted to the church for many of its melodies. Nor was Jewry entirely unaware of the age-old interrelation of church and synagogue music. The famous Jewish poet, Immanuel of Rome, wrote: "What does the art of music say to the Christians? 'Indeed I was stolen out of the land of the Hebrews'" (Gen. 40:15).

JEWISH TUNES IN WESTERN MOLD

The first wave of the great Jewish migration westward broke on the shores of North Africa, Spain, southern France, and Italy. Soon two spiritual centers took shape in Spain and northern France. In these countries two forms of intellectual activity evolved, attracting like magnetic fields all neighboring communities until they included, respectively, a good deal of the Arab countries and the entire Rhineland.[5a] Each cultural

Tropos Spondeiakos

center developed a poetic and musical style of its own, in many respects differing from the other. Not only divergent physical and moral climates account for this bipartition of an originally uniform tradition. Various other factors contributed to the partition. What hitherto had been a whole—the music of Jewry in general—now began to break up into art and folk music. That this cleavage did not result in two completely different styles, as it did four centuries later in European music, was due to the unifying force of a new musical element.

This binding force was what we have come to call the technique of the "leading motif." Although the designation is borrowed from Richard Wagner's vocabulary, the practice was many centuries older, and was a remarkable contribution to European musical structure. The basic idea is to associate a particular holiday, or a particular text characteristic of this holiday, with a special tune or mode, which is used on no other occasion [*neima* or *lahan*]. This principle of leading motifs, assigned to special days or texts, evoked in the listeners clearly defined associations and emotions, even when the tune was detached from its original text or ritual environment. Thus, every Jew will immediately be reminded of the Day of Atonement when he hears the *Kol Nidre*, and, what is more, he will respond emotionally to this experience. The Christian, too, knows certain hymns which are reminiscent of particular occasions and produce corresponding sentiments. It can be proved that this practice of musical association, or leading motif, was borrowed from the medieval synagogue and has since pervaded the liturgies of all churches.

The same centuries (twelfth-fourteenth) also witnessed the opposite interaction, namely, the filtration of Spanish and German elements into Jewish tradition. This musical exchange resulted, especially in the Rhineland, in the creation of some of the most beautiful and noble Jewish melodies. A later generation, ignorant of their syncretistic origin, named these tunes *Missinai, i.e.,* brought from Mt. Sinai, in praise of their outstanding significance and value.

An example of each (on page 967) may illustrate these converse trends. First we have the leading motif, originating in Judaism, entrenching itself in the practice of the church. The opposite direction is shown in a Jewish melody of the same time, demonstrating the adoption of German and French elements.

The Sanctus is a rather late addition to the Gregorian chant and serves as a leading motif for a whole Mass of the Virgin. The *Tal Kaddish* of our illustration is broken up into its constituent parts, some of which have their roots in German folk song, others in the *chansons* of the *trouvères* in northern France. It should be noted that these foreign elements have undergone a considerable transformation, having been adapted to the basic Jewish background and admirably integrated into an organic unit.

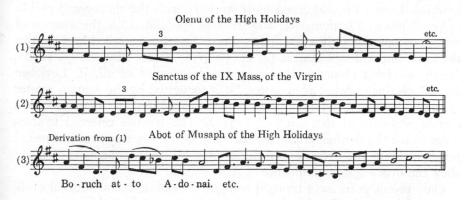

Olenu of the High Holidays

Sanctus of the IX Mass, of the Virgin

Derivation from (1) — Abot of Musaph of the High Holidays

Bo - ruch at - to   A - do - nai. etc.

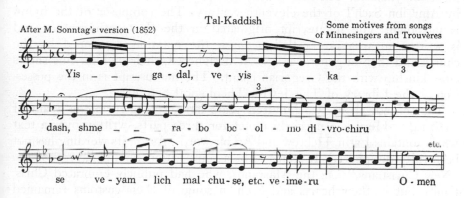

Tal-Kaddish

After M. Sonntag's version (1852)

Some motives from songs of Minnesingers and Trouvères

Yis _ _ _ ga - dal, ve - yis _ _ _ ka _

dash, shme _ _ ra - bo be - ol - mo di -vro-chiru

se   ve - yam - lich   mal - chu - se, etc. ve - ime - ru   O - men

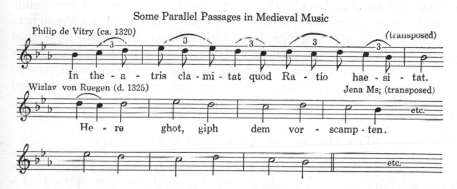

Some Parallel Passages in Medieval Music

Philip de Vitry (ca. 1320)   (transposed)

In the - a - tris cla - mi - tat quod Ra - tio   hae - si - tat.

Wizlav von Ruegen (d. 1325)   Jena Ms; (transposed)

He - re   ghot, giph   dem   vor - scamp - ten.

The Spanish-Arabic center was not quite so rich in fine melodists, but here intellectual life concerned itself strongly with the theory and philosophy of music. Of numerous writers who speculated on the essence of music, we mention only a few who seem to have been studied by Christian theorists: Shem Tob Falaqera (*c.* 1225-1295), Moses Abulafia (*c.* 1250), Isaiah ben Isaac (fourteenth century), and foremost of all, R. Levi ben Gerson (Ralbag), who, as he states, "was requested by the famous master of musical theory, Monseigneur Philippe de Vitry, to demonstrate a certain postulate of that science" (1342). The treatise referred to does indeed give the mathematical foundation of Vitry's new system of musical notation. With the exception of Gersonides, all Jewish theorists of music show the overwhelming influence of Arabic ideas.

Only recent years have brought to light the oldest extant musical documents of Judaism. The first is a hymn upon the death of Moses, a poem by Amr ibn Sach'l of the eleventh century. The composer of the hymn is unknown. The manuscript originated in the thirteenth century and is written in what are called *neumes*, the notation developed by the church and then in general usage. As deciphered, their melodic line shows close kinship with the Gregorian chant.[6] The manuscript is in the possession of the Library of The Jewish Theological Seminary.

The second, about two hundred years later, comes from the Spain of 1460-1480. Here is a masterly motet for three parts, written over a text which contains Latin, Hebrew and Arabic words. As yet its wording has not been fully deciphered. It seems to be a composition for the liturgy of the "New Christians," *i.e.*, the Marranos, who had publicly embraced Christianity but in their hearts and even in some of their customs remained devout and faithful Jews.[7a] The most remarkable feature of this manuscript is the juxtaposition of an ancient Jewish tune—which corresponds to the text (a *Kedusha*, Sanctification)—with a Gregorian hymn, set against the Hebrew tune. One is inclined to believe that the Marrano composer used the extremely enigmatic language as well as the Gregorian tune to camouflage the Jewish character of the piece before the eyes of the dreaded Inquisition.

THE DECLINE OF ANONYMOUS COLLECTIVITY

Approaching the dawn of the sixteenth century, we cannot fail to notice a gradual, but clearly discernible decline of general creativity in the Jewish world. Yet it cannot be said that, from the sixteenth century on, the number of Jewish thinkers or artists decreases or that their accomplishments do not measure up to those of previous generations. Actually, what was languishing was not the creative power itself, but its agency. While anonymous and collective expression of the Jewish group diminishes, individual contribution grows stronger. Judaism had, in the previous ages, conserved its creative vitality through its excellent faculty of transformation and active assimilation. Speaking of music, it had absorbed many elements of Gentile origin, but, capable of complete integration, it had assimilated them, as a plant assimilates air and light into its system. The spirit of the Renaissance, with its emphasis upon the individual, filled the intellectual air of Southern and Western Europe, and its Jewry was not untouched by it. On the contrary, where the opportunity arose, Jews responded powerfully and positively to the new conception of man and his intellectual freedom. Italy, fatherland of the Renaissance and of its frequent concomitant, political tolerance, offered the first opportunity for spontaneous creation by musicians of Jewish birth. The contributions of Judaism cease, those of Jews begin and accumulate. No wonder, then, that the fruits of this new era testify to the irresistible attraction of authors to the culture of their environments, and the gradual loss of Jewish cultural autonomy. Creative power of the individual still remains intact, but in its expression the traditional Jewish substance wanes and weakens.

JEWISH COMPOSERS IN NORTHERN ITALY AND VENICE

The dukes of Mantua and Ferrara, the dynasties of Gonzaga and Bardi, patronized contemporary composers more readily than did the equally music-minded, but conservative courts of the church. Moreover, in a number of cases, the Gonzagas demonstrated a tolerance with regard to Jews which surpassed by far the friendly indifference that was general among Italian nobility. Thus, we find at their court in Mantua a number of Jewish musicians with the high standard of ability demanded by their times. Some of them may be mentioned: Abramo d'all Arpa Ebreo (1525-1566); Isacchino Massarano (1560-1599); Davit da Civita, a composer of madrigals (about 1615), and Allegro Porto, likewise a composer of vocal pieces. The first Jewish composer to reach truly historic stature was Salomone Rossi il Ebreo (1565-1628). For more than forty years he served as court musician at Mantua, and the great number of his compositions demonstrates a prolific creativeness by no means common even in those times. Rossi's significance for the history of music has been clearly established by the great historian, Hugo Riemann, who says: "Rossi is one of the most important representatives of the *stile nuovo* [style of the late Renaissance] in the instrumental field; he was perhaps the first who cultivated the trio-sonata, and his way of treating this form has remained exemplary for a long time . . ."

Rossi was a descendant of an old aristocratic family which traced its ancestry back to King David. As a composer, he enjoyed a great reputation among his contemporaries. Monteverdi, then Italy's outstanding master, held him in such high esteem that he accepted him as collaborator in the writing of portions of the oratorio *Maddalena*. The fields of vocal and instrumental music were tilled by Rossi with equal diligence. He wrote chamber music, suites, madrigals, operatic pieces and music for the church and for the synagogue.

In the Jewish realm, he set a precedent by introducing into the synagogue, hitherto the jealously guarded court of archaic tradition, the style and the technique of his time. This meant four- to eight-part polyphonic choruses without accompaniment, full of the enchanting beauty of the late Palestrina style, and of the same admirably rounded form. It is understandable that soon a sharp reaction against so revolutionary an innovation arose, the more so since, fifty years before, orthodox Catholic circles had raised very similar objections against Palestrina's music. At that time the Council of Trent granted to Palestrina the needed artistic latitude. Now the famous Rabbi Yehuda Leon de Modena, in the company of certain other rabbis, went out of his way to sign an official opinion that there could not be a prohibition of choral art music in the synagogue.

Rabbi Leon de Modena deserves our attention in more than one respect. His incredible versatility—he admits that he succeeded in mastering more than thirty occupations—brought him into closer contact with the general spirit of his time than was heretofore considered befitting a rabbi. A well-trained musician, he founded the first artistic choir in synagogal history, a group of fine singers, named by him *Bezochrenu et Zion* (In Remembrance of Zion). The concerts of this choral society, which he conducted, attracted wide circles of the Venetian nobility.

Rabbi de Modena induced Rossi to write a set of thirty-three liturgical pieces for his synagogue, all of them choral compositions from three to eight parts. The music, though noble in style and beautiful in expression, shows but little trace of Jewish tradition. It deviates in no way from the then current idiom of the Venetian school.

Yet the chain of tradition was not completely broken in northern Italy. Strangely enough, it is other than a Jewish source which documents this fact. The interest in synagogue music displayed by Venetian noblemen in de Modena's time was a contributing factor in the appearance of a famous musical work eighty years later. The *Estro Armonico Poetico*, a collection of fifty psalm compositions for chorus and orchestra, became Benedetto Marcello's *magnum opus*. This talented Gentile composer included eleven melodies of Jewish tradition, quoted together with their original Hebrew texts. He made use of these tunes as *cantus firmi, i.e.,* as nuclei for his own compositions, intending thus to add a certain flavor of authenticity to them.

Intonazione degli Ebrei tedeschi
sopra
Maoz Tzur

From B. Marcello's
"Estro Poetico Armonico".
Two Hebrew Intonations

(1) Ma-oz Tzur ye-shu-a-ti le-cha na-eh le-sha-be-ach

le-et ta-chin mat-be _ _ ach mi-tzar haun-na-be _ _ ach,

as eg-mor be-shir miz-mor, cha-im-Kat ha-mis-be-ach.

Intonazione degli Ebrei Spagnuoli
sopra
Shaar Asher Nisgar

Sha _ _ _ ar a-sher _ _ nis-gar

Ku _ _ _ mah pit _ _ cha _ _ _

hu u-tzvi a-sher ba-rach e _ _ _ lay

shli-cha _ _ _ _ _ _ _ hu.

The first part of our illustration is an old German-Jewish tune of *Maoz Tzur* which displays a certain kinship to the Gregorian chant; but in this case it is wise to exercise utmost caution before assuming Jewish authorship, for here the synagogue seems to have borrowed from the church. The second part shows an old Sephardic song, which, in sharp contrast to the simple German march rhythm, has the intricate, rhythmical pattern usually found in classical Arabic music. Marcello indicated in all eleven cases whether the origin of the piece was Sephardic or Ashkenazic.

The *Maoz Tzur* quoted above is definitely older than the melody with which we are familiar today. Our familiar melody consists of three different German folk songs, the last of which was written around 1620.

In his preface to the *Estro*, Marcello gives a brief history of music in the Bible, expounding the manifold merits of Jewry in the field of musical endeavor. He concludes: "It seems to me most probable (which some Jews assiduously confirm) that the melodies quoted in this work lingered in the memories of the first Jews exiled from Palestine, and that they handed down these tunes by oral tradition to succeeding generations." We see here that Marcello included the traditional tunes for their authenticity and age, not for their beauty. This is the attitude of a scholar, rather than of an artist. In his scholastic concern for the music of the Bible, Marcello by no means stood alone. Since Reuchlin and Boeschenstein edited the first musical transcription of scriptural cantillation, the active interest of theologians had produced many an attempt at reconstructing the ancient, long-forgotten tunes and chords of the Temple.

CHRISTIAN THEOLOGY AND THE MUSIC OF THE BIBLE

A concomitant result of these studies was a revival of the dormant interest in Jewish customs, ritual and history. The masoretic accents of Scripture, as the hypothetical basis of synagogal chant, soon became a favorite topic of Christian scholars. Polyhistors like Bottrigari, Valdensis, Muenster, theologians like Athanasius Kircher, Vitringa, August Pfeiffer, musicologists like Burney, Forkel and the famous Gerbert, all struggled with the problem of scriptural accents, synagogal chant and the Temple music of old.

Their learned endeavors in the field of biblical music were closely watched by many contemporary composers. Time and again we meet the suggestion to reconstitute the music of the Protestant Church after the pattern of an imaginary Temple cult. These intentions frequently led to tortuous and not always unbiased arguments. Thus we need not be astounded to find titles of music collections like *Musae Sioniae, Hymnodia Sionia, Fontana d'Israel* (J. H. Schein, 1586-1630), etc.

Efforts of the scholars to bring the ancient music of Judaism into clear relief were matched by the accomplishments of composers, engaged in the gigantic work of interpreting Scripture in the musical idioms of *their* time. This mutual stimulation reached its glorious climax in the works of Johann Sebastian Bach, George Frederick Handel and a host of lesser, yet still shining luminaries of musical history.

While Judaism cannot claim a share in those extraordinary accomplishments, we should understand that it was the spirit of Hebrew literature as recovered by Protestant ardor that functioned as a catalytic agent, so to speak, between the forces of religion and those of music. Alas, this creative phenomenon was then—in the midst of the eighteenth century— totally remote from the Jewish people.

TWILIGHT BEFORE THE EMANCIPATION

During the decades preceding Emancipation, we notice signs of cultural and spiritual decline in all Jewries of Europe. Not a few Jews, attracted by the glamour of European civilization and eager to participate in it, were convinced that they would have to abandon their ethnic and religious identities before entering the larger world. This might explain why, of the few Jews connected with the history of music shortly before 1800, not one remained faithful to his religion. On the other hand, these individuals demonstrated by their remarkable understanding of all things musical that their original Jewish background, far from being an obstacle, actually deepened their appreciation of the intensive musical culture of their time.[8] We mention here only two converted Jews who made significant contributions to European music: Lorenzo da Ponte and Adolf B. Marx.

Da Ponte (1749-1838), the librettist of Mozart's *Marriage of Figaro*, *Don Giovanni* and *Così fan tutte*, was a Jew of Trieste who, early in life, adopted Christianity and became a priest—"Abbate," as he called himself. Not taking his ecclesiastical vows too seriously, he led the life of a Casanovalike adventurer. Nevertheless, he was a brilliant and, in some respects, an ingenious poet, who fully understood Mozart's genius; and he merits ample credit for the excellent dramatic structure of *Figaro* and *Don Giovanni*.[9]

Marx (1794-1866), son of a wealthy physician, friend of Felix Mendelssohn, founded the *Berliner Allgemeine Musikalische Zeitung*, and later was appointed professor of the history of music at the University of Berlin. He was one of the first representatives of modern musicology, a keenly logical student of musical theory and an outstanding teacher. His creative attempts, the oratorios *Moses* and *John the Baptist*, were failures. His chief merit lies in his clearly defined methodology and in his championship of the great contemporary composers.

These two personalities can be considered typical exponents of the centrifugal forces within Judaism, before the great wall collapsed, that wall which hitherto had separated the old people from its neighbors.

OUTSTANDING JEWISH COMPOSERS IN FIVE GENERATIONS

It is not the purpose of this study to present a complete list of Jewish musicians since 1800. (This must remain the thankless task of a special bibliography to be compiled by an apologete.) Since the musicians of Jewish birth cultivated the style and the forms determined by their environment, it is impossible to trace a consistent line of organic development in their works. Therefore it seems of doubtful value to apply the rigid method of musicology. The general import of these composers has been fully expounded in books on musical history and in monographs.

Instead of a long dull list or a strictly historical disquisition we shall present thumbnail sketches of eight of the most significant Jewish composers, representative of the five generations since Emancipation.

First Generation: Giacomo Meyerbeer (1791-1864)
Felix Mendelssohn-Bartholdy (1809-1847)

An anecdote in lieu of a preface: Abraham Mendelssohn, Moses Mendelssohn's son and Felix's father, was a prototype of the radical assimilationist whose only link with Judaism was forged by his generous philanthropy. Nonetheless, Felix's teacher, old Zelter, Goethe's friend, announced the forthcoming visit of his twelve-year-old pupil to the Olympian of Weimar with the jest: "Indeed, it would be 'some ting raire' [spelled in Yiddish slang *eppes Rores*] if a Jew's son would become an artist." Then he added wistfully, "It is true, he is a Jew's son but not a Jew."

Meyerbeer, son of Jacob Herz Beer, founder of the first Reform synagogue of Berlin, was essentially a showman of genuine dramatic instinct and explosive power. Yet, Richard Wagner, his flatterer to his face and most vicious critic under pseudonyms, was right when he stated that Meyerbeer's music seeks mere effect, and it is "effect without cause." On the other hand, the merits of Meyerbeer in the fields of orchestration and operatic style are undeniable. Often his melodies lack *noblesse*, and his style goes too eagerly after the current fashion. Still, in the history of opera he was a powerful influence to which even his violent critic, Wagner, was heavily indebted, as *Rienzi* and *Tannhaeuser* demonstrate most clearly.

In sharp contrast to the theatrical Meyerbeer, Mendelssohn represented the introvert and aristocratic type of artistry fostered by romanticism. His propensity toward retrospection led him to the study of the great masters of the baroque, chiefly Johann Sebastian Bach. He ardently championed the work of that greatest of all Protestant composers and conducted the first performance of his *St. Matthew's Passion* after the composer's death. By that signal action he started the revival of Bach's then almost forgotten art. In spite of his somewhat archaïc inclinations, Mendelssohn was a composer of distinct originality. The ingenious *Midsummer Night's Dream,* especially the overture written in his seventeenth year, the fiery *Violin Concerto,* his once tremendously popular *Songs without Words* display supreme mastership. No less famous are his oratorios, especially *Elijah* and *St. Paul.* The latter work may, with good reason, be considered his declaration of faith, glorifying the message of Christian universalism.

His fine organ compositions, cantatas and choruses are not so well known, perhaps because of a certain lack of genuine power conditioned by his aristocratic tendencies. Only German racial theorists were able to discover traces of Jewishness in his music. Although from the Jewish point of view such a demonstration would not be unwelcome, there is no real basis for such a thesis. As organizer and first director of the famous Leipzig conservatory, he established the most renowned musical academy of Central Europe. Teacher, organizer, reviver, creative composer, all his activities made him a truly venerable figure in German cultural history— up to 1933.

Second Generation: Jacques Offenbach (1819-1880)

Son of the meritorious cantor, Isaac Judah Eberscht of Cologne, Offenbach showed little if any interest in the musical legacy of his ancestors. He is not unjustly called the "father of the modern operetta." Actually this title reflects but one facet of his complex personality. He was essentially of a polar nature—demonic satirist as well as demonic tragedian. His masterpieces of musical satire, contemporary with and akin to the drawings of Daumier, hold up a merciless mirror to the corruption of the Second French Empire. To this category belong his sharp-witted *Orpheus in Hades, Beautiful Helen, The Duchess of Gerolstein* and many others. The tragic genre is represented only by his unforgettable *Tales of Hoffmann,* his last work. The mocking satirist shed a tear, and it became the fairest memory of him. A charming jester all his life, he showed the profound side of his music only shortly before death took the pen from his untiring hands. While most of his operettas have long since been forgotten, a few live on vigorously, and many of his catchy and witty melodies have lost nothing of their charm in eighty years.

Third Generation: Gustav Mahler (1860-1911)

None of the three composers mentioned thus far can be considered as an embodiment of Jewish ideas or ideals. This is certainly regrettable. The case of Mahler, however, borders on the tragic and must be understood as a woeful symptom of the inner disintegration of the Jewish community. This is so, not only because of the monumental stature of Mahler's genius, which towers far above that of all other Jewish composers, but chiefly because his real spiritual sources ran deeply in emotional and intellectual Jewish terrain.

In many respects he must be viewed as a living anachronism: a prophet burning with the ethical fanaticism of an Amos, a God-seeker of the ecstatic *Saddik* type. A sensitive spirit uttering the words "I shall die to live again for God," though unaware of the Psalmist's similar exclamation, a composer who mysteriously shows distinct kinship with Hasidic tunes,

Mahler, an embodiment of the noblest concepts of Judaism, was entirely estranged from his own people, his own faith!

And yet he felt something of the cleavage in the depths of his being. His ardent love for German folk song, which bore splendid fruit in his first four symphonies, did not fully satisfy his searching soul. He had to go back to medieval poetry (*veni creator spiritus*) and to the mysticism of the second part of Goethe's *Faust*. And in the end he sought and found the real source of his feelings in the poetry of the ancient Far East. In his farewell to life, the immortal *Song of the Earth*, he sings: "I will go home to my abode. No more of roaming far away. Still is my heart, awaiting now its hour."

His influence upon the following generations was extraordinary. Not even now (1946), thirty-five years after his death, can we really measure the full impact of his genius upon modern music. Suffice it to say that no contemporary composer of stature has been left wholly untouched by Mahler's style and technique.

Fourth Generation: Arnold Schoenberg (1874-   )
                           Ernest Bloch (1880-   )

Both of these composers, while vastly different from each other, bear the imprint of Mahler's influence. Schoenberg, the most controversial figure in modern music, shows the keenly logical and technical discipline of a true heir of Mahler, while Bloch represents the "voice crying in the wilderness" of modern musical business; he has not compromised with the concessions generally made to the purely ephemeral demands of the musical market. There is common ground between Bloch and Schoenberg. Both are primarily concerned with the autonomy of melody, and their techniques, despite differences, render harmony almost as a function and a development of melody. Both composers stand today in the forefront of contemporary music. Schoenberg's work began with the consistent disintegration of Wagner's Tristan style and led him to the borders of tonality and beyond them. He was probably the first "atonal" composer, a designation which Schoenberg himself justly abhors. It is interesting to state that this composer has recently found his way back to his people, as the works *Moses* and *Kol Nidre* demonstrate.

Bloch was early attracted by Jewish conceptions: his cello rhapsody *Shelomo* (1912), his great Sabbath liturgy for the synagogue, his inspired *Baal-Shem* suite, his symphony *Israel*, all bear proud witness to Bloch's love of Judaism. He was the first musician of real stature, after the Emancipation, publicly and unmistakably to identify himself with Israel's cause.

Fifth Generation: Darius Milhaud (1891-   )
                          George Gershwin (1898-1937)

The social and musical background of these two composers, even their geographic preconditioning, could not be more completely antithetic. Milhaud is the product of the complex, refined and sometimes decadent tradition of western Europe, Gershwin, the son of plain eastern Jewish immigrants. And yet, in one respect, they are alike: in their love for the folk song of the common man. Both composers erected monuments to the musical lore of their native countries: Milhaud in his numerous Provençal pieces, Gershwin in his *Porgy and Bess*, glorifying Negro lore of the deep South. It was Gershwin's merit to span the gulf between "classical" and "popular" music. By incorporating jazz elements into serious music and by introducing the "classical" technique into popular and dance music, he enriched both realms. Alas, his early death interrupted a promising development; and in the absence of a legitimate heir, the gulf between serious and popular music is widening again. Yet Gershwin's masterpiece, his *Porgy and Bess*, the first truly American opera, will live on as long as America loves her own songs.

Milhaud, the descendant of an old Avignon family, entered on his career soon after the First World War as a strong anti-Wagnerian. A member of the "Group of Six," in the early twenties, he assiduously followed its motto: "Return to simplicity." Later, to his own advantage, he left that narrow path. Moreover, he has become increasingly conscious of his Jewish musical heritage. He has written articles on Jewish folk song, and, what is more, his artistic work has been greatly enriched by this interest. His *Zions-Hymn*, his exultant psalms, his magnificent *Israel Lives* and many other compositions put him in the first line of living composers. That the three greatest living composers of Jewish birth are paying heed and homage to their people's musical tradition is a gratifying sign of the trend of our times.

Thus, lightly etched, we behold the eight most significant Jewish composers since the Emancipation. To say that their importance cannot equal that of a Bach or a Mozart is no indictment or disparagement of their accomplishments. We need only stop for a moment to remember that for fifteen hundred years the Jewish people was excluded from the general growth of music. Nonetheless, this small minority was able in the course of a hundred and fifty years to produce a score of outstanding musicians whose efforts well-nigh reach the highest attainments of creative genius.

On the other hand, not all Jewish composers have wrestled with the highest ideals. The history of popular music, of the operetta, of the "hit song," is replete with Jewish names. It depends upon the reader's system of values as to whether or not he considers this a matter of pride. Musical art may not have experienced any serious advance through their efforts; yet these composers have certainly brought many joyous hours to millions.

Since Offenbach, literally hundreds of operetta composers have flooded the markets of America and Europe with their products. We mention only a few names of that numerous host: Oscar Straus, (1870-   ), E. Kalman (1884-   ), L. Fall (1873-1925), L. Ascher (1880-1942), Sigmund Romberg (1887-   ), Jerome Kern (1885-1946), Irving Berlin (1888-   ). These are genuine talents, and each of them is being imitated and "emulated" by scores of followers. The fashions of popular music change often and unexpectedly. Yet, this kind of composition follows paths of its own, and what was good business yesterday may be a loss tomorrow. Thus, purely commercial music had a course of its own, somewhat removed from the principal thoroughfares of the realm of serious music.

Interpretive Musicians

Even more numerous and at least as well known as the composers are the names of Jewish interpretive musicians. A few outstanding intrumentalists might well be mentioned, for in many cases they have enriched the musical life of entire generations and countries. We list here only those outstanding artists who have influenced the whole course of their art.

Conductors: Ferdinand von Hiller (1811-1885), intimate friend of Felix Mendelssohn, highly meritorious conductor in western Germany, gifted composer and writer. It is interesting to note that this convert had to find an outlet for his Old Testament nostalgia in his oratorios, though none of them attained lasting success.

Hermann Levi (1839-1900), the famous champion of Richard Wagner's work. He was the first conductor of *Parsifal* (!), presumably the reward for his unswerving loyalty to Wagner, in spite of the master's anti-Semitic writings and opinions.

Gustav Mahler (1860-1911), the famous composer. Here it must suffice to note that he was the first representative of a type of conducting since his day frequently imitated. He was an obsessed, demonic idealist, often given to despotic fanaticism. To be sure, he was not an endearing conductor, but proved nonetheless, an ingenious and altogether faithful interpreter of the composer's intentions.

Leo Blech (1871-   ), general music director of the Berlin State Opera, the prototype of fine craftsmanship and reliable solidity.

Bruno Walter (1876-   ), inspiring champion of Bach, Mozart and of the works of his mentor and teacher, Gustav Mahler.

Arthur Bodanzky (1877-1939), disciple of Mahler, conductor at the Metropolitan Opera, a fascinating conductor of fiery temperament.

Fritz Reiner (1888-   ), at present director of the Pittsburgh Symphony; another of the Mahler heirs.

Otto Klemperer (1885-   ), revolutionary director of the Kroll-opera, Berlin; at his best as opera conductor; protagonist of contemporary music.

Eugene Ormandy (1899-   ), director of the Philadelphia Symphony;

a conservative interpreter of a slightly didactic, but intelligent and inspiring nature.

Leonard Bernstein (1914-   ), the youngest in the galaxy of prominent conductors; as a composer displaying creative interest in Jewish matters; for example, his symphony, *Jeremiah*.

Most of these conductors come from Central or Western Europe. When we turn to violinists and pianists, virtuosi of the concert stage, we find the overwhelming majority to be of Eastern Jewish origin. One reason for this seems to lie in the fact that the tradition of Jewish fiddlers (*klezmorim*) in the Eastern countries was still alive in the middle of the nineteenth century, whereas it was completely forgotten and obsolete in Central and Western Europe. These fiddlers functioned as dance bands, and as teachers, furnishing the cultural life of East European Jewry with a strongly artistic element.

Violinists

Most of the outstanding violinists of the past hundred years were directly or indirectly disciples of the two superb teachers of violinistic style: Joseph Joachim (1831-1907), the intimate friend of Brahms, eminent artist and teacher, finally director of the States Academy of Music of Berlin; and Leopold von Auer (1845-1925), the unforgettable master who transplanted the best European tradition to America. Of renowned violinists there are only three who developed outside the orbit of these two great pedagogues: Arnold Rosé (1863-   ), concertmaster of the Vienna State Opera, and primarius of a famous string quartet; Fritz Kreisler (1875-   ), the well known interpreter of the works of the classics. His antagonistic, or at best indifferent, attitude toward contemporary music stands in sharp contrast to the style of the third of this group, Joseph Szigeti (1892-   ), the versatile advocate of modern literature for the violin. Bronislaw Huberman (1882-1947), most inspiring and noble interpreter of serious music, a virtuoso of first magnitude, but ruthless enemy of virtuosity for its own sake, was a *rara avis* among violinists. He had, moreover, the great merit of having founded the Palestine Orchestra at the time Hitler ousted the Jewish members of German orchestras. Huberman defended, proudly and unyieldingly, the honor of Jewish musicians in a revealing correspondence with Wilhelm Furtwaengler, then director of the Berlin Philharmonic Orchestra. As an artist he belongs in the Joachim orbit.

Of Auer's disciples we mention here Mischa Elman (1891-   ) and Jascha Heifetz (1899-   ), the great virtuosi; Yehudi Menuhin (1917-   ), one of the youngest among the eminent violinists, may be considered a spiritual grandchild of Auer, since his training lay in the hands of Auer adepts.

Pianists

The briefest list of pianistic artists reflects the countless facets of the development of European style. Paraphrasing a Latin bon mot: *Quot digiti tot styli!* Beginning with Ignace Moscheles (1794-1870), the elegant friend and epigone of Mendelssohn, there is not one field of piano playing where men of Jewish extraction have not carved out their more or less significant niches. Joseph Fischhoff (1804-1857) and Stephen Heller (1814-1888) belong to the adherents of the Schumann-Chopin romantic school. Anton Rubinstein (1829-1894), friend and champion of Liszt and Wagner, seems to have been of a nature not unlike Mahler's, though scarcely of his depth. Theodor Leschetitzky (1830-1915), master teacher, and Leopold Godowski (1870-1931), both had a flair for virtuoso style, occasionally neglecting the more rigid demands of classic diction. Moritz Moszkowski (1854-1925), a fine pianist and composer of charming miniatures, and Moritz Rosenthal (1862-) are both exponents of late romanticism. So was Ignace Friedman (1882-1947), the great interpreter and editor of Chopin's work, one of the noblest artists of our time. In certain contrast to these neoromanticists stands the figure of Arthur Schnabel (1882-), stanch champion of Mozart, Beethoven and Schubert, at the same time a radical modern composer. To the same ultraclassic category belongs Rudolf Serkin. A remarkable attempt at synthesizing the virtuoso style of the Liszt school with the more severe idiom of the classicists is undertaken by the ingenious and brilliant Vladimir Horowitz (1904-). Modern and ultramodern music has found its faithful and subtle interpreter in Eduard Steuerman (1901-).

As for vocalists, their number is legion. We will not even begin to list them, for in a very real sense the evaluation of singers is largely a matter of personal taste. Nor did singers contribute independently to music's development, being more often the instruments of composers and conductors than autonomous interpreters. Of some significance were the singers of the stage; their story belongs rather to the history of the theater than to that of music.

The Science of Musicology and Its Jewish Students

In antiquity and the Middle Ages music was considered more as a science than an art, and its study was part of the *quadrivium educationis*, together with algebra, geometry and astronomy. This connection with the astronomic-mathematical branch of natural science came to an end when humanism and the Renaissance proclaimed the freedom of the individual and his scientific research. The forms of the opera and of the oratorio, with their emphasis upon spontaneous emotions of the individual, stressed the purely *artistic* side and disregarded the scientific approach of musical endeavors. The ensuing centuries and their characteristic ideologies raised this emotional attitude (at least, where secular music was concerned) to an almost antiscientific individualism. On the other hand, it was emotional romanticism, with its archaic tendencies, that gave new impetus to musical science. The history of music was given a solid standing in the academic curricula of Germany, Austria and, later, of France and England. Mendelssohn and his school consistently cultivated the music of past centuries, especially of the baroque period. Thus, it was hardly a coincidence that Mendelssohn placed A. B. Marx as the first professor of musical history at the University of Berlin. Marx was the forerunner of a group of distinguished musicologists, of whom not a few were of Jewish birth. Bypassing Eduard Hanslick, (son of a Christian and a Jew) Richard Wagner's deadly adversary, the name of Guido Adler (1855-1942) and his Vienna school will for all time be linked with the establishment of musicology based upon sound historic-philological methods. This venerable Nestor of musical science had trained a host of younger scholars, of whom E. Wellesz is of outstanding significance. The Berlin school, meanwhile, had produced such able students as the late O. Abraham, one of the founders of comparative musicology, and Curt Sachs, now of New York University, the greatest authority on musical instruments and their history and at the same time a foremost scholar in the field of the music of antiquity. A specialist in Asiatic music was the late Robert Lachmann, who also published some studies on the music of Oriental Jews. The universalistic tradition of the Riemann school is upheld by so profound a scholar as Alfred Einstein, now at Smith College. We should add here the pioneers of the science of Jewish music, Eduard Birnbaum (1855-1920) and Abraham Z. Idelsohn (1882-1938) who, while in every respect universal scholars, applied the methods of general musicology to the particular problems of the music of Judaism and synagogal tradition. They set an inspiring example for the Jewish musicologists of today.

Epilogue

> "History is change."
> (J. Burckhardt)

A critical evaluation of the Jewish contribution to world music must, of necessity, expound its results in retrospective terms. Nor is it the historian's task to prophesy, however wide the vistas he has opened. The present moment, however, still belongs to the historian; and from this narrow point between past and future we may venture to estimate accomplishments yet to come. We may expect significant attainments in music only where a valuable musical tradition is already in existence. Thus, Jewish contributions may be looked for in Russia, America, perhaps in

Western Europe and Palestine. Individual creations of Russian or French Jews will be acclaimed—and claimed—by their native countries, and the Jewishness of the composers will be of little, if any, significance. Not quite so simple is the American situation, where composers of international stature have drawn originality and power from the eternal sources of their Jewish tradition. Nevertheless, they will remain exceptions rather than become the rule.

Palestine, on the other hand, has no art-music tradition of long standing; but it is building one speedily and, once this prerequisite of musical culture is fulfilled, we may expect significant contributions. Vigorous Jewish life in the Holy Land has already generated a remarkable musical folklore. Art music takes longer than the fifty years Hebrew folk song has had for its new life; a certain intellectual and spiritual homogeneity is likewise required. When this standard will be reached Palestinian compositions will be considered, rightly or wrongly, as the typical output of the Jewish spirit, as an accomplishment characteristic of Judaism, rather than of the personal style of its particular composer. This, then, may become the beginning of a chapter yet unwritten: the role not of Jews, but of Judaism in modern music.

NOTES

[1] *Keilinschriftliches Textbuch zum Alten Testament,* 3rd ed., Leipzig, 1909, p. 45.

[1a] Cf. above the chapter by Elias J. Bickerman, "The Historical Foundations of Postbiblical Judaism."]

[2a] Cf. Judah Goldin, "The Period of the Talmud," pp. 186, 200-201.]

[3a] Cf. above Robert Gordis, "The Bible as a Cultural Monument," pp. 459-460.]

[4a] Cf. above Yudel Mark, "Yiddish Literature," pp. 868-869.]

[5a] Cf. above Cecil Roth, "The European Age in Jewish History (to 1648)," *passim.*]

[6] This oldest document of Hebrew music has been recorded according to the transcription of the writer and its first public rendition is part of the record-album, "Israel Sings," available at the Union of American Hebrew Congregations.

[7a] Cf. Roth, *op. cit.,* pp. 236 f.]

[8] This was especially the case of the *Hazanim*: composers and singers with the ability of a Wolf Bass, Leon Singer (Leoni), A. Beer, etc., absorbed and integrated the musical style of their time.

[9] Da Ponte spent the last thirty years of his life, a miserable pauper, in this country; his American activities deserve new treatment in the light of late research. (Krebiehl's meritorious study of that subject ought to be revised and enlarged.)

Select Bibliography

This is not a complete bibliography; such an undertaking would easily fill a large volume. Only such works are mentioned here as are based upon original research and contain numerous bibliographical notes.

Friedmann, Aron, *Lebensbilder beruehmter Kantoren*. Berlin, 1921-1927.

Hoeeg, Carsten, "La notation ekphonétique," in *Monumenta Musicae Byzantinae*. Copenhagen, 1935.

Idelsohn, Abraham Z., *Jewish Music in Its Historical Development*. New York, 1929.

———, *Thesaurus of Oriental-Hebrew Melodies*. 10 vols. New York and Berlin, 1921-1933.

The Jewish Encyclopedia, New York and London, 1901. Articles on Jewish Music, Accents, Psalms, etc.

Sachs, Curt, *The Rise of Music in the Ancient World, East and West*. New York, 1943.

Saleski, Gdal, *Famous Musicians of a Wandering Race*. New York, 1927.

Schonberg, Jakob, *Die traditionellen Gesaenge des israelitischen Gottesdienstes in Deutschland*. Nuernberg, 1926.

Wagner, Peter, *Einfuehrung in die Gregorianischen Melodien*. Leipzig, 1921, Vol. III.

Werner, Eric, and Sonne, Isaiah, "The Philosophy and Theory of Music in Judaeo-Arabic Literature," in the *Hebrew Union College Annual*, XVI, 251-319. Cincinnati, 1941.

Werner, Eric, "Preliminary Notes for a Comparative Study of Catholic and Jewish Musical Punctuation," in the *Hebrew Union College Annual*, XV, 335-367.

———, "Manuscripts of Jewish Music in the Edward Birnbaum Collection," in the *Hebrew Union College Annual*, XVIII, 397-429.

———, "Prolegomena to a Bibliography of Jewish Music," in *Historia Judaica*, pp. 175-188. New York, 1944.

Zunser, Elyokum, *A Jewish Bard* (Autobiography), edited by A. H. Fromenson. New York, 1905.

CHAPTER 24

JUDAISM AND ART

By Rachel Wischnitzer

In contrast to the general conception of gods in antiquity, Israel saw in the Deity not simply one aspect of nature in preference to others, or an incorporation of a number of gods. The God of Israel transcended the world scene. He was the cause of events in nature and in history. And, being invisible, He could not be identified with any form in "heaven, earth or sea."

The attribute of invisibility was thus fundamental to the Jewish conception of God. To identify Him with any material form whatever would be to confuse the Creator with His creature.

Graven and molten images are usually associated in the Bible with idol worship; but it is quite conceivable that attempts were occasionally made by some dissidents to fashion images of the God of Israel, too. Therefore, the invisibility of God had to be stressed over and over again. When Deuteronomy recalls the circumstances of the Revelation it repeatedly insists that "Ye heard the voice of words, but ye saw no form; only a voice" (4:12). "For ye saw no manner of form on the day that the Lord spoke unto you in Horeb out of the midst of the fire" (4:15).

It is from the imagery of Creation that the Second Commandment (Ex. 20:3-4) drew its vocabulary. Nothing of the created, visible world can possibly represent God, and since "likenesses" of the visible world actually are worshiped in various cults as manifestations of God, they are particularly distasteful.[1]

The Second Commandment in the Book of Exodus reappears in chapter five of Deuteronomy without changes. In chapter four, however, the issue of image making and idol worshiping is taken up more specifically, and there the principal concern of the Lawgiver appears to be over figures "male or female" (Deut. 4:16), not "heaven, earth and sea" and "what is in them." William F. Albright[2] has suggested that the Lawgiver, in pointing to figures, wished to denounce the infamous bloody rites associated with the Canaanite god Baal and the goddess Ashthoreth. The sun was proclaimed the principle of life in Egypt; sex was the principle of life adored in the Asiatic cults. The statues of the human-bodied gods in wood and stone cast a magic spell upon the soul of the people and this spell had to be broken at all cost. Hence again and again it is pointed out that these statues can neither see nor listen to the worshiper, for they are only the works of human hands (Deut. 4:28).

Next the Lawgiver enumerates the animals, birds, snakes and fish (4:17-18). Significantly last come the celestial spheres. The sun, moon, stars and the host of heaven are individually mentioned, the astral cults strictly forbidden. But there is no reference to images associated with the astral cults. The astral cults consisted chiefly in stargazing and incense burning on altars raised on roofs. What was prohibited was "lifting up thine eyes unto heaven" (Deut. 4:19) for purposes of adoration, a practice obviously less offensive than the sanguinary ritual connected with some image cults. The motivation for the prohibition of astral cults reveals the new attitude clearly. Ikhnaton had conceded the celestial Nile as a common possession to all mankind, but the two other Niles, the actual river and the subterranean stream on which the sun was supposed to travel by night back to the east, he reserved as the exclusive property of the Egyptian Empire. But the Lawgiver tells us that the celestial bodies were "divided" by the Lord "unto all nations under the whole heaven" (4:19) and do not belong to the religious sphere of any particular nation.

The attitude of Judaism toward the arts was also affected by the changing function of the arts themselves.

The symbolic significance of an image is not an inherent quality of the image. If in the eighth century B.C.E. ivory plaques with portrayals of Egyptian deities—Horus, Re, Isis, Nephtys—and various symbols were used in Samaria as inlays in furniture, we can be sure that the owners of such furniture did not bother about the significance of the ivory carvings. The few panels that have survived the destruction of Samaria and have been excavated appear to be Phoenician ware. The Phoenician carvers who copied Egyptian models probably did have a vague idea of the subjects depicted, but the Israelite customers in Samaria hardly knew what or whom the small inlay figures were meant to represent.[3] It is interesting to note that the Prophet Amos, when denouncing the upper classes of Samaria for reclining on "beds of ivory" (3:15; 4:4), probably aimed at idleness and luxury rather than the impropriety of the Egyptian figure decoration of the couches. He does not even mention the carvings.

With this in mind, we can better comprehend the cultural background of King Solomon's time (second part of the tenth century B.C.E.) and more easily evaluate the significance of the decoration of the royal palace and the Temple of Jerusalem built by the King.[3a]

The ivory throne in the palace hall was overlaid with gold and flanked by lion statues (I Kings 10:18-20). Lion figures standing guard at a palace gate or a throne were no objects of worship in the Near East; rather they were intended to exalt the authority of the ruler. The winged cherubim in the Holy of Holies of the Temple, carved in wood and paneled with gold (I Kings 6:23 ff.; II Chron. 3:10), were placed on top of the Ark as its crowning part (I Kings 8:6 f.). There is no indication that these cherubim were regarded as cult objects. The interior walls of the main hall of the Temple, the Sanctuary, were decorated with a relief of alternating cherubim, palm trees and open flowers (I Kings 6:29; II Chron. 3:7). There is no suggestion in the Bible that these wall reliefs were associated with any ritual.

Edward B. Tylor has pointed out that the motif of cherubim flanking a palm tree in the Solomonic Temple was derived from Assyrian art, where the palm tree is found flanked by winged human or animal figures.[4] The design is familiar from the ancient Assyrian seals and later wall reliefs in royal palaces in Nineveh. Tylor has been able to interpret the scene. The winged male figures on either side of the tree, carrying a basket and what was supposed to be a fir cone, actually are pollinating the date palm. The fertilization of the date tree in the Near East was described by Herodotus, Theophrastus and Pliny the Elder in his *Natural History*. The Assyrians apparently saw in the achievement of their palm growers an evidence of the assistance of supernatural forces and therefore represented the gardeners as fantastic beings, winged, eagle-headed men, griffins or winged horses. The palm tree became converted into a ceremonial object, a kind of standard set with palmettes or palm-leaf clusters, a symbol of the Tree of Life. Behind the picture there may have been the idea of an actual liturgical performance.

We must determine just what was the relationship of the cherub-palm motif of I Kings 6:29 to the Assyrian ceremonial scene. Since we know that the Temple was built with the help of Tyrian artisans, we have to take into account Phoenician influences in the elaboration of the motif. In Phoenician art the Assyrian "gardeners," who are treated as winged sphinxes, appear in most conventionalized postures, while the tree is simplified and considerably reduced in its form—so much so that it seems rather doubtful that the subject meant the same there as in the original conception. The Phoenician limestone seal from Megiddo[5] may give us an idea of what the design of the cherub-palm tree decoration was like in the Temple at Jerusalem. Since the eatable date fruit is not frequently mentioned in the Bible, we are probably not wrong in assuming that the original meaning of the motif had been lost.[6]

Not before talmudic times do we find reference to the motif of the cultivation of the date palm, that is, to its artificial fertilization. Max Gruenbaum[7] cites Pesahim 56a and records the romantic story of the barren palm tree in Chamtan, wistfully "looking" toward Jericho, which was known from biblical times as the palm city (Deut. 34:3; II Chron. 28:15). A palm grower, the story goes, advises the people how to make the tree bear fruit. Josephus (*Bell. Jud.* IV:8:3) mentions a syrup of a palm fruit, apparently dates, produced in Jericho. The question is, however, was the date a popular foodstuff in biblical times in Palestine? Even more important, what role did fertilization of the date tree play in popular imagination in biblical times? It seems that the poet's mind was inspired by the general symbolism of a tree, its growth, its blossoming, its fruitfulness and beauty, rather than by any specific aspect of its cultivation.

The national tree was the olive. It is this tree which the prophet Zechariah uses as a political metaphor in his fifth vision. The king, Zerubbabel, and the High Priest, Joshua, who are expected to establish firmly the new commonwealth after the return of the exiles in 519 B.C.E., are seen as two olive trees flanking a seven-branched candlestick and furnishing it with oil (4:3 ff.). Here the original Oriental conception underlying the picture can easily be recognized, but the olive substitutes for the date palm.

It is the olive tree again which is used as a metaphor in Psalm 52:8, where the righteous is compared with a "leafy olive-tree in the house of God." In Psalm 92:12 the righteous is promised that he shall "flourish like the palm tree" and the cedar. The reference to the Temple is repeated: Those "planted in the house of the Lord . . . shall flourish in the courts of our God. They shall still bring forth fruit in old age" (vss. 13, 14).

The metaphors used in the Psalms show that the tree had become the symbol of the godly. The cult of the reproductive capacities of mother nature, practiced in Assyria, has been sublimated in Palestine into a figure of speech serving to exalt the faithful. The palm tree flanked by cherubim on the reliefs of the Temple at Jerusalem represents one of the stages in this process of spiritualization; perhaps it is the direct prototype for the literary figure.

H. T. Obbink, the Utrecht scholar,[8] has similarly attempted to explain the purpose of the "golden calves" of Jeroboam. Contrary to the palm-and-cherub reliefs in the Temple, the golden calves erected in the sanctuaries of Beth-el and Dan are expressly said to have been intended as cult objects. Jeroboam, when proclaimed king of the seceded Northern Kingdom after Solomon's death, promptly restored the two ancient sanctuaries in order to prevent pilgrimage to Jerusalem (I Kings 12:26, 27) and gave each sanctuary a golden calf. Suspecting a disparaging tendency on the part of the Judean recorder toward the schismatic king, Obbink doubts that the bulls were actually intended as cult statues. He believes rather that they were meant as supports for the invisible YHWH comparable to the cherubim of the Temple at Jerusalem. For prototypes he points to Near Eastern bull statues used as pedestals for deities.

We know statues of the Sumerian-Acadian Anu and the ancient Semitic god Hadad were represented standing or walking on animals. Hittite deities are found standing on pedestals set on the back of a lion or a bull.

But would a wingless animal of the pedestal type be likely to suggest to the worshiper the invisible presence of God and thus be comparable in its effect to the cherubim of the Temple at Jerusalem? The cherubim set up on the top of the Ark were regarded as flying creatures of the heavenly region, rather than as supports set up on the ground. God communed with Moses "from between the two cherubim" (Ex. 25:22). He "sitteth between the cherubim" (Ps. 99:1). The conception of an uplifted position, a raised throne, seems to be fundamental to the image of the cherubim. It is this idea of an exalted position which inspired the comparison of Tyre, before its fall, with a cherub (Ez. 28:14, 16).

If, then, Jeroboam wished to imitate the cult of Jerusalem he would not have chosen as a model the wingless pedestal type of bull. The suggestion of the Divine Presence produced by a pair of cherubim was hardly possible with a wingless bull. There is, however, a different category of bulls, which fits better into the picture: it is the winged bull of Assyrian art, which can be visualized as a flying creature although it stands on the ground. But George Ernest Wright has pointed out that those huge Assyrian bulls are practically nonexistent in Palestine and Syria.[9]

Assyrian art became an influence in Jewish imagery much later, when the Jews were brought into direct contact with Mesopotamian civilization. It was noticeable in Zechariah's vision and, earlier, in Ezekiel's vocabulary. "By the river of Chebar" in Babylonia, Ezekiel had his vision which carried him back to Jerusalem into the Temple. The Lord appears to the prophet on a "seat" (Ez. 1:1 ff.) placed above four creatures which resemble the cherubim in their function, but possess distinct features of their own. Although winged, these creatures are also wheeled and thus suggest a chariot which can be driven on the ground. The "chariot" actually goes down and up in the interior of the Temple.

While the appearance of the Temple cherubim is not described in the Bible (we can imagine them either as winged sphinxes of Phoenician art, or as winged ethereal angel-like figures of Egyptian divinities, of which a Phoenician version is seen in the ivories of Samaria)[10] Ezekiel's "living creatures" are elaborately described as hybrid figures combining characteristics of a man, a lion, a bull and an eagle. The mystical quaternion implies that Ezekiel had speculated on the meaning of the colossi set up at the gates, and actually carrying the arches of the portals of Assyrian palaces. Assyria at that time was no longer a foe, but a comrade in misfortune, for she had been conquered by the Babylonians a decade before. The composite animals combining the body of a lion and a bull with the head of a man and the wings of an eagle appeared to Ezekiel as similar to the cherubim of the Temple, and the qualities symbolized by the four creatures, the strength of the lion, the virility of the bull, the swiftness of the eagle and the intelligence of man, seemed to offer a key to the comprehension of the mystical nature of the cherubim.

Flying and moving on the ground, Ezekiel's creatures are a blending of two conceptions. The seat of the Lord of Ezekiel's vision is an uplifted throne and at the same time a chariot, a *Merkabah* riding on the floor of the Temple.

The personifications of the four ideal qualities survive in a somewhat modified form in the well-known saying in *Pirke Abot* (V:20): "Be fierce as the leopard, swift as the eagle, fleet as the deer and strong as the lion to perform the will of thy Father in heaven." Originally symbolizing the qualities of faithful doormen guarding royal palaces, the Assyrian animals became converted in Ezekiel's vision into drivers of the Lord's throne-chariot and finally symbols of the pious Jew. The process of spiritualization is strikingly similar to what we observed in the development of the date tree motif.

What do these shiftings in symbolism mean in terms of Jewish art?

On a fragment of a Jewish marble sarcophagus from Rome (in the Berlin Museum)[11] we see a seven-branched candlestick flanked by palm-trees and liturgical symbols, the *etrog*, the *lulab* and some dishes. Ernst Cohn-Wiener, who dated the sarcophagus in the second century c.e., associated it with Zechariah's vision of the leaders of the Restoration. The interpretation is tempting and might be correct in a general sense. However, there are more than two trees flanking the Menorah on the relief, and if we set the date in the late third or fourth century c.e., which is more plausible, a vaguely Messianic interpretation will appear more proper. The *etrog* and *lulab* may allude to a Messianic Feast of Tabernacles in which the pious hopes to have his part.

In a sarcophagus found in a Jewish catacomb on the site of the Villa Torlonia[12] in Rome, the palm-tree motif is abandoned; the Menorah stands alone in the center, flanked by the symbols of Tabernacles. These symbols remain the permanent companions of the candelabrum in Jewish art.

The four animals of *Pirke Abot* became extremely popular in Jewish art. We know them chiefly from the folk art of the eighteenth and nineteenth centuries; they are common in the carved or painted decoration of Torah shrines and *almemars* in Poland, and appear printed on paper flags which children used to carry in the synagogue processions on Simhat Torah. In Germany they were frequently embroidered or painted on linen wrappers of the Torah Scroll.

However, the practice of portraying the four animals symbolic of the pious must be of older origin, since they appear in the magnificent *Arba*

Turim codex of the Vatican (Cod. de Rossi 555) executed by a scribe, Isaac ben Obadiah, in 1436 in Mantua.[13] The manuscript is beautifully illuminated by a first-rate artist of the school of Pisanello. The style, the color scale, the facial types and costumes are extremely close to what we find in the paintings and drawings of this great master of the Italian *quattrocento*.

Among the four larger miniatures of the manuscript there is a synagogue scene with the worshipers in the background and the reader at the *almemar* in the foreground. To the right of the desk, members of the congregation are seen taking out the Scroll from a beautifully carved Torah shrine. In the corner rectangles of the painted frame that encloses the scene are displayed the four animals, the leopard, the eagle, the deer and the lion, in the sequence adopted in *Pirke Abot*, and each animal is accompanied by the appropriate clause written on a scroll. It was a particularly fine idea to frame the synagogue scene with the symbols of piety.

Ezekiel's throne-chariot of God gave rise to esoteric speculations which constitute what is known as the lore of *Maasse Merkabah*. We do not know when the first attempt at pictorial representation of Ezekiel's vision was made by Jews. According to the Talmud (Rosh Hashanah 24b) it is forbidden to portray the four living creatures together. However, the interest in the subject was so great that it could not be entirely ignored. In the thirteenth century prayer book of the Bodleian Library in Oxford (cod. 2373) the *Merkabah* is pictured as an illustration to the portion recited at Pentecost (Mahzor Shabuot).[14] The Divine chariot is treated as a portal carried by two of the fabulous creatures, a twin bull and a twin lion. The eagle and the man are displayed inside the portal, where they are accompanied by other fantastic animals. The inclusion of the *Merkabah* symbolism in the prayer book for Pentecost was not arbitrary since the first chapter of the Book of Ezekiel where the chariot vision is recorded constitutes the *Haftarah* for the first day of Pentecost.

The association with Pentecost brought about an interesting modification in the conception of the *Merkabah*, for in the miniature the "man" of the Ezekiel vision is Moses. Since Pentecost is the Feast of Commemoration of the "Giving of the Torah," the reference to Moses is quite justified, all the more as Moses is depicted in the monologue of the Torah in the prayer book for Pentecost, as the ideal man superior to any biblical figure. In order to emphasize the central motif of the festival, the Revelation on Sinai, the Giving of the Torah is represented on the top of the picture, above the Divine canopy.

The four mystical creatures appear again, this time associated with the prayers for the Day of Atonement. In this conception the portal is literally the "Open Gate of Mercy." In a miniature of the early fourteenth century

Mahzor of the Breslau University Library, the Gate of Mercy is designed as a portal with open wings.[15] The four Merkabah figures are painted on the capitals and bases of the archway which have the form of round medallions. The motif of the archway still retains a relation to the throne-chariot concept, a relation pointed out in the medallions in which the living creatures are displayed. The medallions are meant, of course, to recall the wheels of Ezekiel's vision.

The four wheels, or medallions, enclosing the four mystical figures eventually lose every relationship with the portal which still gave the illusion of a canopied throne. In the *Mahzor* of the Leipzig University Library (second half of the fourteenth century) the four medallions stand unmotivated in a rectangular frame.[16] Rendered in a sort of short-hand style, the four creatures are merely intended to remind us of the Temple, as the text deals with the Temple tax. A pair of scales for weighing the *shekalim* is shown beside the medallions. Beasts and grotesques complete the picture.

The evolution of the chariot motif in Jewish medieval book illustration reveals, then, a tendency to dissolve the visual forms, already considerably disintegrated owing to the talmudic prohibition and the vagueness of *Merkabah* philosophical conceptions. They become immerged in patterns of beasts, foliage and interlaces. The animal decoration of Romanesque and Gothic art afforded a congenial vocabulary for these unrealistic elaborations.

After a glimpse into medieval prayer-book illustration, which uses the nostalgic visions of the Babylonian Exile[16a] as a hieratic background for synagogue liturgy, the contrast with Jewish art in antiquity becomes particularly striking. The climate of the Middle Ages seems much closer to the exalted mood of the Babylonian deportees than to the more realistic attitude of the Jews of the Hellenistic period. The beginnings of the synagogue are still shrouded in obscurity, and we do not know much about the trends in Jewish art before the third century B.C.E. when, suddenly, we meet with synagogue inscriptions.

Judaism was confronted with Hellenism all over the Diaspora, in the West and in the East, and some aspects of Hellenistic culture were necessarily felt by the Jews to be a challenge to their beliefs.[16b] Clashes between what we may call two strongly opposed conceptions of life were unavoidable. It should not be overlooked, however, that a steady process of dissociation of Hellenism from mythology was taking place, a process which made art, in some of its phases at least, tolerable to uncompromising monotheism. Typical of the more realistic and humane approach toward life were, for instance, the late Hellenistic Pergaminian sculptures in Athens, which portray enemy warriors as men endowed with a sense of dignity and pride rather than as mythological monsters.

In Roman art the scope of interests reaches further and portrait, landscape, idyllic animal scenes, subjects of current history, become increasingly important. Reliefs showing the emperor distributing largess to the populace, publicly displayed, were used as means of political propaganda.

Since art, therefore, was shifting toward secular aspects, the Jewish position had to be reconsidered. Jews had their own political concerns, too, and it may be gathered from Rabbinical writings that they were actually re-examining their historical experience in the light of contemporary events, and their discussions of an ideal leader reflected most real political aspirations. And along with the acuteness of political thinking a keener understanding of the culture and the arts of the surrounding population developed.

There is a story in the Mishna which can be regarded as typical of the new attitude. Rabban Gamaliel, the Patriarch (died before 114 c.e.), we are told, once attended the *termae* of Aphrodite at Acco. When asked how he could reconcile his conduct with the Jewish attitude toward pagan art, the Sage dismissed the question with a joke: "I did not come into her domain," he said, "she came into mine," for nobody will maintain that the bathhouse was built for Aphrodite, while it can be said that the statue was set up as an adornment of the bathhouse (Aboda Zara 44b). The debate is striking, for it reflects a most uninhibited attitude of the leading groups of Jewry toward an art which obviously was felt to be no longer a temptation to the Jewish believer.

In discussing the precedent established by the Palestinian Patriarch, a Jewish authority in Babylonia, Rabbah b. bar Hanah (latter part of the third century), ruled that a statue set up for decorative purposes—as may be the case in a large city—would not be objectionable. What was to be avoided were images in smaller places which were likely to be worshiped by the populace (Aboda Zara 41a). The distinction made in this decision is clear. To the educated classes in the big centers, art no longer meant crude idol worship.

Within the more sophisticated Roman civilization, then, emerges a Jewish art. The most important monument of Jewish antiquity is no doubt the synagogue at Dura-Europos on the middle Euphrates in Syria dated by inscription 245 c.e.[17] The entire walls of the synagogue have been found covered with biblical scenes. Dura was a Roman city of recent standing captured from the Persians. The population lived in expectation of a recapture. This actually happened before the decoration of the synagogue was completed. Nothing could possibly reflect more faithfully the feelings of the Jews of Dura than the paintings of their prayer house with their special emphasis on the good old Persian king, Ahasuerus, portrayed seated on Solomon's lion throne (the famous throne which, according to

Rabbinical views, nobody was worthy of inheriting, except possibly the Persian king), and a most detailed rendering of Ezekiel's "Vision of the Dry Bones," showing the scattered tribes reunited and gathered under one king, the resurrected King David.[18] The meaning of the biblical episode portrayed was unmistakable to the members of the congregation who knew that Davidic descendants were still alive, out of reach of the Roman invaders and under the protection of Sapur.

Were these extraordinary paintings unique?

From the mosaic decoration found in synagogues of the fourth to sixth centuries in North Africa[19] and Palestine it can be inferred that this representational art, biblical in content, talmudic in interpretation, was fairly well spread over a large area. The Jerusalem Talmud (Aboda Zara 3, 42d) records that the Samaritans made images of Jacob and Joseph, regarding the latter as their direct ancestor. It would thus appear that in the art of the Jews of the ancient period all the different traditions due to the Judaic, Israelitic and mixed popular elements were represented. The Samaritans revered Joseph as their ancestor and emphasized his story in their art, the synagogue of Dura likewise cherished the memory of Joseph, but was anxious to stress the unity of the nation, the emblem of which—the Temple of Jerusalem—was depicted above the Torah niche. This emblem is common to the floor mosaics of the synagogues at Naaran[20] and Bet Alpha[21] in Palestine, as well as to the gold glasses from Jewish catacombs in Rome. (A fine specimen of the latter can be seen at the Metropolitan Museum in New York.)[22]

It would take us too far afield to discuss the decoration of the ancient synagogue in detail. One more motif should be mentioned, however, because of its controversial character: the signs of the Zodiac, the *mazalot*. The ceiling tiles of the Dura synagogue were decorated with these signs, the floor mosaics of Palestinian synagogues display them. What was the attitude of the Rabbinical authorities toward this pictorial motif, intended to evoke the image of heaven?[23] On the whole, it would appear that they were opposed to its use. However, in the Babylonian Talmud (Aboda Zara 42b) we have a curious concession: pictures of the planets are permissible, but not those of the sun and moon. And the same source (43a) records that Rabban Gamaliel "had a picture of lunar diagrams in his upper chamber in the form of a chart hanging on the wall." There are other talmudic references to astronomical studies carried on by the Rabbis. The prohibition of images has no apodictic character in the sources of the time. What we have in the Talmud are records of discussions, of debates. Thus, in the Babylonian Talmud (Aboda Zara 41a) we find side by side two strictly opposed statements. According to one opinion, all images are prohibited; according to another, an image is not prohibited except when the figure holds a staff or a bird in its hand. What is discussed here is pagan rather than Jewish art, and in particular statues of divinities. Jewish art is also referred to and, significantly, without comment. In the Jerusalem Talmud it is related that "at the time of Rabbi Johanan (third century C.E.) they began to have paintings on the walls and the Rabbis did not hinder them." Are we to suppose that the paintings on the walls were meant to be synagogue paintings? In a fragment of the Jerusalem Talmud (Aboda Zara 3.3) preserved in the Public Library in Leningrad[24] we read: "In the days of Rabbi Abun [first half of the fourth century C.E.] they began to depict designs of mosaics and he did not hinder them." Pavement mosaics referred to in this text can safely be taken to be synagogue mosaics, since such mosaics have actually been excavated in Palestine and the Diaspora.

From the point of view of Judaism it is important to discover that the art practiced by Jews was a national, popular art dedicated to problems of Jewish interest. This art offered a counterpart to the Rabbinical interpretation of Jewish history and Jewish behavior. Art, a companion of literature, shared in the responsibility for the cultural and political education of the community.

Although the Rabbinical leaders seem on the whole to have tolerated art with some misgivings or, at best, without taking issue for or against it, in the case of the Dura murals—of which thirty panels have survived—we have to assume an active part of the spiritual head of the congregation in the planning of the decoration. The murals reveal throughout an intimate knowledge of the vast field of tradition.

As for style, the paintings have the "descriptive" quality of late Roman art, particularly of the provinces. What the synagogue artist was striving for was to convey the meaning, the point of a story, rather than to give the illusion of figures moving and acting in a three-dimensional space. Pompeian paintings had that plastic, illusionistic quality, but it was from later, more vehemently meaningful art that medieval Bible illustration developed. Christian art students evaluate the Dura synagogue paintings particularly from that point of view.

Examining the synagogue mosaics, we notice in the sixth century a tendency to depict liturgical objects rather than figure scenes, and a more conventional, rigid style which reflects restraint, introversion, an attitude due to the deteriorating political and social status under Byzantine domination. There are also to be taken into account general ideological trends, the controversy provoked in the Christian church by the Monophysite doctrine, and later on, in the seventh century, the powerful propaganda of Islam. How the mere threat of an Arab avalanche could affect the cultural policy of a country may be gathered from the bloody iconoclastic campaign initiated by Leo the Isaurian in Byzantium. Aiming at the power of the monastic orders, the emperor, who was of Asiatic origin and spoke Arabic, had understood the signs of the times and knew how to make use of the new slogan.

The East was definitely becoming iconoclastic, and we can safely assume that Jewish art adjusted itself without misgivings to the uncompromising attitude of Islam, which agreed with the moods prevailing in the Jewish community. The *hadit*, in which the Prophet is reported to have declared that those to be punished most severely on the Day of Judgment are the portrayers, was probably approved by the Jews, although they had never denounced art so harshly.

In the earliest preserved Hebrew manuscripts of the tenth and eleventh centuries, executed in Syria, Palestine and Egypt, the process of orna-mentalization and geometrization of real objects of the visible world is found to be completed, and the pictures of the seven-branched candlestick and the Temple utensils appear in Bible illumination, immerged in ornamental design.[25] Nothing is left of other representational topics and the skill of the artist exerts itself in penmanship. Dedications to patrons in huge gold lettering on diapered backgrounds became an outstanding feature of the magnificent parchment codices, and the masoretic notes of the Bible—a running grammatical commentary—in minuscule writing were arranged in marginal and full-page ornamental pieces.

The synagogue walls were decorated in a similar style and were hung with textiles; so, for example, the prayer house in which Maimonides prayed. It is reported that he felt distracted by the ornamental designs on tapestries and synagogue walls and therefore covered his eyes at prayer in order to achieve greater concentration.[26]

Meanwhile, in the European settlements, beasts and birds and all sorts of plants began to creep into the interlaces of the arabesques of the Jewish manuscript decoration. The synagogues were affected by a similar change of style.

The new departure seems to have been made first in the treatment of the masoretic notes, which were now written in animal and floral outlines. Rabbi Judah ben Samuel of Speyer and Regensburg condemned this practice in his *Sefer Hasidim* (twelfth century).[27] A scholar is bound to pay strictest attention to a clear disposition and legibility of the text, while the scribe is too readily inclined to neglect the text for the sake of an elegant flourish. Much of the friction between the writers and the scribes in the Middle Ages was due to this basic conflict. No concerted efforts were made to restrain art in book or synagogue decoration, however, and we cannot even speak of a united front of the Rabbinical authorities on this question.

Very significant is the fact that one of the great authorities of the twelfth century, Ephraim ben Isaac, Rabbi of Regensburg, declared himself a partisan of art.[28] He was consulted by R. Joel b. Isaac Ha-Levi of Bonn about some textiles used in the synagogue, the design of which—birds, fish and horses—seemed to him controversial; and R. Ephraim ruled in favor of animal decoration, pointing to its absolute harmlessness at a time when animal worship was no longer a problem.

The role of animal symbolism in Hebrew manuscript illumination has been touched upon in our discussion of the *Merkabah* motif. We cannot deal with this problem at any length. Suffice it to say that the famous medieval animal book, the *Physiologus,* was much influenced by the Bible and is even traced by some scholars to a Jewish source.

To understand the interest in animals, their habits and appearance, we must also take into account the role of hunting in the Middle Ages. Legend has it that Rabbi Judah ben Samuel spent his youth at archery and at the age of eighteen realized that he wished rather to study Jewish lore.[29] We cannot take this tale too literally; however, it reveals an interest in this sport, at least on the part of the recorder and his public. We do know that Rabbi Ephraim ben Isaac discussed hunting with hound and falcon in a matter-of-fact way, without any unfavorable comment.[30]

It seems that objections to animal decoration appear only after a certain period of toleration, and not as a warning against a newfangled fashion. Thus, Rabbi Isaac ben Moses Or Zarua of Vienna (*c.* 1200) recalled the verdure decoration—foliage with birds—of the Meissen synagogue from his boyhood days. In his old age he felt compelled to disapprove of that sort of thing.[31]

In the Cologne synagogue a controversy was started over some stained-glass windows which Rabbi Eliakim ben Joseph (first half of the twelfth century) wished removed.[32] His attack is particularly interesting because the Cistercian Order had prohibited stained-glass windows in their churches in 1134. The interdict aimed at the luxurious indulgence in colored glass, and was a measure of self-imposed restraint of the senses, proper for a fraternal community. Bernard of Clairvaux (d. 1153) particularly condemned animal decoration (*Patrologia Latina,* vol. 182, cols. 913 ff.). But what was in order for a monastic association was hardly right for a community of men, women and children, and we have Rabbi Judah ben Samuel's words to show that this was actually the Rabbinical view. "Do not say," he warned, "that you want to put on the hairy cloth of the Christian monk, for this would be a sinful way, as you have to deny yourself only what the Scriptures forbid you to enjoy."[33] In fact, Rabbi Eliakim's attitude was dictated by "political anxiety," rather than by religious scruples. He was fearful lest the Jews be accused of worshiping the lions and snakes depicted on those windows, the more so as the windows happened to be on the side the congregation faced at one particular prayer. It may be recalled that the Second Crusade had swept over the Jewish settlements in 1146 and the victims of the first, of 1096, were not yet forgotten. Although the Rabbi tried to associate his objections with some reservations voiced here and there in the Talmud, it was evident that these references were meant only to add some dignity to a restriction provoked by a situation beyond his control.

The last refuge of the artist was the book, for it was less exposed to the public eye than the synagogue. It is true that the Rabbinical authorities did not directly favor book decoration, not to speak of illustration; however, it is significant that while Rabbi Meir of Rothenburg (d. 1293) mildly criticized the animal-and-bird decoration of the prayer books, he did not base his criticisms on religious considerations.[34] The considerable number of prayer books from the thirteenth and fourteenth centuries decorated in this manner is proof that there was no marked opposition to be reckoned with. Perhaps the best evidence of the rather tolerant attitude prevalent is found in the illustrated prayer book (Breslau University Library) executed by a disciple of the Rothenburg Sage.[35]

It is with a sense of profound respect that we examine the huge medieval prayer books, the Bibles and the smaller Haggadas admirably written and illuminated on parchment and exquisitely bound.

Attempts at Bible illustration are found in all the types of Hebrew writings: here it may be an Esther scene, there the "Giving of the Law," or "Abraham in the fiery furnace," an episode from postbiblical literature.[35a]

Continuous biblical picture cycles are rare, however, and there is not one Bible illustrated throughout. Strange to say, an illustration beginning with Adam and Eve is found in Haggadas rather than in Bibles, the most beautiful of them (Codex Add. 27210 of the British Museum) exhibiting an immaculate thirteenth-century French Gothic style.[36] The somewhat later Haggada of the Sarajevo Museum, executed in Spain, opens with the scenes of the six days of Creation—each day represented by the disk of the earth showing the successive improvements, and the seventh day illustrated by the Lord seated on a bench and enjoying His rest.[37] Such a thing would not be possible in a Bible. The Haggada was allowed some measure of freedom and informality. There must have been a certain reluctance to illustrate the Bible codex throughout either because of the immensity of such a task or for religious reasons. At any rate, the most magnificent Bible codex, (Cod. Kennicott I of the Bodleiana completed in La Coruña in Spain in 1476) shows only a few figures: David, Phineas, Balaam and Jonah.[38] Its decoration is chiefly animal and floral.

This particular attitude toward Bible illustration may account for the behavior of Moses Arragel, the Rabbi of Guadalajara, who in 1430 compiled a Castilian translation of the Old Testament for the Order of Calatrava of which he was a vassal.[39] When asked to supervise the work of the illustrators also, Arragel declined, referring to the Decalogue. Did he fear to be involved in problems of interpretation? Possibly so, although in the Bible commentary he furnished he shows an admirable tact in giving credit to Christian and Jewish exegesis alike and siding with none.[40] The alternative is that he honestly opposed Bible illustration as something even the most liberal-minded Jew could not wholeheartedly approve.

With the expulsion from Spain (1492)[40a] the fine Hebrew manuscript production of that country was brought to a standstill. The deterioration of the position of the Jews in Germany throughout the fifteenth century was accompanied by a marked decline in the quality of their books, and the sketchy colored drawings found in their manuscripts of that time reflect haste and carelessness. In Italy alone Hebrew book illumination and, especially, illustration remain on a high level during the fifteenth and sixteenth centuries and show an unparalleled variety and wealth of vocabulary and finesse of execution.[40*] In this art, with its emphasis on balance and mellowness of color—an Italian contribution—there is to be noted also a considerable strain of influences imported by refugees from Spain and Germany.

It has often been said that the Jews had experienced no renaissance, and some students of Jewish history are inclined to extend the medieval period down to the Enlightenment and Emancipation of the eighteenth century. However, the attitude of the Jews toward art in the Renaissance seems to have outgrown the medieval pattern to such an extent that a consideration of that period in distinct terms seems imperative.

The retarding elements that make themselves noticeable during the later Middle Ages in book illumination in Germany and even in Spain are not to be discounted in the appreciation of manuscripts produced in Italy, furthermore, most important is the role of the printed book and the new techniques of illustration, the woodcut and the engraving.

The Jewish scribe and illuminator had no permanent contact with his Christian colleagues, monks or laymen organized in guilds. In the printing presses, however, Jews and Christians were bound to work together. The Jews, frequently forbidden to run presses, had their books printed in Christian printing shops, where Jewish composers had to be employed for Hebrew prints.

The practice of the printers for economy's sake to use the same cuts for various publications and to exchange cuts among themselves, had an effect upon Hebrew printing, too. The new border pieces, title pages and even illustrations turned up in the Hebrew books; and we are not surprised to discover in the Mantua Haggada of 1560 a woodcut from Holbein's Lyons Bible of 1538 as an illustration for the "son who does not know how to ask questions," and Michelangelo's Jeremiah of the Sistine ceiling in the Vatican as one of the Rabbis of Bene Berak.

If this is plagiarism, then we also have to dismiss as plagiarism the famous Renaissance church, St. Francesco in Rimini, since Alberti used the Roman gate of Rimini as a model for the church façade. What we are driving at is not to demonstrate that the whole Renaissance movement was imitative, but to point out the enthusiastic interest in research, in copying and reproducing in various techniques and adapting to various purposes of art works greatly valued. Jews and Christians alike were carried away by this artistic enthusiasm. Jewish and Christian artisans alike reproduced on faïence dishes the biblical scenes of the Loggias in the Vatican painted by pupils of Raphael. Adorned in addition with Passover symbols and illustrations from a Venetian Haggada (first printed in 1609), the Jewish plates were used for the *Seder* meal.[41] Holbein, Michelangelo, Raphael had thus become the teachers of the budding Jewish artist. And later developments were to show how these new influences affected his outlook and sensitivity.

Unfortunately the rapprochement so conspicuous in the keen interest in Hebrew language and literature among the humanists, and the emergence of the Jewish author in Italian literature—one may recall the *Dialoghi d'Amore*, a philosophical treatise by Leone Ebreo,[41a] the son of the Sephardic refugee from Spain, the great Isaac Abrabanel—did not last. That rapprochement was built on an unstable political foundation, and who could better sense the changing "climate" than a native, Italian Jew? It was the poet and grammarian Samuel Archevolti (d. 1609) who uttered the all-familiar warnings. It was clear to him that the first target for anti-Jewish attacks would be refugees, and he was alarmed by what in their customs might irritate the native Jew-baiters. There was that German synagogue at Venice with its quaint interior decoration, nothing particularly disturbing since the Ashkenazic rabbis tolerated it, but somehow inappropriate, perhaps outmoded, not in line with the fashion of the day. Archevolti objected to the "trees and plants" in that decoration, more suited for an inn or a theater, he thought, than a prayer house.[42] He went so far as to admit that he really worried lest the Gentiles accuse Jews of worshiping those images. Had not Apion, centuries earlier, slanderously accused the Jews of worshiping an ass's head?

Another story may illustrate the sense of insecurity and frustration typical of the Jews in the later sixteenth and the seventeenth century. The Jews of Ascoli, when expelled in 1569, went to Pesaro. Among the things they took with them was their synagogue Shrine. In 1639 Rabbi Moses of Trani raises the question whether the lions that adorn the Shrine are compatible with the Jewish view of plastic arts.[43] The rabbi could not know, of course, that someday lion statues carved in the round would be excavated on the site of antique Palestinian synagogues. (I refer to the finds in Chorazin and Kfar Birim.)[44] So he decided in the negative. His view was adopted by Rabbi David ibn Abi Zimra.[45] The argument brought forth was the usual reference to the diverting effect upon the worshiper. However, Abraham Joseph Solomon Graziano of Modena, the great book collector, was of a different opinion. He pointed out (*c.* 1670) that the lions set at the foot of the Shrine could not be well seen from the seats of the congregation and were hardly liable to disturb anyone. Graziano's liberal attitude calls for an explanation. It was Graziano's own great-grandfather, we learn, who had moved the Ascoli Shrine to Pesaro. This Shrine meant something to the man. He gave vent to his indignation in marginal remarks jotted down in his copy of Rabbi Joseph Caro's *Shulhan Aruk*. That is where David Kaufmann found them.[46]

Archevolti's summons to refrain from decorating synagogues was confirmed by the rabbinical court at Safed with some reservations regarding already existing decorations which were not to be obliterated.[47] Every new wave of persecution was followed by pious exhortations to abstain from display of any sort which might bring discredit upon the community. But no wholesale condemnation of art was pronounced by any responsible body in the name of the synagogue.

The Renaissance had released the forces of the individual, Jew and Christian alike, and there was no way back into the narrowness and isolation forced upon the Jews in the Middle Ages. Here and there emerges a name of a Jewish artist associated with some unusual achievement.

Meanwhile in the East, too, there were stirrings. In the medieval period, Western artistic trends had been carried eastward and synagogues of Worms, Regensburg and Cracow were built upon the same scheme. During the Renaissance, Italy began to export to the whole European continent architects, masons, painters, sculptors, many of whom went to Poland and Russia; some occasionally built or remodeled a synagogue. From the blending of these Italian influences with native elements in the Carpathian region, the Ukraine, Lithuania and White Russia, a Jewish folk art developed, which after the Chmielnicki pogrom (1648) was carried by emigrants from Eastern Europe back to the West.[48] Medieval animal decoration was revived in modest country synagogues of the East in terms of a provincial *baroque*. This was actually a survival of a tradition, some links of which were lost. Folk art has a long memory. In this Eastern European synagogue decoration we meet the biblical leviathan, the *behemot*, the hieratic eagle, the fabulous snake of medieval descent, the unicorn familiar from Hebrew illuminated manuscripts in the West as well as from Christian art, the four animals from *Pirke Abot*, and the view of the restored Jerusalem. Regardless of the origin of these pictorial devices—from peasant folk art, imported Oriental textiles, engravings and woodcuts from West and East—the common source of this imagery was the prayer book, with its traditional symbolism.

In a period, then, when Jewish art in central Europe stagnated, a new wave of folklore and artistic conceptions from the East was driven to Moravia, Hungary and farther westward down to the Fuerth region where, scattered in villages and townlets, lived the remnant of German Jewry.

In the seventeenth century there emerged the free republic of Holland, whereto Jews, Sephardic and Ashkenazic, flocked seeking refuge from religious persecution.[48a] Amsterdam superseded the Italian centers of Hebrew printing, and it was again through the medium of the book that Jewish art received its new stimulus.

The Marranos from Portugal, who in Holland returned to their old faith, had a more liberal conception of art, and because of their higher living standard there was among them a certain need for outer display. Family portraits belonged to the amenities of life; and we see Jews portrayed by Dutch artists.

Jewish artists soon began to attempt portraiture also, and it was characteristic of their background that their first attempts in portraiture were intended for books. Thus, in the seventeenth century appear author portraits, designed and sometimes engraved as well by Jews for frontispieces. To be sure, these were portraits of scholars and community leaders. We would hardly expect portraits of women or children in such a dignified and serious company. However, Aaron Chaves, much ahead of his time, designed in the second half of the seventeenth century a portrait of Daniel Levi Barrios with his wife, son and daughter, which was to be appended to a poetical paraphrase of the Bible written by Barrios.[49] The portrait was allegorical and the text was only a version of the Bible; nevertheless, the Portuguese community of Amsterdam refused to give its approbation to the publication of the book.

The Ashkenazim were even more particular about portraits. The portrait of Rabbi Zebi Ashkenazi in the eighteenth century had to be drawn clandestinely, without the rabbi's knowledge. His son, Rabbi Jacob Emden, had serious misgivings about this portrait. He also disapproved of the portrait medal cast for Eleazar Shmelka, the Ashkenazic rabbi of Amsterdam.[50] As late as 1837 Rabbi Akiba Eger in Posen had to be portrayed clandestinely.[51] However, there was a great demand for portraits of prominent rabbis. Whether Adamus Wagner's portrait of Rabbi Jonathan Eybeschuetz (d. 1767), signed and dated 1770, was painted after a drawing from life we do not know. The portrait was exhibited in the Akiba Eger Exhibition in Berlin in 1937.[52] The well-known engraving is a slightly modified version of that portrait. Among others the engraved portrait of Rabbi Ezekiel Landau (d. 1793) should be mentioned. Engravings were later superseded by lithographs. The Jewish Museum in

Berlin had one of the largest collections of portraits of rabbis and scholars, some of considerable artistic value.

The Sephardic community in Amsterdam may be regarded as having practically initiated that type of portraiture among Jews, although some attempts had already been made in Italy. After all, Salom Italia, who engraved portraits of J. J. A. Leon Templo [Jacob Jehudah Leone][53] and of Manasseh ben Israel, came to Holland from Italy. In Amsterdam there was a larger field and a greater demand to tempt an artist.

The Ashkenazic community of Amsterdam, more concerned with religious needs, produced a new illustrated Haggada which was to play a considerable part in the development of Jewish folk art. Compiled for the Ashkenazic and Sephardic ritual, this Haggada was published in 1695 under the patronage of Moses Wesel, an Ashkenazic Jew. The engravings were picked from the immense work of Matthaeus Merian of Basel, who had illustrated a Luther Bible and other popular publications.[54] Children particularly delighted in the many-figured and lively pictures, and it is noteworthy that for Goethe and Heine the Merian pictures were associated with the most cherished childhood memories. However, Heine knew them only from his Haggada—a handwritten and hand-painted version of the Amsterdam Haggada. He never suspected their origin. It is worth reading what he says about those lovely pictures, in his *Rabbi of Bacharach*. Executed in 1723 by Moses Judah Loeb, son of Benjamin Wolf Broda from Trebitsch, Moravia, this Haggada was dedicated to Lazarus von Geldern, Heinrich Heine's great-grandfather.[55] (The Haggada was in the possession of Dr. Heinz Frank in Amsterdam, a refugee from Cologne, when I saw it in 1936.)

The von Geldern Haggada is one of the numerous versions of the Amsterdam print, produced in the eighteenth century. The artists hailed mostly from Moravia, Bohemia and Hungary. In simplifying the composition of the scenes, Judaizing the facial types and costumes, these artists added a popular, provincial flavor to the pictures. Never blindly copying their model, they often introduced scenes or traits of their own invention, thus expanding the picture cycle and adapting it to the tastes and fashions of their own generation. Therefore, those eighteenth-century versions of the Amsterdam Haggada, neatly copied on parchment and illustrated with brightly gouache miniatures, have to be evaluated on their own merit. They offer a remarkable attempt to depict the "Jewish scene." They are in fact the first Jewish genre pictures created by Jewish artists, domestic interiors enlivened with a pot of flowers on the window sill and a bird in the cage, showing charming women, lovely children, men, old and young, gathered around a table, scenes not borrowed from Merian nor necessarily original inventions, yet ably compiled and sometimes exquisitely painted.

With these self-taught, obscure, provincial painters the puritanic spell was broken and Jewish art was at last liberated from its limitations imposed by history rather than "Law."

The painters born on the threshold of the nineteenth century,[56] the miniature-portrait painter Jeremias David Alexander Fiorino of Kassel, the well-known Moritz Oppenheim who was active in Frankfort, and Eduard Magnus, born in Berlin, all have something of the sweetness and lyricism of the Haggada painter of the eighteenth century, despite their formal training, the different background and broader outlook. Their subjects may be Jews or Gentiles; the painters do not engage in any ambitious projects likely to involve them in conflicting situations.

With closer participation in the cultural life of their countries, however, Jewish artists began to join groups organized to carry out definite ideological programs, such as the German Nazarene group in Rome, adherence to which brought about the conversion of the painter brothers, Johannes and Philipp Veit, grandsons of Moses Mendelssohn. Eduard Bendemann, who painted biblical compositions in the classicist vein, also realized soon that he needed a larger audience than Jews could offer and acted accordingly.

The problem of the Jewish artist was that of a man who cannot find an outlet for his activities within his ethnic group and sees himself drawn to the more powerful national audience. At least in Germany, this meant, in the first half of the nineteenth century, desertion of the ancestral faith.

In Austria, Hungary, Poland and Russia things matured more slowly, and serious conflicts could be more easily avoided. In the second half of the century, we meet in these countries an art which caters to the tastes of a cultivated Jewish middle class. This art was dedicated to the Jewish motif, which, as the century wore on, lost most of its lyrical character and struck a more bitter accent.

It is indicative of the social awareness of the promoters of Jewish art in Eastern Europe that a pupil of the sculptor Mark Antokolski, the late Boris Schatz, set out to found in Palestine a school of arts and crafts, the Bezalel School at Jerusalem. The idea of reactivating artistic crafts, metal and woodwork, rug weaving, embroidery and penmanship, had much in common with the program of William Morris. Characteristically, the work of Abel Pann, the outstanding painter of the Bezalel group, was close in style to that of the English Pre-Raphaelites. Whatever the merits of the individual artists associated with the Bezalel movement, they laid the foundation for a freer and more creative art in the future.

A Sephardic Jew, Camille Pissarro, a native of the Antilles, became in the seventies, in Paris, the first exponent among Jews of an experimental type of art, a member of a small group of pioneers which coined its own vocabulary.

Some people may see the significance of the impressionist movement started by Pissarro and his friends in the deheroization of man and the devaluation not only of "studio nudes," but of subject matter in general; others may see that significance in the abandoning of the academic principles of composition and the revolutionizing of painting techniques.

To the Jewish artist this movement meant a release from the sense of inferiority, from the constant awareness of his modest artistic heritage. Here at last was an art which did not claim a noble ancestry; it was a democratic art fitting into modern society, and an art in which the Jew was given a fair chance of achievement. And he accomplished a good deal.

The generation that holds the field now, and which made its first appearance during the First World War, has found a stronger and more universal response than any previous generation. The Jewish artist, like the Jewish writer, addresses himself in our time to the world, to all men. And it would appear that with art surrendering its claim to divinity and exclusiveness, the fight is actually won—for it was this claim to divinity which the Second Commandment had fought.

NOTES

[1] G. E. Wright, "How did early Israel differ from her neighbors?" in *Biblical Archaeologist*, VI, No. 1 (Feb. 1943), pp. 6 ff.

[2] W. F. Albright, *From the Stone Age to Christianity* (Baltimore, 1940), p. 206.

[3] J. W. and G. M. Crowfoot, *Early Ivories from Samaria* (London, 1938), p. 12.

[3a Cf. above Albright, "The Biblical Period," pp. 27-31.]

[4] E. B. Tylor, "The winged figures of the Assyrian and other ancient Monuments," *Proceedings of the Society of Biblical Archaeology,* June, 1890, p. 391.

[5] Ernst Cohn-Wiener, *Die juedische Kunst* (Berlin, 1929), Fig. 23.

[6] G. Dalman, *Arbeit und Sitte in Palaestina* (Guetersloh, 1939), VI, 107 ff.

[7] M. Gruenbaum, *Gesammelte Aufsaetze zur Sprach- und Sagenkunde,* ed. Felix Perles (Berlin, 1901), pp. 202-203.

[8] H. T. Obbink, "Jahwebilder," in *Zeitschrift fuer die Alttestamentliche Wissenschaft und die Kunde des nachbiblischen Judentums* (Giessen, 1929), Vol. 47, p. 267.

[9] G. E. Wright, "Solomon's Temple Resurrected," in *Bibl. Arch.*, Vol. IV, No. 2 (May, 1941), p. 28.

[10] J. W. and G. M. Crowfoot, *op. cit.*, pp. 18 and 24.

[11] W. H. Beyer and H. Lietzmann, *Die juedische Katakombe der Villa Torlonia* (Berlin, 1930), plate 28 and p. 44 where erroneously described under No. 27.

[12] *Ibid.*, plate 26a; see also p. 44.

[13] Erno Munkácsi, *Miniatuermuevészet Itália koenyvtáraiban, heber Kodexek* (Budapest), publication of the Jewish Museum, n.d., Plate VI. 18. The codex was previously in the Derossiana in Vienna and is described in Hans Tietze, *Die illuminierten Handschriften der Rossiana in Wien-Lainz* (Leipzig, 1911), pp. 110-111.

[14] Rachel Wischnitzer-Bernstein, *Symbole und Gestalten der juedischen Kunst* (Berlin, 1935), pp. 27-31, fig. 20.

[15] *Idem.*, "The Messianic Fox," in *Review of Religion*, Vol. V, No. 3 March, 1941, p. 260, plate I.

[16] Robert Bruck, *Die Malereien in den Handschriften des Koenigreichs-Sachsen* (Dresden, 1906), pp. 219-225, fig. 138. The manuscript is summarily described without any attempt at interpreting the illustrations.

[16a Cf. Albright, *op. cit.*, pp. 45 ff.]

[16b Cf. above Elias J. Bickerman, "The Historical Foundations of Post-biblical Judaism," pp. 93 ff.]

[17] H. F. Pearson, C. H. Kraeling, M. Crosby, J. J. Obermann, A. Pagliaro and C. C. Torrey, *Excavations at Dura-Europos*. Report of Sixth Season, Preliminary Report on the Synagogue at Dura (New Haven, 1936).

[18] R. Wischnitzer-Bernstein, "The Conception of the Resurrection in the Ezekiel Panel of the Dura-Synagogue," in *Journal of Biblical Literature,* Vol. LX, No. 1 (March, 1941), pp. 43-55; *idem*, "The Samuel Cycle in the Wall Decoration of the Synagogue at Dura-Europos," *Proceedings of the Amer. Acad. for Jewish Research*, XI (1941), 85-103. For a more detailed discussion of the Dura synagogue paintings see the writer's book *The Messianic Theme in the Paintings of the Dura Synagogue* (Chicago, 1948), with bibliography, pp. 117-124. See also W. G. Kuemmel, "Die aelteste religioese Kunst der Juden," *Judaica*, II, 1 (Zurich, April, 1946), pp. 1-56; A. Grabar, *Martyrium, Recherches sur le culte des reliques et l'art chrétien antique,* 2 vols. (Paris, 1946, Plates, 1943); H. Riesenfeld, *The Resurrection in Ezekiel XXXVII and in the Dura-Europos Paintings* (Upsala Universitets Arsskrift, 1948).

[19] R. Krautheimer, *Mittelalterliche Synagogen* (Berlin, 1927), pp. 68 ff., figs. 14 and 15.

[20] E. L. Sukenik, *Ancient Synagogues in Palestine and Greece* (London, 1934), pp. 28-31, fig. 5.

[21] *Ibid.*, pp. 31-35, fig. 8.

[22] Wischnitzer-Bernstein, "The Sabbath in Art," in A. E. Millgram, *Sabbath, The Day of Delight* (Philadelphia, 1944), pp. 324-327, fig. 19; for a discussion of gold glasses cf. *Idem*, "Die Messianische Huette in der juedischen Kunst," *Monatsschrift fuer Geschichte und Wissenschaft des Judentums*, XXX, 5 (Breslau, 1936), pp. 381 ff.

[23] For the interpretation of the meaning of the Zodiac motif see Karl Lehmann, "The Dome of Heaven," in *Art Bulletin*, College Art Association of America, Vol. XXVII, No. 1, (New York, 1945), pp. 1-27.

[24] J. N. Epstein, (ed.), *Tarbiz*, (Hebrew), Vol. III, No. 19, pp. 15 ff. (Jerusalem, 1931-1932). Cf. also Sukenik *op. cit.*, p. 27.

[25] Vladimir Stassof and David Gunzburg, *L'Ornement Hébreu* (Berlin, 1905). (Plates with summary description.)

[26] Leopold Loew, *Graphische Requisiten und Erzeugnisse bei den Juden* (Leipzig, 1870-1871), Pt. I, p. 34. See also Alfred Freimann, *Responsa of Maimonides* (Jerusalem, 1934) 20 and p. 19.

[27] Sefer Hasidim, (ed. Berlin) 709. Quoted in D. H. Mueller and J. von Schlosser *Die Haggadah von Sarajevo,* with appendix by David Kaufmann, "Zur Geschichte der juedischen Handschriften-Illustration" (Vienna, 1898), p. 257.

[28] Loew, *op. cit.,* p. 33; *Germania Judaica,* I. Elbogen, A. Freimann and H. Tykocinski (eds.) (Breslau, 1934), Vol. I, pt. 2, pp. 289-290.

[29] *Germania Judaica, op. cit.,* p. 293.

[30] *Ibid.,* p. 290.

[31] David Kaufmann, "Art in the Synagogue," in *Jewish Quarterly Review,* IX, 264, (London, 1897).

[32] Carl Brisch, *Geschichte der Juden in Coeln und Umgebung aus aeltester Zeit bis auf die Gegenwart* (Cologne, 1879), I, 39; see also *Germania Judaica, op. cit.,* p. 199.

[33] Loew, *op. cit.,* p. 17.

[34] *Ibid.,* p. 34; Bruno Italiener, *Die Darmstaedter Pessach Haggadah* (Leipzig, 1927), p. 18.

[35] Wischnitzer-Bernstein, "The Messianic Fox," *op. cit.,* p. 263.

[35a] On illuminations of Judeo-Persian biblical manuscripts cf. above Walter J. Fischel, "Israel in Iran: A Survey of Judeo-Persian Literature," p. 833.]

[36] Rachel Wischnitzer, "Illuminated Haggadahs," in *Jewish Quar. Rev.,* Vol. XIII, No. 2, p. 206. (London, 1922).

[37] Mueller and Schlosser, *op. cit.,* plate fol. 2.

[38] Wischnitzer, "Une Bible Enluminée par Joseph ibn Hayyim," in *Revue des Études Juives,* Vol. LXXIII, 146, p. 166. (Paris, 1921).

[39] Samuel Berger, "Les Bibles Castillanes," in *Romania,* XXVIII, 522 (Paris, 1899).

[40] Max Golde, "Die synagogale Kunst im Mittelalter," in *Menorah,* V. 571-584 (Frankfort am Main, 1927).

[40a] Cf. above Cecil Roth, "The European Age in Jewish History (to 1648)," pp. 234 ff.]

[40*] Wischnitzer, "Les Manuscrits à Miniatures de Maimonide," *Gazette des Beaux-Arts,* VI, pér. T. XIII, 869 (Paris, July-August, 1935), pp. 49 ff.

[41] Wischnitzer-Bernstein, "Studies in Jewish Art," in *Jewish Quar. Rev.,* N. S., Vol. XXXVI, No. 1, pp. 58-59 (Philadelphia, 1945).

[41a] Cf. above Alexander Altmann, "Judaism and World Philosophy," pp. 645-647.]

[42] Kaufmann, "Art in the Synagogue," *op. cit.,* pp. 264, 265, 266.

[43] *Ibid.,* p. 258.

[44] Illustrated in E. L. Sukenik, *The Ancient Synagogue of Beth Alpha* (Jerusalem, 1932), figs. 36 and 37.

[45] Kaufmann, *loc. cit.*

[46] *Ibid.,* pp. 255 ff.

[47] *Ibid.*, p. 266.

[48] Some aspects of these eastward and westward trends were discussed in: E. Lissitzky, "The Synagogue of Mohilev," in *Rimon* (Hebrew), III, 9-12 (Berlin, 1923); *idem*, in *Milgrom*, (Yiddish) III, 9-13 (Berlin, 1923); E. Toeplitz, "Wall Paintings in Synagogues of the XVII and XVIII Centuries," in *Rimon, op. cit.*, pp. 1-8; *idem*, in *Milgrom, op cit.*, pp. 1-7; *idem*, "Malerei in den Synagogen" (Besonders in Franken), in *Beitraege zur juedischen Kulturgeschichte* III, 3-16 (Frankfort am Main, 1929). See also Wischnitzer, "Mutual Influences between Eastern and Western Europe in Synagogue Architecture from the 12th to the 18th Century," in *YIVO Bleter* (Journal of the Yiddish Scientific Institute), Vol. XXIX, No. 1, pp. 3-51 (New York, 1947). *Idem*, in English, in *YIVO Annual*, II-III, 1947-1948, pp. 25-68. G. K. Loukomski, *Jewish Art in European Synagogues* (London, 1947).

[[48a] Cf. above. Cecil Roth, "The Jews of Western Europe (from 1648)," pp. 253-254.]

[49] F. Landsberger, "New Studies in Early Jewish Artists," in *Hebrew Union College Annual*, XVIII, 304 ff., fig. 7 (Cincinnati, 1944).

[50] Loew, *op. cit.*, p. 39.

[51] A. Kronthal, "Juedische Bildnismaler der Posener Biedermeierzeit" in *Jahrbuch fuer juedische Geschichte und Literatur*, XXX, 214-215, (Berlin, 1937).

[52] *Akiba Eger Ausstellung* (Catalogue by R. Wischnitzer-Bernstein and E. Pessen, Jewish Museum, Berlin) Hanukkah, 1937, No. 31.

[53] Encyclopaedia Judaica, X, p. 792. "Leon Templo, Jakob Jehuda Arje ben Abraham (1603-1675) . . . Aufsehen erregte das von ihm ausgearbeitete Modell des Salomonischen Tempels . . . Dieser Arbeit verdankt L. den. Beinamen Templo, der auch auf seine Nachkommen ueberging."

[54] Wischnitzer-Bernstein, "Von der Holbeinbibel zur Amsterdamer Haggadah," in *Monatsschrift fuer Geschichte und Wissenschaft des Judentums*, Vol. LXXV, Nos. 7 and 8, pp. 1-18 (Breslau, 1931). For Van Dyck's influence on Jewish illustration: *Idem*, "The Esther Story in Art," in Philip Goodman, *The Purim Anthology* (Philadelphia, 1949), pp. 234 ff.

[55] Elizabeth Moses, "Juedische Kult- und Kunstdenkmaeler in den Rheinlanden," in *Rheinischer Verein fuer Denkmalpflege* (Duesseldorf, 1931), I, 99-200.

[56] For a survey of modern Jewish art see Karl Schwarz, *Die Juden in der Kunst* (Vienna and Jerusalem, 1936, 2nd ed.); *idem, Ha Umanut Ha-Yehudit Ha-Hadashah Beeretz Yisrael* (Jerusalem, 1941); Franz Landsberger, *A History of Jewish Art* (Cincinnati, 1946). Helen Rosenau, *A Short History of Jewish Art* (London, 1948); for discussion of modern synagogue architecture, Wischnitzer-Bernstein, "The Problem of Synagogue Architecture," *Commentary*, III, 3 (New York, March, 1947), pp. 233-241.

BIBLIOGRAPHY

ALBRIGHT, WILLIAM FOXWELL, *From the Stone Age to Christianity.* Baltimore, 1940.

BERGER, SAMUEL, "Les Bibles Castillanes," in *Romania*, Vol. XXVIII. Paris, 1899.

BEYER, H. W., and LIETZMANN, H., *Die juedische Katakombe der Villa Torlonia*. Berlin, 1930.

BRISCH, CARL, *Geschichte der Juden in Coeln und Umgebung aus aeltester Zeit bis auf die Gegenwart*. Cologne, 1879. Vol. I.

BRUCK, ROBERT, *Die Malereien in den Handschriften des Koenigreichs Sachsen*. Dresden, 1906.

COHN-WIENER, ERNST, *Die juedische Kunst, ihre Geschichte von den Anfaengen bis zur Gegenwart*. Berlin, 1929.

CROWFOOT, J. W. and G. M., *Early Ivories from Samaria*. London, 1938.

DALMAN, G., *Arbeit und Sitte in Palaestina*. Guetersloh, 1939.

GOLDE, MAX, "Die synagogale Kunst im Mittelalter," in *Menorah*, Vol. V. Frankfort am Main, 1927.

GRABAR, ANDRÉ, *Martyrium, Recherches sur le culte des reliques et l'art chrétien antique*. 2 vols. and plates. Paris, 1946.

GRUENBAUM, M., *Gesammelte Aufsaetze zur Sprach- und Sagenkunde* (Felix Perles, ed.). Berlin, 1901.

ITALIENER, BRUNO, *Die Darmstaedter Pessach Haggadah*. Leipzig, 1927.

KAUFMANN, DAVID, "Art in the Synagogue," in *Jewish Quarterly Review*, Vol. IX. London, 1897.

KRAUTHEIMER, R., *Mittelalterliche Synagogen*. Berlin, 1927.

KRONTHAL, A., "Juedische Bildnismaler der Posener Biedermeierzeit," in *Jahrbuch fuer juedische Geschichte und Literatur*, Vol. XXX. Berlin, 1937.

KUEMMEL, W. G., "Die aelteste religioese Kunst der Juden," in *Judaica*, II, 1. Zurich, 1946.

LANDSBERGER, F., "New Studies in Early Jewish Artists," in *Hebrew Union College Annual*, Vol. XVIII. Cincinnati, 1944.

———, *A History of Jewish Art*. Cincinnati, 1946.

LEHMANN, KARL, "The Dome of Heaven," in *Art Bulletin*, College Art Association of America, Vol. XXVII, No. 1. New York, 1945.

LISSITZKY, E., "The Synagogue of Mohilev," in *Rimon*, Vol. III (Hebrew) and *Milgrom*, Vol. III (Yiddish). Berlin, 1923.

LOEW, LEOPOLD, *Graphische Requisiten und Erzeugnisse bei den Juden*. Leipzig, 1870-1871.

LOUKOMSKI, G. K., *Jewish Art in European Synagogues*. London, 1947.

MOSES, ELIZABETH, "Juedische Kult- und Kunstdenkmaeler in den Rheinlanden," in *Rheinischer Verein fuer Denkmalpflege und Heimatschutz*, Heft I, Duesseldorf, 1931, pp. 99-200.

MUELLER, DAVID H., and SCHLOSSER, JULIUS VON, *Die Haggadah von Sarajevo*. Vienna, 1898.

MUNKÁCSI, ERNO, *Miniatuermuevésvet Itália koenyvtáraiban, heber Kodexek*. Publication of the Jewish Museum. Budapest, n.d.

OBBINK, H. T., "Jahwebilder," in *Zeitschrift fuer die Alttestamentliche Wissenschaft und die Kunde des nachbiblischen Judentums*, Vol. XLVII. Giessen, 1929.

PEARSON, H. F., and others, *Excavations at Dura-Europos*. Report of Sixth Season, Preliminary Report on the Synagogue at Dura. New Haven, 1936.

RIESENFELD, HARALD, *The Resurrection in Ezekiel XXXVII and in the Dura-Europos Paintings*. Upsala, 1948.

ROSENAU, HELEN, *A Short History of Jewish Art*. London, 1948.

SCHWARZ, KARL, *Die Juden in der Kunst*. 2nd ed. Vienna and Jerusalem, 1936.

———, *Ha-Umanut Ha-Yehudit Ha-Hadashah Beeretz Yisrael*. Jerusalem, 1941.

STASSOF, VLADIMIR, and GUNZBURG, DAVID, *L'Ornement Hébreu*. Berlin, 1905.

SUKENIK, ELEAZAR L., *The Ancient Synagogue of Beth Alpha*. Jerusalem, 1932.

———, *Ancient Synagogues in Palestine and Greece*. London, 1934.

TIETZE, HANS, *Die illuminierten Handschriften der Rossiana in Wien-Lainz*. Leipzig, 1911.

TOEPLITZ, E., "Wall Paintings in Synagogues of the XVII and XVIII Centuries," in *Rimon*, Vol. III, and *Milgrom*, Vol. III. Berlin, 1923.

———, "Die Malerei in den Synagogen," in *Beitraege zur juedischen Kulturgeschichte*, Vol. III. Frankfort am Main, 1929.

TYLOR, E. B., "The Winged figures of the Assyrian and other ancient Monuments," in *Proceedings of the Society of Biblical Archaeology*. London, 1890.

WISCHNITZER (-BERNSTEIN), RACHEL, "Une Bible Enluminée par Joseph ibn Hayyim," in *Revue des Études Juives*, Vol. LXXIII, 146. Paris, 1921.

———, "Illuminated Haggadahs," in *Jewish Quarterly Review*, Vol. XIII, No. 2. London, 1922.

———, "Von der Holbeinbibel zur Amsterdamer Haggadah," in *Monatsschrift fuer Geschichte und Wissenschaft des Judentums*, Vol. LXXV, Nos. 7 and 8. Frankfort am Main, 1931.

———, *Symbole und Gestalten der juedischen Kunst*. Berlin, 1935.

———, "Les Manuscrits à miniatures de Maimonide," *Gazette des Beaux-Arts*, VI, per T. XIII, Nr. 869. Paris, July-August, 1935.

———, "Die Messianische Huette in der juedischen Kunst," *Monatsschrift fuer Geschichte und Wissenschaft des Judentums*, LXXX, Nr. 5. Breslau, 1936. Pp. 377-390.

———, "The Messianic Fox," in *Review of Religion*. Vol. V, No. 3. New York, 1941.

———, "The Conception of the Resurrection in the Ezekiel Panel of the Dura-Synagogue," in *Journal of Biblical Literature*. Vol. XL, No. 1. Philadelphia, 1941.

———, "The Samuel Cycle in the Wall Decoration of the Synagogue at Dura-Europos," in *Proceedings of the American Academy for Jewish Research*, Vol. XI. New York, 1941.

———, "The Sabbath in Art," in A. E. Millgram, *Sabbath, the Day of Delight*. Philadelphia, 1944.

WISCHNITZER (-BERNSTEIN), RACHEL, "Studies in Jewish Art," in *Jewish Quarterly Review*. N.S. Vol. XXXVI, No. 1. Philadelphia, 1945.

———, "Mutual Influences between Eastern and Western Europe in Synagogue Architecture from the 12th to the 18th Century," in *YIVO Bleter*, Vol. XXIX, No. 1. New York, 1947. (Yiddish.)

———, "The Problem of Synagogue Architecture," in *Commentary*, III, 3. New York, March, 1947. Pp. 233-241.

———, "Mutual Influences between Eastern and Western Europe in Synagogue Architecture from the 12th to the 18th century," in *YIVO Annual*, II-III. New York, 1947-1948. Pp. 25-68. (English.)

———, *The Messianic Theme in the Paintings of the Dura Synagogue*. Chicago, 1948.

———, "The Esther Story in Art," in Philip Goodman, *The Purim Anthology*. Philadelphia, 1949. Pp. 222-249.

WRIGHT, G. E., "How did early Israel differ from her neighbors?" in *Biblical Archaeologist*, Vol. VI, No. 1. New Haven, 1943.

———, "Solomon's Temple Resurrected," in *Biblical Archaeologist*, Vol. IV, No. 2, 1941.

CHAPTER 25

THE CONTRIBUTION OF THE JEWS TO MEDICINE

By Arturo Castiglioni

It is very difficult to consider Jewish medicine a chapter with a character all its own in the history of medicine in general.[1a] Our sources for Jewish medicine in antiquity are few and rare. There are available no medical writings which go back to ancient times; there is not even a collection of medical prescriptions or medical stories such as we have for the Egyptians and the Babylonians. The two works that are the sources for the study of Jewish history, the Bible and the Talmud, are chiefly books of laws in which medical subjects are dealt with only incidentally, only in so far as they concern the legislator. In the Talmud some laws on medical matters or problems are discussed, but always from the religious, moral or legal point of view, and evidently medical men have not at all or rarely been consulted. The Rabbis had some general knowledge of medicine, and this was the basis for their judgment or their views.

Jewish medicine of antiquity, at least what has come down to us in the texts of the sacred books, was dominated by the theocratic principle that governed the moral, social and political life of the people. It is easy to understand that this small people, which for centuries was subject to terrible wars, conquests and the influence of mighty neighbors, should in the evolution of its medicine also reveal the results of these circumstances. Unlike Egyptian or Greek medicine, therefore, Jewish medicine cannot be described as something distinctly itself. The first Jewish physicians of whose literary activity we know (seventh or eighth century c.e.) belonged to the world of Arab culture and wrote generally in Arabic, and the most ancient medical work in Hebrew is a collection of prescriptions by the Jewish physician, Sabbatai ben Abraham Donnolo, who lived in Italy in the tenth century and wrote also a mystical commentary on the Book of Creation.

It is even more difficult to speak of Jewish medicine in the period after the destruction of the Temple,[1b] when the bulk of the Jewish people lived in exile. A decisive influence in their medicine was surely the essential character of their religion, and the law which constitutes its basis. This influence is manifest even in the evolution of the thought and activity of the physician, of the hygienist, of the scholar. But the great evolution in medical science, the shift in the Greek schools from magic and dogmatic medicine to clinical medicine and the revolutionary changes in medical doctrine and practice in recent times were not brought about by Jewish scholars; nor did they play any characteristic role in this evolution. The science and scientific activity of the Jews became a part, sometimes more, sometimes less important, of the cultural life of the people in whose midst they lived. Single great scholars accomplished remarkable work, single schools had an important part in the education of scholars and practitioners; it is, however, impossible to say that these scholars or these influences derived from a special character of the Jewish people or of the Jewish mind, and as such stimulated definite action in one or another direction. For many centuries the Jews were concentrated in the Mediterranean countries. Here their medicine had its most important development. A remarkable period of this development is connected with the Arab conquest of the Mediterranean countries. The Jews were the great intermediaries of the Mediterranean; for centuries all commercial goods as well as the treasures of literature and science passed through their hands. The Jewish physicians were philosophers and subtle reasoners, able practitioners, expert diagnosticians and excellent students of botany and pharmacology. They won most important positions at the courts and as teachers, and from this time originate the fame they enjoyed and the role they played in the schools of the Renaissance, especially in Italy, France and Spain. In the following centuries, however, the battle of the European Jews against persecution made their participation in scientific activities difficult and often impossible.

With the emancipation of the Jews in many European countries and the progressive internationalization of science, Jews became more active in medicine and other sciences but no longer did their work have a peculiar character. In later times Jewish scholars held a prominent place as teachers and practitioners, and they made an important contribution to scientific progress. But this contribution cannot be distinguished from that of other great scholars with whom the Jews were in constant contact and from whom they adopted the fundamental concepts and systems of medicine.

We believe, therefore, that this chapter, which attempts to survey the role the Jews played in the history of medicine, may be divided into four parts. The first will be devoted to the medicine of the Bible and Talmud; the second, to the evolution of medicine among the Jews in the Middle Ages and their influence on Arabic medicine; the third, to the role Jewish scholars played in the schools of the pre-Renaissance and Renaissance periods; and finally, a short account of medicine among the Jews in the modern period.

It is not our intention to write the history of the great physicians and scholars and to give their biographies: this has been done in many works at different times and from different points of view. We shall try as far as possible to trace the history of the ideas, the evolution of medical thought, either as it was influenced by the Jews or as it exerted its influence on them, and to give a picture of the role the Jewish scholars and practitioners played in the history of medical science.

The fundamental concept that distinguished the medicine of biblical Israel from that of all other ancient peoples is this: Scripture declares it as a basic doctrine that the One God is the source of life and health; He is also, however, the source of all disease, which comes as a punishment and reproof. "I kill, and I make alive; I have wounded, and I heal" (Deut. 32:39). The animistic concept, the belief in malignant demons, universally accepted among peoples in protohistoric times, was suppressed and all magical practices were forbidden. This is the principle clearly expressed in all canonic books.

The Jewish concept of pathology reveals, however, the belief in a supernatural cause. Humbert states correctly that the origin of disease was attributed by the Jews equally to the Will of God, or to human malediction, or to a fault committed by ancestors (as in the threat of Divine punishment up to the third and fourth generations). As defenses against the hostile influence of individuals, prayers and spells were used. Sigmund Mowinckel and Adolphe Lods have shown that many of the invocations of the Psalms are to be regarded as simple incantations, and that such curses as "Let their eyes be darkened that they see not . . . Let them be blotted out of the book of the living" (69:24, 29) are procedures analogous in their form and scope to the magic preserved in the Assyro-Babylonian texts. According to the earliest narratives, it is not always the One God Who strikes. The plague is carried by an angel of God, who strikes 185,000 Assyrians in one night (II Kings 19:35). The "destroyer" smites the firstborn of Egypt (Ex. 12:23) and the "adversary," one of the Bene Elohim, inflicts malignant ulcers on Job. Angels and malignant demons appear here and there in the sacred books; one of these demons devours the limbs of the dead (Job 18:13).

The concept that tends to attribute chief importance to the blood and a preponderant role in general to the humors is of Sumerian origin. In Scripture, too, will be found the influence of the Egyptian pneumatic concept, that the spirit is the center of life (see Gen. 7:22 "in whose nostrils was the breath of the spirit of life").

In the development of the Jewish concept there is a manifest tendency and practical necessity to concentrate authority and power in the hands of the priestly caste, not because the priests are believed to possess by themselves the power of healing but because they are the interpreters or intermediaries of the will of the One God.

Note the fundamental difference from the medicine of other peoples.

The Jewish priest never plays the role of a physician; he gives his advice according to the religious Law and can help with his prayers. He may be, and really is, an adviser and an expert friend, but he never believes or boasts that he is a healer. When King Asa consulted physicians instead of calling for the help of God through His priests he was promptly punished: he "slept with his fathers" (II Chron. 16:12, 13).

According to this conception it is to God that the sick appeals for the cure of his ills; before Him man prostrates himself to invoke salvation. From the belief in the healing power of God followed the duty to obey all Divine precepts with a scrupulousness no less thorough than that of other nations in their use of magical prescriptions, and to carry out rules of sanitation with the same exactness and fervid faith that had to accompany all religious practices. This was the cause for the rapid development of sanitary legislation, what we may call the first codification of hygienic regulations, among the Jews.

In this recognition of a supreme Divine law and in the abolition of magic beliefs and practices lies the importance of the monotheistic concept for the evolution of medicine in Israel. All the medical practices described in ancient Egyptian and Babylonian texts are originally magic practices, though they may sometimes be rooted in experience; they belong to the religious rites of strange gods and are, therefore, forbidden to the people of Israel. Medicine is poorly represented in early Jewish literature because whenever the magic medicine of Babylonia and Egypt appeared in ancient Judea it was rigorously proscribed and suppressed. Nevertheless, it cannot be denied that in Israel, as among others, some of these practices persisted through the centuries, and it is interesting to see the traces of these practices in the biblical literature. In Scripture, however, they appear under a different aspect: they are made compatible or at least not in conflict with the monotheistic concept.

Traces of magic are evident in the following few examples: The snake was worshiped throughout the Orient as a healing god and was the object of a widespread magic cult; in the Bible he appears in the stories of the Garden of Eden and the brazen serpent. The persistence of this cult is proved by the fact that the serpent had to be destroyed by King Hezekiah to prevent its worship. The Babylonian "Sabbath" is quite likely connected with the magic concept familiar to all Oriental peoples of the unlucky number seven and its multiples. Circumcision was practiced among many primitive peoples and it can probably be explained as an attempt to substitute some bloody rite for human sacrifice. The story of Abraham and Isaac in Gen. 22 is surely connected with the substitution of animal for human sacrifice. Circumcision was prescribed also in Egypt, but only for the priests and upper classes. In Judaism, however, as is repeatedly affirmed in the biblical text, the entire people are regarded as priests, regardless of caste or class; all regulations therefore are imposed equally upon everyone.

The belief in the action of malignant demons (masculine, *shedim*, feminine, *lilit*) which cause insanity, sore throat, asthma and many other ills was prevalent among the Jews. The application of pieces of parchment bearing biblical verses or exorcistic formulae was supposed to aid recovery. A man of God could transfer leprosy from one person to another (II Kings 5:27); with a number of charms the priest could "dry up the thigh and swell the stomach" of the sinful woman after he had made her drink the water in which had been immersed a curse written on a piece of parchment. In epidemics one could obtain relief by sacrificing the sinful person (II Sam. 21:5-6); the prophet Elijah (I Kings 17:21-22) brought a dead child back to life by breathing into its mouth, a rite similar to a Babylonian practice. The proceedings described in Leviticus 14 and the ceremony of the blood of the paschal lamb are founded on analogous practices elsewhere.

In the course of time, after the general acceptance of monotheism, all these beliefs, traditions and customs were absorbed into and filtered through the moral and legislative system of Judaism and the theocratic principle definitely governed the moral, social and political life of the people and the evolution of its medicine. Thus the use of the phylacteries (*tephillin*) and the *mezuzot*, originally ancient apotropaic rites, assumed the character of a religious law of moral importance.

The concept of purity is of eminent importance in biblical legislation. Physical purity is put on a par with moral purity, and it is not admitted that heart and mind can be pure without cleanliness of the body. The aim of Jewish religious precepts, to which the hygienic regulations belong, is purity before God. Hygienic regulations were imposed on the people by law with the authority characteristic of Divine maxims and in the form of religious ceremonies. Some of these regulations existed also in Egypt and in Babylonia, where they had a magic character; but in the Bible the religious distinction between pure and impure is a standard for everyday life. Whoever becomes impure (*tame*) for whatever reason, whether he had committed an evil deed or had contracted a contagious disease, or had touched a corpse, could become pure (*tahor*) with the help of exactly prescribed practices in which bathing was of the greatest importance. The hygienic law of impurity after contact with corpses, of women during and after the menstrual period, of those affected with gonorrhea and leprosy, arise from a purely religious concept. This originally mystic apparatus is important and soon assumes a symbolic character. David prays to God: "Wash me thoroughly from mine iniquity, and cleanse me from my sin" (Ps. 51:4). The sinner is told: "For though thou wash Thee with nitre, and take thee much soap, yet thine iniquity is marked before Me" (Jer. 2:22).

This makes it amply clear that the practice of purification signified to the common mind also a cleansing of oneself from the sin of moral transgression. The well-known passage in the Psalms, "I will wash my hands in innocency" (26:6), takes on symbolic significance, and later the purifying bath is transformed into the symbolic baptism.

No Jew could enter the Temple without being pure, that is to say, without having first taken a bath if he had been in contact with impure persons or things or had done anything which made his body impure. Even before reading the Law, which was regarded as a daily duty for every Jew, a bath had to be taken. The same rite was prescribed after every ejaculation.

The people of Israel did not have professional physicians, although an empirical medicine flourished among the Jews as everywhere else. In ancient times there was no physician (rophe) even on such occasions as that of embalming Jacob's body. For embalming, Joseph called physicians from Egypt. That is why we can derive only fragmentary information on medical cures and medicines from the Bible. The prophets appear to have acted in some cases as wonder-healers, but it is evident that their healing activity was closely connected with an intense moral and religious suggestion.

Later we find mention of physicians and we learn that they enjoyed great esteem. Jesus, the son of Sirach (180 B.C.E.), says, "Honor the physician according to thy need of him with the honor due unto him because verily the Lord hath created him." The physician is always considered as the intermediary, working with the help and carrying out the Will of God.

The Jewish physician who appears in the pages of the Talmud is not a specialist like the Egyptian medical men of whom Herodotus speaks. The physician of the Talmud prescribes cures for internal diseases, but he is also a surgeon who binds the patient on the table and has with him a bag which contains his instruments. He is able to heal wounds with herbs, to give dietetic prescriptions and to give the patient a potion (samme deshinta) for inducing sleep during the operation (Baba Mezia 83b). He opens an abscess and, we are also told, is able to open the skull with a trephine to operate on the brain and to close the wound with the skin of a squash (Tosefta Ohalot 2.6). Amputation of limbs and of gangrenous parts is performed. The physician is expert in the treatment of fractures and it is expected that he be ready to work with knife, plasters, bandages and internal remedies alike.

Gynecological or obstetrical interference of physicians was not admitted, but midwives (meyalledet) played an important role. Some of them are quoted in the Bible; for instance, at the delivery of Rachel (Gen. 35:17) and of Thamar (Gen. 38:28). In the Mishna the midwife is called *hakama,* the "wise woman," like the *sage femme* of the French. Embryotomy was also to be performed by a midwife if a surgeon could not be reached, but not by a pagan because she might kill the child.

Unlike other legislations, the Jewish law holds the physician responsible only if he has intentionally hurt his patient, not if an error occurred. This is commented upon by Pardo, quoted by Preuss, with the observation that "if the physician should be made responsible for every mistake nobody would follow this profession. The judgment and punishment are reserved to God."

There is a clear distinction in the Talmud between the physician, *rophe,* and the bloodletter (*umman*). The latter was considered a worker and had a very low social position. The Talmud regards him unfavorably: he can never become a leader of a community nor take part in the election of king nor High Priest. It may be noted that the profession is despised also among the Arabs. Circumcision, the most frequent surgical operation, was generally practiced by the physician or by a specialist who was called *mahola,* later *mohel.* Circumcision was a religious act of fundamental importance; it was, however, prescribed that children who were sick or bleeders should not be circumcised.

The anatomical knowledge in biblical and talmudic literature was derived only from occasional inspection of corpses and from the examination of the internal organs of slaughtered animals in order to determine their condition. That human dissections should have been practiced in ancient times is very unlikely. The fear of hurting a corpse (*niwwul met*) was certainly the most important reason making dissection impossible. Not even exhumation and inspection of the corpse was permitted. For the same reason embalming was forbidden. A similar attitude is responsible for the custom once general in Egypt of throwing stones at the embalmer as a punishment, after he had performed his work. It is, however, told of the pupils of Rabbi Ishmael (about 100 C.E.) that they boiled the corpse of a prostitute who had been condemned to death, in order to learn what was the number of bones in the human body (B. Bekorot 45a). This method of treating bones seems to have been usual in antiquity, and was expressly forbidden by Pope Boniface VIII in 1301.

In his scholarly work, Preuss has given an exhaustive summary of talmudic anatomy. We may only say briefly that the esophagus, the larynx, the trachea, the lungs, meninges and the genital organs are described, and the spleen, kidneys, liver, heart and intestines are often mentioned. Blood constitutes the vital principle; muscles are referred to as *basar* (flesh) and the tendons as *giddim.* The body was thought to have 248 bones, according to the days of the lunar year, and 365 tendons, according to the days of the solar year. One bone called *luz,* placed somewhere in the vertebral column, was believed to be the nucleus from which the body would be reconstructed at the resurrection of the dead. This ossicle, which was said to be indestructible, was searched for by the anatomists of the Middle Ages without success.

It may be noted that, according to the texts, the liver, the origin of the blood, is the most important organ and the center of life. The heart is not the center of the circulation, but the seat of the soul (Aristotelian doctrine). The anatomical and physiological information about the brain is very poor. During sleep, the brain, they believed, could be removed without breaking any bones, through the nose or, according to the Talmud, through the auditive channel.

The importance of dreams was generally accepted. R. Eleazar stated, "There is no dream without significance," and R. Hisda said, "A dream which is not interpreted is like a letter which is not read." In general the opinion of the teachers is against this interpretation of dreams which, however, are given prominent place in the Bible and Talmud. Very interesting is a statement by R. Joshua b. Hananja that all dreams can be realized according to their interpretation and that for any dream there are not less than twenty-four interpretations which may be correct.

The popular view of etiology of diseases was analogous to that of the Babylonians and Egyptians. The belief in the stars was widespread as was the belief in the influence of the evil eye (*ayyin ha-ra*), which also is probably of Babylonian origin, and is widespread in our times, too, especially among the Mediterranean peoples.

It was generally believed that a mortal disease lasted five days. In therapy the incantation (*lahash*) played an important part, but it was considered part of the occult practices of which no sign can be found in the Talmud. Amulets and charms were very much in use and were not forbidden, probably because this practice was too deeply rooted in the traditional belief of the people. What we know of the spread of epidemic diseases in biblical and later times proves that the idea of contagion, its dangers and the need to overcome them by isolation was well known to the Semitic peoples. In the story (I Sam. 5:1-2) of the capture of the Ark of the Covenant by the Philistines, who carried it to the temple of Dagon, is found the description of an epidemic of bubonic plague (their punishment for the desecration), and when the Philistines decided to return the Ark they offered at the same time a symbolic gift of five golden emerods and five golden mice to the God of Israel. Here is remarkable evidence of the importance attributed to rodents in the spread of the plague in very ancient times. In another epidemic (II Kings 19:35) we are informed of the mortality caused when the angel of the Lord killed 185,000 of Sennacherib's soldiers (705-681 B.C.E.). In the story of this pestilence, which is referred to by Herodotus (II, 141), the rat also plays an important part. In fact, according to Egyptian tradition, the Assyrians were decimated by the god Ptah, who was represented in the temple of Thebes with a rat in his hand. It is probable that the importance attributed to animals as transmitters of disease also had a magic origin.

Leprosy received considerable attention in the biblical books. The Hebrew word for leprosy is *tsaraat*. The number of writings on this subject and of commentaries on the thirteenth chapter of Leviticus, where the diseases are described, is so great that we may easily believe that many discussions took place in order to identify the disease. All the descriptions of the symptoms and of the sanitary measures justify the conclusion that leprosy is meant. Preuss closes his study on the subject with the statement that it is at least a probable identification: we have to admit, however, that the term was often used for other clinical phenomena such as psoriasis, eczema and various inflammations of the skin, perhaps even syphilis. The person suspected of being a leper was brought to the priest; if he found that the *nega*, the affected place, was white and appeared to be deeper than the surrounding skin, he declared that it was really *tsaraat* and that the patient was impure. Note that the symptomatic signs here quoted are the same that the Arabian physicians, especially Avicenna, describe as characteristic of leprosy. It is the white sign, *morphoea alba*, which is recognized as such plus the fact that the hair on the spot turns white.

Among the other more frequent diseases in biblical times were dysentery, dropsy, apoplexy, and mental diseases like Saul's. That certain venereal diseases were common in Judea is apparent from the strict hygienic regulation for those with an "issue" (gonorrhea?). According to certain interpreters, the biblical account of the plague of Baal-Peor should be regarded as the story of a syphilis epidemic as a result of the Hebrews' visit to the brothels of the Midianites. The terrible disease killed twenty-four thousand people. This interpretation, however, is not at all sufficiently proved.

Other diseases like *shehin* (universal eczema), the disease of King Hezekiah (pharynx abscess?), the *baale raatan* (leprosy) are difficult to identify. The information about their symptoms, their course and their recovery is neither clear nor the same in the different accounts; only hypothetical suppositions, therefore, can be advanced.

The sect of the Essenes, which was formed about 150 B.C.E.,[2a] deserves to be mentioned. The Essenes were Jews who lived a monastic life; they included the *Therapeutae* and *Hemerobaptists*, and it seems that the former particularly practiced medicine in some mild form of suggestion. Some believe that the name "Essene" is derived from the Aramaic *Asa* (he healed), corresponding to the Greek Therapeutae. In the therapy of the Essenes prayers and pious formulae were very important and we may compare this medicine with the Christian conventual medicine which arose in the Middle Ages at the time of the foundation of the monasteries.

The Essenes were considered saints, wonder-healers who cured by faith and by words. They practiced medicine in order to perfect the soul and make it more accessible to Divine truth and Divine health. By conjuration they drove hostile spirits out of the patient's body. The Mishna (Bekorot 4:4) refers to Teudas, who was acquainted with conditions in Alexandria as a worthy physician, and Josephus (*De Ant. Jud.* VIII, 2:5) describes the cure of a possessed person in the presence of the Emperor Vespasian by Eleazar, an Essene. A root allegedly recommended by King Solomon and endowed with healing properties was introduced into the nose of the sick man. The Essene pronounced the name of the wise king and a magic formula and the patient recovered. The laying on of hands was practiced and amulets were used.

It is interesting to note that in the Talmud some animal products, in some kind of primitive opotherapy of magical origin, are prescribed. A man bitten by a mad dog was given the omentum of the dog to eat; parts of the liver and the spleen of animals were prescribed for diseases of that organ.

From many biblical passages it is clear that the art of the apothecary was not unknown to the ancient Hebrews. In Ex. 30:22-26 we read: "The Lord spoke unto Moses, saying, 'Take thou also unto thee the chief spices, of flowing myrrh five hundred shekels, and of sweet cinnamon half so much, even two hundred and fifty, and of sweet calamus two hundred and fifty and of cassia five hundred, after the shekel of the Sanctuary and of olive oil a hin. And thou shalt make it a holy anointing oil, a perfume compounded after the art of the perfumer.' "

Mandrake also was a very popular remedy among the ancient Hebrews and it was generally believed to be useful in promoting conception (Gen. 30:14). Nitre was employed as a cleansing agent and oil was used to dress wounds, bruises and sores (Is. 1:6). Many remedies, especially ointments, are referred to by Roman authors as being used by Jews.[3]

Jewish philosophers and physicians participated actively in the flourishing science of Alexandria and, at the time of the Ptolemies, enjoyed a great popularity. The Greeks were then inclined to admire these strange people and to accept them in the schools, in the public discussions, and in the professions; but in the first century C.E. anti-Semitism began to manifest itself and in the Christian empire it took on the form of a social persecution, despite the fact that Julius Caesar and the early Roman emperors followed the policy of the Hellenistic princes to patronize the Jews and grant them full liberty. Jews adopted Greek as their mother tongue and Jewish students inherited the intellectual legacy of Greece.[4a] The inner conflict of the Jewish-Hellenistic intellectual world is reflected in the work of Philo.[5a]

Biblical-talmudic literature permits us to trace the evolution of medical

thought among the Jews from fundamental magical beliefs and conceptions common to all primitive peoples to an empirical and religious
medicine. How great the influence of Greek medicine was is difficult to
determine. The Talmud, as already observed, is a collection of discussions
and of laws and their interpretation but not of medical doctrines. We
may, therefore, pass only a general judgment on the practice of medicine
and believe that the Jewish physicians of those days accepted the diagnostic
rules and therapeutic means prescribed by Greek medicine, but did not care
too much for the clinical doctrines or the theoretical scientific explanations
that were the characteristic elements of Greek science. Jewish physicians
acknowledged the facts, but were cautious and skeptical in adopting
doctrines which appeared to them heterodox from the point of view of
their strong religious faith, whose central belief was expressed by the
words of Divine revelation, "I am the Lord, that healeth thee"
(Ex. 15:26).

In his memorable speech at the International Medical Congress in Rome
(1894) on "Morgagni and Anatomical Thought," Rudolf Virchow said:
"In the Middle Ages the Jews and the Arabs certainly had a definite
influence on the progress of medical doctrine. Recent discoveries have
brought to light Hebrew manuscripts which demonstrate with how great
a diligence and scholarship the Jewish physician of the Middle Ages
was active in the preservation and development of medical thought."

The role played by the Jews during the Arab conquests of the Mediterranean is an impressive one in the history of the Middle Ages and the
pre-Renaissance.[6a] In contact with the Arabs, among whom they were
respected physicians, teachers and counselors, Jews were perhaps the only
aliens able to understand the language and the psychology of the people
whose victorious banners flew over southern Europe for six centuries.
The Jews enjoyed complete freedom in their professional and intellectual
activity. They became the advisers of sultan and caliph and once more
played the historic role to which they seemed destined by the geographical
position of their native country, and by their constant relations with
different races and creeds as a result of war, persecution, dispersion and
exile. These events had surely given the Jews their peculiar orientation of
thought, for they had to adjust themselves to different conditions, laws
and customs, and to adopt or reject new beliefs. Theirs was the passionate
desire to seek out the true and the best everywhere, as far as possible to
placate hostile powers and conciliate opposing opinions. They were, or
tried to be, according to the biblical prescription, the seekers and teachers
of truth, always fighting with others and themselves for their beliefs. They
were acquainted with Greek philosophy and medicine and had felt deeply
the influence of the Alexandrian schools. To the Arabs, a people of
warriors and fanatic believers whose contact with Western civilization was

a violent one at the outset, the Jews gave the first lessons in classic philosophy and science.

At first not only difference in religion but also difference of language was the chief difficulty in the evolution of a Jewish medical literature. The Jews in the Diaspora used Hebrew in their writings, but always needed new words for their scientific vocabulary. These they took from the language of the country they inhabited; and thus the glossaries or dictionaries arose. Later, however, when the Jews in exile forgot the Hebrew language, or used it only in their prayers and in their religious studies, it was necessary for the teacher and scholar who had to address a larger public to write in the language of the country; hence the fact that for the most part Jewish physicians, among them the most illustrious like Maimonides, wrote their medical works in Arabic.

In the evolution of Arabic medicine, the study of classical medical authors went hand in hand with philosophy, and both subjects were entirely free from any religious influence. Thanks to the meticulous researches of Moritz Steinschneider, we now know how great was the service of Jewish translators to science. In their hands was the light of ancient scientific knowledge and by adding it to Arabic culture they saved Greek science for the Occident. The most important classical writings in philosophy, astronomy, mathematics and medicine were translated from Greek into Arabic. Hardly fifty years after the conquest, a Babylonian Jew translated a medical work from Syrian into Arabic.[7] In the latter half of the seventh century Masarjawaih translated many medical texts. These were later retranslated by other Jewish scholars from Arabic into Hebrew and Latin. The activity of Jewish physicians among the Arabs had a decisive influence on the progress not only of Arabic but, later, of Western medicine also.

Although the bulk of Jewish Arabic scholarship consisted of translation from and assimilation of Greek works, it did far more than that. They not only transmitted ancient knowledge, but also contributed to the creation of new knowledge.

The most remarkable Jewish medical writers were Isaac Israeli (850-950 c.e.) and Moses Maimonides (1135-1204). The first was physician to the Caliph Obaid Allah and wrote philosophical works on the elements. According to Harry Friedenwald, Israeli's medical works were the greatest contributions of Arabic Jewish physicians. His full name was Abu Yakub Ishak ibn Suleiman al Israeli, and his works, soon translated into Hebrew and Latin, had widespread fame. He was known among the Arabs as Israeli, in the Western medical world as Isaac Judeus. His works were translated into Latin by Constantinus Africanus, the learned monk who was said to be of Jewish origin. Israeli's most famous books, which are frequently referred to as classics, and which served as textbooks at the school of Salerno, where the books on Urine and Fever, the Opera Isaaci Judaei *"medicorum monarcha,"* were published in Latin in Lyons (1515).

Moses Maimonides (Abu Imram Musa ibn Maimun), born in Cordova in 1135, fled to Fez in 1148 because of the persecutions by the Almohades; later he went to Palestine and finally to Cairo, where he settled in 1165 and soon became famous as philosopher and physician. He was the physician of Saladin and his son, and head of the Jewish community of Egypt; he died in 1204 and was buried in Tiberias. As George Sarton says, his influence was far reaching in space and time. He occupied a prominent place among the great thinkers of the Middle Ages and the forerunners of scientific medicine. That he was the greatest exponent of a new trend of thought is shown by the influence of his work on Albertus Magnus and Thomas Aquinas. He practiced medicine with intelligent observation of his patients, with love and faith, and strictly followed the moral precepts of the Bible. His fame as a healer is still a living tradition throughout the Orient. Even today his synagogue in Cairo is considered an especially sacred shrine, the sick go there to pass the night in order to speed their recovery. And to his tomb at Tiberias, on the shore of the Sea of Gennesaret, a pilgrimage of the sick takes place even at the present time. Many places in different countries enjoy similar fame, but this is the only case in history where the physician himself is regarded, after his death, as a wonder-healer.

This is not the place to estimate the importance of Maimonides as philosopher and religious writer.[8a] We may only say that his profound comprehension and fervid admiration of the scientific achievements of the Greek philosophers and physicians, and, on the other hand, his firm belief in the teachings of the Law, led him to attempt a conciliation between Aristotle and the Bible. This is evident also in his medical works, in his fight against astrology and superstition, in his deep understanding of the importance of a psychological therapy, in his high conception of the duties of the physician. To understand and with a free mind to discuss new currents of thought without abandoning the laws and the traditional beliefs of the Jewish people caused perpetual conflict in the soul of Jewish scholars at all times. In his stupendous activity as commentator of the sacred books, as revered judge in all religious problems, and at the same time as teacher and physician, Maimonides followed the example of the prophets and the great Rabbis. In the evolution of scientific thought in the Mediterranean, which was the center of civilization for twenty centuries, the work of Moses Maimonides had a decisive influence.

Among the distinguished medical translators we may mention the following: Moses ibn Tibbon (*c.* 1283), a Provençal physician who translated many works of Maimonides and Rhazes; Nathan Ha Meati of Cento (Italy), who lived in Rome (1229-1283) and translated, among other books, the *Canon* of Avicenna and the *Aphorisms* of Hippocrates with the *Commentaries* of Galen. Hasdai ibn Shaprut, minister to the caliph of Cordova (*c.* 960), with the aid of a Greek monk translated Dioscorides into Arabic.

Faraj ben Salim was one of the most prominent translators of the thirteenth century. He was very likely connected with the school of Salerno, and must have been in close touch with Charles of France, who ruled Sicily from 1266 to 1285. The Latin translation of the medical work by the Arabic Ali ibn Jazla, which was published in 1532, was dedicated to the king. Faraj was one of the first Jewish doctors to translate from the Arabic directly into Latin. (One of the most popular translators was Gerard of Cremona, who put into Latin the *Canon* of Avicenna [a book which vied in popularity with Aristotle's and Galen's works] and the treatise on surgery by Abulcasis, which was widely read in the Occident until the end of the Renaissance.) The influence of Jewish physicians in Spain and their activity in the schools of southern France (Montpellier), perhaps also in the school of Salerno which many Jewish students attended, was of far-reaching importance.

During the Middle Ages, when dogmatism and Scholasticism hampered the evolution of Western medicine, there occurred an interesting development in Jewish medicine. On the one hand, in certain circles mysticism began to be cultivated with a renewed vigor, and in the *Zohar*, the mystic's Bible, so to speak, appeared its most significant expression. Elsewhere in the present work, the nature of the *Zohar* is discussed.[9a] For our immediate purpose, however, and from one point of view, the work may be described as a mystic-medical book. According to the *Zohar*, the soul, invisible and imperceptible, has its seat above the cortex and governs life through the organs which are divided into two regions separated by a "heaven," the diaphragm. Through channels the Divine grace flows to all parts of the body, but the function of the organs ceases when sin stops the flowing of grace. Different pulses are described and mystically connected with the four elements. A supreme importance is attributed to generation: mysticism and the erotic are closely connected, and each organ receives mystic significance.

Another form of mystic medicine originated in the traditional trust of the devout in the counsel of holy men whose sayings have been preserved for centuries by pious Jews in the East and by the Hasidim. These mystical tendencies were not without influence on Jewish medicine: they introduced the medicine of the so-called wonder Rabbis, who were the revered advisers and medical counselors. Their cures, however, were generally limited to moral or hygienic prescriptions and to the use of certain prayers, formulae or cryptograms. The work of the wonder-healers flourished whenever superstition or belief in the occult was rampant. Generally their medical system was of only the mildest sort; its suggestive therapy was often educational, always fantastic, but certainly not dangerous.

Medicine among the Jews in Eastern Europe, especially in Poland, followed the same mysticism up to our time. In a book published by Jacob Koblenz (Offenbach, 1788) many wonder remedies are recommended, among them incantation with formulae in Hebrew and Yiddish. Throughout the Middle Ages certain prayers and biblical passages were very popular as remedies. The Psalms were often prescribed as cure. In the *Shimmush Tehillim*, which was often printed, we find passages which have to be recited to hasten delivery, passages for protection against eye diseases, against fever. Psalm 22:21 was believed to be especially efficacious against dogbite.

In 1720 a book, *Toledot Adam*, was published whose authors were said to be Elia baal Shem, Joel baal Shem and Simha Rofe; the work contains a great number of cabbalistic prescriptions. The name *baal Shem* was given to those who were believed to be cabbalistic wonder-healers. The most famous of them was the "Besht," Israel baal Shem Tob, the founder of modern Hasidism. It is evident that a continuous line leads from the mystic therapy of the Essenes to the therapeutic system of the wonder practices popular in the East up to the present.

In the schools of the Mediterranean countries, especially in Italy and France, Jewish physicians had always played an important role. The condition of the Jews in the Middle Ages had been one of great hardship and persecution, their activities were restricted; nevertheless, they had maintained an almost continuous line of medical practitioners. Friedenwald, who has written an interesting chapter on this period of Jewish medicine also, says that the history of the Jews in the Diaspora has been the longest in Italy, lasting over more than two thousand years. Already by the end of the fourth century c.e. the Jews had attained great prominence and many of them were official physicians, *archiatri*. Thereafter many church councils forbade Christians to call upon Jewish physicians or be medically treated by them.

However, many exceptions were made. In 1220 Pope Honorius III took under his papal protection Azzachus Avembenist of Barcelona, Jewish court physician to the king of Aragon. Pope Martin IV had at his court a Jewish physician who was a pupil of Rabbi Nathan of Montpellier and his example was followed by many Popes. The attitude of the Popes toward the Jew varied at different times, but in general we can say that the Jewish physicians continued in their prominent position.

In the thirteenth and fourteenth centuries Jewish physicians enjoyed the protection of the rulers and great fame even in Catholic Spain. One of these physicians was Judah Alfachar (d. 1235). He had the title of *Nasi* (Prince) at the court of Ferdinand III in Toledo, and held an important position not only as physician, but also as collector of revenues. Another was Sheshet Benveniste, physician and diplomat at the court of Aragon, with the same position and title. José Orabuena (fourteenth century) was the physician of the king of Navarre and for a long time the treasurer of the court. Both Samuel and Judah ibn Wakar were physicians who enjoyed the confidence of the ruling family.

In many Italian cities, especially in Ferrara, Mantua, and Genoa, many Spanish and Portuguese refugees were received and many Jewish physicians granted the privilege of practicing medicine.

The part that Jewish scholars and teachers played in the old schools is an important one. According to Theodor Puschmann, medicine was probably taught in the ancient Jewish academies of Tiberias, Sura and Pumbedita;[10a] in general, however, medicine was learned by a student serving as apprentice to a physician. Sometimes schools of higher learning grew out of a private undertaking. Dr. Harry Friedenwald quotes a prospectus, published in 1564, by David Provençal and his son Abraham, for a Jewish university to be established in Mantua where not only the sacred laws, but also Latin, logic, philosophy and mathematics were to be taught. Both father and son were physicians. It is not known whether this project was realized, but we do know of an early Jewish school in Paris where medicine was taught; in the fourteenth century, it is said, this school rivaled the university. Many medieval rabbis were physicians as well. The Gaon Hai in his *Moral Admonitions*, about 1000 c.e., urged the study of medical writings.[11a] There were teachers who had a large number of pupils and conducted private schools in which medicine also was taught.

The school of Salerno plays an important role in the history of medical teachings. Salvatore De Renzi tells the well known story of its foundation by four physicians: a Greek, a Latin, an Arab and a Jew (Elinus), each teaching in his own language. This is almost certainly a legend, but it is probably founded on ancient tradition. The Jews played an important part in medical education at this time; Donnolo, who practiced medicine in the tenth century, enables us, as George Sarton says, "to realize how the so-called school of Salerno gradually came into existence. Such men as Donnolo created in southern Italy that focus of medical syncretisms and eventually of medical teaching."

Among the Salernian teachers Benvenutus Grassus (Grapheus) deserves to be mentioned. His book on ophthalmology, translated into English by Casey Wood of Chicago, was very much studied and commented upon in the ancient universities. Benvenutus is believed to have come from Jerusalem and is described by Sarton as the most famous non-Moslem oculist of medieval times. Julius Hirschberg believes that he was Jewish, and in a Parisian codex his name reads *"Biem Venu Raffe."* This name, Hirschberg observes, is very likely only a slight change from the Hebrew *Ha-Rophe.*

His book, *De oculis eorumque egritudinibus et curis,* was the most popular Latin textbook on the subject, as is shown by the number of copies which have been preserved in Latin, English, French and Provençal (twenty-two manuscripts and eighteen printed editions). It also had the distinction of being the first printed book on ophthalmology (Ferrara, 1474). Benvenutus makes frequent reference to his own anatomical studies on the structure of the eye, and his books constituted a notable advance over the work of the Arabic authors. For five hundred years it was regarded as the classical text on ophthalmology.

Salernian uroscopy found in Isaac Judeus, whom we mentioned above, its classic master. According to his book, the urine was carefully examined for color, density and content. For deducing some extremely important conclusions, the different kinds of clouds and precipitates which form after standing for a time were observed. Though this method had no diagnostic value, it was employed for centuries.

In France, in many cities near the Spanish border, where the influence of the Arabic-Jewish physicians was more deeply felt, there were Jewish schools where medicine was taught. Rashi (Rabbi Solomon ben Isaac, 1040-1105), born in Troyes, famous commentator of the Talmud, had a remarkable influence on scientific thought. At Lunel there was a flourishing medical school where Judah ibn Tibbon taught. These schools certainly had an influence on the University of Montpellier, which was perhaps as old as Salerno and for many centuries a leading medical school. Jean Astruc (1684-1766), who studied medicine in Paris and wrote a history of the medical school of Montpellier, stressed the importance of the Jewish participation in the early years of the university.

The first Jewish teacher of Montpellier, Jacob ben Makir ibn Tibbon (Prophatius Judeus), who lived from 1236 to 1304, was, according to Astruc, regent of the university for a long time. Among the outstanding Jewish doctors at Montpellier were the five doctors of the Saporta family, the first of whom, Luis, came from Lerida in Spain, lived first in Arles, then in Avignon, and became professor at the faculty in Montpellier (1506-1529). He was Charles VIII's physician and died at the age of 106. His great-grandson Jean was graduated in 1572 and became professor in 1577 and vice-chancellor in 1603. The Saportas were Marranos[12a] and for this reason were not admitted to municipal office. Friedenwald has suggested that Jean Astruc was also of Jewish origin. It is in any case interesting that the tradition of Jewish instructors and their influence on the development of medical studies at Montpellier survived so long. In the hall of the faculty there is a plaque in honor of Nathan ben Zechariah, master of the medical school in the thirteenth century.

After the Spanish victories and with the end of Arab domination in the Mediterranean, during the renaissance of art and science, the great migration of the Jews began. Among the Jews expelled from Spain were physicians and these now went to the Orient, especially to Constantinople, and to Italy and France.[13a]

The first universities were founded at the end of the thirteenth century; they were under the permanent supervision and control of the Catholic Church, and in 1431 the Council of Basel decreed that no Jew should receive a university degree. However, in many cases Jews were admitted as students to the medical schools, obtained a degree, and sometimes also were permitted to lecture.

With the Bull of Pius IV (1565), it was decided that no Jew should be admitted to any examination for the doctorate. The Venetian Senate, however, eager to protect freedom of learning and teaching at Padua, named a procurator who had the power to grant the degree regardless of the candidate's religion. The non-Catholics had recourse to the Counts Palatine, who had obtained the privilege of conferring academic degrees from the emperor. In 1616 the Venetian Senate decreed the foundation of a collegium which conferred degrees by authority of the Venetian state. Padua had the largest number of Jewish students, not only from Italy, but from foreign countries. Ismar Elbogen, in his article on Padua in the *Jewish Encyclopedia*, says that from 1517 to 1619 eighty Jews obtained the medical degree at Padua, and that in the next century there were about 150. At other universities, *e.g.*, in Rome and Ferrara and Siena, Jewish medical students were admitted and received their degrees.

This is not the place to enumerate all the Jewish physicians who had a part in the history of the ancient universities. Some names should be given, however, particularly those whose works were very popular in the medical literature of the Renaissance and are still considered remarkable contributions to medical progress.

Most interesting was Amatus Lusitanus, born in Castello Branco, Portugal. His parents were Marranos. He studied medicine in Salamanca, went back to Lisbon and later left Portugal for Antwerp. His reputation was so great that he was invited by Duke Hercules d'Este II to occupy the chair of medicine at the University of Ferrara (1540-1547). He lectured on Hippocrates and Galen, enjoyed the friendship of colleagues and scholars and participated in the dissections performed by the famous anatomist Canano. He later went to Ancona, where he finished his first *Centuria* in 1549. Amatus was often called to other cities as consultant; in May, 1550, he was invited to Rome to treat the newly elected Pope Julius III and later to attend the Pope's nephew, the ruler of Ancona. He spent several months in Rome and was very successful. In April, 1551, he finished his *Centuria II*, which was dedicated to Cardinal d'Este. In May, 1551, he dedicated his translation of Dioscorides to the Senate of Ragusa, where he wished to be appointed as city physician. His life was extremely adventurous, and it may be cited as an example of the persecution and the restrictions of Jews and Marranos at this time. In 1555 Pope

Paul IV was elected, and new decrees were promulgated forbidding Jewish physicians to treat Christian patients and ordering the yellow badge for all Jews. The Inquisition began its ruthless program, a great number of Marranos were arrested and subjected to torture, many burned at the stake. The house of Amatus was broken into and all valuables, including books and manuscripts, were looted.

Amatus repaired to Pesaro, where the Duke of Urbino was very friendly toward the refugees; from here he went to Ragusa, where his fame was soon established. But the persecution was not yet ended. In 1558 he left Ragusa for Salonica, where he found a large practice, and wrote the *Centuria VII*. It is believed that he died in 1568 of the plague that was raging in the city. His great work, the translation and comments on Dioscorides, was published in 1553 and contained many criticisms of the book by Matthioli, a famous pharmacologist, who replied to the criticisms in a violent way.

The medical writings of Amatus are interesting chiefly because they cite a great number of case histories, followed by discussion in the form of a dialogue between himself and other scholars. In therapy Amatus stressed the importance of proper diet and general hygiene; he describes more than twenty surgical cases and made an important contribution to the surgical treatment of empyema. He reveals in all his work an extensive knowledge of medical literature and a fine power of observation. He was emphatic in his opposition to superstition and magical treatment. In the history of the discovery of the valves of the veins, Amatus, who worked in Ferrara with the famous anatomist Canano, played an important part.

Another of the great physicians in the medicine of the Renaissance was Abraham ben Samuel Zacutus, also known as Diego Rodrigo, born in Salamanca about 1452. After the expulsion of the Jews from Spain he fled to Portugal and later to Tunis, where he was taken prisoner. He was not only a well-known physician, but also an author of astronomical and historical works of which the *Almanach Perpetuum* and the *Astrolabe* are the best known. It is certain that Vasco da Gama, the first navigator who made the voyage around the Cape of Good Hope, and had a long consultation with Zacuto before leaving, utilized his books during the navigation.[14a]

His great-great-grandson, well known under the name of Zacutus Lusitanus, born in Lisbon in 1575, took the doctor's degree in Salamanca in 1596 and went to Amsterdam in 1625. He published two interesting books of medical history, but he was considered chiefly as a great clinician. He was one of the first to describe blackwater fever, and made an important contribution to the knowledge of syphilis. His *Opera Omnia* were published in Lyons in two large volumes (1642-1644) and were dedicated to Louis XIII of France.

Jewish physicians were among the pioneers in the East Indies. The most illustrious of this group was Garcia da Orta, born in the last years of the fifteenth century in Elvas, Portugal. He studied medicine in Salamanca, then became professor of logic in Lisbon and in 1534 finally sailed for India. He lived in Goa, where he carried on extensive study of medicinal herbs. His work, *Colloquios dos simples e drogas e cousas medicinae de India,* appeared in 1563 and was immediately recognized as the first and most important contribution to the knowledge of Indian flora. The *Colloquios* had a great influence on the study of tropical medicine and of pharmacology. Da Orta's life was one of great affliction: he was tried as a Marrano by the Inquisition, but judgment was pronounced twelve years after his death. In Portuguese literature he is recognized as a most distinguished representative of the natural sciences.

To the same group of medical pioneers in the East Indies belongs Cristoval d'Acosta, a Marrano who was born in Mozambique in about 1515. He embarked for India in 1568 and stayed there four years. He devoted himself to botanical studies and tried to complete the work of his predecessor, Garcia.

Of medical importance in the sixteenth and seventeenth centuries was the family de Castro, of Spanish and Portuguese origin. Many physicians belonged to this family, the first, and one of the most distinguished, being Rodrigo de Castro (1550-1627). He was the author of a book on gynecology, *De Universa Muliebrium Medicina* (Cologne, 1603), which went through many editions.

One of the physicians in this family deserves special mention. Orobio de Castro, born in Portugal in 1620, studied philosophy and medicine in Seville, became professor of philosophy and later took up medical practice. He was very well known and had a large family. He was denounced to the Inquisition by a servant, who had been whipped for stealing, and was thrown into prison and tortured. The story of his suffering, quoted by Friedenwald, is found in the history of the Inquisition by Philipp van Limborch, who had it from Orobio's own mouth: "A linen garment was put over his body and drawn so very close on each side that it almost squeezed him to death. When he had overcome this torture and persisted in his refusal to confess, they tied his thumbs so very tight that the blood spurted out from under the nail." The whole procedure was repeated for a long time and always with new instruments. Finally he was condemned to perpetual banishment. He left Spain, went to Toulouse and then to Amsterdam, where he publicly reverted to Judaism, took the name Isaac and became one of the leaders of the community.

From the Renaissance up to modern times, that is, to the epoch of the Emancipation,[15a] Jewish physicians practiced medicine all over Europe, as we have seen, in great numbers and often with success; however, everywhere, with the exception of Italy, they were persecuted and interrupted in their activity. Some acquired great fame and were also physicians and counselors to kings and princes; sometimes they also had important positions and special privileges; but these were always exceptional cases. In general their life was insecure and it was not possible for them to have an important part in research and in teaching because admission to the great hospitals, the medical schools and general practices was either entirely forbidden or permitted only sporadically for short periods and under the protection of some enlightened ruler.

In the seventeenth century, when religious struggles were raging in Germany, the Italian universities were the only ones where Jewish students could obtain the doctor's degree. For a long time Padua was the school to which they came from all countries of Europe. The first Jewish student, a certain Bonacosa, was inscribed in Padua's medical school in 1255. Elijah Delmedigo (1460-1497) was one of the first among the famous Paduan professors; he taught also in Florence and Perugia. But it was in the sixteenth or seventeenth century that Jews from Germany, Austria and Poland flocked in great numbers to the university. For two centuries all Jewish doctors permitted to practice in Germany and Austria held their degrees from Padua.

It was only in 1782, after the so-called Act of Tolerance by the Emperor Joseph II of Austria, that Jewish students were admitted to the Austrian universities and as candidates for the doctor's degree in the medical schools. However, even when other German universities—such as Giessen, Halle, Goettingen—opened their doors to the students it was very difficult for them to be admitted to the academic profession. Jewish doctors were often referred to as "Italian doctors" because most of them had studied in Italy, and it was only at the beginning of the nineteenth century that a change occurred, that they were free to practice and were given the opportunity to become assistants and professors at the universities.

In the nineteenth century, when emancipation of the Jews was proclaimed after the French Revolution, Jewish students began to attend universities in ever-increasing numbers, and their love for medical studies became intense. Although medical students and professionals faced all kinds of hardship, which made it difficult and sometimes impossible for a Jewish scholar to attain a chair at a university, many distinguished scholars appeared in every branch of medical science.

It is not the purpose of this chapter to list the names of all the eminent physicians who exerted a decisive influence on medical progress. We wish merely to call to the attention of the reader the fact that some specialties, such as immunology, clinical medicine, otology, ophthalmology and psychiatry, seem to be the fields in which the talents of Jewish scholars were particularly noteworthy. In all branches of medicine, however, we find Jews who are prominent.[16a] Especially in the German and Austrian universities there was a growing number of Jewish teachers and students during the era of Enlightenment. In the first part of the nineteenth century three outstanding scientists contributed to the progress of clinical medicine; Moritz Heinrich Romberg (1795-1873), the founder of modern neuropathology who became professor in Berlin in 1838, Robert Remak (1815-1865), professor in Berlin (1859), the founder of microscopic anatomy of the nerves, and Ludwig Traube (1818-1876), who ranks among the greatest clinicians of the period.

Jacob Henle (1809-1885) was among the most famous teachers at German universities. Already in 1840 he postulated the existence of micro-organisms as the cause of contagious diseases. Hermann Lebert (1813-1878), professor in Zurich (1853) and Breslau (1859), was among the first to use the microscope for pathologic-anatomical investigations. One of the greatest clinicians and brilliant teachers of the Vienna school was Heinrich von Bamberger (1822-1888), who taught in Vienna (1872) and was the teacher of Edmund von Neusser. His textbook on diseases of the heart is considered classic. Ludwig Lichtheim (1845-1928), professor in Berlin and Koenigsberg, first described subcortical aphasia, which is named after him; Ottomar Rosenbach (1851-1907) was called to Berlin in 1893 and described the reflex neurosis named after him, as well as the sign of Rosenbach.

Oscar Minkowski (1858-1931) was the founder of modern metabolism research to which Adolf Magnus-Levy (b. 1865) brought an outstanding contribution. Georges Hayem was professor of clinical medicine in Paris (1893-1911) and first described the blood platelets (1878).

In psychiatry Joseph Breuer (1842-1925) was, with Sigmund Freud (1856-1940), the founder of the revolutionary doctrine of psychoanalysis: certainly one of the most famous scientific teachings of the nineteenth century. Cesare Lombroso (1836-1909) gave a new impulse to the study of delinquency and his doctrine has had a mighty influence on legislation in modern times. Among American psychiatrists Adolf Meyer (b. 1866), professor at Cornell University (1904-1909), then and now (1948) professor at the Johns Hopkins University, a great teacher and an excellent clinician, was the leader of the American School of Psychiatry. Abraham A. Brill (1874-1948) of Columbia University was the advocate of psychoanalysis in America and contributed to the development of the doctrine.

In pediatrics Edward Heinrich Henoch (1820-1910) and Heinrich Finkelstein (b. 1865) were leaders in the progress of modern pediatrics in Germany; Max Kassowitz (1842-1913) did basic work on hereditary syphilis and rickets; Bela Schick (b. 1877) is universally known for research in the fields of diphtheria and scarlet fever. The pioneer of pediatrics in America was Abraham Jacobi (1830-1919), and among prominent American pediatricians are men like Isaac Arthur Abt (b. 1867), professor at Northwestern University; Abraham Levinson, with his studies on cerebral spinal fluid; Henry Koplik (1858-1927), the founder of a Children's Pavilion at the Mt. Sinai Hospital in New York, discoverer (1896) of the initial spots in measles (Koplik spots); and Alfred Fabian Hess (1875-1933), with his splendid studies on rickets and scurvy.

Among the founders of modern neurology were Moritz Benedikt (1835-1920) and Moritz Rosenthal (1833-1889) of Vienna. Emil Redlich (1865-1930) discovered the pupillar phenomenon that is named after him. Otto Marburg (b. 1874) of Vienna and New York, pathology of the nervous system, Arnold Pick (1851-1924), with his investigations of the anatomy of the brain, and Ludwig Edinger (1855-1918) are considered among the most eminent research workers and teachers in this field. Hermann Oppenheim (1858-1919) of Berlin was the first to give attention to posttraumatic neurosis.

In dermatology and syphilology the names of the founders of the Viennese school of dermatology, Ferdinand von Hebra (1816-1880) and Moritz Kaposi (Kohn) (1837-1902) immediately come to mind. Paul Gerson Unna (1850-1929), professor in Hamburg, won great fame through his anatomical and biochemical works in the field of skin pathology.

Among the great surgeons of the nineteenth century Anton Woelfler (1850-1917), a pupil of Billroth, was the first to perform gastroenterostomy (1881). To the Vienna school belong also Robert Gersuny (c. 1844-1924) and Julius Schnitzler (1865-1939). James Israel (1848-1926) in Berlin was a leader in urologic surgery and in this field Otto Zuckerkandl (1861-1921) was an outstanding teacher. Mario Donati (b. 1879), professor of surgery at the University of Milan, is generally recognized as the leading surgeon in Italy.

Among the most distinguished gynecologists were Ernst Wertheim (1864-1920) and Joseph Halban (1870-1939), and more recently Bernhard Zondek (b. 1891), whose name became famous through the Aschheim-Zondek reaction (1927).

Among the great ophthalmologists are the names of Hermann Cohn (1838-1906), professor in Breslau, and Harry Friedenwald (b. 1864) of Baltimore who is well known also for his splendid work in medical history. A leader of scientific otology was Adam Politzer (1835-1920), professor in Vienna, founder of a famous school to which disciples came from all over the world. The best known among the pupils of the Vienna school were Heinrich Neumann (1873-1939) and Robert Bárány (b. 1876), professor at Upsala. Among the prominent representatives of laryngology are Karl Stoerk (1832-1899) of Vienna and his pupil M. Hajek (1861-1941), a brilliant surgeon who accomplished a fundamental work. Sir

Felix Semon (1849-1921) occupied an important rank among English laryngologists.

Modern physiology was enriched by the work of Rudolph Heidenhain (1834-1897), Moritz Schiff (1823-1896) of Frankfort, professor in Florence, and Jacques Loeb of Chicago (1859-1924). Among the great research workers in general and experimental pathology were Salomon Stricker (1834-1898), professor of experimental pathology in Vienna, and Arthur Biedl (1869-1938), professor at the German university in Prague, whose book on endocrinology (1910) is of fundamental importance. The revolutionary current of thought that upset the fundamental conceptions in therapy was determined by three great scholars: Carl Weigert (1845-1904), Paul Ehrlich (1854-1915) and August von Wassermann (1866-1925). Weigert introduced new staining methods and wrote a new page in the history of the pathology of the tissues; Ehrlich discovered the doctrine of immuno-biological relations and was the founder of chemotherapy with the introduction of Salvarsan (1910) in the therapy of syphilis, marking a new era in the history of the struggle against that disease. Wassermann's work on toxins and antitoxins was one of the most important contributions to the science of immunity. The reaction that is named after him made his name famous. Still another, Fernand Widal (1862-1929), is well known for the reaction of typhoid fever (1896).

In 1908, together with Metchnikoff, Ehrlich received the Nobel Prize. Robert Bárány received it in 1945, and Otto Meyerhof in 1923 for his work on the physiology of the cell. In 1930 the prize was awarded to Karl Landsteiner of the Rockefeller Institute in New York for his discovery of the blood groups, and in 1931 to Otto Warburg for his work on the respiratory ferment. Otto Loewi of Graz, and now of New York, received the prize in 1936 for his outstanding work in biochemistry.

In the field of the history of medicine two great Jewish scholars did very important work as teachers and leaders: Charles Singer (b. 1876)[17a] of London published a great number of studies on the history of medicine in antiquity and the Middle Ages, and was the leader of the modern English medical historical school, and Max Neuburger (b. 1868), professor of the history of medicine in Vienna, now in London, brought a new impulse to historical studies with his classic book on the history of medicine, with the foundation of the institute for the history of medicine in Vienna, and with a great number of historical works illustrating the relation between the great school of Vienna and the progress of medicine in other countries.

The consequences of the spread of anti-Semitism in the past decade and its terrifying development after the rise of Hitler in Germany, and of the occupation of so great a part of Europe by the victorious Nazi armies, are well known. Jewish professors and physicians who in all the occupied countries had held prominent positions were jailed or exiled; the activity of the medical schools in Germany, in Poland, in France, in Italy and in the Balkan countries was halted; the books of the Jewish scholars were burned. It was a fight which threatened to destroy freedom of science and of opinion, but for many reasons it concentrated first on the Jews, their lives and their activities as professionals and teachers. The end of the war with the victory of the United Nations has changed the situation, but the loss is irreparable. The work that was accomplished by Jews in the European countries was destroyed or wiped out. At the same time, however, what had occurred in the Middle Ages was repeated. The persecuted Jews found a haven partly in Palestine, where scientific medicine began to rise and flourish, partly in other countries, especially in the United States. Just as in the Renaissance Jewish scholars and physicians found a shelter in Italy and the possibility of learning and teaching in the Italian universities, so during World War II a great number of them came from Germany and the occupied European countries to the United States and began here the reconstruction of their life and of their work.

Once more, as in ancient times, during the struggles in the Mediterranean countries and the Arab conquests, the Jewish scholars have been the intermediaries of scientific thought between the East and the West and have upheld freedom of teaching and of learning.

To summarize, then: The evolution of medical thought among Jews followed the line of development to be observed among other peoples, from mystic and magic to empiric and sacerdotal, with this important difference, that the moral and ethical influence of monotheism always predominated in Judaism. The moral and sanitary laws assumed the character of religious prescriptions, and it was among the Jews that hygienic laws were imposed and accepted with the authority of divine commands.

Despite long centuries of persecution in various countries, in two great epochs, during Arab supremacy in the Mediterranean and the Renaissance in certain cities and under certain conditions, the study and practice of medicine flourished. This development of medical studies culminated in the nineteenth century after the Emancipation. In certain periods and regions, particularly in the Orient where Jews were segregated and hounded, the intensive cultivation of traditional mystical beliefs led to a development of medicine like that of the Essenes, the cabbalists, the Hasidim. Note, however, that even when magical practices are suggested and accepted as an escape from misery, as an expression of hope in supernatural salvation, this magic is always practiced with words and scripts, with formulae and sayings, and never degenerates into cruel or obscene acts—a rather frequent and sometimes characteristic phenomenon among other peoples. The mystic medicine of the Jews always had a metaphysical, I might say a literary, character; it involved essentially a subtle discussion and interpretation of words and letters, symbolic signs and numbers. There is not a trace of black magic and its attendant practices in the history of Jewish occult, suggestive medicine.

The history of medicine among the Jews reflects the history of the Jewish people, its sufferings, its struggle for liberty and religious freedom. In this distress the Jews return to the pure virtue of the faith that heals, and which represents the highest and last hope of sufferers. What contribution the Jews made to the science and practice of medicine was made through the centuries by thousands and thousands of believers, of scholars, of martyrs, of teachers and of humble practitioners, obedient to the moral law that constitutes the basis of the Jewish religion. They were inspired by a passionate desire for knowledge and longing for the truth. The Jews have been called the People of the Book: they have been in medicine as in many fields of intellectual activity diligent scholars, great searchers and learned teachers, able to command the respect and the esteem of their pupils and their patients even during the most difficult conditions of their own lives.

NOTES

[1a Throughout this chapter there is material on persons mentioned also below, cf. Charles Singer "Science and Judaism."]

[1b Cf. above Judah Goldin, "The Period of the Talmud," pp. 141 f.]

[2a Cf. *ibid.*, pp. 116-117.]

3 Celsus, Lib. V., 19-22.

[4a Cf. above Elias J. Bickerman, "The Historical Foundations of Postbiblical Judaism," p. 93.]

[5a Cf. above Alexander Altmann, "Judaism and World Philosophy," pp. 627 f.; see also above Ralph Marcus, "Hellenistic Jewish Philosophy," pp. 775 f.]

[6a Cf. above Cecil Roth, "The European Age in Jewish History (to 1648)," pp. 222-224.]

7 Steinschneider, M., *Arabische Literatur.* Introd.

[8a Cf. Altmann, *op. cit.*, pp. 642 ff.]

[9a Cf. above the chapter by Abraham J. Heschel, "The Mystical Element in Judaism."]

[10a Cf. Goldin, *op. cit.* pp. 178 ff.]

[11a Cf. above Julius B. Maller, "Judaism and Educational Theory," p. 907.]

[12a Cf. Roth, *op. cit.*, p. 236.]

[13a Cf. Singer, *op. cit.*, pp. 1064 ff.]

[14a Cf. above Anita Libman Lebeson, "The American Jewish Chronicle," p. 313.]

[15a Cf. above Roth, "The Jews of Western Europe (from 1648)," p. 264.]

[16a Cf. Singer, *op. cit.*, pp. 1086 f.]

[17a Cf. Singer, *op. cit.*]

BIBLIOGRAPHY

The most exhaustive treatise on the history of Jewish medicine is the book of Julius Preuss, *Biblisch-Talmudische Medizin* (Berlin, 1911), which is up until now the most authoritative work on this subject. The history of Jewish hygiene has been dealt with accurately by Max Grunwald (ed.), *Die Hygiene der Juden (mit Bibliographie)* (Dresden, 1911). Mystic medicine of the cabbalists has been studied by Karl Preis, *Die Medizin in der Kabbala* (Frankfort, 1928). An important contribution to the history of Jewish physicians in ancient times and in the Middle Ages has been made by Harry Friedenwald, *The Jews and Medicine* (Baltimore, 1944, 2 vols.), in which the author throws lights upon the work of great scholars, translators, and research workers. An account of the development of ancient Jewish medicine is summarized in Maurice B. Gordon, "Medicine among the Ancient Hebrews," in *Isis* (Bruges, 1941), Vol. 33, Pt. 4. For the history of circumcision see J. Almkvist "Zur Geschichte der Circumcision," in *Janus* (Leyden, 1926), Vol. 30:86, 152, and D. Schapiro, "La Péritomie; étude générale et particulière," in *Janus* (1923), Vol. 27:161, 241, 259 and 1924, 28:120, 193. On the conception of pathology see Adolphe Lods, "Les idées des Israélites sur la maladie, ses causes et ses remèdes," in *Beihefte zur Zeitschrift fuer die Alttestamentliche Wissenschaft*, 40 (Giessen, 1925), pp. 181-193. The prescriptions for contagious diseases have been studied by E. W. G. Masterman, "Hygiene and Disease in Palestine in Modern and in Biblical Times," in *Palestine Exploration Fund, Quarterly Statement* (London, 1918), pp. 13, 56, 112, 156, and 1919, p. 27; also Georg Sticker, *Vorgeschichtliche Versuche der Seuchenabwehr und Seuchenausrottung* (Zurich, 1924). Among the older historians whose works deserve to be consulted, see Thomas Bartholin, *De Morbis Biblicis miscellanea medica* (Frankfort, 1672), and Richard Mead, *Medica sacra* (Amsterdam, 1749). Other subjects of Jewish medicine have been treated by L. Kotelmann, *Die Ophtalmologie bei den alten Hebraeern* (Hamburg und Leipzig, 1910); Max Neuburger, *Die Medizin im Flavius Josephus* (Vienna, 1919); Ludwig Venetianer, *Asaph Judaeus* (Strassburg, 1916-1917, 2 vols.). On the Plague see Otto Neustaetter, "Where did the Identification of the Philistine Plague (I Sam. 5 and 6) as Bubonic Plague Originate?" reprint from *Bulletin of the History of Medicine* (Vol. XI, No. 1, Baltimore, 1942, pp. 36-47). The subject of the ritual food prescription among the Hebrews has been studied by S. I. Levin, and E. A. Boyden, *The Kosher Code of the Orthodox Jew* (Minneapolis, 1940).

CHAPTER 26

SCIENCE AND JUDAISM

By Charles Singer

1. THE GREEK FOUNDATIONS OF SCIENCE

Science has been defined as a search for judgments on which *universal* assent is attainable. Nevertheless, despite this universal element, there is a relation between science and certain particular phases of civilization. The association of science with Judaism is a special case of a general rule, for only in certain periods in the millennia of Jewish history and only in certain localities has there been scientific development. Association of science with Judaism has never been worldwide. In considering these special occurrences we must often dwell on individual achievements; yet much more significance should be attached to those aspects of Jewish thought which have favored the growth of scientific ideas. For this consummation we must await an adequate sociological history of the human vehicles of Judaism.

The first step toward the scientific attitude must be the realization that Nature works in regular and ascertainable ways. Barbarous men, children, even animals, show trust in Nature. They behave as though confident that day will succeed night, that the moons will wax and wane, that summer heat will follow winter cold, that the processes of life will run in certain cycles. But to accept Nature's ways is very different from seeking systematically to know her ways. That form of inquiry appears only late and is always exceptional. It is first clearly discernible among the Greeks of the sixth century B.C.E. Without some consideration of science among them its course among the Hebrews cannot be intelligible.

The Greeks, it has often been remarked, had no sacred writings. The forwardness of their science contrasts with the backwardness of their religion. At a very early stage they concluded that the world is subject to laws that are ever further discoverable. This was the *scientific idea.* Their science and ours grew out of it.

Before the close of the sixth century B.C.E. Greek thinkers were seeking universal applications of conceptions derived from their science. They distinguished as a universal principle *physis,* a word which survives in *physics, physiology, physical,* and *physician.* Physis meant at first growth or development, the essential element of all existence. This, it was seen, always follows definite rules, notably those of development and dissolution, coming into being and passing away, generation and corruption. By transference physis came to be regarded as this rule of change itself, and so something near to what we now call a *natural law*.

As knowledge grew, natural laws were traced more widely. Men tried to discern what lay behind them. It was inevitable that some should see in these laws a common active element. Physis was thus given an independent existence. It was, in fact, more or less personified. Had the religion of the Greeks grown with their other activities, physis would perhaps have reached the rank of a god.

The change in intellectual outlook initiated by Socrates (470-399 B.C.E.) was as fundamental as the spiritual revolution heralded by the Unknown Prophet of the last chapters of Isaiah. Socrates was skeptical as to the validity of all human knowledge, and his thought turned away from physical philosophy. His predecessors, concentrating on the physis of the sensible universe, had developed a system of physics. But his interest, like that of the Hebrew prophet, was in conduct. Seeking guidance for right conduct he concluded that man's soul partook of the Divine. He rejected the whole structure of the physicists and regarded as futile all attempts "to pursue knowledge for its own sake"; instead he stressed "practical wisdom" (*phronesis*), leading to right action. It was *phronesis* against *physis*. Phronesis also tended to personification under various names.

From the conflict between the followers of the Socratic revolution and the physical philosophers arose the main streams of Greek thought. One of them leads on to Plato and to the *doctrine of ideas*. Its ultimate development was the complete indifference to worldly happenings of certain later "Neoplatonists." The physical philosophy, on the other hand, often assumed dogmatic forms, as with the followers of Epicurus (342-270 B.C.E.), the title in Rabbinic writings for the most refractory type of paganism. It is significant that both the Neoplatonic and Epicurean schools ultimately became inimical to science, while neither was friendly to current religion. The development of both science and religion is thus historically associated with other systems of thought which chose a middle way. For science this was the path of Aristotle and his successors which drew heavily on the physical philosophers. For religion it was that of the great Judeo-Christian system of thought, which borrowed not a little from Neoplatonism.

"That nothing," says Aristotle in his *Metaphysics*, "comes to be out of that which is not, but everything out of that which is, is a doctrine common to nearly all the natural philosophers." Only if this is so is investigation of the material universe worth while. Such a view would have found itself in immediate conflict with a religion that had reached the coherent and vocal level of that of the Hebrews. As it was, the inevitable clash among the Greek-speaking peoples was deferred until their philosophy was confronted with Judeo-Christian thought.

But within the philosophic realm itself there was from the first a tension. As this increased it burst its bonds and ultimately brought ancient philosophy to an end. In a world in which, to use the phrase of Lucretius (c. 60 B.C.E.), "nothing is ever begotten of nothing by divine will," it must be that all things act by rules inherent in everlasting matter. What, then, is left that is our real conscious selves?

The question was variously answered. Christians and Jews, as well as those who hovered between the creeds of these, were in agreement in giving the answer—"man's immortal soul." But the Stoic, the most "religious" of the philosophic schools, could, like the Epicurean, only reply with the saintly emperor, Marcus Aurelius (C.E. 121-180): "Thou hast subsisted as part of the whole. Thou shalt vanish into that which begat thee, or rather thou shalt be taken again unto its Seminal Reason, by process of change." Such thinkers could take little interest in Nature. In our day men learn Nature's ways to control her, but that time was not yet. Epicurus would have us know only so much about her as would remove all fear of supernatural interference. Stoic and Epicurean alike show a flagging scientific curiosity. Men were weary of the world. Why seek to know more of Nature, the pitiless, the tyrannical, the irresistible machine? It is better to forget her demonic majesty. We are on the brink of the "Dark Ages." Let us return, then, to the Hebrews and their ideas on Nature.

2. THE BIBLICAL CONCEPT OF NATURE

The earlier parts of the Old Testament know nothing of natural law. Natural events, and especially the more dramatic and destructive, thunder and whirlwind, drought and flood, plague and famine, reveal God expressing Himself. "The voice of the Lord is upon the waters: the God of Glory thundereth" (Ps. 29:3). Even in a less anthropomorphic setting natural events are still acts of Him:

> Who hath measured the waters in the hollow of His hand,
> And meted out heaven with the span,
> And comprehended the dust of the earth in a measure,
> And weighed the mountains in scales . . . ?
> I form the light, and create darkness;
> I make peace and create evil;
> I am the Lord that doeth all these things.
> (Is. 40:12, 45:7 c. 540 B.C.E.)

Such a work as Job of the fourth century B.C.E. shows a definite development. The author dwells on the wonder and intricacy of the rules by which God governs His world. *His* world! If Job does not comprehend them, how can he hope to grasp their purpose?

> Dost thou guide the heavens to know the laws,
> Dost thou establish the dominion thereof in the earth? (Job 38:33.)

These laws are invoked as proof of the power, wisdom and goodness of God, for exactly the same reason as in the famous *Bridgewater Treatises* of more than two thousand years later. The recognition of the natural laws in Job is an echo of the main preoccupation of Greek thinkers when the book was being written.

In the later "Wisdom literature," the contact with Greek thought has become quite evident.[1a] The general features of physical philosophy have been grasped and the concept of the relation of God to the material world has become modified. The laws of nature are now administered by the elusive Wisdom (*Hokmah*) or the awesome Word (*Memra*).

The gracious form of the one or the stern features of the other are almost as difficult to discern as those of *Physis*, whom they both in part resemble. Wisdom has divine attributes, being omniscient and omnipresent. "She reacheth from one end of the world to the other and ordereth all things aright" (Wisdom 8:1). The Word is specially responsible for the catastrophic events. "While all things were in silence . . . Thine Almighty Word leaped down from heaven as a fierce man of war and brought Thine unfeigned command as a sharp sword and filled all things with death" (Wisdom 18:12-16).

This new turn of thought has become self-conscious and polemic. It is set against Greek physical philosophy, wherein various "first principles" had been adopted. Thales proposed "water," Heraclitus "fire," Pythagoras the "circling stars," Anaximenes "air," other philosophers a subtle world essence, or *pneuma*, "winds," while astrological science, coming in from Babylonia, claimed the actual complex mathematical order of the heavenly bodies as the motive power of all things. The Wisdom of Solomon, written by an orthodox Jew in Alexandria about 100 B.C.E., inveighs against all these:

> Surely vain were all men in their natures,
>   and without perception of God
> Who could not, from the good things that are seen,
>   know Him that is.
> Neither by giving heed to the works
>   did they recognize Him who hath wrought them,

But either fire [Heraclitus], or wind [the Pneumatists]
    or the swift air [Anaximenes],
Or circling stars [Pythagoras], or raging water [Thales],
    or the lights of heaven [the astrologers]
They deemed the gods which govern the world.

(Wisdom 13:1-2)

3. NATURE IN LATER JEWISH AND JUDEO-CHRISTIAN THOUGHT

Much of the pseudepigraphic and apocalyptic literature written by Jews of the later pre-Christian or first post-Christian centuries shows the same tendency. This may be traced in the Book of Jubilees, the Apocalypse of Baruch, the Book of Enoch, and the New Testament Book of Revelation.

That this movement, even under philosophic guidance, became indifferent to or contemptuous of scientific spirit is shown by the Alexandrian Jewish thinker Philo, contemporary of Jesus. His trend was Neoplatonic and away from the study of phenomena. He represents a separation of religious Judaism from an interest in phenomena. Judaism and physical philosophy have diverged completely.[2a]

Philo was a conscious "philosopher" in the Greek sense. He betrays this in several ways not found in earlier Jewish writings. The biblical record and Rabbinic doctrine treat God as a separate and very personal existence outside the world, which He had produced by definite acts and continues to guide. But the God of the Hellenist Philo is without emotions or attributes and consequently without name—changeless, imperceptible by man, self-sufficient, simply existent. This God of the Platonic idea could not act upon the world, or create or guide it, though He might set it going once and for all. The old Hebrew view was as incompatible with that of Philo as with that of the Stoics.

Under these circumstances Philo resorted to a new form of an old device. He introduced an existence between God and the world. Physis, Phronesis, Wisdom, the Word (*Memra*) were previous attempts. Philo's device was the Logos. They have now become a regular pantheon! Any of them must turn men's thoughts away from phenomena. Logos and the Memra have other parallels in Rabbinic literature and their further development appears clear enough in the Gospel of St. John, in Acts and in other New Testament works. Science cannot live at close quarters with any of these divine emanations. Judeo-Christian thought lost interest in Nature and her phenomena.

There was yet a further reason for the "flight from phenomena" in later Jewish as in early Christian thought. Since the Socratic revolution some Greek thinkers had regarded the material universe as essentially without worth. They opposed *Nous*, mind, Soul or Spirit to *Hyle*, Brute Matter. The idea of the worthlessness of the material world could be made to fit Hebraic doctrine and the biblical story of the Fall of Man. The view could and did thus enter Jewish and Judeo-Christian thought. Though Philo, like other early Jewish and Judeo-Christian writers, seeks to avoid the conclusion that the world is evil, his efforts, like theirs, are not very successful. His claim, like theirs, is verbal, not real. The "sins of the flesh" became a theological commonplace which passed over naturally, along with the *Logos*, into Christian thought. It is a main theme of apocalyptic literature, Jewish, Christian and intermediate.

Paul's teaching was greatly influenced by this idea, which he extended to include a physical basis of sin. "We know that the Law is spiritual; but I am carnal, sold into the power of sin" (Rom. 7:14). Christianity thus followed Judaism in turning away from phenomena, if for an allegedly different reason. Paul does not conceal his contempt for Greek physical philosophy. It is not so much false as trivial and irrelevant and, before the fearful issue of salvation, therefore impious.

Another common Judeo-Christian thought emphasized this contempt. The end of the world was at hand. Now in much Greek physical philosophy this world is one of a long series. Its end is but the beginning of another like to it, re-formed from its "elements." But in the Judeo-Christian conception the end of the world must involve the destruction of the elements themselves. "The day of the Lord will come as a thief. At that time the heavens will pass away with great violence and the *elements* will be dissolved with heat, and the earth and the works that are in it will be burned up" (II Pet. 3:10) [author's italics]. With that in mind who could regard phenomena? Belief in an imminent Messiah was as deadly for science as was the apocalyptic vision. The combination of the two was instantly fatal. "The day of the Lord" rang the death knell of Greek science. We see it most dramatically in that Jewish work in the New Testament known as Revelation. Judaism, having approached the scientific view of the world, led or escorted Christianity in a retreat therefrom. Opportunity for reunion was not to come again to Judaism for a thousand years and to Christianity for longer.

4. NATURE IN RABBINIC THOUGHT

Thus Jewish thought for the first nine centuries of the Christian era is almost entirely devoid of the scientific element. A certain amount of calendarial debate and discussion on well-worn lines of the physical bases of purity rules covers most of the area. Many have vainly searched the Talmud for evidence of scientific interest or scientific method. The excursions have been unfruitful. Those who have written on science and medicine in Rabbinic literature have merely shown that such studies have left some faint trace on Jewish life in talmudic times. What they have *not* shown is that science took any part, either integral or incidental, in Rabbinic *thought*. It could not have been otherwise. The basic conception of Torah is that every phase of knowledge must be brought into relation with or drawn from an existing and accepted system. Science can exist and even flourish *by the side of* any thought-world, religious, mystic, even magic, but it cannot exist *within* any world but its own. Any attempt to force it to do so is rapidly fatal to it. While science could and later did develop in the same civilization as Torah, it could not and did not take root in a mind or a culture already fully occupied by that concept. A quotation on natural law from the Talmud itself illustrates this incompatibility or rather impossibility:

"*Give ear, ye heavens* (Deut. 32:1). God said to Moses, 'Say unto Israel; Consider the heavens which I made to serve you, Have they ever failed in their duty? [*lit.*, changed their nature.] Does not the sun rise in the east and give light to the inhabitants of the earth? It rises and sets with regularity (Eccl. 1:5), nay, more, it rejoices in doing its Creator's will (Ps. 19:5).' *And let the earth hear My mouth's words (Ibid.).* 'Consider the earth which I created for your service. Has it ever changed its nature? Have you ever sown wheat, and has it yielded barley? Or does the cow not thresh and plough? or the ass not bear his load and walk? Does not the sea observe the limits which I have assigned to it? (Jer. 5:22). If *these* have not changed their nature, these which, unlike you, were created neither for profit nor for loss; if, unlike you, when they do well, they receive no reward, if when they sin, they are not punished: they have no care for their sons and daughters, yet these have not changed their nature: but you if you do well, you receive reward, if you do evil, you receive punishment, and you have care for your sons and daughters. How much more ought you in no wise to change your characters? [*i.e.*, from good to bad, in view of Deut. 32:5, 'You have corrupted yourselves.']' "[3]

Nature, as thus represented, elicits no curiosity and commands no more affection than a machine. There is no hint of the infinite variety and beautiful complexity of the physical world, still less of its exploration as a continual delightful adventure. No scientific interest could be evinced by those whose lives were passed within the talmudic universe of discourse. Scores of Greek names occur in the Talmud, but not one is of a man of science. Even Aristotle is unmentioned. Saadia Gaon (882-942), founder of Rabbinic philosophy,[4a] who had read some Aristotelian works in Arabic, avoids naming him. The discussion of secular science was for many centuries resisted by Rabbinic authority.

Philosophy and science ultimately obtained entry into Israel via Islam.

Christendom was some two hundred and fifty years behind Israel and received the gift largely through Israel. Science, having reached Israel, was certainly seized upon and developed with astonishing vigor. Medicine was followed with particular zeal and success. On this point certain observations should be made on which we shall need to enlarge later.[5a] First, in the Middle Ages science among Jews was almost confined to the Mediterranean area. Second, in Spain, where science first and mostly flourished among Jews, science obtained a foothold before talmudic studies came fully to occupy the Jewish intellect. Third, Jewish devotion to medicine can be explained partly as surrogate for Jewish interest in conduct, partly as a way of livelihood for those interested in science, partly as a result of social pressure which excluded Jews from other professions. There is, in fact, hardly a Jewish scientific personality before the nineteenth century that did not practice medicine.

The question remains why within Judaism scientific interest declared itself only on certain occasions. These were (a) within Islam and neighboring countries from the tenth to the thirteenth century with a trailing off into a mainly translatory period from the thirteenth to the fifteenth; (b) as part of the Marrano incident in the sixteenth century and (c) in north-western Europe for about a hundred years from shortly before the mid-nineteenth century. The answer must cover not only these phenomena but also certain others, notably the substantial absence of the scientific element within Judaism at other times and places, the late entry of science into the Jewish orbit, the intensity of Jewish application to certain sciences, and the character of the non-Jewish cultures associated with the three main scientific outbursts among the Jewish people. Discussion of these matters is best deferred till the incidents themselves have been reviewed.

5. Hebrew-Arabic Science

Until the ninth century scientific interest is hardly encountered in Jewish writings. Only the Egyptian astronomer Masha alla ("What God wills," c. 770-820), known to Latins as Messahalla, has left any impression on later ages. He was the first Jewish man of science (if he was a Jew) to write in Arabic. There is little evidence that before him Jews were especially prominent even in medicine. The great scientific movement within Judaism arose as part of the renaissance of learning in the Arabic-speaking world.

The Arabic language was cultivated by Jews as a consequence of the Saracen conquests. From the mid-ninth century it was familiar to all who dwelt in Moslem lands. Arabic writing rapidly replaced Aramaic, which from about 300 c.e. till that time had been used for both secular and sacred purposes. For centuries scientific works were written by Jews in

Arabic. Yet while Jews spoke Arabic throughout the Islamic world they did not everywhere develop science. The overwhelming Jewish interest was talmudic throughout the Asiatic Arabic-speaking world. Science took no root there. But the Talmud did not effectively reach the West till the tenth century and by then science was established among the Jews of Tunis and Egypt and was appearing in Spain.

In Spain, Arabic continued in general use among Jews, even in the Christian zone, till the end of the twelfth century. Spanish Jews preserved some living acquaintance with the language till the fourteenth century. Even then, when Arabic had ceased to be spoken by Spanish Jews, it was still used for learned purposes by Western Jewish scholars. But from the beginning of the thirteenth century, the output of original literature in Arabic by Jews ceased to have value. Original scientific works in Hebrew, however, continued to appear, while Jews were actively translating into Latin from both Arabic and Hebrew until the sixteenth century.

We must not expect in the Hebrew-Arabic scientific literature that vast variety and range associated in the twentieth century with the word "science." The experimental and the biological sciences were absent from the whole Western medieval scheme, both Latin and Arabic. In effect we meet but three kinds of works that can be called scientific: (a) cosmological, passing into philosophy, (b) mathematical often associated with astronomy and astrology, and (c) medical with rare excursions into biology.

Science of its very nature tends to become superannuated. The cosmology of the Middle Ages is now an interesting fossil that has left some quaint remains in our language. But our own mathematical and medical systems are natural outgrowths of the mathematical and medical systems of the Latin Middle Ages, which were in their turn not only influenced by the Hebrew-Arabic material but were actually founded and based upon it and extended very little beyond it. The transmission of this material and its development were largely the work of Jews. Indeed, it is fair to present medieval European mathematics and medicine as special developments of the Hebrew-Arabic system. The cosmological systems of the Latin Middle Ages also bear constantly the impress of Jewish thoughts.

6. The Kairouan School, Ninth and Tenth Centuries

Of the departments in which Jews have attained distinction, medicine comes first. The ancient Jewish contribution to hygiene, both social and individual, has often and rightly been stressed. But, although highly important, it was not made by the scientific method or presented in the scientific spirit. Therefore, it does not concern us here. But during certain periods from the ninth century Jews have contributed to scientific medicine to a degree out of all proportion to their numbers.

This phenomenon is first observable in Tunis under a local dynasty that ruled from Kairouan for more than a century from 800. One of these sultans invited to his capital the Egyptian Jewish (?) physician Isaac ibn Amram (d. 908). His writings show a definite scientific interest. He had Jewish pupils and a most distinguished Jewish successor, Isaac ben Solomon Israeli (c. 855-c. 955), Isaac Judeus of the Latins. He is the first Jewish scientific figure whose life course is known.

Isaac Judeus, like Isaac ben Amram, who was perhaps his teacher, was born in Egypt and like him may have received direct some remnant of the Greek scientific tradition of Alexandria. He practiced as an oculist in Egypt where he served the sovereign. Later at Kairouan he was physician to several of its rulers. A Moslem historian describes him as a man of the loftiest character and worthy of the highest respect, for, though much occupied about the court, he was quite indifferent to wealth and personal advancement. He lived childless and unmarried—a most unusual thing among medieval Moslems or Jews—and died at over a hundred.

This able and saintly man wrote many philosophical treatises. That *On Definitions* introduced some of the favorite terms of the Latin Scholastics which they adopted from it. Isaac's larger philosophic work expounds Aristotelian physics. Beside these he wrote *On Diet, On Urine, On the Pulse, On Simples,* and above all his great book *On Fevers.* This last, perhaps the best clinical treatise of the Middle Ages in any language, was widely read until the seventeenth century.

Isaac's medical works early influenced the Latin West. His pupil's pupil was Constantine the African, who began life in a Jewish environment at Kairouan. When that city was sacked by the Bedouins in 1057 he made his way to Sicily. There he became the Oriental secretary of the Norman invader, Robert Guiscard, who afterward conquered Salerno, in the shin of Italy. At Salerno, alone in Christian Europe, there was the remnant of a medical school in the reawakening of which Jews had some part. Constantine spent the last ten years of his life as a monk at Monte Cassino, turning into Latin the writings of Isaac and of one of Isaac's pupils. They were the first Arabic medical works to be translated into Latin and introduce the long supremacy of Hebrew-Arabic medicine in Latin Europe.

Isaac's *On Fevers* was, for centuries, the constant companion of every European physician and was, in fact, one of the most genuinely useful in his library. Isaac's work influenced the Persian Avicenna (987-1037), whose vast *Canon of Medicine* was and is extremely popular among the Arabic-speaking peoples. Through it certain of Isaac's views can be traced throughout the world, for the *Canon* was early translated into every literary language, and several times into Hebrew.

The centuries from the tenth to the twelfth are the flowering time of the scientific movement within western Islam. In this Jews had a large share. Science had come to Spain in the ninth century, when the life of Spanish Jews was still isolated from that of their fellow countrymen. The entry of Jews into science opens, as might be expected, with medicine.

7. THE IBERIAN SCHOOL, TENTH TO TWELFTH CENTURIES

Of medical writings of classical antiquity the most popular, during the first Christian millennium, was that *On materia medica* of the Asiatic-Greek Dioscorides (first century c.e.). In 948 the Byzantine emperor sent to the Spanish caliph a finely illustrated manuscript of this work. Since no one in Spain knew Greek the caliph asked the emperor for an interpreter. In 951 he sent him a learned monk Nicholas who gave open instruction in Greek at Cordova to many physicians and scholars. Among them was the Andalusian Jew, Hasdai ibn Shaprut (915-970).[6a] He joined Nicholas in translating the Dioscorides manuscript into Arabic. These two were thus the first Westerners to introduce Greek writings directly to the Arabic-speaking world. Their version of Dioscorides still circulates in the Orient.

Ibn Shaprut was a man of great and varied activity. The shift of the Jewish intellectual center from Babylonia to Spain came in his time and was largely his work. He is the first of the brilliant Jewish scientific school that lasted till the thirteenth century. He was also instrumental in establishing talmudic study in Spain (*c.* 945).

A member of the scientific school initiated by Hasdai was another Andalusian—Jonah ibn Biklarish ("man of Biclar" or Valleclara) of Almeria. About 1080 he produced a dictionary of drugs in Syriac, Persian, Greek, Latin and "vulgar barbarian" (Spanish). It is the earliest of its kind. Jonah was one of the first Jewish scholars to learn Latin, which, it must be remembered, took with Christians the place of Hebrew with Jews. His knowledge of Greek probably reached him in a direct tradition from his fellow countryman and coreligionist ibn Shaprut.

A very different figure was Jonah's contemporary, Moses Sephardi. He was born in 1062 at Huesca in Aragon, then in Moslem hands. In 1096 Pedro I recovered it for the Christians and it became the Aragonese capital. Pedro was succeeded in 1104 by his brother Alfonso to whom Moses became physician. In 1106 Moses was baptized as Petrus Alfonsi (Alfonso's Peter), Alfonso being godfather. He wrote two astronomical works and another which makes a plea for astronomical observation. Alfonsi visited England, became physician to Henry I, and was intimate with Walcher, prior of Malvern, an ardent astronomer. In 1120 Walcher issued a work which introduces the use of degrees, minutes and seconds and contains certain exact observations. All are in the Arabic manner and had evidently been learned from Alfonsi. This represents the first impact of Arabian learning in England.

A figure as important for Jewish culture as Hasdai ibn Shaprut was the

Catalan Abraham bar Hiyya (d. *c.* 1150), known to the Latins as Savasorda, that is, *Sahib al schurta,* "chief of the police," which was his office. Until his time the Sephardic and the Ashkenazic Jews had been almost isolated from each other. They were in geographical but not social contact on the frontier between Catalonia and Provence. In 1112 these territories came under one ruler. Thus Savasorda could contact the Provençal Jews, among whom Arabic was unknown. To them he opened secular studies by translating Arabic scientific works into Hebrew. He was the first Arabic speaker to prepare works specifically for a non-Arabic speaking audience. Writing always in Hebrew, he and his successors gave to that language a special interpretive value which it retained for centuries. His chief scientific work was an encyclopedia of mathematics, astronomy, optics and music. In it he wrote: "I have not entered on this work of my own wish or for my own honor, but because in all the land of France there is no book on these sciences in the holy tongue. Therefore I have summarized what follows from the Arabic." A treatise by him on practical geometry (1116) was translated into Latin by his friend Plato of Tivoli (1145) as the *Liber embadorum.* It is the first introduction of Arabic trigonometry and mensuration to the Latin West and contains the oldest table of chords in a Latin work. It made a special impression on Leonardo of Pisa, the ablest mathematician of the Middle Ages, who embodied large sections of it in his *Practical Geometry* (1220).

Savasorda also left a treatise *On the Form of the Earth* which was turned into Latin and French. He wrote in 1123 the first Hebrew treatise devoted to the calendar and also Hebrew astronomical tables based on Ptolemy. His *Scroll of the Revealer* is an extensive treatise on the courses of the stars, treating Arabic astronomy with understanding and acuteness. In it he concludes that the Messiah will come in 1358! Savasorda, with his Christian friend, Plato of Tivoli, translated at Barcelona a whole series of Hebrew and Arabic works into Latin (1133-1145). The most important of them was Ptolemy's *Quadripartitum.*

The famous Abraham ibn Ezra (1092-1167), poet and scholar, was born in Toledo. In 1140 his life was devastated by the conversion of his son to Islam. Thenceforth he led a wandering life, first in Italy, where he composed many works, and then in Provence, where he was enthusiastically received. In 1158 he went to London, where he wrote an account of the intellectual state of the Jews in England. After much journeying he died at Calahorra in northern Spain. He has permanent importance as a fore-runner of biblical criticism, and Spinoza derived much from him. Ibn Ezra seconded Savasorda in translating Arabic writings into Hebrew, thus opening secular literature to his coreligionists and especially to the Ash-kenazim outside Spain. His wanderings helped to distribute manuscripts of his works.

Among Abraham ibn Ezra's scientific achievements is the introduction into Hebrew science of a decimal system of numeration with place value for the integers. This he did through his commentary on al-Kwarizmi's tables (Narbonne, 1160). He made certain other real additions to mathematics. Several of his astrological treatises became extremely popular. Among the works that he translated into Hebrew from Arabic were two treatises on astrology by Messahalla (Lucca, 1148). Incidentally, ibn Ezra provides some important information as to the passage of the decimal place-value system from Indian to Arabic mathematics.

The advent of Latin translations of Arabic scientific works aroused the emulation of Latin Christians. A number sought a knowledge of Arabic. All worked with Jewish aid. The pioneer was Adelard of Bath (*c.* 1090-1150) who visited both Spain and the Sicilies. His great achievement is the Latin translation of the astronomical tables of al-Kwarizmi. They included a table of sines and, with Savasorda's *Liber embadorum* of about the same date, introduced Arabic trigonometry to the Latin world. Adelard also made a version of Euclid. His popular *Natural Questions* is a compendium drawn from Arabic sources and largely from a debased "Aristotelian" work. The French-Jewish scribe Berachiah Ha-Nakdan (Benedictus Punctator), who was in Oxford in 1194, translated it from Latin into Hebrew. It was the first work so treated. This Hebrew version has since been translated into English. Parts of it have thus passed from Greek into Syriac, from Syriac into Arabic, from Arabic into Latin, from Latin into Hebrew and from Hebrew into English!

Throughout the medieval period the Latin West was eagerly seeking the treasures of Arabic learning. Jews, as translators and interpreters, played an overwhelming part in this effort. The best known of the native Spanish translators was Johannes Hispalensis, whose Arabic name, ibn Daud (ben David), was corrupted by the schoolman into Avendeath (*c.* 1090-1165). He was born at Toledo, soon after that city fell into Christian hands (1085). He translated a whole host of astronomical and astrological works, among them those of Albumasar (786-886) of Bagdad, of Omar ibn al-Farrushan (d. *c.* 932) the Persian, of Thabit ben Kurra (826-901) the "Sabian" of Harran, of Messahalla (d. 815) the Jew of Egypt, of Messahalla's pupil Albohali (d. 835), of Alfraganus (d. *c.* 880) of Fargan in Transoxania, and the *Centiloquiam* of Ptolemy (*c.* 180). Avendeath provided an appreciable proportion of the mathematical, astrological and astronomical works in the medieval Latin library.

Notable among Avendeath's versions was the pseudo-scientific, pseudo-Aristotelian *Secretum secretorum*. This extremely popular work he prepared for a Spanish queen. There are copies and variants in hundreds of manuscripts in many languages, Hebrew included. It influenced serious scholars, and Roger Bacon wrote a commentary on it.

Most important of Avendeath's translations is the *Liber Algorismi de practica arismetrica*. This is an elaboration by Avendeath of an elaboration by a Moslem writer of the work of the Persian Muhammad ibn Musa al-Kwarizmi (fl. *c.* 830). In it our so-called *Arabic* numerical notation, in which the digits depend on their position for their value, is fully used in a Latin work for the first time. It is professedly based on Hindu knowledge. The "Arabic" numerals displace the clumsy Latin forms. The method was but slowly accepted. The whole of modern mathematics may be said to date from this translation but incorporation into our system was hardly complete until the sixteenth century. The word *algorism*, used in the Middle Ages for what we now call arithmetic, conceals the name al-Kwarizmi, *i.e.*, "the man of Khiva."

The most active translator from the Arabic was Gerard of Cremona (1114-1187). As a young man he came to Toledo to acquire Arabic that he might read Ptolemy's *Almagest*. He remained for life and superintended the translation of no less than seventy-one works, many, such as the *Canon of Medicine of Avicenna*, of great length. He worked with a whole school of Arabic-speaking Jews and Christians. They translated many scientific works by Jews such as Messahalla and Isaac Judeus. Perhaps the oddest work from his school is that of "Alchandrius." It is an astrological treatise which contains a number of Hebrew words. It seems based on a very early pre-Arabic original showing remnants of the ancient classical astrology. It may be the earliest scientific work of Jewish origin.

8. MAIMONIDES. SECOND HALF OF THE TWELFTH CENTURY

Contemporary with the twelfth-century Jewish movement in science in Spain and the West there was in Africa a comparable activity, for which Jews were almost entirely responsible. Several were physicians to the caliphs and published genuine clinical observations—a very unusual thing at that time. The letter of one to Saladin (d. 1193) has survived. Incomparably the most important of this school was the great thinker Maimonides, with whom Jewish philosophy culminates.

Moses ben Maimon, called Maimonides (1135-1204), was born at Cordova, and educated by a learned father and Arabic masters. When he was thirteen Cordova fell to the fanatical Almohades. Maimonides fled and, after wandering in Spain, Morocco and Palestine, settled in Cairo (1155) where he passed the rest of his life. He was a very successful physician and was attached to the court. His works, both medical and philosophical, became widely known, not only among Arabic-speaking peoples, but also among the Latins and Jews. He used Arabic for nearly all his writings.

Maimonides held that there can be no conflict between truths discerned by reason and those inculcated by revealed religion. The former are to be sought primarily in the Aristotelian writings, the latter in the Torah. He was convinced that both written and oral Torah contain philosophical material which harmonizes with Aristotle. We can here discuss neither his philosophical nor his religious views,[7a] but we are concerned with his presentation of the structure of the world. This had a share in determining both Latin and Jewish beliefs. With certain closely similar schemes it provided the framework within which alone medieval science could develop. It is set forth in his *Guide for the Perplexed*.[8a]

The universe in the Maimonidean-Aristotelian system is spherical, with earth fixed in the center, and the heavens revolving round it. The matter of our world is composed of the four elements, *earth, air, fire* and *water*. These, however, are not seen in their pure form on our imperfect globe. Each has in it an admixture of the other three. The three lighter elements tend to range themselves in concentric hollow spheres around the spherical earth. *Earth* being heaviest is naturally lowest, that is, at the center. Remove it from the center and its natural motion is in a straight line toward its own place, that is, downward toward the center; hence gravity. *Water* is next heaviest; its natural place is just above earth; like earth it tends toward the center. Above the water, which laves earth's surface, is the hollow sphere of *air*, concentric with that of earth and water. The natural motion of air is opposite to that of earth and water, straight outward, that is, upward, toward the circumference of the world. It cannot, however, go beyond the sphere of the lightest and purest element *fire*. The natural place of this is outside the other elements but like air it tends outward, that is, upward. Fire, too, forms a hollow sphere, the *Empyrean*.

All things formed by combination of the elements in this our lower world are subject to generation and decay. While nothing here is permanent, there is yet no annihilation, for all material change is but recombination of the four elements. Causes of all this generation and decay are the motions of the heavenly bodies that occupy spheres outside the sphere of the outermost element. Lowest of these heavenly bodies is the moon, next the other planets, next the fixed stars. The heavenly bodies are composed of a fifth substance, something purer than the elements, namely, the *quintessence* or *ether*. Heavenly bodies differ from things composed of the four elements in that they are not subject to generation, save at the Creation, or to decay, save at the final consummation and then at God's will. Their only change is *movement*, but this movement differs from that of things in our lower world and notably of the elements there. These have their natural movement of falling or rising in straight lines, but the heavenly bodies circle eternally round the center, for the circle is the perfect figure. They are set in a series of concentric transparent spheres which revolve and carry them in their movement:

> For ever singing as they shine
> The Hand that made us is Divine.

The world thus pictured is finite in time as well as in space. God Himself set the outermost sphere in motion, or rather is the eternal cause of its motion. Similarly each of the many circular motions, of which the composite movements of the heavenly bodies are the resultant, is produced by its own proper mover, which is pure form or spirit. Hence the absurdity of astrology, for it is these spirits, acting under God, that cause the movements of the stars and not *vice versa*.

One aspect of the physics of Maimonides affected scientific development. Maimonides perceived that the difference between belief in an eternal and belief in a created world may ultimately be resolved into a difference between belief in impersonal mechanical law, as an explanation of the universe, and belief in an intelligent being acting with a particular design. Maimonides admits that Aristotle's resolution of all motions below the lunar sphere in terms of an impersonal mechanical law is successful. It is in the outer spheres that Aristotle fails, though we need not follow Maimonides into details of his failure. Yet, since outer and inner spheres are intimately connected, failure in explaining the one involves failure in the other. The mechanistic view of the world, which excludes free will, miracle and efficacy of prayer, must, he claims, therefore be rejected.

For the mechanistic hypothesis Maimonides substitutes the intelligent purpose and design so dear to the heart of Galen (130-200 c.e.), physician to the philosopher-emperor Marcus Aurelius (121-180 c.e.). With the works of Galen, Maimonides, as a physician, was very familiar. For Maimonides, as for Galen, *design*—God's plan—is expressed in *natural law* and continues to be directed by intelligence. That there were rules of wide application in nature Maimonides fully realized; that these rules depended for their working on certain underlying series of events he also accepted. But ultimately these rules depended, he held, on the action of an intelligence working to intelligible ends. By avoiding the enormous claims of Galen that these ends were wholly known or immediately discoverable by man, he leaves far more room for scientific discovery than does Galen and far less room for the comparable claims of astrology.

The actual scientific efforts of Maimonides do not compare in profundity with his philosophic studies. They can, perhaps, hardly be expected to exhibit great originality—a quality to which his age attached a negative value—but they do nevertheless reveal him clearly as a highly competent, sensible, trusted and effective physician. He knew no Greek and relied entirely on Arabic versions of Galen and Aristotle and on Arabic writers who in their turn relied on Galen and Aristotle. His medical writings have exercised much influence on both Eastern and Western medicine. It is reasonable to claim for them that they kept Hebrew-Arabic medicine sane and levelheaded. Most of his medical works have been translated into both Hebrew and Latin.

Maimonides must have been a very busy man. He thus describes his day's work in a pleasant letter written in 1199, a vivid picture of the life of the best type of medieval physician:

I dwell at Fostat but the sultan at Cairo; these places are two Sabbath days' journey [about one mile and a half] from each other. My duties to the sultan are very heavy. I have to visit him daily early in the morning; and when he or any of his children, or inmates of his harem, are indisposed I dare not leave Cairo, but must spend most of the day in the palace. If any of the royal officers fall sick, I must attend them. Hence I usually go to Cairo very early in the day, and can hardly return to Fostat until afternoon. Then I am tired and hungry. I find the antechambers filled with people, Jews and Gentiles, nobles and common people, judges and bailiffs, a mixed multitude, awaiting my return.

I dismount from my animal, wash, and beg my patients to bear with me while I eat, the only meal I take in the day. Then I attend to my patients, write prescriptions and directions for them. Patients come in and out till nightfall, and sometimes, I assure you, until two hours and more in the night. Sometimes I converse with and prescribe for them while lying down from sheer fatigue, and when night falls I am so exhausted that I can scarcely speak.

Thus none converse with me [on religious matters] except on the Sabbath. Then the whole congregation, or at least most of them, come to me after the morning service, when I advise them as to the work of the week. We study together a little until noon, when they leave. Some return and read with me after the afternoon service until evening prayers. Thus I spend the days. I have related to you only a part of what you would see if you were to visit me.

Late in the twelfth century Maimonides received an inquiry from the Rabbis of Provence asking his views on astrology. He replied in Hebrew that he regarded it as superstition. This attitude was rare in the Middle Ages, for astrology then stood for rationalism. Astrology was therefore often condemned as impious but seldom for the reasons that Maimonides gave. Though he wrote no work on astronomy, his views on the subject can be traced in his other works. They were conservative, rejecting the doctrine of epicycles as contrary to the view of Aristotle.

Almost exactly contemporary with Maimonides was ibn Ruschd (1126-1198) of Cordova, Averroës of the Latins. He held the office of a judge but studied and practiced medicine. He was a Moslem and his writings earned him the bitter enmity of orthodox Moslems, just as those of Maimonides were long abhorrent to orthodox Jews. Averroës had immense influence on Jewish thought.[9a] The opponents of Averroës regarded him as a Judaizer. The general contents of his writings were similar to those of Maimonides though his opinions were very different. The works of Averroës, like those of Maimonides, were almost immediately translated into Hebrew. The widely read Latin versions of Averroës were rendered not from Arabic but from Hebrew. Averroan works and doctrine were forbidden in the universities and regarded by the church as presenting the utmost spiritual danger.

9. Provençal and Sicilian Translators, Thirteenth Century

The end of the twelfth century and the death of Maimonides (1204) saw the close of the brilliant period of Spanish and Egyptian Jewish science. There were several important figures in the centuries to come though none to measure by Hasdai ibn Shaprut, Abraham bar Hiyya and Maimonides. Nevertheless, the demand for translations from Arabic and Hebrew increased with the development of the universities. Jews played the main part in providing these. Why, then, did their original output fall in quality and quantity?

The full answer is complex but the major factors are plain enough. The thirteenth century was the great period of foundation of universities. Those at Palencia, Valladolid, Salamanca, Lerida and Coimbra in the Iberian Peninsula and, outside it, Paris, Montpellier, Salerno, Bologna, Padua, Naples, Rome, Oxford and Cambridge all began effectively in the thirteenth century. From all these Jews were excluded. As the learned output of the universities rose, that of the Jews fell in relative importance. Jews were thrown back on their own resources. Moreover, the Inquisition was established in Spain and the position of Spanish Jews was steadily deteriorating.[10a] The Jews of Provence and Italy were losing such hold as they had on the Arabic language. Outside the Mediterranean area secular science had hardly reached any Jewish group. Among the Ashkenazim, outside France and Italy, talmudic studies remained all-absorbing. The Golden Age of Jewish science was over.

Prominent among the translators of the Silver Age were members of the Provençal family Bene Tibbon of Spanish origin. Samuel ben Judah ibn Tibbon (c. 1160-1232) of Lunel and Marseilles[11a] introduced Aristotle to Hebrew readers by his Hebrew version of the *Meteorology* from the Arabic. He made it at sea during a voyage from Alexandria (1212). He also rendered a commentary on Galen, but he is chiefly remembered for his diffusion of the Maimonidean philosophy in the West and his development of the Hebrew philosophical language.

Jacob Anatoli (c. 1194-1256) of Marseilles was a disciple and son-in-law of this ibn Tibbon. The Emperor Frederick II invited him to Naples (1231), where he possibly met Thomas Aquinas and certainly Michael Scot. Anatoli turned the work of Averroës into Hebrew and thus took the first step toward Averroistic heresy among both Jews and Latins. Equally influential was the help that he gave to Michael Scot (d. c. 1235) to render into Latin a conflation of the great biological works of Aristotle, the first work of ancient biological science that became available to the West.

In the same region and period there worked the Sicilian Moses Farrachi (Ferrachius). He was specially employed as one of a band of Jewish translators by Charles of Anjou (1220-1285). His great achievement is his Latin version (*c.* 1275) of the enormous *Liber continens*, a medical work by Rhazes (d. 932). Another Jewish Sicilian translator, Moses of Palermo, was engaged by Charles to learn Latin. He afterward translated a veterinary work from Arabic.

The most active of all the translators from Arabic into Hebrew was Moses ben Samuel ibn Tibbon of Marseilles. In addition to Aristotle's philosophical works, he translated many mathematical and medical treatises including Geminus's *Introduction to Hipparchan Astronomy* (Naples, 1246), Euclid's *Elements* (Montpellier, 1270) and Theodosius of Bithynia's *Spherica* (Montpellier, 1271), medical works by a pupil of Isaac Judeus 1259), Rhazes's *Antidotary* (1257), Avicenna's *Canticum* (1260), and many others.

10. CASTILIAN AND ARAGONESE ASTRONOMERS AND CARTOGRAPHERS, THIRTEENTH CENTURY

In Spain there were some noteworthy translations from Arabic in the thirteenth century. Alfonso X of Castile (1252-1284), called "the Wise," came to the throne when the transference of Eastern thought was very active. He directed the translation of some of this material into the vernacular and so influenced the development of the Spanish language. He was himself an author, interested in philosophy and astronomy, and employed a number of Jewish translators. The most remarkable scientific work of his reign was the so-called *Alphonsine tables*. These lists of planetary movements are the basic documents of modern astronomy and continued in repute for centuries. They were prepared under the wise king's direct command between 1262 and 1272 by two learned Jews of Toledo, Judah ben Moses Cohen, a physician, and Isaac ben Sid, a synagogue precentor. They are based on the tables of a Cordovan astronomer of the eleventh century and the last edition for practical use appeared at Madrid in 1641! They were consulted by Kepler and Galileo. The tables on which they were based were themselves rendered into Spanish by another Jewish translator for Alfonso X.

The preface of the Alphonsine tables tells that, since computed positions often differ from those observed, the king had collected instruments and directed observations to be taken at Toledo. The writers, Moses Cohen and Isaac Hazan, therefore observed the sun for him through an entire year, particularly at the equinoxes and solstices, and at the middle of the signs of Taurus and Scorpio, Leo and Aquarius. They also observed conjunctions of planets both with each other and with fixed stars, and took observations of lunar and solar eclipses. Both authors produced many other important astronomical, mathematical and mechanical works in Spanish, and constructed many astronomical instruments.

Alfonso's patronage of learning was copied by his neighbors, the monarchs of Aragon. The Jew Astruc Bonsenior of Barcelona was secretary and interpreter to King Jaime I of Aragon (1208-1276) in his campaigns. His son Judah Bonsenior became interpreter to Alfonso III (reigned 1265-1291) and Jaime II (reigned 1291-1327). In 1287 Alfonso III took him on his expedition to Minorca. In 1294 Jaime II arranged that he review the translation into Spanish of all Arabic business documents.

A scientific department in Aragon that was largely officered by Jews was that of mapmaking. For Aragonese merchants sailing books of the Mediterranean known as *portolani* were prepared. These contained descriptions of coasts, harbors, anchorages and so forth. Toward the end of the thirteenth century they began to be provided with charts. The *portolano maps* give the outline of the Mediterranean and have the directions of and distances between different ports. The best were made in the island of Majorca, where an important school of Jewish mapmakers sprang up. They relied largely on the Arabic geographers.

At Las Palmas in Majorca the Jew Cresques drew up in 1375 the first map that set forth the discoveries of Marco Polo. This was sent as a gift from the king of Aragon to Charles VI of France. Cresques long continued his cartographical activities. In 1419 he was summoned to Portugal by Prince Henry the Navigator (1394-1460), to assist in establishing an astronomical observatory.

11. RISE OF NORTH ITALIAN SCHOOL, THIRTEENTH CENTURY

By the mid-thirteenth century the two original gates of entry of Arabic science into Europe—the Spanish Peninsula and the Sicilies—were ceasing to function. In the former, organized into Christian kingdoms, the vernaculars Catalan, Castilian and Portuguese began to be used even for learned purposes. The cultural and political importance of the Sicilies was waning. The universities of north Italy and France had determined the intellectual centers of gravity. Islam was in retreat in the West, and at its heart had sustained the irreparable blow of the Mongol invasion and sack of Bagdad (1227). The great period of translation from the Arabic was past although the process continued for centuries. Yet the prestige in Europe of Arabian science was still undiminished. Padua had become an important medical school, linked to Venice, the portal of Eastern trade, and Paduan learning had stamped itself on the philosophical and medical thought of Italy and soon spread to Montpellier.

Jews were numerous at Padua and there one of them, Bonacosa, made the first important north Italian contribution to the library of Arabic-Latin medical translations, the *Colliget* (Arabic *Kulliyyat, i.e.,* "General [medical] rules") of Averroës (1264). It was long studied at Padua and the last edition appeared there in 1560. It was translated twice into Hebrew.

Another product of the Paduan Jewish school was a Latin translation from the Hebrew version of the *Theizir* (Arabic *Taysir, i.e.,* "Aid to health"), of the Spanish Moslem, Avenzoar (d. 1162), written for his friend Averroës. It was widely read in Hebrew, whence it was turned into Latin by the Jew Jacob of Capua, an immigrant from the south. He also rendered into Latin from Hebrew the *Hygiene* of Maimonides, and a book of Indian stories, the so-called *Kalilah wa-Dimmah.* This collection became extraordinarily widespread, largely through Jewish agency. It is said to have been translated into thirty-eight languages and to have passed into about one hundred and eight editions. The English version was derived from the Spanish, which was taken from Latin, which was taken from Hebrew, which was taken from Arabic, which was taken from Pehlavi, which was taken from Sanskrit!

Another strange document of the Paduan school is the most popular of all the medieval books on remedies, the *Canones generales* of "Mesue." This is the name of a well-known Arabic medical writer, but the book is a compilation from the Hebrew. At the end of the thirteenth century one Samuel ben Jacob of Capua, son of the above, composed this drug list, or part of it, in Hebrew. From this the Latin version was prepared. It became very popular and was printed scores of times, the last occasion being in 1581. It was the chief pharmaceutical work of the Renaissance and has influenced the modern pharmacopoeias, including that of England.

A translator who links north Italy with north Spain and south France was Abraham ben Shemtob of Tortosa, whose father, Shemtob ben Isaac of Marseilles, was a well-known translator into Hebrew from Arabic. In 1290, with the Christian Simon Cordo of Genoa, Abraham produced in Latin the popular drug list associated with the name of *Serapion junior.* This mysterious figure is unmentioned by the Arabic historians. He was invented, perhaps by Cordo and Abraham, to cover a work of miscellaneous Arabic and Hebrew origin. *Serapion* was frequently printed. It, too, has influenced the modern pharmacopoeias. The partnership between Cordo and Abraham Shemtob produced several other medical translations.

12. FRENCH CHRISTIAN AND JEWISH HEBRAISTS, THIRTEENTH AND FOURTEENTH CENTURIES

In southern France, Jews were particularly active in the practice of medicine, notably at Avignon. There were many Jewish physicians at

Montpellier, which had been a medical center since the early twelfth century. In the thirteenth century it received a new medical tradition from Bologna and Padua. In 1263 John of Brescia, who had migrated to Montpellier from Bologna, collaborated with the Jew Jacob ben Makir in translating from Arabic into Latin certain important astronomical tables.

This Jacob ben Makir (d. 1308) was born at Marseilles, studied at the great talmudic seminary in Lunel, married the daughter of Moses ben Samuel ibn Tibbon and practiced actively as a physician at Montpellier. After assisting John of Brescia he busied himself in presenting the philosophy of Maimonides in Hebrew. He is best known for a Hebrew work that he wrote in 1288 on the astronomical quadrant, into which he introduced certain improvements. The form he advocated was known as the "Jewish quadrant" (*quadrans judaicus*). This important work was turned into Latin no less than three times, on the first occasion by an Englishman, who was making a stay at Montpellier about the year 1308, and on the second occasion about 1314 by the Christian Hebraist Armengaud of Montpellier. The well-known surveying instrument usually called *Jacob's staff* is probably named after this Jacob ben Makir. The first description of it that we have is, however, by his countryman and coreligionist Gersonides. An *Almanach* of Jacob ben Makir was used by Dante in the *Divina Commedia*.

Jacob ben Makir made many translations of scientific works from Arabic into Hebrew, such as Euclid's *Elements* and Alhazen's *Astronomy*, the works of Autolycus and of Menelaus *On the Sphere*, and Aristotle's *De partibus animalium* and *De generatione animalium* in the version of Averroës. His work was appreciated in both Latin and Hebrew circles and he is quoted by Copernicus and Kepler.

With Jacob ben Makir is associated the equally accomplished Christian Hebraist and physician Armengaud Blasius of Montpellier (d. 1314). He rendered many Hebrew works into Latin including writings of Maimonides. He was always helped by Jacob ben Makir or by his pupils. In 1305, while at Barcelona in attendance on Jaime II of Aragon, he occupied his spare time in Latinizing from the Hebrew the very curious *Cantica* of Avicenna and the medical work of Maimonides *On the Treatment of Poisoning*. His reliance on Hebrew rather than Arabic for these works exemplifies a widespread practice in the Scholastic ages. The reciprocal relationship of Jacob ben Makir and Armengaud is typical and was much commoner in the later Middle Ages than appears on the surface.

In 1305 Armengaud was displaced in his attendance on Jaime II by Arnald of Villanova (1235-1311), than whom few medieval figures would give a better opportunity to a romantic writer. Arnald, after a youth of hardship, studied at Naples and Salerno, traveled in Italy, Sicily, France and Spain and taught at Montpellier. Both there and at Barcelona he was associated with Armengaud. He was one of the earliest European alchemical writers and he also wrote voluminously on philosophical subjects in a heretical vein. He had some knowledge of both Hebrew and Arabic, and had ample access to those who had such knowledge. He was medical adviser to the papal court both at Rome and at Avignon, was employed as ambassador on more than one special mission, and he ended a very eventful life at sea. He translated from the Arabic a work of Avicenna on the heart and from the Hebrew a work of Avenzoar on diet. Both were effected with Jewish help. On the other hand, Arnald's own works were much read in Hebrew into which language about ten of them were translated.

By the second half of the thirteenth century activity in translation from Arabic had spread northward, and had reached Paris and Flanders. The earliest patron of these northern translators of whom we have tidings was the Fleming, Henri Bate (1244-*c.* 1310), a disciple of Albertus Magnus (1206-1280) at Paris. He was intimate with William of Moerbeke (d. 1285), the translator from the Greek employed by Thomas Aquinas (1227-1274). Bate received an ecclesiastical benefice at his birthplace at Malines in 1273. Next year a French Jew, one Hayyin, translated into French works of Abraham ibn Ezra in Bate's house at Malines. These influenced Bate's later writings, notably a treatise on the astrolabe, produced in 1274 on William of Moerbeke's suggestion. Bate later went to Italy and translated other works of ibn Ezra at Orvieto (1281 and 1292). Other works of ibn Ezra were translated by the heretical Paduan professor Peter of Abano (1250-1318), one of the most picturesque of the Scholastics whose natural death saved him from a more violent one, for his body was exhumed and burned.

During the first half of the fourteenth century the French Jews displayed much philosophic and scientific activity. The leading representative of this movement is Levi ben Gerson, known as Gersonides (1288-1344).[12a] He lived at Avignon and Orange, and is important in the general history of philosophy and especially for the thought of Spinoza. He was a courageous man of outstanding scientific ability, but as a writer Hebrew was his only medium. The extent, variety and depth of his knowledge bear testimony to the qualities and possibilities of medieval Hebrew literature.

Gersonides was an enthusiastic Aristotelian, who fearlessly interpreted what he regarded as the view of his master in opposition alike to current Judaism and to the Averroism of the schools. He regarded himself as a complete rationalist and his philosophy was largely banned by his own people. His work that most stirred the world in which he lived was astronomical. A passage from it dealing with "Jacob's staff" was translated into Latin in 1342 during his lifetime by order of Pope Clement VI as *The Instrument That Reveals Secrets.* Later the whole work was Latinized. It demonstrates the falseness of the current view that all the heavenly bodies move round the same center. It thus in a sense leads on to Copernicus. It deservedly enjoyed a high reputation and was still esteemed in the seventeenth century, when Kepler was at pains to secure a copy. Kepler quotes Gersonides several times and refers to three separate works by him.

Mention should perhaps here be made of the very important French Hebrew fourteenth-century writer Hasdai Crescas. He had nothing to say on science in the modern sense but he is philosophically important as opposing Aristotle as represented by Maimonides. Thus he anticipates the reaction against Aristotle that later introduced the scientific movement to the Latin world.[13a]

13. Decline of Hebrew-Arabic Science, Fifteenth and Sixteenth Centuries

In the later fourteenth century the long decline of the Jewish scientific intellect began. The political and social conditions of Jews were steadily deteriorating, culminating with the expulsion from Spain, Sicily and Sardinia in 1492. Yet it was long before the Hebrew-Arabic element that had already entered Latin thought began to lose importance. The main philosophical reading of the West continued to be affected by Hebrew-Arabic literature far into the time of printing, and even to the seventeenth century. In this connection it must be remembered that the revival of Greek learning affected science much later than literature and philosophy.

Among the later Jewish translators of the period of decline, mention should be made of Elijah Delmedigo (1463-1497) of Padua. A good Hebrew, Latin and Italian scholar and a physician as well, he applied himself to philosophy and took part in the activities of the university. Padua, alone among the universities, occasionally granted a medical degree to Jews and that from as early as 1409. Among Elijah Delmedigo's students was Pico della Mirandola (1463-1494), at whose request some of his translations were undertaken. Delmedigo's writings are mostly Latin renderings of various treatises by Averroës. He also produced original philosophical works. He differs from Pico in having a strong bias against cabbalism.

In contrast to Delmedigo is Judah Verga of Lisbon, where he died under torture in 1490. He was a cabbalist but his secular work was of an exclusively scientific nature. Among his scientific writings, which are all in Hebrew, is a description of an astronomical instrument which he invented to determine the sun's meridian. The account of it was written at Lisbon about 1457.

It may seem strange that cabbalistic and scientific learning should occur in the same individual. In fact, however, this was often the case. Thus Guglielmo Raimondo of Girgenti, who was converted to Christianity in

1466, and later became a bishop, had both these interests. From him we
have a translation of an astronomical work of the Arab mathematician
Alhazen of Basra (965-1038). The dedication cites the Talmud and ibn
Ezra. About 1477, Raimondo also prepared a number of eclipse tables.

A similar combination of interests was exhibited by Paolo Ricci, a converted Jew of German origin who acted as physician to the Emperor
Maximilian. He translated cabbalistic treatises from Hebrew and later
became professor of medicine at the University of Pavia. He is mentioned
favorably by Erasmus. In 1519 he issued the only edition that we possess
of the medical treatise of the Spanish physician, Albucasis (1013-1106).

Bonet de Lattes was of a family from Lattes near Montpellier and he
himself was from Carpentras. He achieved an excellent reputation for
himself as a physician and was medical attendant to two successive Popes,
Alexander VI (d. 1503) and Leo X (d. 1513). In 1493 in a work dedicated
to Pope Alexander VI he described in Latin an astronomical instrument
for taking solar and lunar altitudes and thus determining the hour. It
gained much popularity. A pleasing description of Bonet, his house, his
instruments and his mode of life has been left by a Christian scholar who
visited him at Rome (1507). Some remains of this house were recovered
half a century ago.

By the sixteenth century translation of scientific works into Latin directly
from the Arabic had ceased, but translation into Latin from Hebrew
continued, mostly in the spirit of the New Learning. The last of the Jewish
translators who can rightly be termed medieval, Jacob Mantino (d. 1549),
was also connected with Padua. He was born in Spain, whence, on the
Expulsion, his parents brought him as an infant. He studied philosophy
and medicine at Bologna and Padua, and devoted most of his life to
translation into Latin. He settled in Venice and attracted the attention of
Clement VII as well as that of many scholars. His eventful life was marked
by office as physician to Pope Paul III and by disputes with the Messianic
visionary, Solomon Molko (1500-1532).

Mantino rendered into Latin from Hebrew works of Averroës, Gersonides, Maimonides and Avicenna. He is best remembered, however, as
editor of the monumental standard Latin edition of Averroës published
at Venice in 1552, soon after his death. It was the basis of the Averroistic
philosophical school that flourished among Christians and Jews at Padua
well into the seventeenth century and had some distinguished exponents.
William Harvey (1578-1657), discoverer of the circulation of the blood,
was affected by it. The ultimate representative of the medieval Hebrew-
Arabic movement in Italy was the Averroist, Cesaro Cremonini (d. 1637),
professor of philosophy at Padua till his death.

The decline of what we may call the Hebrew-Arabic-Latin scientific
movement is contemporary with the advent of a Jewish element in the new

"Renaissance" of science. The movement was short lived. It is illustrated by the careers of two Jewish astronomers, Abraham Zacuto and Joseph Vecinho who were involved in the explorations of Vasco da Gama and Columbus. So far as Hebrew-Arabic science in the Iberian Peninsula is concerned, theirs is a swan song.

Abraham Zacuto (1450-1510) taught astronomy at the universities of Salamanca and Saragossa. Leaving Spain he settled in Lisbon as astronomer to John II. He was consulted on the expedition of Vasco da Gama, whose vessels were fitted with astrolabes designed by him and provided with improvements that he introduced. In 1473, while still at Salamanca, Zacuto wrote in Hebrew a *Perpetual Almanac*. This was translated into both Latin and Spanish by his pupil Vecinho and issued in 1496 at Leiria in Portugal by a Jewish printer. Manuscript copies of it were carried in the fleets of Vasco da Gama, Cabral, João de Nova, and Albuquerque.

This Joseph Vecinho was also in the service of John II of Portugal, who sent him to the coast of Guinea to measure the solar altitude. When the plan of Columbus for Western exploration was laid before King John he submitted it to a committee of five, of whom Vecinho was chief. The other members were the Bishop of Ceuta, the court physician, the German cartographer Martin Behaim, and a Jewish mathematician named Moses. The committee reported against the expedition but Columbus retained a high respect for Vecinho and wrote in the margin of one of his books: "In the year 1485, the king of Portugal sent Master Joseph, his physician and astronomer, to determine the altitudes of the sun throughout Guinea, all of which he performed. He reported to the king, in my presence, that he found the Island of Idols near Sierra Leone to be exactly five degrees distant from the equator. Afterward the king often sent to Guinea and other places, and always found the results accord with those of Master Joseph." In another marginal note Columbus states that during voyages to Guinea he had taken solar altitudes of the sun, which always agreed with those of Vecinho.

Columbus (1446-1506) had, in fact, much intercourse with Jewish men of science and was acquainted with Zacuto as well as with Vecinho. Almost the first financial assistance that he secured was from the Jewish statesman and Bible commentator, Isaac Abrabanel (1437-1508), and in his will Columbus left a legacy to a Lisbon Jew. At least five Jews accompanied him on his first expedition, especially as interpreters. The first landing was effected on October 15, 1492, and on November 2, Columbus sent out his first expedition on American soil. It consisted of two men, one the Jew Luis de Torres. Torres was one of the first Europeans to tread American soil and the first to experiment with the effects of tobacco, using himself as guinea pig. He settled and died in Cuba.

Many have thought that Columbus was himself of Jewish origin and there is much to support that view. One point that might be made is that Columbus, though born and bred in Genoa, never employs an Italian word in any of his documents. Spanish is the only vernacular that he uses. This language was and is the lingua franca of Mediterranean Jews. For a Genoese to write only Spanish would in itself suggest a Jewish origin.

This is perhaps the place to mention the remarkable figure of Pedro Nunes (*c.* 1492-1577). He was born of a Marrano family in Portugal and studied medicine at Lisbon and mathematics at Salamanca. He went to the East Indies as an official in 1519 but was soon recalled as professor of philosophy at Lisbon. In 1529 he became cosmographer royal. In 1544 he was called to the chair of mathematics at Coimbra. Nunes devoted himself to investigation of figures and lines on spheres other than "great circles." He is a founder of scientific navigation and his *Treatise on the Sphere* (Lisbon, 1537) and *On the Art and Science of Navigation* have an assured place in the history of cartography. He himself escaped the direct attentions of the Inquisition but his grandchildren paid the penalty.

14. THE MARRANO EPISODE[14a]

In the world of intellect the persecution of Jews in Spain had certain surprising implications, some of which have been insufficiently recognized. Toward the end of the Jewish Iberian period there was, especially in Portugal, a remarkable number of Jewish writers touched by the spirit of the New Learning. The works of Judah Verga (d. 1490), Abraham Zacuto (d. 1510) and Joseph Vecinho (d. *c.* 1495) were the swan song of Jewish science in the Peninsula. With the migration their tradition was continued by such men as Elijah Delmedigo (d. 1497), Abraham de Balmes (1423-1523) and Jacob Mantino (d. 1549). But from then onward Jewish science, outside medicine, is mute until the nineteenth century. No important Jewish name appears in scientific literature, except in medicine, for nearly three centuries. The revival is not then with the Sephardim but with the Ashkenazim of Central Europe. This very fact adds significance to the immense number of physicians of the Marrano migration.

For much of the sixteenth, seventeenth and even the eighteenth centuries an astonishingly high proportion of important physicians of Europe was of Marrano descent. The phenomenon needs explanation, which is not yet perhaps fully forthcoming. Many factors may be suggested. Doubtless it was an advantage to possess the full clinical tradition of the Hebrew-Arabic medical system. Social pressure certainly left few avocations open to foreign refugees. Perhaps the mental detachment that comes of insecure social position may not be without its uses to the medical observer. Surely a natural channel of the Jewish tradition will always be humane social service. Assuredly it was no small thing to acquire early a respect for learning. Moreover, the minds of the Marranos were free in a sense in which those of professing Jews were not, for their very circumstances and history implied release from Rabbinic limitations.

There is something to be said for all these as factors of the intellectual outburst, which was almost exclusively among those of Sephardic and Iberian origin. The period coincides with the movement of the center of gravity of the Latin intellect from the Mediterranean area to the northwest. Thither the Marranos largely followed it. The northern Ashkenazim, however, were still in a pre-Scholastic stage. They were neither in a social nor an intellectual position to develop secular studies and there is no significant scientific figure among them before the nineteenth century. The determining elements in the outburst of Marrano intellectual activity will be a matter of opinion. The general situation bears resemblance to that of the Jews of Central Europe during the past hundred years. A culture hunger is aroused by the breakdown of the Rabbinic environment. This is most easily satisfied by the rising enthusiasm for science in a changed social milieu. The New Learning of the sixteenth century was to the Marranos what the New Science was to central European Jewry.

In both cases importance must be attached to the freeing of the mind from talmudic preoccupation. This sounds like a truism since a mind preoccupied by any line of thought obviously cannot at the same time admit another line. But it is a special feature of talmudic preoccupation that it tends to occupy the whole area of thought as do few other studies; for the Talmud is not only a subject of study, it is a habit of thought, a cast of mind, a way of life. The practical test lies in the historic record. Very few if any talmudists have made contributions to science. Why should this be? The answer must be in terms of Jewish sociology or psychology where it cannot be followed in this place.

It is difficult to give a picture of the medical activity of Marranism as a whole. It represents no definite school. The groups with which we are concerned are almost entirely disconnected. It is precisely this division among themselves that prevented the Marranos from developing a separate religion and so from having a history in any proper sense. But an account of the lives of a score of Marrano physicians over these three hundred years reveals the impetus of a remarkable intellectual movement working itself out until it becomes extinct in the nineteenth century. Not all the figures here selected are of great medical eminence. Some are selected as helping to complete the patchwork picture of the Marrano intellect. Some, too, were not Marranos themselves but descendants of Marranos.

Belonging to the first generation of the migration were two physicians bearing the name Leo, whose widely different careers illustrate the diversity of the Marrano activities. The better known was Leo Hebreus or Judah Abrabanel (c. 1470-1535), son of the famous statesman Isaac

Abrabanel. In 1492 his son was taken from Leo and baptized and he himself was expelled from Spain. He practiced in Naples and was physician to the successive kings of the "Sicilies." That realm being invaded, he sought a home successively at Venice, Corfu and Genoa, where his famous *Dialogues of Love* was written (1502) for his friend the philosopher Pico della Mirandola. Leo was a Neoplatonic dreamer and his work is a discussion between *Sophia*, Wisdom, and *Philo*, Love. Despite its esoteric character it contains matter of medical interest and Leo's medical services were always highly esteemed. The book is an Italian classic. It was printed nineteen times in the sixteenth century and has been translated into many languages, including Hebrew and English.

The other Leo, less known to fame, was a pioneer in a different sense. He was of Venice and ventured to Russia in 1490 in the train of an ambassadorial mission to Moscow, the first Western European medical man to enter Russian territory. He was called to treat a local prince, who unfortunately died. The physician was accordingly executed and Russia had naturally to wait some time for her next Western medical adviser.

Francisco Lopez de Villalobos (1472?-1549) was one of the very few great physicians who remained in sixteenth-century Spain. His surname is that of a place near Zamora but it is uncertain whether he was born there or at Toledo. He studied at Salamanca, was much occupied about the court of King Ferdinand (1509-1516) and of the Emperor Charles V (1518-1542), retiring at the age of seventy. He came early under suspicion of the Inquisition and was incarcerated for eighty days but managed to clear himself. He was forced on later occasions to be a witness to the burnings of heretics. Villalobos has a definite place in the history of medicine. He provided the clearest early account of syphilis in the form of a poem published at Salamanca in 1498. He wrote other important medical works which are still of interest.

Dionysius Brudo (c. 1470-c. 1540), son of a medical man, occupied an excellent post as physician to the crown in Lisbon. He was a controversialist on bloodletting, the method of which was a subject of violent debate at the time. In 1534, despite his eminence, he found reason to leave suddenly for Antwerp and a pension from the crown ceased to be paid him. His Jewish sympathies had been discovered. His son Manuel Brudo is said to have declared himself a Jew at Venice. Manuel practiced in England for a time about the year 1540. A work by him on the treatment of fevers (Venice, 1544) was widely read. It contains many references to his English cases and his English experiences and to English customs.

Although not medically important, one of the more remarkable of the Marrano physicians was another member of the London Marrano group, Hector Nunez (c. 1520-c. 1595). He was born at Evora, graduated at Coimbra, came to England about 1550 and joined the minute colony of Judaizing Marranos in London of whom there were about a hundred.

He became their leading spirit during the reign of Catholic Mary (1553-1558), despite the rigidly anti-Jewish attitude of her husband, Philip of Spain. Hector had widespread connections in the government and continued to enjoy the confidence of Elizabeth's great ministers, Burleigh and Walsingham. He was the first Jew or Marrano to be admitted as a fellow of the Royal College of Physicians (1554). He was esteemed within the college, holding the title of censor in 1562 and 1563. The college books show that he was still living in 1589 but that he was not then in England.

The most striking medical figure of the sixteenth century was the Belgian professor at Padua, Andreas Vesalius (1514-1564), founder of the study of anatomy. For both of his anatomical works (1538 and 1543) he had Jewish assistants. He speaks of the chief of these in the most cordial way as his friend and guest. He needed their help to explain to him the meaning of Arabic and Hebrew anatomical terms.

Of the medical men of the sixteenth century few were better known in their own time than Juan Roderigo who usually called himself Amatus Lusitanus (1511-1568).[15a] He was born at Castello Branco in Portugal, son of Marrano refugees from Spain. He took a medical degree at Salamanca and practiced for a while in Lisbon. About this time complaints were raised in the Cortes that almost all physicians and apothecaries were "New Christians," that is, Marranos. There was much truth in this. Anticipating the entry of the Inquisition into Portugal (1536) Amatus left for Antwerp. There he established a reputation based partly on his *Index to the Remedies of Dioscorides* (1536). In 1540 he was called to the chair of medicine at Ferrara, then one of the most tolerant places in Europe. It was a center for anatomical study, a subject entirely neglected in Spain and Portugal. At Ferrara he performed a considerable number of dissections and witnessed more. He was invited to become court physician in Poland and town physician in Ragusa. Owing to some miscalculation concerning the latter he moved to Ancona (1547), where he carried on a very successful practice and wrote the first of his seven *Centuriae* (1549) of medical observations. This was issued at Rome in 1551 during a long visit there. In 1555 decrees issued by the new Pope, Paul IV, placed restrictions on medical practice by Jews and Marranos. A number in Italy were arrested by the Inquisition and twenty-four burned at the stake. Amatus fled first to Pesaro and then across the Adriatic to Ragusa. Finally he reached Salonica, 1558. There he wrote his *Centuria VII* (1561) and died some years later.

Amatus wrote an important book on *materia medica* (Venice, 1552) that contains many original botanical observations. The works by which he is rightly remembered, however, are his *Centuriae*. These are clinical records of actual cases, the first major collection of the kind ever made, and are of great historic and scientific importance.

Garcia da Orta (1498-1568) was one of the most distinguished medical men of the sixteenth century. He studied at the universities of Salamanca and Alcalá. In 1534 he sailed for India and settled finally at Goa. He was the pioneer of the study of tropical diseases and one of the fathers of botanical science. His valuable and interesting *Colloquies on the Simples and Drugs of India* (Goa, 1563) was the first book printed in that country. It is still consulted as the earliest authority on the subject. Da Orta traveled much in India and his observations were outstanding. One of his famous sayings expresses the true spirit of science: "In Spain I would never have dared to affirm anything contrary to the Greeks and particularly to Galen, but in India, free from convention, in the midst of luxuriant vegetation, it matters little what Dioscorides, Pliny, Avicenna and Galen have said. Do not frighten me with them. I have seen." What was in effect an illustrated edition of Da Orta's book was produced in 1578 by another Marrano, Cristoval d'Acosta.

Many of Garcia da Orta's relatives suffered from the Inquisition and his sister was burned at the stake in the year of his death. In 1580 the Inquisition found that he was a Jew and ordered his remains to be burned. He had been dead for twelve years.

Continuity of medical tradition in a Marrano family is illustrated by the Saportas. The Catalonian Luiz Saporta was born at Lerida (*c.* 1460-1565). After nine years of medical practice there he left for Provence and started practices first at Arles, then at Avignon, and then at the ancient university town of Montpellier. He did much military service, received many signs of royal approval and is said to have died at Marseilles, age 106. His son Louis Saporta II (*c.* 1490-*c.* 1580) took his degree at Montpellier and practiced at Toulouse, where he acquired a great reputation, dying at the age of ninety. His son Antoine Saporta (*c.* 1510-1573) was born at Montpellier, took his medical degree there in 1531, became professor of medicine there in 1540, dean in 1551 and chancellor in 1566. His son Jean Saporta (*c.* 1550-1605) also became professor there (1577) and later vice-chancellor (1603).

Rodrigo de Castro (1546-1627) came of a well-known Marrano medical family, many members of which, including his own brother, suffered from the Inquisition. He was born at Lisbon, educated at Salamanca and practiced first at Evora and then at Lisbon. He earned a great reputation and was offered a post in India to continue the work of Garcia da Orta. He decided, however, to leave Portuguese territory, fearing the inquiries of the Holy Office. He settled in Hamburg about 1590 and there became one of the most respected and sought-after physicians in northern Europe, being called upon to attend a number of sovereigns and high notables. De Castro's own reputation was greatly increased by his steady refusal to leave his post in plague-time. About the beginning of the seventeenth century the very small band of Marranos in Hamburg began openly to profess the Jewish religion. Official sanction was given to their residence in 1611. De Castro wrote two books of considerable medical importance, one the earliest original modern treatise on gynecology and the other on the relation of the doctor to the state. He had two sons who also were physicians.

At the end of the sixteenth century the grand dukes of Tuscany sought to attract a higher type of professor in reorganizing the University of Pisa. One of their captures was a young man named Galileo Galilei. For the medical department distinguished Marranos were available. Among those secured was Estevão Rodrigues de Castro (1559-1637), a native of Lisbon. He was a prolific writer who made pioneer observations in pathology. A gifted teacher, he was called in 1615 to Padua, the leading medical school of the time. He was followed at both Pisa and Padua by Antonio Rodrigues da Fonseca (d. 1632), another native of Lisbon and also a voluminous writer, whose achievement lay in having helped to check the practice of excessive bleeding.

Abraham Zacuto (1575-1642) the Portuguese (Lusitanus) came of a long line of physicians, perhaps the longest on record, for his great-grandfather of the same name was already the third of his line. Our Zacutus was born at Lisbon, studied at Salamanca and Coimbra and took his degree at Siguenza. After practicing for thirty years (1596-1626) in his native town with noteworthy success, he was forced to flee and headed for Amsterdam. He joined the Jewish congregation there and at once began a long and voluminous series of publications which ended only with his death. Zacutus was a strong medical conservative. Although he had passed beyond the "Arabist" phase he was obstinately Galenist in the mood of the previous generation. Living till almost the middle of the seventeenth century this attitude was certainly backward but he was nevertheless an excellent clinical observer. His work on the infectious diseases is still occasionally consulted and he was one of the first to describe the deadly blackwater fever.

A physician who is immortalized for adventitious reasons is Dr. Ephraim Hezekiah Bueno (d. 1665). He came of a Spanish family that included many physicians. His father, Joseph Bueno, arrived in Amsterdam from Bordeaux, where he had taken a medical degree, and was a doctor of good repute. Ephraim was very friendly with Manasseh ben Israel, whose first work he published, but he will always be remembered by the delightful picture of him by Rembrandt known as "The Jewish Doctor." His features represent the best Spanish type, with gentle, pitiful, sadly thoughtful eyes; a typical Sephardi. Beneath the contemporary engraving by Lyrius is inscribed, "A second Avenzoar, distinguished in medicine and a pupil of a distinguished father." He was a kind and charitable man, an efficient doctor and a good son of the synagogue.

John Lumbrozo (d. 1665) was a refugee from Portugal to Holland. Thence in 1656 he came to the palatinate of Maryland, where he practiced medicine with much success. In 1663 he secured letters of denization. He was the first Jewish inhabitant of Maryland of whose faith there is documentary evidence. One of the earliest trained practitioners there, he was probably the earliest ex-Marrano to practice medicine in the territory of what is now the United States. His career is of interest in relation to the development of religious toleration in Maryland. After two years of undisturbed quiet as a recognized Jew, as a consequence of his own indiscretion zealots obtained his arrest for "blasphemy," that is, for denying the doctrine of the Trinity. He was released under the general amnesty proclaimed a few days later by the Protector, Richard Cromwell.

Balthasar Orobio de Castro (1620-1687) was the child of Marrano parents living in Seville. He studied at Alcalá and became a teacher of philosophy at Salamanca. Later he studied medicine and practiced successfully at Seville, attending relations of the king. He was denounced by a servant to the Inquisition as an adherent of Judaism, but persistently denied the truth of this through two years of imprisonment and torture. In view of his later history it is evident that this treatment turned him toward Judaism in at least the sense that it turned him against Christianity. On his release he left Spain (1663) and became professor of medicine at Toulouse. Finally he migrated to Amsterdam (1666), where he embraced Judaism openly. There he practiced medicine until his death. He is known chiefly for his theological writings and for his friendship with Spinoza. His wife died at Amsterdam in 1712. Members of his family continued to be victims of the Inquisition far into the eighteenth century. An Orobio de Castro was writing medical works at Amsterdam toward the end of the nineteenth century.

Fernandez Mendez (c. 1645-1725) was born in Portugal and was graduated from Montpellier in 1667. He reached London in 1669 and became physician in attendance on Queen Catherine of Braganza (d. 1705). In 1687 he was admitted a fellow of the Royal College of Physicians. He married a lady of the migration, a Jewess, and a child was born to them in the royal palace of Somerset House. He was one of those in attendance on Charles II in his last illness. There is no reason to suppose that Mendez was a man of any special medical ability. The fact that the queen should choose this ex-Marrano illustrates the poorness of non-Jewish medical personnel in Portugal. The great tradition of Marrano medicine was itself petering out.

Daniel da Fonseca (1677-c. 1745) was born in Portugal. His grandfather had been burned as a Marrano and his father escaped as one when Daniel was only eight years old. He was baptized, brought up in the Catholic faith and entered the priesthood, nevertheless secretly adhering

nnmer⁹ annornꝫ	nomina menſiuꝫ	dies	digiti	feria	bore	minut	finis eclipſis bore	minu

Ʒab eclipſis luminariuꝫ et primo de ſole

nnmer⁹ annornꝫ	nomina menſiuꝫ	dies	digiti	feria	bore	minut	bore	minu
1493	octob	10	9	5	0	0	1	20
1502	ſepteb	30	8	6	17	28	19	12
1506	Julii	20	3	2	1	49	3	3
1513	martii	7	4	1	23	49	1	9
1518	Junii	7	10	2	18	22	19	17
1524	fannar	23	9	2	3	12	4	6

Ʒabla de eclipſib⁹ lnne

1494	ſepteb	14	17	1	17	5	2	33
1497	fannar	18	17	4	3	50	7	18
1500	noueb	5	13	5	10	17	13	30
1501	maii	2	10	1	15	33	19	6
1502	octob	15	14	7	10	15	12	9
1504	februa	29	16	5	10	47	14	13
1505	ang⁹	14	15	5	5	42	9	6
1508	Junii	12	23	2	15	21	19	0
1509	Junii	2	7	7	9	29	2	3
1511	octob	6	13	2	9	11	2	25
1514	fannar	29	16	2	14	20	16	3
1515	fannar	19	15	7	5	0	6	42
1516	Julii	13	14	1	10	0	12	30
1519	noueb	6	20	1	5	50	6	48
1522	ſepteb	5	15	6	11	22	12	4
1523	martii	1	17	1	7	30	9	14

A PAGE FROM THE *Almanach Perpetuum* OF ABRAHAM ZACUTO, LEIRIA, 1496

Christopher Columbus used Zacuto's computations. As is well known, Columbus learned from them of the moon's eclipse on February 29, 1504 (listed in the page above), and used the information to overcome the hostility of the Indians on the Island of Jamaica.

to the Jewish religion. This being suspected, he fled to France, where he studied medicine. He then made his way to Constantinople, where he openly embraced Judaism, practiced medicine, successfully obtained the confidence of high officials and showed himself consistently pro-French and anti-Austrian. He was appointed physician to the French embassy and later to the sultan himself. He retired about 1730 to Paris, where he spent his last years in the delightful society of the salons, a friend of Voltaire, who regarded him as the only Jewish philosopher.

Samuel Nunez (c. 1680-c. 1750) was a Marrano physician of great distinction who was born in Lisbon, where he was educated and practiced in high circles. He was denounced to the Inquisition, however, and he and his family were imprisoned. His services were in such demand that he was released but had to submit to the permanent residence in his house of two officers who would make certain that he did not relapse into Judaism. He succeeded in persuading the captain of an English ship to take his family and himself to England secretly. There they joined other Marranos and a small party of German Jews. They set sail in 1733 for Georgia. Despite attempts to prevent them from settling, most of them, protected by Oglethorpe, were able to remain, Nunez among them. He became a substantial landowner and was an ancestor of Mordecai M. Noah.

Jacob de Castro Sarmento (1691-1761) was born at Braganza, studied at Evora and Coimbra, taking his medical degree in 1717. He left his country to escape the Inquisition, settled in 1720 in London, was admitted to the Royal College of Physicians in 1725, became a fellow of the Royal Society in 1729 and of the college in 1739. He was one of the earliest advocates in England (1721) of the protection against smallpox by "variolation," that is, by inoculation with a mild form of the disease (to be distinguished sharply from vaccination, which came into use eighty years later). It is possible that he may have brought the idea with him from Portugal as he did a preparation of quinine, which he introduced. He published in Portuguese in London a work of some importance on mineral substances used in medicine (1731-1758). He openly professed Judaism and equally openly corresponded with Jesuits on scientific matters. He always retained his connections with Portugal and translated Newton's works into Portuguese. He left the synagogue in 1758.

Of the later Marranos perhaps the most important scientifically was Jacob Rodrigues Pereira (1715-1780). He was born in Spain of Marrano parents. On his father's death his mother was in danger of denunciation to the Inquisition. She and her son fled, settled in Bordeaux and embraced Judaism. From about 1737 on, the young man devoted himself to the experimental study of deaf-mutes. He thus slowly elaborated a method of teaching them to speak and gradually his method was accepted. His achievements have been generally acknowledged in modern times and his scientific reputation now stands very high. His interest in deaf-mutes was inherited by his great-grandson.

It would be very easy to extend this description of the pageant of Marrano life with a whole series of romantic figures. It would be equally easy to include in our illustrative list many scores of physicians distinguished in their day but short of eminence. Again the series might be made to include many theologians or other thinkers who, in the Jewish manner, had practiced for a time as physicians or had medical degrees. But by the mid-eighteenth century the Marrano impetus was failing. The migration had ceased. The Iberian Peninsula had become, as it remains, the most backward and illiterate region of Western Europe. The Marranos themselves were largely absorbed in the general population. The Jewish people of the eighteenth century, whatever their interest in the sociologist and social historian, provide little for the historian of science.

15. A HUNDRED YEARS OF CENTRAL EUROPE

The role of Jews in the drama of modern scientific progress has been noteworthy in several Western countries. In central Europe it has been overwhelming and a discussion of the entire situation would be interminable. Here the consideration of the historical elements must suffice, omitting contemporary figures. Moreover, in order to keep within reasonable limits, we must confine ourselves, for the most part, to the German-speaking region. In that area Jews have played an ever-increasing part in intellectual life. Something must, therefore, be said of the history of Central European science, which is, in effect, German science. Furthermore, the German-speaking area is the effective center of the modern Jewish people. It is true that by the beginning of the twentieth century the relative importance of the German language and of German culture from the Jewish standpoint was rapidly declining. Nevertheless, Germany remained, until the rise of Nazism, the center of Jewish intellectual life.

A characteristic of German cultural history is the lateness of its scientific development. The great scientific movement of the sixteenth, seventeenth and eighteenth centuries, beginning in Italy, spread to northwestern Europe. For a long time the German area was little affected by it. There were a few eminent early German scientists but no outstanding school of scientific thought in a German environment. The real German scientific contribution was scarcely begun until the end of the eighteenth and did not reach impressive proportions until the nineteenth century. The first important native school of scientific thought was the mathematical, astronomical and physical movement linked with the great names of Karl Friedrich Gauss (1777-1855), and Wilhelm Eduard Weber (1804-1891) and associated largely with Goettingen.

Both this tardy arrival and rapid development are rendered partially understandable by the history of the universities and of the technical industries of Germany. German scientific technique has, like German learning, always been in the hands of university professors. The brilliant amateur, so frequently a figure in French and English science, has seldom appeared on the German scene. On the other hand, a significant role has been played by the "doctoral dissertation," a feature always greatly stressed in German university life. Until well into the nineteenth century German custom demanded that these dissertations, like lectures, be formal and in Latin. When this tradition, with its associated turgid absurdities, was finally abandoned, the system so developed as to provide German professors with what were, in effect, considerable staffs of trained but unpaid assistants. The officers of German universities have always been under state control and, given judicious state support, it was easy for a professor to introduce a high degree of organization into research.

Neither institutes nor organizations create science. Men of science are unique and beyond all valuation. Looking back upon the history of science as a whole, taking into consideration the proportion of people in Europe who use the German tongue, the high state of their material culture, and realizing that a large proportion of German scientific writings are products of non German or part-German influences, it may fairly be said that Germans have been distinctly less successful than several other peoples in producing creative work of the first rank. But the situation in the second half of the nineteenth century had special features. Much of the significant scientific advance in German in that period was related to skilled co-operative effort. There are phases in the development of the sciences for which a high degree of organization is especially favorable. Such a phase was traversed for certain sciences between the years 1860 and 1920. It happened to coincide with the industrialization of Germany. The rise of industrialism and the development of great scientific institutes were of mutual assistance, notably from 1882 to 1907, when the extremely able Friedrich Althoff reigned tyrannically in the Prussian Ministry of Education.

In the later nineteenth century private benefaction in the United States, England and France had not yet enabled research to be organized on anything like the scale that we see today [1946]. Moreover, universities in these countries shunned industrial contacts, sometimes even depreciating the sciences. Hence the German universities had advantages in certain disciplines. In Germany many scientific departments, ably officered and with numerous highly trained and well-disciplined staffs, were in a position to concentrate directly on specific problems to a degree unknown elsewhere. All this fitted the state-directed industrialization under the Prussian hegemony, some of the profits from which were skillfully diverted to the needs of fundamental research. The development of scientific interests among Jews in Germany must be considered with this background in mind.

The nineteenth- and twentieth-century outburst of Jewish intellect reveals both contrasts and parallels to that of the earlier Marrano episode. In contrast it was almost entirely among Ashkenazim, for Sephardic activity has progressively waned. Its external accompaniments were those liberating, liberalizing, humane forces that both produced and emerged from the French Revolution. The atmosphere of this emancipation was totally different from the extreme Catholic nidus that bred the Iberian Marranos. Moreover, the political emancipation of Jews in central Europe resulted, and was designed to result, in their assimilation to the normal social environment.[16a] This, too, was quite unlike the designedly extrusive process of the Spanish and Italian Inquisitions. Furthermore, the Emancipation coincided with and was partly dependent on a general recession of the power of the churches.

Despite these differences in origin, the two movements had analogous features. Both arose among people in whom the breakdown of talmudism had left the tension produced by a spiritual vacuum. It is not remarkable that in the resulting cultural hunger the intellectual products should bear traces of this. The Marranos, like their later counterparts, carried some residue of the old Jewish culture and, like them, they had not quite completely absorbed the culture of their environment. The double maladjustment, not so great as to constitute a spiritual conflict of the gravest kind, was yet enough to give an independence of approach, a philosophic detachment to the entrant into the newly accessible scientific field. This was certainly an advantage. An impartial outlook is a significant part of the equipment of the man of science. The circumstances that may induce it are worthy of further attention from the social psychologist.

It is not easy to depict the rise of science as a part of the history of western European Jews. Science, in the modern sense, is truly no part of their heritage. How could it be rooted in the history of a people to whom the renaissance of literature and of learning, of art and of science, had brought nothing except heavier bonds? The Renaissance has little place in Jewish history. On the other hand, the development of science itself cannot be said to be distinctive of any people. How could it be, since science is, of its nature, universal? It is neither Jewish nor Christian, neither national nor racial, but a product of a particular philosophic outlook. If we use language exactly we cannot speak at all of Jews or of Judaism in science. We do so in this place only by making several elipses and assumptions.

As with the Marrano episode, we can thus but present an imperfect panorama, emphasizing here and there those activities in which Jews have especially distinguished themselves. And even for such a partial account of the part that Jewish individuals have played in science it is necessary to correlate the record with that of the admission of Jews to universities.

In the sixteenth century the only university to which Jews had any easy access was Padua. In the seventeenth, Leyden began to take its place both in scientific eminence and in the freedom with which religious tests were waived. This great Dutch school achieved even greater prominence in the eighteenth century. In the central European universities professing Jews could hardly obtain admission until the mid-nineteenth century, while important posts, and notably full professorships, were almost entirely denied to them until well into the twentieth century. In the ancient English universities it was not possible for a Jew even to take a degree until the passing of the Universities Test Act in 1871.

Under these circumstances there arose in the German-speaking countries a movement closely resembling Marranism. Among nineteenth-century Jews, as among Christians, only a small proportion were "believers" in any profound sense. Many, both of Jewish and of Christian parentage, to whom religion meant little, found the formal profession of Christianity no unbearable strain on the conscience. In all countries, but especially in the Germanic, facile "converts" passed readily enough into the prevailing formal Christianity. Naturally they carried with them some elements of their traditional habits of thought. Of such persons it may be said that, except for the fact that their environment was happier and safer, their spiritual outlook did not and does not differ vastly from that of the earlier Iberian Marranos.

But while these German Marranos differ in some respects from their neighbors of non-Jewish origin, these differences did not and do not unite them. They have no common outlook. These nominal Christians of Jewish origin represented, and still represent, no organized or effective movement. As with the Iberian Marranos, their separateness was the result of external pressure rather than of internal force. This absence of internal force, this failure of and even resistance to organic development, has been the real basis of the Jewish tragedy. Even Jewish nationalism is basically of external origin, part of the nationalist pandemic that has swept the world for a century. Moreover, the withering of the religion, the only possible unifying element in the Jewish intellectual revival, happened to be contemporary with certain scientific developments. Jewish emancipation coincided with an era of enormous scientific advance, the result of extreme fragmentation in the scientific field resulting from the natural product of increasingly complex techniques. As with the finest craftsmanship, the very exercise of technique provided an outlet for self-expression. The frustrated and culture-starved German Marranos eagerly occupied this new field. They gave to it a certain spiritual significance that they drew from their half-forgotten religious heritage.

There is another and contrasting side to this scientific movement corresponding to the natural variety of character found in every social aggregate. Those of the reflective type sought immediate substitutes to fill the religious gap. They rapidly became part of the philosophic movement at the German universities. With this we are hardly directly concerned, except for the significant effect it had on the scientific movement itself. In fact, some of the greatest Jewish exponents of science in the early nineteenth century were men of the widest scientific grasp. Let us glance at the effects on Jews of these new sources of inspiration.

Before World War II Jews formed roughly one per cent of the population of Europe, which was roughly five hundred millions. But the Jewish five millions was far from evenly distributed. In the Iberian Peninsula it was next to nothing. In Scandinavia it was about one-tenth of one per cent. In parts of Russian and Rumanian territory it was a hundred times as much. The special area of Jewish intellectual success, though not of density of Jewish population, was German-speaking. In that region Jews formed about one in a hundred of the entire population. To a lesser extent Italian-speaking Europe, with a Jewish population of about one in a thousand, presented similar phenomena. These were less marked in the French- and English-speaking worlds. For obvious reasons Jewish intellectuals played hardly any part in the old Russian Empire and Rumania. Jewish scientific development was thus confined to a relatively small part of the European area in which Jews were settled.

These phenomena are capable of comparatively simple historical and demographic explanation. Jewish activity in the scientific realm has been particularly notable in the mathematical and medical fields. Mathematics relies less on apparatus and on organization than do other departments of science. In its development the solitary worker is less handicapped than in most departments. Those debarred from normal social, literary and scholastic contacts naturally throw themselves into this most abstract discipline. Jewish addiction to medicine again requires little explanation. Its pursuit is in the full Jewish tradition. Moreover, the social developments of the time and the constitution of the universities made it simpler for Jews to enter this than any other profession.

But when all is said there remains an essential something that is a real source of wonder. A people scattered, disunited, numerically less than one of the smallest nations of Europe, has for a century provided from an effective German-speaking population of some two millions an ever-increasing proportion of the best scientific exponents in central Europe and Italy. Put the matter numerically and in the roughest way. In pre-Nazi Germany Jews formed about three-quarters of one per cent of the population. Of distinguished German mathematicians, physicists and medical researchers, they provided something like thirty times their due proportion, for at least twenty-five per cent of these were Jews. In Italy, where the Jewish population was only one per thousand, Jewish intellectual supremacy was even higher in certain departments. Well above fifty per cent of the distinguished Italian mathematicians were Jews.

We turn to glance at some individual achievements in the different sciences, beginning with mathematics.

Karl Jacobi (1804-1851), son of a Jewish merchant of Potsdam, was the first prominent German mathematician of Jewish origin and among the greatest mathematicians of modern times. A prolific writer and able teacher, he profoundly influenced the entire realm of mathematical thought of his age; there is hardly a branch upon which he did not leave an imprint. His greatest contribution was his development of the theory of elliptic functions. Very important was his work on the theory of numbers and of determinants and, especially, of functional determinants ("Jacobians"), of the calculus of variations, of differential equations and of the theory of mechanics. In the last two fields his achievements form the basis of modern mathematical physics.

Jacobi's pupil Leopold Kronecker (1823-1891) of Liegnitz in Silesia entered the business world but by the time he reached his early thirties had saved enough to give all his energies to mathematics. He became the recognized leader of the "Berlin school." His chief work was on the theory of numbers. His theory of equations was based on the idea of the theory of groups of Galois. Kronecker tried to "arithmetize" the whole of mathematics.

Among the greatest mathematicians of all time, whose ideas revolutionized the whole area of mathematics, was Georg Cantor (1845-1918). Though born at St. Petersburg, he was of German origin, speech and culture and spent nearly the whole of his life in Germany. Despite the greatness of his achievement he was a tragic figure. Misunderstood by his contemporaries and exhausted by the struggle to defend his views, he passed into depression mounting to insanity. It would be hardly possible to overestimate the value of his idea of sets or aggregates, which is fundamental to the study of the philosophical foundations of mathematics. Of prime importance, too, is his notion of transfinite numbers by which he overcame the *horror infiniti* of his predecessors. The notations of the so-called "transfinite cardinal numbers," represented by the Hebrew symbol ℵ, remains his monument. The whole of modern analysis and theory of functions is based on Cantorian principles and his activity marks a period in the history of mathematics.

A distant relation to his namesake was the German scholar Moritz Cantor (1829-1920) who wrote an unsurpassed history of mathematics and organized much research in the subject.

At the age of eighteen, Hermann Minkowski (1864-1909) of Alexotas in Lithuania submitted his solution of a problem in the theory of quadratic forms to the Academy of Sciences at Paris. It earned the Grand Prix des Sciences Mathématiques. He became a professor at Goettingen, long a leading mathematical center. His introduction of the new notion of geometrical illustration into the theory of numbers created the so-called "Geometry of Numbers" and made his reputation international. No less important were his works relating to the new mechanics of Albert Einstein. His name must always be connected with the scientific revolution of the theory of relativity of time and space.

Felix Klein (1849-1925) was the recognized head of the Goettingen "universalists." He was a model professor both as teacher and as organizer of research. During the last forty years of his life his was the foremost mathematical influence in Germany. His many-sidedness is especially noteworthy. He held that all the various geometries should be regarded from the standpoint of the theory of groups. He was a very able propagator of Georg Friedrich Bernhard Riemann's theory of functions and his own researches in allied departments are of lasting value. A strong adversary of one-sided specialization, he dealt with all the branches of mathematics, seeking to link them more closely and to treat them as a unit. Klein played an important part in the planning and editing of the famous *Mathematical Encyclopedia*, and its success is largely due to his fascinating personality.

In addition to such men, whose genius is admittedly of the highest rank, there were and are scores of very eminent German-Jewish mathematicians whose distinction cannot yet be estimated. It is not possible here to list even their names. Of special interest, however, is Emmy Noether (1882-1936), the very gifted daughter of the well-known mathematician Max Noether (1844-1922). She was one of the most brilliant modern algebraists and perhaps the ablest woman mathematician since Hypatia. Through her numerous works she gave a new direction to the theory of algebraic fields, initiated by Evariste Galois and developed by Richard Dedekind and Kronecker. She laid down the foundations of the theory of ideals, of great importance in modern algebra. Expelled by the Nazis, she found refuge in the United States, where she died soon after her arrival.

Luigi Cremona (1830-1903), one of the outstanding Italian mathematicians, was the founder of the modern "synthetic" geometry. The "Cremona transformation" has proved of importance. In addition to this achievement, he was a senator and minister of education. Another Italian, Vito Volterra (1860-1940) was largely instrumental in the creation of a new branch of mathematics, the theory of integral and differential equations. He stands among the great mathematicians of modern times. Tullio Levi-Civita (1873-1942) died in the Vatican during World War II, having been dismissed in 1938 from his professorship in accordance with the Fascist anti-Jewish policy. With Gregorio Ricci (Curbastro) he laid the foundations of absolute differential calculus. This, as Einstein has recognized, made possible the formulation of the mathematical theory of general relativity. Levi-Civita's work in mechanics and theoretical astronomy is no less valuable. Gino Loria (1862-   ) has contributed greatly to the theory of curves and is of the highest distinction as a historian of mathematics. Federigo Enriques (1871-1945) earned great regard as a mathematical philosopher. There have been several other eminent modern Italian-Jewish mathematicians. When one recalls that only one Italian in a thousand is a Jew, the contemporary existence of at least five eminent Italian-Jewish mathematicians is, in itself, a matter of note.

Several of the most prominent figures in French mathematics have been of Jewish origin. The most notable are Georges Halphen (1844-1889), Paul Appel (1855-1930) and Jacques Hadamard (1865-   ). In general Jewish eminence in mathematics has been a special feature of the German scene. In the English-speaking world, however, a mathematician of the first rank was James Joseph Sylvester (1814-1897). As a loyal Jew he was unable to take a degree at Cambridge and still less to hold a fellowship. Nevertheless, he adorned the chair of mathematics successively at London, at the Royal Military Academy, Woolwich, at Johns Hopkins and at Oxford. In brilliance of conception, in acuteness of penetration, in fluency and richness of expression, Sylvester has had few equals among mathematicians of any age or nationality. At an earlier date Benjamin Gomperz (1779-1865) of London, though occupying no official position, helped to lay the foundation of modern vital statistics.

Success in astronomy usually demands official status and Jews, especially in the German zone, have thus been more handicapped than in mathematics. Nevertheless, there have been among them some able exponents of astronomical science.

One of the greatest of all astronomers, Sir William Herschel (1738-1822), was born at Hanover, his family being of remoter Jewish origin, and settled early in England. His discovery of the planet Uranus in 1781 brought him immortality. He conducted valuable researches on double stars, nebulae and star clusters and is the founder of modern stellar astronomy. His theory of the general structure of the universe still holds the field. His sister Caroline (1750-1848) was his very able research assistant, detecting some remarkable nebulae and many comets. His son Sir John (1792-1871) has a rank among astronomers second only to his father.

Wilhelm Beer (1797-1850), brother of the well known Parisian musician Giacomo Meyerbeer, having secured a competence in business, devoted himself to astronomy. With Needler he produced a great chart of the moon which marked an epoch in works of its kind. The Viennese Maurice Loewy (1833-1907) settled in Paris and with the support of Urbain Jean

Joseph Leverrier made researches on comets and on the photosphere of the sun. He became president of the French Academy of Sciences and, as so often, German loss was the world's gain. Samuel Oppenheim (1856-1928), a Moravian, president of the Astronomical Society of Vienna, was a master of astronomical calculations. His writings are devoted to the motion of stars, double stars and calculation of orbits of comets.

Despite the early death of Karl Schwarzchild (1873-1916)—the result of service in the German army during World War I—he was one of the greatest astronomers of his day. As a schoolboy he published two articles on determination of orbits. In later years he originated in photographic photometry a new method depending on measurement of density of star images. He introduced the use of a color index for stars, which has yielded information on their spectral types and surface temperatures, and is well remembered for his *Goettinger Aktinometrie*, a catalogue of 3,500 stars completed in accordance with his newly invented method. No less influential have been his mathematical study of star movements and of the structure of the solar system and his contributions to physical theory, especially in optics.

A German-Jewish astronomer who had a remarkable career was Hermann Goldschmidt (1802-1866) of Frankfort. After years in his father's warehouse he migrated in 1836 to Paris, where he earned distinction as a painter. In 1847 he turned to astronomy and in 1852 discovered a minor planet which he called Lutetia, the ancient name of Paris. He continued his researches and revealed the presence of fourteen previously unknown asteroids. Of Jewish origin also was Adolf Marcuse (1860-   ), who made numerous astronomical expeditions and, like Fritz Cohn (1866-1921), was director of the Royal Observatory at Berlin. German-Jewish astronomers who worked in Switzerland were Adolf Hirsch (1830-1901) of Neuchâtel, remembered for his services to the International Commission for Measurement of the Earth, and Rudolf Wolf (1816-1893) of Zurich, the accepted historian of astronomy.

Experimental physics, even more than astronomy, is dependent on that free access to a laboratory which only university status can provide. Nevertheless, many Jews have distinguished themselves in this field. The earliest was Moritz Jacobi (1801-1874), brother of the great mathematician. He was an architect but devoted much attention to the electrical deposit of metals, or electroplasty. The first Jew elected to the Prussian Academy of Sciences was Peter Riess (1805-1883), who devoted himself to the study of frictional electricity. But during the second half of the nineteenth century the number of German-Jewish physicists became so large that we can mention only a few of fully recognized distinction.

Eugene Goldstein (1850-1930) of Gleiwitz (Silesia) was one of the most skillful experimental physicists of modern times. His name is especially associated with the discovery of gamma rays. Great scientific men cannot be arranged in order of merit. Yet it is safe to say that Heinrich Hertz (1857-1894) is among the ten physicists of most influence during the past hundred years. He wrote little during his short life but every line was significant. He measured the length and velocity of electromagnetic waves and showed that they are the result of transverse vibration and are subject to reflection, refraction and polarization, like those of light and heat. He demonstrated that electromagnetic oscillations are propagated with the same velocity as light and finally demonstrated the electromagnetic nature of light. He adumbrated the principles of wireless and of X rays. It is pitiful to recall that Hertz's pupil, successor and literary executor, Philipp Lennard, himself a recipient of the Nobel Prize, shamed his old age by devoting himself to violent anti-Jewish Nazi propaganda directed largely against the teacher whose works he had edited and whose biography he had written.

Outstanding work in solar physics was done by Ernst Pringsheim (1857-1917) of Breslau. Certain other of his investigations led naturally to the quantum theory later enunciated by Max Planck.

Lise Meitner (1878-) of Vienna is among the small band of great women physicists of whom Madame Curie is the best known. Like hers, Lise Meitner's name is connected with radioactivity. She is especially remembered for her discovery in 1918, along with Otto Hahn, of the element protoactinium with atomic number 91. Her name will always be connected with the development of the theory of atomic energy.

Jews played a large part in the development of the classical physics of the nineteenth century. It may fairly be said that their contributions to the physics of the twentieth century based on relativity have been overwhelming in proportion to their numbers. The mention of Albert Einstein, Niels Bohr, James Franck, Ludwig Hertz must suffice. At the time of the Nazi seizure of power the general development of theoretical physics was greater at Goettingen than in any other university in the world. The dismissal of teachers under the "Aryan" edicts left the two great institutes of physics in that university almost entirely depopulated.

Few Jewish physicists distinguished themselves in the classical period outside the German zone. The most eminent was probably the American Albert Michelson (1825-1919), whose parents were driven from Germany when he was two years old. Between 1879 and 1882 Michelson made measurements of the velocity of light. In 1886, along with Edward Williams Morley, he made experiments on the relative motion of ether and matter, showing that the ether within a transparent medium is carried forward when it moves, but at a lesser velocity. In 1887 he had suggested the wave length of sodium light as a standard unit. This was put into effect in a very delicate experiment performed by him in Paris in 1892.

Since this unit depends only on the properties of vibrating atoms it is probably one of the most constant dimensions in nature. In 1900 he showed that spectral lines are tripled when the radiations emanate in a magnetic field. Michelson was the first American to be awarded the Nobel Prize.

Jews have perhaps been less successful in the practical development of physical principles than in investigating the fundamental properties of matter. In other words, they have excelled more in pure than in applied science. Nevertheless, there have been some very eminent inventors among them.

In 1851 the American Isaac Singer (1811-1875) produced the first practical sewing machine. Siegfried Marcus (1831-1897) of Mecklenburg, a very gifted and versatile inventor, produced the first electrical instrument for regulating temperature and the first effective means of estimating earth movements. He is, however, particularly remembered as father of the internal-combustion engine, of which he constructed a model in 1864. By 1875 he had made a practical engine which he was able to drive in the streets of Vienna, where it was still preserved in 1937. The scheme of lighter-than-air dirigibles was first developed by the German David Schwarz, who built his first airship at St. Petersburg in 1892. His patents were afterwards purchased from his widow by Count Zeppelin.

Philip Reiss (1837-1874), born in poverty near Frankfort, began experiments on hearing apparatus in boyhood which ultimately developed into what was in effect a telephone (1861). This was exhibited in 1864. It was on his principle that Alexander Graham Bell and Thomas Edison perfected their device (1876). Emil Berliner (1851-1929) of Hanover settled in the United States in 1870 and there developed several inventions, among them the microphone.

Hermann Aron (1845-1913) was professor at the Artillery School at Berlin and developed an effective electrometer (1888). Leo Arons (1860-1919) was a picturesque figure who was dismissed from his post at Berlin University (1899) because of his Socialist sympathies. He did much to advance the practical applications of electricity. Notably he invented the first mercury vapor lamp (1896). Gabriel Lipman (1845-1921) of Luxembourg passed his scientific life in Paris, where he held a chair of physics. His development of color photography earned him a Nobel Prize in 1908.

Arnold Berliner (1862-1939) was put to death by the Nazis. A man of extraordinary scientific versatility, he rendered great services to German science as editor for many years of *Naturwissenschaften*, a journal for the general exchange of scientific views.

Chemistry was for long largely extra-academic. Thus Jews had opportunities that were denied them in physics. An early Jewish arrival in the chemical field was Heinrich Magnus (1802-1879), a pupil of Berzelius at Stockholm and of Gay-Lussac in Paris. He made many technical contributions of importance, perhaps the most significant being his determination of the coefficient of expansion of gases. He described a large number of new compounds, one of which, his "green salt" (a platinum-ammonia compound), is still known by his name. He ultimately became rector of Berlin University.

Charles Gerhardt (1816-1857) of Strasbourg was a pupil of Justus von Liebig and did most of his scientific work in Paris. He has a distinguished place in the history of chemistry, for his name is associated with the doctrines of valency and of chemical equivalents. He developed the molecular theory and made the first effective classification of organic compounds.

There is nothing more remarkable in the history of modern Germany than the rise of her chemical industry. Without this she could not have become a great power. There were so many and such able chemists of Jewish origin associated with this process that it is safe to say that without them her industrial development would have been impossible.

Adolf Frank (1834-1916) was the founder of the potash industry of Germany. He instituted the first potash factory (1861) at Stassfurt near Magdeburg, obtaining it from the local mineral deposit. Until then potash had been extracted from ashes burnt in or under pots, hence the name. With the Polish Jew, Nikodem Caro (1871-   ), he took the first step toward the nitrogen-fixation industry by forming calcium cyanide from nitrogen and calcium carbide. This industry was to be epochal not only for Germany but for the world.

Equally important for German economic development was Adolf von Bayer (1835-1917), professor at Munich whose mother was a Jewess. Just as Frank founded the German heavy chemical industry so did Bayer found that of fine chemicals. He was one of the foremost organic chemists of his day, the discoverer of the phthalein class of dyes (1874) and the first to synthetize indigo (1878). Synthetic indigo came entirely to take the place of the natural product. His patents passed to the Badische Anilin und Soda Fabrik, which formed the nucleus of the giant I. G. Farbenindustrie. Other patents absorbed by that combine were those of Heinrich Caro (1834-1910) of Poznan, the discoverer of methylene blue and of many other aniline dyes and of Carl Liebermann (1842-1914) of Berlin, who made important discoveries among the aniline compounds. German chemical industry was, in fact, substantially based on Jewish genius and Jewish enterprise.

The name of Victor Meyer (1848-1897) of Berlin is one of the greatest in the history of organic chemistry. At Heidelberg he was the favorite pupil and personal assistant of Robert Wilhelm von Bunsen. He succeeded Friedrich Woehler at Goettingen (1882) and Bunsen (1889) at Heidelberg, where he died by his own hand. His comprehensive researches on nitro compounds of the fatty series, upon isonitrous compounds and upon thiophene are among the most remarkable of the nineteenth century. The method he devised for estimating vapor density has become standard.

To give an account of all the German chemists of Jewish origin would be to write an appreciable part of the history of German chemistry from about 1860 onward. There have also been many distinguished Jewish chemists outside the German zone, but only a few can be mentioned here.

Henri Moissan (1852-1907) of Paris is remembered for several achievements. He succeeded in isolating fluorine, long a main problem in chemistry. He invented the electric furnace for very high and steady temperatures, which is known by his name. He demonstrated the nature of the diamond by producing it artificially.

Another brilliant chemist was the Englishman Raphael Meldola (1849-1915). He made the first oxazine dyestuff (Meldola's blue, 1879) which has become important for cotton dyeing, and worked much on naphthalene and azo compounds. He was very versatile, took much interest in biology, was a friend and correspondent of Charles Darwin and experimented with the coloration of animals.

A rather special place is occupied by Edmund Lippmann (1857-1942) of Vienna. He was the leading authority on the chemistry of sugars and the sugar industry and introduced the strontium process into sugar refining. He extended his researches into the history of the subject and finally became an authority on its alchemical aspects.

The name of Fritz Haber (1868-1934) will always be associated with the opening up of new industrial possibilities by a practical method of nitrogen fixation, the "Haber process" for the synthetic production of ammonia. It proved of the utmost importance to Germany's supply of nitrates both for agricultural and for military purposes. Nevertheless, in 1933 he was forced by the Nazis to leave Germany. This great benefactor of his country died in exile while Germany made war with the processes he had invented.

Richard Willstaetter (1872-1942) of Karlsruhe, a very great biochemist, discovered several forms of chlorophyll in plants. He demonstrated relationships between this green coloring matter and the red coloring matter in the blood of animals. He also produced the anesthetic avertin.

Mineralogy, as a science, has few exponents but among them the most distinguished were several who were Jewish. The first of them, the Parisian Armand Lévy (1794-1841), who spent many years in England, was a skilled mathematician and did much to introduce mathematical notation into crystallography. Harry Rosenbusch (1836-1914) of Heidelberg became head of a new school that dealt with the microscopy of minerals. Auguste Michel Lévy (1844-1911) of the Collège de France and of the French geological survey was among the founders of the modern science of petrography. Edward Suess (1831-1914), born in London, son of a German merchant, was long professor of geology in Vienna. His monumental *Face of the Earth* (1885) has been translated into many languages and gone into many editions. Many tendencies in modern geology have stemmed from it. Victor Goldschmidt (1853-1933), for many years a professor in Heidelberg and afterwards at Oslo, was one of the greatest exponents of crystallographic science. He introduced the binocular goniometer. His monumental work summarized the knowledge of the subject and his home became the recognized meeting place of the crystallographers of the world. His son succeeded him as professor of crystallography at Oslo.

Turning to biology, it might be thought that age-old urbanization of Jews would deprive them of interest in what were primarily countrymen's subjects. That this has not proved to be the case is doubtless due to the fact that the traditional Jewish attitude toward medicine has always involved contact with the problems of living things. In fact, since the German universities have been opened to them Jews have always been prominent in biology.

The name of Nathaniel Pringsheim (1823-1894) is especially connected with the study of algae. He demonstrated the reproductive processes of many kinds and showed that they were exhibited in an alternation of sexual and asexual generations (1856), both of which he elucidated. He produced a classic work on the life of the fern (1862) and later turned to plant physiology, doing much to explain the action of chlorophyll (1874). He subsequently demonstrated that light itself may have a lethal effect on plants (1879).

Ferdinand Cohn (1828-1898) of Breslau, a pupil of Johannes Mueller, was a peculiarly skilled microscopist particularly interested in the minute fungi. As author of the first monograph on bacteria he is the father of bacteriology. He rendered a great service by his encouragement of an unknown young man, Robert Koch (1843 1910). The latter's demonstration of the relation of anthrax bacteria to the disease was publicized by Cohn (1876); it contained the first evidence of the production of a specific human disease by a known species of bacteria.

Perhaps the most influential botanical teacher of the nineteenth century was Julius Sachs (1832-1897) also of Breslau and professor for many years at Wuerzburg. After applying himself to the study of the structure of forms of plants he turned to physiology and from 1857 became immersed in the problems of nutrition. He became convinced that chlorophyll is not diffused in tissues but is contained only in special bodies, the "chloroplasts." He showed that sunlight plays the decisive role in determining their action in reference to the absorption of carbon dioxide. Further, chlorophyll is formed only in light and, moreover, in different variations of light the process undergoes different degrees of activity. Sachs's researches covered every aspect of botany and he became a kind of botanical dictator.

Edward Strasburger (1844-1912) worked at Bonn, where he laid the foundations of the knowledge of the phenomena of nuclear division (*Mitosis*, 1875), clarifying the relation of nuclear changes to the sexual process. He was an encyclopedic botanist and his textbook is still in common use. Demonstrating that the chromosomes are individually recognizable and traceable from cell to cell (1905-1908), he thus laid the foundations of the modern science of genetics.

Approaching the medical field we are overwhelmed with names. From the beginning of the nineteenth century the number of distinguished Jewish names in the German-speaking countries have progressively increased in this their own traditional field. During the century interest became most intensely focused on the minute analysis of structure and its correlation with function. In this field Jews played a particularly prominent part.[17a]

The earliest influential Jewish figure in this movement was Karl Friedrich Canstatt (1807-1850) of Ratisbon, who made a study of the finer structure of the eye. Perhaps his greatest discovery was his pupil at Erlangen, Robert Virchow, accounted with Henle the founder of modern pathology.

Jacob Henle (1809-1885) of Fuerth near Nuremberg was the greatest German microscopic anatomist of his time and one of the greatest anatomists of all time, comparable only to Vesalius. He was professor of anatomy at Zurich (1840), Heidelberg (1844) and Goettingen (1852). His achievements in his special field were enormous and his work in histology was the first of its kind. He was a most versatile genius, for he was a poet, artist, orator and a very great teacher. And he was in his way a prophet, for he saw, as in a glass darkly, the microbic origin of infectious disease.

Benedikt Stilling (1810-1879), a skilled surgeon, introduced a new technique for the microscopic examination of the nervous system in the manipulation of which he was extremely expert. Structures in the nervous system are still identified by his name. He also instituted important advances in nervous physiology.

Ludwig Traube (1818-1876) of Ratibor worked in Berlin for thirty years, and was a founder of experimental pathology and of the scientific investigation of the action of drugs. He was an outstanding clinician and a particularly successful teacher. Gustav Valentin (1810-1883) of Breslau accomplished much in the physiology of muscle and nerve and in the digestion of carbohydrates. Gottlieb Gluege (1812-1898) of Brakel in Westphalia migrated to France and was thence called to Brussels. He did excellent physiological work, wrote the first treatise of pathological histology (1839-1841), began the study of parasitology and gave the earliest account of the essential cause of trichiniasis.

Robert Remak (1815-1865) of Posen worked in Berlin, where he had a distinguished reputation as a microscopist. His most eminent service was perhaps to demonstrate the true nature of the multiplication of cells. In 1842, long before Pasteur and Koch, using himself as guinea pig, he showed that certain skin diseases are caused by microscopic organisms. He was also a pioneer in electrotherapy.

Moritz Schiff (1823-1896) of Frankfort began as a zoologist and turned afterwards to physiology, which he taught at Florence and Geneva. He was a man of restless energy, almost prophetic insight and infinite originality, who covered too many fields to be a complete master of one. He anticipated Pavlov in the conception of conditioned reflexes, Claude Bernard in that of vasodilator nerves and much later work on the thyroid. He was a pioneer in many aspects of brain physiology and his experiments in the artificial production of diabetes via the nervous system (1856-1859) are classics.

Rudolph Heidenhain (1834-1897) of Breslau is especially associated with the interpretation of secretion in cellular terms. His research projects on the secretion of various organs and his stains and methods of staining are daily recalled in every biological laboratory. Julius Conheim (1839-1884), while professor at Breslau, revealed the true nature of suppuration, proving that the corpuscles of pus are formed from those of the blood. Despite his short life his contributions to pathological knowledge were numerous and very important.

Hugo Kronecker (1839-1914) of Liegnitz in Silesia, professor of physiology at Berne in 1885, distinguished himself particularly by his work on the fatigue and recovery of muscle, by his proof that the heart muscle can pass into a tetanic state and by his investigation of the mechanism of swallowing. He invented many ingenious physiological devices, and he is especially remembered for his demonstration that the heart's motto is "all or none," that is, that it will either contract to its fullest extent or not at all.

Carl Weigert (1845-1904) was perhaps the most eminent microscopic anatomist of the later nineteenth century. He introduced many new methods and was responsible for the highly important technique of bacterial staining which is one of the most valuable aids to modern scientific medicine. He also greatly added to the knowledge of the structure and function of the nervous system.

Elie Metchnikoff (1845-1916) was a Russian half-Jew who worked most of his life in Paris. His most important experiments, begun on the water flea, showed how amoeboid cells act as scavengers in the body, engulfing and digesting solid particles and notably bacteria. He showed that inflammation is accompanied by the gathering of swarms of these scavengers or policemen to the site of the injury.

Oscar Minkowski (1858-1931) brother of the mathematician, demonstrated the relation between the pancreas and diabetes and thus led to the study which culminated in the discovery of insulin.

Jacques Loeb (1859-1924) left Germany for America in middle life and ultimately became head of the department of experimental biology at the Rockefeller Institute. His research projects were of varied character. Many of them were designed to demonstrate that much "vital" action can be explained as response to chemicals or physical stimuli and do not involve the intercurrence of "mind."

These are hardly more than a random sample of those of central European Jewish origin who made distinguished contributions to nineteenth-century medicine. The mind of any well-informed medical man will react to the names of the members of this list.

The most characteristic development of modern medicine is the interest in the vast complexity of the functions and minute parts of the body and their reactions to its environment and especially to the organisms of disease and to their products. In this field the Jewish contribution is overwhelming. There is Alexander Besredka (1870-1940) of the Pasteur Institute, Ludwig Brieger (1849-1919), who initiated the study of toxins, Albert Neisser (1885-1916), discoverer of the gonococcus, Albert Frankel (1848-1916) and Carl Friedlaender (1847-1887), discoverers of the organism causing lobar pneumonia, Fernand Widal (1862-1929), elucidator of the nature of blood reactions, Paul Ehrlich (1854-1915), the greatest of biochemists, who made chemotherapy a science, Waldemar Haffkine (1860-1930), introducer of protection against plague and cholera, Alexander Marmorek (1865-1923), whose serum provides protection against streptococcal infection, Casimir Funk (1884-   ), one of the discoverers of vitamins and originator of the name, Ernst Salkowski (1844-1923), father of clinical pathology.

In the investigation of the functions of the nervous system a high place is taken by Wilhelm Erb (1840-1921), who introduced electrodiagnosis by induction, revealed the significance of the knee jerk and, along with his contemporary Hermann Oppenheim (1858-1910), described many unrecognized pathological conditions.

Anatomy, in the old sense of the term, is regarded as one of the "completed" sciences. Such significant contributions as were made to it in the past generations were largely the work of Jews, among them the Viennese Julius Tandler (1869-1910), last of the great anatomists, and Emil Zuckerkandl (1849-1910), also of Vienna, whose account of the structures of the parts of interest to otorhinologists is likely to remain the standard work of reference.

Space fails even for the names of eminent exponents of clinical practice of central European origin, but we mention Wilhelm Ebstein (1836-1912) of Goettingen, and the great authorities on drugs Matthias Liebreich

(1838-1908) of Berlin, Oswald Schmiedeberg (1838-1921) of Dorpat, and Moritz Romberg (1795-1893) of Berlin.

Psychology in its medical applications may be said to be almost a Jewish science. Since our list must be brought to an end we do so with the names of Alfred Adler (1870-1937) of Vienna, Viktor Adler (1852-1918) of Prague, Alfred Binet (1857-1901), the experimental psychologist of Paris, Sigmund Freud (1856-1939) of Vienna, Bernard Hollander (1864-1934) of London, and Emil Kraepelin (1856-1927) of Dorpat. These men have not only introduced new methods of treatment but they have changed the whole direction of medical thought, practice and education. They have done more, for they have taught us a great deal about ourselves and changed the outlook of modern philosophy.

As one contemplates the galaxy of talent at which we have but glanced, two reflections arise. First, it is a tragedy for the Jewish people that the stream of life and thought that this implies has been broken. The break is more than that of the inevitable death of individuals, for the stock from which they have arisen has ceased to reproduce itself adequately. This is a loss to humanity as well as to the Jewish people. And secondly, it is a tragedy for the German people that, at the urging of a perverted outcast, it has extruded from its body politic a main source, perhaps *the* main source, of its claim to respect from the world of intellect. So far as the products of the intellect are concerned we must write *Germania fuit*, for henceforth German will be a language of secondary importance in the field of learning.

The intellectual future of the Jews themselves must depend, in this writer's opinion, upon many factors that are at present indeterminable, but most of all on one that *is* determinable. We live in a world in which religions and religious sanctions are breaking down. Religion is the one link that can unite the Jewish people. The problem is whether the Jewish religion can or cannot develop in a non-Jewish environment as one of the great world religions. If it can, the future of a special Jewish intellectual atmosphere is secure. If it cannot, Judaism will continue as a fossil fragment of the ancient Syrian civilization and, like other fossils, it will slowly but surely disintegrate.

Notes

[1a Cf. above Elias J. Bickerman, "The Historical Foundations of Postbiblical Judaism," pp. 97-99; see also above Robert Gordis, "The Bible as a Cultural Monument," pp. 482-487.]

[2a Cf. above Alexander Altmann, "Judaism and World Philosophy," p. 627; see also above Ralph Marcus, "Hellenistic Jewish Literature," pp. 775 ff.]

[3] *Sifre, Deuteronomy* Haazinu, 306, f. 131 a. (Quoted from Montefiore and Loewe, *Rabbinic Anthology*, London, 1938.)

[4a] Cf. above Judah Goldin, "The Period of the Talmud," pp. 194 ff.; see also Altmann, *op. cit.* pp. 636 ff.]

[5a] Cf. also the chapter above by Arturo Castiglioni, "The Contribution of the Jews to Medicine."]

[6a] Cf. above Cecil Roth, "The European Age in Jewish History (to 1648)," pp. 222-223.]

[7a] Cf. Altmann, *op. cit.*, pp. 642 ff.]

[8a] Cf. above Abraham S. Halkin, "Judeo-Arabic Literature," pp. 811-813.]

[9a] Cf. Altmann, *op. cit.*, pp. 644-647.]

[10a] Cf. Roth, *op. cit.*, pp. 237 ff.]

[11a] Cf. Halkin, *op. cit.*, p. 814.]

[12a] Cf. Altmann, *op. cit.*, p. 645.]

[13a] Cf. *ibid.*, pp. 645-646.]

[14a] Cf. Roth, *op. cit.*, p. 236.]

[15a] Cf. Castiglioni, *op. cit.*, pp. 1028-1029.]

[16a] Cf. above Roth, "The Jews of Western Europe (from 1648)," pp. 264-265.]

[17a] Cf. Castiglioni, *op. cit.*, pp. 1031 ff.]

BIBLIOGRAPHY

General Works

For the general scientific background: Charles Singer, *Short History of Science to the Nineteenth Century* (Oxford and New York, 1941, and later editions). For an objective study of Judaism and the Jewish people in world history: A. J. Toynbee, *A Study of History (abridgement by D. C. Somervell)* (Oxford and New York, 1946). For estimate of the contribution of Judaic thought to modern civilization: Edwyn R. Bevan and Charles Singer (eds.), *The Legacy of Israel* (Oxford and New York, 1927, and subsequent editions). For a general account of the contribution of Jews, as distinct from Judaism, Cecil Roth, *The Jewish Contribution to Civilization* (Cincinnati, 1940). Much material is to be found in that mine of well-arranged learning, George Sarton, *Introduction to the History of Science* (Baltimore, 1927).

Specialized Works

For the Rabbinic attitude toward nature: C. G. Montefiore and H. Loewe, *A Rabbinic Anthology,* selected and arranged with Comments and Introduction (London and New York, 1938). The entire Hebraeo-Arabic period with bibliography is treated by Aldo Mieli in *La Science Arabe et son rôle dans l'évolution scientifique mondiale* (Leyden, 1938). The specifically Hebraic aspect of Arabic science is treated with superb comprehensiveness, but for reference only, in Moritz Steinschneider, *Die hebraeischen Uebersetzungen des Mittelalters und die Juden als Dolmetscher* (Berlin, 1889-1893). For the translation of this literature into Latin, etc., Moritz Steinschneider. *Die europaeischen Uebersetzungen bis Mitte des 17. Jahrhunderts* (Vienna, 1904-1905), also only for reference. For the Marrano episode: Cecil Roth, *A History of the Marranos* (Philadelphia, 1941). For the Central European century: Louis Gershenfeld, *The Jew in Science* (Philadelphia, 1934); Ernst Heppner, *Juden als Erfinder und Entdecker* (Berlin, 1913); Felix A. Theilhaber and Ernst Heppner in *Juedisches Lexikon,* Vol. 2, cols. 462-467 (Berlin, 1928); *L'Apport d'Israel à la Civilisation: Conférence donnée à l'Hotel de la Paix, à Lausanne, le 8 fevrier, 1939, sous la Présidence de M. le Prof. Henri L. Miéville,* containing "La Médecine" by Professor Dr. Maurice Muret, and "La Philosophie et les Sciences," by Marcel Reymond (Lausanne, 1939); H. Newman (ed.), *The Real Jew, Some Aspects of the Jewish Contribution to Civilisation* (London, 1925), containing "The Jew and Scientific Research," by S. Brodetsky, "The Jew and Medicine," by Lester Samuels, and "The Jew and Chemistry," by Philip Blackman; Madison C. Peters, *Justice to the Jew* (London, 1899), Ch. VII: "The Jew in the Sciences."

For Medicine

Harry Friedenwald, *The Jews and Medicine* (Baltimore, 1944, 2 vols.), Sidney Osborne, *Germany and Her Jews* (London, 1939), Ch. 3: "The Jews as Physicians"; Ch. 4: "German Jews as Scientists and Inventors." Felix A. Theilhaber, *Schicksal und Leistung, Juden in der deutschen Forschung und Technik* (Berlin, 1931). *Cahiers Juifs,* Alexandria-Paris, Nos. 5-6, September-November, 1933: *L'Apport des Juifs d'Allemagne à la Civilisation Allemande,* contains "Le Progrès des Sciences Naturelles," by Horace Goldie, "Médecine, Chirurgie, Pathologie," by Ernst Fraenkel, "Mathématique, Physique," by Bernard Kwal and "Techniciens et Inventeurs," by E. Aisberg. The *Jewish Review,* No. 5, June-September (London, 1933). *The Jewish Contribution to Modern Life and Thought in Germany* contains "The Physical Sciences," by H. Levy; "Applied Science," by F. Adler, and "Medicine," by Samson Wright.

CHAPTER 27

JUDAISM AND THE DEMOCRATIC IDEAL

By Milton R. Konvitz

JEWISH AND DEMOCRATIC IDEALS

In this chapter we shall take as the essence of the democratic ideal the belief in equality. An explication of this belief in equality leads to cultural and religious pluralism; to constitutional government, with effective checks on the agencies of government; a wide and equitable distribution of property; universal education and emphasis on reason, rather than super-stition and force, as instruments of social control and progress; freedom of speech, freedom of the press, and freedom of assembly.

Just as a sharp distinction must be made between the accidental and the essential aspects of democracy, so the same distinction must be made among the various aspects of Judaism. Judaism, too, has had its highest insights, which, though they may have been conditioned by historical events, deserve perpetuation on their own account. On the other hand, like all other social institutions, Judaism has frequently needed to accommodate itself to the accidents of time and place in ways which did not at all times exhibit its own highest ideals. As in the case of democracy, it is the deeper motivation, the profounder insights, rather than the superficial aspects, that have kept alive Judaism as a way of life and as a philosophy of life.

Living in the middle of the twentieth century, we, of course, face problems radically different from those faced by the prophets thousands of years ago, or by the great Rabbis responsible for the Babylonian and Palestinian Talmuds.[1a] Freedom of speech must mean something sharply different to a people with a press than it did to a people who prohibited reduction of their learning to writing. This means only that the branches of democracy are different; the root is the same: it is the same wherever and whenever people live together in a community, wherever and when-ever people constitute a society. The problem of human freedom is always the same: though at one time, to achieve more of it, we must fight a civil war to abolish economic and physical slavery; at another time we must fight to abolish racial distinctions in immigration policy; at one time, to achieve more of freedom, we must carry on a fight for woman suffrage; at another time the fight is against the white primary and the poll tax;

at one time the fight is for freedom to teach Torah in Jabneh; at another time the fight is for freedom to teach the theory of evolution in Tennessee. The scenes change; the characters and the plot are pretty much the same. This does not mean, necessarily, that the history of mankind can be written in terms of the history of liberty. We are not here concerned with the degree of truth in a Crocean philosophy of history. All we mean to say is that, whatever liberty may have meant at different times in the history of mankind, its essential character, as we have stated it, has been always pretty much the same. The struggles have been variations on a theme. The theme has been: human equality and freedom.

THE DEMOCRATIC IDEAL: RACIAL AND NATIONAL EQUALITY

Almost at the outset of our discussion we must face the obvious question of the consistency of the concept of the chosen people with the democratic ideal. How can a people that considers itself elected of God as His special inheritance, find its institutions and ideals consistent with democracy? Some have met the question by a denial that Jews today consider themselves God's chosen people.

This is one answer. Most Jews, however, assert that, when rightly understood, there is no inconsistency between the doctrine of the chosen people and democratic ideals. The doctrine of the chosen people may lead to exclusiveness, physical and spiritual isolation, haughtiness of spirit; but this happens only when the doctrine is adhered to by a person with a narrow heart and mind, who has no real comprehension of the meaning and utility of the doctrine. When taken on a higher ground, it is said, the concept has great value in furthering the ideals of both Judaism and democracy.

An excellent statement of this point of view is to be found in the philosophical writings of Rab Saadia Gaon.[2a] "All creatures are His creatures," said Rab Saadia Gaon, "and we may not say that He has taken to Himself one to the exclusion of the other or to a greater degree than another." For, "if God hath chosen but one man and one city, who would remember the rest of mankind?"

In the same way, said Rab Saadia Gaon, we must consider allusions to God as the God of Abraham, Isaac and Jacob. "For when the Psalmist exclaimed 'O Lord, the portion of *mine* inheritance and *my* cup,' did he alone want to possess the master of the worlds?"

"We hold," said Rab Saadia Gaon, "that He is the God of all mankind" and that "the worth of each man and his lot are equally precious before Him." The doctrine of the chosen people to Rab Saadia Gaon was nothing more than an expression exalting and praising God; for he who feels himself especially touched by God's love describes himself as the recipient of God's grace and special favor. But it carries no implication that God does not stand in the same loving relationship to all men, and that others may not designate that relationship in the same or similar terms.

It is probable that today most Jews accept the doctrine of the chosen people as the Jews' explanation of the possession by them "of a spiritually unique literature and philosophy." The Jews are the chosen people only because God has chosen them from among all peoples to give them the Torah.[3a] The supreme treasure is not the Jewish people but the Torah; and the former are important in God's universal scheme only as the recipients and bearers of this great treasure. Israel was selected and made the custodian of the Torah only so that he might share his inheritance with all other men. It is the duty of Israel to be the model and guide to all nations; but this he can accomplish only by living in accordance with the dictates of the Word of God in the Torah. In brief, Israel was "chosen" only in the sense that he was selected by God to transmit the Torah to all the peoples of the earth—to be a light unto the nations. When the Exile was considered from this standpoint, the Rabbis said that it was not intended as a punishment of Israel, but as an opportunity to spread the Word of God among the nations of the earth: the Jews are deprived of a home and the security it offers because they are God's servants. Viewed in this light, the doctrine of the chosen people offers the Jews no privileges denied to others; on the contrary, it imposes on them a mission, loyalty to which must bring them suffering, humiliation, agonies of pain and death; the Jew must suffer persecution, so that of him one might say in truth: "He is despised and rejected of men; a man of sorrows, and acquainted with grief." In this aspect, the doctrine implies no superiority inherent in the Jewish people, apart from the superiority that is attached to one who is charged with the duty to carry an important message. It is the message and not the messenger that is superior; so that one might speak really of the *Chosen Message* rather than of the *Chosen People*; the people are not endowed with superiority, but charged to be humble; humility, rather than riches or glory, must clothe them.

This interpretation of the concept points away from the particularism that is frequently charged against Judaism, and points to the universalism of which the Prophets were the leading spokesmen. Judaism, then, is a universalistic religious faith. Its truths are not to be kept under lock and key. In the first place, the truths of Judaism are to guide the Jewish people at every step and at every moment: Israel must obey God's law; he must strive to attain the purposes of mankind, as directed by God, *within his own community*. But he must do more: he must strive to attain that purpose in the *entire community of mankind*. If the Jew is particularistic at all, it is only that he wants to make of himself a *worthy* messenger, *one who himself lives by the message he carries*.

Jews, it has been said, are actually "an ethnic group with a universalistic religious faith which transcends the values of a single people but which they are forced to use as an instrument of survival. in an alien world." This is the irony of Jewish existence: devotion to a universalistic faith marks the Jews off as a "peculiar" people, a "chosen" people! But God's "covenant" with this people is binding on God only so long as Israel himself observes the letter and spirit of the "covenant." To quote from Reinhold Niebuhr:

The first religious apprehension of a universal and unlimited moral obligation was achieved in prophetic monotheism, which had its inception in the prophet Amos's conception of a universal history, over which the God of Israel presided as sovereign but of which the history of Israel was not the center and end. Amos thought of the "Holy One of Israel" as a transcendent God who would both use and reject the special mission of Israel in his universal designs and who could taunt his own people with the words, "Are ye not as children of the Ethiopians unto me?"

This is not, I submit, only a Christian's view of the mission of Israel; it is the view of Israel, the view of Israel's prophets. The "chosen people" are not at the center of the world; they are charged with the duty to live by, and transmit, the highest moral ideals, in deep humility and in a spirit of charity. But God's ways are inscrutable; the Torah was written in the words of man, so that man might understand it, but there are errors and sins at every step and in every moment of the life of a mortal man; there is the finiteness of the intelligence, and the contingency of the will. Who, then, knows what is the ultimate truth? or what is the way or the plan of God? All one can do is walk humbly; and if one does this, he may trust that he is walking humbly with his God.

This is what is meant by the doctrine of the chosen people. Admittedly, it is a statement of ideals and not a description of the way Jews live. To live by these ideals would make it very dangerous to be a Jew. But during the past thousands of years many Jews have lived dangerously. The ideal, at any rate, is not an impossible one; and even if it were, it might, from the moral point of view, still be a relevant one.

When men are judged by any empirical test they are not equal: some are richer than others, some wiser, some swifter, some more beautiful. Yet the essence of democracy is equality. Men reject the empirical tests and assert their equality notwithstanding the evidence adduced by their eyes and ears and other senses. "All men are created equal," said Jefferson in the Declaration of Independence; and he had no footnote references to statistical tables by way of documentation. The belief in equality is a transcendental belief, if you wish; it makes an assertion which may be true only in the world of noumena. But no matter: it is the cornerstone of the democratic faith and the essence of moral idealism. "The basis of democratic development," says Harold Laski, "is therefore the demand that the system of power be erected upon the *similarities* and not the *differences* between men." Here we have the clue to the problem of democracy: differences are not to be eliminated, for it is good that one man paint better than another, that one woman cook better than does her neighbor, that one surgeon operate better than another; yes, and even that one man legislate better than another. But the system of power (political power, economic and social power) must be based on the similarities and not on the differences between men. The demand for equality manifests itself in many relations: there is the demand for equal suffrage; for economic equality; there must be no privilege by birth; there is the demand for educational equality; there must be equality in participation in the results of social developments and improvements; equality before the law (real and not merely formal equality).

At bottom the democratic faith is a moral affirmation: men are not to be used merely as means to an end, as tools; each is an end in himself; his soul is from the source of all life; a man is born "trailing clouds of glory behind him"; no matter how lowly his origin, a man is here only by the grace of God—he owes his life to no one but God. He has an equal right to pursue happiness: life, liberty and the pursuit of happiness are his simply by virtue of the fact that he is a live human being. He has his place in the sun, and neither the place nor the sun was made by men.

This faith finds its essence in what Henry Michel called the "eminent dignity of human personality." One of the chief sources of this faith is in the wellsprings of Judaism.

It may be possible to arrive at the philosophy of equality within the framework of secular thought, as, *e.g.*, in the systems of John Dewey and Bertrand Russell and in socialist Marxism. Within the framework of a religious system, however, it is probably impossible to arrive at the philosophy of equality in the absence of a belief in ethical monotheism.

For as long as one believes in the existence of a multiplicity of gods, each expressing his own biases and partialities, loving his friends and hating his enemies, and no one supreme god above all others, there is no room provided for accommodation of the beliefs in the fatherhood of God and the brotherhood of man. In ethical monotheism, however, these beliefs are basic. Judaism conceived of God as the creator and ruler of the entire universe: "In the beginning God created the heavens and the earth." He created Adam and Eve, from whom all mankind have sprung. Humanity lives, therefore, in "One World"; one world in every sense of the term; the laws of physical nature are the same everywhere; the laws of human nature are the same everywhere: the heavens and the moral law are the same everywhere.

Not only are the physical laws the same everywhere, but the laws of righteousness too. For God is not only *ehad*, One, but He is God "sanctified in righteousness." He is the judge of all the earth, as Abraham said, and cannot act unjustly. "Thou art not a God who hath pleasure in wickedness; evil shall not sojourn with Thee; Thou hatest all workers of iniquity." God, as the prophet said, wants to loose the fetters of wickedness, to undo the bands of the yoke, to deal bread to the hungry, to cover the naked, to shelter the homeless—He wants to see all this, and more, accomplished—but through the free agency of man.

Implicit and explicit in the ethical monotheism that is Judaism are, then, the beliefs in the fatherhood of God and the brotherhood of man. Thus Malachi cried out: "Have we not all one Father? Hath not One God created us?" Thus is posited the fatherhood principle. But in the same breath the prophet added: "Why do we deal treacherously every man against his brother?" The fatherhood and brotherhood principles go together; they are inseparable: if two men have the same father, are they, then, not brothers?

"God," said the Rabbis, "is on the watch for the nations of the world to repent, so that He may bring them under His wings." When the nations will accept the reign of righteousness, the Kingdom of God will have become established; and God wants this to happen above all else.

The most graphic expression of the fatherhood of God and the brotherhood of man is the statement in the Bible that man was created in the image of God. The Rabbis did not tire of creating homilies on this figurative expression of the oneness of the human family. Thus, R. Joshua b. Levi said: "When a man goes on his road, a troop of angels proceed in front of him and proclaim, 'Make way for the image of the Holy One, blessed be He.'" The following passage from the Mishna is especially revealing of the universalism of Judaism:

Only one single man was created in the world, to teach that, if any man has caused a single soul to perish, Scripture imputes it to him as though he had caused a whole world to perish; and if any man saves alive a single soul, Scripture imputes it to him as though he had saved a whole world. Again, but a single man was created for the sake of peace among mankind, that none should say to his fellow, "My father was greater than your father"; also that the heretics should not say, "There are many ruling powers in heaven." Again, but a single man was created to proclaim the greatness of God, for man stamps many coins with one die, and they are all like to one another; but God has stamped every man with the die of the first man, yet not one of them is like his fellow. Therefore every one must say, "For my sake was the world created."

In another passage there is the same emphasis on the transcendent importance of human life, any man's life:

"By ten sayings the world was created." To teach you that him who fulfills one command, or keeps one Sabbath, or preserves one human life, the Scripture regards as if he had preserved the whole world. And him who commits one sin, desecrates one Sabbath, and destroys one human life, the Scripture regards as if he had destroyed the whole world.

It is related that Ben Azzai quoted the verse from Genesis, "This is the book of the generations of Adam," and remarked that this is the greatest principle in the Torah. The same point was made by Rabbi Akiba but in a different statement. He said that the greatest principle in the Torah is "Love thy neighbor as thyself." Rabbi Tanhuma put the matter in a third way. He said that one should not say to himself, "Because I am despised, so may my neighbor be cursed with me"; for if one acts in this way he despises a being made in the image of God.

In the Talmud the question is raised why man was created a solitary human being, why were there not created several Adams and several Eves at one time? The answer given is this: "So that it might not be said that some races are better than others."

The injunction against shedding blood is repeated frequently in the Bible and in the writings of the Rabbis, and the law was declared that the life of one man may not be sacrificed to save the life of another man. The law is illustrated by the following passage from the Talmud:

A man came to Raba and said, "The prefect of my town has ordered me to kill so and so, or he will kill me." Raba said, "Let him kill you; do you commit no murder. Why should you think that your blood is redder than his? Perhaps his is redder than yours."

In the Midrash it is stated that the falling of rain is an event greater than the giving of the Torah, for the Torah is for Israel only, but rain is for the entire world. According to the Mekilta, however, even the Torah is for the entire world: "The Torah was given in the wilderness and in fire and in water. As these three are free to all the inhabitants of the world, so are the words of the Torah free to all the inhabitants of the world."

Are only the righteous among Israel the elect of God? Not at all; for righteousness, like sin, is the great leveler; the sinners among Israel are no better off than the evil ones among the non-Jews; and the righteous Israelites are not preferred to the righteous among the non-Jews. "The just among the Gentiles are the priests of God," says the Midrash. "I call heaven and earth to witness that whether a person be Jew or Gentile, man or woman, manservant or maidservant, according to his acts does the Divine Spirit rest upon him." Just as the acknowledgment of idolatry is a repudiation of the Torah, so repudiation of idolatry is an acceptance of Torah.

The injunctions in the Bible relating to the treatment of a brother were not construed as being directed only to the treatment of Israelites (though all Israelites are brothers) but of all mankind (for all men are brothers). Thus it was said: "The heathen is thy neighbor, thy brother. To wrong him is a sin." The point is made graphically by the following incident in the Midrash:

Simon ben Shetah was occupied with preparing flax. His disciples said to him, "Rabbi, desist. We will buy you an ass, and you will not have to work so hard." They went and bought an ass from an Arab, and a pearl was found on it, whereupon they came to him and said, "From now on you need not work any more." "Why?" he asked. They said, "We bought you an ass from an Arab, and a pearl was found on it." He said to them, "Does its owner know of that?" They answered, "No." He said to them, "Go and give the pearl back to him." "But," they argued, "did not Rabbi Huna, in the name of Rab, say all the world agrees that if you find something which belongs to a heathen, you may keep it?" Their teacher said, "Do you think that Simon ben Shetah is a barbarian? He would prefer to hear the Arab say, 'Blessed be the God of the Jews,' than possess all the riches of the world . . . It is written, 'Thou shalt not oppress thy neighbor.' Now thy neighbor is as thy brother, and thy brother is as thy neighbor. Hence you learn that to rob a Gentile is robbery."

In the same spirit it is said in the Talmud that an idolator who studies the Torah is like the High Priest; that a Gentile who lives a godly life is like the High Priest. It is related that Rabbi Judah told the Emperor Antoninus that he would have a share in the world to come even though he was a Gentile; for all men have a share in the world to come as long as they desist from acts of violence. In the spirit of Simon ben Shatah the Talmud states:

In a city where there are both Jews and Gentiles, the collectors of alms collect both from Jews and Gentiles, and feed the poor of both, visit the sick of both, bury both, comfort the mourners whether they be Jews or Gentiles, and restore the lost goods of both.

The Bible begins the story of man not with the birth of Abraham but with the creation of Adam and Eve; and the Rabbis said that Adam was made from dust gathered by God from the four corners of the earth; so that no people should later be able to say that he was made from the dust gathered only in their own corner of the world. And wherever one turns in the writings of the Jews this motif of equality, the fatherhood of God and the brotherhood of man, appears irresistibly. Thus, at the Passover *seder* a drop of wine is to be spilled from the cup at the mention of each of the ten plagues with which the Egyptians were afflicted, the reason being, say the Rabbis, that one's cup of joy cannot be full as long as there is suffering somewhere in the world. And Purim, when the names of the sons of Haman, as they are hanged, are read in the synagogue, the reader must try to read them all in one breath; for it is painful to consider the torture of even Haman and his sons. Again, at the Passover *seder* the head of the household reads of the drowning of the Egyptian hosts in the Red Sea; and the Rabbis comment on the passage by relating that when the drowning was taking place, angels in heaven commenced to sing the praises of the Lord, but He rebuked them, saying, "My children are drowning, and you would sing!"

These sayings of the Rabbis are in the spirit of Amos, who cried out: " 'Are ye not as children of the Ethiopians unto Me, O children of Israel?' saith the Lord. 'Have I not brought up Israel out of the land of Egypt? and the Philistines from Caphtor, and Aram from Kir?' " (9:7).

So, too, according to Isaiah, The Lord says: "Blessed be Egypt My people and Assyria the work of My hands, and Israel Mine inheritance" (19:25). And when Jeremiah speaks of the afflictions that must be visited upon the sinful people of Moab, he says that God wails: "Therefore will I wail for Moab; yea, I will cry out for all Moab; for the men of Kir-heres shall my heart moan" (48:31). And the Book of Jonah, which occupies so prominent a place in Jewish ritual, relates of God's concern for the salvation of the inhabitants of the city of Nineveh—a city of Gentiles, not of Jews.

It is clear, we believe, that Judaism, or the ethical monotheism elaborated by the Old Testament and the Rabbis, posits as one of its fundamental precepts the equality of all men before God: all men who share righteousness share the grace of God. And righteousness is not considered from the standpoint of ritual observance: works of benevolence, says the Talmud, form the beginning and end of the Torah; or, as Micah expressed the truth:

> Wherewith shall I come before the Lord?
> And bow myself before God on high?
> Shall I come before Him with burnt-offerings?
> With calves of a year old?
> Will the Lord be pleased with thousands of rams,
> With ten thousands of rivers of oil?
> Shall I give my first-born for my transgression,
> The fruit of my body for the sin of my soul?
> It hath been told thee, O man, what is good;
> And what the Lord doth require of thee;
> Only to do justly and to love mercy
> And to walk humbly with thy God (6:6-8).

THE DEMOCRATIC IDEAL:
SOCIAL AND POLITICAL EQUALITY AND FREEDOM

That the ideals of equality and freedom which one finds at the heart of Judaism were not projected merely for "the end of days," but were principles of daily conduct, becomes clear when one examines some of the institutions that are characteristic of Judaism. In their relations with Gentiles the Jews could speak of equality and freedom only as ends to be achieved after a long struggle: both the Jews and the non-Jews will need to realize the nature of righteousness and strive for it together before they lie down together in equality, no one a lion and no one a lamb, but all children of the One Father, brothers who have issued from the same source of life. The ideal was always there; Israel could preserve itself only by loyalty to its universalistic religion; its mission was never to be treated lightly, let alone forgotten; and every opportunity was to be taken advantage of to elicit from the non-Jew a blessing for the One God, and thereby to bring him closer to righteousness. The incident about the pearl found on the Arab's donkey dramatically illustrates the consciousness of the obligation to win adherents for God and His ethical laws. That is what *Kiddush ha-Shem* means. The same awareness of this mission is illustrated by the dictum in the Talmud that to cheat a Gentile is even worse than to cheat a Jew, for besides being a violation of the moral law, such conduct brings Israel's religion into contempt and causes a *Hillul ha-Shem* (a desecration of the Name).

In relations among themselves the Jewish people had an opportunity to give the ideal of equality "a local habitation and a name." The keystone of the Jewish community was the precept that "all Israel are responsible for one another." The Rabbis relate that when Moses summoned all Israel before God, he said, "Your captains, your judges, your elders." But God made him add the words: "all the people of Israel." This passage receives clarification by the statement of the Rabbis that Moses did not stop with "all the people of Israel," but went on to add: "your little ones, your wives, and the stranger that is in thy camp"; for, said the Rabbis, "God's mercies are on male and female alike, on the wicked equally with the righteous, as it says, 'From the hewer of thy wood to the drawer of thy water.' All are equal before God; hence it says, 'All the people of Israel.' " Rabbi Akiba said that even the poorest in Israel are looked upon as freemen who have lost their possessions, "for they are the sons of Abraham, Isaac and Jacob." In other words, all *men* are equal because all are the children of Adam and Eve; all *Israelites* are equal because all are the children of Abraham, Isaac and Jacob—not to mention Adam and Eve.

The hereditary character of the priesthood in ancient Israel[4a] has led to the charge that Judaism recognized a class of privileged persons whose rights were obtained by birth: a hereditary aristocracy. But this is due to a misunderstanding. The priests were not permitted to consider themselves the heads of the community; they were a class whose status was determined by function; they were servants of God in a special sense; but being such servants, they carried obligations rather than privileges. People were not to stand in superstitious fear of them; they had no superior spiritual powers. The Rabbis had freed themselves from almost every trace of sacerdotalism. The priesthood was maintained because the Torah required it; but it was not the priests who blessed Israel; it was God Who bestowed the blessing; the priests were not intermediaries, like angels or saints.

It says at the end of the priestly benediction, "and it is I that will bless them." One might think that if the priests choose to bless the Israelites, then they are blessed, and if they do not choose, they are not blessed. Therefore it says, "And it is *I* that will bless them. *I* will bless my people."

Nor did the Rabbis themselves constitute a privileged caste. Three crowns were recognized, the crown of the Torah, the crown of the priesthood, and the crown of the kingdom.

Aaron was worthy of the crown of the priesthood and obtained it, David was worthy of the crown of the kingdom and obtained it. The crown of the Torah remains, so that no man shall have the pretext to say: "If the crown of the priesthood and the crown of the kingdom were yet available, I would have proved myself worthy of them and have obtained them." For the crown of the Torah is available for all. For God says: "Of him who proves himself worthy of *that* crown, I reckon it to him as if all the three were yet available, and he had proved himself worthy of them all. And of everyone who does not prove himself worthy of the crown of the Torah, I reckon it unto him as if all three crowns were yet available, and he had proved himself worthy of none of them."

The crown of the Torah is not inherited; it was worn by men who earned their living by cobbling shoes, weaving flax or making candles. Ben Azzai said: "If any man humiliates himself for the Torah, eats dry dates and wears dirty clothes, and sits and keeps guard at the doors of the wise, every passer-by thinks him a fool, but at the end you will find that all the Torah is within him"; and if the Torah is within him, he may wear the crown of the Torah. A famous passage in *Pirke Abot* is the following:

This is the way that is becoming for the study of the Torah: a morsel of bread with salt thou must eat, and water by measure thou must drink, thou must sleep upon the ground, and live a life of trouble, the while thou toilest in the Torah. If thou doest thus, "Happy shalt thou be and it shall be well with thee"; happy shalt thou be in this world, and it shall be well with thee in the world to come. Seek not greatness for thy self, and crave not honor more than is due to thy learning; and desire not the table of kings, for thy table is greater than theirs, and thy crown greater than theirs; and faithful is He, the master of thy work, to pay thee the reward of thy labor.

As water is priceless, said the Rabbis, so is the Torah priceless; and as water is free for all, so is the Torah free for all. But the Torah was also compared to wine: as wine cannot keep in vessels of gold and silver, but only in cheap earthenware vessels, so the words of the Torah are preserved only in him who makes himself lowly. "The greater the man," says the Midrash, "the humbler he is." Man, especially one who wears the crown of the Torah, must be as humble as is God Himself; wherever you find the greatness of God, there, too, you will find His humbleness. For "God loves nothing better than humility." Said Rabbi Johanan: "The words of the Torah abide only with him who regards himself as nothing." The Torah was not to be used as an ornament with which one might adorn himself; nor was it to be used as a spade with which to dig; knowledge of the Torah was its own reward; it is only to study the Torah that God created man: study of the Torah is his purpose, his end, his happiness and his reward.[5a] "Do the words of the Torah for the doing's sake; speak of them for their own sake. Do not say: 'I will learn Torah so that I may be called wise, or sit in the College, or gain long days in the world to come.'" Nor may one charge fees for teaching the Torah; for the words of the Torah are free; God gave the Torah free: "he who takes a fee for the Torah destroys the world."

The humility with which the greatest of the three crowns was to be worn is illustrated by the following incident related in the Talmud:

One day, at the close of the fig harvest, Rabbi Tarfon was walking in a garden, and he ate some figs which had been left behind. The custodian of the garden came up, caught him, and began to beat him unmercifully. Then Rabbi Tarfon called out and said who he was, whereupon they let him go. Yet all his days did he grieve, saying, "Woe is me, for I have used the crown of the Torah for my own profit." For the teaching ran: "A man must not say, I will study so as to be called a wise man, or rabbi, or an elder, or to have a seat in the College; but he must study from love. The honor will come of itself."

The Rabbis did not constitute a caste; they generally were not supported by the community but had to carry on a trade or calling from which they might support themselves and their families: "I call heaven and earth to witness," says the Midrash, "that every scholar who eats of his own, and enjoys the fruits of his own labor, and who is not supported by the community, belongs to the class who are called happy; as it is written, 'If thou eat the fruit of thy hands, happy art thou.'" They were teachers, but received no compensation for their teaching; they had to make a living by spending a part of their day in some occupation for which there was a monetary reward: "He who occupies himself with the study of the Torah only is as if he had no God." A man was counseled to spend as little time as possible, however, at his trade or work: only long enough to earn sufficient money to keep body and soul together. It was the duty of everyone to study the Torah at some time during each day: at least two ordinances in the morning and two in the evening; but the more study, the greater the reward (in the world to come). "If a scholar engages in business and is not too successful, it is a good omen for him. God loves his learning and does not want to enrich him." The greatest calumny was to call one an *am ha-aretz*, a boor; to be poor was to be blessed, but to be ignorant was to be cursed. No *"mitzva"* was greater than study: the study of the Torah was superior to all other things—all other things except one: teaching Torah. "He who learns receives but one-fifth of the reward that goes to him who teaches."

It is evident, then, that the crown of the Torah did not carry with it social privileges: the most learned man still needed to continue at his cobbler's bench or carpentry work. On the contrary, it imposed the obligation to teach. The social ideal of Judaism was a community of scholars, where all would be companions. This is what it means to have been created in the image of God: to fulfill the obligation or commandment to study the words of God. This commandment was imposed on *every* Jew equally; it had to be fulfilled by himself, and not by a surrogate.

The schools were commanded not to engage in strife one with the other. Tolerance in scholarly dispute was an obligation. "If a scholar has no *derek eretz* [good taste, refinement], he is lower than an animal." It is related that Rabbah would open his discourse with a jest, and let his hearers laugh a little. For years the schools of Hillel and Shammai[6a] maintained a dispute over a matter of law, finally a Voice descended in Jabneh and cried out: "The words of both are the words of the Living God, but the decision should follow the School of Hillel." It was asked, why, if the words of both are the words of the Living God, was the decision granted to Hillel's school? The reply was: "Because the members of the school of Hillel are amiable of manner and courteous; they teach the opinions of both schools; and furthermore, they always give the opinion of their opponents first." This teaches, said the Rabbis, that whoever abases himself is exalted by God. One was not to assume that the Divine Wisdom rested with him alone and that those who differed from him uttered words of no worth. One was to be a constant fount of tolerance and humility; one must be conscious of the relativity of his own statements even when, or perhaps especially when, the statements related to ultimate truths; for one was always subject to error and sin; all statements of truth were subject to finiteness and contingency. "One says its meaning is this, and another says its meaning is that. One gives such an opinion, his fellow a different one. But they all were given from one shepherd—that is from Moses, who received the teaching from Him who is One and unique in the world." This spirit of tolerance, mutual respect, profound religious humility, is perhaps best expressed in the following favorite saying of the Rabbis of Jabneh:

I am a creature of God and my neighbor is also His creature. My work is in the city and his is in the field. I rise early to my work and he rises early to his. He cannot excel in my work and I cannot excel in his. But perhaps you say, I do great things while he does small things. We have learnt that it matters not whether a man does much or little, if only he directs his heart to heaven.

Judaism is not merely a matter of beliefs and ceremonies, it is a way of life; and the economic aspect of human existence was not a matter of indifference to the prophets and Rabbis. The Bible was not considered a mere theological treatise; it was viewed as a document with the greatest social significance; for in its teachings one could find the ways by which to enter into intimate relation with God, and find joy and freedom in His service; also the ways by which to enter into proper social relations, so that the perfect social order, the kingdom of heaven, might be established on the earth. Today we might be tempted to say that one aim was religious while the other was social; but Judaism would reject the distinction. Judaism recognizes no profane virtues; all virtues are sacred; the social function is as religious as the religious function is social. "Rabbi Judah said in the name of Rab: 'A man is forbidden to eat anything until he has fed his beast.'" Was this considered a religious law or a social law? The distinction would not have been comprehensible to either Rabbi Judah or Rab. In Judaism all duties are divine commands. While several duties appear to be arbitrary, nearly all are expressed in laws which our conscience recognizes as obligatory on free will. Economics and ethics are the same; ethics and religion are the same.

In a word, there was no distinction between the social conscience and the religious conscience. The study of the Torah was chiefly the study of social relations, individual and communal problems. The Torah taught that "if two men claim thy help, and one is thy enemy, help thy enemy first"; and the same Torah taught that "he who gives food to a small child, must tell its mother"; and the same Torah taught that one must permit the poor to glean after the reapers, and that one must not take interest on a loan.

Perhaps it was the experience of the Israelites in Egypt that compelled them to project the ideal of social equality and freedom. For in Egypt they saw that when great wealth and political power are in the hands of the same group, the welfare and happiness of the rest of the people are greatly imperiled. Political and economic power must be spread out among all, with little if any disparity in the distribution. If this is not accomplished, and men are unjustly exploited—used as mere means and not as ends; when it is forgotten that every man bears the image of God—physical, spiritual and social pestilence will spread, and insurrection will follow, shaking the community to its very foundations. Masters cannot exploit their workers and God should not see. The excessive wealth of the masters leads to luxury; derived through injustice, wealth breeds further injustice; luxury corrupts what may have been left untouched by the injustice of exploitation. In the end the system collapses; blind injustice leans against the pillar of its palace and is destroyed with it.

Furthermore, as Charles Foster Kent has well pointed out, the experience of Moses showed him that violence does not avail in correcting industrial evils. The only true method is that which he used:

Education and organization of those industrially oppressed; clear presentation of their claims and rights; patient, persistent agitation in order to educate public opinion; and efficient organization to protect their interests.

The Israelites did not win their freedom merely to duplicate among themselves the system they had rejected. They were to build their own community on a basis of moral idealism, ethical religion and social justice. There was to be in the Promised Land no form of political or industrial oppression; for always the Jews were commanded to remember, at every turn, in every crisis, at every temptation to commit an injustice: "Remember that thou wast a slave in the land of Egypt, and that the Lord thy God brought thee out from there by a mighty hand and an outstretched arm." Future generations, after the exodus from Egypt, were commanded to look upon themselves as though *they*, and not merely their forefathers, had been rescued from the hand of the Egyptian taskmaster. The *freshness* of their freedom was constantly to be before their eyes.

Moreover, they were commanded to remember in humility that it was not by their own strength that they won their freedom, but because God is One Who watches over the poor, the fatherless, the afflicted, the helpless, the outcast: He is a just Judge; He loves justice and mercy and righteousness, and requites evil with evil. God has created a world in which the moral law is as implacable, as impersonal, and as imperative as is a physical law: there is no escape from it.

In ancient Israel the atmosphere was a thoroughly equalitarian one: all were practically equal and free. Each was represented in the council of the clan or tribe.[7a] While slavery was tolerated (it is to be remembered that the United States retained this institution until only three generations ago), the harshness of the master-servant relationship was in many ways mitigated. The biblical fugitive-slave law, unlike the laws passed by Congress before the Civil War, protected the fugitive; for in Deuteronomy it is provided:

Thou shalt not deliver to his master a bondsman that is escaped from his master unto thee. He shall dwell with thee in the midst of thee, in the place which he shall choose within one of thy gates, where it liketh him best; thou shalt not wrong him (23:16-17).

While the institution of private property was recognized, and there were laws against theft, clear recognition was given to the fact that property is fundamentally a social object, that property is subject to social control, that society may direct as to how much property a man may possess, how much of his income he may retain for his own use, for how long a period he may divest himself of title to property allotted to him, and so on. Thus it was provided that "when thou comest into thy neighbor's vineyard thou mayest eat grapes until thou have enough at thine own pleasure . . . when thou comest into thy neighbor's standing corn, thou mayest pluck ears with thy hand . . ." (23:25-26). Among the first laws to protect the rights of laborers are those found in the Bible. The Sabbath was instituted as a social institution, as a day of rest: "in it thou shalt not do any manner of work, thou, nor thy son, nor thy daughter, nor thy man-servant, nor thy maid-servant, nor thine ox, nor thine ass, nor any of thy cattle, nor thy stranger that is within thy gates . . ." (5:14). Wages were to be paid promptly:

Thou shalt not oppress a hired servant that is poor and needy, whether he be of thy brethren, or of thy strangers that are in thy land within thy gates. In the same day thou shalt give him his hire, neither shall the sun go down upon it; for he is poor, and setteth his heart upon it; lest he cry against thee to the Lord, and it be a sin in thee (24:14-15).

The well-off were forbidden to oppress the impoverished citizen:

No man shall take the mill or the upper millstone to pledge, for he taketh a man's life to pledge . . . When thou dost lend thy neighbor any manner of loan, thou shalt not go into his house to fetch his pledge. . . . And if he be a poor man, thou shalt not sleep with his pledge; thou shalt surely restore to him the pledge when the sun goeth down, that he may sleep in his garment, and bless thee (24:6,10,12-13).

Bankruptcy laws were instituted, so that a man shall not be borne down by his debts forever, but shall, instead, have an opportunity for a fresh economic start. "At the end of every seven years shalt thou make a release" (15:1); the creditor shall not exact the debt from his debtor. At the same time, he who hath must not close his heart to the importunities of him who hath not, and say to himself that "the seventh year, the year of release, is at hand" (15:9), and refuse to lend to the poor; for if this happen, God will hear the cry of the poor man, and the rich man will be guilty of a crime. "Thou shalt surely give him and thy heart shall not be grieved when thou givest unto him" (15:10). The owner of the land was not to think that the land was *really* his, to do with as he pleased;

for the land is the Lord's; and the Lord commanded that every seventh
year the land must lie fallow; it must not be abused, lest it become a waste
place, and all the land a dustbowl. A share of a man's income had to be
turned over to the communal authorities for the relief of needy persons.
Even when a man builds a house for himself, he must take into consideration the duties he owes his neighbors; he must make a parapet for
his roof, so that no one will fall from it.

Time and again the prophets cried out against the economic inequalities
that resulted in loss of freedom, injustice and oppression. Men became too
rich and too powerful for their own and the community's good. Such rich
men were declared enemies of the people and the chief sinners against God.
The accumulation of such wealth and the exploitation it entailed were
condemned in the strongest terms possible:

> Because they sell the righteous for silver,
> And the needy for a pair of shoes,
> That pant after the dust of the earth on the head of the poor,
> And turn aside the way of the humble . . .
> And they lay themselves down beside every altar,
> Upon clothes taken in pledge,
> And in the house of their God they drink
> The wine of them that have been fined (Amos 2:6-8).

Amos foretold such as these what their destiny would be:

> Hear this word,
> Ye kine of Bashan, that are in the mountains of Samaria,
> That oppress the poor, that crush the needy,
> That say to their lords, "Bring, that we may feast."
> The Lord God hath sworn by His holiness:
> "Lo, surely the days shall come upon you,
> That ye shall be taken away with hooks,
> And your residue with fish-hooks . . ." (4:1-3).

Isaiah brought severe charges against the oppressors of the common man:

> It is ye that have eaten up the vineyard;
> The spoil of the poor is in your houses.
> What mean ye that ye crush My people,
> And grind the face of the poor? . . . (3:14-15)
> Woe unto them that join house to house,
> That lay field to field
> Till there be no room and ye be made to dwell
> Alone in the midst of the land! (5:8).

Just as Judaism posits the ideals of social equality and economic equality,
so, too, it posits political freedom and equality. Israel was to be a holy
nation, each Israelite was to be a member of "a kingdom of priests, a
holy nation." God alone is ruler over Israel. What need is there of a king?

No one was permitted to make laws for the nation; for God had given His Torah to His people Israel—to every Israelite; there was no room left for a king. Not even David or Solomon[8a] could abrogate the laws of the Sabbath, or of the seventh year, or make oppression of the needy just. Israel was different from all other peoples: its legislation came from God. If a king cannot make laws, of what use can he be? God was the Lawgiver, the Ruler and the Judge. When the Jews asked Samuel to appoint over them a king, he told them of what use a king could be:

"This will be the manner of the king that shall reign over you: he will take your sons and appoint them unto him for his chariots, and to be his horsemen; and they shall run before his chariots. And he shall appoint them unto him for captains of thousands, and captains of fifties; and to plow his ground, and to reap his harvest, and to make his instruments of war, and the instruments of his chariots. And he will take your daughters to be perfumers, and to be cooks, and to be bakers. And he will take your fields and your vineyards, and your oliveyards, even the best of them, and give them to his servants. And he will take the tenth of your seed, and of your vineyards, and give to his officers, and to his servants. And he will take your men-servants, and your maid-servants, and your goodliest young men and your asses, and put them to his work. He will take the tenth of your flocks; and you shall be his servants (I Sam. 8:11-17).

The Jews never forgot this lesson of Samuel's; even though they took upon themselves the yoke of a kingship, they would not tolerate oppression and despotism. The king was to be a servant of the people and not their master; he was to rule under God and not as a substitute for Him. Thus the Jews became a "rebellious" people; for they would not tolerate a tyrant even if he were of the seed of David. When Solomon died, the northern tribes rose in protest against a perpetuation of oppressive measures by Rehoboam, whom Solomon had nominated as his successor.[9a] It is related that Rehoboam and the Israelites met at Shechem, where he was asked if he would make lighter their yoke. The king took counsel with the old men who had served Solomon, and they said to him: "If thou wilt be a servant unto this people this day, and wilt serve them, and answer them, and speak good words to them, then they will be thy servants forever" (I Kings 12:7). The king would not follow their advice; he "gave no heed to the people." When the Israelites saw that he disregarded their petition, they said to him:

"We have no portion in David
Neither have we inheritance in the son of Jesse;
Everyman to his tents, O Israel" (II Sam. 20:1).

Even if it meant breaking up the kingdom, Judaism's democratic ideals had to be asserted and reasserted. Thus it was throughout Israel's history in Palestine. The people, and sometimes the prophets speaking for the people, constantly submitted the moral presuppositions of the ruling caste to scrutiny and re-examination. The freedom of the private moral judgment was always kept alive. When Ahab, misguided by Jezebel, his queen, showed his disloyalty to the democratic ideals, a popular uprising ended his dynasty. Elijah spoke for the conscience of Israel.[10a] When Naboth refused to sell his vineyard to the despotic king, and the king, through a perversion of justice, had him murdered, Elijah spoke out against the king, and when the king heard his words, "he rent his clothes and put sackcloth upon his flesh and fasted, and he lay in sackcloth, and went softly" (I Kings 21:27). For the king knew that he could reign only under and within the law; and he was not above the Torah.

And this brings us to our final point, namely, that no people can be free, no democracy can continue to exist, if the rulers selected by the people do not consider themselves bound by the law. There must be limitations on rulers if the individual's rights are to be preserved. The citizen's rights are measured by the restrictions on government. There must, in other words, be a constitution which defines clearly how far the government may go in this matter or that delegated to its authority. Israel had such a constitution in the Torah. No one was above it. Only under the Torah could kings rule and judges judge. As God is righteous, so must the king be; as God defends the weak, so must the king. Only justice is the foundation of a people's happiness and stability. Psalm 72 expresses this thought:

> Give the king Thy judgments, O God,
> And Thy righteousness unto the king's son;
> That he may judge Thy people with righteousness,
> And Thy poor with justice . . .
> May he judge the poor of the people,
> And save the children of the needy,
> And crush the oppressor . . .
> He will have pity on the poor and needy,
> And the souls of the needy he will save.
> He will redeem their soul from oppression and violence . . .

This, in part, is the picture of the ideal king.

Indeed, how could Israel view the status and function of government otherwise; for does not God Himself govern in accordance with law? Judaism is a law-centered religious civilization. All that God does, said Rabbi Akiba,[11a] He does by justice; "the procedure in the heavenly court is governed by law as in an earthly court." The day has twelve hours, said Rabbi Judah in the name of Rab, and in the first three God sits and busies Himself with the Torah! God Himself is bound by the Torah, by His own laws. He made the world "by law," not arbitrarily. Why, then, should He not spend His time teaching the Torah to the righteous in heaven? When Moses went up to heaven, he found God sitting and weaving crowns for the letters, little flourishes on some letters of the Torah to ornament the Scroll of the Law. The imagination of the Jewish folk could devise no occupation more worthy of God than the writing and study of His own Torah; because Israel found such a delight in the Law: "But his delight is in the law of the Lord; and in His law doth he meditate day and night" (Ps. 1:2). The ordinances of the Lord are to be desired more than gold, yea, than much fine gold; they are sweeter than the honey and the honeycomb. "I have rejoiced in the way of Thy testimonies . . . I will delight myself in Thy statutes." The Lord's commandments apply to every significant act in life; as Rabbi Phineas said, one must think of the commandments when one builds a house, when he makes a door, when he buys new clothes, when his hair is cut, when his field is plowed, when his field is sowed, when the harvest is gathered, "even when you are not occupied with anything, but just taking a walk . . ." And the commandments are for *all* the people to observe: "All are equal before the law. The duty of observance is for all. For the Torah is the 'inheritance of the congregation of Jacob.' It does not say 'priests' or 'Levites' or 'Israelites,' but 'the congregation of Jacob.' " No one can be above the Law—whether he wear the crown of Torah, or the priestly crown, or the royal crown— because all men are equal, all are equally bound by the Law and subject to it, alike at every point; more than this, the world itself is subject to the Law; God made the world in accordance with the Law. Is not then even God Himself bound by the Law? "God created the world by the Torah: the Torah was His handmaid and His tool by the aid of which He set bounds to the deep, assigned their functions to sun and moon, and formed all nature. Without the Torah the world falls." The same Torah sets bounds to man's greed, man's injustice; assigns functions to this man and that, and forms civilization.

Without law there is no freedom. Unless a people meditate on the statutes and delight in the Law, they will not be able to walk at ease; unequal strength will lead to unequal justice; and when justice is dead, said Kant, it is better not to be alive. If Judaism projects a *rechtlichbuer gerliche Gesellschaft*, it is to be borne in mind that this law-centered society is also an *ethischbuergerliche Gesellschaft*, for the law is within as well as without; and at the center of the ethico-legal system is the injunction of God: "For unto Me are the children of Israel slaves; they are not slaves unto slaves."

Not all democratic institutions were foreseen by the prophets and Rabbis; such agencies are evolved by societies of men as the need for them is felt to be irresistible even by those who would prevent their emergence. But the spirit, the inner values, the energies of democracy are right at the very heart of Judaism.

NOTES

[1a Cf. above Judah Goldin, "The Period of the Talmud," pp. 172-179.]
[2a Cf. ibid., p. 194.]
[3a Cf. below Louis Finkelstein, "The Jewish Religion: Its Beliefs and Practices," pp. 1340-1342.]
[4a Cf. above Robert Gordis, "The Bible as a Cultural Monument," pp. 464-465.]
[5a Cf. Finkelstein, pp. 1331 ff.]
[6a Cf. Goldin, op. cit., pp. 129-133.]
[7a Cf. Gordis, op. cit., p. 477.]
[8a Cf. above William Foxwell Albright, "The Biblical Period," pp. 24 ff.]
[9a Cf. ibid., pp. 29 f.]
[10a Cf. ibid., pp. 34 f.]
[11a Cf. Goldin, op. cit., pp. 156-158.]

BIBLIOGRAPHY

The literature on the subject is meager. Following are a number of essays suggested for further reading:

BOKSER, BEN ZION, "Democratic Aspirations in Talmudic Judaism," in Science, Philosophy and Religion (Second Symposium), published by the Conference on Science, Philosophy and Religion. New York, 1942.

——, "Rabbinic Judaism and the Problem of Egoism," in Conflicts of Power in Modern Culture, (Seventh Symposium), ed. by Lyman Bryson, Louis Finkelstein and R. M. MacIver, published by the Conference on Science, Philosophy and Religion. New York, 1947.

BURROWS, MILLAR, "Democracy in the Hebrew-Christian Tradition: Old and New Testaments," in Science, Philosophy and Religion, op. cit.

FINKELSTEIN, LOUIS, "The Beliefs and Practices of Judaism," in The Religions of Democracy, by Louis Finkelstein, J. Elliot Ross and William Adams Brown. New York, 1941.

——, "Foundations of Democracy—Hebrew Sources: Scriptures and Talmud," in Foundations of Democracy, ed. by F. Ernest Johnson, published by the Institute for Religious and Social Studies. New York, 1947.

——, "The Ideal of Religious Liberty—A Jewish View," in Wellsprings of the American Spirit, ed. by F. Ernest Johnson, published by the Institute for Religious and Social Studies. New York, 1948.

KAPLAN, MORDECAI M., The Future of the American Jew. New York, 1948. Chapter 15 on "Basic Values in Jewish Religion."

A number of pamphlets in the series Popular Studies in Judaism published by the Tract Commission of the Union of American Hebrew Congregations and the Central Conference of American Rabbis, Cincinnati, are relevant:

CRONBACH, ABRAHAM, *The Social Outlook of Modern Judaism.*
FELDMAN, ABRAHAM J., *Contributions of Judaism to Modern Society.*
HELLER, BERNARD, *The Jewish Concept of the Chosen People.*
SCHULMAN, SAMUEL, *Jewish Ethics.*
TARSHISH, JACOB, *Judaism and Socialism.*
WITT, LOUIS, *Judaism and Democracy.*

CHAPTER 28

THE INFLUENCE OF THE BIBLE ON ENGLISH LITERATURE

By David Daiches

I

It has long been a commonplace among teachers of English in British universities that a proper understanding of English literature is impossible without a thorough knowledge of the Bible and of the Latin and Greek classics. These have been the great twin sources of inspiration for English writers at least from the latter part of the sixteenth century, and to a lesser degree and in a somewhat different way in earlier centuries also. Both these influences operated in a twofold manner: they were used rhetorically, as a teacher of style and literary devices of all kinds, and they also provided a set of stories and ideas which were incorporated, in an infinite number of ways, into the content of the later literature. While the Latin and Greek classics exerted this twofold influence on all the literatures of Europe, it was only in English literature that we find the Bible working similarly in both ways—and this because only in England was there produced a translation of the Bible acclaimed by successive generations as among the very greatest masterpieces of that country's literature. "Among the greatest" is perhaps too mild a phrase, for, while the Authorized Version of the Bible is generally ranked with the works of Shakespeare by literary critics, there can be no question that of the two the Bible has always been the more widely read and the better known among the English people as a whole. The fact, therefore, that the English Bible existed as a great literary work in its own right, as well as constituting a popular source of stories and moral ideas, meant that in England the Bible had a rhetorical, or purely literary, influence in addition to its influence as a rich storehouse of tales and ethical principles. In other European countries the Bible had only the latter kind of influence, for its translation into the vernacular never achieved the position among national literary masterpieces that was achieved by the English translation of the Bible known as the Authorized, or King James, Version.

It is true that in the seventeenth century it is often impossible to distinguish the rhetorical from the ideological influence of the Bible, for familiarity with the diction of the Authorized Version came to be regarded by many as implying an acceptance of certain religious doctrines. There are occasions when the experienced reader can infer from the kind of biblical English used by a writer (for there are many kinds of biblical English) to what particular Protestant sect he belonged. It is also true that in the eighteenth century it is sometimes difficult to distinguish a writer's use of the classics as a source of imagery and other stylistic devices from his acceptance of certain Greek or Roman ideals. In other words, though both the Bible and the classics have two distinct kinds of influence on English literature, there are periods when enthusiasm makes a writer deliberately exhibit one kind to show that he has also been affected by the other. Yet this is true of only certain limited periods, for on the whole it can be fairly said that both the Bible and the classics have had a continuous stylistic influence even in quarters where agreement with the ideas expressed in the models imitated has been of the slightest.

That a Protestant people, encouraged by all the religious controversies of the Reformation to turn to the text of the Bible as their main weapon of attack and defense, should come to know the Bible well is easy enough to understand. But the full extent of the purely *literary* influence of the Bible on English literature can only be explained when we realize the number and variety of literary forms that the Bible contains.[1a] A writer like Milton thought of the Bible both as the fundamental document of his religion and as a collection of literary models comparable on aesthetic grounds with the great classics of Greece and Rome. History, short story, lyric, epic, ode, elegy, tragedy, comedy—these are all displayed in some form in the Old Testament. If we think for a moment of the differences in style and literary form between the simple narrative of Exodus, the lyrical directness of the Psalms (which themselves display a wide variety of poetic expression), the slow-moving, plangent eloquence of the fortieth chapter of Isaiah, the poetic elegies of Jeremiah, the variety of narrative styles shown in the Books of Kings, Ruth, Jonah and Esther, the extraordinary quality of the Book of Job (which Milton called a "brief epic")— to mention only a few examples—we can see how the Bible struck the imagination of a generation of writers still wrestling with the problem of literary "forms" and the kinds of style appropriate to different kinds of subject matter. This is what makes the seventeenth century such a pivotal period in English literature; for it was during this century that the struggle was waged with equal intensity both on the religious and on the literary plane. Whereas in many other European countries the religious struggle was fought out on the battlefield, in England it was on the whole a battle fought with texts and pamphlets, and each side produced its triumphs, which include Hooker's *Laws of Ecclesiastical Polity* at the end of the sixteenth century and Bunyan's *Pilgrim's Progress* in the latter part of the seventeenth century—neither of which books could have been written if there had been no English Bible.

It should be remembered that, although it was the acceptance of the Authorized Version as the definitive English translation that made possible the tremendous literary influence of the English Bible, that influence was already beginning to be exerted long before 1611, for the style of the Authorized Version—a style already antique when that translation was made—had been building up for generations, from Tyndale's earliest efforts in 1525, through the work of Coverdale and others for almost a century before the Authorized Version was published. English biblical prose was not born in the seventeenth century: indeed, by the time the Bible of 1611 appeared the people long had fairly fixed ideas of the kind of language appropriate for the English Bible, and they judged—and accepted—the Authorized Version accordingly. Coverdale's Bible, Matthew's Bible, the Great Bible, the Geneva Bible, the Bishop's Bible—each of these versions had played its part in developing biblical English. By 1604, when the Authorized Version was begun, the standard of style had long been set, and the only problem that remained was that of greater accuracy of rendering.

There is another point to be remembered. The achievement of the English biblical style was taking place during the very period when modern (*i.e.*, postmedieval) English literature was entering on its first great phase. When we talk of "the Bible and Shakespeare" (a collocation of a kind possible only in English literature) we are referring to two different kinds of English literary achievement; we are referring also to two contemporary achievements. The Authorized Version was being prepared during the period when Shakespeare was producing his final masterpieces. This was the fine flower of generations of noble experiment with style and language, in both poetry and prose. The fact, therefore, that English Bible translation was fortunate enough to grow up with this great phase of English literature helped both to ensure that it would profit to the utmost from the exciting literary experimentation that was taking place at this time and to produce a counterinfluence from the Bible translation already achieved on the secular literary works being produced. Thus the fanatical attitude of the more extreme Puritan sects to the letter of the biblical text as they understood it was tempered by the simultaneous consideration of the English Bible as a secular document, which contained important lessons for the writer and the literary critic. If this happy conjunction had not taken place, the Puritan suspicion of the arts would have done more damage in England than it actually did. Just as the medieval Church combined sacred and secular activities in the Miracle Plays (which brought the Bible into literature in a very different manner from the way in which it entered literature after the Reformation in England), so the seventeenth-century Puritan was led, often in spite of himself, to an appreciation of literary art even while denouncing the arts as pastimes of the devil. Milton, artist and Puritan, is the great symbolic figure here, but it is also worth considering whether the extraordinary work of Spenser—Platonist, Protestant, and at the same time a "poet's poet"—or the poetry of a Puritan such as Andrew Marvell could have existed were it not for the resolution of Puritanism and aesthetics made possible by English Bible translation. Only in the work of that Greek Puritan, Plato, the poet who denounced poets, is a similar phenomenon to be observed.

2

Before the sixteenth-century English Bible translation had brought the Bible to the people as a literary as well as a religious document, the ordinary Englishman, like his contemporaries all over Europe, had a sporadic knowledge of the Bible from pictures in stained-glass windows, sermons which quoted and elaborated biblical texts, and popular biblical paraphrases. In medieval Europe, therefore, the Bible could be known only for its stories and its doctrine, never for its literary qualities. Even the translations of single biblical texts made by individual members of the clergy in sermons were always made in the preacher's own words, not in the words of such translations as existed. Translations of the Bible did exist in Europe in the Middle Ages, but at least until the end of the fourteenth century they were translations made for individual members of the nobility or by some solitary scholar for his own private use, and they never achieved any circulation. The Church, during this period, took the view that ordinary folk should not read the Bible themselves, but should have appropriate portions of the Vulgate (Jerome's Latin version, the authorized text of the Church) interpreted to them by properly trained experts. "It was not without reason that Almighty God decided that Holy Scripture should be secret in certain places, lest, if it were clearly apparent to all men, it might perhaps be little esteemed and be treated disrespectfully," wrote Pope Gregory VII to the king of Bohemia in 1179 in a letter refusing the latter's request that his monks might be allowed to recite the divine office in Slavonic. It was this principle that underlay the persecution of sects like the Waldensians in southern France and the Lollards in England, both of which groups advocated the rendering of the Bible into the vernacular so that it could be understood by the people. Innocent III's letter to the archbishop of Metz in 1199 made the same point as Gregory had made earlier. Innocent was concerned with another heretical Bible-reading sect, the "Vaudois," and he expressed the view that "the secret mysteries of the faith ought not to be explained to all men in all places," stating his fear "lest any simple and unlettered person should presume to attain to the sublimity of holy scripture." In concluding his letter Innocent asked the archbishop to find out the social and educational status of those who indulged in vernacular Bible reading, the implication being clear that permission to read a translation of the Bible would depend on the status and intentions of the reader. The local applications of this theory (later embodied in the *Decretal* of Gregory IX and thus becoming of universal canonical application) made it clear that the clergy as a whole understood it to imply a general prohibition of biblical translation as such, particularly when any popular circulation was aimed at.

The Anglo-Saxon church in early medieval England, though it had formally accepted the Roman discipline at the Synod of Whitby in the seventh century, never wholly lost those qualities of humanitarian common sense and quiet individualism characteristic of the Celtic church which had been originally responsible for the conversion of Britain. The limited but definite interest in Bible translation in England during Anglo-Saxon times derives to some extent, perhaps, from these qualities. Bede is said to have translated the Gospel of St. John into English, though it has not survived. More definite evidence is the ninth-century *Vespasian Psalter*, which contains the Psalms in Latin together with an Anglo-Saxon "gloss," or literal word-for-word translation, written above. Such a translation was not, of course, intended for the general reader: it was to assist the less well educated of the clergy. The *Paris Psalter*, another Anglo-Saxon version of the same period—the time of King Alfred—contains a slightly different Latin text of the Psalms together with an Anglo-Saxon version, in parallel columns. It is also significant that in the preface to the code of laws drawn up by King Alfred there is an Anglo-Saxon translation of chapters 20 to 23 of Exodus—the account of the giving of the Law to Moses and of the Ten Commandments. Anglo-Saxon versions of the Gospels also exist, the earliest (if we exclude the "glosses") probably dating from the year 1000.

The most famous name in Anglo-Saxon Bible translation is that of Aelfric, abbot of Eynsham, who is known for his interest in promoting the translation of the Bible among English scholars. His sermons are full of biblical texts, translated by himself, and he produced the Anglo-Saxon *Heptateuch*, a somewhat abbreviated version of the first seven books of the Old Testament. Aelfric seems to have been the first English translator to have made some attempt to achieve an appropriate literary prose style for his biblical translations.

In an age when the distinction between literature and scholarship was obscure, and secular literature as a worthy contemporary activity had not yet achieved recognition, it was inevitable that a high proportion of written works should be biblical or at least religious. It should be remembered that by far the great majority of literary works produced in the Middle Ages are religious works. Thus we cannot infer from the Anglo-Saxon record any real "influence" of the Bible on literature, for literature in its modern sense was not yet adequately differentiated from any other activity of "clerks." And when we find numerous paraphrases of Bible stories, such as the Anglo-Saxon poems *Genesis, Exodus* and *Daniel*, attributed to Caedmon, we must not forget that these works were produced by the clergy primarily as religious documents and not by secular poets as "literature." The authors of these poems wrote for the instruction and edification of the tiny minority of the population who read them, and not, as the seventeenth-century religious poets wrote, in order to produce works of art which were at the same time religious in content and feeling. It is of course true that many religious documents were not written as "art" though they have later come to be regarded as such. The Bible itself, as the sixteenth- and seventeenth-century English critics were so excited to discover, contains many individual works of literary art, though it is doubtful, to say the least, if they were originally produced as such. But if we are to deal with "influences" at all we must first distinguish the factor that influences from that which is influenced. In an age when writing is the prerogative of the clergy and art is to a large extent (though by no means wholly) a by-product of religion, the question we are discussing becomes chiefly one of terminology.

The position becomes a little clearer in the Middle English period, for an age which produced the medieval lyric, the romances, and the works of Chaucer and his followers can hardly be said to have been without an ideal of secular literature. It is thus possible to make some useful generalizations about the influence of the Bible on English literature from the beginning of the thirteenth century to the middle of the fifteenth. As in Anglo-Saxon times, we have in this period a considerable number of biblical paraphrases, but we also have a variety of secular works which make use of biblical story for purposes of illustration or embellishment and, in addition, some ostensibly religious works which deal with biblical themes in a purely secular manner. There are, too, religious poems such as *The Pearl* which, like the religious poetry of the seventeenth century, were written as works of literary art rather than as religious documents. In the main, however, we are able to say that during this time a general knowledge of biblical story, acquired by the people through nonliterary means, had made it possible for writers to refer to biblical characters in their works with confidence that the significance of the reference would be apparent not only to those who could read the work but also to the much larger number of those to whom the work was read. The more picturesque of the Old Testament stories were frequently so used, sometimes with dramatic effect. While in the Middle Ages, as in later times, the more emotional type of religious poetry drew its inspiration more from the New Testament than from the Old, the Old Testament was the main source for secular writers in search of effective analogies and images, as well as the paraphrasers.

To the medieval Englishman, as to his contemporaries throughout Europe, the Bible was a Latin book[2a]—the Vulgate—and all translations were of course made from the Vulgate, not from the original texts. Neither Hebrew nor Greek was to any extent known in medieval Europe—Greek was acquired in some degree by a few scholars, and the merest rudiments of Hebrew only by the tiny minority of clerics who found Jewish teachers.

It was in the Middle English period that it first became clear that the historical portions of the Old Testament were—at least the earlier parts— fairly widely known and were accepted as authentic history. Thus almost all the medieval histories that are more than chronicles of individual reigns begin with the Creation and accept the Book of Genesis as their starting point. At some stage or other in their narrative these histories link up the story of the nation with which they deal with the biblical account—just as in the romances of this period there is so often a link with Greek and Roman history. The link with the Bible in the medieval histories is in a sense closer than that with the classics in the romances, for the Vulgate was accessible and known, while the texts of Homer and Virgil were known only by repute and even those who referred to these ancient writers had the vaguest ideas of the contents of their works. Indeed, Virgil throughout most of the Middle Ages was known simply as an ancient magician—and this in spite of the fact that his "Messianic" eclogue had long been interpreted by the Church as a prophecy of the coming of Christ and he had therefore won for himself a special place among the classical writers. The "matter of Rome" with which so many of the medieval romances dealt is very difficult to associate with anything found in the Latin or Greek writers, and though the story of Troy haunted the medieval imagination in an almost uncanny fashion, it is not the story that Homer told or Virgil used, but a series of strange, passionate incidents in which figures who are casually mentioned only once by Homer play the dominant parts. But the origins and nature of medieval romance are hardly relevant to this discussion. All we need point out here is that the link between medieval romance and the classics (best exemplified, perhaps, by the characters of Troilus and Cressida and their development up to Chaucer) is less direct than the link between medieval history and the Bible. These medieval histories were almost all written in Latin, however, and cannot be said to be wholly a part of English literature.

The influence of the narrative portions of the Old Testament is thus to be seen in Middle English writing and the Latin works of the period in several ways. Bible characters and events are used for purposes of comparison and illustration. And in the histories biblical events are actually used in the opening portions. There are also paraphrases and glosses of parts of the Bible, including two versions of the Psalms. One might add a less tangible kind of biblical influence, an intense moral feeling about justice and retribution, which one finds in such works as Chaucer's *Pardoner's Tale* and which pervades much of *Piers Plowman*. Such a feeling is directly or indirectly traceable to the Hebrew prophets (though the prophets were little known in the Middle Ages), just as in certain medieval devotional works the influence seems to be that of the Psalms together with parts of the New Testament. But here we come to cases in which we are dealing with the influence of Christianity rather than of the Bible, and this raises questions far beyond the scope of this chapter. There is, however, yet another direct kind of biblical influence noticeable in Middle English literature and conspicuous in such poems as *Cleanness* and *Patience*, in which biblical stories (taken of course from the Vulgate text) are woven almost whole into the narrative. While the function of the biblical stories in these poems is illustrative, the author is not content merely to allude to the story by way of example but proceeds to tell it in his own words. Thus *Patience* illustrates the nobility of that quality by giving a versified version of the story of Jonah.

Finally, before proceeding to say something about actual biblical translations in the Middle English period, we must touch on the most striking of all examples of the use of biblical story in medieval English literature. This is to be found in the Miracle Plays, which, having their origin in antiphonal chants as part of the church service, developed into crude ecclesiastical dramas and finally into full-dress though primitive plays more secular than religious in feeling. The plays as they eventually developed are often lively, if naïve, dramatizations of scriptural story. Some show a boisterous humor and even a flagrant coarseness that testify to the extent to which they had moved away from the spirit of their origins. *Noah and the Flood*, one of the best known, exists in various forms, the version in the Wakefield group being full of lively humor while that in the Chester Cycle contains humorous and realistic details of animal life combined with more serious religious scenes. The famous quarrel between Noah and his wife in the Wakefield *Noah* is a purely original, realistic treatment of an aspect of the Bible story done in contemporary terms. The later the date of these plays the more the elements of humor and realism have ousted the original religious feeling, the mid-fifteenth-century Wakefield Cycle being the furthest advanced on this road. The plays of the late fifteenth-century Coventry Cycle, however, revert to a serious didacticism, drawn almost entirely from the New Testament. The most effective of all the Miracle Plays is the Brome play, *Abraham and Isaac*, a genuinely dramatic version of the biblical story maintaining a high level of serious expression without any contemporary comic relief.

These, then, are the ways in which the influence of the Bible manifested itself in medieval English literature without benefit of any vernacular version. The Bible thus made use of by writers was the Vulgate, a text accessible to all who could read Latin—that is, to the greater number of the relatively large class of "clerks," all of whom were members of the clergy—but inaccessible to the unlearned. The story of the fight for Bible translation, which arose in England in the fourteenth century, shows that even at this period there were forces working for the extension of biblical knowledge among the people. These forces eventually produced a wholly new situation as far as the influence of the Bible on English literature is concerned.

3

The first complete English version of the Bible was the direct result of a challenge to the authority of the Church in matters of practice and doctrine. John Wycliffe, who instigated if he did not actually translate the Vulgate in the early 1380's, was moved by his determination to make the original source document of Christianity available to the people. This attitude, which was to become one of the main elements in Protestant thought, regarded the Bible as the final court of appeal in matters of doctrine. The orthodox view had been that it was the duty of the priests to explain selected scriptural passages in their sermons, relating parts of the Bible story in their own words and adding "the usury of their own minds," *i.e.*, the moral to be drawn. Wycliffe and the movement with which he was associated took the view that the people ought to have direct access to the Bible themselves and ought not to be dependent on the fancy interpretations of preachers—"for some by rhyming, and others by preaching poems and fables, adulterate in many ways the word of God." If the Bible was to be generally accessible, it had to be translated into the vernacular.

We need not here go into Wycliffe's social and theological theories, which led him to formulate his demand for Bible translation and to take steps himself to satisfy that demand. Suffice it to say that Wycliffe and the Lollard movement, which spread many of his ideas, argued for Bible translation that the people might have ready access to the one original source of their religion, and that out of this movement developed the two translations of the Bible from Latin into English associated with Wycliffe's name. The Church opposed the Lollard attitude as it had opposed that of the Waldensians and other groups in Europe who had advocated vernacular Bible translation on a large scale. The Wycliffite translations, like the Lollard movement in general which developed the Wycliffite tradition, remained suspect as heretical, and as late as 1528 Sir Thomas More condemned them as such, though ignorant of their nature. The immediate climax of the controversy about Bible translation was reached in 1408 when the provincial council at Oxford forbade the translation of the text of the Bible into English without specific episcopal license.

The literary quality of the Wycliffite translations is not impressive: the second is better than the first, less literal and wooden, but even it hardly constitutes a great monument of English prose. These two versions, especially the later one, enjoyed a certain popularity, as the number of surviving manuscripts prove, though their popularity cannot, of course, compare with that of later printed Bibles (the Wycliffite versions were made before the age of printing) made after the principle of vernacular translation had been generally accepted.

The Lollard heresy was suppressed at the beginning of the fifteenth century, but the idea that the Bible, as the one original source of Christianity, should be available to the people in their own language did not die. As the criticism of the Church that was eventually to bring about the Reformation spread in England as elsewhere, the demand for Bible translation also grew. The Church shifted its ground somewhat in the face of this growing demand and began to object to the Wycliffite translations because they were erroneous rather than because they made the Bible readily accessible to the public. When Sir Thomas More, for example, was discussing Bible translation in 1528 he made it clear that in his view the Church could only have condemned the Wycliffite versions if they were textually corrupt and contained heretical notes, and he accordingly assumed that these versions did in fact have these faults. Thus there had been a radical shift in orthodox opinion some time before More wrote: earlier, the opinion had been that the text of the Bible should not be made accessible to ordinary people, who were not qualified to interpret it properly, while the later view was that translations for whatever purpose were permissible if they were accurate and contained no heretical notes. This change was the measure of the success of the growing popular demand.

The development of large-scale Bible translation in England is bound up with the development of the Reformation, and the development of the Reformation is in turn inseparable from the growth of the "New Learning." The revival of the study first of Greek and then of Hebrew in the fifteenth century and later made available a critical apparatus for the examination of the original texts of the basic documents of Christianity. This put a new weapon in the hands of the reformers and they lost no time in using it. The work of Reuchlin and Erasmus—who fought obscurantism in the Church without leaving the fold—made the scholarship of the Renaissance available to the zeal of the Reformation, and from this marriage the Golden Age of English Bible translation was born.

The story of that Golden Age has been often told. William Tyndale, profiting by recent developments in Greek and Hebrew studies, began his work on Bible translation from the original texts in 1524 and spent the rest of his life in this activity. He was unable to do his work in England, and for thirteen years worked secretly in exile until he was brought back to England by a trick and burned as a heretic in 1536. Tyndale was an open reformer and attacked not only the abuses of the Church but its doctrine. His zeal for Bible translation was bound up with his interest in Church reformation and his theological ideas; like Wycliffe before him, he wished to have the one original source of Christianity laid open to all. "I defy the Pope and all his laws," Tyndale is said by Fox to have declared, "and if God spare my life, ere many years I will cause a boy that driveth the plow shall know more of the scripture than thou [a 'learned man' to whom he was talking] dost." Tyndale was here echoing words which the humanist Erasmus had uttered earlier in his *Exhortation to the Diligent Study of Scripture*, a work which Tyndale translated.

Tyndale translated the whole of the New Testament and a considerable portion of the Old, and his work is the foundation on which all subsequent English Bible translation is built. Shortly after his death the atmosphere in England grew more favorable to Bible translation. While the rise of humanism and the Renaissance movement in general had put new and stronger weapons in the hands of those who argued in favor of Bible translation, and helped to produce a series of significant changes in European thought and culture, the invention of printing had enabled these changes to develop with unprecedented rapidity and had also made it increasingly difficult for the authorities to prevent the circulation in large numbers of prohibited works. The abuses of the Church, the new attitude to religion that was in part produced by these abuses, the rediscovery of forgotten aspects of the ancient world, the development of a new Greek and Hebrew scholarship and the invention of printing—these were the factors that combined to speed the pace and improve the quality of English Bible translation. At the time of Tyndale's death his victory was already assured.

In England the situation was further helped by the changing political situation. Henry VIII found the Reformation helpful in his personal difficulties, and throughout the many changes in the theory and practice of Church government in England for which he was responsible the cause of the English Bible steadily progressed. In 1530, while strongly condemning Tyndale's translation and prohibiting Bible translation, Henry nevertheless affirmed his intention of providing for an authorized translation when the time was appropriate. Five years later the first complete printed English Bible appeared, the work of Miles Coverdale, a man inspired by the same ideals as Tyndale but milder in his views and more compromising in character. This was not the authorized version for which the English bishops were preparing, but Coverdale assumed that his work would be acceptable to the king. A later edition of Coverdale's Bible, published in 1537, bears the legend: "Set forth with the Kynges moost gracious licence." The main battle had been won, and the 1537 quarto edition of Coverdale's Bible was the first "authorized version" of the Bible in English. Henceforth the fight was to be concentrated not on the right to translate but on the improvement of the translation.

Coverdale's was not an original translation from the Hebrew and Greek but a version derived from later Latin and German versions. Though his style lacked the fine simplicity of Tyndale's, it was smooth and free flowing and contributed substantially to the rhythms of later English renderings. From now on translations followed closely on one another's heels. The same year that Coverdale's first authorized version appeared saw the publication of Matthew's Bible, also "set forth with the King's most gracious licence," and strongly supported by the bishops. Matthew's Bible was a composite version, made up of Tyndale's translation of as much of the Old Testament as he had translated, Coverdale's translation of the remainder of the Old Testament and Tyndale's New Testament. It was this Bible that was the basis for the series of revisions that culminated in the King James, or Authorized, Version of 1611. Its imperfections were freely admitted by the bishops, even though Archbishop Cranmer promoted it as strongly as he could, and the Great Bible, a revision of Matthew's Bible made by Coverdale at the instance of Thomas Cromwell, was published in April, 1540. By this time public Bible reading had become widespread and the readings were often accompanied by scenes almost riotous in their enthusiasm. Thus we find that, while the Great Bible was ordered to be set up in every parish church, provisions were made against the misuse of Bible reading, readers being enjoined not to read "with loud and high voices" or in a disputatious frame of mind, but "humbly, meekly and reverently."

By this time citations of biblical texts in English were freely used to challenge specific practices of the Church. Fox, for example, tells the story of a young man refusing to kneel down before the crucifix and quoting from the Bible in justification, "Thou shalt not make any graven image, nor bow down to it, to worship it." The English Bible was rapidly becoming a familiar part of the ordinary Englishman's intellectual equipment. Further, while in the Middle Ages only the Psalms and the more picturesque narratives were generally known of the Old Testament, from this time on the Hebrew prophets, almost unknown earlier, began to influence men's minds and imaginations.

The Great Bible ran into many editions, but there were continuous suggestions of a further revision. On the death of Edward VI the progress of English Bible translation was temporarily halted. Queen Mary was a

Catholic, and on her accession the printing of vernacular Bibles in England came to an abrupt stop. Many of the Protestants most interested in Bible translation went into exile, and it was at the colony of these exiles at Geneva that the next English translation of the Bible was made. The Geneva Bible, published at Geneva in 1557, was a thorough revision of the Great Bible after the original texts with the help of such other versions and aids to translation as had recently appeared on the Continent. The most accurate and scholarly English translation yet made, the Geneva Bible is not in the direct line of succession of the Authorized Version, though it was fairly heavily drawn upon by the King James translators. On the whole, the Geneva translators sacrificed style to accuracy, and there is a pedantic flavor about the work, particularly noticeable in the spelling of proper names.

The accession of Queen Elizabeth marked a reversion to middle-of-the-road Protestant policy. The Great Bible was once again ordered to be set up in churches (the Geneva Bible, being the work of more extreme Protestants who were considerably to the "left" of Elizabeth's Anglican Church, was not officially recognized). In 1568 the Great Bible was superseded by a further revision made by a company of bishops, and hence known as the Bishops' Bible. This version was not, however, altogether successful. A combination of the work of different revisers working with little common policy or discipline, it is patchy and uneven, and in accuracy considerably behind the Geneva Bible, which continued to be the most popular translation in England until after 1611. Finally, when James I ascended the throne in 1603 he appointed a company of learned men consisting of the most competent Hebrew and Greek scholars available (excluding, however, those who were definitely antagonistic to the Anglican Church) to prepare a great new revision. This work, begun in 1604 and completed seven years later, after meticulous and carefully co-ordinated labor, has remained *the* English Bible ever since. There have been more scholarly versions made in the past three-quarters of a century, but none has rivaled the Authorized Version of 1611 in literary quality and none has had the great literary influence of that extraordinary work.

It has often been remarked that the Authorized Version was the work of a syndicate, yet is a total work of art with all the marks of individual genius. This mystery becomes less baffling when we realize that the diction of the English Bible was forged in almost a century's experimentation and was an organic and not a mechanical development. The Authorized Version was the culmination of that development. And when we further realize—as has already been noted—that this development took place during the most brilliant experimental period in the whole history of English literature, we can understand something of what lies behind the diction of this translation.

By the time the Authorized Version appeared the English Bible had been accepted for several generations as the great basic document of English civilization. Theologians, moralists, philosophers, poets, political thinkers and economists turned to it for inspiration, for historical facts, arguments, images, principles and theories. The extent to which the great debate on the nature of political freedom, which raged in England throughout the Civil War and indeed throughout almost the whole of the seventeenth century, drew its inspiration from biblical sources has never yet been fully appreciated by political historians. Anyone who has studied the debates in the Long Parliament and the innumerable pamphlets and tracts of a sociologico-religious or politico-religious nature that fell in a tremendous flood from the printing presses of the period cannot have failed to notice the underlying biblical inspiration. There was an inspiration both in style and in ideas. The various Puritan sects which advocated different types of democratic organization and whose discussions of the nature of liberty contributed more than has yet been conceded to the development of British democratic ideals, were trying to apply biblical principles to the modern world. And though with the Restoration this kind of activity subsided, its effect was by no means lost, and it continued in a milder form throughout subsequent ages. It might further be pointed out that behind the American Constitution and the American Bill of Rights lies the English Bill of Rights of 1689 and all those theories of individual liberty so fiercely debated by Puritan students of the Bible in the seventeenth century and later, given more polished and equable form in the writings of philosophers such as Locke. The influence of the English Bible here will bear much further investigation.

4

We have not mentioned all the English translations made before the Authorized Version, nor have we discussed in any detail the kinds of biblical style developed between 1523 and 1611. A full treatment of these aspects of the subject would require a volume. The main point for our present discussion is that the Authorized Version represents at the same time the culmination of almost a century's work in English Bible translation and one of the greatest literary masterpieces in the language. This twofold aspect accounts in part for the strength of its influence. For a great body of Protestants, both Puritans and Anglicans and, later, a variety of nonconforming sects, the English Bible was the authentic voice of God and could be appealed to, quoted, and directly and indirectly referred to in innumerable ways. Hundreds of biblical texts in the Authorized translation became proverbs and household words in English homes. And though there was a great deal of what their opponents called "canting" among

Puritan quoters of the Bible, among the majority of the people such quotation became a natural embellishment of serious speech. And while the English Bible was working among the people this way and enriching popular speech, which in turn enriched the speech of writers like Bunyan, literary men irrespective of religious belief were assimilating its stylistic riches. The English Bible thus came into English literature both directly and indirectly—indirectly through its influence on popular speech and directly through the conscious utilization of biblical rhythms, images or diction by writers from Milton to Ruskin and beyond.

That this influence was making itself felt before the Authorized Version had become the accepted translation is made clear by the attitude toward the Bible of writers who used other versions. Shakespeare, for example, used the Geneva version, drawing upon it freely for illustration and allusion and taking for granted that his audience would immediately see the references. In this he was typical of a host of writers of his own time and later who often achieved some of their most brilliant effects by such use of biblical sources. The actual vocabulary of the English Bible introduced many new words and familiarized many others which had been in little use previously. Nothing exercises a developing language more effectively than its use in translation. Words and phrases such as "loving-kindness," "tender mercy" (both first introduced by Coverdale), "beautiful" (not found before Tyndale) and numerous others, both gentle and stern, pastoral and passionate, realistic and highly figurative, entered into the English literary language through English Bible translation. The rich imagery of the Song of Songs, the melancholy lyricism of *Kohelet*, the pithy aphorisms of Proverbs—their influence is everywhere in English prose and poetry. In one short piece alone, David's lament for Jonathan, there are half a dozen phrases that have become part of the English language: "how are the mighty fallen," "in their death they were not divided," "swifter than eagles, stronger than lions." One could write a volume on the influence of the Book of Job alone, and a whole treatise on the use of the word "shepherd," both as noun and as verb, deriving from the first verse of Psalm 23. The use of the words prompted by the Bible does not confine itself to the serious use of the original context: the treatise on the use of "shepherd" would have to take up, for example, the ironic and humorous use of the term as applied by Tony Weller to the Reverend Mr. Stiggins in Dickens's *Pickwick Papers*. Too much "canting" by Puritans led to a secondary use of such words, an ironical use which, though only indirectly attributable to the Bible, has had a great deal of influence on English speech and in English fiction.

As far as actual influence on style is concerned, the Psalms, the Prophetic books and the "Writings" had much more influence than the Pentateuch, whose narrative style is extremely primitive (any number of short sentences linked by "and") and whose influence manifested itself through the use of biblical stories rather than through any imitation of rhythm or cadence. But the passionate rhythm of the Hebrew prophets is to be found in much nineteenth-century prose, just as the cadences of the Psalms can be found in both prose and poetry in that century. And as there is some evidence that the translators of the Authorized Version made an attempt to preserve something of the Hebrew rhythm (or what they conceived to be the Hebrew rhythm) in their English rendering, especially in the Prophets, the link with the original text here is more definite than might be thought.

Seventeenth-century English literature is so rich in works showing biblical influence of every kind that it is impossible to deal with this influence in short compass. Though the prose of the period is often more influenced by Latin and Greek models than by the prose of the English Bible, and writers like Robert Burton, Sir Thomas Browne and Jeremy Taylor turned to the classics for their literary inspiration, biblical influence on the poetry of the period and on the controversial tracts on religious and political subjects was continuous. But here, as we have seen, it is difficult to separate religious from purely biblical influence: the two become so intertwined in the religious poetry of the century (and so much of the best poetry of the century was religious) that one cannot isolate the influence of the Bible as a book from that of the Bible as the source document of the Christian religion. Yet in the poetry of George Herbert, for example, there is found that combination of gravity and simplicity which, as a quality of *style*, clearly owes something to English biblical prose. A line like, "But thou shalt answer, Lord, for me," could not have been written if the Psalms had never been translated into English. As a rule it is in those poets whose emotion is more restrained and whose passion is under control that the biblical influence is most clearly discernible: we can see it in Herbert but not in Crashaw, in Vaughan and Marvell more than in Donne. And we can see it in a different sense in the great satires of Dryden, which drew on biblical characters and incidents with a confidence that amounts to nonchalance.

Milton perhaps more than any other English poet was conscious of the twofold value of the Bible—its moral teaching and its literary qualities. Though by no means a typical Puritan, he had the typical Protestant attitude toward the Bible as the final court of appeal for all Christians: "Let them chant what they will of prerogatives, we shall tell them of Scripture; of custom, we of Scripture; of Acts and Statutes, still of Scripture . . ." He also recognized the number of literary forms contained in the biblical writings, and deliberately modeled his own *Paradise Regained* on the Book of Job. A humanist as well as a Puritan, a lover of the Latin and Greek classics as well as the Scriptures, Milton was able to reconcile the

religious and the aesthetic aspects of the Bible just as he reconciled classical
with biblical imagery. Early Christian practice had long established the
tradition of retaining classical gods as Christian devils, and Milton saw the
advantages of this combination for poetic expression. As a result, he gives
us, from his earliest period, examples of combined biblical and pagan
allusions done with complete confidence:

> *Peor,* and *Baalim,*
> Forsake their Temples dim,
>   With that twice batter'd god of *Palestine,*
> And moonèd *Ashtaroth,*
> Heav'n's queen and mother both,
>   Now sits not girt with tapers' holy shrine,
> The Lybic *Hammon* shrinks his horn,
> In vain the *Tyrian* Maids their wounded *Thammuz* mourn.
>
> And sullen *Moloch,* fled,
> Hath left in shadows dred,
>   His burning Idol all of blackest hue;
> In vain with cymbals ring,
> They call the grisly king,
>   In dismal dance about the furnace blue;
> The brutish gods of *Nile* as fast,
> *Isis* and *Orus,* and the Dog *Anubis* haste.
>   —Ode on the Morning of Christ's Nativity—The Hymn
>   [Author's italics]

Throughout all of Milton's prose and poetry Bible names and images
recur. The fact that his greatest works are on biblical themes makes this
the more appropriate. But in general the style as such is influenced more
by classical than by biblical models, though in *Paradise Regained* and
Samson Agonistes he deliberately cultivated a less ornate style closer to
at least one kind of biblical style than to that of classical epic.

John Bunyan's use of the Bible was more direct and more naïve than
that of Milton. He adopted the Bible's simpler narrative style, making
frequent use of the actual language of the Authorized Version. Bunyan's
clear prose narrative played its part in the simplification of English prose
that went on in the late seventeenth and the early eighteenth century, and
thus we can trace some connection between biblical English prose and the
prose of Sir William Temple and Joseph Addison, which in turn laid the
foundations for generations of later English prose writers.

The growth of hymn writing in the eighteenth century, attributable in
large measure to the Wesleyans, did not, as might have been expected,
bring the language of the English Bible more and more into English
diction, for hymns were by nature nonbiblical—they were the alternative

to Scripture reading and biblical paraphrases, using more everyday speech and, often, exhibiting more sentimental attitudes. Even the hymns of William Cowper, often based on specific biblical texts, can hardly be said to be in any sense biblical in their language except for the actual references to the texts used. On the whole, the influence of the English Bible in the eighteenth century took the form of unconscious assimilation of the images and expressions of a familiar text. The direct and conscious influences were almost always classical—and because they were so direct and conscious not always so happy in their results, perhaps, as the less deliberately sought influence of the Bible. At any rate, it is worth remembering that the style of Johnson and Gibbon and the less successful styles of their imitators are classical and not biblical in their inspiration, though, of course, by this time no writer (and least of all Johnson) could have written at length in prose without displaying in his work some of the effects of generations of Bible reading.

"Generations of Bible reading"—the phrase is worth pondering. For the English, perhaps more than any other people in Europe, were Bible *readers*. The Bible was read, both silently and aloud, in innumerable families throughout the country from the late sixteenth century until the late nineteenth, and even today there is much more knowledge of the English Bible among the people of Britain than there is in the United States, in spite of the fact that there are in the latter country whole areas and communities where a lively evangelical tradition has kept Bible reading very much alive. The effect of this continuous Bible reading among the people of Britain was to acquaint all classes with a vocabulary and a number of literary styles (for, as we have noted, the Bible has many styles) that were constantly working on both the spoken and the written English language.

The English poets of the eighteenth and nineteenth centuries drew as naturally on the English Bible for imagery and allusion as if the book had been an original English masterpiece bearing the same relation to later literature as the *Iliad* and the *Odyssey* did to later Greek writing. Some, like Byron, drew deliberately on Old Testament stories and ideas. Among the nineteenth-century prose writers Ruskin was perhaps the most influenced by the Authorized Version. He was brought up to read it regularly, and he more than once testified to the effect this reading had on his literary taste and prose style. Knowing much of the English Bible by heart, he wrote, "it was not possible for me, even in the foolishest times of youth, to write entirely superficial or formal English." Ruskin was also one of those who was profoundly influenced by the ideals of social justice proclaimed by the Hebrew prophets, and in this he was typical of his age, for as the nineteenth century advanced there was a distinct tendency to turn away from those aspects of the Bible which had most influenced earlier writers and to dwell on those books which had been less dwelt on previously. The tendency was, as far as the Old Testament was concerned, away from Law and toward the Prophets. Isaiah, Amos, Hosea and Malachi became more popular than the Pentateuch and the historical books, and their words were often consciously echoed by the increasing number of those who were preoccupied with the problems of social and economic reform. Among English writers and thinkers today this tendency continues to be strong, and there are many who, while turning away from the more specifically theological formulations of religious doctrine, have sought inspiration for a creed of humanistic reform from the passionate and noble utterances of the Hebrew prophets. Among adherents of all religious faiths and of none, the Bible thus continues to exert influence, and to the various kinds of influence the English Bible has had in the past—influence as a source of images and symbols, as a source of literary forms, as a series of models in prose style, as a storehouse of moral and religious ideas— there is now to be added its contribution toward the formulation of a dynamic social philosophy.

Brief though this discussion has been, and few and sketchy as have been the illustrations of the argument, enough has perhaps been said to make clear the extraordinary way in which the Bible has worked in English literature. Because English Protestantism drew equal strength from the humanistic scholarship of the Renaissance and the individualism of the Reformation, insisting equally on broad learning and on the popularizing of the fruits of that learning, the English Bible became at the same time a moral and an aesthetic force. That strange but significant old Hebrew phrase "the beauty of holiness" thus found a new interpretation in the history of English literature, whose development illustrated time and again that wisdom and beauty were bound up with each other. There was a classical ideal at work here too, the Socratic identification of virtue with knowledge and the implied Platonic association of the aesthetic with the moral. In a sense it can be said that the English tradition at its best and most characteristic always tended to interpret the Bible in the light of classical humanism, and thus to avoid pedantry in its view of either. English literature is, on the whole, moral without being didactic and humanistic without being pagan. In the first of these qualities it differs from the German, and in the second from the French. It is not extravagant to see the basis of this English *via media* in the fact that the Bible became known to Englishmen in a book which was regarded at the same time as a great religious and a great literary document. Thus the Puritan read it for its doctrine and fell under its literary spell, and the skeptic read it as a work of art and imbibed its morality. Which of the two profited more is a question that can be debated forever.

NOTES

[1a Cf. above Robert Gordis, "The Bible as a Cultural Monument," pp. 490 f.]

[2a Cf. below Frederick Lehner, "The Influence of the Bible on European Literature," pp. 1134-1135.]

SELECT BIBLIOGRAPHY

BAIKIE, JAMES, *The English Bible and Story: Its growth, its translators, and their adventures.* London, 1928.

BOWEN, FRANCIS, *A Layman's Story of the English Bible considered in its Literary and Secular Aspect.* New York, 1885.

BUTTERWORTH, CHARLES C., *The Literary Lineage of the King James Bible, 1340-1611.* Philadelphia, 1941.

COOK, ALBERT, S., *Biblical Quotations in Old English Prose Writers.* London, 1898.

————, *The Authorized Version of the Bible and its Influence.* New York, 1910.

DAICHES, DAVID, *The King James Version of the English Bible.* Chicago, 1941.

DEANESLEY, MARGARET, *The Lollard Bible and other Medieval Biblical Versions.* Cambridge, 1920.

GRIERSON, SIR HERBERT, *The English Bible.* London, 1943.

LOWES, JOHN L., "The Noblest Monument in English Prose," in *Essays in Appreciation.* Boston and New York, 1936.

McAFEE, CLELAND B., *The Greatest English Classic: a Study of the King James Version of the Bible and its Influence on life and literature.* New York and London, 1912.

McCLURE, JAMES G., *The Supreme Book of Mankind: The Origin and Influence of the English Bible.* New York, 1930.

McCOMB, SAMUEL, *The Making of the English Bible, with an Introductory Essay on the Influence of the English Bible on English Literature.* New York, 1909.

MOULTON, RICHARD G., *The Literary Study of the Bible.* Boston, 1899.

NOBLE, RICHMOND, *Shakespeare's Biblical Knowledge.* London and New York, 1935.

POLLARD, ALFRED W., *Records of the English Bible.* Oxford, 1911.

SANDS, P. C., *Literary Genius of the Old Testament.* Oxford, 1924.

WESTCOTT, BROOKE F., *A General View of the History of the English Bible* (3d. ed. rev. by W. A. Wright). London and New York, 1905.

WORK, E. W., *The Bible in English Literature.* New York, 1917.

CHAPTER 29

THE INFLUENCE OF THE BIBLE ON EUROPEAN LITERATURE

By Frederick Lehner

It is nothing new to consider the Bible not only as a religious document but also as a great work of literature, an anthology containing historical reports, poetry, short stories, one philosophical drama and illuminated, apocalyptic writings. As literature, it follows the laws of all great literary works: it is a creation of lofty imagination, and it influences writers of the following generations and centuries to appropriate from its content whatever they decisively may feel as new, startling, impressive, stimulating thought and provoking imagination. Indeed, as an anthology of literature, as a source of stories, forms and ideas, the Bible became bread and meat for centuries to come. To be exact, the Bible did not enter the mind of continental Europe as a Jewish document; it became influential as a part of the Old and New Testament, and it took centuries before its specific essence was recognized. First it became a part of the intellectual property through the channels of Christianity.

Thus it was not the Hebrew original—even though the study of the original never was discontinued—it was not even the first Latin translation that created the miracle, that interested nations in Hebrew stories and history and philosophy; it was rather the Latin version of the Hebrew Bible by Jerome (fifth century) that helped the Oriental tales to shine and sparkle in a new setting. At first, of course, its influence was not wide, but when the monasteries sent out missionaries to win over native tribes to Christianity, especially in the eighth, ninth and tenth centuries, the Jewish legends went along with the Christian legends. Soon the Hebrew report about the Creation replaced the report of the Icelandic saga, the story of the tree Yggdrasil. Soon the tragic stories of the Fall, the First Murder, Sodom and Gomorrah, the Flood, the Tower of Babel appeared in many variations, sometimes distorted, more naïve than the original. Then the first epics and plays about Joseph were written, about Moses, Judith, Solomon, Daniel, Susanna and the Elders. Topics and forms abounded. And soon we can perceive several different trends. We can see how topics were discovered and used, how the Psalms became an essential part of the Christian service, how the many apocalyptic dreams in the Bible provoked new utterings and new mystical outbursts, far from the mystical world of Jerusalem.

What could the Bible offer other than what was offered by the other major traditions or legacies of imagination, fiction and folklore? The four great traditions which influenced and formed European literature in its various manifestations were the Hebrew, the Greek, the Germanic and the Celtic. The Germanic tradition (*Edda*) and the Celtic (*Les Chevaliers de la Table Ronde*) appeared and disappeared again, as well as the Hebrew and the Greek, but they did not have the general appeal, the great and persistent influence on *all* Continental literatures; they did not have the extraordinary and absolute value of the Greek and Hebrew legacies. These two, certainly, were responsible for the spirit of Western civilization; they served as its pillars of beauty and intellectual strength. They formed our world, though in different ways, sometimes alternately, sometimes together, and each according to its special essence, inherent in its spiritual body. If "the governing idea of Hellenism is spontaneity of consciousness,"[1] that of Hebraism is strictness of conscience. Where one legacy stated the problem, the other made it ethical. "It is in the confluence of the Hellenic stream of thought with the waters that flow from Hebrew sources that the main direction of world's progress is to be sought."[2] In this report we are concerned only with one part of the problem. We shall try to observe the influence of the Bible on Continental European literature, to follow this influence, and to analyze its aspects and importance.

Such an influence can be found in many regions and sections of what we call literature. We can easily discover that certain stories, topics, tales of the Bibles were taken out of their (religious) context, and told, retold, changed in many curious ways. There is, however, to begin with, the problem of the language itself, a fact that should not be neglected.

In an essay contained in the Oxford *Legacy of Israel*,[3] Laurie Magnus cites good English material to make this point clear. He quotes a poem by Matthew Arnold (*Sohrab and Rustum*) and another poem by Alfred Lord Tennyson (*Ulysses*), and shows rather clearly that, when we analyze their language, the structure of their thoughts, the images and similes, we discover that the Oriental poem by Arnold owes its poetical structure to Greece, while the Greek poem by Tennyson is full of biblical echoes.

This influence of the Bible on the interior construction of a poem, the molding of its expression, the selection of its comparisons, for instance, can be exemplified by the authors of other nations as well: Dante, for instance. In general it can be said that from single words to images, from images to the entire mode of the expression, from expression to topics, philosophy— every kind of influence can be detected in the European languages and literatures. "Sodom and Gomorrah," to cite some examples, the "Tower of

Babel," the "Hueter meines Bruders," "the keeper of my brother," the "calf of gold," a whole world of words, images and ready-made thoughts have remained alive and have been added to the languages of Germanic, Romance and Slavic roots as well. Magnus, in his contribution to the *Legacy of Israel*, proves even more, on the same level. He shows how not only in English, but in other languages as well, "the Hebrew simile has become naturalized." To explain his point he states that the Greek writer compares one element with another, and elaborates the second. The Hebrew simile elaborates the first element as it speaks of it in terms of the second. ("*He* shall be like a tree, *his* leaf also shall not wither.")[4] And the Continent imitates the example.

The historical development of this phenomenon follows a common trend. Often-quoted material influences our thinking to the very expression of thoughts: the Bible, obviously, was often quoted. And as this material found its way to European minds, first mostly through the medium of Latin, the perennial language of the Church, the phenomenon of this influence became genuinely visible only with the Reformation, when Luther's Bible in the German vernacular created the German *Schriftsprache*. This translation and the King James Version[4a] in English-speaking countries and the corresponding efforts in France, in Italy and in Spain popularized the original text and wording of the New and the Old Testament in a tremendously successful and efficient way. The original text became known not only to scholars or priests, not only to educated laymen, but to everyone who could read. And not only certain basic books dealing with scientific topics became afterwards a "Bible" whose pronouncements were law; the Bible itself became a "Bible" in this respect and was consulted, quoted and understood. Let us now proceed to its influence on topics.

The so-called *Wiener Genesis*—the manuscript is of the twelfth century —is the oldest of the many religious poems written in the Austrian Carinthia and based on the Bible.[5] It was written because the Roman Church demanded in its *Breviarium* that the *lectiones* during the time from Septuagesima Sunday to Tuesday after Quadragesima be based on chapters 1 to 14 of Genesis.[6] Thus the poem, as it was preserved for us in the different manuscripts, contained especially two lessons, the Creation and the Fall. (Another chapter, however, added to those two, deals with Cain and Abel, and others with Noah, with Abraham, with Isaac and his sons, and with Joseph in Egypt.) To the same epoch, about 1220, belong two other manuscripts, two epics about Exodus, as described in the first fifteen chapters of the Second Book of Moses.[7] The poem followed the text of the Itala. We have also a separate poem dealing with Moses, a Balaam, two Judiths (mostly to be found among the manuscripts of the Vorau monastery), a *Lob Salomos*, the *Juenglinge in dem Feuerofen*, fragments of a book about the Maccabees, an Esdras, an Isaiah, and a Song of Songs translated in 1276 by Brub von Scombeck, constable of Magdeburg.

These stories and poems taken from the Hebrew Bible were also stories in the medieval tradition. Wherever there was an opportunity to adjust the foreign context to the surrounding European and Christian world, it was done. When the plants of Paradise were described, the poet found his material in the description of a model garden as it was given in Charlemagne's *Capitulare de Villis.*[8] In the *Exodus* we have an elaborate presentation of a medieval army, even the grasshoppers, frogs and flies were enemy armies and described as such. But to summarize, if we take the German epics mentioned above as an example of what happened in all civilized districts of continental Europe, we may correctly conclude that an essential part of the Hebrew Bible was known to every educated man of the twelfth century. But it came to him as a part of the Christian legacy, and the ethical or philosophical content of the Jewish stories was taken purely as a forethought of what was expressed with greater clarity in the Gospels of the New Faith. At any rate, this first approach proved not only stimulating; it was also carried over as a durable element into European literature.

The topics from the Hebrew Bible, of course, were not only chosen by the monks in Austria and Franconia, who described them in hymns or epics or songs. In France, too, the Bible attracted creative minds. If we follow the report given by Bédier and Hazard, we learn that translations of parts of the Bible in prose or in verse, poems taken from this or that chapter of the Scriptures were done in the twelfth century.[9] There are translations of the Psalms, the first of them in the first half of that century; there is a version in verse of Genesis (by Everat for the Comtesse Marie de Champagne) from 1190. In the same year the Hebrew and the New Testament were put into verses by Herman de Valenciennes; and other attempts of this kind followed. And here and there in Europe the *fratres* imitated the French and German example.

In the twelfth century, however, another type of literature, *the drama,* also discovered the treasures hidden in the Hebrew Bible. The oldest drama written in French dates from the twelfth century. It is called *Représentation d'Adam*[10] (author unknown), and again we are back to our topic. This *mystère,* as the religious tragedies were called, presents first the *Paradis terrestre,* then the Temptation and the Fall of Adam and Eve. We see the murder of Abel, after which the prophets parade by and announce the arrival of the Messiah. It is a lively play, and really dramatic, truly medieval and truly French, especially in the scenes of the temptation. This play, however, was only a beginning. The end of the development can be found in the *Cycle de l'Ancien Testament,* a compilation into one great work which was made in the course of the second half of the fifteenth century.[11] The opus is composed of fifty thousand verses. This play was performed in Paris in 1542 by the *Confrères de la Passion* in the Hôtel de Flandres, and proved to be a great success. "*L'entrée coûtait deux sous par personne; et une loge, trente sous pour toute la durée de la représentation qui remplit environ vingt séances.*"[12] But this tradition was stopped by the Arrêt du Parlement de Paris (November 17, 1548), which banned *all* religious plays from the stage, including the *Mystère du Vieux Testament*. Nevertheless, it was not very long before the specific value of the topic overcame the ban, and the colorful and thrilling stories of the Bible reappeared on the stage, this time no more as *mystère* nor as *moralité*, but as plots of Renaissance tragedies, climaxed in *Les Juives* by Robert Garnier (1580) and in *Esther* by Jean Racine (1688-1689). Before we proceed to describe this change and new life, however, we have to see what happened in other European countries, especially in Spain.[12a]

In the Iberian Peninsula there was no parliament that forbade the performance of religious plays. The great flowering of these plays was never interrupted by decree. Unfortunately, we do not know too much about their beginnings. But we do know that in the first half of the sixteenth century Diego Sanchez wrote a *Farsa de Salomón*, a *Farsa de Isaac*, a *Farsa de Abrahám, de Moysén, del Rey David*, topics chosen again because of their "close symbolic relationship to Christ's sacrifice."[13] In the second half of the century Micael de Carvajal wrote a *Tragedia Josephina* which deals with the sale of Joseph by his brothers, with his stay in Egypt and the death of Jacob. The most important document, however, is the great Codex at the Biblioteca Nacional (1550-1575) containing ninety-six religious plays, twenty-six of which deal with material taken from the Hebrew Bible.[14] If we look into details, two of these plays treat Adam, one treats Cain and Abel, three deal with Abraham, four with Jacob, two with Joseph and three with Moses, the lawgiver. The ratio is, as we see, twenty-six to ninety-six; that is to say, one-fourth of the entire corpus was taken from the Hebrew Bible, which proves how useful the plots seemed to be for dramatists, and how well they lent themselves to the special treatment of playwrights. We find here, for instance, an *Aucto de los hierros de Adán*, and an *Aucto de la lucha de Jacob con el ángel*, or an *Aucto de la deposório de Moysén*, an *Aucto del rey Nabucdonosor cuando se hizo adorar*, an *Aucto del sueño de Nabucdonosor*, religious plays with familiar topics. And here, too, the subjects correspond to the *lectiones* in Septuagesima, Sexuagesima and the Quadragesima season of the Catholic service, as we had observed when we looked into the epics of the German Middle Ages. And at the time when the religious epic in Central Europe began to lose its appeal, when the religious drama reached its climax in

Spain with Lope de Vega and Calderón de la Barca, the religious epic found its most perfect fulfillment in Italy; the Bible proved again to be a stimulating force demanding respect, offering stories, characters and philosophical insight even into the modern life of the fourteenth century.

If we follow Vossler in his *Medieval Culture*,[15] which is an introduction to Dante and his times, we are soon convinced that the great Italian poet considered the Bible not only a religious document. It was not only Divine truth for him; it was Divine poetry as well. The *Divine Comedy* may be called a summary of the ethical, religious and aesthetic tendencies of the Middle Ages ("the voice of ten silent centuries"). Thus we find in it all the features that belong to such a representation. And the Bible meant for Dante not only the specifically Christian, but the Hebrew Scriptures as well. We find here indeed an extreme reverence for the word and the letter of the Hebrew legacy, we find an almost jealous effort to extract from the pictures in the biblical stories and from their poetic contents more or less general philosophical concepts. We find also that Dante deduced from them moral commandments, and we find mystical significance. It is again Vossler who points out the tremendous influence of the language of the Bible in Dante's work.[16] He shows how Dante's memory was full of biblical reminiscences and pictures. And, true, the Bible is the most-quoted book in his writings. "He [Dante] had it in his head and heart better than many professional clerics."[17] Dante took over unchanged whole sentences, figures, comparisons, similes, especially in his early works. In the *Divine Comedy* this method, this *hantise*, reached its climax. Dante presents the whole cast of the Bible; he presents Adam and Eve, Cain and Abel, Abraham, Rachel, Rebecca, Sarah, Isaac and Esau, Jacob and his sons, the kings, the prophets, the Maccabees, Esther, Ruth, and so on. He presents Cain in the first part of the poem, in *Inferno*, then he lifts him up into *Purgatorio* and we meet the sinner finally even in *Paradiso*, Dante's heaven. But this lavish use of heroes, patriarchs, personages from the Hebrew Bible must not obscure the fact that here again the Jewish men and women are taken from the Christian Bible, of which the Old Testament is a part. Their presence has to be justified. Dante does this very soon, in the beginning of the poem. He crosses a rather Greek landscape in order to enter the Inferno, and among the first people he meets there are the great persons belonging to Jewish antiquity. They are to be found in the first Circle already, in the Limbo, or the borderland of the Unbaptized.[18] It is true, admits Dante, that they have their merit, but to have merit is not enough so long as you have not been baptized. Thus we meet the shades of the First Parent, of Abel, of Noah and Moses, of Abraham, David, Israel with his father and his children and Rachel. If anything is comforting in this picture it is this: we meet them in good company, for soon after them we see Homer, the sovereign poet,

Horace, Ovid, Lucan, Plato, Socrates, Orpheus, Hippocrates and Saladin. And when Dante uses some striking picture taken from the Hebrew Bible, Jacob's dream, for example, he soon shapes the tale into a new form, and the ladder into heaven becomes a representation of contemplative monasticism. But the beginning of the poem is pure Jeremiah. There is the wilderness in which we find ourselves, "midway upon the journey of our life"; there is the lion out of Jeremiah's forest ("which will slay them"); there is the wolf of Jeremiah of the evening ("which will spoil them"); there is the leopard ("which shall watch over their cities") and "everyone that goeth out thence shall be torn to pieces." A good example of the method Dante used to transform the biblical picture and text is given in the passage quoted by Vossler to prove the same point. Of the mysterious tree in Paradise, he says:

Two shoots from this plant first appear on the sixth cornice of the Purgatorical mountain: first, as actual means of punishments, second, as magical mouthpieces of moral admonition and warning. Thirdly, we find on the summit of the mountain the tree of knowledge itself, as a comprehensive allegory, full of philosophic, ethical, and political instruction. All the transformations from sensuous materialization to moralizing, and even to intellectualizing, are here passed through, and according to its needs the Biblical tree receives the most varied and marvelous environment.[19]

Dante, however, not only quoted and transformed the Bible and transplanted its content into the ideas and symbols of the medieval world. His work reveals also that in his soul there slumbered a more deeply rooted affinity with that part of the biblical tradition which comes from the Prophets. He starts with Jeremiah, as we saw. He possessed not only the voice but also the spirit of a prophet himself.[20] This "inward genuineness" was certainly one of the reasons why Dante often attained a real prophetic style of his own

which is both classic and thoroughly Florentine, wherein the Hebrew elements acquired fresh and eloquent life and were all but recognizable. The single sermon of wrath, *Ahi serva Italia, de dolore ostello,* suffices to convince us that the Old Testament prophets' language of moral indignation is the mightiest of all artistic treasures which the Bible bestowed upon our poet.[21]

In Chapter 1 we meet the four apocalyptic beasts of Jeremiah. In the fourteenth canto of *Inferno* we have Nebuchadnezzar's dream. In *Purgatorio* 29 we meet Ezekiel, in *Paradiso* 15, Isaiah. They certainly live in Dante's work, as stimulants and even more. In his *Divine Comedy*, then, the influence of the Bible reached its climax, as far as the medieval approach is concerned. But with Dante and some minor disciples the trend to quote the Hebrew Bible, to transform its stories and to interpret them so that they might prove the events in the New Testament, also came to an end.

The reason for this change has to be sought in the general development religion went through in the sixteenth century, when the Renaissance introduced Luther's Reformation and Protestantism as its religious counterpart. Not only in Germany, but in France and England also, the ideas of Protestantism proved to be a liberating force.

Through the Reformation the Bible became common property and the new era of its influence can now be detected. Especially in German-speaking countries, where Luther's translation was a sensational event, the social group of the *Buerger* could now read the story of the Creation, of Joseph and of Moses in the vernacular. In the mind of Luther the different tales of the Bible did not have the same value, so that he in a sense overlooked their importance for writers and poets. Thus he was enthusiastic about the Fifth Book of Moses, but he was less interested in the Book of Proverbs. The reason for this is obvious. The *Liber Proverbium Salomonis* is for him *"ein schoenes Buch, denn darin sieht man, wie es in der Welt zugeht"* (a beautiful book, for one can see in it what the world looks like). Further, he disliked the Books Ezra, Judith and Tobias, while Job again was classified as a *"sehr gutes Buch."*[22]

At any rate, his translation proved to be influential and stimulating, even more than his remarks in letters or in his *Tischreden*, although these remarks also opened the way to deeper understanding and appreciation. And to those who believed that the Old Testament was entirely superseded by the Gospels, he answered in clear language: "Ob aber jemand wollte vorgeben, das alte Testament sei aufgehoben und gelte nicht mehr . . . antworte ich: Das ist nicht so . . ." (If someone should think the Old Testament discarded and of no further value, I say: It is not so.)[23] There was no religious epic of importance, however, in the sixteenth century, and it took almost two hundred years before Protestantism in Germany dared to follow the English example given by Milton. Only as late as 1748 was Klopstock ready to publish the first part of his *Messiah*. The reason for this is easy to detect. The people could now read the thrilling stories in the vernacular, and there was no immediate need to rewrite them as tales or poems. The drama, on the other hand, was strongly influenced through Luther's translation and also by his remarks. Translation included not only the Greek but the Hebrew of the Bible. The dramatists, however, ostensibly preferred the Jewish tradition, as these stories could easily be adapted to modern sixteenth-century life.

In France, as we have seen, the presentation of medieval religious plays was forbidden by law; the ban struck also the *mystère* of the Old Testament. In Spain, on the other hand, the Golden Age of the drama, of Lope de Vega and Calderón de la Barca (who used very few tales from the Hebrew Bible), kept the Bible more than ever on the stage. But these authors closely followed the medieval tradition in which the Old Testament had to "prove" the New. In Germany now, through Luther, and after him without interruption, the dramatists of the laymen's *Buerger-spiele* and the writers of the laymen's school theater, in colleges and universities, with enthusiasm and almost incredible haste, appropriated the rich material offered to them by the Bible in the vernacular. All reports show conclusively that now, as no outspoken religious purpose stood behind the undertaking, and nothing had to be proved but moral, ethical issues, the authors of the *Schuldrama*, of the *Buergerspiele*, preferred the colorful tales of the Hebrew Bible to all the other material at their disposal. It is almost unbelievable, notes one authority, to observe what material was taken as a pretext for a drama. The Fall, of course. Then the first murder, the story of the Patriarchs, Moses, the Judges, Susanna and the Elders, the three men in the fiery furnace, the golden calf. In these dramas, certain characters had become typical of certain problems: passionate and criminal love appeared in Joseph; the mad passion of old men for a young woman was depicted in Susanna; harmonious life in the bosom of the family was presented in Rebecca, in Tobias. But there were also Judith and Holofernes, and another Joseph by a Dutch educator, and another Susanna in German and Latin. In brief, after Luther the dramatists preferred the biblical stories above all; they liked the interesting plots as they found them in the new translation of the Old Testament. The Hebrew Bible became secularized.

But there is also another reason why Luther is featured in this report. He translated not only prose and the historical parts of the Bible, he also translated the Psalms and contributed thereby to a renewal of Hebrew poetry.

His translations of certain psalms were not the first. We have already mentioned French attempts to put Hebrew poetry into the vernacular. From the tenth century we have a free Bavarian translation (or adaptation) of Psalm 138, a poem written in the *althochdeutsch* vernacular. No other part of the Bible was taken over so completely and so uniformly as the Psalms: from the beginning they were a part of the Christian service. What Luther added was a new, strong and productive emphasis, a new evaluation of this part of the Bible. And the genuine poetical feeling of his translation in the vernacular transformed certain Hebrew songs (Psalm 46:6: "Eine feste Burg ist unser Gott . . .") into German poems of unusual brilliance. That is to say, before Luther the songs in the Church (including the *Stabat Mater* and the *Dies Irae*) were influenced by Solomon's psalms. Luther brought the tradition closer to the Bible when he tried his hand at Psalms 2, 14, 46, 67, 124, 128, 130. And there was Clément Marot in France, who published a very successful, but poor translation of the Psalms (1541, *Trente Psaumes de David;* 1543, *Cinquante Psaumes*). The Huguenots especially praised him for his work, for the songs *"qu'ils entonnaient en marchant au combat."* The Huguenots needed a hymnbook. This explains the vogue, the immense success of the book. But it was read by the Catholics also. And, according to Bédier, the courtiers at the court of Navarre and the court of France hummed the *Chants de David*, even though the Sorbonne banned the translation. Thus it became a part of the Protestant liturgy, it deeply influenced the development of French poetry in the following centuries, and was followed by another translation, that of Théodore de Bèze (1563). The Catholics soon tried to compete: Le Baïf's attempt dates from 1578. And there were the German Protestant and Catholic poets in the seventeenth century following his example. A new sphere of influence remained active.

The very program of French classicism—the next trend in modernism—seemed to exclude biblical topics; Greek costumes (more than Greek thoughts and philosophy) outlawed all else. All the more, therefore, is it interesting to see how the Jansenist Jean Racine came back to the Bible when he wrote *Esther* for Madame de Maintenon's school for girls in Saint-Cyr. In *Esther* the play follows the Bible closely, except for the smoother, less bloody ending of the French tragedy. It is a hymn to Israel, and not merely superficially, for it owes its plot as well as its style and philosophy to Hebrew tradition. It is true, the *chœur des Israélites* is a chorus in the manner of Greek tragedy. It follows the tradition and the purpose of Greek drama, but the philosophy and the wording come from the Hebrew legacy, from the Psalms. And when we analyze this chorus we find, for instance, the very words of Psalm 121. But the *Esther* of Racine shows still another interesting change. The biblical story is related to prove its own objective, its own philosophy, not—as in the Middle Ages—to prove Christianity. The process of secularization has gone so far that there is not the slightest allusion to another religion. The play is, furthermore, the perfect amalgamation of Greek form and Hebrew content. The king in the play, however, is Louis XIV.

In the eighteenth century, the Protestants, that is to say, Klopstock, Bodmer, Herder and Goethe, lead us to another and different sphere of influence. The reasons for this change are rather complex. As we saw, there was a readiness to reinterpret the Bible, a readiness that came from Luther and the Reformation. But there was also the influence of Jean Jacques Rousseau, whose social philosophy found its way even into the field of literature. The *"retour à la nature"* in literature meant indeed a new flowering of folklore, of original poetry and ideas, an attitude which soon was used in respect to the Hebrew Bible. Rousseau was—in the beginning—less successful with this idea in France than in Germany. The German disciples of Rousseau—Herder above all, and with him the outstanding disciple of Herder, namely Goethe—looked at Hebrew folklore with new eyes. They were no longer interested in the Bible as a religious document (overcoming thereby the Middle Ages, and Luther too), they discovered in the secularized text the loftiest piece of "original" literature. Goethe was so much enchanted by the Bible, so strongly influenced by its stories and ideas, that he asked his father's permission to study Hebrew in order to be able to read the Bible in the original. Remarks about his interest in the Hebrew text abound in his work. The *Jahrmarktsfest in Plundersweilen* includes a playlet dealing with Haman, Mordecai and Esther. In *Dichtung und Wahrheit*, his autobiography, sixty-year-old Goethe expresses rather extensively and in clear words how deeply he is and was influenced by the Bible, meaning the Hebrew text. The same can be said about certain paragraphs in the novel *Wilhelm Meisters Lehrjahre*. The influence continued the older the poet and thinker himself grew, as we can see in the appendix to the *Westoestlicher Divan*, where Goethe's admiration for the Hebrew contribution is expressed. The debt to a great influence reached its climax in the greatest drama the poet conceived. The final stage of Faust's life and his death is clearly developed after the greatest model in the Bible, after Moses' last years and death. The lawmaker Faust closely follows the lawmaker Moses in his last experiences, and the end of Faust's life and his salvation is certainly influenced by the Bible on the highest, the spiritual, level.

All over Europe they soon followed Goethe, even in France where the Age of Enlightenment drove religion underground. A student of details and catalogues will easily find how strong was the influence of the Bible on the French writers, poets and dramatists in the nineteenth century. He has only to search the work of Chateaubriand, Lamartine, Alfred de Vigny, Victor Hugo. The characters, whom Chateaubriand borrowed from the Bible, are no more the *belles infidèles* of Robert Garnier or Racine; they are taken from the Bible itself. The words of the young Eudore in *Les Martyrs* come directly from the Song of Songs: *"Que vous êtes belle, mon amie . . . que la myrrhe et l'aloès couvrent votre lit embaumé!"* And finally, according to a subtle remark of the French poet, André Spire, *"la découverte de la valeur de la Bible par Chateaubriand fut l'origine d'une profonde transformation de la langue littéraire française."*[24] And Lamartine writes: *"Lorsque mon âme enthousiaste ou pieuse ou triste, a besoin de chercher un écho à ses enthousiasmes, à ses piétés, ou à ses mélancholies . . . je n'ouvre ni Pindare, ni Horace, ni Hafiz . . . j'ouvre les psaumes et j'y prends les paroles qui semblent sourdre des siècles et qui pénètrent jusqu'au fonds de l'âme des générations."* And in his tragedy *Saul*, and in other works of inspiring importance, Lamartine rediscovered the lyrical *élan* of the prophets: *"La Providence divine est toujours présente, la pitié pour les pauvres et les déshérités, les appels des opprimés à la miséricorde et à la pitié de Dieu."*[25] And Alfred de Vigny left six biblical poems among the thirty he wrote.

Thus, a student of literary influences will find biblical themes, quotations from biblical material, interpretations of certain tales, biblical similes, images and characters in the works of Michelet, Quinet, Lamennais, James Darmesteter (*La Légende Divine*), Leconte de Lisle. He will discover the unbroken influence of a great legacy in the poems and works of French symbolists, Remy de Gourmont (*Lilith*), Gustave Kahn, Edouard Dujardin. In Germany—where the harvest is less abundant than in France—he will find Hebbel's *Judith*, Gutzkow's *Koenig Saul* and Otto Ludwig's *Makkabaeer*, to mention only writers and plays of great importance.

In France the twentieth century witnessed the *Saül* of André Gide, a play sparkling with intellect; so, too, we have *Judith* by Jean Giraudoux, where the biblical story lends itself to a brilliant play of sophisticated spirit. We have *Semaël* by André Spire, a serious philosophical fantasy. And we have *La première famille* by Jules Supervielle, a biblical farce, surrealist in style, full of that *esprit gaulois*. We have tragedy, comedy, farce. The great Viennese Jewish dramatist and poet, Richard Beer-Hofmann, published his biblical tragedies (*Jakobs Traum, Der junge David*), which enjoyed great success. Stefan Zweig wrote his *Jeremias*. We could point furthermore to the influence of Hebrew poetry—I mean the Psalms—on two French Catholic poets, Péguy and Claudel. But there I should first mention the influence of the Psalms on the *vers libre* of Walt Whitman, and on other forerunners of Claudel. At any rate, we hear an echo from Solomon in the *Grandes Odes* of Claudel, in his dramas, and in the *Mystère d'Eve* by Charles Péguy.

Thus we have reached the climax of a development which began with an old French play, an old German epic. The old sacred story is employed not merely for its narrative, as in the period before Luther; it is adopted not only as a form convenient for moderns. Its potentialities as a symbolic frame for a twentieth century idea or problem are discovered. We turn, therefore, to Thomas Mann's *Joseph* novel. What could a writer of the twentieth century find in the Bible? In a former work Thomas Mann had described successfully the rise and fall of a nineteenth-century bourgeois family; in another novel he described the intellectual, moral and political situation of Europe before the 1914 war. His style was patterned after the style of Goethe, dramatist, novelist and poet of the eighteenth and the early nineteenth century, and his world was seen with the eyes of a naturalist, that is to say, with the eyes of a man who reveals even romantic feelings as "natural" as possible; and his imagination found its expression and its symbols in the intellectual language of a modern twentieth-century thinker. What could he find in the Bible? Well, in a later work he intended to describe, above all, the problems of the twentieth century. He looked around for some *durable* material in which to express his ideas. And as he looked he could find no more adequate a frame for his picture than the one he discovered in the Bible: the adventures of young Joseph, Joseph in Egypt, Joseph the Provider. The reason for this choice was, of course, not superficial; it was a special and inescapable one. In his own words: "The selection of the Old Testament subject was certainly not mere accident." He found in the story of Joseph and his brothers something which could not be expressed in another material, which could not be presented through another symbol, in the same defiant spirit, with the same convincing clearness. The defiant spirit states: "To write a novel of the Jewish spirit was timely, because it seemed untimely,"[26] a remark which reveals more of the author's mood than of his search for a creative theme. And Thomas Mann knows this as well as we do. As a creative spirit he has to follow his own rules, his own inner law. Therefore, he adds to his first statement, that he did not intend to write a hymn of a tradition, a political tract or a religious essay. He was influenced by a great legacy, he was overwhelmed by it, but he was not sold to it. Thus his story follows the report in Genesis, in Thomas Mann's own words, only "with semijocular faithfulness, and often it reads like an exegesis and amplification of the Torah, like a Rabbinical Midrash," and "all that is Jewish, throughout the work, is merely foreground, only *one* style element among others, only one stratum of its language . . ."[27] But even if we do not overlook the self-imposed limitation expressed in these words, we see that such an approach to the original story, to the original spirit of the sacred text, has never been undertaken or dared before. The *Wiener Genesis* was a Hebrew report, but did not show Jewish spirit at all; and Racine's *Esther* celebrated in a Jewish story the glory of King Louis XIV. The Jewish spirit was only the setting, the décor, the costume in those works. Here we discover that it is at least one stratum of its language. And when Thomas Mann was asked what "made [him] turn to this remote, out-of-the-way subject and induced [him] to transform the biblical legend of the Egyptian Joseph into a broad cycle of novels," he answered that he was "delighted" when he read the original, which means that his imagination was caught by the text. Then, "a preliminary probing and productive searching began in [his] mind as to what it would be like to renew and reproduce this charming story in fresh narrative with all the modern means."[28] This final success and reawakening of a centuries-old story would not prove very much if this reawakening were a single fact. Thomas Mann, however, helps us here, too, when he reveals how "almost immediately, these inner experiences [mentioned above] significantly associated themselves with the thought of a tradition: the thought of Goethe, in fact, who relates in his memoirs *Truth and Fiction* how he, as a boy, had dictated the Joseph story to a friend and, in doing so, had woven it into a broad narrative . . ." As an explanation of this youthful and premature adventure, the sixty-year-old Goethe observes, "This natural story is highly amiable, only it seems too short, and one is tempted to carry it out in all its details." And it seems also to be revealing of the attitude of a twentieth-century man who is influenced by the Bible.

"As a man," confesses Thomas Mann, "and as an artist, I must somehow have been in readiness to be productively attracted by such subject matter, and my Bible reading was not mere chance." This readiness has to be explained more elaborately.

The various stages of life have different inclinations, claims, tendencies of taste—as well as abilities and advantages. It is probably a rule that in certain years the taste for all purely individual and particular phenomena, for the *individual case,* for the "bourgeois" aspect, in the widest sense of the word, fades out gradually. Instead, the typical, the *eternally human, eternally recurring, timeless,* in short, the *mythical steps into the foreground of interest.* For, after all, the typical is already the mythical, in so far as it is pristine pattern and pristine form of life, timeless model and formula of old, into which life enters by reproducing its traits of the unconscious.[29]

How far we have come! To take an illustrious example: the Jewish story of Joseph and his brothers appeared and reappeared again and again, as stimulating form and thought-influencing material in European—French, Spanish, German and Italian—literature. It was an epic in the twelfth century in Germany; a play in the thirteenth century in France and Spain; its characters appeared in Italian and Portuguese works of literature; it was a *moralité* in the Germany of the Protestant Reformation, then again (Goethe), and finally an opera and a ballet and a novel. In brief, it was a sacred story in the original text and became a symbol of humanity in the provisional present form.

By this the circle is rounded again. The Bible, a religious work, has proved its inspiring value in the field of literature, too, as an influence on language, images, thought, as a storehouse for fairy tales, moral stories, ethical legends, as a model for new forms in poetry, and as a gold mine for mythical symbols. Its lasting charm has worked on the greatest occasions—in the *Divine Comedy,* in the *Esther* of Racine, in Goethe's *Faust,* in Mann's *Joseph*-novel   as a genuine, sparkling and influential source of inspiration.

NOTES

[1] E. R. Bevan, and C. Singer (eds.), *The Legacy of Israel,* p. 504.
[2] *Ibid.,* pp. 540 f.
[3] *Ibid.,* p. 483.
[4] *Ibid.,* p. 486.

[[4a] Cf. above David Daiches, "The Influence of the Bible on English Literature," p. 1126.]

[5] P. Piper, *Die geistliche Dichtung des Mittelalters,* pp. 87 ff.

[6] *Ibid.,* pp. 91-191.

[7] *Ibid.,* p. 194.

[8] *Ibid.,* p. 12.

[9] J. Bédier and P. Hazard, *Histoire de la littérature française illustrée,* I, 4.

[10] L. Petit de Julleville, *Le Théâtre en France,* p. 3.

[11] *Ibid.,* p. 19.

[12] *Ibid.,* p. 71.

[[12a] For the development in English literature cf. Daiches *op. cit.*]

[13] J. P. Crawford, *Spanish drama before Lope de Vega,* pp. 41 ff.

[14] *Ibid.,* pp. 142-147.

[15] *Medieval Culture,* II, 99.

[16] *Ibid.,* II, 100.

[17] *Ibid.,* II, 100.

[18] Dante, *Divine Comedy* (Inferno, canto IV).

[19] K. Vossler, II, 103.

[20] Dante, canto I.

[21] Vossler, *op. cit.,* p. 104.

[22] *Luthers Werke* (ed. Buchwald), VIII, pp. 191, 195.

[23] *Ibid.,* VII, 241.

[24] *Pour la Victoire.* New York, March 13, 1943.

[25] *Ibid.,* quoted by André Spire.

[26] Thomas Mann about his *Joseph*-novel (printed report of a lecture delivered at the Library of Congress), p. 17.

[27] *Ibid.,* p. 18.

[28] *Ibid.,* p. 5.

[29] *Ibid.,* p. 7.

BIBLIOGRAPHY

BEDIER, JOSEPH, and HAZARD, PAUL, *Histoire de la littérature française illustrée.* 2 vols. Paris, 1923-1924.

BEVAN, EDWYN R., and SINGER, CHARLES (eds.), *The Legacy of Israel.* Oxford, 1927.

CRAWFORD, J. P. WICKERSHAM, *Spanish drama before Lope de Vega.* Philadelphia, 1937.

PETIT DE JULLEVILLE, LOUIS, *Le Théâtre en France.* Paris, 1923.

PIPER, PAUL, *Die geistliche Dichtung des Mittelalters.* Berlin, 1888. Vol. 3.

ROTH, CECIL, *The Jewish Contribution to Civilization.* Cincinnati, 1940.

VOSSLER, KARL, *Medieval Culture,* An Introduction to Dante and his times. 2 vols. New York, 1929.

III

THE SOCIOLOGY AND DEMOGRAPHY
OF THE JEWS

CHAPTER 30

WHO ARE THE JEWS?

By Melville J. Herskovits

I

The problem of drawing definitions precise enough to permit the setting up of acceptable and workable categories of human types has from the earliest days plagued students of man. As in the other natural sciences, the difficulty arises primarily out of the fact that in nature categories are never sharply differentiated from each other. Rather, we find that one type merges imperceptibly into the next. The definitions by means of which delimitation is sought, though in a broad sense inherent in the materials, in their precise statement lodge primarily in the mind of the student. It follows, then, that unless there is agreement as to where the lines of demarcation are to be drawn, the validity of a classification will be a subject of endless debate.

The differentiation of human groups according to their physical characteristics for the most part stands where taxonomy, the science of classification, stood in the other biological sciences at the turn of the century. It will be recalled that until then, the attention of biologists was so focused on the need to distinguish species from species, subspecies from subspecies, race from race, that there was little consideration of problems of a more dynamic character. It is hardly necessary to repeat here how, when Gregor Mendel published his findings concerning the mechanisms of heredity in 1865, the discovery was to all intent ignored, and continued so for almost four decades.

It is important that we understand why classification presented the difficulties it did and resulted in long debates between specialists, since the point is crucial for any discussion of human types. In essence, it was because the attention of students was so centered on the problem of differentiating types that the factor of variation was quite neglected. Yet, in truth, we know today that there is no "real" type specimen of any living form except by agreement, since no two examples of a given class are exactly alike. They can only be said to approximate each other more closely than either will resemble a form that belongs to a different category.

Nor is this all. Classifications based on measurements and description have classically employed the end products of a process of change that for the group is described in their biological evolution and for the individuals is encompassed by the processes of their hereditary endowment and the influence of the natural setting in which they live their lives. But it is these dynamic problems, involving change, that bulk so large in the thought of present-day biologists and have brought the revolutionary concepts of the nature and functioning of the organism, and of the reasons for the rise and maintenance of the many different forms, to be distinguished in the plant and animal world, that are today basic in the biological sciences.

In the study of human physical type, the fact of variability is, in the main, today taken into account; but what may be termed the genetic point of view is by no means as prevalent as its importance in the study of the lower forms would seem to warrant in the study of man. It is true that the difficulties of method in the study of human genetics are so great as to be discouraging; yet with the proper biometric techniques they can and are being attacked, on the basis of statistical analysis rather than through the laboratory controls it is possible for animal geneticists to maintain. Even to recognize the approach as valid when applied to man is fruitful, however. A race becomes not an aggregate of individuals, but an aggregate of genetic lines that breed true to produce certain types. Conventional studies of race—something which, perverted to serve racist rather than scientific ends, has caused such misery in the world—become almost pointless; it is studies of local types, population formation, stability of physical traits under crossing and the plasticity of the organism under different environmental conditions that come to have meaning and lead to significant results for the study of human biology.

Yet a serious complicating factor faces the human biologist that the student of other forms need not take into account. This arises from the fact that man is the only member of the biological series who possesses speech, and who can use tools. This in turn induces an element operative in the case of none other than the human animal, the factor of culture. Man is the only culture-building animal that exists in the world, and the multitude of differing ways of life he has devised as a result of differing traditions have influenced his physical types in their ultimate form by protecting him against the elements, giving him a stable habitation, assuring him the kinds of food his tradition demands, and above all in setting up conventions which, all unconsciously, function as controls over his mating and make for social rather than natural selection. It is significant that the only types that resemble man in living under such conditions are the domesticated animals, and they alone are as variable in physical form, species for species, as is the species *homo sapiens*. Nor is it without further significance for an understanding of the nature of human racial differences

that the traits in which these animals vary most markedly are the characteristics of coloring, size, hair form, among others, the very traits that,
since they comprehend the outstanding differences between men, have
been most employed in differentiating human races.

2

Of all human groupings, there is none wherein the problem of definition
has proved to be more difficult than for the Jews. Even when all possibilities seem to have been exhausted—race, people, nation, religion, cultural
entity, historic group, linguistic unit—we find students casting about for
other, more precise, more comprehensive designations. That this is a fact
does not mean that it is the less important to continue the search for
adequate delimitation, for though the establishing of categories can never
be an end of scientific investigation, it is an essential beginning.

It is instructive to set forth some of the attempts that have been made
to draw definitions of the term "Jew." Thus Haddon and Huxley (1936)
say:

> Ripley, in his classic *Races of Europe* (1900), concludes by affirming that
> "the Jews are not a race but only a people after all." We believe him to be
> right. The Jews can rank neither as nation nor even as ethnic unit, but rather
> as a socio religious group carrying large Mediterranean, Armenoid and many
> other elements, and varying greatly in physical characters. Like many other
> groups its members are held together by external pressure of various kinds,
> partly by a long historic memory, partly by a sense of common suffering,
> partly by a religion. These factors, acting through long ages, have produced a
> common consciousness which is relaxed when the pressures are relaxed and
> intensified with the reverse process.[1]

Coon (in 1939), in one of the most elaborate studies of human taxonomy
that has been published to date, gives his concept of what constitutes
Jews in the following terms:

> ... the Jews form an ethnic group; ... like all ethnic groups they have their
> own racial elements distributed in their own proportions; like all or most
> ethnic groups they have their "look," a part of their cultural heritage that
> both preserves and expresses their cultural solidarity. And since the ethnic
> solidarity of the Jews is remarkable for its strength and constancy, so the
> Jewish look seems to be one of the most noticeable and most easily dis-
> tinguished of characteristic facial expressions found within the family of
> white people.[2]

In a subsequent consideration of the problem (in 1942), he states:

> ... not only are the Jews different to a measurable degree from the other
> people among whom they live, but they are a *population*, just as the Vol-

hynians and Swabian villagers are populations. The Jews, therefore, are not a race . . . They are a group of people as united biologically as is the average intermarrying social or geographical unit found among white peoples; they have racial peculiarities which serve to differentiate the majority of them anthropometrically from their non-Jewish compatriots and neighbors.[3]

Krogman (1945), after pointing out that "centuries of injustice and of rigorous competition" have forced the Jew so to "compensate . . . by a tremendous drive," says, "this fact . . . has given him a set of behavioral attitudes and responses that are often characteristic to the point of recognition and group definition . . . [but] that . . . are *cultural, not biological*." He summarizes his position with the statement: "A Jew belongs not to a race but to a Jewish community."[4]

Seltzer (1939), presents this definition:

For our purpose we shall define the word Jew to include all individuals of the so-called "White" races of mankind who, by virtue of family tradition, do practice or whose ancestors did practice the religion of Judaism.[5]

This is in line with Parr's conclusion (1934), based on the study of blood types, that: "There is serological evidence that the Jews are a religion rather than a race."[6]

Wider in its limits is the racio-religious definition implicit in the categories set up by Joseph Jacobs, in an early study of the anthropometry of the Jews aimed at describing what he held to be a Jewish race, and presented in a paper read before the Royal Anthropological Institute of London (1886).[7] In a table giving the numbers "of various classes of persons now living, who may claim to be Jews by religion or by birth, or both," he includes:

A. Jews both by religion and by birth
   Ashkenazim, Sephardim, and Samaritans (?)
B. Jews by religion, but not by birth
   Falashas of Abyssinia, Karaites of the Crimea, Kaggatouns, etc., of the Sahara, Beni-Israel of Bombay, and the Cochin Jews of Cochin
C. Jews by birth, but not by religion
   Chuetas or Anussim of the Balearic Islands, the Maiminen of Salonica, and the G'did al Islam of Khorasan.

He adds, "Besides this, there exist a large number of persons, mostly in Europe, who have Jewish blood in their veins as Jewish converts . . . especially . . . in Spain."[7a] He insists that "The anthropology of Jews can never be satisfactorily settled till careful examination of these various data has shown their resemblances and differences. From the common qualities of classes A and B we can determine qualities due to religion; from those common to A and C, but differing in B, we might draw valuable conclusions as to the influences of race," and expresses regret that because "for the second and third classes we have practically no data to work with," such analyses must be deferred. In all this we find adumbrated a recent dictionary definition of the Jew: ". . . any person of the Hebrew race or whose religion is Judaism."[8]

All the definitions that have been cited, while recognizing the existence of both biological and cultural factors, have because of their anthropological character been directed primarily at the problem of whether or not the Jews comprise a racial entity. Students who approach the problem from the sociological point of view, however, are likewise no clearer or more agreed on proper terms to be employed. A case study of this conflict in definition is to be had in the summary given by Max Weinreich (1945) of replies received by the Yiddish Scientific Institute from social scientists to a questionnaire concerning the desirability of having the classification of "Jew" on United States Immigration and Naturalization Service forms retained or deleted.

Bram (1944), in a discussion of the problem of definition, notes that "countless attempts to place the Jews in clear sociological categories have still left them an undefined social phenomenon," and documents his statement with these examples:

Louis Wirth has said that "the elementary question as to whether the Jews are a race, a nationality or a cultural group remains unsettled." Other writers who have tried to find a proper definition for them have expressed the difficulties in very characteristic terms. They refer to the Jews as "an unusual type of nationality," "a social anomaly," "a peculiar people." Talcott Parsons considers them "a unique social phenomenon," Carl Mayer calls them "a chimeric people" leading "a life of unreality."[9]

Kennedy (1942), striving for preciseness in characterizing the group status of the Jews in the United States, says: "The Jews are a religio-national group occupying the status of a quasi-caste in American society." Earlier in his paper, after stating that "our focus can shift at once from the biological to the social and cultural plane," he provides the basis for the "religio-national" element in the definition just quoted in these terms:

We see then that the Jews manifest traits characteristic of a nationality in their common traditions, common patterns of ideas and behavior, and common ethnocentrism or consciousness of kind, and that these transcend whatever other nationality affiliations they may assume. Most of these traits are closely intermeshed with their religion, so much so that some readers may insist that it is enough to call them a religious group rather than stress the point of nationality. . . . The issue can be resolved by designating the Jews as a "religio-national" group.[10]

It must be clear from this sampling of the many attempts that have been made to define the term "Jew" and to arrive at some formula to describe those who are to be placed in the category of Jews that there is certainly no agreement. The failure to obtain a consensus of opinion would seem to derive, in part at least, from the difficulty of drawing a definition when the very terms that must apparently be employed so lack preciseness. What, for example, is an "ethnic group"? It is obviously not a race, yet it is stated to have subracial status, with certain distinguishing physical characteristics and certain ways of life. And how does an "ethnic group" differ from a "people," or "a socio-religious group," terms accepted by students of competence who specifically state that Jews are neither to be ranked "as nation nor even as ethnic unit"? What does it mean to say they are a "population," or that they are those who belong to "a Jewish community" or that they are a "religio-national group"? What, even, does it mean to state that Jews are "a religion," when the views of the nature and functioning of the universe held by those included in a Jewish "ethnic group," "population" or "community" are so heterogeneous that, as one Jewish wit has said, "Where there are two Jews, there are three opinions!"

Let us refer to certain broad principles in the scientific study of man that may help us understand the dilemma in which those who would define the term "Jew" have found themselves. Outstandingly, it is essential to remember the basic fact that, though man is both a biological and a culture-building animal, and that while these two aspects may and on occasion do interact, man's physical type and his culture represent different dimensions of his existence which must be regarded as independent even when they are interrelated variables. Physical traits are inherited through the genetic mechanism that determines the limits within which a given form, in its development, will eventuate in the kind of adult human being it proves to be. Culture, on the other hand, in all its many manifestations, is learned, and is thus of a different order of causation.

But if we turn not only to the definitions that have been cited, but also take into account the many others that have been drawn and continue to be heard, we find that they almost invariably attempt to encompass both dimensions of man, physical and cultural. That is, Jews are held to have delimitable physical traits, like other groups we designate as nations, or peoples, or tribes, or races; and they are also held to be marked by certain beliefs, or habits, or traditions, or points of view, or values that mark them off from other peoples. Hence any attempt to draw a logically valid definition, it is felt, since it must describe as well as delimit, has to include two terms which, because they vary independently, rarely, if ever, exhibit a one-to-one correspondence. We may merely refer to the categories of Joseph Jacobs that have been cited, to realize that no such order of correspondence holds for the Jews.

It is instructive to scrutinize the following description of the Jews of

Cochin, India, with the definitions that have been cited, in their two-dimensional form, in mind:

At present the Jews of Cochin number, in all, some fourteen hundred. As are their Hindu neighbors, the Jews are divided into castes which do not intermarry or interdine with each other. There are three Jewish castes . . . The white Jews, who are at the head of the Jewish caste hierarchy, range in skin color from a pale white to a medium brown . . . The skin color of the other two castes is like that of the natives of Cochin, ranging from a light brown to a deep brownish-black. The white Jews have their own synagogue, where the brown Jews are also allowed to worship. The black Jews, who are by far the most numerous, have seven synagogues.

The life of the Cochin Jews is conducted strictly according to the precepts of the *Shulhan Aruk*, the orthodox codex. While the mother tongue of the children is Malayalam, the Dravidian dialect of the country, yet all, boys and girls alike, learn to read Hebrew; the men whose single garment is a waist-cloth, inevitably have a small skullcap of gaily colored cloth perched atop their heads, from which two earlocks often drop; rice and curry, the diet of the South Indian, is also their staple food, but meat curries are never mixed with milk curries. An orthodox Jew from Warsaw or the Bronx might find the Sephardic liturgy of the Cochin synagogues a bit odd at first, but the devotion of the Cochin Jews to Jewish law and learning would soon make him feel at home.[11]

The matter of definition is especially baffling because there is enough similarity in physical type between enough Jews to permit the development of a stereotype that in the minds of the laity receives daily reinforcement and even justifies certain scientific classifications for certain Jewish subgroups. There is, also, enough of a least common denominator of belief, a certain minimum of traditionally accepted values, a certain sense of historic continuity held by enough Jews to make these aspects of Jewish life loom large in the minds of those concerned with definition. Yet whether on the level of physical type or of culture, the exceptions remain, exceeding any limits that can seemingly be drawn. This is undoubtedly the reason why it is far easier to say what Jews are not than to describe what they are.

Even so tentative a discussion as that of Bram does not elude the common dilemma. Admitting the "picture of the Jewish people" to be "one of heterogeneity . . . of a changing people interacting with diverse national societies and whose social identity is constantly subjected by both sides to fluctuating interpretations," he still frames his concept of his task as an understanding of "the problems of social and ethnic identity" of the Jews. "The two extreme groups," he says, with insight, "those who want to be Jewish and those who cannot escape being Jewish, have, for a common denominator, only common ancestry and the recurrent hostility of the surrounding world."[12]

In the remainder of this chapter we shall attempt to describe the physical characteristics and trace the differentiation of the various types of Jews that have been distinguished, and to raise again the question of their unity, referring to anthropometric analyses except where cultural— that is, historical—factors must be taken into account to explain the observed facts. As for the delimitation of the Jewish groups with which we are concerned, we shall face our dilemma in the only way possible, by utilizing the flexibility and realism of an operational definition to permit us to follow the data wherever they lead. In the manner of a definition advanced some years ago (Herskovits, 1927) which stated, "A Jew is a person who calls himself a Jew or who is called Jewish by others,"[13] we shall seek to describe the antecedents and physical traits of those who, over the world, are held to be Jews.

3

There is today general agreement among anthropologists that the Jews, in their biological and historical antecedents, stem primarily from that special type of the Mediterranean subrace of the Caucasoid race—or, as others put it, of the Mediterranean race included in the Caucasoid stock of *homo sapiens*—formed several thousand years ago in the eastern littoral of the Mediterranean Sea.[13a] The most recent findings have been summarized by Krogman (1945), who describes the "historic nucleus of Jewish origins" as follows:

The earliest Jews in their Euphrates homeland soon mixed with the Canaanites of the lowlands, the Amorites of the highlands, and with the Hivites, Amalekites, the Kenites, the Egyptians and the Hittites—mostly long-headed peoples, but round-headed peoples as well. By about 2000 B.C., the "Semitic Empires" of Palestine centered the Jews in western Asia Minor.[14]

Some disagreement exists among students as to the component populations from whom the early Jews were derived. Haddon (1925)[15] designates partial Hittite descent as the source of the "so-called 'Jewish' nose" thus accepting von Luschan's position[16] which is unacceptable to Coon (1939).[17] Seltzer,[18] on the other hand, lays stress (1939) on the influence of the "Iranian Plateau type" described by Field (1935) whose significance he maintains derives largely from the fact that "the most outstanding feature of this race is its nasality." He therefore holds that the Jews are the descendants of early inhabitants of Palestine "predominantly of Mediterranean stock with a definite element of the convex-nosed Iranian Plateau type."[19]

The modern descendants of these early Jews achieved their dispersal in three historic periods, until their final expulsion from Palestine. Coon[20] gives these as, first, the period of the captivity of the Jews in Babylonia beginning 586 B.C.E.,[20a] when considerable numbers were removed to the East, to Mesopotamia and Iraq, where they took root and where, as in Iraq, their descendants live to the present. The second dispersion was during the period of Hellenistic influence, from the time of Alexander and continuing through the Byzantine Empire,[20b] when substantial centers of Jewish population were established in Egypt, Syria, Asia Minor, the Crimea and the Balkans. The third and final distribution of Jews, throughout the Roman world, was a long process, covering more than two centuries. It was primarily in a westward direction, and when it ended the Jews were not only established in Rome itself, but had taken part in the settlement, along with Romans, of Spain, France and Germany west of the Rhine.[20c]

In most discussions of Jewish types, two principal groups have been distinguished, the *Ashkenazim*, or German, Russian and Polish Jews, and the *Sephardim*, the Spanish and Portuguese Jews, as Fishberg (1905)[21] puts it. These latter, in the Balkans, are also called "Spanioli," after the dialect they use, which is derived from the Spanish their ancestors spoke before their expulsion from Spain in 1492, and which distinguishes the Sephardim from the Ashkenazim, who speak Yiddish, a tongue based on German. This dual designation has attained prominence only because so much attention has been given to European Jews. It will be remembered that the first category of Jacobs[22] includes, besides these two, the Samaritans, though they are queried. Today, however, the Samaritans, said by Coon to be "generally supposed to represent the indigenous Palestinian Jewish strain more faithfully than any other,"[23] are held to appertain to a third category, the *Oriental* Jews, who inhabit Palestine, the Yemen, Iraq, Iran, Turkey and the Caucasus.

Krogman (1945)[24] holds that the Oriental Jews are in physical form closest to their "Mediterranean prototype," then the Sephardim, then the Ashkenazim. The most striking anthropometric differences, however, are between the first two, on the one hand, and the third. The resemblance between Oriental and Sephardic Jews is such, indeed, that Coon (1939), while distinguishing them, says, "On the whole the Jews of the entire Mediterranean racial belt, from Persia to Morocco, and including those whose ancestors once lived in Spain, are remarkably constant in their racial unity."[25]

The differences between these groups and the Ashkenazim is customarily discussed in terms of variations in head form, the trait that has been most studied by anthropologists. In recent years this problem has been posed as the "brachycephalization" of these Central European Jews—that is, their conversion from a long-headed Mediterranean type to a short-headed form that characterizes the Alpine subrace of Caucasoids. Such a formulation, which assumes an aboriginal long-headed type (though there are difficulties here, as in the case of the Nablus series of Samaritans discussed by Huxley [1905], who found much short-headedness among them), was first sketched in terms of this process of brachycephalization by Dixon (1923).[26] Later Coon made of it a principal point of his study of European "races" (1939), stating that the study of what he terms "the brachycephalized Jews" of Asia and Central Europe is "an intimate part of the problem of Central European brachycephaly."[27]

"The contrast between the Ashkenazim and the Sephardim," writes Krogman (1945),[28] "is really one between an Alpo-Dinaric (or Armenoid) and a Mediterranean racial type." He cites F. Wagenseil's figures (1923), which show an average in the ratio between length and breadth of the head of male Spanish Jews to be 78.1, as against 82.5 for male Russian Jews, the figures for females being 78.9 and 82.4, respectively. This means that the Spanish Jews are strikingly longer headed than the Russian Jews measured, since the lower the ratio the longer the skull in relation to its breadth. This is also seen in the distribution of this ratio, the *cephalic index*, when all the members of each series, irrespective of sex, are considered together:

	Spanish Jews (Per cent)	Russian Jews (Per cent)
Long-headed	19.7	1.0
Medium-headed	65.5	29.0
Short-headed	14.8	70.0

Comparable results are to be found in a table given by Fishberg (1911)[29] for the head form of Jews of differing areas, which may be rearranged to afford greater clarity than in the original:

	Yemen (Per cent)	No. Africa (Per cent)	"Jews in Europe" (Per cent)	Caucasus (Per cent)
Long-headed	71.80	25.97	2.89	—
Medium-headed	24.35	57.15	48.65	10.80
Short-headed	3.85	16.88	48.45	89.20

Similar findings are at hand for a trait of a quite different order, blood type, despite the fact that, according to Parr, from whose work these data are taken, any general "correlation between blood types and anthropometric features . . . can hardly be justified." As an example of this, he says, "Recently we examined twenty-eight members of an American Jewish family of three generations and found that the blood type percentages (O, 17.8, A, 82.1) would give a race index of infinity, distinctly different from the race index for the group (1.85), yet these twenty-eight people are beyond question typical of their race."

It is impossible here to explain in detail the serological techniques or genetic assumptions underlying the study of blood groups, but relative percentages of the four types (O, A, B and AB) for Ashkenazic and Sephardic Jews, Arabs (who are long-headed Mediterraneans) and Armenians (short-headed Alpine-Dinaric types), suggest how basic are the distinctions between the two categories of Jews, and how close is their taxonomic affiliation with the subraces represented by these two other non-Jewish populations:[30]

Population	Blood-group			
	O	A	B	AB
Arabs	43.6	32.4	19.0	5.0
Sephardic Jews	41.1	28.5	23.4	7.0
Ashkenazic Jews	37.2	34.1	18.1	10.6
Armenians[a]	27.0	53.0	14.0	6.0
Armenians[b]	36.3	40.3	16.6	6.8

[a] 653 cases, typed by Parr.

[b] 380 cases, typed by Kossovitch.

It is thus not strange that students, in the light of these and the many other facts concerning differences in physical type, no longer regard the Jews as a "race." With this has also gone the tendency of earlier days to speak of Jews as "Semites." The word "Semitic," it is now realized, describes a linguistic phenomenon, so that at most Jews might be termed descendants of one of the "Semitic-speaking peoples" much in the way that, for want of a better designation, the inhabitants of the heart of the African continent, a heterogeneous grouping of local types, are referred to as "Bantu-speaking peoples." The lack of validity of such a phrase as "Semitic race" is to be seen from the following statement by Ariëns-Kappers (1934):

The expression "Semitic race or races" . . . is one of the most inappropriate expressions occurring in anthropology, just as confusing as the word Aryan. Although taken in the biblical sense it means to indicate people that are mutually related (being all descendants of Sem) practically the term only indicates people that speak a Semitic language . . . What then is the anthropological meaning of the expression "Semitic people"? None at all.[31]

This would seem to put a capstone of specific refutation on the structure of critical analysis exemplified in von Luschan's Huxley Memorial Lecture for 1911:

Combinations of Philology with Anthropology have in former times, especially through Friedrich Mueller and his school, often led to serious mistakes. One spoke of Aryan races instead of people with Aryan languages, and one went so far as to speak of Aryan skulls and of Aryan eyes, so that Max Mueller formally protested against the intrusion of linguistics into ethnology, stating that one might just as well speak of a brachycephalic grammar as of an Aryan skull.[32]

Granting, then, that the Jews are no race, but in the main belong to sub-races of the Caucasoid grouping of mankind, we may in so far as possible sketch the types that are envisaged by students of human taxonomy. The Sephardim and Oriental (Mediterranean) Jews, according to Coon (1939),[33] are brunet in coloring of hair and eyes, and "brunet-white" in skin color. Two subtypes are distinguished, both slender, but one heavier than the other. One has a short and moderately broad face, the other a face long and narrow. The nose type of the former is short and straight "with a tip of medium thickness and nasal wings usually medium, seldom com-pressed or flaring"; of the latter, the nose is "extremely long with com-pressed wings, the nasion depression slight, the nasal tip somewhat depressed, the nostrils highly set on the sides," with convex nasal profile, and a high, but not unusually high nasal bridge. The fact that the Sephardic and Oriental Jews are as distinctly Mediterranean as they are, that they are no more heterogeneous than they are, is undoubtedly caused by the fact, also recognized by most students, that they have lived among peoples who belong to this same subrace, and with whom they could mix without unduly disturbing any physical characteristics that marked their forebears among the early Israelites.

To describe any single set of physical traits that mark off the Central European Jews is quite another matter. The relative homogeneity of the Mediterranean type of Jew gives way, in Europe, to a divergence of type that makes it necessary to set up a series of local forms, each for separate analysis, rather than envisage any single category. Seltzer has indicated the complexity of the task in no uncertain terms. "The Ashkenazic Jews are extremely composite in physical characteristics," he says, "which indicates a very heterogeneous racial background."[34] A favorite quotation employed by Fishberg[35] from Renan, "Il n'y a pas un type juif, il y a des types juifs," to underscore the results of his study of the physical form of European Jews, aptly summarizes the matter. Boas's statement (1923), that "the assimilation of the Jews by the people among whom they live is much more far-reaching than a hasty observation might suggest,"[36] implies the mechanism whereby the marked variation in physical type within the category of European (Ashkenazic) Jews may have been brought about, as well as why this division stands in such striking contrast in homogeneity when compared to the Sephardic and Oriental Jews in this respect. We must, therefore, next address ourselves to the significance of this.

4

Homo sapiens constitutes a single species,[37] and its members, as with all other similar categories in the animal world, whatever their subspecific (racial) affiliation, are mutually fertile. This biological fact has been implemented in the historical development of the human race by the widespread amount of intermixture that has occurred between all groups of men who have come into contact. Not only on the level of crossing between representatives of those major aggregates of mankind we term races has this been continuous, but also between subracial types and groups of smaller order, such as local communities. So universal has this been over the ages man has been on earth, even in early prehistoric times,[38] that it takes on the aspect of an axiom in the study of man when we say that any two human groups, whatever their differences in physical type or way of life, will under contact produce offspring of mixed parentage. This is why anthropologists have rejected the concept of a pure human race as a fiction, why it is stated that man is the most mongrel of all animals.

In the case of the Jews, this fact of mixture between peoples in contact is given almost a laboratory demonstration. If, as seems reasonable to assume, the early Jews were a Mediterranean type whose dispersion took them into areas where they were in contact with indigenous populations also of Mediterranean stock with whom they mixed, then the mixture with these other Mediterranean populations would result in the maintenance of type and the relative homogeneity in physical traits that marks the Sephardic and Oriental Jews as compared to the Ashkenazic Jews, who mingled with Alpine, Nordic and Dinaric populations. As Coon has put it (1942):

Among the Ashkenazim one can pick out Palestinian types that could readily be drawn from the courts of Solomon and David; Nordics to delight the eye of Julius Streicher, if he were to see them without their passports; Alpines who could yodel in any Hofbrauhaus; and Dinarics who could be Tyrolese skiers or Parisian policemen.[39]

We can see how, statistically, this is manifest by citing some comparisons that have been made between Jewish and non-Jewish populations living in the same countries. Fishberg, whose studies even today provide the most inclusive documentation for questions of the physical anthropology of the Jews, has several tables that show how average head form, expressed as cephalic index, is manifested among Jews and non-Jews living together:[40]

	Jews	Non-Jews
Lithuania	81.05	81.88
Rumania	81.82	82.91
Poland	81.91	82.13
Hungary	82.45	81.40
Little Russia	82.45	82.31
Galicia	83.33	84.40

When the above table is scrutinized it becomes evident that the head form of Jews varies, in the main, as does that of the non-Jewish populations with whom they are in contact. This is also apparent in a similar table of average indices for Jews and non-Jews gathered together by Coon (1942):[41]

	Jews	Non-Jews
England	80.0	78.0 (English urban population)
Bosnia	80.1	85.3
Frankfort	80.8	81.4 (Rhineland)
Karaites, Lithuania	81.0	82.6 (Lithuania)
Lithuania	81.7	
Galicia	81.7	83.5
Poland	81.9	82.9
So. Russia	82.5	83.2 (Ukraine)
Poland	82.8	82.9
Warsaw	82.9	82.0
Ukraine	82.9	83.2
Bavaria	83.5	84.1
Bukovina	84.3	86.3

Here, again, a correlation is apparent. But it is also true, as Coon points out, that if we compare the range of values in the Jewish column (80.0-84.3) with that of the non-Jewish (78.0-86.3) the differences manifest among the latter are greater than those among the former. This brings Coon to the following conclusion: "That the Jews of all European countries have more in common anthropometrically than do the non-Jews of these countries." He also feels that "there are no clear general trends in correspondence between local Jewish and non-Jewish means," but this is not nearly so evident from inspection of the table as the other, nor is it supported by Fishberg's data given above.

We must be fully aware of the implications that lie in the fact that only cephalic index has been considered in these tables, since the form of the head is but one of many traits used in analyzing relations between populations, traits which do not by any means always vary in the same way. Thus Fishberg, many years ago, found that the hair and eye color of Jews was distinctly darker in both characters than of non-Jews in the same country (1905),[42] a finding confirmed recently by Morant (1939).[43] On the other hand, when comparative figures for stature are given[44] they confirm "in a striking manner the similarity of the stature of the Jews to that of their non-Jewish neighbors."

Let us approach the matter from another point of view, and consider the degree of variation found within European Jewish and non-Jewish populations. For this, we may abstract from a table presented by Coon (1942)[45] the statistical constants that indicate variability (technically, the mean square deviations, or *sigmas*) of the series of Eastern European Jews measured by Fishberg, of seventy-nine series "chosen from many parts of the world" by Howells, and of an average of six series of "small, geographically unified, isolated village communities" in Germany, for various traits:

Group	St.	H.L.	H.B.	F.H.	F.B.	N.H.	N.B.	Av., 6 Meas. in mm.
E. European Jews	6.6	6.1	5.5	6.6	6.2	4.0	3.0	5.2
"79 Series"	5.8	6.2	5.2	6.4	5.3	3.8	2.9	5.0
6 German Series	5.7	6.0	5.8	6.7	5.5	4.0	3.0	5.2

Group	Cephalic Index	Facial Index	Nasal Index	Av. 3 Indices
E. European Jews	3.2	5.8	8.1	5.7
"79 Series"	3.4	5.1	7.8	5.4
6 German Series	3.2	5.0	6.7	5.0

(St., stature; H.L., head-length; H.B., breadth of head; F.H., facial height; F.B., facial breadth; N.H., nasal height; N.B., nasal breadth; Cephalic Index, ratio between length and breadth of head; Facial Index, ratio between height and width of face; Nasal Index, ratio between height and breadth of nose.)

This table is presented by Coon to show that the variation within Jewish groups is no greater than in non-Jewish populations, so that "the Eastern European Jews measured by Fishberg deserve the rank of a biological population as truly as do most central and eastern European communities united, as the Jews are not, in space."

The problem of relative variability of Jews and non-Jews may be attacked from a dynamic point of view which is often overlooked. This approach, devised by Boas (1916) is essentially an analysis in terms of the genetics of population formation, and can be stated simply, and in summary, as follows: A population is composed of a series of family lines, the end results of which are at any given moment its individual members, some of whom are related more closely than others, some quite unrelated. These individuals differ in their physical traits from one another, but less so when they are related than when they are not. Gross variation of a population is thus to be divided into the *variability of family lines*, manifest in the differences between families, and *fraternal variability*, or the average range of variation found to exist within the families that make up this population. The lower the former the more inbreeding there has been; the lower the latter the more homogeneous the stock from which the population was derived. Free mating in a population of mixed origin would thus produce high family *and* fraternal variation; an inbred community descended from the same stock would have low values.

Comparative findings, which include Eastern European Jews, are instructive; they concern cephalic index:[46]

	Variability of family lines	Variability within families
Potenza, Italy	2.41	2.52
Central Italians	2.39	2.72
Bohemians	2.37	2.61
Worcester, Mass.	2.36	2.36
East European Jews	2.29	2.52
Scottish	2.17	2.66
New York mixed Negroes	1.85	2.93
Blue Ridge Mountaineers	1.85	2.09
Chippewa Indians	1.77	3.32
Bastaards (So. Africa)	1.26	2.52

Inbreeding among the Blue Ridge mountaineers, New York Negroes, and an Indian tribe with mixed ancestry, caused by geographical and sociological isolation, give low values for variation of family line, while free intermingling of short- and long-headed Italians, or absence of selective factors in such a city as Worcester, Massachusetts, makes for high values. It is interesting that the Jews occupy a middle position in the variability of their family lines, but that they show a higher figure for fraternal variation both in comparison with their own family variability and with such an inbred population of homogeneous ancestry as the Kentuckians.

Yet this is what we should expect on the basis of what we know about the biological history of the Jews. With a tradition of endogamy and under pressure from outside their own group Jews have inbred more than the surrounding populations. Yet the "axiom" of crossing as a result of contact, the historical fact of proselytizing which brought non-Jews into the Jewish religious group, the gradual lifting of discriminatory legislation during the nineteenth century, made for interbreeding between Jews and non-Jews that gives those called Jews—to say nothing of those non-Jews of partial descent from families called Jewish—anything but a homogeneous ancestry. Hence we find that Jewish populations differ from each other as do those among whom they live, yet that each has a degree of homogeneity that comes from a tradition of marriage within the group reinforced by majority pressures; and with this, an overall variability that has completely denied scientific validity to the concept of a "Jewish race."

What of the "Jewish look"? Is it "nasality," as Seltzer claimed (1939), thus giving present-day assent to Jacobs's thesis expressed in 1886? Or is it some "quality of looking Jewish,"[47] some "characteristic facial expression" that still makes of the Jews, for all their anthropometric heterogeneity and historical divergence of derivation, a recognizable unit?

Stereotypes die hard. "Nasality" was considered, and dismissed as an identifying trait of the Jew many years ago. Topinard's conception of the "hooked," or aquiline, nose as Jewish was later analyzed by Fishberg (1905),[48] who gave the following figures for nasal profile in Jews of European origin living in New York City:

	Males (Per cent)	Females (Per cent)
Straight	58	59
Hooked, aquiline	14	13
Retroussé (snub)	22	14
Flat and broad	6	14

The aspects of the trait that figure in the stereotype may, of course, be other than profile—Fishberg himself felt that it might be a matter of "nostrility." But to date no device for measuring this exists, so that, on the basis of other studies, and until data to the contrary are presented, it can be regarded as a stereotypical rather than typical "Jewish" characteristic.

Is the "Jewish look" contained in the gestures the Jew employs when he talks? That Jews "talk with their hands" is a fundamental element in the Jewish stereotype, and one that is not easily susceptible of objective analysis. The study made by Efron (1941) does, however, throw considerable light on the matter. With the aid of an artist and using motion pictures, he analyzed the gestures of Italians and Jews, dividing each group into "assimilated" and "traditional" categories. The findings demonstrate how little validity there is in the assumption that the Jewish type is to be described in terms of patterns of gesturing:

Both from the standpoint of number of people gesturing and of frequency and manner of gesticulation in those people who do gesture, the assimilated Eastern Jews and the assimilated Southern Italians in New York City (a) *appear to differ greatly from their respective traditional groups,* and (b) *appear to resemble each other.*[49]

The quality of "looking Jewish" was further tested in an ingenuous study, instituted by the late Franz Boas two decades ago and carried on with the co-operation of various universities over the country. Its purpose was to discover how far racial or national origin could be determined through inspection. Freshmen, grouped in sections of large classes, were asked during the first week of sessions, before they knew one another, to indicate on forms provided for the purpose their places of birth, that of their parents and grandparents, the language they spoke at home, their "race"— however they might wish to define this term—and its characteristics as they conceived them. Then each student, in turn, called by number only, stood before the class while his fellows wrote what they thought his origin to be, their degree of certainty in drawing this judgment, and why they classified him as they did.

The results of this study were never published, but in conversation Professor Boas stated that at one of the New York colleges forty per cent of the Italians were taken to be Jews, and the same percentage of Jews were adjudged Italians. This would seem to argue that if there is a "Jewish look" it is also in a large number of cases an "Italian look"—quite possible, since South Italians, like stereotyped Jews, are of Mediterranean stock. Midwestern judgments, where the northern European population is predominant, were also of interest. Some of the replies from students at Northwestern University may be given. One lad of Scottish birth was designated as belonging to all Northern European groups, and to be of French and Italian origin as well; three blond Jews were similarly assigned, while four brunet non-Jews, only one of whom was of southern European origin, were designated as Jews by some of their fellows.

5

It is thus apparent that it is neither race, nor such an aspect of physical type as nasality, nor a "Jewish look" that affords terms in which the question "Who are the Jews?" is to be answered. In some regions some aboriginal Mediterranean traits have been retained, but by no means everywhere. In like manner, language, culture, belief all exhibit so great a range of variation that no definition cast in terms of these concepts can be more than partial. Yet the Jews do represent a historic continuum, have survived as an identifiable, yet constantly shifting series of groups. Is there any least common denominator other than the designation "Jew" that can be found to mark the historical *fait accompli* that the Jew, however defined, seems to be? It is seriously to be questioned. A word can mean many things to many people; and no word, one may almost conclude, means more things to more people than does the word "Jew."

NOTES

[1] J. S. Huxley and A. C. Haddon, *We Europeans; a Survey of "Racial" Problems,* (New York and London, 1936), p. 147.

[2] Carleton S. Coon, *The Races of Europe* (New York, 1939), p. 442.

[3] *Ibid.,* "Have the Jews a Racial Identity?" in *Jews in a Gentile World* (Isacque Graeber and Stewart H. Britt, eds.) (New York, 1942), p. 35.

[4] Wilton M. Krogman, Anthropology, physical (ms. of article prepared for the *World Encyclopedia Institute,* 1945).

[5] Carl C. Seltzer, "The Jew—His Racial Status," in *Harvard Medical Alumni Bulletin,* Vol. 13, No. 3, 1939, p. 68.

[6] Leland W. Parr, "Isohemagglutination Studies on Near East Race Groups," in *An Introduction to the Anthropology of the Near East in Ancient and Recent Times* (Amsterdam, 1934), p. 195.

[7] Joseph Jacobs, "On the Racial Characters of Modern Jews," in *Journal of the Royal Anthropology Institute,* Vol. xv, 1885, pp. 24-25 (London).

[7a Cf. above Cecil Roth, "The European Age in Jewish History (to 1648)," p. 236.]

[8] Webster's Collegiate Dictionary, 1943, s.v. "Jew."

[9] Joseph Bram, "The Social Identity of the Jews," *Trans. N. Y. Acad. of Sci. Ser.* II, Vol. vi, No. 6, 1944, p. 194.

[10] Raymond Kennedy, "The Position and Future of the Jews in America," in *Jews in a Gentile World, op. cit.,* pp. 419-420.

[11] David G. Mandelbaum, "The Jewish Way of Life in Cochin," in *Jewish Social Studies,* Vol. I, 1939, p. 424.

[12] Bram, *op. cit.*

[13] M. J. Herskovits, "When Is a Jew a Jew?" in *Modern Quarterly,* Vol. iv, No. 2, 1927, pp. 109-117.

[13a Cf. above William Foxwell Albright, "The Biblical Period," pp. 3 ff.]

[14] Krogman, *op. cit.*

[15] A. C. Haddon, *The Races of Man and their Distribution* (New York, 1925), p. 25.

[16] Felix von Luschan, "The Early Inhabitants of Western Asia," in *Jour. Roy. Anth. Inst.,* Vol. xli, 1911, p. 244.

[17] Coon, *op. cit.,* p. 435, n. 41.

[18] Seltzer, *op. cit.,* p. 72.

[19] Henry Field, "Arabs of Central Iraq, their History, Ethnology and Physical Characters," *Anthropology Memoirs* (Field Museum of Natural History, Chicago), Vol. iv, 1935.

[20] Coon, *op. cit.,* pp. 435 ff.

[20a Cf. Albright, *op. cit.,* pp. 31 ff.]

[20b Cf. above Elias J. Bickerman, "The Historical Foundations of Post-biblical Judaism."]

[20c Cf. Roth, *op. cit.*]

[21] Maurice Fishberg, "Materials for the Physical Anthropology of the Eastern European Jews," in *Annals New York Academy of Sciences,* Vol. xvi, No. 6, Pt. II, p. 157.

[22] Jacobs, *op. cit.,* p. 24.

[23] Coon, *op. cit.,* p. 439.

[24] Krogman, *op. cit.*

[25] Coon, *op. cit.,* p. 443.

[26] Roland B. Dixon, *The Racial History of Man* (New York and London, 1923), p. 174.

[27] Coon, *op cit.,* pp. 638 ff.

[28] Krogman, *op. cit.*

[29] Fishberg, *op. cit.,* p. 50.

[30] Parr, *op. cit.,* pp. 188-189.

[31] C. U. Ariëns-Kappers, *An Introduction to the Anthropology of the Near East in Ancient and Recent Times* (Amsterdam, 1934).

[32] Von Luschan, *op. cit.*, p. 244.

[33] Coon, *op. cit.*, p. 440.

[34] Seltzer, *op. cit.*, p. 74.

[35] Fishberg, *op. cit.*, p. 160; also Fishberg, *The Jews: a Study of Race and Environment* (London and New York, 1911), p. 506.

[36] Franz Boas, "On the Variety of Lines of Descent represented in a Population," in *American Anthropologist* (Lancaster, Pa.), (n.s.), Vol. xviii, No. 1, 1916, p. 5

[37] Cf. Th. Dobzhansky, "On Species and Races of Living and Fossil Man," in *American Journal of Physical Anthropology* (n.s.), Vol. ii, No. 3, 1944, pp. 254-255.

[38] Cf. Franz Weidenreich, "The Skull of Sinanthropus Pekinensis; a Comparative Study on a Primitive Hominid Skull," *Palaeontologia Sinica* (Lancaster), (n.s. D.) No. 10, 1943, pp. 238 ff.

[39] Coon, "Have the Jews a Racial Identity?" p. 32.

[40] Fishberg, *op. cit.*, p. 52; also *ibid.*, "Materials for the Physical Anthropology of the Eastern European Jews" (p. 164) for more detail and for sources.

[41] Coon, *op. cit.*

[42] Fishberg, *op. cit.*, p. 269.

[43] G. M. Morant, *The Races of Central Europe, a Footnote to History,* (London, 1939), pp. 80-83.

[44] Fishberg, *op. cit.*, pp. 186-187; Morant, *op. cit.*, pp. 72-74.

[45] Coon, *op. cit.*, p. 36.

[46] Boas, *op. cit.;* also Herskovits, *The American Negro, a Study in Racial Crossing* (New York, 1928), p. 28.

[47] Coon, *The Races of Europe,* p. 441.

[48] Fishberg, *op. cit.*, p. 257.

[49] David Efron, *Gesture and Environment* (New York, 1941), p. 136.

BIBLIOGRAPHY

ARIËNS-KAPPERS, C. U., *An Introduction to the Anthropology of the Near East in Ancient and Recent Times.* Amsterdam, 1934.

BOAS, FRANZ, "On the Variety of Lines of Descent Represented in a Population," in *American Anthropologist* (Lancaster), (n.s.), Vol. xviii, No. 1, 1916, pp. 1-9.

———, "Are the Jews a Race?" *World Tomorrow,* Vol. vi, No. 1, 1923, pp. 5-6.

BRAM, JOSEPH, "The Social Identity of the Jews," *Trans. N. Y. Acad. of Sciences* Ser. II, Vol. vi., No. 6, 1944, pp. 194-199.

COON, CARLETON S., *The Races of Europe.* New York, 1939.

———, "Have the Jews a Racial Identity?" in *Jews in a Gentile World* (Isacque Graeber and Steuart H. Britt, eds.), pp. 20-37. New York, 1942.

DIXON, ROLAND B., *The Racial History of Man*. New York and London, 1923.

DOBZHANSKY, TH., "On Species and Races of Living and Fossil Man," in *American Journal of Physical Anthropology* (n.s.), Vol. ii, No. 3, 1944, pp. 251-265.

EFRON, DAVID, *Gesture and Environment*. New York, 1941.

FIELD, HENRY, "Arabs of Central Iraq, their History, Ethnology, and Physical Characters," *Anthropology Memoirs*, Vol. iv. Field Museum of Natural History, Chicago, 1935.

FISHBERG, MAURICE, "Materials for the Physical Anthropology of the Eastern European Jews," in *Annals New York Academy of Science*, Vol. xvi, No. 6, Pt. II, 1905, pp. 155-297.

———, *The Jews: a Study of Race and Environment*. London and New York, 1911.

HADDON, A. C., *The Races of Man and their Distribution*. New York, 1925.

HERSKOVITS, M. J., "When Is a Jew a Jew?" in *Modern Quarterly*, Vol. iv, No. 2, 1927, pp. 109-117.

———, *The American Negro, a Study in Racial Crossing*. New York, 1928.

HUXLEY, J. S., and HADDON, A. C., *We Europeans; a Survey. of "Racial" Problems*. New York and London, 1936.

JACOBS, JOSEPH, "On the Racial Characters of Modern Jews," in *Journal Royal Anthropological Institute*, Vol. xv, 1886, pp. 23-56.

KENNEDY, RAYMOND, "The Position and Future of the Jews in America," in *Jews in a Gentile World, op. cit.*, pp. 418-432.

KROGMAN, WILTON M., Anthropology, physical (ms. of article prepared for *the World Encyclopedia Institute*), 1945.

VON LUSCHAN, FELIX, "The Early Inhabitants of Western Asia," in *Jour. Roy. Anth. Inst.*, Vol. xli., 1911, pp. 221-244.

MANDELBAUM, DAVID G., "The Jewish Way of Life in Cochin," in *Jewish Social Studies*, Vol. 1, 1939, pp. 423-460.

MORANT, G. M., *The Races of Central Europe, a Footnote to History*. London, 1939.

PARR, LELAND W., "Isohemagglutination Studies on Near East Race Groups," in *An Introduction to the Anthropology of the Near East in Ancient and Recent Times, op. cit.*, pp. 178-196.

SELTZER, CARL C., "The Jew—His Racial Status," in *Harvard Medical Alumni Bulletin*, Vol. 13, No. 3, 1939, pp. 67-75.

WAGENSEIL, F., "Beitraege zur physischen Anthropologie der spaniolischen Juden und zur juedischen Rassenfrage," in *Zeitschrift fuer Morphologie und Anthropologie*, (Stuttgart), Vol. xxiii, 1925, pp. 33-150.

WEIDENREICH, FRANZ, "The Skull of Sinanthropus Pekinensis; a Comparative Study on a Primitive Hominid Skull," in *Palaeontologia Sinica* (n.s. D), No. 10. Lancaster, Pa., 1943.

WEINRICH, MAX, "Summary and Conclusions," in *The Classification of Jewish Immigrants and its Implications* (Yiddish Scientific Institute), pp. 106-154. New York, 1945.

CHAPTER 31

SOURCES OF JEWISH STATISTICS

By Uriah Zevi Engelman

There are two sources of Jewish population statistics: the government population census and the researches of private Jewish agencies. Not all government censuses collect Jewish statistics, while the private Jewish statistical agency, wherever it was organized, proved a poor substitute for census taking. As a result, Jewish population statistics are incomplete and defective.

The governments that gather Jewish population statistics do so by means of the general religious census of individuals. Its aim is to enumerate, individually, the members of each separate creed. The individual religious census usually makes up part of the general population census and is taken simultaneously with it. The question bearing on religion appears in the form of a separate item on the general population schedule. It is addressed to every individual, who is asked to state his religion in his own words, irrespective of whether or not he attends a church, belongs to it, or observes all its tenets.

A deep-rooted antagonism, however, against the inclusion of a religious query on the population census prevents many governments from collecting statistics about Jews as well as about other religious groups in their countries. This antagonism is very common in democratic countries, and is shared by legislators, census statisticians, liberals of all types and leaders of religious minorities. It is based on the conviction that religion is the intimate, private concern of an individual and must suffer no public probing by census takers. The opponents also claim that the individual religious inquiry will not only violate the principle of freedom of conscience but, by arousing in the enumerated a suspicion of bias, will have an adverse effect on the accuracy of the answers to all questions on the schedule. Leaders of religious minorities advance added reasons against the individual religious census. They are afraid that information gathered about them by the census will be interpreted in an unfavorable light, or that in the presentation of the final census reports they will not be allowed proper space, that their numbers will be published under a miscellaneous heading or be thrown into the total of some major creed.

Historically, these fears are justified. In the past, in most autocratic countries, the religious census was frequently followed by the enactment of antiminority legislation.

The situation is, of course, different in the modern democratic state. The census is no longer feared as the source of discriminatory legislation. The religious question on the schedule, phrased simply "What is your religion?" allows the individual to state the particular creed he believes in, while the final published tables classify the answers as given on the original schedules.

And, finally, the answers to the religious question on the population schedule in all democratic countries are optional. There is no penalty for refusing to answer the question, while the answers to the other items on the schedule are obligatory.

But old suspicions die hard. There are at present many countries where a direct, even though optional, request to state religious profession is considered undesirable. Great Britain, France, Belgium, Spain, Portugal and Italy belong to this category of states. The United States and most countries of South and Central America are in this group. The United States, however, independently of the general population census, collects information about the membership, property and expenditures of the organized churches. Canada, on the other hand, regularly gathers information about Jews through its decennial religious population census.

The U.S.S.R. forms a notable exception. It collects comprehensive statistics about Jews, not by means of the religious item on the schedule but by the question on the ethnic background of the enumerated.[1a]

In Asia, Jewish population statistics are gathered for the Russian-Asiatic provinces and Palestine. Most of the other countries in Asia conduct no censuses at all.

In Africa, official statistics on the Jews are available for Egypt, British South Africa, Algiers, Tunis and Tripoli. Australia and New Zealand also gather Jewish statistical information in connection with their general population censuses.

The scope of the published government-population statistics of Jews varies greatly. Russia, Germany, Poland, Palestine have, in the past, given a comprehensive demographic description of Jewish population numbers, male and female, urban and rural distribution, occupations, age groupings. Switzerland and Canada classified the Jewish inhabitants by sex and by rural and urban residence only.

THE CENSUS OF RELIGIOUS BODIES

The United States conducts a unique religious census, not of the religious profession of every individual but of the membership and wealth of organized denominations. The survey is not general, it reaches only those who are officially affiliated with some house of worship. The source of the data is secondary; it is either supplied by the head of the organization or copied from denominational sources. This census is known today as the Census of Religious Bodies. It was first instituted in 1850 under the name of the American Census of Social Statistics, and for five decades was taken simultaneously with the general population census. At the turn of the century, however, it was detached from the latter and has since been carried on separately during the intercensal interval, on the sixth year of each decade (1906, 1916, etc.).

At the first three censuses of 1850, 1860 and 1870 the religious inquiries sought to determine the number of houses of worship, value of church property and number of sittings for each denomination. Under the last heading, the census was to record the number of seats for individuals in church structures and halls hired for worship, or the number of people they could accommodate.[1] It was only in 1890 that statistics on communicants or membership were collected for the first time.[2] And as members or communicants, the instructions of 1890 considered "all those, without distinction of sex, who were permitted to partake of the Lord's Supper in denominations observing that sacrament and those having full privileges in denominations like the Friends, the Unitarians and the Jews";[3] in a word, affiliated, dues-paying members. Obviously, since not all Jews are affiliated synagogue members, the Census of Religious Bodies could not claim to have enumerated all Jews in the land.

In order to realize how inadequate the Census of Religious Bodies was as a general census of the Jewish population, one need but state that for 1906 it reported 101,457 and in 1916 it reported 357,135 members of Jewish congregations. The Jewish population for these years respectively was estimated at fifteen and ten times these figures.

In 1926 the Census of Religious Bodies extended the definition of a member of a Jewish synagogue to include "all persons of Jewish faith, residing in communities where there was a congregation."[4] This definition also held for the census of 1936. It substituted population statistics for church membership. The latter it ascertained, not through a government-conducted, general population census but through private efforts, which involved a variety of scientific and pseudo-scientific calculation methods.

PRIVATE SOURCES OF JEWISH STATISTICS

There are few Jewish statistical research organizations in the world. There was one in Germany. Vilna was the seat of the Yiddish Scientific Institute (YIVO), which had a valuable statistical section. Following the occupation of Vilna by the Nazis, the YIVO was transferred in 1940 to New York City. The Jewish Agricultural Association in czarist Russia engaged in extensive statistical studies. The Jewish communities of France and England made sporadic attempts at organizing statistical bureaus. In Canada the American Jewish Congress recently established one. In the United States the American Jewish Committee for a number of years in the past helped support the Jewish Statistical Bureau.

The private Jewish statistical research bureau has proved useful for intensive studies of population data published by governments. However, it turned out to be a defective instrument for carrying out enumerations of large population groups. For this task extensive and expensive machinery is needed so that everyone in the country may be reached. Such machinery the private Jewish bureau lacks. Nor does it command the authority to enforce general compliance with its requests. Whenever, therefore, a private research agency attempts a canvass of a widely distributed population it must resort to estimates. These may range from mere guesses to elaborate statistical studies based on one or more demographic factors. Thus, in some places, the number of Jewish births, deaths, marriages, or the number of people affiliated with synagogues was used as a statistical clue in determining the Jewish population; in others, the proportion of popular Jewish names in the city directory (Cohen, Levy), the number of absentees in the public schools on the High Holy Days, or the number of contributors to the Jewish Federation was used as a basis for estimating the number of Jews.

The main agency for estimating the Jewish population in the United States is the Jewish Statistical Bureau, whose findings are published in the statistical section of the *American Jewish Year Book* and in the United States Census of Religious Bodies. For a number of years the Jewish population statistics for separate cities and states were personal estimates by prominent residents. The total Jewish population was then arrived at by combining these estimates. Joseph Jacobs, one of the earliest pioneers in the field of American Jewish statistics, rightly considered these estimates as little better than guesses because "few persons are aware how large a few hundred of human beings bulk in the real or imaginary eye."[5]

In 1910 an improvement was made in the method of evaluating the Jewish population in the United States. The improvement consisted in determining the percentage increase in the population of fifty cities—by comparing their estimated Jewish populations in 1907 and 1910—and then assuming that the entire Jewish population in the country had grown proportionately. It is obvious even to the least statistically trained that basing one estimate upon another may be but a compounding of errors. A more earnest attempt at estimating the Jewish population in America was made by Joseph Jacobs in 1914. Realizing that estimates even by well-informed people might be misleading, he conducted the inquiry "on as many divergent lines as possible, so that the figures to which they all converge may be reasonably supposed to vary but little from the truth."[6] These lines were: (1) the number of Jewish immigrants, (2) the census data bearing on "mother tongues" of the "foreign white stock," including Yiddish, which was spoken by a large number of Jews who migrated to this country, and (3) estimates of the Jewish population by the Industrial Removal Office for a number of cities to which it had been planning to direct immigrants.

In 1917 Dr. Alexander Dushkin[7] made a new contribution to the techniques of estimating the Jewish population in the United States. He estimated the total number of children in New York City on the basis of attendance statistics on the High Holy Days and on a sample study of Jewish names in the continuous school census kept by the Bureau of Attendance of the Board of Education of New York City. Having determined the number of Jewish children of elementary school age (five through fourteen), he then assumed that its proportion to the total Jewish population of New York City is similar to that given by the United States Census Bureau for the general elementary school population of the city in relation to the city's general population.

This method, which came to be known as the Yom Kippur absentee method, was later used in estimating the Jewish population in a number of cities. The major defect of this method is that it assumes that the Jewish child age distribution is similar to that of the general population: an assumption entirely unwarranted by Jewish demographic experience.

In 1926 the Jewish Statistical Bureau took a new step in the development of American Jewish statistics. It undertook a comprehensive survey of the Jewish population in connection with the Census of Religious Bodies, which adopted for that census (1926) an enlarged definition of what constitutes a member of a Jewish congregation. According to this definition, as pointed out above, all Jews living in localities having one or more congregations were reported as synagogue members.

Dr. Harry S. Linfield, director of the Jewish Statistical Bureau, who was in charge of the population survey, was also appointed United States government special agent to gather Jewish religious statistics for the 1926 Census of Religious Bodies. In making the two surveys, Dr. Linfield utilized most of the techniques for estimating the Jewish population that were in vogue at the time. The Jewish population of the cities of New York, Newark, Boston, Detroit, Philadelphia, St. Louis, was estimated on the basis of school attendance on the Day of Atonement; of Cleveland and Pittsburgh, on the basis of a roster of all Jewish children prepared by local social workers. The estimates were supplemented and corrected in the light of government census statistics bearing on the number of people who reported Yiddish or Hebrew as their mother tongue.

The number of Jews in the remaining fifty-seven cities of 100,000 population or over and in the 219 cities of 25,000-100,000 population was determined "chiefly on the basis of the local estimates, examined in the light of the number of Jews that reported Yiddish or Hebrew as their mother tongue in the census of 1920, and in the light of the number of Jewish children enrolled in the religious schools of the respective cities."[8]

Before 1927 estimates of the number of Jews in the country were made only for states and divisions. But in 1926, for the first time, Dr. Linfield used a statistical method for sampling "the 15,700 incorporated cities, towns and villages of the various sizes and the 45,000 rural unincorporated areas in the country"[9] to determine how many of these had Jewish residents and what the number of such residents was.

The use of many methods does not of course assure the accuracy of a survey. If each method is defective, the survey must necessarily suffer from the sum total of all the defects. And that the methods used for determining the Jewish population in 1926 and later in 1936 were defective becomes apparent when one considers that they were based on (1) guesses (personal local estimates), (2) estimated child population, and (3) random sampling.

The defectiveness of the data is not the only criticism one may advance against the statistics gathered by the Jewish Statistical Bureau. Another equally important objection is their very narrow scope. These statistics only offer totals for states, cities and other geographical divisions. There is no classification by sex, age groups, civil status, occupations, etc. Consequently, the data are of little value as material for social, economic and demographic studies. The lack of any significant body of sociological information about the Jewish group in America can be traced directly to deficient and meager Jewish demographic statistics.

In the past decade, a serious attempt has been made to correct the defective American Jewish statistics. Under the auspices of the Conference on Jewish Relations, organized by Morris R. Cohen, censuses, based on total or partial counts of the Jewish population, were made for a number of cities. These censuses were the first to gather information on sex and age distribution, marital status, occupations, size of family, etc. These studies have been published in a volume of *Jewish Population Studies*, which is the first important work on Jewish demography in America.

The Biblical Period[9a]

The Bible is one of the earliest repositories of statistical data. It contains records of three major censuses taken of the ancient Hebrews. The first two were ordered by Moses: one, at the foot of Mt. Sinai, a year and a month after the Exodus; the second, after forty years of wandering in the desert. The third was ordered by King David.

Dr. Salo W. Baron painstakingly scrutinized the statistical data in the Bible.[10] He examined the figures mentioned more than once in the original Hebrew Scriptures and in the early translations, and found few discrepancies. He also analyzed the factors that could possibly influence Jewish population growth in antiquity: infanticide, polygamy, slave economy, economy of scarcity, spread of disease, size of families, famine, wars. This analysis and the inner consistency discovered in the figures, he rightly concludes, testify to the accuracy of the biblical census population statistics. King David's census, which related to adult males able to bear arms, would indicate, according to Professor Baron, a total population well over four million in the days of the Kings. But since the enumeration was made with a view of ascertaining both the number of people in the military class and those subject to taxation, Professor Baron thinks the census included also people of non-Jewish tribes. Deducting the latter, he arrives at an estimate of a Jewish population of 1,500,000-1,800,000 in the days of the Kings.

About one hundred years before Professor Baron, Moreau de Jonnés, a famous statistician and member of the French Academy of Science, analyzed the statistical records in the Bible and found them trustworthy. "Mankind," said Moreau de Jonnés, "may take pride in realizing that more than 4,000 years back, in a remote corner of Asia, there lived a small nation which gathered population statistics of great scientific accuracy, and for the very reasons modern nations do it today, for the purpose of governing the country, conducting wars and regulating the people's economy."[11] The Jewish population of Palestine in the days of King David, according to his estimate, numbered 3,757,000. His reasoning sheds interesting light on Jewish population trends of that period.

According to the biblical record, four hundred and thirty years elapsed from the time Jacob arrived with his "seventy souls" in Egypt, until the enumeration at the foot of Mt. Sinai. During this period Jacob's family grew to be a people of apparently 1,500,000. They lived in peace, in a salubrious place, and had an abundance of food. It was an increase of one person per every 430 individuals a year. Many European countries in the nineteenth century enjoyed a rate of increase twice or three times as high. Only as we go back into antiquity, when modern arts and sciences were unknown, do we encounter the slow rate of increase of Israel in Egypt. During the forty years of wandering in the desert the Jewish population declined slightly. Scarcity of food, plagues and civil war, it seems, destroyed that part of the population which comes from an excess of births over deaths. During the centuries between the conquest of the land and the reign of King David, the population more than doubled to 3,757,000 individuals. The annual proportional increase was one person per 770, or about one-half of the relative increase recorded by them in Egypt. France within an equal period tripled her population, and England increased her population sixfold. In Canaan the Jews were no longer primitive shepherds. They were soil cultivators and city dwellers. They had a well organized military and civil organization. And this, apparently, retarded their rate of natural growth as much as high standards of living do today.

THE CLASSICAL PERIOD

During the millennium following the reign of King David the little country of Palestine was twice completely devastated, several times overrun by invaders, ravaged by prolonged wars of extermination and laid waste by civil strife and bloody revolts.[11a] While no authoritative figures are available, the writer estimates that in the first century of the Common Era, the Jewish population, according to various authoritative estimates, numbered between five and seven millions. This population increase was made possible because: (1) Jews encouraged population growth. (2) They were a useful, productive and valuable economic element in Roman society. Hence, Jews were allowed to live in relative security. (3) They voluntarily migrated and spread over the lands and islands of the Mediterranean Basin. Especially numerous were these migrations during and following the Hellenistic period. (4) Greek and Roman rulers valued Jews as colonists for their skill, industry and dependability; frequently they were employed for opening up new territories. (5) The Jewish practice of ransoming captive brethren and Jewish proselytizing [a practice characteristic of this period] also were factors in the growth and spread of the Jewish population. (6) Last but not least, Jews manifested a remarkable ability to resist assimilation. This resistance was rooted in their deep loyalty to a nomocracy, to a book of laws, and it was not confined to any one locality. Such loyalty was everywhere to be seen.

In the classical world, the Jews formed between eight and ten per cent of the population. It was the highest density ever achieved by a large Jewish population group scattered over so wide a territory. Had the Jews retained today the same proportion to the total population, there would have been more than ten times as many Jews in the lands that were once part of the Roman Empire. And this empire, it is well to recall, did not include Russia, Poland and the United States, where today the majority of world Jewry is to be found.

THE FEUDAL PERIOD

In the centuries following the breakup of the Roman Empire, the Jewish people was decimated. These were centuries of vast population movements.[11b] In their wake cities shrank in size, decayed, ceased to be centers of population, government and trade. Commerce vanished, government disintegrated and all orderly means of communication broke down. The Jews found their old urban occupations, trade and crafts, no longer serviceable for earning a living. Together with the non-Jews who formerly lived in cities, they now settled on the land. For about five or six centuries the soil became the chief and almost only source of livelihood for the Jewish population. But this radical occupational readjustment resulted in a severe dwindling of their numbers. The non-Jewish population was relatively less affected by this change, since it had had a very small urban element in the classic world.

How much the Jewish population declined during this period we have no way of telling, until we come to the twelfth century, and read the diaries of Benjamin ben Jonah of Tudela, a Jewish traveler, who preceded Marco Polo by a century and a half. According to his testimony and additional information which he did not include in his report, the Jewish population in the then known world was probably less than a million and a half.[12] But the decline still continued in the coming three centuries.

From the evolving manorial economy, the Jews were gradually eliminated. They were removed from the soil, shut out of the guilds, and barred from all lucrative economic occupations offered by church and monastery, the only great medieval employers of labor. The Jews were thus forced to gain a living outside the manorial economy. This meant earning a livelihood through trade in goods and in money. But trading in the medieval period was a nonsanctioned, highly hazardous occupation. Besides, there was little of it. Medieval trade did not require the services of a large middle class. Even if it were largely in Jewish hands, trading could support only a small number of people. The fact is, however, that non-Jewish merchants—Syrians, Armenians, Lombards, Portuguese—outnumbered the Jews. The Jewish masses had no big share in medieval trade. Removed from soil and manor, they could find no means of gaining sustenance and, as a result, their numbers diminished.

It was at this time also that the Crusades, and the intolerance they unleashed, played havoc with the Jewish population.

THE PERIOD OF COMMERCIAL EXPANSION

Extinction loomed real on the Jewish horizon. This danger was partly offset. Jews married early, and meticulously observed a sanitary religious code of life which probably reduced mortality rates among them. These measures, however, were of little avail. Jewish populations continued to decline as long as they were treated as superfluous within the social-economic body of the countries they inhabited. This decline reached its nadir by the fifteenth century. On the entire European continent there were probably fewer than 300,000 Jews; in the entire world there were fewer than a million, most of whom were concentrated in the Near East. But the following century marked a turn of affairs.[12a] Crusades were ended and with them the wanton destruction of Jewish life. The feudal order, which forced the Jew into the interstitial zone of feudal economy, had about spent itself. There was a vigorous revival of city life, a substantial increase in the volume, variety and number of commodities for trade. A large trading class was emerging. The highly restrictive town economy, in which the Jew was considered an alien intruder, yielded to a system of intercontinental trade with international trading corporations and exchanges where the Jew was accepted as a member. The importance of commerce and handicrafts for the development of a country had become apparent even to the most backward ruler. Increasingly, countries were being linked closer to each other. It was an interlinking due to the greater mutual dependence of trades and markets. This was of tremendous influence on the growth of Jewish population in the next few centuries. The Jews, whom feudal disabilities a few centuries ago had forced to engage in trade, now found themselves in the vanguard of an evolving commercial era. Their expulsion from any one place could no longer be the sole concern of a ruler's or class's arbitrary whim. A massacre, an expulsion of the Jewish trading group, might disrupt the normal economic activities of a city, and might unfavorably affect its relations with other commercial centers. The period of expulsions was ended; the era of readmission had begun. One of the first effects of the Commercial Revolution was to check the decline of Jewish population.

Another favorable demographic factor at this time probably operated within the Jewish, as contrasted with the general population. Medieval cities had been nests of disease. Yearly, they had had a large excess of deaths. Only by drawing on the countryside population had the cities been able to grow in size and replenish their losses.

The Jews lived in the unsanitary medieval cities because they were forced off the land in the early feudal period. During the centuries they probably developed a relative biologic immunity to the city. And it was at this time that the city took on added importance.

The expanding commercial activity on the Continent naturally resulted in a sudden increase of aggregate wealth. Such an increase, according to demographic experience, has always been correlated with an increase in population growth. And what happened generally happened to Jews too. They shared in the increase of aggregate wealth; their population also increased. According to available fragmentary information, Jewish numbers probably more than doubled by the time the Commercial Revolution had become the Industrial Revolution. It has been estimated that at the end of the eighteenth century the Jewish population of the world was between two and two and a half millions.

JEWISH POPULATION IN THE NINETEENTH CENTURY

During the nineteenth century the Jewish population increased more than fourfold. This large increase, part of a general increase of world population, was the consequence of technical, industrial, economic and social processes, partly initiated and partly accelerated by the advance of industrial capitalism.

TABLE 1

Jewish Population Growth in the Nineteenth Century

Year	Population
1800	2,500,000
1825	3,280,000
1850	4,750,000
1880	7,650,000
1900	10,600,000

Source: Jacob Lestschinsky, "Die Umsiedlung und Umschichtung des juedischen Volkes im Laufe des letzten Jahrhunderts," *Weltwirtschaftliches Archiv*, Jena, 1929, II, Band 30, p. 155.

What were these processes? Among others, they were the rise in the number, prestige, differentiation and power of the middle classes; the shift in the center of economic activity from village to town; the enormous increase in the opportunities for gaining a livelihood—a consequence of the

TABLE 2

Growth of Jewish Population

1825-1900

Countries	1825	1850	1880	1900
Western and central Europe	458,000	693,500	1,044,500	1,328,500
Eastern and southeastern Europe	2,272,000	3,434,000	5,726,000	7,362,000
Europe	2,730,000	4,127,500	6,770,500	8,690,500
America	10,000	65,000	250,000	1,175,000
Asia	300,000	320,000	350,000	420,000
Africa	240,000	250,000	280,000	300,000
Australia	1,000	2,000	12,000	17,000

Source: *Schriften fuer Wirtschaft und Statistik* (in Yiddish), Juedisches Wissenschaftliches Institut, Berlin, 1928, Band I, p. 6.

introduction of mass production; the division of labor and the vast development of transportation and communication; the abolition of the legal limitations on Jewish marriages; the vast improvement in the sanitary conditions of city life; the opening up of new centers for colonization, especially in North America.

Political emancipation played a minor part in the expansion. The major increase in the Jewish population occurred in eastern Europe, which remained politically unemancipated. The countries that abandoned anti-Semitism as a state policy in the nineteenth century, the highly industrialized western countries and the Americas, shared only indirectly in the growth of the Jewish population by accepting the population overflow from eastern Europe.

How Fast Did the Jews Multiply?

The fourfold increase of the nineteenth-century Jewish population, remarkable as it seems, was in keeping with the general population trends of the period.

The nineteenth century was one of tremendous population expansion. "For half a million years since mankind rose up on its hind legs and made a bid for world supremacy . . . its natural increase was so slow that in the year 1800 there were less than 850 million people."[13] But in 1938 there were over two billion people in the world. In 138 years mankind not only exceeded the growth achieved by it in the preceding half million or million years, but had added more people to the human total than in the entire previous span of its existence. Dr. Henry Pratt Fairchild rightly considers these figures the most amazing statistics in the world, while all other statistics "may quite accurately be regarded as mere embroideries upon this great central pattern."[14]

When the Jewish population increase is compared with another that might be analogous, namely, that of the English-speaking peoples—who, like the Jews, are distributed over several continents—one finds that the Jewish rate of natural increase in the nineteenth century was quite slow. A United States Census report is revealing on this point.

The population of Great Britain in 1712 is estimated to have been but 9,000,000. During the succeeding century, the eighteenth, Great Britain contributed from the small population the stock which formed the larger part of the white population of the United States in 1790, and which increased by 1900 to approximately 35,000,000 souls. In 1801 the population of the United Kingdom was 16,200,000, by 1900 it had increased to 41,000,000. But during the nineteenth century the mother country also contributed, even more freely than she had contributed during the eighteenth century to North America, to the population of the United States and to that of a score of younger colonies

... It is possible that a population growth similar in character may have occurred upon a small scale in connection with some of the colonies established
by ancient cities along the Mediterranean, but in magnitude there appears
to be no parallel in history for this population achievement of the British race
from 1700-1900.[15]

Nor does the growth of Jewish population seem exceptional when compared with the growth of separate countries, as is shown in Table 3.

TABLE 3

	1580	1680	1780	1880
England	4,600,000	5,532,000	9,561,000	35,002,000
Prussia	1,000,000	1,400,000	5,460,000	45,260,000
Russia	4,300,000	12,600,000	26,800,000	84,440,000
France	14,300,000	18,800,000	25,100,000	37,400,000

It is well to note that the world population increased also prior to the
sixteenth century, "an increase of possibly 33 per cent in one hundred years
was reached by the seventeenth century and of 50 per cent by the
eighteenth."[16] The Jewish population following the disintegration of the
Roman Empire declined until almost the sixteenth century.

THE HINTERLAND OF JEWISH POPULATION GROWTH

A population as a whole may grow only by an excess of births over
deaths; in any one specific area, however, it may increase by an excess
of births and a difference between immigration and emigration. Viewing
world Jewish population as a unit, one learns the remarkable fact that
practically its entire natural increase during the nineteenth century was
supplied by those in eastern Europe. This area comprised the Ukraine,
White Russia, Lithuania, Poland, Rumania, Galicia and Hungary. It
constituted the hinterland of Jewish population expansion. It served as a
reservoir of people, the kind of reservoir which in all countries the rural
communities provide. Culturally, it was backward; socioeconomically, it
was just about to emerge from an economy based on serfdom. It had, in
the nineteenth century, higher Jewish birth and death rates, a higher rate
of natural increase, and a lower standard of living than any of the other
Jewish population groups of western and central Europe, or America.

The advance of industrial capitalism into this hinterland, the introduction of the steel plow, the opening up of numerous small factories, the
increase in trade, resulted in augmenting the opportunities for livelihood.
These opportunities were not followed by an increase in individual well-
being but by a large expansion of the population and a sinking standard of
living. It seems that as soon as the frontiers of starvation were pushed

back the area left open was filled by new births. For once Malthus's theory was vindicated! This experience of the Jewish hinterland was not unique. It followed the pattern set by England and other European countries in their early stages of capitalist development.

And as the pressure for bread and space became acute in the hinterland, its population pushed out into the western countries and overseas, replacing with its members the dwindling urban Jewish communities.

TABLE 4

Showing Absolute and Relative Increase of Jewish Population in the Countries of Western and Eastern Europe, 1825-1900[17]

	1825-1850 Absolute Increase	Percentage Increase	1850-1900 Absolute Increase	Percentage Increase
Western Europe	235,000	51.3	635,500	91.7
Eastern Europe	1,162,000	51.1	3,928,000	114.4

The figures in Table 4 do not reveal the full extent of the natural increase of the Jewish population in western and eastern Europe. To determine the natural increase of the Jews in eastern Europe one must add to its given population the number of the east European immigrants and

TABLE 5

Growth and Distribution of the Jewish Population in the Hinterland

1825-1900

Country	1900	1880	1850	1825
Prewar Russia	5,175,000	3,980,000	2,350,000	1,600,000
Poland without Posen	1,325,000	1,005,000	575,000	400,000
Ukraine, New Russia, Bessarabia	2,200,000	1,600,000	925,000	625,000
Lithuania, White Russia	1,450,000	1,225,000	800,000	550,000
Other provinces of Russia	200,000	150,000	50,000	25,000
Galicia	811,000	687,000	450,000	275,000
Hungary	852,000	638,000	352,000	200,000
Rumania	267,000	200,000	130,000	80,000
Bukovina	96,000	67,500	15,000	8,000
Bulgaria	34,000	20,000	10,000	7,000
Other provinces of southeastern Europe	92,000	77,000	52,000	37,000

Source: *Schriften fuer Wirtschaft und Statistik, op. cit.,* p. 6.

their descendants, who lived at the time in western Europe, in the Americas and in the other countries. What their number was one cannot tell precisely. But that it was large may be gauged from this: By 1900, more than one million East European Jews had settled in the Americas, and about a quarter of a million in western Europe and other lands. Eastern Europe, on the other hand, received no Jewish immigrants.

Similarly, in order to evaluate the natural increase of west European Jews in the nineteenth century, one would have to add, on the one hand, about 250,000 west European Jewish immigrants and their descendants who migrated to America and other countries and, on the other hand, deduct at least 200,000 east European Jews who settled in western Europe.

NINETEENTH-CENTURY VITAL BALANCE SHEET

Leroy Beaulieu makes a pointed observation in his book *Israel Among the Nations* in regard to Jewish population growth in the nineteenth century. "They [the Jews] bring fewer children into the world, but they bring more of them to maturity. It would seem as if, with their characteristic cleverness at calculations, they have instinctively solved the difficult problems of population in the manner most advantageous to themselves and most satisfactory to the economists." This observation held true for every country in Europe, as is shown by Tables 6 and 7.

The Jewish birth rates in the eastern countries of nineteenth-century

TABLE 6

Jewish and General Birth Rates in Europe at the End of the Nineteenth Century

Place	Year(s)	Jewish Birth Rates	General Birth Rates	Jewish Birth Rates Lower by
Rumania	1896-1900	40.1	40.1	—
Galicia	1895-1900	40.4	44.3	3.9
Bulgaria	1891-1895	37.5	37.5	—
Russia	1896-1897	35.9	50.2	14.3
Budapest	1891-1900	29.5	34.6	5.1
Vienna	1900	22.2	31.7	9.5
Prussia	1900	19.4	36.2	16.8
Hamburg	1900	19.1	28.8	9.7
Frankfort on the Main	1900	18.0	30.3	12.3
Trieste	1891-1900	17.2		
Padua	1891-1900	13.2		

Based on the following sources: B. Bienstock and S. Novoselski, *Dvijenie Eureiskavo Naselenia v Europeiskoi Rossii*, Petrograd, 1915; Robert R. Kuczynski, *The Balance of Births and Deaths*, The Institute of Economics, The Brookings Institution, New York, 1928, II; Jacob Lestschinsky, "Probleme der Bevoelkerungs Bewegung bei den Juden," *Metron*, Padova, 1926, VI; *Zeitschrift fuer Demographie und Statistik der Juden*, 1905; *Blaetter fuer Demographie, Statistik und Wirtschaftskunde der Juden*, Berlin, 4.

Europe were higher than in the western countries. This difference increased with the distance from the hinterland. The physical distance was probably of minor importance. The major cause for the differential was the higher degree of modernization in the western lands. In all countries, the Jewish birth rates were much lower than those of the general population.

TABLE 7

Jewish and General Death Rates at End of Nineteenth Century

Country	Years	Jewish Death Rates	General Death Rates	Jewish Death Rates Lower by
Bulgaria	1891-1895	23.1	27.9	4.8
Rumania	1896-1900	21.4	27.4	6.0
Galicia	1895-1900	20.8	28.4	7.6
Russia	1900-1904	16.7	31.0	14.3
Warsaw	1901	18.2	21.6	3.4
Hungary	1896-1900	16.8	27.6	10.8
Prussia	1900	14.9	21.7	6.8
Vienna	1900	12.9	20.7	7.8
Trieste	1891-1900	17.6		

Based on the following sources: Kuczynski, *op. cit.*; Bienstock and Novoselski, *op. cit.*; *Mouvement de la Population de la Ville de Varsovie*, Publié par le Service Statistique de la ville de Varsovie, Varsovie, 1902; Lestschinsky, *Metron, op. cit.*; *Zeitschrift fuer Demographie und Statistik der Juden*, 1905, Heft 5, Heft 6.

The Jews, who, historically, became urbanized earlier than their neighbors and were more sensitive to the inroads of industrialization, led the decline in Europe both in birth rate and in death rate. Jewish death rates began to decline much sooner than their birth rates. The difference in birth rates between Jews of the western countries and of the hinterland, held also for death rates. The Jews of eastern Europe had higher birth rates, they also had higher death rates. As in the case of birth rates, the Jewish death rates were lower than those of the general population.

JEWISH POPULATION IN THE TWENTIETH CENTURY

The great increase in mankind's population in the nineteenth century was, in Dr. Fairchild's words, the resultant, among others, of man's ability to "spread himself over the entire globe without breaking up into more than one species." In the twentieth century, the Jews literally found themselves spread throughout the world, yet, on the whole, retained their spiritual ties with one another.

Between 1900 and 1938, according to the estimate of Dr. Arthur Ruppin, in his book *Jewish Fate and Future*, the Jewish world population increased from 10,600,000 to 16,717,000.

But in the twentieth century new demographic tendencies became apparent, whose origin could be traced to the latter part of the nineteenth century and whose cumulative effect was a sharp slowing up of the rate of increase. The Jewish population felt the impact of these influences both earlier and more strongly. As a highly urbanized minority, living most of the time under severe social pressures, it developed a higher sensitivity to social change than did other urban groups. This higher sensitivity was revealed in its continued lead in the twentieth century of a decline in birth rates; in its being first to mark a sharp rise in death rates in a number of countries; in its rate of natural increase and in the size of its families, which were shrinking faster than those of the general population.

THE DRYING UP OF THE RESERVOIR OF JEWISH POPULATION GROWTH

Early in the twentieth century it became clear that many Jewish communities in western, northwestern, southern Europe, and also in America, could not continue to maintain themselves through natural increase. Their birth rates were declining, their death rates rising; intermarriage increased, and the Jewish proportion in the total population diminished. The Jewish population of these countries, however, was replenished and in fact increased through immigrants. Yet as the twentieth century advanced the hinterland lost its function as a reservoir for supplying Jewish people.

Wars, revolutions, secession meant dismemberment for Jews; a sinking rate of natural increase reduced the relative Jewish population density in the entire area and its separate provinces, even before the outbreak of the Second World War.

In the Soviet Union, which comprised the major part of the hinterland, the Jewish population was subjected to economic and intellectual influences which weakened its historic consciousness of uniqueness as an ethnic group.

Before the First World War half the world Jewish population lived in czarist Russia, where it formed 4.2 per cent of the population. In the Soviet Union in 1926 it numbered 2,600,000, and had a relative density of 1.8. The Jewish density of the Soviet Union will continue to sink because the Jewish rate of natural increase is lower than that of the other population groups. Thus in 1926, for the entire territory of all the Soviet Republics, the rate of natural increase for the White Russians was 26.91, for the Ukrainians, 24.31, for the Great Russians, 22.64, and for the Jews, 14.97. Also the growing number of mixed marriages is an added factor in diminishing the Jewish proportion in the population of the Soviet Union.

This latter fact is especially significant, since, according to a study made by the present writer, there is a direct relationship in the Soviet Union between the rate of natural increase and the density of the Jewish population, and an inverse relationship between Jewish population density and intermarriages.[18]

Poland and Rumania, the other two important sections of the hinterland, were occupied for over four years by the Nazis. Most of the Jews in this area were slaughtered. Not much better is the situation in Austria, especially in Galicia, or in Hungary. Eastern Europe as a hinterland of world Jewry has thus ceased to exist. It is questionable whether the Jewish communities outside the hinterland will be able to maintain themselves by natural growth.

TABLE 8

Jewish and General Birth Rates in the Twentieth Century

Countries	Year	Jewish Birth Rates	General Birth Rates	Jewish Birth Rates Lower by
Rumania	1901-1905	32.6	39.5	6.9
	1930	15.8	35.8	20.0
Bulgaria	1904-1907	34.2	43.2	9.0
	1930	20.2	30.1	9.9
Poland	1928	20.4	26.5	6.1
	1933	18.7	26.5	7.8
Galicia	1901-1902	38.1	43.9	5.8
	1928	20.8		
Lithuania	1925	15.9	29.6	13.7
	1928	17.1	28.7	11.6
Hungary	1896-1900	33.9	38.5	4.6
	1929	12.0	25.8	13.8
Prussia	1900	19.4	36.2	16.8
	1929	9.1	19.1	10.0
	1931-1935	6.1	18.0	11.9
Vienna	1900	22.2	31.7	9.5
	1929	6.5	9.4	2.9
Amsterdam	1899-1900	25.2	30.4	5.2
	1919-1922	19.2	21.7	2.5
Leningrad	1910-1913	17.6	27.7	10.1
	1920	17.2	21.8	4.6

Tables 8 and 9 based on the following sources: Jacob Lestschinsky, "Probleme der Bevoelkerungs Bewegung bei den Juden," *op. cit.; Information de L'Office Central de Statistique*, Varsovie, 1932, XX, Fasc. 2; *Résultats Généraux du Recensement de la Population dans le Royaume de Bulgarie*, 1926, I; *Lietuvos Respublica, Statistikos Biuletenis* (Statistics of the Lithuanian Republic), Kaunos, 1928-1929, 6, 56; *Zeitschrift fuer Demographie und Statistik der Juden*, 1905; Arthur Ruppin, *Sociologia shel Hayehudim*, Tel-Aviv, 1931-1932; *Idem, The Jews in the Modern World*, London, 1934; *Idem, Jewish Fate and Future*, London, 1940; Kuczynski, *op. cit.*, I, II; *Digest of Jewish Statistics*, published by the Jewish Statistical Bureau of New York, I and II.

Twentieth-Century Vital Balance Sheet Birth Rates

During the first three decades of the twentieth century, both Jewish and general birth rates declined in all the lands for which statistics are available. In the hinterland the Jewish birth rates declined faster and in the western countries slower than the general birth rates. As a result, during the first three decades the differential between the Jewish and the general birth rates widened in the hinterland and was narrowed outside of it. As in the nineteenth century, the birth rates were lower the farther the country was from the hinterland.

In eastern Europe Jewish death rates declined during the first three decades of the present century; in western Europe they rose. They were lower than the general death rates in all countries, except for Prussia, where the Jewish death rates were higher than those of the general population.

In the nineteenth century, east European Jews had higher death rates than their coreligionists in the western countries. In the twentieth century the situation has been reversed. Interesting to note is this: the countries farthest from the hinterland now have the higher death rates; in the nineteenth century this was true of the countries in the hinterland.

TABLE 9

Death Rates of Jewish and General Population in the Twentieth Century

Country	Year	Jewish	General	Jewish Greater or Lower by
Rumania	1901-1905	21.2	25.7	−4.5
	1930	10.1	19.7	−9.6
Poland	1927	11.2	19.6	−8.4
	1933	10.0	14.2	−4.2
Bulgaria	1904-1907	13.7	21.9	−8.2
	1925-1928	11.1	18.5	−7.4
Budapest	1925	13.4	17.2	−3.8
	1929	15.0	18.8	−3.8
Vienna	1900	12.9	20.7	−7.8
	1929	13.2	14.4	−1.2
Prussia	1900	14.9	21.7	−6.8
	1929	15.4	12.9	+2.5

INTERMARRIAGES

Intermarriage has become a serious factor in reducing Jewish numbers in politically emancipated countries. Two circumstances contributed to that. The Church withdrew the medieval ban against mixed marriages; moreover, cultural assimilation, which follows political emancipation, leads frequently to mixed marriages. In many cases intermarriage is a prelude to baptism.

Assimilation affects Jewish population growth in yet another way. The upper professional, intellectual, artistic and financial classes are usually unable by their reproductive powers to maintain their ratio to the population as a whole. This gap in the upper ranks creates a movement from the lower classes into the upper ones. But in the upper economic and professional classes the influence of assimilation is unusually strong. That influence sometimes insulates the members from all Jewish influence, and may even result in intermarriage and baptism.

Julius Drachsler pointed out in his *Democracy and Assimilation* that in America a high degree of mental and social assimilation coexisted with a low proportion of intermarriages. Whether this is still so today we do not know; in Germany, however, assimilation always went hand in hand with mixed marriages and baptism. During the past three decades of the twentieth century there were in Germany 109,544 homogeneous marriages and 37,507 mixed marriages. The latter formed 34.2 per cent of all endogamous marriages.

In the Soviet Union, the number of mixed marriages increased from 2,987 in 1924 to 3,198 in 1925, and to 4,361 in 1926. The number of homogeneous Jewish marriages during the same period decreased by 800.

The rate of Jewish intermarriages in the Soviet Union varies inversely with the density of the Jewish population. White Russia has the highest Jewish population density, 8.2 per cent of the total White Russian population, and the lowest record of Jewish mixed marriages. In 1926 it reported sixty-five mixed per thousand Jewish homogeneous marriages. In the Ukraine, where Jewish density is slighter, 5.4 per cent of the Ukrainian population, the rate of Jewish mixed marriages was 106 in 1926. The highest rate of Jewish intermarriages was reported for the European part of R.S.F.S.R. (Russia Proper) where the density of Jewish population is only 5 per cent of the total population of the republic. In 1926, for every thousand unmixed Jewish unions there were 532 that were intermarriages.

In Hungary the number of mixed Jewish marriages formed over 32 per cent of the homogeneous ones. Thus during the years 1931-1933 there were in Hungary 9,420 endogamous marriages and 3,059 mixed Jewish marriages. In Bohemia the number of Jewish marriages has been rapidly mounting. During the first year after World War I, ten out of every hundred marriages were contracted out of the fold. In 1927, 300 mixed against 500 homogeneous marriages were reported. In Austria mixed marriages formed 24 per cent of all Jewish marriages of 1929-1931.

Likewise, Switzerland has reported a growing number of intermarriages. The ratio of mixed per every thousand homogeneous marriages has increased from 57 in 1888 to 74 in 1900, to 97 in 1910, to 132 in 1920, to 190 in 1930.

In Copenhagen, for the 1889-1899 decade, the average yearly number of intermarriages was sixty-eight for every hundred unmixed marriages; the average rose to eighty-two for the 1900-1905 period.

URBANIZATION OF JEWS

Jews massed into cities earlier than other population groups and at a faster tempo. In the Middle Ages, Jews settled first in cities along the trade routes. Later, in eastern Europe, where navigable rivers were few and roads bad, each district was economically self-sufficient and had its own markets. Jews, who were artisans and small traders, spread very thinly over the countryside because no one village could support more than several of them.

The church records of the number of Jews in the 5,019 villages of the diocese of Olck for the year 1775 offer a graphic illustration of the wide distribution of the Jews in the eighteenth century.

TABLE 10

Distribution of the Jewish and Non-Jewish Rural Population of the
Diocese of Olck[19]

	Number of Villages	Number of Christian Inhabit.	Aver. No. of Christian Inhabit. per Village	Number of Jewish Inhabit.	Aver. Number of Jews per Village
Olck	595	33,332	56	2,460	4.1
Maszovien	2,688	129,467	48.1	10,332	3.8
Rawa	44	3,172	72	114	2.6
Wyszogorod	176	9,222	52.4	1,211	6.9
Dobrzyn	365	24,631	67.4	1,235	3.4
Wizk	265	17,408	73.2	1,486	5.6
Zawskrzyn	595	20,464	34.4	1,052	1.7
Zakzosczyn	291	15,197	52.2	904	3.1

In the nineteenth century Jews shared fully in urbanization, which had become a universal concomitant of the Industrial Revolution and the rapid development of modern means of transportation and communication.

In the hinterland, which in the nineteenth century contained more than 60 per cent of Jewish world population, this movement was accelerated by anti-Jewish legislation, which barred Jews from rural areas. Jewish urbanization entailed moving from villages and smaller towns to larger ones. But at the end of the nineteenth and the first decades of the twentieth, it entailed moving to the capitals and the large industrial centers of the world. "One may thus speak," aptly remarks Professor Salo Baron, "of the metropolization rather than urbanization of the Jewish people."[20]

In 1925 more than a fourth of all Jews in Europe and America lived in the fourteen cities with a million population or more, while only 5.7 per cent of the total population of the two continents lived in them.

Before the outbreak of the Second World War this process was so far advanced that more than half the world's Jewish population lived in forty-two cities having 100,000 inhabitants or more; each had upwards of 50,000 Jewish residents; while 35 per cent of the world's Jewish population lived in communities with more than 100,000 Jews. In America only 21.7 per cent of the total population lived in cities of more than 100,000 people, while 83.7 per cent of the Jewish population lived in such cities.

The urbanization of the Russian population, coming in the wake of the five-year industrialization periods, was phenomenally rapid. During the years 1928 to 1932, Russia's city population increased 40 per cent. Jewish participation in this urbanization process was equally amazing.

Urbanization retards population growth. In the cities birth rates are lower, death rates higher, families smaller and the population "older" than in the rural areas or in the smaller towns. Many cities have only an apparent natural increase—apparent because migration has resulted in a population whose age composition is favorable to low death rates and high birth rates.

But for many, if not most, urbanized Jewish communities of the world, even before the outbreak of World War II, there was no longer an apparent natural increase. For these there was an actual natural decrease.

Of all Austrian Jews 91.9 per cent were in Vienna. For the decade 1928-1938 the city's Jewish birth rates were insufficient to balance the yearly number of Jewish deaths. Likewise Budapest, which contained more than half of Hungary's Jews, registered 2,526 more Jewish deaths than births for 1931-1932. The situation was similar in most European capitals and large cities.

The major portion of the Jewish populations of England and France was in London and Paris. London had, in 1932, a natural increase of only two per thousand population and Paris recorded even a lower natural increase. Since Jewish birth rates were everywhere lower than those of the general population, one may safely assume that Jews did not share in the small surpluses recorded by either capital. And this trend is prevalent not only in the old capitals of Europe, it is asserting itself also in the United States. There are no birth or death statistics for American Jews. However, the several studies of the size of the American Jewish family and of the age composition of the Jewish population, recently made for a number of cities, tell that their Jewish population is not reproducing itself.[21]

The Effect of the Decade 1936-1946 on Jewish Population Numbers[21a]

World War II cut into Jewish population in a double sense. It killed, literally, millions of Jews, and it contributed to the aggravation of the dysgenic demographic trends that were observable before its outbreak.

The European phase of the war was waged in an area which contained almost 60 per cent of world Jewish population. The actual annihilation of the Jewish population was one of the main ideological and military objectives of the German Nazified war machine. And this objective was to a large extent achieved.

Eugene M. Kulisher estimated in his study *The Displacement of Population in Europe* that by the beginning of 1943 over four million Jews were expelled, deported and uprooted. The number perished is variously estimated from 25 per cent and up.[22] But during the years 1943 and 1944 the toll mounted. As the Nazi machinery of death was forced to roll back under blows of the Allied armies, it slaughtered or carried off the surviving Jewish populations.

But wars, massacres, expulsions are aberrations of an age. They do not decide the ultimate destiny of a population. The latter is determined, in the long run, by the vital processes, which work constantly and persistently at shaping its size, course and composition; upon these processes wars are only superimposed.

At the beginning of the war, there was a general rise in the number of first and second births, but a decline in the number of consecutive births. The average size of the family has not been materially altered. And the low Jewish birth rates of the prewar period will probably sink still more. A further decline will of necessity be followed by a rise in the death rates and the fast "aging" of the population.

NOTES

[1] "At the census of 1870 the inquiry headed 'number of churches' was divided into two parts (*a*) number of church organizations and (*b*) number of church edifices. This was done because on the previous two censuses it was not possible to feel assurance in any particular case whether church organizations or church edifices, were returned."

[1*] On the 1926 U.S.S.R. population census schedule, the question used for gathering information on the multi-national character of Soviet society was "narodnost" (an ethnographic category); in 1939 the question was "natsionalnost" (nation). The wide difference in the terms used on the two censuses makes the statistics hardly comparable.

U. S. Census of 1870, 9th census, Vol. I, "Population and Social Statistics," (Washington, 1872), p. 502.

[2] At the census of 1880 statistics of religious bodies were collected but never published. Dr. Henry Randall Waite, who was at the time head of the Department of "Statistics of Churches, Schools and Libraries" ascribes "this misfortune for which there is no excuse . . . to the failure of appropriations; also to an indisposition on the part of the then superintendent of the Census (Colonel Seaton) to give to these statistics the attention . . . they should have received." (*Lutheran Quarterly*, [Gettysburg, Pa.] Vol. XIX, No. 3, July, 1889, pp. 413-414.)

[3] *A Compendium of the Ninth Census,* (Washington, 1872), p. 261.

[4] *Jewish Congregations,* Statistics, History, Doctrine and Organization, Census of Religious Bodies, 1926 (U. S. Government Printing Office, Washington, 1929), p. 6.

[5] Joseph Jacobs, "Jewish Population of the United States," Memoir of Bureau of Jewish Statistics of the American Jewish Committee (*The American Jewish Year Book,* 1914-1915), pp. 339-378.

[6] *Ibid.*

[7] Alexander M. Dushkin, "A Statistical Study of the Jewish Population of New York," *The Jewish Communal Register of New York City, 1917-18* (New York, 1918), pp. 77-79.

[8] Harry S. Linfield, *The Jews in the United States,* A Study of their Number and Distribution (New York, 1929).

[9] *Ibid.*

[9a For background material cf. above William Foxwell Albright, "The Biblical Period."]

[10] Salo W. Baron, *Uklusei Yisroel bimei hamelakim* (Population of Israel in the days of the Kings), in *Abhandlungen zur Erinnerung an Hirsch Perez Chajes* (Vienna, 1933).

[11] Alexandre Moreau de Jonnés, *Statistique des peuples de l'antiquité, les Egyptiens, les Hébreux, les Grecs, les Romains, et les Gaulois,* 2 vols. (Paris, 1852).

[11a Cf. above Judah Goldin, "The Period of the Talmud," and Elias J. Bickerman, "The Historical Foundations of Postbiblical Judaism."]

[11b Cf. above Cecil Roth, "The European Age in Jewish History (to 1648)."]

[12] Benjamin of Tudela, *The Itinerary of Rabbi Benjamin of Tudela,* translated and edited by A. Asher, 2 vols. (London and Berlin, 1840-1841.)

Benjamin of Tudela's data add up to 989,475. For five places which he visited he gives no figures, stating only that he found there Jewish congregations. His data for western Asia are probably exaggerated; on the other hand, he did not include in his itinerary the Jewish communities of central Europe, of Russia and of Poland.

[12a Cf. above Roth, "The Jews of Western Europe (from 1648)."]

[13] Edward M. East, *Mankind at the Crossroads* (New York, 1923), p. 66.

[14] Henry Pratt Fairchild, *People, The Quantity and Quality of Population* (New York, 1939), p. 3.

[15] *A Century of Population Growth from the First Census of the United States to the Twelfth, 1790-1900.* United States Bureau of the Census (Government Printing Office, Washington, 1909), p. 91.

[16] W. S. Rossiter, "The Adventure of Population Growth," *Journal of the American Statistical Association,* March, 1923, p. 563; see also A. B. Wolfe, "Fecundity and Fertility of Early Man," *Human Biology,* 1933, Vol. 5; pp. 35-60.

[17] Jacob Lestschinsky, "Das juedische Volk im Wandel der letzten hundert Jahre" (in Yiddish), in *Schriften fuer Wirtschaft und Statistik* (Juedisches Wissenschaftliches Institut, Berlin, 1928), Band I, p. 10.

[18] Uriah Z. Engelman, "Vital Statistics in the Soviet Union in 1926," in *American Journal of Sociology,* Vol. XXXVIII, No. 3, November, 1932, pp. 437-440.

[19] Konotacya Parafii I, Handschrift 806, S. 651-673, quoted from *Zeitschrift fuer Demographie und Statistik der Juden* (Berlin, 1919), pp. 61-64.

[20] Salo W. Baron, *A Social and Religious History of the Jews,* 3 vols. (New York, 1937), II, 226.

[21] ". . . The Buffalo Jewish Family is so small as to be below the size necessary for the perpetuation of the Jewish group." *A Study of the Size of Families in the Jewish Population of Buffalo,* University of Buffalo Studies, (Buffalo, 1938), Vol. XVI, No. 1.

"Although the percentage composition of the Jewish population is such as is associated with a positive crude rate of natural increase, the net reproduction rate of 64 for native and 68 for foreign-born Jewish women forecasts a decrease in the future."—A. J. Jaffe, *A Study of Chicago Jewry Based on Death Certificates,* p. 144. *Jewish Social Studies,* Publication No. 3, Edited by Sophia M. Robison, Conference on Jewish Relations, New York, 1943.

[21a] Cf. above Arieh Tartakower, "The Problem of European Jewry (1939-1945)."]

[22]   Jewish Losses in Nazi-Occupied Countries of Europe

Country[1]	Jewish Population September 1939	Number of Jews Lost	Percentage of Jews Lost
Poland	3,300,000	2,800,000	85.0
Soviet Union (Occupied area)	2,100,000	1,500,000	71.4
Rumania	850,000	425,000	50.0
Hungary	404,000	200,000	49.5
Czechoslovakia	315,000	260,000	82.5
France[2]	300,000	90,000	30.0
Germany	210,000	170,000	81.0
Austria	60,000	40,000	66.6
Lithuania	150,000	135,000	90.0
Holland[2]	150,000	90,000	60.0
Latvia	95,000	85,000	89.5
Belgium[2]	90,000	40,000	44.4
Yugoslavia	75,000	55,000	73.3
Greece	75,000	60,000	80.0
Italy[2]	57,000	15,000	26.3
Bulgaria	50,000	7,000	14.0
Miscellaneous[3]	20,000	6,000	30.0
Totals	8,301,000	5,978,000	72.0

[1] Considered within prewar borders.

[2] Figures for Holland, France, Belgium and Italy include refugees.

[3] Denmark, Estonia, Luxembourg, Norway, Danzig.

Balance Sheet of Extermination, by Jacob Lestschinsky, Jewish Affairs, Vol. I, No. I, Feb. 1, 1946, issued by the Office of Jewish Information, American Jewish Congress.

BIBLIOGRAPHY

ENGELMAN, URIAH ZEVI, "The Need for Jewish Population Statistics," in
Menorah Journal (New York), November, 1927, pp. 464-479.
A discussion of the methods used in collecting Jewish population sta-
tistics.

LESTSCHINSKY, JACOB, "Das wirtschaftliche Schicksal des deutschen Judentums," in *Schriften der Zentralwohlfahrtsstelle der Deutschen Juden,* No.
7. Berlin, 1932.
An analysis of the social-economic position of German Jews prior to the
advent of the Nazis.

LINFIELD, HARRY S., *The Jews in the United States.* New York, 1929.
A study of the distribution of the Jewish population in America by
larger and minor divisions.

RUPPIN, ARTHUR, *Sociologia shel Hayehudim* (Hebrew), 2 vols. Tel-Aviv,
1931-1932.
The most comprehensive sociological study of the world Jewish population.

———, *The Jews in the Modern World.* London, 1934.
———, *The Jewish Fate and Future.* London, 1940.
Dr. Ruppin's books in English offer in condensed form the material con-
tained in the *Sociologia shel Hayehudim* and brought up to date.

Tzentral'noye Izdatelstvo Narodov USSR (Russian). Documents and Studies
about the Jewish population. Moscow, 1929.
Based on the data of the 1926 census of U.S.S.R.
Much demographic statistical material is found scattered in various publications in several languages.

The American Jewish Year Book. Published by the American Jewish Committee, Philadelphia, 1899- .

Blaetter fuer Demographie, Statistik und Wirtschaftskunde der Juden (Yiddish). Berlin, 1923-1925.

The YIVO Blaetter. Schriften fuer Yiddischen Wissenschaftlichen Institut.
New York, 1939- .

Zeitschrift fuer Demographie und Statistik der Juden. Vols. 1-15. Heraus-
gegeben vom Bureau fuer Statistik der Juden. Berlin, 1905-1919.

CHAPTER 32

JEWISH MIGRATIONS, 1840-1946

By Jacob Lestschinsky

1. Migrations in General and Jewish Migrations in Particular

It is doubtful whether certain historians and sociologists are correct in saying that the whole of world history is contained in the history of mass migrations. No one will deny, however, that migrations play a colossal role in human affairs—and this is especially evident in the period of capitalism.

One need only glance at the American continent, at its weighty role in human history from the beginning of the nineteenth century to the middle of the twentieth, to appreciate the significance of migration. The immense growth of this continent has revolutionized the lot of all the peoples of the world. At the beginning of the nineteenth century, there were on this continent hardly twenty million people, representing no more than 2½ per cent of world population; now this continent numbers almost three hundred million people, practically 15 per cent of the world's population. When these figures are properly understood, however, it is clear that they signify much more than 15 per cent of the life, the conditions, the perspectives of the world.

From Europe alone, during the past century and a half, sixty-five million people have migrated into the various American countries. These sixty-five million have become hundreds of millions, of which the United States received approximately half. And the transplanting of sixty-five million people from the most civilized and cultured region of the world to an almost free and uncultivated area altered the appearance of the earth, changed the entire trend of world history. The center of gravity of world history shifted from Europe to America. The American continent has about 75 per cent of the world's iron supply, 80 per cent of the nickel supply, 60 per cent of the copper and naphtha supplies, 35 per cent of the coal and about 50 per cent of the cotton supplies. So much for material wealth. Now, it can be safely assumed that, as far as spiritual-cultural resources are concerned, the center is also shifting to America, primarily, of course, to the United States. Thousands of European leaders of the highest positions in art and science have settled during recent years in the Americas, mainly in the United States. The destruction of the cultural institutions of

Europe and the pauperization of Europe as a whole make, therefore, for a new distribution of power, not only in the political and economic sense, but also in the spiritual and cultural sense.

The destruction of Europe is the fault of the European peoples, but the extraordinary progress of the American continent is the work of those same peoples—of those splinters of the European nations who were compelled, for various economic, political and religious reasons, to leave their old homes and seek their happiness across the sea. Splinters of scores of nations of aged Europe revealed on the virgin soil of the new continent new strength, almost entirely unsuspected in the forsaken Old World. The nations of course remained where they were, on their historic territories; but they sent off their youngest, most energetic and most creative children to the Americas. The fate of these nations was henceforth bound up not with the fortune of their émigrés, now identified with new national groups, but with the development of the American continent. Even for Englishmen, who of all peoples furnished the greatest number of emigrants, the national center remains on the European isle. The United States is an English country in language only; it does not belong to the English people. Nationhood is a much broader concept than language. In the United States the number of people of British descent is perhaps not less than in England itself. And without a doubt, the number of people of Irish descent in the States is greater than in Ireland. Yet the homeland remains the national home, the national center of the *Volksgeist*. The same is true of all other European nations. Each may have given huge numbers to the American peoples—from ten to twelve million Italians, eight to nine million Poles, and so on; nevertheless, they remained as nations, as national groups, in the old home, in historic Europe.

Regardless of the absolute or relative number of the various European peoples in the New World, they do not feel themselves to be Englishmen, Germans, Frenchmen, Swedes, Italians, Spaniards, Poles. They regard themselves as Americans, as Americans of the United States, as Argentinians, as Brazilians, as Mexicans, and so on. Despite their European descent the immigrants are unable to resist the pressure of their new countries. Memories of origin soon yield to the need to strike root in a new world.

The nature of the émigré's ties with his native land varies. Such ties are either strong or weak, of long or short duration, depending upon the well-being of the "old country." Hence the paradox that immigrants from highly developed countries, Swedes, Englishmen, Norwegians, Danes, are less closely attached to their mother countries than immigrants from backward, impoverished lands, Poles, Ukrainians, Lithuanians, Letts, etc. Apparently the former, children of rich and free peoples, are confident of the survival of their original national groups; when they migrate they cease to worry about the future of their historic group. On the other hand, the latter emigrants, children of poor and less free peoples, take with them the unrest of their early homes and even in their new country bear for quite a long time the yoke of battle for freedom for the native land.

Many additional factors, of course, determine the degree of affiliation to the new land and new people. One must also take into account time, distance, remigration, cultural kinship between land of origin and new land and a host of other influences.

As with Christians, so with Jews—and yet this is not altogether true. The position of Jews is peculiar, unique, so that certain phenomena acquire a new dimension, a new character, in their case. The intensity of Jewish migrations; the concentration in certain regions, on the one hand, and, on the other, a vast dispersion over the whole world; the consequences of migration for the fate of the entire people; for those remaining in the old country and those in the new settlements; adaptation to new cultural environments and attachment to the older heritage—externally all these are no different from what confronts all or many Europeans; essentially, however, the case is very different with the Jews.

Of sixty-five million people who emigrated from Europe, in a century and a half about four million were Jews. This represents about 6 per cent of the entire emigration from Europe. The percentage of Jews in Europe at the beginning of the nineteenth century was not more than 1½, never more than 2. The intensity of Jewish emigration was, therefore, three to four times as great as that of the general emigration from Europe. If we consider only those sections of Europe from which Jews emigrated, i.e., middle eastern and southern Europe, the intensity of Jewish emigration is not three to four times, but six to seven times as great as that of the general emigration. Western and northern Europe (France, England, the Scandinavian countries, Belgium, Holland and Switzerland) had so few Jews at the beginning of the nineteenth century that for Jews they became lands of immigration, although there was quite an exodus of non-Jews from these countries to America. It is safe to say that the sixty-five million who migrated from Europe during the past century and a half comprise a third of Europe's population at the beginning of the nineteenth century, while the approximately four million Jewish migrants outnumber the total Jewish population of the world at the beginning of that century. Even if we grant that not all of the four million were from Europe (two to three hundred thousand were Sephardic and Arabic Jews from middle eastern Asia and north Africa), there would still remain about three million and seven to eight hundred thousand Jewish emigrants from Europe: this is still greater than the number of Jews in the entire world at the beginning of the nineteenth century.

No other people among all the immigrants into the various American countries so concentrated itself in urban centers, especially in the large cities, as did the Jews. In the United States, 98 per cent of the Jews live in urban centers, 86 per cent in cities of more than 100,000 population; 58 per cent are in the three largest cities (New York, Chicago and Philadelphia) and 43 per cent are in one city, New York. Approximately the same is true in all countries where Jews have migrated. And yet none of the other migrating European peoples spread itself out over as many continents and isles. The Vienna community, in its migration report for the year May, 1938, to May, 1939, listed eighty-four countries to which 104,000 Viennese Jews had gone. There is now actually no corner of the world where a Jew cannot be found. This is, however, a result of the past hundred years, and especially of the past ten to fifteen years, when the need for new places of settlement was constantly on the increase, for the gates of the formerly hospitable lands where Jews had concentrated in the first stages of their great migrations were being closed more and more tightly.

Regardless, however, of the world-wide nature of Jewish dispersion, the center of the Jewish people shifted from one continent to a second—from Europe to America. And if for a thousand years the Jews were first an Asiatic-European people and later a European-Asiatic people, they have become, as a result of the migrations of the last hundred years, an American people.[1a] If in the past two to three hundred years the bulk of Jews was found mainly in the sphere of Slavic-Arabic culture, now the majority of the Jewish people finds itself in an English sphere of influence.

Table 1 will illustrate the organic transplanting of the center of the Jewish people, and at the same time reveal the relative growth of the new center, as a result of the catastrophe that befell European Jewry.

TABLE 1. *The Number of Jews on the European and American Continents at Different Times during the Past Hundred Years*

YEAR	EUROPE		AMERICA	
	Absolute Numbers	Percentage of World Jewry	Absolute Numbers	Percentage of World Jewry
1840	3,950,000	87.8	50,000	1.1
1900	8,800,000	80.0	1,200,000	11.0
1939	9,500,000	56.9	5,540,000	33.2
1945	3,000,000	27.3	6,000,000	54.6

The American continent, which a hundred and five years ago had one seventy-ninth the Jewish population of Europe, now has twice as many Jews as the latter. From one per cent of the Jewish people, American Jewry jumped to more than half the entire Jewish population. The first three lines of the table show clearly the results of the migrations—as we shall see later, from 1840 to 1945, in round numbers, about 3,300,000 Jews (approximately 85 per cent of all Jewish migrants) migrated into all American countries. Through natural increase, the 3,300,000 immigrants became more than five and a half million. The fourth line shows the results of the European catastrophe. Although the absolute number of Jews on the American continent increased little from 1939 to 1945, in all about 460,000, and although that increase is the result more of natural increase than of immigration, still the relative weight of American Jewry increased. What was formerly one-third of world Jewry has now become more than half of the Jewish people. This is due to the destruction of six million Jews on the European continent.

The important fact, however, is that Jews are now an American people. We must also take into account the fact that the Jews of America have a natural increase of approximately fifty thousand per year, while European Jews in the next ten to fifteen years will undoubtedly suffer a biological decline, for the mortality rate of the physically and mentally wearied European Jews will certainly be high. It is impossible to hope for many births, because the material conditions in which European Jews find themselves make family life impossible. And no matter how small immigration into American countries may be, there will still be some Jews immigrating and large numbers in flight from Europe. The conclusion is inescapable: in the next ten years European Jewry will lose numbers heavily, and there will be an increase of American Jews. Quantitatively, therefore, Jews are becoming decidedly an American people.

Parallel with a world-wide dispersion, as we noted, a concentration of Jews has taken place. The chief concentrations are in American countries, particularly the United States, Canada and Argentina. In these three lands live 5,700,000 of the 6,000,000 American Jews, in other words, 93 per cent of all Jews on the American continent. More than 87 per cent of all American Jews live in the United States alone. But Jews migrated not only to the Americas; they migrated to many other lands, only two of which may be characterized as centers—Palestine and South Africa. Of approximately more than 600,000 Jewish migrants to countries besides America, about 400,000 (easily two-thirds) went to Palestine and about 75,000 to South Africa. Of all the countries admitting Jewish immigrants, the Americas included, the United States takes first place and Palestine second. Of course, in the past one hundred years, the United States admitted seven times as many Jewish immigrants as Palestine; but Palestine received a greater number of Jewish immigrants than all the other countries. Since Palestine exerts more of a spiritual than an economic or political influence, it figures prominently immediately after the great "quantitative center" of the United States.

We have been contrasting Europe with America. Actually, however, Jews on each continent had a specific area which could be regarded as their center. In America it has been the United States, and in Asia it has been Palestine. In Europe it was the eastern part of the continent. This region was almost a territorial center for Jews for several centuries. Till the middle of the twentieth century, in those countries which lie between the rivers Vistula, Niemen, Dvina, Dnieper and Danube (Poland, Ukrainia, White Russia, Lithuania, Latvia, Hungary, Rumania, Slovakia and Carpathia), there lived about seven million Jews; eight million if we include Russia proper. The Jews in all these lands were geographical neighbors and, until the First World War, the great majority belonged to two empires—Russia and Austria. To geographical proximity and common citizenship are to be added common language, traditions and habits. These people had behind them a history and legacy of many centuries and together constituted, until World War II, the principal quantitative and spiritual center of world Jewry. But it would be an error to think that Hitler alone destroyed that center. Its decline had begun much earlier.

Table 2 reveals how emigration caused the decline of eastern Europe as a center, and how, as if directed by a national providence, it prepared two substitute centers: the quantitative one in the United States and the spiritual one in Palestine. (We have added Canada to the States, because Canadian Jewry is an integral part of the North American Jewish center.)

TABLE 2.   *The Development of the Three Centers of World Jewry*

PERIODS	EASTERN EUROPE*		U.S.A. & CANADA		PALESTINE	
	Absolute Numbers	Percentage of World Jewry	Absolute Numbers	Percentage of World Jewry	Absolute Numbers	Percentage of World Jewry
1840	3,200,000	71.1	40,000	0.9	10,000	0.2
1900	7,400,000	67.3	1,100,000	10.0	50,000	0.5
1939	7,000,000	41.9	4,900,000	29.5	480,000	2.9
1945	1,000,000	9.1	5,400,000	49.0	580,000	5.3

* Figures exclusive of the Jews in Russia proper.

For the first three periods, the results of the migrations are conclusively expressed—the relative importance of the East European Jewish center continued to decline. From 1900 to 1939 even the absolute numbers of Jews in that historic center decreased. Relatively, its weight fell from over 71 per cent in 1840 to a mere 42 per cent in 1939. The decline was a significant one, but despite that, this center still played an enormous role in the life of the entire Jewish people. It was this center which supplied the human material for the upbuilding of Palestine and the spiritual and political leaders for Israel in all countries. The Hitler catastrophe completely liquidated this center. Of seven million before the war, there remained only one million. This remnant, however, is broken physically and spiritually, and most likely it will exert all its efforts to leave Europe. The migrations that brought millions of Jews to America and hundreds of thousands to Palestine saved, therefore, the Jewish people from oblivion. Thus the significance of migration for the fate of the Jewish people is unique; for no other people has migration played so decisive a role. Elsewhere emigration eased the economic conditions of the masses, often distracted them from political revolt; in the case of Jews it made survival itself possible. For all other peoples, despite migration, national centers remained in their original European countries; so far as Jews were concerned, the situation in this respect was entirely different. Even now no one can tell how the development of the two new immigration centers will proceed: to what extent the Palestinian spiritual center will become quantitatively strong and to what extent the American center will assume also spiritual leadership in Jewish life. The Jewish people is today at the crossroads; both immigration centers are still young.

Although in speaking of Asia we have concerned ourselves only with the Yishuv in Palestine, we must add that in Soviet Asia during recent years a great number of Jews have been admitted. One hundred years ago, there were no more than several hundred Jews in Asiatic Russia. Today the region must contain about half a million. While this increase is a result of migration, it does not enter into our account for this migration is within the confines of the Russian state. We are here concerned only with trans-oceanic movements. If we were to include in our survey the migrations within the borders of Europe and within the boundaries of any one state, we would have to conclude that in the past hundred years about six million Jews changed their place of habitation—more than twice the number of Jews in Europe at the beginning of the nineteenth century. About half a million Jews migrated from eastern Europe to England, France, Germany, Austria, Belgium and the Scandinavian countries. Several hundred thousand migrated from the Russian-Ukrainian, Russian-White Russian and Russian-Lithuanian provinces to South Russia (the provinces of Kherson Ekaterinoslav, Bessarabia and Taurien). In the twenty-five years after the Russian Revolution and the abolition of the Pale of Settlement, about half a million Jews migrated from Soviet Ukrainia and Soviet White Russia to the central areas of Russia proper.

At present there are half a million Jews in Asiatic Russia. In Biro-Bidjan, however, which has the right of a Jewish autonomous district, there are no more than 25,000 Jews, newcomers from 1928 to 1939. This may be inconsequential, but Biro-Bidjan is already assuming the character of a center. The remaining Jews of Soviet Asia are scattered over many districts, cities and villages. Of the half million, about 225,000 were already in Asia prior to World War II; the remainder are Jews evacuated in 1940-1941 and stranded there.

2. MIGRATIONS AS A FACTOR IN JEWISH HISTORY

The historic common fate of the Jews, manifest in various countries under various economic, political and cultural conditions was once again affected by these migrations. The stronger the ties between the Jewish communities of various lands the easier was reunion. The Jews of the various East European countries, of Russia, Poland, Galicia, Rumania, Carpathia, etc., who had already begun to adjust themselves to various foreign tongues and cultures, very soon banded together in the American countries. This was more difficult for the younger generation, because it had already adopted another language, the language of *its* native country. Disregarding the language question, however, we must definitely assume that even between German Jews and East European Jews an amalgamation has taken place. And in the most recent tragic years, there is a marked tendency on the part of Sephardic Jews to declare their oneness with the larger communities of the Ashkenazim. This could happen only through the coming together in the lands of immigration.

One hundred years ago, on the steamers traveling to the New World there had already taken place a commingling of Jewish migrants from Germany and North Africa, Poland and England, Lithuania and Hungary, etc. Especially colorful was the meeting of Jews on the ocean liners in the past ten to twelve years. Never before in the sufficiently sad history of the Jews had there come together so many hunted and harried Jews from so many different countries and from so many different social and cultural levels. They fled from practically all the countries of Europe—and the exceptions can be counted on the fingers of one hand. Jews with earlocks and *zizit* prominent, and Jews whose fathers had already forgotten that they were the seed of the Patriarchs, fled together. Ships with financiers of Vienna and Paris and poor shopkeepers and artisans from Poland and Rumania; ships with rich land magnates from Hungary and uprooted beggars and peasants from the Carpathians; rich manufacturers from Warsaw and Lodz and beggarly junk peddlers from the Galician villages; professors and artists and scientists along with old fashioned *heder* teachers and modern Hebrew pedagogues from Poland and Lithuania—this kaleidoscopic mass testified, on the one hand, to the fact that not one or two European countries, but almost all of Europe was in the throes of a profound social and economic convulsion and, on the other hand, that "all Israel are brethren," that in a violent age Jews of all groups are victim, and there is "neither wisdom nor shrewdness" which can prevail against anti-Semitism.

"All Israel are brethren and all Jews are responsible for each other"— in transit, and in the first difficult years of adjustment to the new life this becomes clear for all the scattered individuals. No matter what Jews live in this or that remote land, or how small the settlement happens to be, when Jewish immigrants arrive the care for their lives and the provision for their support begin at once. There is even concern over the immigrants' conduct, for it is often but too true that the common fate that Jews share is more the result of anti-Semitism than of national interests.

The longer a Jewish community is settled in a country the deeper, obviously, is its attachment to that country, to its language and culture. This has generally meant that that particular community also drifted away from other Jewish communities. Such isolation from other Jews, however, is interrupted as soon as immigration gets under way on a large scale. An awareness of kinship is once again established.

An excellent illustration of this phenomenon is provided by the development of Yiddish. Jews came to the Germanic countries in very small groups, often family by family. Naturally, to be able to communicate with the local population, they were forced to adopt the language of the land. But they did not take over the language mechanically. Instead they transformed and adapted it to their own religious and national requirements. They punctuated German with Hebrew words and concepts. Nevertheless, the structure of this adopted language and its whole spirit remained very close to the original idiom of the surrounding alien environment. Had the Jews remained in Germany uninterruptedly it is doubtful whether the language would have acquired the typical form and spirit that it acquired in the Slavic countries. When Yiddish finally departed from its original source and became an independent vehicle of expression it experienced a noteworthy development.[2a] Jews of Germany came to Poland in great numbers and found there most favorable conditions for remaining isolated in culture and language from the environment, and for developing further the language they had brought with them. Though the first Jews in Slavic countries had begun to adopt the languages of their neighbors, the new large migrations of German Jews put a halt to that cultural assimilation. Yiddish then became the language of the East European Jews, even of those who had previously used Slavic languages.

As a result of conditions that prevented the Jews from taking root in any one country for long, two significant facts emerged. On the one hand, Jews could not altogether lose their identity, the process of assimilation never became thoroughgoing. On the other hand, whatever Jews did adopt from their environment they integrally converted into their own; that which had been foreign became organically an element in their culture.

What we have said of language is true in other respects, too. Any number of alien customs and forms found themselves naturalized in Jewish life.

So long as the religious tradition was strong in Jewish life, the Jewish immigrant, for his own well-being and happiness, had to participate actively in the life and habits of the Jewish community to which he had come. Not only did his new neighbors make possible the *minyan* which he required for public prayer, not only did the community own the cemetery where he would have to purchase his burial plot, but daily and in a thousand ways he was dependent upon his new milieu. Hence integration in the community was the only choice open to the immigrant, and migration reinforced a sense of kinship.

In our own day, however, the story is entirely different. A generation had grown up which had no knowledge of Yiddish. These Jews spoke the language of their respective countries; and although in the recent upheaval they all met in flight and their fate was the same, the Hungarian Jews did not understand the Rumanian, the Rumanian could not understand the Polish, the Polish could not understand the French. Since piety had languished, there was little the religious tradition could do to emphasize for the immigrants their interdependence. True enough, in the haven of refuge the German Jew came closer to the Polish and Lithuanian Jew, estranged Hungarian and French Jews showed deeper interest in Jewish affairs than they had in their native lands. But in this era of assimilation migration ceased to achieve positively what it could accomplish in days gone by.

3. THE CAUSES OF THE JEWISH MIGRATIONS 1840-1946

If one studies the migrations of the nineteenth century, one is amazed by what at first appears paradoxical: the modern period of emigration begins much earlier and is of longer duration in the wealthier countries than in the poor lands. And by "wealthier" we mean not only material riches, but cultural resources, resources which contribute to the individual's initiative and enable him to risk danger in search of happiness and fortune. The greatest number of emigrants came from the wealthiest continent, Europe. Of all European countries, the richest (England, Germany, Sweden, Norway) supplied the greatest mass of emigrants, numerically and relatively. And emigration from these countries began much earlier than from the poorer East European countries.

This phenomenon can be observed also in the case of Jews—the Jews of Russia in the time of Nicholas I certainly suffered more politically and were economically poorer than the German Jews; yet Jewish mass emigration began first from Germany; only later did it occur in the poverty-stricken Ghettos of eastern Europe.

Poverty, apparently, is not alone sufficient to dislodge masses and set them into movement. Indeed there is a poverty so acute that it makes one indifferent and resigned. To be sure, those who emigrated from the rich countries were the poorer elements; nevertheless, they had lived where horizons were broader, concepts loftier, knowledge of the world greater than in the backward countries of eastern Europe, where feudalism reigned until late in the nineteenth century. At a time when the feudal lords of Russia and Poland were still beating their serfs to death, there was already in England a complete legal code concerning obligatory support of poor families by the civic communities.

The industrial machinery which, at the beginning of the nineteenth century, was responsible for the well known English unemployment sharpened the appetites of the masses for better living conditions. Decades passed before this machinery had like effect on the appetites of the eastern and southern European masses, before it gave them the mental initiative, cultural courage and self-confidence necessary to pull up stakes. Only then did the great emigrations from those countries of Europe, where the number of Jews was great, occur.

Here are some figures to tell the story: 6,700,000 Europeans came to the United States from 1820 to 1870. Of these immigrants only seventy thousand, *i.e.*, 1 per cent were from eastern and southern Europe, although these countries had one-third of the entire European population. From 1870 to 1930, 25,558,000 European immigrants entered the States; fourteen million, or 54 per cent, were from eastern and southern Europe.

The partition of Poland in the second half of the eighteenth century and, simultaneously with it, the decline of business and urban life in general shook the foundations of Jewish life. Before the partition, fully half the entire Jewish people lived in Poland, from two-thirds to three-quarters of all Ashkenazic Jews, in other words, of all European Jews. The poverty of the Jewish masses in the Polish towns of that time was so serious that the Polish government was forced to establish commissions to find some means for its alleviation. Solomon Maimon, in his autobiography, paints a vivid picture of that tragedy. The Jewish masses were not only materially poor, but culturally they were provincial, backward. The few rich arendars and merchants who traveled to the Leipzig fairs and had some knowledge of the distant world were an inconsequential percentage of the Jewish population. Yet the Jewish masses exhibited initiative, and we find that in 1776, 1777 and 1778 several Polish communities appealed to the consulate of the recently founded New Russian province (later the provinces of Kherson and Ekaterinoslav) for permission to emigrate and settle there. This was fully forty years before the colonization program was organized by the Russian government, after it acquired great numbers of Jews from partitioned Poland. Jewish migration to New Russia from the erstwhile Polish districts began, then, before the Russian government took the initiative.

But at approximately the same time—only a few years later—a German Jew turned to the President of the Continental Congress with a request for land for a large group of Jews who wished to emigrate from Germany to America. The letter was first made public in the June, 1783, number of the German journal *Deutsches Museum*; it appeared in pamphlet form in 1787, in Frankfort and Leipzig as *Schreiben eines deutschen Juden an den Amerikanischen Presidenten.* The author of the work remained, unfortunately, anonymous, but the document, which portrays, on the one hand, the tragic situation of the German Jews and, on the other, the desire to emigrate, presents great interest and we shall permit ourselves to quote from it at length.

After the writer has expressed his joy at the peace which the States have at last made with England, and after observing that the States have so much land that even after a hundred years it will probably not be as thickly populated as Germany, he goes on to say:

Your religion cannot prohibit you from leaving these deserts to us for cultivation; besides, for a long time you have been tolerating Jews near you. Whether policy might forbid you that, I do not know. At all events you have the legislative power in your hands, and we ask no more than to be permitted to become subjects of these thirteen provinces, and would gladly contribute twofold taxes for their benefit, if we can only obtain permission to establish colonies at our own cost and to engage in agriculture, commerce, arts and sciences. Do we not believe in the same God as the Quakers do? Can our admission become more dangerous and precarious than that of the Quakers? Supposing that two thousand families of us would settle in a desert of America and convert it into a fertile land, will the old inhabitants of the provinces suffer by it? Let the conditions be stated to us, gracious President, under which you will admit us; we will then consider whether we can accept and keep them.

You would be astonished, most mighty President, at the perseverance of a German Jew, if you could witness it. The great, nay, perhaps the greatest part of them, spend almost their whole life on the highway in the pursuit of retail business, and the trader consumes for his own person nothing but a herring and a penny loaf; the nearest brook or well has to supply his drink. All that he earns besides he conscientiously lays aside in order to bring it home on Friday to supply food and clothing for wife and children. During these one and a half days when he enjoys somewhat better food and rests in the bosom of his family he forgets the wretched life which he is compelled to take up again on the next Sunday. And would you believe it, this wretch, who has to strain all his wits to convert a capital of fifty florins nearly as many times during the year, if he wants to live by it with his family, is nevertheless not infrequently envied by many Jews? . . . Granted that a Jew has at last become possessor of a capital that would suffice to support a family, still he will not be able to marry the woman he loves. Most of the time and in most of the German provinces he is obliged to acquire protection money for a sum which reduces his property to a half or a third. But love overcomes this difficulty too. He strains his energies anew, again completes his capital and then seeks permission to marry. If he obtains it, the experience just described is repeated, for he has to pay dearly for this permission, and the expenses of a wedding are not less among the Jews than among the Christians.[3]

A few German and even Polish Jews were in the States as early as the eighteenth century. Newport, which in the second half of the eighteenth century had the largest Jewish community in America (over a thousand of approximately three thousand Jews), certainly included Ashkenazic Jews. But they were few in the literal sense of the word; one can hardly speak of migration of European Ashkenazic Jews before the nineteenth century. Jewish migration into the United States and the other Americas until after the Napoleonic Wars was Sephardic, though in absolute numbers the Sephardim did not represent a large mass. In relation to the total number of American Jews, however, they were the largest majority, and the period up to 1820 bears their stamp.

Mass emigration of Ashkenazic Jews began in the years following the Napoleonic Wars. It is perhaps characteristic that within eight years there appeared in Russia two Yiddish translations of Joachim Heinrich Kampfe's famous work, *The Discovery of America*: the first, *Zafenat Paaneah*, by the well-known *Maskil*, Chaim Horowitz, in 1817, and the second in 1823 by the Hebrew writer, Mordecai Aaron Ginsburg.[4a]

The history of the Jews in Europe in the first half of the nineteenth century reveals two developments. On the one hand, political reaction grew stronger in Germany and Russia, the two countries with the majority of European Jewry. Ruined and impoverished by the Napoleonic Wars, which, for the most part, were fought in those regions where masses of Jews were concentrated, these countries let loose on the Jews unremitting restrictions and persecutions. In 1827 the Russian recruiting policy began, the military conscription of Jewish children for twenty-five years, which practically meant conversion. Several years later came the edict driving the Jews out of the border provinces. In 1845 recruiting of Jews was made law in Poland also. Russian Jewry was in a quandary. Philippson, the editor of the German *Allgemeine Zeitung des Judentums*, wrote a series of articles about the frightful plight of Russian Jewry, in which he said: "The persecutions have reached that borderline where even human cruelty must end—unless one were yet to take the slaughtering-knife into one's hands. The victim—Jewry—stands at the brink of the grave, its blood already flows."[5] In Germany, the *hep-hep* pogroms of 1818 and 1819[6a] were accompanied by a spread of anti-Semitic literature, which called for new restrictions and renewed expulsions.

On the other hand, in both countries Jewish communities bestirred themselves. The German Jews began to battle mightily for equal rights. Germany was then at the height of its transition from feudalism to capitalism. In this transition Jews played a principal role. In the seventeenth century the Prussian king invited wealthy Viennese Jews to settle in Berlin in order to develop industry and commerce. In Berlin, in the eighteenth century, there was a Jewish community of three (later four) thousand, although Jews had no right of residence in the Prussian capital. Already a significant Jewish bourgeoisie, for whom there was great need, had arisen; so, too, a Jewish professional intelligentsia and a Jewish propertied middle class appeared. Germany's economic development actually dictated equal rights for Jews—Jews were, after all, the biggest and ablest bankers in the country; they created capital funds and organized foreign loans; they first connected Germany with world markets and possessed the initiative necessary to develop the German domestic market.

In Russia also significant economic developments were taking place, altogether opposed to the backwardness of Nicholas's regime. In the provinces of erstwhile Poland commerce was exclusively in Jewish hands. The efforts of the Russian government economically to absorb Polish territory into the Russian Empire was impossible without the participation of Jews, who in many areas were the majority of the urban population and, as already stated, the only tradesmen. Export of grain, which was on the increase and which was necessary for the awakening Russian capitalism, was almost exclusively managed by Jews. Despite the above-mentioned persecutions and pogroms, therefore, there developed in the first half of the nineteenth century large Jewish communities in Warsaw, Odessa, Berdichev and many other cities. The Jewish village and rural masses threw off their lethargy and began to seek sources of income in the larger cities.

Along with this general awakening, along with the rising discontent with the *status quo* and feverish search for new opportunities in life, began also the stream of migration. The masses of poor, who in the first half of the nineteenth century constituted the outstanding majority of German Jewry, grew more enterprising; in their search for a new life they were prepared for a number of risks. If one brother moved from Posen to Berlin and opened a tailor shop which in ten years developed into a clothing factory, the other brothers also contemplated settling in Berlin. If there were no opportunity for them in that city, they might think of the prospects in England, or other distant lands. The same occurred in Bavaria, where the Jewish masses were poorest, even though the country might already boast of a few wealthy Jewish bankers. Even in Germany there was at that time no strong middle class between upper bourgeoisie and the poor masses; there was only a very narrow margin of more or less wealthy people.

This phenomenon—economic progress of the few along with impoverization of the many to the point where they feel they must move on to other countries—confronts us, *mutatis mutandis,* in every other European country, with this difference, however: elsewhere it appeared about half a century later than in Germany, because there capitalism developed later than in Germany. In Russia, in the Polish provinces, in Hungary and in all other East European countries capitalism became intensive only in the second half of the nineteenth century. Only then did the great awakening of the Jewish masses take place. In the first half of the nineteenth century, therefore, German Jews emigrated in great numbers but East European Jews in driblets. In the second half of the century the wave of Jewish emigration from Eastern Europe rose higher and higher, while the number of emigrants from Germany decreased.

Because in Eastern Europe capitalism came very late, its development was slow and weak. Here, however, lived the great Jewish masses. The contrast between increasing poverty as a result of a dying feudalism and the new opportunities as a result of a rising capitalism was much greater than in Germany—where Jews were few and capitalism was well advanced. No wonder, therefore, that in the eighties of the nineteenth century—the peak was reached in the first years of the twentieth century—there was little emigration *from* Germany but considerable migration *into* Germany by Polish and Russian Jews.

In contemplating the reasons for emigration, it is not enough to consider the factors that lead one to leave the homeland. One must also take into account the conditions in the lands of immigration, which may attract and also repel newcomers. If the need to emigrate from Europe had not been accompanied by a phenomenal economic progress in America, emigration would certainly not have reached such heights. Toward the beginning of the twentieth century American industry developed so rapidly and impressively that it became one of the most significant factors in attracting all those who wished to quit Europe. The Jewish weaver from Lodz, who earned barely two dollars a week and received a letter from a former fellow countryman or relation saying that in Paterson one earns seven to eight dollars a week and that living costs are only twice as high as they were in the old country, hurried to America even if in Lodz he was sure of work. The same was true everywhere: the letters from the first émigrés were the best agitation for emigration.

One further point. The poor Jew who in 1850 or '60 knew of the New World and its magnificent opportunities, particularly for his children, often lacked the funds to travel; hence he was compelled to remain where he was though he saw his doom plainly. At the beginning of this century, however, there were already more than one million Jews in the Americas, and they subsidized the emigration of their European kin.

This was particularly the case in Russia, where the greatest concentration of Jews was located.[7a] On the one hand, for the sake of economic interests the czarist government had to make concessions and grant rights of residence in all of Russia to certain Jews, rich merchants, manufacturers of the first and second guilds (a kind of commercial franchise), individuals with an academic training, qualified artisans; on the other hand, it expelled Jews from the villages even in the Pale of Settlement, instituted quotas in the universities and high schools, and interfered with the economic Jewish institutions of mutual and self-help and with Jewish communal and charity institutions. Add to this the fact that in 1871 there was a pogrom in Odessa, in 1881 and 1882 a whole series of pogroms with many dead and wounded, in 1903 the Kishinev pogrom, and in 1905, during the October Revolution, over five hundred pogroms in five hundred places; it becomes clear why emigration from Russia continued and increased.

In Rumania the situation for Jews was no better, if not much worse. In the seventies conditions there were so frightful that the American government deliberately appointed a Jewish public servant, Benjamin Franklin Peixotto, as general consul with a special mission to help the local Jews. And these were the words of President Grant to the consul: "The reports concerning the sufferings of the Rumanian Jews deeply stir our humane sentiments. That which reaches us from Rumania is a chain of malice and barbarity without measure."[8] As is known, Peixotto presented a project for an organized Jewish mass migration from Rumania. Evidently Peixotto found no hope for improvement there. Today it is clear to everyone that the American Jew was far more farsighted than the philanthropists of Paris and Berlin, who discarded this plan and staked the fortune of the Rumanian Jews on the card of the struggle for equal rights.

It would, however, be an error to assume that all classes of the Jewish population were treated equally in Rumania. The Jewish commercial and industrial bourgeoisie, most active in the creation of what little modern economic life Rumania possessed, was generally and for a limited time not disturbed. But at the same time the impoverished Jews were so mercilessly treated that hundreds of them organized in groups and journeyed afoot to Vienna in the hope of meeting with sympathy there and finding the opportunity to emigrate to America.[9]

This dual policy—exploitation of Jewish intellectual forces, Jewish commercial abilities, Jewish psychological awareness and international connections, on the one hand, and, on the other, driving of the Jewish impoverished masses to despair and emigration—operated only when there was a more or less intensive development of capitalism and an ever-increasing emigration of the broad masses. Capitalism created new sources of income for those who abandoned the villages because there was not enough land for the growing rural population, and emigration drained off those who found no place in the urban economy.

But the crisis of lack of land and employment, already manifest before World War I, grew far more acute after the war. Emigration became less and less possible because countries to which immigrants had come in the past would not admit an unlimited number of new settlers. Such restrictions, however, applied universally and affected non-Jews as well as Jews. What complicated matters for Jews was their specific minority status.

The stream of Jewish emigration from the small towns was accompanied by a corresponding one of the Gentile population from villages and hamlets, in all the central and eastern European countries. The number of Gentiles moving from country to town was of course much larger than that of the Jews; but it was smaller in proportion to the total population. The Jews entered business, liberal professions, labor and small industries, established factories, and engaged in domestic and foreign trade, preparing the way for the large numbers of Gentile migrants who came to the city, and became part of the culture of the towns. The large group of non-Jews that flocked from the villages entered the factories or became unskilled laborers. The children of large and middle class landowners became public officials, or professionals, with some few entering commerce and industry. But the second generation of the cityfied Gentiles was more dynamic, businesslike, and ambitious. Yet as a result of the first stage of development, it turned out that in all the lands of eastern Europe—Poland, Rumania, Hungary, Lithuania, and Latvia (Russia must be excluded, as the First World War led to distinctive situations there) the Jews constituted the majority in trade and particularly in foreign commerce and big business. They also provided between 35 per cent and 50 per cent of the physicians and members of liberal professions, i.e., those callings in which personal talent and initiative play an important role.

All the above-mentioned countries became politically independent after the First World War. This gave the ruling national majority a weapon against which the Jews were helpless. In the open market the Jew was victorious, even when the surrounding Christian merchants, artisans and doctors called for a boycott of their Jewish colleagues; but against the governments' measures, which placed higher taxes on Jews than on Christians, which expelled all Jewish doctors from the national and city hospitals, which limited credit to Jews but granted enormous concessions to Christian entrepreneurs—such official anti-Semitic politics,[10a] which were not merely formal but actual, rendered the Jews helpless.

Added to the general economic crisis and the diminishing emigration was the program of thorough elimination of Jews from all business. The aggressiveness of the general population grew with the encouragement of the governments. Finally force was resorted to: people began to beat Jews in the universities, picket their stores and keep out Christian customers, demolish Jewish market stalls and prevent Jews from coming to the markets and fairs, forbid Jewish stores to open in Christian sections of the city. Then came pogroms, which were everywhere of one pattern and purpose—not so much to kill as to make the lives of the Jews so miserable that they would flee in great numbers. Emigration of Jews was the objective not only of these governments but of numerous elements of the populations, especially those competing with Jewish businessmen. The members of the professional classes, particularly doctors and jurists, led the anti-Semitic agitation that more and more spread over the countries of eastern Europe; behind them were the merchants; then followed the manual laborers and the youth of all strata, including the peasantry, who had received a modern education.

Thus was created the inferno in which the majority of European Jews lived from 1925 to 1939. With Hitler's rise to power all these governments became either entirely or partly Fascist and therefore more arrogant and aggressive in their anti-Semitic policies. Naturally, that element of the general population which was in the anti-Semitic vanguard until 1933 grew even more violent. In those prewar years Jews did try to find some corner in the world where they might live in peace, but, as is well known, they were not very successful.

What we have tried to describe is that "normal" conditions compelled European Jewry to emigrate in order to survive. To dwell on the result of Hitler's triumph in Germany and the occupied countries is superfluous. Even in Jewish life this is an unprecedented experience; strictly speaking, such a chapter is not of immediate concern.

4. The Extent of Jewish Migrations in the Nineteenth and Twentieth Century and the Division of the Migrants According to Countries of Immigration

If one wishes to visualize the extent of Jewish migrations in the past hundred years, one must go to the countries to which the immigrants went, for the information about the respective emigrant peoples was, up to the present, scanty. Unfortunately we do not possess official data on the dispersal of immigrants, according to religion, for the whole century. In the United States the rubric "Hebrew" was adopted only in 1899; for Palestine we have official data from 1919, for Canada from 1925; and there is information also for a few small countries, such as South Africa and Australia. These official data include, however, about 70 per cent of all Jewish emigrants. If to the official sources we add the data of ICA on the South American countries and of the philanthropic organizations of the United States on the years until 1899, we get sufficient correct data for over 90 per cent of the Jewish migrants of the past century. For the other countries, the only alternative is a rough estimate.

Tables 3a and 3b give us the total of Jewish migrations for one hundred and two years, in absolute and relative figures. One must remember that until 1914 migration was determined exclusively by the free will of the

TABLE 3A

Jewish Migrants According to Countries of Immigration
1840–1942
Absolute Numbers

Years	U.S.	Canada	Argentina	Brazil	Uruguay	Other Countries of America	South Africa	Palestine	All Other Countries	Total
1840–1880	200,000	1,600	2,000	500	——	1,000	4,000	10,000	2,000	221,100
1881–1900	675,000	10,500	25,000	1,000	——	1,000	23,000	25,000	4,000	764,500
1901–1914	1,346,400	95,300	87,614	8,750	——	3,000	21,377	30,000	10,000	1,602,441
1915–1920	76,450	10,450	3,503	2,000	1,000	5,000	907	–15,000	5,000	89,310
1921–1925	280,283	14,400	39,713	7,139	3,000	7,000	4,630	60,765	10,000	426,930
1926–1930	54,998	15,300	33,721	22,296	6,370	10,000	10,044	10,179	10,000	172,908
1931–1935	17,986	4,200	12,700	13,075	3,280	15,000	4,507	147,502	20,000	238,250
1936–1939	79,819	900	14,789	10,600	7,677	15,000	5,300	75,510	60,000	269,595
1940–1942	70,954	800	4,500	6,000	1,000	2,000	2,000	35,000	10,000	131,954
1840–1942	2,801,890	153,150	223,540	71,360	22,327	59,000	75,765	378,956	131,000	3,916,988

TABLE 3B

Jewish Migrants According to Countries of Immigration
1840–1942
Relative Numbers

Years	U. S.	Canada	Argentina	Brazil	Uruguay	Other Countries of America	South Africa	Palestine	All Other Countries	Total
1840–1880	90.5	0.7	0.9	0.2	—	0.5	1.8	4.5	0.9	100.0
1881–1900	88.4	1.3	3.3	0.1	—	0.1	3.0	3.3	0.5	100.0
1901–1914	84.0	5.9	5.5	0.5	—	0.2	1.4	1.9	0.6	100.0
1915–1920	85.6	11.7	3.8	2.2	1.1	5.6	1.0	−16.6	5.6	100.0
1921–1925	65.6	3.4	9.3	1.7	0.7	1.7	1.2	14.0	2.4	100.0
1926–1930	31.7	8.9	19.5	12.9	3.7	5.8	5.8	5.9	5.8	100.0
1931–1935	7.6	1.8	5.4	5.5	1.4	6.3	1.9	61.7	8.4	100.0
1936–1939	29.7	0.3	5.4	3.9	2.8	5.5	2.0	28.1	22.3	100.0
1940–1942	53.7	0.4	3.3	4.6	0.7	1.5	1.5	26.6	7.7	100.0
Total	71.5	3.9	5.7	1.8	0.6	1.5	1.9	9.7	3.4	100.0

TABLE 4.   *Average Yearly Migration in Various Periods*

Years	Average Migration
1840-1880	5,393
1881-1900	38,225
1901-1914	114,460
1915-1920	14,885
1921-1925	85,386
1926-1930	34,551
1931-1935	47,650
1936-1939	67,400
1940-1942	43,985
1840-1942	38,029

emigrants and by the laws of the countries of origin. One may say that until 1914 there were no limitations on emigration; even in Russia, where travel out of the country was forbidden and entailed many formalities and difficulties, in actuality the Jewish population was openly and freely allowed to organize and plan emigration. Fortunately also only few and exceptional persons—the sick, criminal, anarchist and such—were denied admission to the countries immigrants flocked to. Consequently the data of the Jewish emigration until 1914 reflect more or less accurately the emigration needs of Jews. And this was the yearly average:

1840 to 1880	5,393
1881 to 1900	38,225
1901 to 1914	114,460

Such were Jewish migrations under free conditions. Obviously, to understand such migrations fully one must remember that the countries to which immigrants came were at the same time experiencing an economic growth. Now, from the first period to the second, Jewish immigration increased sevenfold while at the beginning of the present century it increased threefold in the short interval of fourteen years. The war years do not enter into our account; the 15,000 emigrants per year indicated merely that the Jewish need even in the dangerous war years was so great that Jews hazarded everything in order to escape the European Gehenna. No sooner was the war over than Jewish emigration spiraled upward—in 1921 into the United States alone came close to 120,000 Jewish immigrants. If we include immigration into Palestine and South America the figure, for the first normal year after the war, is over 150,000. Had it not been for the quotas that were soon enacted, Jewish immigration in the postwar era would have risen higher and higher.

Nevertheless, Table 4 reveals that from 1921 to 1925 there was an average emigration of over 85,000 per year. The fact is that the tragic halt to migrations did not take place before the adoption in 1925 of the second quota system. It was directed principally against eastern European countries whence came 95 per cent of the immigrants.

From 1926 to 1930 emigration dropped from the more than 150,000 of the year after the war and from the yearly average of over 85,000 during the first five normal years, to less than 35,000 per annum. But despite the crisis in the Americas and the high restrictions that the consulates of all countries established, the Jewish masses, driven to a new low of insecurity by economic persecution and physical attacks, swept aside all migration barriers and penetrated into the remotest corners of the world, particularly into Palestine—a country unprepared economically for a mass immigration, but the land of Jewish dreamers nonetheless. Gradually it received the greatest number of Jewish immigrants, surpassing even the United States.

This is clear to us from Table 3b, which furnishes the relative numbers of the different countries. The United States, which, until the end of the nineteenth century took about 90 per cent of all Jewish emigrants, admitted less than 8 per cent from 1931 to 1935—fewer than 4,000 immigrants yearly. In the same five years Palestine admitted an average of 30,000 annually and almost two-thirds of all Jewish immigrants.

Tables 3a and 3b give us a clear picture of the role of the various countries in Jewish migration. Of about four million Jewish emigrants, the United States received more than two-thirds, 71.5 per cent; next comes Palestine, which in the entire period received close to one-tenth (9.7 per cent); third is Argentina, with over 5 per cent of all Jewish migrants. The other countries admitted only small numbers of Jews.

Within larger limits of time, the picture is even more striking. Contrast, for example, Palestine with the United States. We have used round numbers for the sake of convenience.

Years	Total Jewish Migration	Immigration into the U. S.		Immigration into Palestine	
		Absolute	Per Cent	Absolute	Per Cent
1840-1900	985,000	875,000	88.8	35,000	3.6
1901-1925	2,119,000	1,703,000	80.4	76,000	3.6
1926-1942	813,000	224,000	27.5	268,000	33.0
1840-1942	3,917,000	2,802,000	71.5	379,000	9.7

Here we see the development more strikingly. In the past years the United States has taken second place to Palestine in respect to Jewish immigration. In the most tragic years of Jewish history, from 1926 to 1942, the United States admitted only 224,000 Jewish immigrants, only 27.5 per cent of all Jewish immigration, while Palestine admitted 268,000, 33 per cent.

Of great interest is the range of Jewish immigrant dispersion. Here is a table of Jewish immigration into all countries besides the United States, Palestine, Canada and Argentina:

	Absolute Numbers	Per Cent
1840-1900	36,000	3.6
1901-1925	89,000	4.2
1926-1942	234,000	28.8
1840-1942	359,000	9.2

In general, in over a hundred years, 359,000, less than a tenth of all Jewish emigrants, scattered to tens of countries. Within certain periods, however, the situation is even more tragic. In the sixteen years from 1926 to 1942 more than 28 per cent of all Jewish migrants were dispersed in tens of countries where no firmly established Jewish communities existed.

For a more thorough understanding of the character of the mass of Jewish immigrants, we must analyze all available data on the various countries. Inasmuch as 80 per cent of all Jewish immigration of the past hundred years was taken care of by the United States and Palestine, we shall study carefully the characteristic streams of immigrants into these two countries.

5. THE CHARACTER OF THE JEWISH IMMIGRANT MASS IN THE UNITED STATES

A. Jewish Immigration into the United States in the Nineteenth Century

Jewish immigration into the United States may be divided into two large periods for a purely technical reason: we possess official and exact information only for the twentieth century. For the earlier period we are obliged to be satisfied with private sources, and therefore with much sparser content.

Nineteenth-century immigration into the United States was made up of two basic streams: (1) the German Jewish, from about 1820-1825 to 1870; it moved slowly and was never very large until 1880, when it was almost completely stopped, though a few businessmen continued to come occasionally for commercial purposes; (2) the East European Jewish, which began a little later than the German; it grew intensive in the middle of the century and immediately after the first large wave of Russian pogroms in 1881 and 1882 developed into a great mass movement.

The tempo of immigration of both German and East European Jews can best be gauged by the rise of the Jewish communities in the States. The famous traveler, J. J. Benjamin, who traveled through the States in the fifties, lists the founding dates of fifty congregations. The following tables, which we have drawn up, will give the information at a glance.

Year in Which Congregation Was Founded	German Jewish	Polish Jewish	Portuguese Jewish	Others	Total
1730	—	—	1	—	1
1782	—	—	1	—	1
1791	—	—	1	—	1
1802	1	—	—	—	1
1819	—	1	—	—	1
1823	1	—	—	—	1
1828	1	—	—	—	1
1830	1	1	—	—	2
1840	2	1	—	—	3
1841	2	—	—	—	2
1843	1	—	—	—	1
1845	1	—	—	1	2
1846	—	2	—	1	3
1847	1	—	1	—	2
1848	1	—	2	1	4
1849	2	1	—	1	4
1850	2	2	—	—	4
1851	1	1	—	—	2
1852	1	2	—	1	4
1853	1	1	—	2	4
1854	—	—	—	2	2
1855	—	1	—	—	1
1856	—	—	1	—	1
1858	—	1	—	—	1
1859	—	—	—	1	1
	19	14	7	10	50

Here we have in dry figures the tempo of immigration of different groups of Jews. One must not forget that a congregation is not founded by a negligible number of people or heads of families; often it is not founded even when there is the minimum required to create institutions. A cemetery alone—the first thing Jews generally acquire to begin their communal life—does not yet make a congregation. In the eighteenth century only three congregations were founded, all of the Portuguese ritual. But this does not mean that over the country there were not individual or tens of German Jews, even Polish Jews. All it means is that these had thus far not organized into a community. The first German Jewish congregation was founded in 1802 and the first Polish Jewish congregation in 1819. It is safe to say that this is the time difference that separates the German from the Polish Jewish mass immigration (by

"Polish Jewish" we mean all East European Jews). Further, this was the development:

        1820 to 1830, 4 congregations, of which 3 were German and 1 Polish
        1831 to 1840, 3 congregations, of which 2 were German and 1 Polish
        1841 to 1850, 22 congregations, of which 10 were German and 5 Polish
        1851 to 1859, 16 congregations, of which 3 were German and 6 Polish

The greatest number of congregations of the German ritual were founded between 1841 and 1850. Evidently, then, in the preceding ten or twenty years there had taken place an intensive immigration, and by this time the immigrants had been sufficiently rooted to establish communities. Between 1851 and 1859, however, more congregations of the Polish than of the German ritual were already founded—evidence that in several cities there were enough Polish Jews to found a congregation of their own. And in those last eight years there were founded six "other" congregations, of Hungarian and Bohemian Jews.

Despite the fact, therefore, that the first important period of Jewish migration into the United States was German in character, it is well to remember that other elements also were then present. This is particularly so in the years between 1860 and 1881, when a good many East European, Hungarian and Bohemian Jews arrived. These may even have outnumbered the German Jewish immigrants. Already in 1869, at a conference in Berlin called by the *Alliance Israélite*, the question of East European Jewish immigration was taken up, with particular attention paid to the Jews of Kovno, where a famine was raging. From 1870 on, East European Jews came to the States in ever-increasing numbers, and their great migration should perhaps be dated from then rather than from 1881. This is the record according to the official data of the United States:

Years	From Russia and Poland	From Austria-Hungary
1820-1870	7,550	7,800
1871-1880	52,254	72,969
1881-1890	265,088	353,719

According to official Austrian data from 1881 to 1890, the Jewish emigrants from Galicia constituted 59.7 per cent of the total emigration. In the emigration from Poland and Russia the percentage of Jews was still higher.

On the basis of various calculations, we have reached the conclusions that in general, during the nineteenth century, approximately 850,000 to 900,000 Jews entered the United States. Of these about 750,000—700,000 at the least—were from eastern Europe and about 150,000 from Germany and the German portion of Austria.

In comparison with the total immigration into the United States, the Jewish immigration was approximately as follows:

1820 to 1870	....	0.4 per cent
1871 to 1880	....	2.5 per cent
1881 to 1890	....	3.8 per cent
1891 to 1900	....	10.8 per cent

In the first fifty years Jewish immigration constituted less than one-half of one per cent of the total immigration. These were the years of the great migration from western and northern Europe—from England, France, the Scandinavian countries, etc. The percentage of Jewish immigrants rose continually in the last thirty years of the century, until at the end it represented almost 11 per cent of the total immigration. This was the highest percentage point of Jewish immigration. Here it remained, with rare exceptions which we shall discuss below, in the twentieth century.

From the material published in the German Jewish press we get a clear picture of the nature of Jewish emigration from Germany.

For example, the *Israelitische Annalen* (Frankfort) of 1839 (pages 213-214) presents in German the following very interesting and characteristic description of an emigrant group:

Until now we often read reports about Jews emigrating from Bavaria (our neighbor) to the Free States of North America. Now I have something similar to tell you about a community of Royal Wuerttemberg, although the causes and conditions are different.

On Sunday, June the 16th, fifty souls of the Mosaic faith (some of whom were young people who had already started a few weeks ago), left Ebenhausen (a parish eight hours from Stuttgart) to emigrate to the United States of North America.

A large crowd of bystanders had come from far and near, for the leave-taking. There was no eye without tears, all hearts were filled with sorrow, for this time it was not only the young, but fathers of families, women and children. It was really touching and heart-breaking when an old man of eighty (out of whose twelve children eleven will have emigrated), said good-bye to three of his children and fourteen grandchildren, the youngest of whom was two months old.

The cause of this strange happening in Wuerttemberg is partly that, for the past thirty years, many people had left this place to go to the United States, where they found free work and made a good living; those people invited their relatives (who had stayed behind), provided them with the necessary travelling expenses and prepared everything for their arrival across the ocean.

The religious community here counts 500 Jews. As the number of the emigrants has grown to be ninety-two souls, this makes one-fifth of the community; it is a situation which presents palpable gaps.

This quotation is rich in content. First, it tells us that for thirty years Jews had already emigrated from Wuerttemberg. So, too, we learn that no less than a fifth of the Wuerttemberg population had already migrated to America, and this in 1839, before the emigration of German Jews became intensive. Our correspondent also tells us that the pioneers of this emigration did remarkably well in the United States; and they invite relatives and friends and take care of their needs even before the latter arrive at their new destination. Clearly, then, there were some who did not possess enough for expenses. This is well corroborated by the famous Dr. Lillienthal, who wrote in the *Allgemeine Zeitung des Judentums* of 1847 (page 24):

We have in this city [New York] a great number of retail merchants who own business concerns which amount to 100 or 200 thousand dollars—and these people, upon their arrival six years ago, had not a penny in their pockets. They first carried 100 to 120 pound packs on their backs all day, in order to earn a trifle. When they had already earned this "trifle," they began to peddle goods with horse and buggy. Later they opened small stores in the villages and now they have concerns in New York which are regarded highly by all and which have good credit.

The social-economic background of the Jewish emigrants from Germany is difficult to determine, but there is no doubt that the large majority came from the commercial class—German Jewry had few artisans. In Prussia, no more than 7 to 8 per cent of the Jews were artisans; in Posen, about 15 per cent; and in other parts of Germany there were fewer than in Prussia. Among the emigrants from Germany after the revolution of 1848 there was already no small number of Jewish intellectuals, but a really great percentage could not have been educated, for there were not yet many Jewish professionals in Germany then.

We have a bit more information about the emigrants from eastern Europe in the nineteenth century. The minimum of 700,000 Jews who entered the United States may be divided, according to period, as follows:

1820 to 1870	30,000
1871 to 1880	70,000
1881 to 1890	200,000
1891 to 1900	400,000
Total 1820 to 1900	700,000

Whoever is at all acquainted with the East European scene will agree that, both economically and politically, conditions, in the last ten years of the century, were better than in the entire period from 1820 to 1870; yet in the decade from 1890 to 1900 thirteen times as many Jews as in the fifty years from 1820 to 1870 emigrated. We have already explained this phenomenon: (1) only in the second half of the nineteenth century did the Jewish masses shake off their lethargy and go off in search of better living conditions; (2) the first immigrants were now subsidizing the later emigration.

According to countries of origin, this is how the immigrants into the United States are roughly divided:

From Russia and Congress Poland	72.0 per cent
From Galicia and Hungary	23.0 per cent
From Rumania	3.5 per cent
From South European countries	1.5 per cent
Total	100 per cent

Already in the closing years of the nineteenth century Jewish immigration into the United States meant not an individual but a family migration, with the intent to settle permanently in the new country. This was the percentage of women:

1886-1888	37.1
1889-1896	44.0

The percentage of children was as follows:

1886-1888	27.9
1896-1898	44.0

Among these East European immigrants the percentage of artisans was certainly higher than among the immigrants from Germany, but even among the former this percentage was not so high as it was to be later, in the twentieth century.[11a] The first large wave of East European Jewish immigration included very many vocationless elements, without craft or trade to their name. Here is what one immigrant of the 1880's, who had lived among the masses all his life, had to say:

Happy were they who knew a trade in the old country. The tailors, the joiners and other artisans would obtain employment very quickly. But the bulk of the Jewish immigrants had no vocation.[12]

And there is hardly an exaggeration to the picture which Dr. Hoffman presents in his history of the cloak operators union:

Former Yeshiva students, sales clerks, insurance agents, semi-intellectuals, teachers, bookkeepers, sons-in-law of the well-to-do, storekeepers, merchants, etc., became cloak operators.[13]

We can therefore say that socially the East European Jewish immigration was made up of an enormous vocationless lower middle-class mass, of approximately 25 per cent handworkers, and of altogether common people, porters, wagoners, peddlers and the like. The percentage of intellectuals was negligible; its influence, however, was great. But we must also remember that among the vocationless lower middle-class mass there were quite a few who had attended not only a good *heder*, where they already studied Talmud, but also a *Yeshiva*. Although this group was without knowledge of worldly matters, it adjusted itself quickly to the new environment and culture, and very quickly, too, learned to speak English. And this group of educated Jews, with talmudic acuteness and Jewish energy, soon began to produce modern intellectuals who became the leaders of Jewish movements and the founders of Jewish institutions. Not a few likewise quit the Ghetto to take their place in the general cultural life of America.

B. Jewish Immigration into the United States in the Twentieth Century

Jewish immigration into the United States in the first forty-four years of this century was also made up of two principal streams, the East European and the German. With this difference, however: Until 1933, 95 per cent of the Jewish immigrants from Europe were East European; some of course came via Germany and France, England and Belgium; they may even have been registered as coming from these countries; but in fact they were East Europeans who stopped temporarily in those countries until their funds permitted them to go on. From 1933 on, however, German Jews predominated—at least they represented half of all Jewish immigrants. It is not that East European Jews gave up their wish to emigrate in these terrifying years. On the contrary, they would have given anything to emigrate from Poland, Rumania, Hungary and the rest of Eastern Europe; but no country would admit them. In this respect the German Jews were fortunate: Germany had a high quota of over 27,000 immigrants per year, while Poland had a quota of only over 6,000, Rumania of barely 377, and Hungary of 869. But even these small quotas could not serve Jews exclusively, for non-Jews, too, were in flight from the Old World. According to law, the consul was not obliged to issue all available visas. The quota figure constituted the maximum at his disposal, and all consuls were dedicated to the proposition that "the more sparing the more praiseworthy."

For technical statistical reasons also we must divide these forty-four years into two periods. Until 1925 the immigration data present an accurate picture of the character of the immigrant mass, they provide us with the individual's sex and age as well as social and economic background. The subsequent data reflect quotas and privileged groups like clergymen, students and others. In the distribution of visas altogether different factors begin to operate in 1938. Henceforth Jewish immigration becomes more a matter of sheer physical rescue than of economic need. A proper understanding of the normal character of the Jewish immigrant mass requires, therefore, an analysis of the official data up to 1925.

As already observed, Jewish immigrants arrived everywhere with the intent to settle permanently. This was especially true with regard to the United States, to which Jews came not only from Europe but also from other American countries. Yearly, for example, thousands of Jews come from Canada. This is confirmed by official figures from the year 1908 on.

From 1908 to 1925, 1,018,878 Jews entered the States and only 52,585 Jews emigrated, barely 5.2 per cent. Compare this Jewish remigration with the remigration of other European peoples (remigration, by the way, implies not only a departure of people but also the export of funds saved by the immigrant during his sojourn):

TABLE 5.   *The Remigration of Various Peoples from the United States (1908-1925)*

	Remigration	
Peoples	Absolute	Percentage Relative to Immigrants
Rumanians	65,554	67.0
Magyars	150,936	64.2
Italians	1,167,407	55.8
Russians	111,903	50.6
Poles	324,493	40.0
Lithuanians	35,513	25.4
Czechs	18,366	21.2
English	161,914	19.0
French	65,104	17.3
Ruthenians	29,124	16.7
Germans	125,738	15.3
JEWS	52,585	5.2

Now note: in the case of four peoples, more than half the immigrants returned to their native land; the percentage of remigrants of two of these peoples reached two-thirds. Of six of the twelve peoples more than one-fourth of all immigrants returned. The highest percentage of remigrants are for the agrarian peoples: the role of the American dollar in the Italian or Hungarian village is sufficiently well known. Even one-sixth of the French and English remigrated—three times as much as Jewish remigration. Rumanian remigration was thirteen times as much, Magyar twelve times as much, Italian eleven times as much, and so on.

A serious factor of even greater weight than the export of funds saved is presented by remigration. There is considerable difference in mentality between the immigrant who, from the moment he boards ship on his way to a new country, resolves unqualifiedly to settle in his adopted land and to raise his children there and the immigrant who is ever contemplating return to his native land.

Especially striking in this connection are the data on remigration in the

years just after the First World War. Poland, which became independent
after the war, shall serve as a model. Polish Jews fought heroically and
wholeheartedly for the liberation of Poland. Now, not only Poles and
Jews lived in Poland but also Ukrainians. Let us therefore compare the
remigration of the three peoples. Between 1919 and 1922 there returned
from the United States to Poland:

Peoples	Absolute Numbers	Percentage Relative to Immigrants in the Same Year
Poles	89,959	369.5
Ukrainians	428	56.5
Jews	528	0.5

Truly eloquent figures. Almost four times as many Poles returned to
Poland as came from Poland; more than half the number of Ukrainian
immigrants went back to enjoy their status as a territorial minority in the
resurrected Polish state. What about the Jews? Hardly one-half of one
per cent relative to the number of immigrants chose to return to the
resurrected Polish state! The pogroms even in liberated Poland during
the honeymoon of liberation were hardly an inducement.

One more fact is particularly illuminating. During the critical years
1932-1935, when economic conditions in the United States were difficult
and insecure, more people emigrated from than immigrated into the
country—138,911. In other words, the natives of Europe were going
home, although in the homelands too, as we recall, livelihood was far
from certain. But "there is no place like home," after all. In these very
years, however, 13,911 Jews entered the States.

The permanent-settling character of Jewish immigration is corroborated
also by the data on the sex and age range of the respective immigrants. Of
every hundred immigrants from 1900 to 1925, the percentages of women
were:

> Jews ....45.8 per cent
> Non-Jews ....32.9 per cent

the percentages of children under fourteen were:

> Jews .... 25.3 per cent
> Non-Jews .... 12.3 per cent

Very interesting, too, are the places to which the Jewish immigrant went.
These were not always the same and a comparison between 1900 and 1925
reveals the distribution of Jews over the land during those twenty-five
years, for one naturally goes to a place where he has relations or
landsleit.

At the beginning of the century hardly one-half of one per cent of all Jewish immigrants went to California and Michigan; in 1925 almost one-tenth went there. Seventy per cent of all Jewish immigrants used to go to New York; in 1925 only half went there. In the case of non-Jewish immigrants the same tendency prevailed, but not in the same proportion.

TABLE 6. *Destination of Jewish and Non-Jewish Immigrants (in Per Cent)*

People	New York	Philadelphia	California	Michigan
Jews:				
1900	70.0	9.7	0.1	0.4
1925	50.4	9.0	4.3	5.1
Non-Jews:				
1900	29.3	21.3	2.9	2.7
1925	21.7	6.3	8.1	8.9

And now for the most important point in the character of the Jewish migrant mass. A country may not only attract a large or small number of immigrants but also affect their professional status. This was certainly true of the United States, which not only absorbed tens of millions but in its melting pot converted huge masses of one profession into another. On the other hand, the majority of immigrants continued at their former occupations even in the New World. The Italian, Polish, Ukrainian peasant was attracted to husbandry or to the kind of labor with which he was more or less acquainted. The skilled German, English or Swedish mechanic or technician sought employment in heavy industry. The Jewish tailor or cobbler looked for his opportunity in the Ghettos of the city, where the manufacture of commonly used articles was concentrated. This has been true of the immigrants of the past fifty years, for American economy had by then been highly developed and the immigrant saw little pioneering to be done. He looked for the path of least economic resistance, for work which resembled what he had done in the Old World. Kinship and friendship also played their part in determining the occupation of the immigrant; and so, too, did United States demand for certain types of labor.

Concretely: (1) In Russia, which contributed more than two-thirds of all Jewish immigrants to the States during the first quarter of this century,[14a] a complete revolution in the occupational structure of the Jewish masses occurred in the last quarter of the nineteenth century. The transition from various middleman occupations to labor, especially to handicrafts, assumed mass proportions. This was especially true of the younger generation of the middle class; up to the age of fourteen or fifteen they studied in the small town *heder* and then went to Lodz, Warsaw, Odessa, Ekaterinoslav, Vilna or Bialystok, to the workshop or factory to learn a trade. These small-town boys and girls formed a large percentage of the Jewish émigrés from Russia at the beginning of the century.

(2) Simultaneously, industry, and particularly the clothing industry, developed intensively. Here are some figures of the number of workers employed by the ladies' garment industry: 1879—25,192; 1899—83,739, more than three times the number twenty years earlier; 1919—165,649, the figure is again doubled, and it is seven times what it had been in 1879. These were the wages that the industry paid out: 1879—$6,661,000; 1919—$195,296,000, thirty times the first amount. This extraordinary advance in wages, rumors of which penetrated into the Ghettos of Russia, Poland, Rumania, Hungary, Lithuania and Latvia, influenced not only experienced tailors to come to New York, where more than 90 per cent of the clothing factories were then located, but young Jews, too, children of the upper middle class. They now took sewing lessons to be equipped for America.

Let us now look at the occupational structure of the Jewish and non-Jewish immigrants.

TABLE 7. *Occupational Structure of the Jewish and Non-Jewish Gainfully Occupied Immigrants into the United States (1900-1925)*

Occupational Groups	Jews		Non-Jews	
	Absolute Numbers	Percentage	Absolute Numbers	Percentage
Industry	596,043	60.1	1,719,361	14.9
Commerce (Trade)	100,147	10.1	475,822	4.1
Husbandry	24,792	2.4	3,059,798	26.6
Liberal professions	19,620	2.0	261,033	2.3
Unskilled laborers	102,739	10.4	3,760,213	32.7
House servants	123,220	12.4	1,779,218	15.4
Miscellaneous	25,769	2.6	456,111	4.0
Total	992,330	100.0	11,511,556	100.0

Almost two-thirds of all gainfully employed Jewish immigrants belonged to the industrial class, the highly productive class of immigrants. For non-Jews, this group comprised only one-seventh of all gainfully employed immigrants. The percentage of farming and unskilled labor among non-Jewish immigrants was the same as that among Jewish skilled labor. One-tenth of all Jewish and 4 per cent of non-Jewish immigrants were merchants. In general merchants comprise only a small proportion of Jewish immigration—Jews brought to America not only six times as many skilled workers as traders, but also more menial laborers and domestic servants.

Here is a table of the distribution of craftsmen according to branches of industry:

Clothing industry	362,642	60.8 per cent
Lumber and building	84,683	14.2
Metal work	46,336	7.8
Food industries	42,501	7.1
Jewelry and watchmaking	9,582	1.6
Printing	9,282	1.6
Leather workers	8,017	1.4
Miscellaneous	33,000	5.5
	596,043	100.0

The role of the Jewish immigrant mass in the general immigrant mass can be seen from the following table (1900-1925). In percentages Jews represented

Of the total immigrant mass	10.3
Of the industrial immigrants	25.8
Of the clothing workers	48.8
Of the wood workers	16.4
Of the metal workers	12.8
Of the food workers	12.8
Of jewelers and watchmakers	49.7
Of printing workers	34.1
Of the leather workers	41.4
Of shopkeepers and merchants	22.2
Of farm workers	0.8
Of the liberal professions	7.0
Of domestic servants	6.5

This table is instructive. It reveals that one-fourth of all immigrant and skilled industrial labor in the United States was brought by Jews. The many millions of non-Jewish immigrant farm workers and menial laborers became, in large measure, industrial workers because of the intensive development of industry; but for this development on their part the country had to expend energy and funds. Jews, on the other hand, arrived in large measure as industrial workers. For two crafts—tailoring and watchmaking—Jews brought almost half the immigrant craftsmen. Jews constitute less than one-fourth of immigrant merchants and shopkeepers, but more than a third of all printing workers and more than 40 per cent of all immigrant leather workers.

This distribution of the Jewish immigrant mass during the greatest Jewish immigration period not only makes clear what Jews went through in adjusting themselves to the New World and its opportunities, but also belies the widespread notion that immigrant Jews were mostly merchants and vocationless persons. The Jewish immigrant was a laborer, a skilled craftsman, capable not only of keeping himself employed and helping those who remained in the old country, but also of taking his place in industry, which was then in need of skilled labor.

Beginning with 1933 the social structure of the Jewish immigrants changed radically. The entire immigration was stamped with the features of the German Jew's social and economic character. The more than 75,000 gainfully employed Jews who immigrated into the United States from 1933 to 1943 were distributed occupationally as follows:

Trade	31,724	41.9 per cent
Skilled workers	20,798	27.5
Liberal professions	15,047	20.0
Maids and menial labor	4,848	6.4
Miscellaneous	3,180	4.2
Total	75,597	100.0

More than twice the number of those of the first quarter of the century are now in trade. The percentage of persons engaged in the liberal professions is three times what it was, and correspondingly there is a decrease in the percentages of skilled workers, now less than half of the former numbers.

It is still too early to determine the results of the immigration of over 15,000 Jewish intellectuals, hundreds of whom were first-rate scholars, scientists and artists. In an editorial the *New York Times*, April 9, 1943, declared that in the future chronicle of World War II one of the most glorious pages will have to be devoted to the contribution of the many talented mathematicians who escaped from Germany prior to the war. The influence of tens and hundreds of talented and creative individuals will be manifest in the coming generation.

These are the occupations of over eleven thousand Jewish intellectuals who entered the United States from 1938 to 1943:

Physicians	2,693	24.0
Professors and teachers	1,470	13.0
Lawyers	1,306	11.7
Engineers	1,218	10.9
Clergy (rabbis)	487	4.3
Miscellaneous	4,047	36.1
Total	11,221	100.0

That the doctors were very useful to this country in the war years is beyond a doubt. The contribution of tens of first-class professors of medicine and world-renowned specialists in various branches of medicine to medical science in America is difficult to appraise. Among the approximately 1,500

Jewish scholars were tens, if not hundreds, of internationally famous mathematicians, philosophers, sociologists, economists, psychologists, natural scientists; their influence in American institutions of learning is already being felt and will be more apparent in later years. Among the more than four thousand various intellectuals there are many first-class writers, poets, actors, journalists, etc.

6. THE CHARACTER OF THE JEWISH IMMIGRATION TO PALESTINE

According to the table of migrations 379,000 Jews entered Palestine from 1840 to 1942. If we include the immigrants of 1943, 1944 and the first six months of 1945 the total rises to over 400,000. In 1943, 8,507 Jews arrived, 14,500 in 1944, and 8,000 by July, 1945. Since at the end of the First World War there were in Palestine no more than approximately 50,000 Jews, it is clear that more than four-fifths of all Jewish immigrants came in the past twenty-five years. This is the reverse of what occurred in the United States, where the largest number of Jewish immigrants arrived in the first fourteen years of this century.

All the figures given below about the character of Jewish immigration will not be in accord with the data of the above-mentioned table because we have taken the net immigration. The data on sex, age, as well as occupation in the old country, is included in the gross immigration figures which are those registered by the Palestine immigration office. On the

TABLE 8.   *The Distribution of Immigrants into Palestine According to Country of Origin 1919-1943*

| | Immigrants | |
Countries	Absolute Numbers	Percentage
Poland	139,756	42.2
Soviet Union	30,926	9.4
Germany	44,635	13.5
Rumania	18,737	5.6
Czechoslovakia	10,555	3.2
Lithuania	9,908	3.0
Yemen	9,813	3.0
Austria	9,772	3.0
United States	8,043	2.4
Greece	6,739	2.0
Iraq	5,842	1.8
Latvia	4,982	1.5
Turkey	3,929	1.2
Hungary	3,555	1.1
Miscellaneous	23,430	7.1
Total	330,622	100.0

other hand, we have everywhere omitted the unknown rubric and have taken only the exact figures in order that the relative numbers shall correspond more accurately.

TABLE 9.   *Distribution of Illegal Immigrants According to Countries of Origin*

Countries	Immigrants Absolute Numbers	Percentage
Czechoslovakia	4,557	30.6
Poland	2,450	16.4
Austria	2,187	14.7
Germany	1,714	11.5
Rumania	1,318	8.7
Hungary	1,300	8.9
Bulgaria	769	5.2
Miscellaneous countries	460	3.1
Stateless	132	0.9
Total	14,887	100.0

Immigration into Palestine took on a mass character only after the First World War. Before that generally only a highly idealistic, ideologically committed element went there, namely, Zionists. The rest were ordinary folk seeking a livelihood, but also possessing a nostalgia for the Holy Land, with its ancient memories, and its rural life.

To be sure, even in the past twenty-five years a goodly number of enthusiastic Zionists left for Palestine. But it is difficult to distinguish these from the large mass of immigrants. Although a majority of the illegal immigrants were young Zionists, illegal immigration became a mass movement only when remaining in one's native land proved even more terrible than sailing on the Black Sea and not being admitted into any port. This is easily seen from Table 9. Polish Jews who, during normal migration, contributed (Table 8) over 42 per cent of all immigrants, were but little more than 16 per cent of the illegal immigrants. Czechoslovakians, on the other hand, who in normal migration were only slightly more than 3 per cent, constituted almost one-third of the illegal immigrants. The same is true of the Austrians: normally they represented only 3 per cent of the immigrants; among illegal immigrants they were almost 15 per cent.

There are figures in Table 8, however, which remind us that eight thousand and more immigrants went into Palestine from the United States. Considering that the United States was the land to which above all immigrants flocked, the land of which millions of Jews over the world dreamed, eight thousand is no small number.

From Table 8 we see that Palestine is really "a gathering place of the exiles." To it people have come from every corner of the world. Poland

and Germany together contributed more than half the entire immigration. From Soviet Russia also came no small number of immigrants; one must remember, however, that this immigration occurred only in the first years after the Bolshevik revolution. Later emigration was prohibited and the prohibition stands to this day.

If we divide the immigrants into Palestine according to historic back‑ground, we get the following (in percentages):

Ashkenazim	88.8
Sephardim	5.1
Yemenites	2.9
Miscellaneous	3.2
Total	100.0

The percentage of women among Palestinian immigrants is similar to that of the immigrants into the States—from 1919 to 1942 it amounted to 47.6.

The age groups reveal that a markedly large percentage of young and middle-aged people went to Palestine, in other words, the most able workers and the most productive element of the Jewish people. The following table tells the story for the period from 1919 to 1942:

0 to 9	10.7
10 to 20	21.7
21 to 35	41.8
36 to 50	12.8
51 and over	13.0
Total	100.0

Almost three-fourths of all the immigrants are younger than thirty-five and all of 87 per cent are younger than fifty.

The data on the percentage of women and children among the illegal immigrants testify to the pressure to emigrate and to their choice of Palestine: 33.9 per cent of all illegal immigrants were women and 7.2 per cent, or 1,116, were children under sixteen. When the sword is at your throat you risk everything. Under such circumstances Jews fled from Europe to Palestine. They sought refuge in other countries, too; in these, however, they were not only refused admittance, but it was unthinkable to seek admittance forcibly. Yet this was done in Palestine and several tens of thousands of Jews were thus rescued from the Hitler massacre. Of course, there were many tragedies—the *Struma* with her 700 Jewish passengers drowned, the *Patria* with her 250 passengers drowned, the 1,585 illegal immigrants mercilessly packed off by the English to the island of Mauritius, where they languished for almost five years, from November, 1940, to August, 1945, and many others. Nevertheless, the number rescued is much greater than those sacrificed—who would have suffered far more in the Hitler Gehenna than on the waves of the sea.

The uniqueness of the Palestinian immigrants is even more strikingly brought out by their occupational distribution. The fact that during these years at least several tens of thousands *halutzim* entered Palestine—young people trained especially for agriculture or physical labor of various kinds —itself put a special stamp on the social structure of the immigrants. But even among the immigrants of the recent war years who were running for their lives the percentage of workers was higher than among immigrants into other countries.

TABLE 10. *Distribution of Gainfully Occupied Immigrants According to Their Occupations in Their Native Countries*

Occupation	Absolute Numbers	Percentage
Industry and crafts	38,066	33.0
Building and unskilled labor	23,618	20.5
Agriculture	19,075	16.5
Trade	15,114	13.1
Liberal professions	11,300	9.8
Officials (or executives)	4,364	3.8
Religious leaders	1,906	1.6
Transport workers	1,318	1.1
Miscellaneous	657	0.6
Total	115,418	100.0

The higher percentage (16.5) of those engaged in agriculture—seven times what it is among the immigrants into the United States—strikes one immediately. In addition, one must take into account the fact that in the past ten years the proportion of German and Austrian Jews among the immigrants was great, and that in the last five years almost all of the preparatory training in the Diaspora for work in Palestine was all but halted. Only 13.1 per cent were engaged in trade, almost half of what it was among the immigrants into the States. The percentage (9.8) in the liberal professions is high, five times that among the immigrants into the States during the first quarter of the current century; but it will probably not be higher than the percentage of United States immigrants in the liberal professions from 1932 to 1943.

We also possess trustworthy knowledge of the amount of private capital which Jews managed to rescue in the five war years (1940-1944). In these years Jewish immigrants brought into Palestine £21,450,000, or, over $85,000,000. The national capital brought into Palestine during the same period was £12,000,000, or, $48,000,000. Private capital, therefore, is almost twice as much as public capital. Estimates were also made of the capital which the refugees brought into the States from the beginning of the war until 1944. These estimates ran between $800,000,000 and a billion dollars; but in this figure is also included the wealth of Christian refugees from France, Belgium, Holland, Norway and other countries.

Notes

[1a Cf. above Anita Libman Lebeson, "The American Jewish Chronicle,"¹ and Moshe Davis, "Jewish Religious Life and Institutions in America."]

[2a Cf. above Yudel Mark, "Yiddish Literature."]

3 Dr. Ch. Kayserling, "A Memorial sent by German Jews to the President of the Continental Congress," *Publications of the American Jewish Historical Society*, No. 6, 1897.

[4a Cf. Mark, *op. cit.*, p. 870.]

5 *Allgemeine Zeitung des Judentums* (Leipzig, 1845), pp. 46-50.

[6a Cf. above Cecil Roth, "The Jews of Western Europe (from 1648)," p. 266.]

7a Cf. above Uriah Zevi Engelman, "Sources of Jewish Statistics," pp. 1188-1189.]

8 Joseph Kissman, *Studien zu der geschichte fun rumenische yiden in ninezenten yahrhundert* (New York, 1944), p. 22.

9 *Ibid.*

[10a Cf. Roth, *op. cit.*, pp. 273 ff.]

[11a Cf. below Nathan Reich, "The Economic Structure of Modern Jewry," pp. 1240 f.]

12 Bernard Weinstein, *Yiddische Yunions in America* (New York, 1929), p. 44.

13 B. Hoffman, *Fufzig yahr klokmacher yunion* (New York, 1936), p. 22.

[14a Cf. Reich, *op. cit.*, pp. 1243-1244.]

Bibliography

In addition to the official statistical publications of the United States, Canada, Palestine and the Latin-American republics, and the reports of ICA (Jewish Colonization Association) and *Hicem* the following works have been utilized in this study:

The American Jewish Year Book. New York, 1920-1944.

Bulletin of the Economic Research Institute of the Jewish Agency for Palestine. Jerusalem, 1945.

Davie, Maurice R., *World Emigration.* New York, 1939.

Ha-Aliah, ha-Yishuv, ve-ha-Tenuah ha-Tivit shel ha-Oklosiah be-Eretz Yisrael. Jerusalem, 1945, Shenaton, Tel-Aviv, 1945.

Joseph, Samuel, *Jewish Immigration to the United States from 1881-1910.* New York, 1914.

LESTSCHINSKY, JACOB, *Die anheben fun emigratzie bei yiden in ninezenten yahrhundert.* Berlin, 1929.

———, "Die berufliche Zusammensetzung der juedischen Einwanderung in die Vereinigten Staaten," in *Weltwirtschaftliches Archiv,* January, 1948.

———, "Die juedische Wanderung, ihre Ursachen und ihre Regelung," in *Archiv fuer Wanderungswesen.* Leipzig, 1930.

———, "Dos soziale ponim fun dem Americaner yudentum" in *YIVO Bleter* (Journal of the Yiddish Scientific Institute), Vol. XVII. New York, 1941.

———, "Emigratzie in der kapitalistischer tekufeh" in *Yiddische Ekonomik,* Nos. 2 and 3. Warsaw-Vilna, 1937.

———, "Juedische Wanderungen im XIX. Jahrhundert" in *Internationaler Congress fuer Bevoelkerungsforschung.* Rome, 1932.

———, *Wuhin gen mir? (Yiddische wandrungen amol und heint).* New York, 1944.

———, *Yiddische wanderung in die letzte fuenf und zwanzig yahr.* Berlin, 1927.

LEVINE, LOUIS, *The Women's Garment Workers.* New York, 1924.

ROSENBERG, LOUIS, *Canada's Jews.* Montreal, 1939.

TAFT, DONALD R., *Human Migration.* New York, 1936.

TARTAKOWER, ARIEH, and GROSSMAN, KURT, *The Jewish Refugee.* New York, 1944.

Yiddish Scientific Institute, *The Classification of Jewish Immigrants and Its Implications.* New York, 1945.

CHAPTER 33

THE ECONOMIC STRUCTURE OF MODERN JEWRY

By Nathan Reich

A discussion of the economics of modern Jewry must be preceded by several preliminary remarks. First, it is important to bear in mind that there is no independent Jewish economy; Jews have become an integral part of the economies of their respective countries. A thorough analysis of the occupational stratification of the Jewish communities throughout the world would require a discussion of the economic development of practically the entire modern world—a task which would clearly transcend the confines of one chapter. The second limiting consideration is the lack of accurate information, particularly in countries where the census does not classify the citizens on the basis of religious or ethnic affiliation. Third, even where census data are available for individual countries, they are not always strictly comparable as between different countries, inasmuch as different census authorities follow different bases of occupational classification. Summary generalizations of occupational structures of Jews belonging to many countries may not always, therefore, meet the requirement of scientific precision. Finally, one should bear in mind that because of the enormous dislocation of Jewish life in Europe during World War II it is necessary to limit the discussion primarily to the conditions as they obtained at the outbreak of the war, with only tentative references regarding post-war trends.

The economic career of modern Jewry was shaped by two main factors: political emancipation and the Industrial Revolution. The first freed Jews from the political and legal restraints of the Ghetto; the latter offered them the opportunity to use their freedom to the best of their ability. The effectiveness with which the Jews availed themselves of this newly won freedom has been remarkable indeed. In the course of a little over one hundred years the Jewish people transformed themselves from a people concentrated primarily in the economically backward area of eastern Europe and Asia into a people inhabiting, in substantial numbers, the economically advanced areas of the Western world; and from an undifferentiated mass of petty traders with a sprinkling of artisans into a people engaged in a wide variety of significant economic activities.

Yet, while the Jews on the whole have integrated themselves into the economies of their respective countries and while there is hardly an occupation in which Jews are not present, the Jewish economic structure of today still retains a number of characteristics which differentiate it from the general economic structure of the countries in which Jews live.

First, the Jews are an overwhelmingly urban people. Before World War II almost half of world Jewry lived in cities with a population exceeding 100,000, and over one-fourth lived in cities of one million or more inhabitants;[1] of one hundred Polish Jews seventy-six dwelt in cities; of one hundred non-Jews in Poland, only twenty-two. In Germany the proportions were eighty-four and forty-nine and in Rumania sixty-nine and eighteen, respectively.[2] Of the 3,020,100 Jews in Soviet Russia 87 per cent lived in cities; only 13 per cent in rural areas.[3] In the United States practically the entire Jewish population is urban. In Canada over 96 per cent of the Jewish population is urban according to the census of 1931.[4]

Moreover, Jews are not merely urban; they tend to be metropolitan. In the United States about 40 per cent of Jewry reside in New York City. London houses over 60 per cent of the English Jews, Berlin comprised 32 per cent of German Jewry, and Vienna 90 per cent of Austrian Jewry. Montreal has about 37 per cent of Canadian Jewry and Buenos Aires claims about half the Argentine Jews. In eastern Europe the degree of metropolitan concentration was less pronounced. Thus in Poland, where 36 per cent of the Jews lived in cities of 100,000 inhabitants and over,[5] Warsaw claimed only about 11 per cent of Polish Jewry. In Soviet Russia, Moscow, in which under the czar only a few thousand privileged Jews were permitted to live, attracted since the revolution over 400,000, or about 14 per cent of Russian Jews. Even in Palestine, where a determined effort has been made to direct Jews into agricultural pursuits and to effect a balanced distribution of population, Tel-Aviv and Jerusalem contain almost half of Palestinian Jewry.

The second characteristic of modern Jewry is its concentration in several areas of economic enterprise. Broadly speaking, the bulk of Jews draw their sustenance from commerce, industry, professions and clerical occupations. Within these broad areas there is a further concentration in the various subdivisions. Thus in commerce large numbers of Jews are engaged in retail trade; within industry Jews are concentrated primarily in consumer goods industries, such as clothing, furs, shoes and food, with little representation in the producer goods industries, such as steel, coal, heavy transport. Within the professions, law, medicine, dentistry and pharmacy claim the overwhelming proportion of Jewish professionals. It is generally known that very few Jews devote themselves to agriculture.

The following tables give a quantitative picture of the occupational composition of Jews. Table 1 reveals the marked contrast in the proportions

TABLE 1

Percentage Distribution of Gainfully Employed Jews and Non-Jews in Selected Countries
(Agriculture)

Country	Year	Jews	Non-Jews
Poland	1931	4	66
Germany	1933	1.3	24.9
Rumania	1930	4.1	75.6
Hungary	1930	2.7	54.1
Czechoslovakia	1930	8.3	35.6
Latvia	1930	1.1	68.5

Source: Except for the figures on Poland, which are estimates, the data are from the
Universal Jewish Encyclopedia, Vol. 8, p. 268.

of Jews and non-Jews engaged in agricultural pursuits in various countries of Europe. The relatively high proportion of Jews engaged in agriculture in Czechoslovakia is due to the large number of Jewish peasants in Carpatho-Ruthenia. The contrast is less marked when we compare the occupational distribution of Jews and non-Jews outside of agriculture. An analysis of Table 2 reveals that, while differences exist in many areas, they are sharp only in commerce and in some countries also in industry. Thus, of one hundred Jews in Poland forty-five were engaged in industry and handicraft, as compared with forty-nine among one hundred non-Jews. In countries where the Jewish population was small, as in Germany and Czechoslovakia, the divergence in the industrial group is larger. The sharpest contrast, however, is noted in the commerce group, in which the proportion among Jews is several times that prevailing among non-Jews. Among Jews in Poland the number of those engaged in commerce was four times as high as among non-Jews; in Germany, over three times as high; in Hungary and Czechoslovakia, over four times as high. The proportions are reversed in the transport and communication group and in the domestic service group. Conditions which prevailed in Germany were roughly typical of other industrialized countries of Europe.

An analysis of the occupational distribution of Jews in the United States offers special difficulties, for at least two reasons: (1) the census does not classify the American people on the basis of religious or ethnic origin; (2) because of the sharp occupational changes between the generation of the immigrant and native groups. Because of the lack of accurate census data it is necessary to rely on private studies which are fragmentary in nature. Moreover, as these individual studies were made by different persons at different times using different methods, the data are not strictly comparable. It cannot, therefore, be too strongly emphasized that the

Table 2

Percentage Distribution of Gainfully Employed Jews and Non-Jews
(Outside of Agriculture)

Country	Year	Industry and Handicraft		Commerce and Credit		Transport and Communication		Public Service and Liberal Professions		Domestic Service		Independent Maintenance*		Others	
		Jews	Non-Jews	Jews	Non-Jews	Jews	Non-Jews	Jews	Non-Jews	Jews	Non-Jews	Jews	Non-Jews	Jews	Non-Jews
Poland	1931	45.4	49.0	38.2	9.3	3.5	7.3	6.1	12.0	3.3	10.9	2.6	9.2	0.9	2.3
Germany	1933	18.7	45.6	49.8	15.1	0.3	5.5	9.4	8.3	1.3	5.3	20.5	20.2	—	—
Rumania	1930	34.8	47.5	51.5	18.1	2.6	10.1	2.9	13.4	—	—	—	—	8.2†	10.9†
Hungary	1930	32.8	49.5	46.2	10.0	2.0	6.2	8.4	10.4	1.5	11.6	7.4	8.9	1.7	3.4
Czechoslovakia	1930	22.2	51.7	46.7	10.1	2.2	6.0	8.3	6.7	1.7	6.9	17.8	16.4	1.1	2.2
Latvia	1930	29.1	41.1	49.2	11.8	2.2	10.6	13.0	17.0	2.0	10.5	—	—	4.5‡	8.0‡

Source: Data taken from the *Universal Jewish Encyclopedia*, Vol. 8, pp. 268-269.

* Includes pensioners, capitalists, inmates of institutions.

† Includes domestics and those not engaged in gainful occupations.

‡ Includes those not engaged in gainful occupations.

statistical data are at best approximations and should be accepted in the most tentative mood.

One important factor in the occupational scene of American Jewry is the rather sharp contrast between the vocational distribution of the Jewish immigrant population[5a] and that of their sons and daughters born in this country. Table 3 presents the results of a study on the occupational distribution of Jewish immigrants from Russia.

TABLE 3

Occupational Distribution of Immigrant Jews Born in Russia and Living in American Cities of 250,000 and Over in 1900

Occupation	Per Cent
Manufacturing	59.6
Trade	20.6
Domestic and personal service	8.0
Clerical	6.7
Professions	2.6
Transportation and communication	1.7
Agriculture, fishing, forestry and mining	0.5
Public service	0.3

Source: Nathan Goldberg, "Occupational Patterns of American Jewry," *Jewish Review.* Vol. III, No. 1, p. 11.

Table 3 reveals that the majority of immigrant Jews were engaged in industry. This is understandable. The immigrant came to America without means, frequently without skill. He did not know the language of the country; he consequently flocked to the shops, primarily to the clothing shop where he could with little delay acquire the necessary skill and establish himself economically in the quickest possible way. It should also be remembered that many immigrants were tailors or other craftsmen in the countries of their origin. But in time, as they acquired the language and managed to save some money, many of the former immigrants took advantage of the expansion of commercial opportunity, left the workshop and entered the trade group. Studies made of the occupational distribution in the years 1924-1925 reflect the shift of American Jews from industry into trade, professions and clerical occupations. A survey of thirty-six cities made by the American Jewish Economic Commission of Aleph Zadik Aleph, B'nai B'rith Youth Organization, estimates the proportion of Jews engaged in industry at 16.3 per cent, in trade at 47.4 per cent, in professions at 10.1 per cent and in clerical work at 16.8 per cent.[6] Another survey covering ten cities puts the proportion of Jews engaged in industry at 42.8 per cent, in trade at 30.8 per cent, in professions at 9.6 per cent and in clerical work at 8.4 per cent.[7] While the figures are not comparable with those contained in Table 3, they nevertheless reflect an unmistakable shift from manufacturing to trade, professions and clerical occupations.

One of the difficulties in appraising the present occupational distribution of American Jews is the wide variation between the large cities and small towns. A survey of numerous recent studies reveals that the percentage of Jews engaged in manufacturing is larger in big cities which house industrial plants than in small towns without industrial opportunities and where the majority of Jews are engaged in commercial pursuits. Table 4 presents the results of a survey of New York City made by the Conference on Jewish Relations in 1938.

TABLE 4

Percentage Distribution of Gainful Jewish Workers in New York City (1937)

General Division of Industry	Jewish Gainful Workers* (Per Cent)	All Gainful Workers (Per Cent)
Trade	25.7	16.9
Manufacturing Industries	25.4	19.8
Domestic and personal service	10.9	14.2
Professional service	7.4	6.6
Construction industries	5.2	9.9
Transportation industries	2.7	5.7
Finance	2.4	5.4
Amusements	2.4	1.7
Public service	2.2	2.9
Public utilities	0.5	3.6
Other	1.7	2.3
Unemployed	13.5	11.0

Source: *Industrial Classification of Jewish Gainful Workers in New York City,* New York: Conference on Jewish Relations, 1938, 31 pages (mimeo.).

* The term "workers" includes both employer and employee.

The table reveals that about one-fourth of New York's Jews were engaged in manufacturing and trade respectively. A comparison with the column referring to all gainful workers discloses the rate of divergence between the occupational distribution of Jewish workers and all New Yorkers: the proportion among Jews was higher in industry, trade, professions and amusement trades, and lower in domestic and personal services, transportation, public utilities and finance. The low proportion of Jews in public utilities and finance probably reflects discriminatory employment policies in these occupations. It should be remembered that these figures are based on estimates and should be accepted as mere approximations.

The differences between the occupational distribution of New York Jews and that of Jews living outside the metropolitan area are brought out in Table 5.

TABLE 5

Occupational Distribution of Jewish Gainful Workers in Selected Cities

(in Per Cent)

	Dallas, Texas	Detroit, Mich.	New London, Conn.	Norwich, Conn.	Passaic, N.J.	Stamford, Conn.	Trenton, N.J.
Divisions of Industry	1939	1935	1938	1938	1937	1938	1937
Trade	51.9	54.1	54.5	50.8	43.2	56.2	53.7
Manufacturing and mechanical	11.4	23.3	16.2	22.7	22.5	16.1	11.7
Professional services	11.7	9.5	13.7	9.4	12.3	13.5	12.3
Clerical occupations	20.2	—	4.7	9.2	14.6	—	12.4
Domestic and personal services	1.6	9.6	5.6	3.9	4.6	5.5	5.3
Transportation and communication ..	1.3	2.2	2.2	1.6	2.3	—	2.9
Public service	—	0.9	1.0	1.3	0.4	0.9	0.9
Others	1.9	0.4	2.1	1.1	0.1	7.8	0.8

Source: Adapted from tables in *Patterns of Jewish Occupational Distribution in the United States and Canada*, Jewish Occupational Council, New York, 1940.

Because of the different bases of classification and different method of collection of data these figures are not strictly comparable with the figures given for New York City. Allowing for certain discrepancies, the figures nevertheless disclose that outside the New York area the proportion of Jews in industry declines and that of trade and professions increases. The results of a more extensive survey made by various individuals and organizations during the years 1934-1939 and covering sixty-five cities are summarized in Table 6.

TABLE 6

Percentage Distribution of Gainfully Employed Jews

Occupations	61 Communities	4 Communities
Manufacturing	12.4	34.8
Trade	47.3	33.3
Professions	11.9	11.3
Clerical	15.7	—
Domestic and personal	6.8	12.4
Public service	2.9	2.6
Transportation and communication	1.9	3.7
Other and unknown	1.1	1.9

Source: Nathan Goldberg, "Occupational Patterns of American Jews," *Jewish Review*, Vol. III, No. 3, p. 172.

The first column covers sixty-one communities mostly of small or medium size; the second column refers to New York, Detroit, New Orleans, and Stamford, Connecticut. Except for Stamford the cities are large and all four are the homes of extensive industries. The larger proportion of Jews engaged in industry in the second group of cities reflects the great local variations in the occupational structure of American Jews. Here again the reader should be cautioned regarding the tentative nature of conclusions based on incomplete and not always comparable studies.

It is, of course, difficult to give a precise account of the over-all occupational distribution of American Jewry. On the basis of all estimates it would be fair to conclude that of one hundred American Jews, between thirty-five and forty-five draw their sustenance from commercial pursuits; about fifteen to twenty are in manufacturing industries; from ten to twelve in professions and about fifteen in clerical professions. Comparing these figures with those for the American population at large we may conclude that Jews are three times as heavily represented in commerce; perhaps twice as heavily represented in professions; while the proportion of Jews engaged in manufacturing is smaller by one-third, and the proportion of Jews engaged in agriculture is merely a fraction of the proportion of all Americans so engaged.

Although the Jewish community of Canada is relatively small, its occupational distribution deserves consideration for two reasons: (1) Canada is the only country in the Western Hemisphere which classifies the occupations of her residents on the basis of religious affiliation and for which information about occupations of Jews is complete. (2) Because of the substantial similarity in the origins and traditions of Jewish immigrants to Canada and those who flocked to the United States, the Canadian picture may throw valuable light on the occupational pattern of Jews in the United States. Table 7 gives the occupational distribution of Canadian Jews as revealed in the last three census enumerations. The table is interesting for its comparison between the occupations of Canadian Jews and those of all Canadians. Thus, while the proportion of Jews in trade is four times greater and in agriculture one-twentieth that of all Canadians—an experience common to most Jewish communities the world over—the proportion of Jews engaged in industry is twice that of the general population. The larger proportion of Jews engaged in manufacturing and the lower proportion engaged in trade and professions, as compared with the corresponding proportions among Jews in the United States, reflect the more recent immigrant origin of Canadian Jews as compared with the older American Jewish community. In this regard the occupational pattern of Canadian Jewry in 1941 resembles that of American Jews at the close of World War I when large-scale immigration to the United States was drastically restricted.

TABLE 7

Occupational Distribution of the Jewish and Total Population of All Origins in Canada
(in Per Cent)

| | 1921 | | 1931 | | 1941 | |
	Total Population	Jews	Total Population	Jews	Total Population	Jews
Agriculture	32.82	2.35	28.82	1.26	25.24	1.19
Fishing, logging*	3.66	0.19	3.83	0.10	4.88	0.17
Manufacturing	12.83	30.45	12.10	29.62	16.73	31.24
Construction	5.11	3.36	5.17	3.20	4.86	2.25
Transportation	6.34	2.94	7.67	2.84	6.57	2.64
Trade	8.39	38.22	7.99	35.94	8.54	34.86
Finance	0.27	0.13	0.28	0.21	0.29	0.28
Insurance	0.58	0.74	0.66	1.17	0.35	0.92
Professional service	5.38	3.61	6.07	5.06	5.79	5.62
Personal service	6.50	2.61	9.09	3.44	9.94	4.10
Clerical	6.87	8.82	6.14	10.16	8.04	14.20
Laborers	9.63	5.23	11.13	2.69	6.51	1.45
Others	1.62	1.35	1.05	4.31	2.26	1.08
Total	100.00	100.00	100.00	100.00	100.00	100.00

Source: Louis Rosenberg, "The Jews of Canada," *Jewish Review*, Vol. II, Nos. 2-3, p. 136.
* And mining.

There is little precise information on the occupational distribution of
Jews in Latin-American countries. Argentina, Brazil and Mexico are the
only countries with sizable Jewish communities. In Brazil and Mexico, as
well as in the other countries, the bulk of Jews are engaged in commercial
occupations and in industry in the capacity of employers. In Argentina,
which contains the majority of Latin-American Jewry, an estimate made a
few years ago places the proportion of Jews engaged in industry at 23
per cent; in trade at 60 per cent; in agriculture at 13 per cent, with the
remainder in professions and other activities.[8] A more recent report puts
the number of Jewish colonists in Argentina at 27,448 persons representing
3,946 families.[9] Because of the growth of the Jewish population in
Argentina and the relatively stationary agricultural population, the proportion of Jewish agriculturists among Argentine Jews is now probably less.

The occupational distribution of Russian and Palestinian Jewries deserves special consideration, the former because of the different basis of
social and economic organization of the country, and the latter because of
the unique ideological factors that have shaped the economic structure
of the young Palestinian community. The occupational distribution of pre-
revolutionary Russian Jewry followed the usual pattern characteristic of

Eastern European Jewry. According to the 1897 census, of one hundred Russian Jews thirty-six were engaged in industry and crafts, thirty-one in commerce, eleven in personal services and about five in professions.[10] The virtual disappearance of private enterprise under the impact of the successive five-year plans has changed the very basis of occupational classification. According to the 1939 census the socioeconomic structure is given as follows:[11]

	Per Cent
Workers and salaried employees	71.2
Collective farmers	5.8
Artisans in co-operatives	16.1
Independent artisans	4.0
Others	2.9

The largest group consists of workers and salaried employees. As the ratio of workers to salaried employees is given as 3:4, it follows that over 30 per cent of Soviet Jews are workers and over 40 per cent salaried employees.[12] Of greater relevance to the subject of occupational distribution is the distribution of workers and employees among the various branches of the economy as shown in Table 8.

TABLE 8

Distribution of Gainfully Employed Jewish Workers and Salaried Persons in the Most Important Branches of Social Economy and Culture in 1936-1937

(in Per Cent)

Branch	Ukraine	White Russia
Industry	36.2	45.1
Construction	4.4	2.4
Agriculture	2.5	1.1
Transportation	1.9	3.6
Communication	0.4	0.5
Communal economy	2.3	3.8
Trade	11.6	11.1
Food	4.5	2.4
Education	16.3	13.2
Art	1.5	3.3
Health protection	9.7	6.4
Institutions	8.7	7.1

Source: Lev Singer, *Dos Banaite Folk*, Moscow, 1941, p. 62.

The Jews in the Ukraine and White Russia comprised about two-thirds of Soviet Jewry in 1939. Industry claimed the largest proportion; education the second largest, followed by those engaged in trade. True to the pattern of Jewish economies elsewhere, construction, transportation and agriculture absorb insignificant percentages of the Jewish population in the U.S.S.R. Of further interest is the distribution of those engaged in industry; the three groups claiming the largest proportion are machine building, needle trades and food industries. With the exception of machine building the industrial distribution does not deviate much from the pattern followed by Jewish workers in other countries. Jacob Lestschinsky estimates the economic structure of Soviet Jewry in 1940 as follows:[13]

	Per Cent
Salaried employees	32.2
Liberal professions	17.8
Wage workers	21.5
Artisans	14.3
Farmers (collective and individual)	7.1
Others	7.1
Total	100.0

The occupational structure of Soviet Jewry differs markedly from that of all Russians; on the other hand, it does not differ radically from that of Jews in other lands, except that, in conformity with the basic social organization, Soviet Jews, of course, exercise their economic functions primarily through state institutions.

The occupational distribution of Palestinian Jewry comes closest to that of a modern independent national economy. The economic experience of this youthful and vigorous branch of Jewry must be viewed in the light of the powerful extraeconomic ideological impulses that have inspired migration and settlement in Palestine.

TABLE 9

Occupational Distribution of Gainfully Employed Jews in Palestine

	Estimates for 1939		Estimates for 1945		+
	Earners	Per Cent	Earners	Per Cent	—
Agriculture	37,000	19.3	24,000	10.7	− 8.6
Industry, handicrafts	36,000	18.7	66,000	29.3	+10.6
Transport, communications	9,000	4.7	12,000	5.3	+ .6
Building & public works	14,000	7.3	14,800	6.6	− .7
Trade & finance	33,000	17.2	43,000	19.2	+ 2.0
Liberal professions	20,000	10.4	23,000	10.2	− .2
Clerks and civil servants	19,000	9.9	15,200	6.7	− 3.2
Services (domestic, etc.)	14,000	7.3	17,500	7.8	+ .5
Various	10,000	5.2	9,500	4.2	− 1.0
Total	192,000	100	225,000	100	+10.4

Source: *Palestine and Middle East*, August, 1944, p. 151, and *Statistical Handbook of Jewish Palestine*, 1947, pp. 66-68.

A glance at Table 9 discloses that in 1939 almost one-fifth of the Jewish people worked the soil, a slightly smaller proportion was engaged in industry and crafts, over one-eighth in trade and one-tenth in professions. The figures for 1945 show a marked shift from agriculture to industry. It is at this point difficult to gauge the extent to which these changes express the universal and enduring trend from rural to urban occupations or merely reflect the war-induced crisis in the citrus industry and heavy war demand of industrial goods. Symptomatic, too, is the distribution of industrial workers among the various industry groups. Jewish workers in Palestine are heavily represented in the metal, chemical and machinery industries as well as in the needle and food trades.

More significant than the existent occupational pattern would be an examination of recent occupational trends among Jews. Unfortunately there is only the most inadequate information on the subject. Scattered references have been made to the trend toward professions and clerical work among the native American and Canadian Jews. In the occupational studies of the Jewish population in Trenton, New Jersey, and Stamford, Connecticut, the foreign-born were separated from the native Jews. A comparison reflects the wide variations between the two groups. Thus in Trenton the native group showed a smaller proportion in manufacturing and trade but a threefold relative increase in professions and a fourfold increase in clerical professions; the trend was roughly the same in Stamford. An extremely wide occupational divergence between foreign-born fathers and native sons is disclosed in a study of the economic characteristics of Baltimore Jewish youth.[14] The study shows that, while among the fathers 4.7 per cent were engaged in professional or technical work, among the sons 13.4 per cent were in and almost half aspired to professional careers. Characteristic, too, is the marked reluctance of American-born young Jews to follow in the footsteps of their parental store- and shop-keepers: While among the fathers 45.9 per cent were proprietors, only 4.9 per cent of the sons were in and only 6.4 per cent aspired to this economic career. On the other hand, only 6.7 per cent of the fathers were engaged in office and sales work, but 53 per cent of the youth were in that group and 25.6 per cent showed preference for this group. Significant, too, is the trend away from skilled labor; this category claimed 32 per cent among the fathers but only 2.4 per cent actual and 7.1 per cent aspirants to skilled labor. In interpreting the significance of these findings it is important to make allowance for the age difference. Proprietary occupations are usually common in the middle-age group, while clerical and office work is associated with youthful age. With all allowances for these qualifications, however, the figures indicate a marked occupational shift into professions and clerical work. These changes are also reflected in the findings of the Canadian census. A comparison of the 1921, 1931 and 1941 censuses (given above) shows a steady decrease in the proportion of farmers among Jews, a slight decrease in the trade category, a very marked drop in the category of laborers, while increasing proportions are noted in the manufacturing group with substantial increases in the professional and clerical groups. The increase in the last two groups reflects the fact that the bulk of Jewish immigration into Canada occurred in the years preceding World War I and the children of these immigrants are now entering the labor market. On the basis of existing evidence it would appear that in the United States we are now in the third phase of occupational adjustment: during the period of active immigration the proportion of industrial workers among Jews was on the increase; after a period of economic acclimatization many of the erstwhile immigrants left the bench and workshop for the counter of the store; the sons of these immigrants, however, are turning their backs on their fathers' stores and press into professions, commercial employment and clerical jobs.

The occupational shifts in the American Jewish scene are not typical of all other countries. The picture in Soviet Russia is not clear. Many Jewish workers have found their way into Soviet industry, but there is also evidence of heavy pressure on the professional and clerical workers; and the proportion of agricultural workers among Russian Jews has declined in recent years. In Poland the tendency in recent years was away from trade into industry and crafts, and because of the deplorable economic conditions and discriminatory barriers placed before Jews in many walks of life there was an increase in the ranks of laborers among Polish Jews in the years preceding World War II.

In Palestine, the ideological orientation of a large number of the immigrants, combined with the objective conditions characteristic of a pioneer economy, converted many traders and professionals and sons of traders and professionals into agricultural and industrial workers. Interesting light on this remarkable occupational transformation is thrown by the figures in Table 10 on page 1252.

The table shows that almost half the workers in Palestine were sons of traders; and, while among the fathers only 3.8 per cent were engaged in agriculture, the proportion among their sons in Palestine was 23.4 per cent. Whether the sons of the present generation of farmers and workers will continue in their fathers' footsteps or whether they, too, will follow the trek into commerce, professions and clerical work, depends upon the general economic conditions in the Palestine to be.

Closely related to the occupational structure is the socioeconomic status. Here, too, there is a marked difference between Jews and the general population, particularly in European countries. Because of Jewish concentration in retail trade and in consumer industries—areas of economic enterprise in which small-scale operation predominates—the proportion of independent proprietors among Jews is on the whole higher than in the general population.

Thus in Poland, in the nonagricultural sector of economy, the percentage of "independents" among Jews is 62, among non-Jews 18.2; in Germany the percentages are 43.1 and 13; and in Hungary 35 and 16.4, respectively. Correspondingly, in the case of salaried employees and workers the proportions are reversed. On the basis of fragmentary statistical evidence in the United States between 60 and 70 per cent of gainfully employed Jews are in the category of wage earner or employee.[15] In Canada, where we have comprehensive census data, of one hundred gainfully employed Jews about 70 per cent are in the categories of clerks, skilled and semiskilled workers working for hire. The trend points to further increase in the proportion of employees.

TABLE 10

Occupational Distribution of Palestinian Jewish Workers and Their Fathers Abroad

(in Per Cent)

	Occupations of Fathers Abroad	Occupations of Workers in Palestine
Agriculture	3.8	23.4
Building	1.8	10.6
Transport and heavy industries	8.5	21.6
Consumer industries	7.5	7.5
Traders	48.2	—
Factory owners	2.3	—
Undefined occupations	12.6	2.5
All others	15.3	34.4
	100.0	100.0

Source: Data from Horowitz and Hinden, *Economic Survey of Palestine*, 1938, p. 185; figures based on Labor Census of 1937.

The discussion thus far has centered on the occupational distribution among Jews. The degree of occupational concentration is further reflected in the extent of Jewish participation in the various branches of economic enterprise. Except for Palestine, the share of Jews in total agriculture of the respective countries is insignificant. The share of Jews in commerce and industry, however, is quite substantial—in some countries dominant. Thus in Poland, where Jews formed less than 10 per cent of the total population, they comprised almost 20 per cent of all engaged in industry and handicrafts and over 52 per cent of all engaged in trade. In Hungary, where Jews numbered about 5 per cent of the population, they formed 7.4 per cent of all in industry and 35.8 per cent of all engaged in commerce and 8.9 per cent of all active in professions. In Germany, with a Jewish population which had amounted to less than 1 per cent of the total population, they formed 3.3 per cent of all engaged in commerce. In Canada, where the Jews form 1.5 per cent of the population, they form 2.7 per cent of all engaged in industry and crafts and 6.8 per cent in commerce.[16] A more detailed breakdown into the various subdivisions would undoubtedly reveal a dominant Jewish position in selected branches such as clothing, textiles and other branches of consumer goods production and distribution.

In the United States, too, the distribution of Jewish economic effort is highly uneven. In New York City, for instance, where of one hundred gainfully employed New Yorkers twenty-seven are Jews, the latter constitute 41 per cent of all engaged in trade, 39 per cent of all employed in the field of amusement and 35 per cent of all employed in manufacturing industries; but Jews constitute only 14 per cent of all construction workers, 13 per cent of all transportation workers, 12 per cent of all engaged in finance and 4 per cent of all employed in public utilities. Within the manufacturing industry Jews form 35 per cent of the total, but their share in the various industrial subdivisions ranges from a low of 4.2 per cent of all gainfully employed in machine shops to a high of 82.2 per cent in the fur industry. Likewise in the trade group, where Jews are 41 per cent of the total, their share ranges from 80 per cent of all engaged in apparel stores to a low of 12.4 per cent in the automotive group.[17]

These figures refer to employers and employees. The share of Jews in terms of ownership and management has been considerably higher in practically all countries. In Poland, for instance, it is estimated that over 27 per cent of all industrial establishments employing twenty or more workers were owned by Jews.[18] In the textile industry the proportion was 52 per cent. This estimate does not include enterprises of mixed ownership, nor enterprises employing fewer than twenty workers in which Jews in Poland figured to an even greater extent. The number of Jewish commercial establishments was estimated in 1926 and 1928 to have amounted to 65 per cent of all commercial establishments in Poland. Roughly similar conditions prevailed in other agrarian countries of eastern Europe. It should be added, however, that throughout this area Jewish participation in commerce had been gradually reduced by the relentless pressure of non-Jewish merchants aided by government action. That the share of Jewish ownership in commerce and industry in countries of central and western Europe was greater than their numerical proportion is well known.

In the United States the degree of economic concentration in terms of ownership is perhaps greater than in terms of employment. According to the study made by the editors of *Fortune*,[19] Jews operate about 95 per cent of the women's dress factories, 85 per cent of the men's garment industry, 95 per cent of the fur industry and a large proportion of the millinery industry. Jews owned three of four leading cigar-manufacturing establishments but are a decided minority in cigarette manufacturing. Jewish ownership controlled 50 per cent of distilleries, 30-40 per cent of the boot and shoe industries, 15 per cent of the silk and 16 per cent of the rayon yarn industries and 5-10 per cent of wool textile and 5 per cent of cotton textile industries. Jews loom large in the motion-picture industry. In centers of large Jewish habitation Jews have a substantial share of the independent retail trade. According to estimates made in 1937, in New York City Jews owned in whole or in part almost 70 per cent of the retail shops, ranging from 87 per cent ownership in the furniture group to a low of 7.5 per cent of the automotive group.[20] Jews are, however, a decided minority in the chain-store field. Jewish representation in the steel industry (except in the scrap iron division), the coal industry, railroads and automobile industry is negligible. The *Fortune* study also dispelled the widely held notion of Jewish financial control. Except for some Jewish participation in the field of investment banking and brokerage business, the Jewish role in American banking is negligible. The economic activities of the Jews in Canada follow substantially the same pattern.

Present information about the Jewish economic role in the countries south of the Rio Grande is inadequate. While it is impossible to give a quantitative estimate of the share of Jewish enterprise in the economy of the various countries, qualitatively Latin-American Jews are active in the "traditionally" Jewish fields of economic activity. In all nonindustrial countries they are engaged primarily in various branches of trade in capacities ranging from the ubiquitous peddler to the owners of large establishments. In some countries, like Mexico, Brazil, Chile, the Jew was instrumental in the introduction of industries especially in the field of consumer goods. In Argentina, Jews, besides being active in agriculture, are prominent in the lumber and furniture industry, clothing, knitting, silk weaving, the small-metal industry, and substantial numbers are engaged in trade.

These dry bones of statistics do not, of course, reveal the vast amount of energy and initiative displayed by Jewish enterprise, the pioneering role of Jewish entrepreneurs in the industrialization of countries of central and, more especially, eastern Europe, where in the midst of a stagnant, overwhelmingly agrarian economy the Jews had been for a long time virtually the sole carriers of economic progress. Nor do they reveal the extent of the resourcefulness displayed by the millions of Jewish immigrants in effecting a successful adjustment to the American scene; the degree of ingenuity and adaptability displayed by the more recent immigrant to the countries of Latin America; and the amount of devotion, effort and sacrifice embodied in the inspiring record of the upbuilding of Palestine—a modern economic oasis in the midst of Oriental stagnation.

These statistics do not reflect the difficulties which had been placed in the face of Jewish endeavor by unfriendly segments of population in various countries, frequently backed by hostile governments, and the amazing tenacity shown by Jews in their struggle for existence. Neither do they reflect the amount of suffering and poverty that came to many in the wake of industrialization—accentuated in the case of Jews by unfriendly acts of some governments. The record of the economic career of modern Jewry—a record going beyond the array of impersonal statistics and bringing to life the story of dynamic achievements as manifested in the lives of industrial and commercial entrepreneurs, the masses of artisans and industrial workers, the vast net of trade organizations, co-operatives, trade unions, developed by the Jews in many lands in the furthering and safe-guarding of their economic life—is yet to be written.

The paucity of Jews in agriculture and heavy industries and the con-centration in consumer industries, commerce, professions and clerical work have caused grave concern among many Jews. Many view the Jewish economic structure as "abnormal"; the literature devoted to lament over and to the solution of this "abnormality" would fill a sizable library. This apprehension was greatly accentuated in recent decades, first, by the devastating effect of the Bolshevik revolution upon the fortunes and lives of the masses of Jewish traders and by the economic disfranchisement of hundreds of thousands, members of the "bourgeois" class in Russia and, second, by the continuous deterioration of the economic position of Jews in central and eastern European countries during the interwar period.

This concern is inspired by a variety of considerations: some economic, others sociopolitical. Some believe that Jewish preference for commercial, clerical and professional occupations is to be deplored and actively com-bated on the ground that they are not "productive," at least not as pro-ductive as work on the bench or work behind a plow. Others have a vague feeling that the types of occupations preferred by Jews are more subject to the vagaries of the market and consequently less secure. Still others, while regarding "Jewish" occupations as productive as any other and not any less secure, argue that the concentration of Jews in large urban centers heightens Jewish "visibility," helps arouse envy and adds fuel to the flame of anti-Semitism. These urge a program of economic restratification on grounds of sociopolitical expediency, to silence the anti-Semitic camp. Finally, some feel that the normal and balanced development of a group depends upon a diversified economic structure and that undue concentra-tion in a few areas of economic activity accentuates certain traits and attitudes at the expense of a well-balanced group character.

Is the economic structure of modern Jewry abnormal? The main difficulty in answering this question is the lack of a clear concept of economic "normality." A comparison of the economic structure of various

peoples reveals wide differences; as, for instance, when comparing the
English people, of whom only a little over 6 per cent are engaged in
agriculture, with the people of Poland, of whom 60 per cent are so engaged. In fact, when the economic structure of the Jews the world
over, of whom over 4 per cent are engaged in agriculture, is compared
with that of people in England, the differences are not so great as
is generally supposed. The Jewish economic structure differs, of course,
markedly when compared with that of the total population within each
country where Jews reside. Such comparisons, however, are not very
helpful, as a breakdown into ethnic components of heterogeneous countries
frequently would prove that all such groups follow occupational patterns
differing from composite averages. Thus the economic structure of the
Slovak and Ruthenian minorities in Czechoslovakia differed markedly
from that of German and Czech groups, and the Ukrainian minority in
Poland from the Polish group. In the United States the descendants of the
various racial and ethnic strains certainly show economic structures differing from that of composite United States. Immigrants coming to America
did not choose their occupations on the basis of some statistical occupational
quotas but rather on the basis of their experience and skill and the requirements of the local labor market.

If we apply this last test—perhaps the only rational test of economic
normality—the occupational structure of modern Jewry is far from
abnormal. The economic structure of the Jews is not a matter of Jewish
design to capture and control this or that area of economic activity. Nor is
it due to some special trait which predisposes Jews to commercial activity.
Rather, it is the product of the objective political and economic conditions
that prevailed during the past hundred and fifty years, on the one hand,
and, on the other hand, the crystallized historical experience, the traditions
and the aptitudes that characterized the Jewish people at the beginning of
this modern period of history.

The past century and a half have witnessed a remarkable measure of
economic expansion, an ever-widening movement of industrialization, an
almost uninterrupted shift of the center of economic gravity from rural
areas to urban centers and from rural occupations to urban trades. Because
of the crucial bearing of this factor upon the character of the Jewish occupational structure, it is worth while to look closer into this most remarkable
occupational transformation. Modern occupations fall broadly into three
categories: primary industries, comprising agriculture, fisheries and forest
products; secondary or converting industries, which comprise all manufacturing industries; and tertiary or servicing industries, such as commerce,
transportation, professions, personal service and public service. An analysis
of census reports reveals a sharp and steady relative decline of the proportions of people employed in the primary industries; a rise in the proportion

of those engaged in secondary industries during the early phase of industrialization followed by a stabilization of that proportion once the country had built up its industries; and a steady rise in the proportion of gainfully employed in the tertiary or servicing industries—a rise which still continues in practically all economically advancing countries.

In the United States, for instance, the proportion of people engaged in agriculture, forestry and fishing declined from 72 per cent in 1820 to about 18 per cent in 1940; in England from 11.3 per cent in 1881 to 6.4 per cent in 1931; in France from 63 per cent in 1827 to 24.5 per cent in 1931; in Germany from 39.1 per cent in 1882 to 20.4 per cent in 1933; in Canada from 48.3 per cent in 1891 to 25.2 per cent in 1941; in Australia from 44.2 per cent in 1871 to 24.4 per cent in 1933. Decreases of varying degrees were registered for practically all other modern countries. The secondary industries, that is, manufacturing and building industries, have remained remarkably stable. In the United States they have oscillated between the low of 25.6 per cent in 1890 and the high of 30.6 per cent in 1920; in England around 38-40 per cent; Germany at 36-46 per cent; and in France around 40 per cent. The sharpest relative increases occurred in trade, professions and personal services. The proportion of those engaged in the tertiary industries increased in the United States from 15.3 per cent in 1820 to 45.8 per cent in 1930 and has registered a further increase since that time; in England from 44.8 per cent in 1881 to 49.7 per cent in 1931; and in France from 19 per cent in 1866 to about 40 per cent in 1931.[21]

In terms of absolute numbers one can say that employment in the primary industries fell far behind the population increase, the secondary industries merely kept pace with the growth of population, while the group engaged in the tertiary industries increased at a rate many times faster than that of the increase in the population. In the United States, for instance, the total number of employed was quadrupled between 1870 and 1940. But during this period employment in the primary industries increased by little more than one-half; the manufacturing group quadrupled, that is, increased in the same proportion as the total population; but those engaged in trade increased more than elevenfold, the professional group more than tenfold, the clerical group more than seventeenfold and the public service group more than twenty-onefold.

This occupational morphology is not a historical accident, nor is it merely the consequence of the capitalist system of production. It is rather the result of basic factors inhering in the nature of demand, on the one hand, and technical conditions of production, on the other. Simple observation tells us that the demand for food does not increase in proportion to the increase in income and wealth. In economic parlance we speak of the *inelastic* demand for agricultural products. Simultaneously the rapid technological advance and the application of scientific method to agriculture have made it possible for an ever-decreasing proportion of workers to turn out increasing amounts of food. The demand for manufactured products is more *elastic* and tends to increase with increased economic welfare, but here again the application of labor-saving devices enables increased output without a relative increase in the labor force devoted to the manufacturing process.

Simultaneously the very characteristics of the primary and secondary industries provide the conditions for the sharp expansion of the tertiary servicing industries. Thus growing specialization and scale of production necessitate the employment of a larger number of people in the process of bringing the product to the consumer. The progressive reduction of cost of manufacturing due to technological cost-saving devices releases buying power for the purchase of professional, educational, recreational and other personal services. The demand for these services is quite elastic and can expand almost indefinitely. Moreover, the application of machinery to the service trades is quite limited, and increased demand is usually translated into increased employment of men and not, as in the case of manufacturing, in the application of better machines. The occupational changes in modern times are thus rooted in the very rationality of the economic process itself. In fact, in a study on the occupational morphology of our times Colin Clark, a distinguished Australian economist, established a close correlation between the rate of flow of labor from primary to secondary and from secondary to tertiary groups and the growth of economic prosperity, and terms this movement "the most important concomitant of economic progress."[22]

In view of the evidence given above the flow of Jewish labor and enterprise into the tertiary group appears in a completely different light. Far from being an abnormal manifestation, it appears to be the perfectly natural and obvious development. It should be remembered that these occupational trends began to manifest themselves at about the time when Jews were being gradually freed from the legal and political restraints. The Jews entered upon the modern world at the time when certain areas of economic activity began expanding at a faster rate than others. It was their good fortune that by tradition and experience Jews were excellently equipped precisely for those activities which were at the threshold of greatest expansion. Jews had had a long record of commercial experience. They showed a high degree of literacy. Many of them had been living in towns and cities—the new centers of economic gravity—and were attuned to the tempo and pattern of city life. Free from deep attachments to "native" soil, they possessed a high degree of geographical mobility and readily shifted to new areas of economic opportunity. Unburdened by holdings of real property they held their wealth in liquid form and could quickly shift their activities to new profitable areas of enterprise. Schooled in the hard struggle for survival in the unfriendly atmosphere of the Diaspora, they developed a remarkable degree of adaptability to new environments and to ever-changing economic and social conditions. In short, Jews entered upon the modern scene equipped with precisely those experiences and aptitudes which were required by the objective conditions of economic development. That Jews took excellent advantage of this favorable juncture of circumstances is a perfectly normal reaction of an energetic and long-restrained people to newly found opportunities.

Evidence cited above should also dispose effectively of the charge that the tertiary industries, in which perhaps more than two-thirds of the Jews concentrate, are not "productive." If this were true then the whole economic world of the past hundred years was becoming less and less productive, which is patently absurd and flies in the face of all experience. It is precisely in countries where the relative decline in primary industries, *e.g.*, agriculture, was greater and the transfer of labor and resources to tertiary industries, *e.g.*, trade, professions and services was greatest, that the rate of economic progress and the level of economic welfare has been most impressive. The attempt to narrow the concept of productivity to agriculture and physical labor in the turning out of material goods has a long and respectable history but is nevertheless fallacious. Anything that creates economic value, that is, creates something that people desire and are willing to pay for, be it material goods or services, is productive and, in the economic sense, valuable and useful. It is elementary economics that value does not inhere in the object or service but in the person's desire to possess the particular object. A pound of coffee on the overglutted coffee plantations in Brazil is of little value there; it is made valuable only when brought and deposited at the door of the housewife's kitchen. Anybody who in any way contributed in this long process—the shipper, the warehouse owner, the insurer, the wholesaler, the salesman, the retailer—actually adds to the value and thus performs a productive and useful occupation. These as well as the other auxiliary groups—the clerks, the professional groups, the public servants—are all indispensable to any progressive economy.

Moreover, the rapid growth of this tertiary group is independent of a particular economic system and is as characteristic of Soviet Russia as of capitalist countries. It is true that during the early period of the Soviet regime the Jews suffered economic dislocation, but the reason for it lay in the peculiar Russian conditions rather than in the nature of socialist economy. Russian Jewry was engaged predominantly in consumer goods industries and in trade. It was exceptionally hard hit, through the general breakdown of industry and trade and through the later development of heavy industries for which few Jews were trained. Once the foundations for the development of basic industries were laid and the Soviet planners began paying attention to the production of consumer goods and to the development of the distribution apparatus, the Jews were easily absorbed into the economy of the country.

Neither was the economic deterioration in Poland, Rumania and other countries of eastern Europe due to the alleged "nonproductivity" of Jewish occupations. The functions that had been performed by Jews were not abolished; they were simply taken over by non-Jews. The charge thus that Jews, by concentrating on consumer goods, manufacturing, and in tertiary industries, are not making productive contributions to society, is without foundation. It occasions no surprise that the charge is assiduously cultivated by anti-Semitic propaganda, though strangely enough the argument is not directed against non-Jews in similar occupations. It is, however, striking testimony to the power of propaganda that such charges not infrequently emanate from friends and well-wishers and even from Jews themselves.

Nor is there any justification for assuming that agriculture and heavy industries offer greater stability. It is true that a system of small-scale self-sufficient peasantry is less vulnerable to the cyclical fluctuations. But this is paid for by a low level of productivity and low standard of living. The efficient American farmer who produces specialized crops for the market, however, is exposed to the vagaries of the market no less than is the manufacturer. In fact, agriculture and heavy industries usually show the greatest cyclical fluctuations: the former in terms of prices and income, the latter in terms of output and employment. The perennial "farm problem" in the United States is a case in point.

There remains the argument that, while "Jewish" occupations may be productive and economically sound, the relative absence of Jews from agriculture and basic industries and their overwhelming concentration in trade and nonmanual occupations provide ammunition to the arsenal of anti-Semitic propaganda. This argument finds wide acceptance among Jews and others. It is argued that the concentration of Jews in nonmanual work makes them conspicuous; their success arouses general envy; and their competitive strength earns them the hatred of other merchants and professionals. In support of this argument it is frequently pointed out that the middle classes are the main carriers of modern anti-Semitism. Consequently, if Jews should quit their present occupations in favor of agriculture or other forms of manual work, they would remove or at least blunt the most important anti-Semitic weapon.

The validity of this argument depends upon the acceptance of the basic premise of the rational and economic causation of anti-Semitism. At the risk of treading upon the slippery ground of human motivation there is ample reason to doubt that anti-Semitism is *caused* by economic factors.

The mainsprings of anti-Semitism are rooted in the realm of irrationality and do not spring from the particular pattern of Jewish occupational distribution. True, anti-Semitism frequently is clothed in the language of economics but this is merely a rationalization of an already present prejudice. The choice of the argument depends frequently upon the particular intellectual climate. In the medieval religious atmosphere religion was given as the cause of anti-Judaism and conversion was held out as the price of acceptance. In the age of rising nationalism national assimilation was demanded as the condition of equality. In the race theory of nazism racial incompatibility is given as the justification for Jewish extermination. In our age, preoccupied with economic problems, the argument is adorned with economic terminology.

It is of course undeniable that anti-Semitism has found a wide response among the middle classes—a response influenced without doubt by the competitive position of the Jewish businessman and professional. But are we justified in assuming that other social groups will not respond in the same spirit should Jews attempt a large-scale entry into any other occupation? The competition of the highly successful Japanese farmers on the West Coast has been resented by other farmers quite independently of the status of Japan as an enemy. Many Polish workers have stubbornly resented attempts of Jews to enter factory work. In the United States, some sections of employers and unions have maintained an effective color bar, and resisted attempts of the government to introduce Negroes into "white" fields of industrial employment. In a prejudice-ridden world a member of a minority group will be resented and resisted be he in business or in industry. In a world based on understanding he will be judged solely on his productive contribution to society regardless of the field chosen by him.

The arguments of leaders and rulers who justify their anti-Semitism in terms of Jewish occupational idiosyncrasies are frequently belied by the very actions of these leaders. Thus it would appear only reasonable that if Jews are resented because they tend to crowd the commercial and professional world, then they should be encouraged by all means to enter agriculture and manufacturing industries. Yet, among the first acts of anti-Semitic governments in Europe was to put obstacles in the way of Jewish artisans, to oust Jewish factory workers from industries taken over by the state and to deny Jews the benefits of agrarian reform. Among the first acts of the Hitler regime was to oust the few Jews who were engaged in agriculture. It is significant that the country that seems perilously close to anti-Semitism on the American continent is Argentina—a country which has a sizable Jewish agricultural population; and that anti-Jewish excesses are conspicuous in the province of Entre Rios, the center of Jewish agricultural colonization. To assume, therefore, that one can cure anti-Semitism by a dose of occupational restratification is highly unrealistic. The acceptance of occupational restratification under pressure of anti-Semitic propaganda must be emphatically rejected. It would not solve the problem of anti-Semitism; it would imply the acceptance of the charges advanced by anti-Semitic spokesmen; it would cause economic hardship to the Jews, and it would, moreover, be harmful to the economy of the countries that would exchange good businessmen and professionals for indifferent and perhaps economically "unneeded" farmers and coal miners.

The question as to whether occupational restratification is warranted on purely economic grounds is less easy to answer. In the light of occupational trends it would seem that, except for Palestine, where occupational restratification is dictated by national considerations, drastic occupational restratification is neither warranted nor feasible. All evidence points to the fact that agriculture will not experience expansion in the immediate future and, even assuming that many Jews will be willing to turn to agricultural activities—an assumption which is quite unwarranted—it will not be able to absorb large numbers of Jews.

As to the prospects for industry's capacity to absorb large numbers of newcomers, a distinction must be drawn between countries which have already attained a large measure of industrialization and those which are now in a stage of incipient industrialization. In the former countries, the proportion of people engaged in industry has become stabilized and is not likely to grow in years to come, although the ratio of the number of persons engaged in heavy industries to the number engaged in consumer goods industries may experience a shift, most likely in favor of the second group. But it is in the consumer industries that Jews are already operating in substantial numbers, and additional numbers of Jews could, if necessary, easily enter these industries. The most promising field of expansion, however, is offered by the tertiary industries. As stated above, this group of occupations has experienced a steady and almost uninterrupted expansion during the past hundred years. There is every indication that this trend will continue. As Jews tend to congregate in this occupational sector, they seem to be favorably situated with regard to the potential expansion of employment opportunities.

This, however, does not imply that Jews do not face problems of vocational reorientation within the broad sector of tertiary occupations. Modern economy is a dynamic one. Old skills become obsolete and new ones emerge. Within the tertiary area there are many divisions and subdivisions; some with expanding, others with contracting opportunities. Thus in the United States the legal profession is overcrowded, but "newer" professions are increasing. Because of the trend toward geographical decentralization of industry employment opportunities may be better in the midwestern, western and certain southern states, than in the overcrowded eastern states.

A comprehensive system of vocational guidance based on a careful and continuous observation of occupational trends would facilitate economically desirable vocational adjustments in the industrialized countries. Conditions may be different, however, in countries which are on the threshold of industrialization and in which the demand for industrial workers is likely to be considerable. Thus in the countries of eastern Europe and Latin America the outlook for greater industrial employment among Jews is favorable. A program of vocational training and retraining to enable large numbers of Jews to enter expanding industry in these areas would contribute greatly to the improvement and the strengthening of the economic position of Jews in these countries.

In all countries, however, Jews face occupational problems arising from changing forms of economic organization. The trend toward industrial concentration, that is, concentration of production in the hands of a decreasing number of enterprises of increasing size, narrows the area of small business—an area in which many Jews operate; an increasing number of young Jews will consequently have to turn to big business for a livelihood. The growth of governmental control and the expansion of public enterprise introduce new factors into the employment situation. The last factor is of particular importance in countries of eastern Europe—Czechoslovakia, Poland, Hungary, Rumania, Yugoslavia and Bulgaria—which comprise over sixty per cent of surviving Jews of continental Europe outside of Soviet Russia. Unlike western Europe, where there has been no sharp break with prewar economic institutions, the countries of eastern Europe now within the orbit of Soviet Russia have experienced a fairly rapid shift to economic collectivism. The nationalization of industry and trade has already rendered the economic functions of many Jews, *e.g.*, private traders, obsolete. Thus among the Jews who re-established themselves in Poland after World War II relatively few have entered or re-entered private trade. Moreover, a large proportion of those who entered industry have chosen the co-operative form of enterprise as the more congenial type of enterprise in the present political climate. The situation is similar in the other countries of that area. In order to integrate the Jews into the state-controlled economies of the respective countries a program of vocational reorientation has become essential. The local Jewish communities as well as the American relief organizations, such as the American Jewish Joint Distribution Committee (J.D.C.), and the ORT have developed comprehensive programs aiming at a speedy adjustment of Jews to the new economic conditions.

In many cases the economically displaced Jews have faced the necessity of acquiring new skills. In many other cases the collectivization of economic life does not involve so much a change in the nature of occupations as a change in the institutional forms through which the economic functions are being performed. Men will still sell groceries but may have to do it in the capacity of clerks, in a chain store, co-operative or government food-distribution center. Doctors will continue to practice but perhaps as salaried physicians in the public health system. The problem involved here is not economic, in the sense that particular skills or services will become obsolete, although there is involved a shift in psychological orientation and economic outlook. The problem is, however, political from the point of view of safeguarding the rights of competent individuals to continue in their work without fear of losing their jobs due to ill-will toward them on the part of the decision-making authority. The attitude of the manager or public official toward the political, racial or religious background of an individual becomes an important factor in the economic status of a person. With reference to Jews, these economic changes bring into sharp relief the problem of job discrimination. Thus the paramount problem that faces Jews in all lands is not so much, as is widely held, that the economic functions exercised by Jews are growing obsolete and that Jews must, therefore, redistribute themselves among radically new occupations, but rather that the opportunity to exercise these functions may be denied them by discriminatory policies of private and public enterprises. The economic future of the Jews thus depends on the effectiveness with which access to economic opportunity will be kept open to all regardless of creed, color and national origin.

NOTES

[1] Salo W. Baron, *A Social and Religious History of the Jews* (New York, 1937), II, 266.

[2] *Algemeine Entziklopedia* (New York, 1945), 2nd ed., Vol. Yiden Alef, p. 320.

[3] Lev Singer, *Dos Banaite Folk* (Moscow, 1941), p. 39.

[4] Louis Rosenberg, *Canada's Jews* (Montreal, 1939), p. 27.

[5] Jacob Lestschinsky, *Yiden in der Shtotischer Bafelkerung fun Umophengikn Poiln* (New York, 1943), p. 5.

[5a] Cf. above Jacob Lestschinsky, "Jewish Migrations, 1840-1946," pp. 1230-1233.]

[6] Nathan Goldberg, "Occupational Patterns of American Jews," in *Jewish Review*, Vol. III, No. 3, 1945-1946, p. 163.

[7] *Ibid.*

[8] *ORT Economic Review* (New York), Vol. III, No. 2, April, 1942, p. 18.

[9] *Jewish Colonization Association: Its Work in the Argentine Republic, 1891-1941* (Buenos Aires), p. 16.

[10] Singer, *op. cit.,* p. 8.

[11] *Ibid.,* p. 49.

[12] *Ibid.*, p. 50.

[13] *ORT Economic Review,* Vol. II, No. 4-5, p. 17.

[14] Jewish Occupational Council, "Some Characteristics of 408 Baltimore Jewish Youth" (New York, 1939-1940), p. 14.

[15] Oscar I. Janowsky (ed.), *The American Jew* (New York, 1942), p. 166.

[16] *The Universal Jewish Encyclopedia* (New York, 1942), VIII, 272.

[17] Conference on Jewish Relations, *Industrial Classification of Jewish Gainful Workers in New York City* (New York, 1938), (mimeographed).

[18] I. Schiper (ed.), *Zydzi w Polsce Odrodzonej* (Warsaw), II, 505.

[19] Editors of *Fortune, Jews in America* (New York, 1936), pp. 39 ff.

[20] Industrial Classification of Jewish Gainful Workers, *op. cit.*

[21] Colin Clark, *The Conditions of Economic Progress* (London, 1940), Chap. V.; H. Dewey Anderson and Percy E. Davidson, *Occupational Trends in the United States* (Stanford University, 1940), pp. 16-17.

[22] Clark, *op. cit.,* p. 176.

BIBLIOGRAPHY

ANDERSON, H. DEWEY, and DAVIDSON, PERCY E., *Occupational Trends in the United States.* Stanford University, 1940.

Algemeine Entziklopedia. 2nd ed. Vol. Yiden Alef. New York, 1945.

BARON, SALO W., *A Social and Religious History of the Jews.* 2 vols. New York, 1937.

CLARK, COLIN, *The Conditions of Economic Progress.* London, 1940.

Conference on Jewish Relations, *Industrial Classification of Jewish Gainful Workers in New York City.* New York, 1938 (mimeographed).

Editors of *Fortune, Jews in America.* New York, 1936.

GOLDBERG, NATHAN, "Occupational Patterns of American Jews," in *The Jewish Review.* Vol. III, No. 3, pp. 3-24, 162-186, 262-290. New York, 1945-1946.

JANOWSKY, OSCAR I., *People at Bay.* New York, 1938.

———, (ed.), *The American Jew.* New York and London, 1942, pp. 161-182.

Jewish Colonization Association: Its work in the Argentine Republic, 1891-1941. Buenos Aires.

Jewish Occupational Council, "Some Characteristics of 408 Baltimore Jewish Youth." New York, 1939-1940.

———, *Patterns of Jewish Occupational Distribution in the United States and Canada.* New York, 1940.

LESTSCHINSKY, JACOB, *Dos Sovietishe Yidntum.* New York, 1941.

———, *Yiden in der Shtotischer Bafelkerung fun Umophengikn Poiln.* (Yiddish). New York, 1943.

———, (ed.), *Shriftn far Ekonomik un Statistik.* 2 vols. I, Berlin, 1928. II, Vilna, 1932.

NATHAN, ROBERT R., and others, *Palestine: Problem and Promise.* Washington, 1946. Pp. 101-338.

ROSENBERG, LOUIS, *Canada's Jews*. Montreal, 1939.

——, "The Jews of Canada," in *Jewish Review*. New York, 1944. Vol II, Nos. 2-3, p. 136.

RUPPIN, ARTHUR, *The Jews in the Modern World*. London, 1934. Pp. 109-226.

SCHIPER, IGNACY (ed.), *Zydzi w Polsce Odrodzonej*. Warsaw, n.d. Vol. II.

SEGAL, SIMON, *The New Poland and the Jews*. New York, 1938. Pp. 95-152.

SINGER, LEV, *Dos Banaite Folk*. (Yiddish). Moscow, 1941.

Universal Jewish Encyclopedia, Inc. New York, 1942. Vol. VIII, pp. 268 f.

CHAPTER 34

THE JEWISH COMMUNITY

By Samuel C. Kohs

1. JEWISH COMMUNITIES AND ORGANIZATIONS

Earliest Jewish Communities

If we define "community" as an association of people with similar backgrounds and objectives, whose aim is to satisfy common social, economic, physical and spiritual needs, then no Jewish community existed in the United States until a small band of Jewish men, women and children set foot in New Amsterdam in September, 1654. We do have records of individual Jews active in trade, commerce and exploration before 1654, but they were not members of any existing Jewish "community."

The second Jewish community to be founded in this country was that of Newport, Rhode Island, possibly sometime between 1660 and 1670. Most of the Newport Jews apparently came from the earlier Jewish settlement of New Amsterdam to the south. One of the factors which stimulated the movement from New Amsterdam northward was the more favorable attitude of Roger Williams and his fellow colonists toward the Jewish people. The obstacles toward political and social integration in New Amsterdam did not exist in Newport. Before the Revolutionary War, Newport represented the most significant and, commercially, the most important Jewish community in this country.

The Jewish community of Philadelphia crystallized between 1720 and 1730. It remained small in number during the early years but grew considerably during the American Revolution, when many Jews from New York City moved to Philadelphia.

The fourth Jewish community established was that of Savannah, Georgia. The few original settlers were about the same in number and background as those in New Amsterdam. The Jewish settlers of Savannah followed closely upon the heels of General Oglethorpe's arrival and designation as governor of the Georgia Colony in 1732. The following year a number of German Jews arrived. Whereas in the northern Jewish communities already established the German Jews or those of English extraction had no difficulty being accepted and participating in the general life of the Jewish community as a whole, in Savannah there was a distinct cleavage between the Spanish Portuguese and German Jews in local Jewish communal life.

The fifth Jewish community of North America was organized in Charleston, South Carolina, sometime around 1741. This community came into being as a result of the quarrels and strife over the slavery issue and the differences in cultural background of the two groups of Jews in Savannah. The British destruction of Newport during the Revolution made the Charleston Jewish community the largest and most important one in the United States at the beginning of the nineteenth century. It was in Charleston that the first Reform congregation was established.

From these major centers[1a] other small Jewish communities grew. These communities were established in seaport cities and in communities along the highways of transportation which then consisted primarily of rivers and major post roads.

Jewish historians frequently make the mistake of dating the establishment of Jewish communities by the establishment of the first synagogue or cemetery. It should be remembered that in many communities common worship was begun as soon as a *minyan* was available. Rarely is a formal report of such an event carefully recorded for historical purposes. On what date a group first came together to discuss common problems of housing, land purchase, civil rights, business and so on is not so easily established as is the date when the first Jewish cemetery was purchased or the first formal synagogue board meeting was held. As a result, our dating is at best approximate.

From 1800 to 1850 Jewish communities followed the growth and development of new communities and new frontiers. This was true not only for the communities along the Atlantic seaboard but also for those along the Gulf of Mexico, the Great Lakes, America's major rivers and the Pacific Coast.[2]

Earliest Jewish Organizations

In attempting to understand the nature and variety of the earliest Jewish organizations in America we should remember that the Jewish settlers on this continent came here with a rich heritage of ideals and practices dating back thousands of years. This, of course, is true not only for the Jewish group but for other groups as well.

In the seventeenth and eighteenth centuries the religious elements in Jewish communal life were extremely important and very powerful. The three cornerstones of Judaism—worship, learning and righteousness—were fundamental in the content of every Jew's daily life. Consequently, the earliest communal organizations to be created were a synagogue, a Hebrew and religious school for the children, various philanthropic services and especially a Jewish cemetery.

Synagogue

The early Jewish settlers in the United States were not confined to Ghettos. The synagogue, however, though in its first period it functioned without a full-time paid rabbi, served as the center of Jewish life.[3a] The religious tradition was universally Orthodox, and the most learned men in the community (some had been trained for the rabbinate in the old country) were chosen as rabbis with all the attendant authority.

In the earliest days, before buildings could be converted into synagogues or erected for that purpose, the *minyan* would assemble in the home of some prominent member of the community and hold services. In not a few instances the small local Jewish community would rent some communal hall for its Sabbath services. As soon as possible, of course, efforts were made to establish a synagogue, either by purchasing land and erecting a building specifically for this purpose or by remodeling an already existing structure.

The minutes of the early synagogues read like the minutes of some present-day federation of philanthropic agencies in small communities: finance, supervision and control of the synagogues, the Hebrew and religious schools, and the philanthropic organizations of the community were discussed. The synagogue board was interested in every phase of Jewish community life, secular as well as religious. Excommunication was still effective, although it was no longer so powerful a discipline as it had been in European countries. It was the synagogue and its learned men, the community leaders, that determined policy, not only on internal matters but also on matters relating to other Jewish communities in America and elsewhere, and on matters relating to other groups in the United States. Since all the members of the community were more or less on the same economic level wealth played little part in leadership.

Hebrew and Religious Education

Two major factors should be kept in mind with reference to the early establishment of Hebrew and religious schools. First, there was the ancient tradition to teach the youth not merely prayers and religious precepts, but also something of Jewish history and Jewish hopes. Second, there were then no public educational institutions as we know them today. Public education in the United States dates from the early nineteenth century, and it was achieved only after a severe struggle. The necessity, therefore, of providing Jewish children with a secular as well as religious education made the establishment of Jewish day schools inevitable.[4a]

The secular curriculum of these schools generally included, in addition to the English language and the three R's, the language of the country from which the parents of the children had come. Thus, in New York

City, the earliest Jewish schools taught Spanish. When later Jewish schools were established by the immigrants from Germany, German became the required language in these schools. This foreign-language program was abandoned after two or three generations.

One great advantage of these schools was that they had a unified curriculum—unlike today when separate curricula exist for the public school, Sunday school, community center and so on. Today, generally, only 25 per cent of the Jewish children in a Jewish community receive a Jewish education at any one given time, although it is estimated that 75 per cent receive a Jewish education of some sort before they reach maturity. In the early days of Jewish settlement in this country virtually 100 per cent received such an education.

Philanthropic Activities

Only within comparatively recent times has the paid professional social worker emerged. Formerly all the philanthropies of the community were in charge of volunteers or specially designated philanthropic "secretaries."

From time immemorial seven distinct and principal branches of philanthropy were carried on by Jews and Jewish communities:

1. Feeding the hungry. This has always been one of the prime responsibilities of organized Jewish life and of the individual Jew, whether he was a member of an organized community or not. The obligation to feed the hungry covered particularly those periods during which Jews celebrated their religious festivals, and the methods used in extending relief were such as to preserve the dignity and self-respect of the recipient. Such methods also characterized every other form of philanthropy.

2. Clothing the naked.

3. Sheltering the homeless. This involved not only caring for transients who needed overnight lodgings not available in private homes, but also providing homes for the orphaned and the aged.

4. Visiting the sick. This was a communal obligation. When Jewish communities grew large and complex this responsibility was assigned to specially designated visitors. Needless to say, the concern for the sick was also the responsibility of close relations.

5. Burying the dead and comforting the mourners. Jewish ritual prescribes specific religious ceremonials attending the death of a Jew. The guarantee that all religious observances would be assured and that burial would be in a Jewish cemetery was a communal responsibility.

6. Redemption of captives. When a Jew was either kidnapped or held for ransom, it was the duty of his coreligionists to redeem him. Along with this might perhaps be mentioned the *are miklat*, the cities of refuge, which in earlier times were set up as sanctuaries. Here certain offenders might begin life anew. In modern times such concern is expressed by

organizations interested in the welfare of Jewish prisoners. Members of these welfare organizations visit prisons, reformatories and similar institutions and try to help their inmates.

7. Dowries for poor maidens. When girls needed dowries in order to get married the community in olden days provided the funds from a treasury set up for this specific purpose. Although the institution of dowry has almost entirely passed away, in the larger Jewish communities one may occasionally find organizations still interested in making provision for the marriage of orphans and children of the poor.[5a]

It is on these traditions that the philanthropic activities of the early Jewish settlers of this country were built. As communities grew in size and additional synagogues were established, duplication of philanthropic activity inevitably developed. In time, therefore, many communities created a *central* Jewish welfare organization; thus duplication gave way to co-ordination. Down through 1850 Jewish communal organizations were set up in the following order: (1) the synagogue; (2) the Jewish school; (3) the burial ground; (4) aid societies for the local poor and transients; (5) orphanages; (6) free-loan agencies; (7) Jewish hospitals (at first in remodeled quarters, later in buildings specially constructed for the purpose).

In the early days of American history Jewish communities along the Atlantic seaboard were deeply interested in each other. In a sense, the Jews were better informed of their own problems, needs and development than were the colonies, in general, of theirs. This was undoubtedly due to the centuries-old practice of Jews to keep in touch with and come to the assistance of their coreligionists whenever and wherever possible. Thus, the traditional solicitation of funds throughout the world for building a synagogue helped establish synagogues in the New World. Not only were funds supplied but also Torah Scrolls and other sacred articles. Similar interest and co-operation were manifested in connection with Jewish education and commercial ventures. The latter was made possible especially because Jewish merchants used to send representatives from one city to another and into the "hinterland" to make connections and to find more and more markets for their goods. These traveling merchants not only contributed to the expansion of commerce and trade but also were instrumental in bringing all kinds of news to the scattered and more or less isolated regions of the country.

Despite common interests and efforts, differences existed in Jewish communal life then as well as today. The earliest Jewish settlers in this country were of Sephardic background. Later, and not so secure economically, came the Ashkenazic Jews. Differences in religious practice, economic status, and origin created friction. When livelihood or security was at stake, the differences among Jews disappeared. When security had been achieved, however, and complete civil and political rights were won, the differences led to disagreement and rivalry which interfered with Jewish community life.

Conversion to Christianity and mixed marriages were serious problems in early Jewish community life in America. The absence or the weakness of community disciplines—such as operated in the Old World—no doubt accounted for this condition.

Although civil rights were generally granted to Jews equally with all others, political rights were in some states and communities limited even after the American Revolution. In Maryland, for example, until 1825 only professing Christians were eligible for political office.

The participation of Jews in the early life of America is summarized by Anita Libman Lebeson:

A methodical person attempting to chart the pattern of the Jew's place in the social scheme of things in the eighteenth century, would have to give up the attempt. The result, try as one will, is a crazy-quilt arrangement. One cannot say of the Jew, he is a merchant, a scholar, a craftsman. One of the most learned men of Surinam, Isaac Nassi, was a dealer in old clothes, as well as its foremost scholar. He had a discriminating knowledge of history, knew a number of languages, and in his spare moments compiled a dictionary of one of the Indian dialects. Many a learned scholar, as well as a number of rabbis turned to business to earn a living, while the greatest zeal and passion of their lives was lavished on book learning. This versatility, this separation of vocation and avocation has come down to the Jew with the ages.

These men whose interests were largely financial or mercantile had so many irons in the fire that they are not to be pigeonholed. The same man may be a broker, merchant, ship owner, land speculator, Indian trader, venturer, importer and exporter, and manufacturer. He may be found running a lottery in his spare time. His name is likely to be attached to those educational philanthropic, fraternal institutions which are found in his community. He is often a patron of fine arts. Gilbert Stuart, Sully, Malbone were some of the prominent American portrait painters who were commissioned to paint the prosperous colonial Jew, his wife, and his children.

He may be found owning and selling slaves or ardently opposed to the institution. He may be a Tory or Patriot, conservative or liberal. He may be a successful doctor, lawyer, scientist, while at the same time cherishing the ambition of becoming a member of the landed gentry, like Dr. Lumbrozo of Maryland, and Dr. Nuñez of Georgia.

He is found in and out of the army. He may be called upon to finance campaigns, to act as commissary and to furnish equipment for the army. Numbers of Jews are found bearing arms during war; Jewish soldiers usually exceeding their population quota. On the other hand, there are frequently Jewish pacifists pleading the cause of peace.

The Jew may be regarded as an alien, an outcast, a foreigner, a curiosity, an anomaly, a social pariah, yet individuals apart from the group are frequently welcomed as useful and integral members of their community.[6a]

In 1800, there were fewer than three thousand Jews in the United States. Since this small number was scattered among some fifteen or twenty Jewish communities, Jewish communal needs were small and large social service and philanthropic agencies were unnecessary. At this time, as indicated before, the Jewish community in Charleston, South Carolina, was the largest of its kind in the country. It was the "New York City" of its day. Its Jewish population in 1816 was over 600, approximately 150 to 200 families. It was natural, therefore, for the first organized "charity" or social service organization to be created there. In 1801 the Charleston Jewish community established the first Jewish communal institution to care for "orphaned" children. Of course, compared with modern institutions, it was a modest affair.

The first Jewish family welfare society in the United States was the Hebrew Benevolent Society, organized in New York City in 1822. There was no really serious relief problem in New York City at that time. But funds collected to assist a disabled veteran of the War of 1812 were available; these formed the nucleus for larger sums later turned over for the care of needy persons and families.

The first known institutionalized program for medical care was set up in 1850 (some sources give the year as 1845) in Cincinnati. By that time the Jewish population of the United States had grown considerably, Jewish communities of size and importance had been established in the Midwest (east of the Mississippi), and the Jews of Cincinnati were an enterprising and farsighted group. This first hospital was located in a remodeled residence and was a rather modest affair. It served those patients who either had no homes of their own or required treatment outside the home.

No precise date can be given for the formal establishment of the first Jewish educational institutions. Whatever institutionalized Jewish education there was before 1800 was largely in the form of classes or schools closely attached to and supported by the one synagogue serving the whole community. In 1811 the state legislature permitted the municipality of New York City to grant a subsidy to Shearith Israel Congregation for the education of "poor children." This school was separated from the synagogue and was established as the "Hebrew and English School." The first Jewish school established on a philanthropic basis was that in New York City in 1833. It made provision for the religious and secular education of Jewish children, whether or not their parents were members of the synagogue; children of Jewish families too poor for membership in the synagogue or to support the school were admitted free.

Care of the aged presented no problem in the early days. Jewish populations were small; families were well knit. Those who reached advanced years had already achieved some competence and their own families or relations continued to provide for them. Immigration consisted largely of able-bodied persons in their younger years or not much beyond middle age.

Not until the mass migrations of the middle of the nineteenth century and later did the care for the indigent aged prove pressing.

The first Jewish Community Centers came rather late. The very first organization of this kind was the Young Men's Hebrew Association, established in New York City in 1874 by a group of young men interested in spending time together in a place of their own for discussion of current affairs and for a variety of social activities.

Federations of Jewish philanthropies, as we now know them, had no real basis for existence until after the immigration of hundreds of thousands of Russian and Polish Jews into the United States. The first such federation was established in 1895 in Boston, and it was followed the succeeding year by another in Cincinnati.

The first Jewish Community Council (the Kehilla) was established in 1909 in New York City.[7a] The purpose of the Kehilla was so to organize New York Jewish activities that Jews might solve more effectively, as a united body, various problems which affected all phases of Jewish life in the community. Although with the outbreak of World War I, the Kehilla went out of existence, it left behind a number of constructive Jewish agencies that have continued to function down to the present time, although in some instances they have been absorbed by reorganized agencies. Quite some time elapsed between the establishment of this first community council in the United States and the present, when approximately fifty such councils function in various communities throughout the country.

Jewish Welfare Funds are of comparatively recent growth. The need for reducing the multiplicity of campaigns for funds for local needs not taken care of by local Community Chests, for national Jewish organizations, and for agencies serving Jews overseas, resulted in centralization of all fund-raising. One campaign once a year is conducted and allocations are then made to the sundry institutions. The first such welfare fund was established in Oakland, California, in 1925—although previously some six or seven communities had experimented with joint fund-raising but not with the formal organization of a "welfare fund."

Before we proceed to a description of the contemporary Jewish community and its manifold functions, it might be well to call attention to those factors which brought a change in the form, organization and character of the Jewish community in the eighty-five years from 1850 to 1935. While there is no attempt here at an exhaustive treatment of the subject, ten chief developments call for comment.

1. Population Changes

Elsewhere in the present work changes in the number and the composition of the American Jewish population have been traced.[7b] The relation of these fluctuations to conditions in Europe and those in the United States is obvious.

These waves of immigration which affected the pattern of Jewish community organization, the variety of Jewish social agencies and their functions, and the control and operation of these activities, were themselves influenced by the character of the new immigrants, their European origin, the conditions under which they migrated, the nature of their community organization in Europe, and the attitudes and patterns of behavior of the already settled American Jews.

Although a substantial proportion of all Americans are immigrants, second-, third- and fourth-generation families tend to look coldly upon newcomers, and the tension between the "in group" and the "out group" (as the sociologist would say) soon manifests itself—even though both groups may constitute one ethnic stock. This was true in the early days of Jewish settlement in the United States when the Spanish Portuguese Jews had to mingle with the English and German immigrants in their midst. Until 1820 German Jewish immigrants were not too cheerful about the kind of welcome they were receiving. It was the Spanish Portuguese Jews who occupied high places in Jewish community life and in the general community. The earlier settlers were suspicious of the newcomers, their religious practices, their general behavior, and feared that these "ill-bred" German Jews might jeopardize their social standing.

The later German Jewish immigration, which began in the late forties of the nineteenth century, did not have so difficult a time in becoming adjusted because the first Germans who had come a generation or two earlier were inclined to be more sympathetic than the older Spanish Portuguese Jews.

By 1890 the German Jewish immigrants of the forties had had considerable opportunity to make their adjustment to American Jewish life. These Jews brought Reform Judaism into being; and many of them were now well established in business, had taken over the direction and support of Jewish philanthropies and were equipped to help the later Russian and Polish immigrant adjust to American life.

The unprecedented migration of Jews into the United States from 1880 to 1915 overwhelmed and strained every Jewish communal organization and all resources for relief and adjustment. The older German Jewish element had its own conception of the type of American the Russian and Polish Jew should become. On this subject, however, the Russian and Polish Jew had somewhat different ideas. German Jews felt keenly that the new immigrant should forget as quickly as possible all his Old World ways and become "American." Russian Jews were expected to drop their interest in Yiddish, to cease publication of their Yiddish newspapers and magazines and to acquire rapid and increased facility in English. The presumably ungrateful immigrant refused to abandon Yiddish, which he regarded as his mother tongue; he never would concede that Yiddish was a jargon German. There was considerable bitterness over this issue, as well as over the Russian Jew's political and economic notions and theories.

Another illustration. German Jews were very sympathetic in their understanding that many Jewish immigrants would require financial assistance before achieving independence and self-support. Consequently, societies raised more and more funds for relief and the number of "visiting committees" increased. This was the "Lady Bountiful" period not only among Jews but also among non-Jewish voluntary agencies. But the new immigrants did not like the approach. They preferred free-loan societies, "relief" or assistance on the "loan" basis without interest, expecting the beneficiary to repay his debt in time so that similar assistance might be available to others in later years. Practically all the free-loan societies were established at the initiative of the new immigrants, although they were also liberally supported by the German Jewish population.

Again, in religious matters the older element was moving rapidly in a Reform or Conservative direction; the new immigrants, on the other hand, were either strongly Orthodox or altogether hostile to religion. In any event, here, too, there was no lack of friction.

When the east European Jews finally acquired stability and self-confidence, they began to create institutions of their own, corresponding more to their philosophy and habits. Inevitably this led to further multiplication and diversification of Jewish communal effort.

2. Increased Urbanization

Although everywhere in the United States there was a speedily increasing movement from the farm to the city, among the Jews the pace was more rapid. Recently arrived immigrants insisted upon remaining in large centers of population. "Jewish neighborhoods" quickly developed in such large cities as New York, Chicago, Boston, Philadelphia, St. Louis, Cleveland and to a smaller degree in other cities. Although the efforts of the Jewish Agricultural Society and the general farm settlement movement, together with the activities of the Industrial Removal Office, were of some value, the urbanization of Jews could not be halted. (Nevertheless, over 100,000 Jews are settled on farms throughout the United States; in many small communities throughout the country families remained on the land.)

Increased urbanization of the Jewish population is reflected in occupational distribution.[8a] Industrialization soon followed; the development of the clothing industry is a case in point. So, too, came an increasing profession-

alization and the tendency to join the white-collar industrial and commercial groups.

These deviations from the normal, or so-called normal, occupational
distribution have brought certain advantages and disadvantages to Jews,
with certain corresponding results for the types and varieties of Jewish
social service. On the one hand, the urbanization of the Jew made possible
a somewhat higher economic status and therefore a rather liberal support
of Jewish and communal agencies. On the other hand, frictions and mis-
understandings have arisen with which vocational guidance has had to deal.

3. Professionalization of Jewish Social Work

In the early years social service or philanthropic activity was conducted
by the rabbi, several members of the congregation and some benevolent
ladies. But somewhat different problems confronted the German Jews who
later assumed leadership in the Jewish community. Not only did they have
to deal with a larger mass immigration, but the problems of adjustment
were more complex. Especially during the large Russian-Polish Jewish
immigration, philanthropic work could not be handled entirely by volunteers. There was too much to do. Consequently, people were hired to
serve as secretaries of philanthropic organizations. They would devote
their time exclusively to the agency. Many of these early workers were
rabbis who had decided to go into Jewish philanthropic work rather than
into the ministry proper. Other organizations were run by "sympathetic
and understanding" women. They were not particularly trained in psychology, sociology, education or any of the social sciences; but with sympathy
and common sense they attempted to meet the particular needs of their
clients. Occasionally, too, a man who had failed in every other kind of
employment was given the job of "superintending" the Jewish communal
agency. Between 1910 and 1915, however, through the interest and
co-operation of distinguished laymen and a few outstanding Jewish social
workers the question of professional training for social work was raised.[9a]
The deliberations culminated in 1925 in the establishment of the Graduate
School for Jewish Social Work, which after some fifteen years went out
of existence.

Interest in the professional training of Jewish social workers has not
diminished. The lack of action is a result of the general disorganization in
which "organized" Jewish philanthropy in the United States finds itself
at present. Jewish social agencies have to depend upon Catholic, Protestant
and nonsectarian schools of social work for the training of men and women
for Jewish social service. How soon this problem will receive the proper
attention of the Jews of America is uncertain at the moment.

However, what has been achieved in the professional training of Jewish
social workers by either Jewish or non-Jewish agencies has been influential
in determining the character and direction of Jewish social work today.

4. *Increased Interest in Co-ordination and Central Fund-Raising*

When some forty years ago the Federation movement was first launched, few appreciated what was involved. After about ten years, however, co-ordination of all philanthropic work under one centralized agency and one fund-raising program gained momentum. Although in communities like Chicago, there were two separate federations, one presumably for the non-Orthodox and the other for the Orthodox Jewish community, in time these united, and every Jewish community in the United States with five or more communal agencies set up one centralized organization known as Federation or United Charities, Federated Philanthropies, or something similar.[10a] What prompted federation was above all the belief that thus the great number of campaigns in the community would be eliminated and perhaps philanthropy might be carried out more economically and efficiently.

In a number of communities, the federated agency did not provide for Jewish education either because of the feeling that each Jewish family should provide a Jewish education for its children out of its own resources (compare the early American attitude on public education) or because of the unwillingness of many Jews to continue the traditional education in an American milieu. These attitudes still persist, although today they may not be so severe and so antagonistic as they were a number of years ago.

Likewise, Federations would not provide for Y.M.H.A.'s and Jewish Centers—on the one hand, because many of the Community Center leaders did not regard their institution as a charitable undertaking; on the other hand, Federation leaders looked upon Jewish Centers as a luxury, and funds, they felt, ought to go principally to the poor, the orphaned, the sick, the aged and other economically dependent persons.

The development of the Community Chest in the United States after 1915 also contributed to the federation of local Jewish organizations. One federation could more effectively appeal to the Community Chest trustees for assistance for its respective agencies' needs than could each agency separately. In some communities where the Jewish Federation was in existence before the Community Chest, the general feeling was that the Federation should become a member organization of the Chest. Where this has been done there is now some regret because, with its independence gone, the Federation can no longer expand or develop on its own or according to its own needs. Where the Jewish population and its needs have increased more rapidly than those for the community as a whole, it is extremely difficult for the Federation to withdraw from the Chest although the current situation makes such a move well nigh imperative.

In 1927 the National Appeals Information Service was established to assist local Federations and existing Welfare Funds in more effective budgeting for national and overseas agencies. The National Appeals Information Service gathered its information from the various national and overseas agencies and made it available to member Federations and Welfare Funds. After three years as an independent agency, the Information Service combined with the former Bureau of Jewish Social Research and became the present Council of Jewish Federations and Welfare Funds. The Council of Federations and Welfare Funds offers guidance and service to local communities in the organization, administration and financing of communal programs. Upon request it makes local surveys of existing or necessary philanthropic services and recommends personnel for executive positions in communal enterprises. Periodically the Council summarizes trends in Jewish social welfare and submits reports on the needs and expenditures of national and overseas agencies. Recently it has been interested in developing a program of national budgeting for national and overseas needs. This plan has met with considerable opposition because of a fear that some particular ideology might bias recommendations toward certain agencies and against others. Some have been suspicious of the auspices under which such a program would be conducted. Others fear that many Jewish communities would feel committed to these recommendations and would not exercise sufficient interest and initiative of their own to determine what was to be done with the national budgeting recommendations.

The Jewish Community Council is something new. It attempts to organize and operate Jewish community activities on a thoroughly democratic and representative basis. This is so radical and important a development that its more complete discussion is deferred for a later section of this chapter.

The co-ordination of certain national agencies has already occurred. The Y.M.H.A. and the Jewish Center movement may be said to be co-ordinated through the National Jewish Welfare Board, and Jewish education through the National Association for Jewish Education. Efforts to co-ordinate national Jewish health services have thus far failed. Although there is a certain degree of clearance and consultation through the Council of Federations and Welfare Funds and through the National Conference of Social Welfare, the special functional fields of Jewish philanthropy—family welfare, child care, medical care, care of the aged and so on—have not been co-ordinated on any national basis. An exception perhaps is the Jewish Occupational Council, which acts more or less as an advisory body to the vocational guidance and placement services in various communities throughout the United States. Perhaps, too, the American Jewish Committee, in organizing local chapters throughout the United States, may in time take the position that it democratically represents the opinion of all American Jewry.

B'nai B'rith, which claims to have a membership representing all groups and levels of American Jewish society, declares that it expresses Jewish public opinion because of that membership, and because of its large number of lodges scattered all over the United States. In fact, in some places the B'nai B'rith lodge is the only formal organization of the Jewish community.

5. The Rapid Increase of Anti-Semitism after World War I

Perhaps one of the most powerful influences on the character of Jewish communal work has been the rapid increase of anti-Semitism since 1919. The *Dearborn Independent*,[11a] the millions of booklets on the "Protocols of the Elders of Zion," the canards of blood libel, falsehoods about Jewish monopolies and other evils, the rapid growth of the Ku Klux Klan—all these have made Jewish Americans acutely sensitive to anti-Semitism. This curse, and the sensitivity to it, Hitler and nazism only intensified. Future historians may be able to determine how seriously Jewish life has been thrown off balance by anti-Semitism.

Unfortunately, thus far no comprehensive study of anti-Semitism in the United States from a sociological, psychological and statistical viewpoint has been made. We are likely to be overwhelmed by specific case histories without realizing that the proportion of philo-Semites may be as great as, if not greater than, the proportion of anti-Semites in the general population. The tendency on the part of those who continually warn the Jews of America against anti-Semitism is to neglect emphasizing the fact that the United States, in many important particulars, is not the same as Germany and other Fascist countries. Germany had neither the tradition of liberty nor the history of one hundred fifty years of democratic government.

To dwell further on this question is perhaps out of place here. Nevertheless, the increasing concern of American Jews with anti-Semitism, be the concern adequate or not, has definitely affected many Jewish communal services in the thirty years since 1916.

6. Breakdown of Class Stratification

As the country shut its doors to immigration, the Jewish lower classes moved more rapidly into the upper classes. This was the result of various economic and social forces.

It is well to remember that some of the oldest Jewish families of the United States have already largely been assimilated into the general population. However, association, marriage between socially prominent Jews and Jews of other classes is perhaps more frequent than it is between the elite and the middle classes in the country generally. It is no longer unusual for children of Russian Jewish families to marry into a family of old German Jewish stock. B'nai B'rith, at one time an organization exclusively of those of German-Jewish background, has a predominant membership of Jews of Russian and Polish descent. Large and exclusive Reform congregations, which once either refused admission to Russian or Polish descendants or granted them membership on condition that they pay dues but expect no voting rights, are rapidly discontinuing such practices. In fact, many Reform temples are predominantly "Russian" Jewish in their membership and leadership. The same is true of various Jewish private social clubs. The more the east European Jew has prospered or won recognition for his achievements the more have class lines disappeared, despite occasional incidents to the contrary.

The effect of such restratification is to be seen also in Jewish communal work. A new leadership often appears in the community and a new emphasis occurs with reference to various phases of Jewish communal effort.

7. Overseas Needs

Before World War I, Jewish communal effort in the United States was largely concentrated on local and American needs. The only major overseas interest was Palestine; American Jewry was then devoted primarily to increasing the membership of the Zionist Organization and, through the Jewish National Fund, to providing funds for the purchase of land in Palestine.

After World War I, the HIAS, which had come into being during the days of the heaviest east European migration into the United States, greatly expanded its European services. The Joint Distribution Committee also was created to meet the needs of European Jewry whose economic, cultural, religious and social life had been thoroughly demoralized by the ravages of the war. To hundreds of thousands of Jews it was also apparent that Palestine must be not only a haven of refuge for the oppressed Jews of the world but a cultural center of Judaism as well. Within a comparatively short time a host of organizations (ORT, HICEM, OSE and others) appeared, and these undertook to minister to the many needs of the helpless Jews of Europe.

All this activity was intensified by World War II. The effort to raise $100,000,000 in 1946, $175,000,000 in 1947 and $250,000,000 in 1948, for the overseas needs of the Joint Distribution Committee, the United Palestine Appeal, and for the needs in this country of the United Service for New Americans, is in itself an index of what has occurred. Some of those associated with the United Jewish Appeal have even insisted that all funds raised in this country for any purposes other than those of the United Jewish Appeal be frozen at the 1945 levels, thus making certain that every penny over that year's amount be deposited with the United Jewish Appeal.

This redirection of funds overseas, beginning with World War I, has definitely affected the nature of local and national Jewish philanthropic work. Some pessimists predict that a continuation of this trend will make it impossible in the future to raise similar funds, for by an emphasis on relief to an almost sad neglect of other needs, the Jewish American will ultimately forget his Judaism and the very tradition of lovingkindness and service that it impresses upon him.

8. Increasing Conflict Between Jewish Nationalists, "Integrationalists" and Assimilationists

Differences among Jews in the United States on such matters as assimilation, a Jewish state in· Palestine, religion—although in existence between 1850 and 1935—have been greatly sharpened since World War I, and the antagonisms have grown most intense since 1940. The roots, however, go back to basic differences in ideology: there are those who believe in the melting-pot theory of American life, and others who are convinced that only in Palestine can Jewish life have that setting and enthusiasm which alone make survival and further creativity possible. The conflict between these two groups is not merely academic. Not only has it broken out in the open, to the astonishment of many non-Jews, but these differences have begun to disrupt the forces making for the integration and democratization of American Jewish life.

9. Changes in the Influence of Religion

Despite the poverty of precise data, it is generally recognized that the synagogues of the Orthodox, Conservative, Reform and others (e.g., Jewish Science) have lost some of their influence on the population.[12a] This is quite a departure from the past.

At one time, as we have seen, the synagogue, structurally and functionally, represented the nucleus of all activities of organized and individual Jewish life. The organization of the Jewish community, although in a sense "democratic," experienced a certain ecclesiastical domination; its values and program were determined primarily by the religious leaders and later, in the pre-Emancipation period, by religious and secular lay leaders of influence.

But with the coming of the Emancipation,[13a] especially in countries where state and church were separate, and government activities were limited to secular and nonreligious matters, the structure of the Jewish community changed, too. Thus, in the United States the synagogue and religious leadership have increasingly been relegated to a secondary and relatively unimportant position in Jewish communal affairs. The rabbi is looked upon merely as a spiritual minister for such Jews as feel the need of religion. He is not expected to interfere with the "business" of running community affairs. This especially in the larger Jewish communities of the country. In the smaller communities rabbis may still act, more or less, as communal leaders; they may continue to exercise their influence on the direction of local Jewish communal work. Since some eighty per cent of the Jewish population of the United States resides in large cities, the influence of the rabbis on the *bulk* of American Jewry is small.

That is why Jewish philanthropies are being increasingly secularized, why more and more they begin to resemble and become indistinguishable from Protestant or so-called nonsectarian institutions.

A special case in point are the past (1946) thirty or forty years' changes in the character and the content of Jewish family welfare agencies. It is a fact that Jewish family welfare agencies are taking on for service an increasingly larger Christian case load. They disclaim, most emphatically, that there are any specifically Jewish factors in case-work practice, and through the rapidly developing fee-charging services in which they take great pride these agencies are really abolishing the basis for continued Jewish financial support. And what we observe in the Jewish family welfare field is increasingly evident in other Jewish social services.

10. *The Organization of Jewish Life*

The manifestation of a desire for democratic organization of Jewish communal life goes back to the earliest days of the history of the Jewish people. Jewish life has not always been organized and conducted along democratic lines. Changing conditions, settings, stresses, threats, the mechanization of industry, the growth of capitalism, the power of wealth— all these and more contributed to lapses of democracy in Jewish community life. Jews throughout their history have gone so constantly from one crisis to another that the opportunity for democratic organization came only at intervals.

The urge toward Jewish survival has frequently meant abandoning democratic forms, developed in periods of security, to meet the needs of a life-and-death struggle. At such times (and tragically they have been too frequent) strong personalities arise who take leadership and carry the "folk" along until another period of security emerges, to await the next crisis.

Then, too, the power that comes through the organization of an aggressive minority, or of wealth, occasionally upsets the democratic applecart. But the desire for democratic organization has been a perpetual longing and pursuit of the masses of the Jewish people.

What complicates matters at the present time is the presence of such a multitude of organizations that it is difficult to work out some feasible plan for equitable representation. First, what is this cry for unity which is so frequently raised? To what extent, for example, will differences still be possible once all the organizations in a field are united or amalgamated? Second, what does constitute authentic democracy? There is hardly any

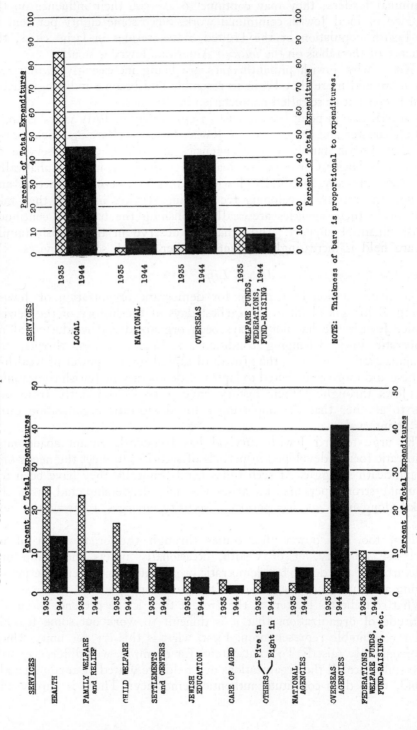

CHART 1   *How the Jewish Philanthropic Dollar was Distributed in 1935 and in 1944*

agreement on what is or is not democratic. Cliques, classes, vested interests (of leadership and professional social workers) have given Jewish community organization a jumbled over-all appearance, bewildering to Jews no less than to non-Jews.

Here, then, are the major forces operating in contemporary Jewish communal effort. With this background, the description of the programs and activities in various functional fields of Jewish communal work may become more intelligible; perhaps, too, the analysis may be of value in contemplating future developments.

Local, National and Overseas Jewish Organizations

In 1917 Dr. Boris Bogen reported that "1,191 separate and distinct Jewish organizations—not including mutual benefit societies, cemeteries, burial societies, trade unions, Zionists, Territorialists and other organizations doing work of an international character" were in existence in 1909. The distribution of these organizations in various groupings was as follows:

National Organizations	7
Relief Societies, including federated charities, sewing societies, etc.	809
Institutions, including hospitals, dispensaries, orphan asylums, convalescent homes, sanitaria, nurseries, etc.	148
Educational institutions, including institutes, settlements, trade schools, etc.	227
Total	1,191

Unfortunately, Dr. Bogen did not at that time collect any figures on the expenditures of the various organizations.

In 1936 the Council of Federations and Welfare Funds issued a table which we reproduce here as Table 1 with some minor modifications.

The table and allied chart reveal that in 1935 approximately 86 per cent of the known expenditures for local, national and overseas philanthropy was spent in the United States in connection with local and regional social welfare activity. Only 8 per cent was devoted to national organizations engaged in health work, civic protection, cultural and educational activities and other nation-wide programs, and barely 7 per cent of all funds raised to overseas services covered by organizations such as the Joint Distribution Committee, the United Palestine Appeal, the HIAS and others.

It is also noteworthy that of the funds spent nationally in 1935 for ten different functional fields, six consumed over 98 per cent. In the order of amount expended these were: (1) hospitals and other health services, approximately 46 per cent; (2) Jewish education, slightly over 14 per cent; (3) child welfare, 13 per cent; (4) family service and relief, somewhat over 10 per cent; (5) Jewish Community Centers and settlements, almost 10 per cent; (6) care of the aged, somewhat over 5½ per cent. All the

TABLE I

Expenditures of Local, National and Overseas Jewish Social Service Agencies in 1935

Field and Type of Service	Number of Agencies	EXPENDITURES	
		Amount	Percentage
Local and Regional			
Health..............................	67	$18,786,222	39.0
Family Service and Relief...............	113	4,179,713	8.7
Child Welfare..........................	94	5,422,521	11.2
Aged..................................	60	2,322,609	4.8
Homeless and Unattached...............	15	93,677	0.2
Employment and Vocational Guidance....	10	237,516	0.5
Remedial Loans........................	12	89,796	0.2
Vacation Service.......................	22	270,323	0.6
Centers and Settlements................	216	4,000,000	8.3
Jewish Education......................	2,200	5,825,000	12.1
Subtotal..............................	3,909	41,227,377	85.6
Others			
National Agencies......................	26	2,477,673	5.1
Overseas Agencies......................	11	3,251,988	6.8
Administration of Federations, Welfare Funds, Comm. Councils, Fund-Raising, etc.................................	89	1,200,000	2.5
Subtotal..............................	126	6,929,661	14.4
Grand Total......................	4,035	$48,157,038	100.0

other services combined, namely, services for the homeless and unattached, for employment and vocational guidance, for remedial loans and vacations did not quite total 1½ per cent.

As far as is known, there has never been any discussion—certainly no decision by any competent group—to suggest what might be a normal type of distribution of Jewish community funds, in order to meet the legitimate requirements of a normal Jewish population. True, "normality" would inevitably have to be related to the nature and composition of the Jewish population in a given locality. Even so, few Jewish communities have so much as attempted a properly balanced budget to meet equitably all local needs and the requirements of all the members of the community. The current and almost universal practice is to depend almost entirely on various pressure groups and vested interests of the community.

Proper studies and adequate recommendations are the responsibility either of the National Conference of Jewish Social Welfare or of a national assembly of Jewish communities that would be representative and competent to deal with this kind of problem. That the need for such a group is present is amply testified to by the general desire for national budgeting, although the current recommendations submitted through the Council of Jewish Federations and Welfare Funds have not received universal acceptance.

In order to picture the changes of emphasis that have occurred in the distribution of Jewish communal funds between 1935 and 1945, the Council of Federations and Welfare Funds was requested to provide a table of expenditures for local, national and overseas needs for three different years, 1935, 1940 and 1944 (or as close to those years as possible). The Council prepared Table 2; it is most interesting and significant.

The following cautions should be observed in reading the percentages on this table and in making year-to-year comparisons:

1. Note that a different number of cities is listed reporting for local and national and overseas expenditures. Because of this, actual fluctuation of total dollars from year to year would be incorrect and would lead to wrong conclusions. Under these circumstances percentages have been utilized and related to their respective bases: the total amount reported by these communities for allocation toward specific purposes.

2. Likelihood of more complete and more accurate reporting on some items than on others.

3. It has been assumed, without real investigation and analysis, that the seventy-four communities reporting their expenditures in 1935, the 102 in 1939 and the 133 in 1944, represented in their respective years a satis-factory cross section of Jewish communities throughout the country and of the allocation of Jewish funds for various purposes. But there are considerable local variations in allocating funds for local, national and overseas purposes. New York City is the largest Jewish community in the United States, and its expenditures for any given functional purpose may fall into a range of thirty to fifty per cent of all moneys raised for a similar purpose all over the United States. This may result in undue overrating or underrating of the averages. The functional services, rep-resented by allocations made through the Federation of Jewish Philan-thropic Societies in New York City, are more nearly in line with the total figures of the table. However, for the contributions to national and overseas agencies, the figures are likely to be askew. New York City has no central fund-raising machinery comparable to the Welfare Funds in other communities. One is therefore unable to detail what the multifarious fund-raising activities in that city actually produce for other than a few major causes. Yet, despite these limitations, the figures in the table are significant.

4. It is extremely difficult to relate the actual dollars expended to a base of reference, or total, which increases rapidly from year to year. What

TABLE 2

*Expenditures of Local, National, and Overseas Jewish Social Service
agencies in 1935, 1939, and 1944**

Field and Type of Service	1935		1939		1944*	
	No. of Cities	Per-centage	No. of Cities	Per-centage	No. of Cities	Per-centage
Local and Regional						
Health	29	25.9	27	17.7	31	13.7
Family Service and Relief	67	23.8	80	16.4	83	7.8
Homeless and Unattached	41	0.4	43	0.3	77	0.1
Immigration and Refugee Service	—	—	57	3.3	52	0.9
Child Welfare	53	16.9	65	10.4	82	6.9
Care of Aged	39	3.2	53	2.1	58	1.8
Employment and Vocational Guidance	6	1.0	10	0.9	14	1.1
Remedial Loans	16	0.7	16	0.4	16	0.3
Settlements and Centers	32	7.2	46	5.5	92	6.3
Vacation Service	12	0.8	16	0.8	27	0.6
Jewish Education	29	3.8	46	3.2	60	3.7
Civic Protection	—	—	33	0.8	58	1.1
Soldiers and Sailors Welfare	—	—	—	—	77	0.7
Other	14	0.3	15	0.1	43	0.3
Subtotal†	71	84.0	100	61.9	130	45.3
Others						
National Agencies	55	2.3	98	3.1	133	6.1
Overseas Agencies	38	3.4	94	27.2	132	40.8
Administration of Federations and Welfare Funds, Fund-Raising, etc.	66	10.3	88	7.8	132	7.8
Subtotal†	74	16.0	99	38.1	133	54.7
Grand Total†	74	100.0	102	100.0	133	100.0
Total Expended	$12,312,124		$20,328,812		$34,127,501	

CJFWF, April 4, 1946 (prepared by Mae Dauer)

*Data used represent budgetary allocations for 1944—not expenditures.

†The totaled figures for "No. of Cities" represent the number of cities that sent in replies to questionnaires. Thus, in 1935, seventy-one cities sent in replies on local and regional social services. However, only twenty-nine supplied information on health expenditures. The absence of information from the other forty-two cities might be due either to the fact that no expenditures for organized or specific health services were being made or, if they were, no systematic way of reporting these expenditures had been developed up to that time.

may seem a relatively lower percentage of allocation for a specific functional field may, in actual dollars, represent an increase. The approximately $22,000 increase in one item from 1935 to 1944 does not necessarily represent that much increased giving. On the contrary, approximately sixty more communities reported their expenditures in 1944 than in 1935. It is therefore necessary to compare percentage changes rather than fluctuations in the amount of dollars.

5. There may be local differences in classifying expenditures. What one community may list separately for "care of the aged" or "child care" may be included by another community under "family service and relief."

The standardization of cost-accounting procedures, definition of terms, consistency in financial record-keeping are still goals to be achieved in the over-all reporting for the Jewish communities of the country. The Council of Jewish Federations and Welfare Funds should be given a great deal of credit for having stimulated and encouraged the progress that has already been made. But there is still much to be done.

6. Although percentages may show a decrease, this should not be construed as *smaller* expenditure. Actually, the income may have remained fairly constant or may have been greatly increased. The percentages should be related to the total amount expended each year.

7. It should be noted that the 1944 figures represent allocations and not actual expenditures. No figures for expenditures in 1944 were available; nevertheless, since the allocations may not differ materially from the funds actually expended, these figures were utilized for purposes of comparison.

8. Finally, it is important to remember that the comparisons made are to be of two kinds: first, of percentage relationships to all moneys raised; second, of percentages in their relationships to moneys used locally and to moneys used nonlocally. Perhaps the administrative expenditures of local federations for operation, promotion and fund-raising might be shifted to the extralocal section of the table. But there are good reasons why they should be listed as part of local expenditures.

And now for an analysis of the table:

1. The six local functional fields which from 1935 through 1944 received the largest allocations were, respectively, health, family service and relief, child welfare, settlements and centers, Jewish education and care of the aged. In 1939, owing to the increased local requirements for care of refugees, immigration and refugee service took fifth place, while Jewish education and the care of the aged went to sixth and seventh places. In 1944, however, these six functional fields were restored to their 1935 positions.

2. These six functional fields received almost 81 per cent of all funds raised, slightly over 96 per cent of all moneys expended for local services.

In 1944, however, the allocations to these six fields represented only a little over 40 per cent of all moneys allocated for local work ten years ago, and almost 89 per cent of the funds appropriated to local organizations. Although there was a reduction of 7 or 8 per cent in the share these groups received from the community, they still held on to the bulk of local funds because of existing needs, pressure of contributors. the inability of new and in some instances extremely valuable services to overcome the competition of the established older organizations, and the general inability of the community to recognize and support new projects.

3. If we adopt the sum total of dollars for all purposes as a base, we see that the percentage for health services decreased about 50 per cent between 1935 and 1945. If the subtotal of the percentages spent locally is the base, however, it appears that, whereas in 1935 the health services received about 30.8 per cent of all local allocations, in 1945 the decrease was very slight; then the allocation was 30.2 per cent.

In the case of family service and relief, we have a somewhat different picture. The decrease from 1935 to 1945 on the basis of all sums raised was about 67 per cent (from 23.8 per cent to 7.8 per cent). The reason for this change will be explained below. In terms of proportions of local funds available for this work, in 1935 family service and relief received 29.3 per cent of the money for local purposes; in 1945 it received 17.2 per cent.

The support for child welfare in this ten-year period dropped from 16.9 to 6.9 per cent of all local funds. However, if we take into account the percentage of local allocations to various agencies involved in child care work, the drop is not serious. In 1935 child welfare agencies received 20.1 per cent of all local funds for such services; in 1945 they received 15.2 per cent. When compared with the percentage figures calculated on the basis of sums raised for all Jewish philanthropies during these ten years, the difference is not considerable.

As far as settlements and centers are concerned, although there seems to be a slight falling off of allocations in the ten-year period this is true only when the allocations are set against the total of all funds raised locally. Note, however, that if the percentages are related to the amounts available and distributed locally, against 8.6 per cent allocated to settlements and centers in 1935, there has been an increase of almost 14 per cent of all local funds for settlements and centers in 1945. (The difference here is an excellent example of the need for caution in interpreting statistical data.) A similar feature is evident in the field of Jewish education. The table might suggest a static condition of allocations for local programs of Jewish education. Actually, in 1935, 4.5 per cent of all local funds were allocated to Jewish education. In 1945, however, this proportion rose to 8.2 per cent—almost double the amount of ten years before.

Although the table indicates a reduction of almost 50 per cent in the funds contributed for the care of the aged between 1935 and 1945, actually this is true only in so far as total funds raised for all purposes are concerned. When one examines the proportion allocated locally from available funds, however, it becomes evident that allocations for the care of the aged have remained constant, perhaps increased slightly—3.8 per cent in 1935; 4.0 per cent in 1945.

These six fields of community service, by the way, have quite a monopoly of local Jewish communal funds. Some services, *e.g.*, research, the development of diagnostic procedures, community education, social prophylaxis, are lost under the headings of specific functional agencies. This is unfortunate. On the one hand, it obscures the nature and extent of these vital phases of community effort; on the other, the services may be so insignificant that their general and permanent value is negligible.

It is also noteworthy that during the past seven or eight years local expenditures for civic-protective work have increased rapidly. These are supplementary to the national programs of B'nai B'rith, American Jewish Committee, American Jewish Congress and the Jewish Labor Committee. In some instances the expenditures may include local disbursements by Jewish Community Councils toward developing democratic forms and organization of local Jewish community life, which disbursements, however, many regard as part of civic-protective programs.

4. Most interesting are the comparisons of the proportion of local funds distributed to national and overseas agencies during these ten years. As against 5.7 per cent of all funds for national and overseas agencies in 1935, the figure for national agencies and agencies doing work overseas in 1945 is 47 per cent, of which the overseas agencies absorb by far the greater share of the increase. What these ratios may be in 1948, will perhaps, be self-evident.

In 1935, national agencies were given 14.4 per cent of all local funds for non-local purposes; the overseas agencies, 21.2 per cent; and the local federations, for their administration, fund-raising and other expenditures, 64.4 per cent. In 1944, however, the allocations to the national agencies of funds for nonlocal distribution amounted to 11.2 per cent; the federations absorbed 14.3 per cent, but the overseas agencies received 74.6 per cent of all funds reserved for nonlocal use. (The situation for 1946, 1947 and 1948, is even more extreme than this.) From a 16 per cent of local funds for national, overseas and local administration, fund-raising and general overhead in 1935, we come to approximately 55 per cent in 1945, with the needs of overseas agencies of course absorbing the bulk of this increase.

To summarize: American Jewry has three foci of interests—local needs, national needs, needs of Jews overseas. The shift of community interest and emphasis has been as follows:

Period 1, up to World War I: concentration on local community needs and building local community agencies and functional services.

Period 2, between the two World Wars: shift of interest from the local to the national scene. Problems common to all Jewish communities— fund-raising, national civic-protective work, national health agencies, etc.— received major interest and attention.

Period 3, since World War II: the interest and funds have shifted largely to overseas requirements.

What the chief interest will be ten years from now is difficult to predict. A great deal will depend on the extent to which American Jewry scientifically studies its local, national and overseas needs, and provides the finances necessary for efficient operation of all its essential services.

One further reference to Table 2. The table reports an almost 200 per cent increase in the amount expended. But this should be discounted for the increase in the cities reporting expenditures was almost 100 per cent. The increase represents mostly that of the smaller Jewish communities, however; the increase in expenditures, therefore, is relatively larger than the difference between 100 and 200 per cent. In other words, although the number of communities reporting their expenditures almost doubled, the expenditures between 1935 and 1945 probably tripled. In 1948 it may increase tenfold without either the increase in the Jewish population or in Jewish economic status to account for it.

If we study the data on each functional field by itself we find not only interesting developments in expenditure but also (perhaps more so) in fundamental thinking.

1. *Health*

The changes during the ten-year period are as follows:

a. A departure more and more from the observance of *kashrut*.

b. Increased services to non-Jews.

c. Increasing emphasis on maternity wards and on hospital provisions for paying patients.

d. Greater concern for experimentation and research.

e. Growing interest in community education on matters pertaining to health.

f. A deepening concern over and desire to serve other functional fields of Jewish social service, such as child care, psychiatric service, care of the aged and chronic invalidism.

2. *Family Service and Relief*

a. The most noteworthy change within the past ten to twenty years has been in the great reduction of the relief load and the emancipation of the agency for more constructive work with individuals and families.

b. There has been increasing interest in making family welfare services available to those better off economically in the community, and in the provision for fee-paying services.

This development brings with it not only a new clientele from the Jewish community but many Christians too. In this respect, many Jewish welfare agencies function, both in philosophy and in method, exactly like the so-called nonsectarian, or Protestant, agencies.

c. More service to and alignment with organized labor. This development is paralleled by the appointment of labor and union representatives to the directorates of Jewish family welfare agencies.

d. With few, if any, exceptions, continued indifference to Jewish content in the programs and contacts with Jewish families, and an inability to comprehend, an unwillingness to encourage the utilization of cultural values in Jewish family life. Since about 1911 Jewish family welfare agencies have been institutions in search of their souls.

e. An increasing desire to interpret changing methods and ideology so that the average Jewish contributor might understand what the Jewish family welfare agencies are about. This is yet to be fully realized.

3. Child Welfare

a. In the past ten years there has been growing interest in the development of centralized communal bureaus for the planning and conduct of community-wide child care activities.

b. Greater emphasis on the placement of children in foster or private homes as against institutions. It has been increasingly recognized, however, that some children thrive best in an institutional environment. This means that much more careful diagnostic, psychological and educational work is necessary before a child can be returned to its own home or turned over to a foster home or some institutional setting.

c. Wider recognition of the need for psychiatry and psychoanalysis in the treatment of children.

d. Realization that the war has contributed to an increase in child dependency and delinquency. This has been accompanied by an awareness that our agencies and facilities, our procedures and our personnel, are not adequate to meet the critical situation in every community.

4. Settlements and Centers

a. Shifts of population make it necessary either to dispose of community centers and settlements or to turn them over to other groups in the community which have displaced the former Jewish families in the area.

b. The army USO programs have developed a deeper interest in the establishment of community centers and a desire to make existing centers more serviceable and meaningful.

c. Greater interest in developing center programs which have more meaning for the individual, which improve the Jew's relations to his fellow Jews and make him a better American citizen.

d. A stronger desire for the development of community center services as an extension of the center—either extension centers as such, or, in rural and small communities, professional guidance and assistance by neighboring large Jewish communities and Jewish Community Centers.

e. An increased interest in the center as representing a "movement," and an increase in the "Jewish content" of Jewish Center programs.

5. Jewish Education

a. The creation of national, centralized organizations interested in Jewish education has greatly stimulated the further development of Jewish education programs in various cities throughout the country. A greater number of Jewish communities have begun to establish bureaus of Jewish education. These bureaus attempt to organize the program of fund-raising, allocation, supervision, teacher training, teaching standards, personnel practices, and community accounting.

b. More and more it is recognized that there is no one single pattern that may be called "Jewish education." In view of the different backgrounds and interests of Jewish community groups, certain essential minima, on which membership in a Bureau of Jewish education is contingent, must be adopted. A school is required to meet certain curricular requirements if it expects community funds.

c. Growing awareness on the part of communities that without an effective program of Jewish education the future of the Jewish community and of Jews in America is threatened.

6. Care of the Aged

a. There has been considerable change in the care of the aged since funds have become available from federal, state and local governments through Social Security.

b. Increasingly, old-age institutions have tried to place the aged in private homes where they can take care of themselves and meet other than just aged persons; the institution itself is reserved for those who are chronically ill, who require frequent medical attention.

c. Jewish communities are paying more attention to the fact that American Jewry is a rapidly aging group—because of the low birth rate the proportion of the aged among Jews is increasing more rapidly than among others in the country as a whole. This presents now, and will present in the future, serious problems for the Jewish communal agencies, both medical and institutional. A number of Jewish communities are already devoting themselves to this question in terms of fact finding and community planning.

7. The Other Local Functional Fields

In the larger communities there is a wide variety of services that are highly specialized. Among the most significant are vocational guidance

agencies geared to the local occupational scene and demands. As a service
to other Jewish communal agencies they are most helpful.

National Agencies

National agencies as distinguished from local social service agencies are
organizations that serve all Jewish communities either directly or through
an existing local agency or committee. This service may be for individual
local residents or their families. Again it may be in the form of advice,
guidance and direction for a specific program.

Although the table on page 1286 indicated that probably only twenty-six
national agencies were in existence in 1935 and that they spent approximately $2,500,000, it is quite likely that there were many more, and that
by 1940 they numbered fifty and spent close to $6,000,000. Exact informa-
tion is not available. (That, however, is typical of a great deal of information on Jewish life in this country.)

The national agencies to be discussed may be placed in the following
categories:

1. Health agencies
2. Cultural and recreational agencies
3. Civic-protective programs
4. Rescue, immigration and readjustment services
5. Fraternal organizations
6. Representative organizations
7. Occupational organizations
8. Religious organizations
9. Research organizations
10. Palestinian organizations

Before discussing these ten categories it might be of interest to remark
that the 1946-1947 issue of the *American Jewish Year Book* includes a list
of approximately 268 organizations under the heading "Jewish National
Organizations." These national organizations report a total membership
of approximately two millions. Naturally, there are many duplications of
membership and many of these national agencies did not submit their
membership lists for analysis. All but fifteen were founded since about
1900, and forty-seven have come into being since 1940.

1. Health Agencies

The major institutions in this field are those devoted to the care of
Jewish tubcrculars—although non-Jewish patients also are admitted. The
hospitals include: the National Jewish Hospital for Consumptives in
Denver; the Ex-Patients Tuberculosis Home in Denver; the Jewish
Consumptive Relief Society in Denver; the National Home for Jewish
Children in Denver; and the Jewish Consumptives and Ex-Patients
Relief Association in Los Angeles. Another Jewish hospital, founded by
B'nai B'rith, is the Leo N. Levi Memorial Hospital in Hot Springs,
Arkansas. It serves patients, predominantly non-Jewish, suffering from
rheumatic, arthritic and blood diseases.

Within recent years a National Council of Jewish Tuberculosis Institutions has been established to deal with problems common to the National Jewish Hospital, the Ex-Patients Tuberculosis Home in Denver and the Jewish Consumptive and Ex-Patients Relief Association in Los Angeles. The Denver Jewish Consumptive Relief Society has kept out of the Council.

2. Cultural, Educational and Recreational Agencies

One of the most significant agencies in this field is the National Jewish Welfare Board, created in 1917 as a result of a merger between the former National Association of Y.M., Y.W.H.A.'s and kindred organizations and the Jewish Welfare Board, a war-service organization serving Jewish men and their families during and after World War I.[14a] Its purpose is, therefore, twofold: (1) to serve and promote the interests of Jewish Community Centers and the Jewish Community Center movement in the United States, Canada and elsewhere; (2) to function as liaison between the Jews of America and the federal government in ministering to Jewish men and women in our armed forces and to veterans. During World War II the National Jewish Welfare Board was one of the member agencies of the United Service Organizations (USO).

Through its initiative it has launched and is supporting the Jewish Book Council and the Jewish Music Council. J.W.B. has conducted many Jewish community studies which have not only encouraged the establishment of Jewish Community Centers but have also had a bearing on other aspects of Jewish community life.

Another group in this field are the Hillel Foundations of B'nai B'rith. These are social and cultural centers established on the campuses of various colleges and universities throughout the United States. At the present time (1946) approximately fifty such units are in operation under full-time directors and some seventy-five under counselors. B'nai B'rith launched this movement in 1924.

Antedating the Hillel Foundations as an organization of Jewish college students was the Menorah Society established in 1913. It publishes the *Menorah Journal*.

Another national organization serving colleges throughout the country is the Jewish Chautauqua Society. It provides lecturers for scheduled forums in the colleges. At present the society is a project of the National Federation of Temple Brotherhoods associated with the Union of American Hebrew Congregations.

A number of cultural and educational organizations are religiously motivated. Among these may be included the National Academy for Adult Jewish Studies sponsored by the Jewish Theological Seminary of America. The Academy serves congregations whose rabbis are members of the Rabbinical Assembly. Another is the United Yeshiva Foundation, organized to foster the establishment of *Yeshivot* (Hebrew Day Schools) in the United States and to assist in their financial support. The National Council of Young Israel, organized in 1912, has some seventy branches with a membership of about 25,000 and is devoted through its clubs and societies to the perpetuation of traditional Judaism. Young Judea, established in 1909, now numbers some 750 clubs and clubleaders with a membership exceeding 17,000. Although it has no official connection with any of the larger synagogue movements, it is Conservative in tradition and is strongly tied, ideologically, to Zionism and to the development of Palestine as a Jewish national home.

The two institutions of higher learning whose emphasis is secular as well as religious are Yeshiva College in New York City and Dropsie College in Philadelphia.[15a] Of the two, the former undoubtedly exercises a wider influence and reaches a larger number of Jews throughout the country.

Middlesex College in Waltham, Massachusetts, has been reorganized as Brandeis University which was formally inaugurated on October 7, 1948, when Dr. Abram Leon Sachar was installed as president. Its first student body consisted of 107 including Catholics and Protestants as well as Jews.

The Jewish Theological Seminary of America has announced plans for a University of Judaism. These include schools for the training of social workers, of a center for the interpretation of Jewish ideals in art, music and letters, for a school of Jewish sacred music, as well as the expansion of the present facilities of the Seminary for the training of rabbis and teachers. At the present time (1946) it appears that the University of Judaism contemplated by the Jewish Theological Seminary of America will be established on the West Coast, in Los Angeles.

Among the organizations issuing books or magazines are the following: The Jewish Publication Society, the outstanding publisher of Jewish books in the United States. It also issues regularly the *American Jewish Year Book* sponsored by the American Jewish Committee. The American Jewish Committee publishes a monthly magazine, *Commentary*, which incorporated the former *Contemporary Jewish Record*. The Conference on Jewish Relations publishes a quarterly, *Jewish Social Studies*, which is devoted mainly to technical papers on Jewish history or to Jewish statistical studies. The Yiddish Scientific Institute through its *YIVO Bleter* publishes articles drawn from its rather active research program of Jewish life all over the world. The Jewish Teachers' Seminary and People's University issues the *Jewish Review*, which carries articles like those in the *YIVO Bleter*. Both these magazines are bilingual (Yiddish and English). There are other important magazines, such as the *Jewish Frontier*, published by the League for Labor Palestine, *Congress Weekly*, published by the American Jewish Congress, *Die Zukunft* published by the Forward Association in New York City, the *New Palestine*, published by the Zionist

Organization of America, the *Jewish Social Service Quarterly,* published by the National Conference of Jewish Social Welfare. Mention has already been made of the *Menorah Journal* published by the Intercollegiate Menorah Association. A large number of publications is issued by national agencies (*e.g., National Jewish Monthly* of B'nai B'rith).

The Jewish Reconstructionist Foundation issues a magazine, the *Reconstructionist,* along with other publications, as a medium for teaching American Jews the basic philosophy and program of the Reconstructionist movement.

The *Histadruth Ivrith* is a national organization interested in promoting Jewish education along Hebrew lines and in developing close ties between the creative Hebrew work in Palestine and that in the United States.

The Jewish Braille Institute of America was organized in 1931 to help the Jewish blind throughout the United States by means of books and other materials, so that these people might continue their interest in Jewish religious life and culture.

A large number of organizations such as the B'nai B'rith, the National Council for Jewish Women, the Zionist Organization of America, through the organization of young people's groups (or, as they call them, "juniors"), provide cultural, educational and recreational programs in order to develop an interest in each organization's program and philosophy. Such activities are intended to stimulate participation in the activities of the senior organization when the young people achieve maturity.

In general, a tremendous amount of cultural, educational and recreational activity is carried on for both adult and subadult groups. These are very poorly co-ordinated, however. There is no criterion of "fitness," and what is "fittest" is determined by the availability of funds and local pressure, rather than by what is of greatest value to the greatest number of Jews, or by what may contribute most effectively to the survival of the Jewish people.

3. *Civic-Protective Programs*

The following national agencies are interested in one aspect or another of this program in American Jewish life: B'nai B'rith, through its Anti-Defamation League, the American Jewish Committee, the Jewish Labor Committee, the American Jewish Congress, the Jewish War Veterans, the National Jewish Welfare Board and the Jewish People's Committee for United Action against fascism and anti-Semitism. This last organization was formed in 1936. It now has some forty-four branches and claims an affiliated membership of some 300,000.

The American Jewish Committee is the oldest American institution established for the protection of Jewish civil and political rights wherever they may be threatened. The B'nai B'rith through its Anti-Defamation League has limited itself to counteracting individual and group anti-

Semitism on the American scene, while the American Jewish Committee has dealt with such manifestations both in America and abroad. Both agencies have been involved in programs of education, social action and legislation. As the policies and programs of these agencies are determined by their constituencies, there have been differences of emphasis and of procedure, depending upon the preferences for varying approaches. Since the Second World War there has been an increasing amount of close co-operation and co-ordination between these agencies.

The American Jewish Congress believes that it must rise to the defense of Jews when they are discriminated against by legislative act or by individuals or organizations. It has made numerous studies of anti-Semitism and on specific problems has frequently acted either alone or in co-operation with other national agencies.

The Jewish Labor Committee, representing a large number of organized labor groups throughout the country, has recognized its stake in this field too. The Jewish War Veterans, by virtue of their participation in the armed forces of this country, also feel that they should deal with this difficult problem.

The National Jewish Welfare Board through its Bureau of War Records, through its contacts with men in the service who experienced real or alleged anti-Semitism, through community contacts, has also been drawn into civic-protective work. In addition, the Welfare Board's access to community centers, community center programs and professional personnel and membership, may be able to exert desirable influence on the study of the problem and on the development of a program of co-operation.

Some five years ago the National Community Relations Advisory Council came into being to co-ordinate the plans and programs of the various civic-protective organizations and to plan for the assignment of new projects to one agency or another. Each organization is represented on the governing board.

4. *Rescue, Immigration and Readjustment Services*

The four principal organizations operating in this area are the American Jewish Joint Distribution Committee, the HIAS, the National Council of Jewish Women and the United Service for New Americans. Of these, the Joint Distribution Committee is by far the most prominent. We shall have the opportunity to discuss further the fund-raising program of the J.D.C. during the past ten years. J.D.C. grew out of a merger of the American Jewish Relief Committee, the Central Relief Committee and the People's Relief Committee, representing respectively the Reform, the Orthodox and the radical, or labor, groups in the United States. As one organization, J.D.C. surpasses by far any previous organization in history in terms of funds expended, professional staff and geographic coverage.

It represents the major medium through which the Jews of the Western world, including North and South America, have combined to raise the funds necessary to save the survivors and fugitives of war-torn Europe.

HIAS carries on a parallel program but without the resources, the financial backing and the professional staff available to the Joint Distribution Committee.

The National Council of Jewish Women has been interested for years, in fact since its establishment in 1893, in the immigrant and in service to the foreign-born. At the height of Jewish migration into the United States some thirty or forty years ago, the Council had regular visitors or workers at ports of entry and did yeoman service in the Americanization and naturalization of the newcomers. During the period of refugee resettlement in this country the Council once again did superb work. With the change of name of the National Refugee Service to United Service for New Americans, it took over the port work and other overseas activities formerly carried on by the Council.

The United Service for New Americans, founded originally in 1937 as the Co-ordinating Committee for Aid to German Jewish Refugees which in turn became the National Refugee Service, came into being with Hitler's rise to power; it was responsible for the resettlement and readjustment programs for German, Polish and Austrian refugees who arrived in the United States by the thousands from 1931 to the outbreak of World War II. Since the end of World War II, it has had added responsibilities for the resettlement of Jews from China, as well as from the DP camps in Europe.

In addition to these organizations there is an American Biro-Bidjan Committee interested in the resettlement of displaced Jews in the Biro-Bidjan area in Eastern Russia. There is also an American Jewish Joint Agricultural Corporation and the Dominican Republic Jewish Settlement Association interested in the resettlement in the Dominican Republic of homeless Jews. The former organization is also interested in a colonization project in Bolivia. In addition to these we have ORT (the initials of the organization in Russian and in French), which emphasizes more definitely trade, the agricultural and occupational retraining in European countries, and the economic adjustment of the immigrants in America.

Other organizations are the OSE and TOZ, both promoting health measures for the European Jewish population. They have been absorbed by the J.D.C. program. The ICOR Association, organized in 1924, was one of a series (*e.g.*, the Agro-Joint and KOMZET) interested in Jewish farm settlement in Biro-Bidjan and elsewhere in Russia. Now ICOR has added to its interests "information on the economic, cultural and social life of Jews the world over."

5. *Fraternal Organizations*

Undoubtedly, the outstanding Jewish fraternal organization is the Independent Order of B'nai B'rith, known as B'nai B'rith. Established in 1843, it now numbers approximately 230,000 members: about 143,000 in men's lodges, 61,000 in women's auxiliaries and 25,000 in B'nai B'rith youth organizations. It lists 733 lodges, 681 of which are in North America and fifty-two in Europe, South America, Asia and Africa. It has sponsored the establishment of hospitals, orphan asylums, Jewish Community Centers and other philanthropic agencies on a national, regional or local basis throughout the United States. Through its "Wider Scope Program" it launched a much-intensified Anti-Defamation League program, provided subventions for colonization in South America and Palestine, assisted in the development and co-ordination of vocational guidance services, the exten-sion of Americanization efforts, the establishment of the Hillel Founda-tions. In 1944, B'nai B'rith created the B'nai B'rith Youth Commission, the governing body of the B'nai B'rith youth organization embracing AZA, B'nai B'rith Girls, B'nai B'rith Young Men, B'nai B'rith Young Women, and it has sponsored various publications under the auspices of the Anti-Defamation League and other units. It publishes the *B'nai B'rith Monthly* magazine, which is perhaps one of the most widely circulated Jewish publications in the United States.

Other fraternal organizations are the Independent Order B'rith Abra-ham, B'rith Sholom, Free Sons of Israel, B'nai Zion (which has a distinctly Zionist and Palestinian aim), and the United Order of True Sisters.

Other organizations of a similar order are the Workmen's Circle, (*Arbeiter Ring*), the Jewish National Workers Alliance (*Verband*), and the International Workers Order.

The *Arbeiter Ring* was the first fraternal organization for the Jewish working classes. It has developed an extensive cultural and educational, as well as a social service program, for its members. It has established many *Arbeiter Ring Folkshulen*, Jewish educational institutions for youth, throughout the country. It is also responsible for the various Jewish Centers known as Workmen's Circle Centers. The Jewish National Workers Alliance developed as a protest against the lack of interest in, or opposition to, Zionism and Palestine on the part of the Workmen's Circle. Like the *Arbeiter Ring*, the Alliance has established Jewish educational institutions and various services for its members. The International Workers Order came into being with the rise of the Union of Soviet Socialist Republics and contains a membership sympathetic to Soviet political and national philosophy. This Order has established Jewish educational programs in harmony with its tenets.

Other national associations of Jews for specific purposes are those of the Jewish War Veterans, the Jewish Theatrical Guild of America and a large·number of fraternities and sororities, some of which are general in character while others are specialized—for physicians, dentists, pharmacists, lawyers, artists, etc.

In addition to these, there are federations (associations of *Landsmannschaften*) of Polish, Galician, Rumanian, Lithuanian, Sephardic and other groups of Jews.

6. *Representative Organizations*

In this group are included national agencies which regard themselves as spokesmen for the bulk of American Jews or for the majority of the organized groups whose views should determine American Jewish policy.

It is extremely difficult to give any of the organizations priority because of the keen competition between them and because of the fact that the only widely representative organization, the American Jewish Conference (in 1947 designated "the American Jewish Assembly"), is still uncertain of its future.

The American Jewish Assembly was called into being in 1942 and held its first sessions in 1943. Its constitution provides for representation through delegates appointed by national Jewish organizations which have a national membership or a membership through local community units; in addition, other representatives of local communities, elected by popular vote either through local inclusive organizations such as Jewish Community Councils, or through a committee or organization that is widely representative of all members of the Jewish community who wish to participate in the conduct of its affairs, are included. Currently there are over 100 delegates representing sixty national Jewish membership organizations and about 380 selected by local community organizations.

Many of those originally associated with this enterprise wished this "assembly" to concern itself with domestic as well as foreign problems. But this was not to be. The forces opposed to the creation of such a central body were too strong to overcome. The name of the Conference itself created a great deal of controversy; the name finally accepted was "American Jewish Conference," with emphasis on the word "Conference," in order to underscore that this body was merely "a platform" with no authority to bind any single individual or organization on any action over which there might be the slightest disagreement, either in principle or in method. For various reasons many Jewish communal leaders are irreconcilably opposed to any organization that will represent itself as the "voice" of American Israel. This was evident at the time the United Nations Organization was established in San Francisco in 1945. Sydney H. Zebel, in a review of international events for the *American Jewish Year Book*, writes:

Despite this concern, however, efforts to unite American Jewish organizations working in this field in support of a unified post-war program met with no success. In February, 1945, invitations were issued by the American Jewish Committee to Agudas Israel, the American Jewish Conference, the American Jewish Congress, and the Jewish Labor Committee to participate in an informal conference to consider formulation of such a program; but favorable replies were received only from Agudas Israel and the Jewish Labor Committee. The Conference and the Congress, its constituent, declined the invitation, stating that a positive program could best be achieved through the Conference, which, they claimed, was the sole "representative body of American Jewry."

To date the American Jewish Conference has held three sessions. The first was from August 29 to September 2, 1943, in New York City; the second session December 3-5, 1944, in Pittsburgh, Pennsylvania; the third February 17-19, 1946, in Cleveland, Ohio.[16]

At the second session the question was raised whether the American Jewish Conference should include within its interests domestic Jewish problems, that is, problems of "the American scene." For various reasons the Conference decided to look one way only, to devote its energies to overseas problems exclusively.

At the third session of the Conference the question of the "emergency" character of the American Jewish Conference was raised—had not the time arrived to liquidate the Conference altogether? The upshot of the discussions was to direct the new Interim Committee "to continue and intensify the work of the Conference within the purposes defined in the Pittsburgh proposals." It was also decided that a fourth session of the Conference should be called not later than fifteen months after the date of the third session. Throughout the meetings of the third session there was general recognition of the fact that there is a fairly widespread demand for a permanent American Jewish organization which would speak authoritatively for the Jews of America, which would genuinely register the will of the overwhelming majority of American Jewry. The Interim Committee of the Conference was directed to explore the possibility of bringing such a democratically constituted organization into permanent being.

[According to an article that appeared in the *New York Times*, January 1, 1949, "The American Jewish Conference, which dealt with post-war Jewish problems since 1943, closed its offices at 521 Fifth Avenue yesterday, it was announced by Louis Lipsky, chairman of the Conference Executive Committee."]

What may ultimately come of all this is a matter of guesswork. Much no doubt depends on the integrity and decency of American Jewish professional workers and lay leaders, on the capacity of existing national Jewish organizations to think more of the larger good of Israel than of selfish interests, and on the willingness to re-estimate the ideologies of present organizations.

First constituted in 1917, reconstituted in 1922, and reorganized in 1938, the American Jewish Congress has appealed largely to the Russian Jewish element and the middle-class groups of American Jewry. The Congress has never had the upper-class standing that the American Jewish Committee enjoys.

In time, however, the democratic base of the American Jewish Congress became less and less obvious. More and more the Congress became a movement with local supporters who by their character and make-up were presumed to represent a cross section of the entire Jewish community. In this respect, the Congress was regarded as representative of American Jewry. Actually no local "congresses" or "assemblies" were developed. The local American Jewish Congress committees speak for the American Jewish Congress and help provide local backing and funds for the national organization. There is no local program which is developed by the local congresses of the American Jewish Congress; nor are there any local expenditures for American Jewish Congress programs and activities, except as these are directed from the national office. These programs are mostly promotional, propagandistic, educational. No mandate exists for a local action program to parallel that of the national organization for the national and international scenes; nor do the local Congress committees compete with existing Jewish community councils, which do represent, as nearly as possible, the local democratic organization of the Jewish community. In every instance the local Congress committee is represented in the Jewish Community Council; it is nowhere regarded as a competitor of the Community Council itself.

In its early years the American Jewish Congress was somewhat confused for lack of a significant program. It was more or less like a fire department waiting for an emergency to develop. Since 1938, however, it has come to life and become much more combative. Just as the American Jewish Committee is now going through rapid expansion so, too, the American Jewish Congress is rapidly developing in a number of directions: in public relations, defense programs, Jewish public education, vocational guidance and placement, publication, issuance of pronouncements on specific Jewish problems requiring public or governmental attention, individual organizational action in defense of Jewish rights, watching and counterattacking the enemies of Palestine, and so on and on.

In the period before World War I, the plan and leadership of the American Jewish Committee developed. It was created to do something about the rising dangers to Jewish economic, social and political security—primarily overseas and only incidentally in the United States itself. A parallel development in France was the creation of the *Alliance Israélite* through the initiative of Adolphe Crémieux.

Originally, since its national board and regional representatives represented the upper classes and more or less assimilated German Reform

Jews, the Committee's attention was naturally focused on the larger question of Jewish minority rights, and showed little concern over the local internal questions of American Jewish life. However, this situation has changed during the past six or seven years. At present the American Jewish Committee program extends over every area and aspect of Jewish community life.

Two other organizations, quite different in origin, history and function, have a bearing on the question of who represents the will of organized American Jewry. These are the National Conference of Jewish Social Welfare (originally known as the National Conference of Jewish Charities —later the National Conference for Jewish Social Work) and the Council of Jewish Federations and Welfare Funds. The Council of Jewish Federations and Welfare Funds was an outgrowth of an original National Appeals Information Service (N.A.I.S.), which in turn was a service made available through the former Bureau of Jewish Social Research. Late in 1932 the representatives of some fifteen federations met in Cleveland, Ohio, and organized the Council, whose aims and objectives have already been outlined.

At the present time the Council has associated with it approximately 250 member organizations in approximately 200 communities throughout the country. In many communities these member agencies may represent the local Federation or Welfare Fund or Jewish Community Council or various combinations of these three. Under the circumstances, since it is both the only single national agency to which federations, welfare funds and a large number of community councils look for direction, and exercises great influence on these major organizations, the Council is regarded by many as the most representative and the most democratic organization of American Jewry. Many admit that its board of directors and those who represent the local communal organizations do not necessarily come from all ranks in the community in proportion to respective numbers. Nevertheless, many contend, by virtue of the status of these leaders in their respective communities, their recognition by Jews and by non-Jews, their familiarity with all phases of Jewish communal life, that they are most representative, and that they should have the power and authority to undertake commitments for the communities they represent. As long as they represent the will of their local population (some may say, what *should* be the will of their local Jewish community), democracy in a practical sense has been achieved.

In its earliest days the National Conference of Jewish Social Welfare represented the only Jewish national organization providing an opportunity to laymen, professionals and rabbis to meet annually and discuss local Jewish community problems and to devise means of handling them effectively. True, no religious, economic or social sanctions could be imposed upon a violator; nevertheless, basic rules for the conduct of Jewish philanthropies were promulgated. Consider, for example, the "Transportation Rules." These grew out of the evil of communities passing on dependents from one to another without consulting or asking permission of the receiving community. This practice created tremendous difficulties for all cities, small and large, and proved no less unjust and cruel to the persons who were so assisted. Numerous controversies broke out between communities. The evil was removed by the Transportation Rules. Penalties were assessed and collected. The only force was that of universal and accepted opinion of the decencies in social work practice.

Today, however, the National Conference of Jewish Social Welfare is less than what it was. The creation of the Council of Jewish Federations and Welfare Funds took from the Conference its major *raison d'être*. The great increase in the number of rank-and-file workers, their demands for union recognition and for a more sympathetic attitude toward Russia in the pre-World War II period, unsatisfactory program planning that gradually eliminated the participation of laymen and rabbis, and finally the restriction of the Conference to mere discussion and no action, have all finally reduced it to an organization limited to professionals who get together annually for discussions without real impact on Jewish social work in the United States. What has happened to the National Conference of Jewish Social Welfare is a symptom of American Jewish life as a whole. Despite the extraordinary demands upon the Jews of America during the past ten years, there has not been a single committee of the Conference, appointed or called into existence, to offer the best professional help and guidance of organized Jewish professional social work.

At the present time the National Jewish Welfare Board is an association representing some three hundred to four hundred Jewish Community Centers throughout the United States. In addition, there are a number of Federations and other central community agencies that look to the National Jewish Welfare Board for the kind of guidance and direction other central Jewish organizations receive from the Council of Jewish Federations and Welfare Funds. The membership of these affiliated local organizations is reported to be approximately 425,000.

Another national agency is the American Association for Jewish Education. In April, 1939, representatives of a number of already existing bureaus of Jewish education in various cities met in Atlantic City in order to create a service and co-ordinating agency on a nation-wide basis. This became the American Association for Jewish Education.

At present (1946) there are thirty-seven central agencies for Jewish education. Twenty-eight are local, two are regional and seven are national in scope. Since the establishment of the American Association for Jewish Education thirteen bureaus of Jewish education have come into existence.

The Association has been involved in twenty-three educational surveys throughout the country. It played an important part in securing local community recognition for Jewish education; contributions to Jewish education from federations and welfare funds rose from $800,000 in 1942 to approximately $1,200,000 in 1944.

Also created in 1939 was the Jewish Occupational Council. Though at first it offered considerable promise and effectiveness, its work in the past three years has been on the decline, partly as a result of the decrease in financial support from the co-operating agencies originally instrumental in the Council's establishment. It was organized to provide advisory and co-ordination services to all national and local Jewish organizations interested in vocational guidance, placement, training, occupational research, or the battle against discrimination in industry and the professions. The Council's most recent report indicated an affiliation of twelve national organizations and a membership of twenty-eight local agencies in twenty cities.

Somewhat like the National Conference for Jewish Social Welfare, the National Association of Jewish Center Workers and the National Council for Jewish Education represent the organization of professional workers in these two specialized fields. It is the aim of both these organizations (they meet generally in association with the National Conference of Jewish Social Welfare) to advance the professional work in centers and in Jewish education.

On occasion there have been attempts to bring about a merger of these three organizations but this has not yet come to pass.

Another organization which falls in this area of specialization for service and co-ordination is the National Community Relations Advisory Council. The Advisory Council is of recent origin; it specializes in the area of publicity and community relations. It is an association of six national agencies and community-wide committees, in some nineteen cities, concerned with the public relations aspect of Jewish communal work, with problems of anti-Semitism and other related questions. As its title indicates, its functions are primarily advisory, and include research, clearance, co-ordination and guidance; the activity programs in public relations it leaves entirely to the six associated national organizations, the Anti-Defamation League of B'nai B'rith, the American Jewish Congress, the American Jewish Committee, the Jewish Labor Committee, the Jewish War Veterans and the Union of American Hebrew Congregations (the Synagogue Council, at this writing, has been added as a seventh constituent organization).

Mention should also be made of agencies offering service and co-ordination in specialized fields of some national organizational activity. These include the American Zionist Youth Commission, the B'nai B'rith

Youth Commission, the *Histadruth Ivrith* Youth Commission and the Synagogue Council of America, in the fields, respectively, of Zionist work, B'nai B'rith activities and interests, Hebrew education and religious activities.

The Central Sephardic Jewish Community of America, with headquarters in New York City, is devoted to the activities of Sephardic Jewish communities scattered throughout the United States. Although this organization has been in existence for some time, it is only lately, with the appointment of a professional executive director, that the organization has moved into a position of effectiveness in its area of work. It is regrettable that in a large number of Jewish communities with a substantial Sephardic Jewish population—persons coming from the Mediterranean Basin, and not necessarily of the original Spanish-Portuguese stock in the early history of this country—little has been done to bring these Jews more effectively into the community scene. The differences in religious practice and in general psychological and sociological orientation between this group and the Russian, Polish and German Jewish elements have been responsible for the Sephardic isolation. The Central Sephardic Jewish Community of America hopes not only to strengthen the Sephardic groups so that they may meet their own particular needs more effectively, but also to put an end to this isolation.

Another national agency which may be included in this survey is the National Desertion Bureau. It was organized at the peak of the Russian Jewish migration into this country. The Bureau serves family welfare organizations, federations and other local Jewish communal agencies in their efforts to bring relief to a family when its head has disappeared. Its services have been unique and most effective. The organization was created through the promotional efforts of the National Conference of Jewish Charities.

The above organizations include practically all types of service which attempt to co-ordinate and serve intelligently Jewish communal and philanthropic work, and Jewish social service.

7. *Occupational*[17]

B'nai B'rith established a Vocational Service Bureau a number of years ago; it is still active and increasing in effectiveness. It specializes in stimulating co-operation on programs of vocational guidance and service activities, and has published a large series of pamphlets on the possibilities in specific fields of industry, trades and the professions, in an attempt to guide young people toward an intelligent choice of vocation.

Owing to the great interest of a number of Jews in encouraging farming, both the Jewish Agricultural Society and the National Farm School serve in this field of work.

The Jewish Agricultural Society has been in existence since 1900. In its initial years it was heavily subsidized by the Baron de Hirsch Fund. Throughout these years the Society has given every encouragement to Jews with the potentialities and the basic interest to farm. It has advanced loans; it has offered technical service and advice. According to certain estimates, a substantial part of the 100,000 Jewish farmers either came to their farms through the stimulation and the help of the Jewish Agricultural Society or have been served in one way or another by its various departments.

The National Farm School movement represents a program for developing the interest of Jewish youth in agriculture during their high school and college years, to prepare for farming in adult life. The National Farm School was organized in 1896; it is located near Doylestown in Bucks County, Pennsylvania; its alumni association has over a thousand members. The National Farm School trains not only Jews but a good number of non-Jews as well.

These are the obstacles to the normal development of a centralized Jewish vocational guidance organization:

1. Fluctuating economic trends, business cycles, alternating periods of prosperity and depression, have all influenced the rise and fall of interest in vocational guidance and placement. When there are labor shortages and the demand for workers is high, the problems of vocational guidance and placement are not acute. On the other hand, in periods of depression, of an overcrowded labor market, increased anti-Semitism, the whole problem of Jewish occupational distribution and Jewish unemployment becomes serious. The question has then been raised: Are Jewish young people going into the right occupations? Under these circumstances long-term planning is extremely difficult.

2. The Jews of America have neither adequate nor valid statistics to indicate the occupations Jews enter. Occasionally communities make studies, some valid, some not, to determine the occupational distribution of Jews in that specific community.[18a] It has been found, however, that there are such wide variations from community to community that no generalizations can be made for the country as a whole. Unfortunately, there are many Jews who vigorously oppose the gathering of data to determine the occupational stratification of Jews. The absence of such data locally and nationally makes it impossible to develop a constructive program.

3. The lack of adequate recognition that in matters of vocational guidance the parents are at least as much of a factor influencing the children as the children themselves.

4. The absence of a persistent lay and professional leadership to promote this important program.

5. Another major reason why this field has not progressed toward the growth and effectiveness it deserves has been that concern with Jewish vocational guidance and occupational problems has been "everybody's

business." The Jewish Occupational Council was organized to bring some order into this field. Organizations will go along on a co-operative basis, however, only as long as they think it necessary. It is likely that this condition will be with us for some time because there is nothing on the horizon to indicate any change in point of view on the part of national agencies with a stake, small or large, in this important field of Jewish communal effort.

8. *Religious Organizations*

The three major religious groups in the United States, Orthodox, Conservative and Reform, have five major theological institutions serving their needs. They are: the Hebrew Union College, primarily for Reform and incidentally for Conservative congregations; the Jewish Institute of Religion, primarily for Reform, incidentally for Conservative and occasionally or rarely for Orthodox congregations; the Jewish Theological Seminary of America, primarily for Conservative but also for other traditional congregations; the Rabbi Isaac Elchanan Theological Seminary, primarily for Orthodox and secondarily for Conservative congregations; finally the Chicago Hebrew Theological College primarily for Orthodox and, less frequently, for Conservative congregations. There are other seminaries of minor character and importance, all serving the Orthodox Jewish community of the United States.[19a]

The associated rabbinical groups for the Reform, Conservative and Orthodox religious fields are, respectively, the Central Conference of American Rabbis, the Rabbinical Assembly of America and the Rabbinical Council of America. In addition, there is another Orthodox rabbinical organization known as the Union of Orthodox Rabbis, and a third, the Yeshiva Synagogue Council, which is especially associated with the Rabbi Isaac Elchanan Theological Seminary.

The congregational organizations associated with these religious groups are the Union of American Hebrew Congregations (Reform), the United Synagogue of America (Conservative) and the Union of Orthodox Jewish Congregations of America. Each of the denominational groups has its respective sisterhoods, women's auxiliaries, men's clubs, brotherhoods and youth councils.

Mention should be made of the Agudas Israel, which is a separate organization, with its own women's organization and youth council; it is concerned with the preservation and advancement of religious orthodoxy all over the world.

The Synagogue Council of America is the union of all Jewish religious bodies in the United States (exclusive of Agudas Israel) for common action on religious matters. The Council's most recent notable activity was the sponsorship and direction of the Committee on Army and Navy Religious Activities of the National Jewish Welfare Board.

For the Sephardic Jews of America, who are Orthodox in their religious practice, there exists the Union of Sephardic Congregations.

9. *Research Organizations*

One of the major omissions of the Jews of America has been in the field of Jewish social research. This may be due, first, to the fact that the importance of research has not been appreciated by the leaders of Jewish life. A crisis, an emergency and the emotional appeal, rather than careful study, have dictated the content and direction of Jewish research programs. Another factor may be the absence of properly trained personnel in the field of Jewish social research. The greatest contributions in Jewish social research have come either from non-Jewish research organizations or from Jewish research organizations located outside the United States. From both these sources the entire Jewish lay leadership has been isolated: from the first, because of the technical publications in which the data appear, from the second, because the European organizations have published their works in Yiddish, a language to which a substantial number of American Jewish lay leaders have a pathological aversion.

Perhaps a third factor has been the pathetic and unfounded fear of some Jews that Jewish social research might uncover unsavory facts.

Jewish social research certainly suffers as a result of the unco-ordinated activities of the various agencies and institutions. There is not a single national Jewish organization of any prominence which does not carry on some program of research, surveys, studies. It is shameful that some of these efforts, fostered by local communities and organizations, are characterized as "research." Some national Jewish organizations carrying on research are: the Conference on Jewish Relations, the Jewish Statistical Bureau, the American Jewish Historical Society, the American Jewish Committee (through its Department of Scientific Research), the American Association for Jewish Education, the National Jewish Welfare Board, the American Jewish Congress, B'nai B'rith, the Yiddish Scientific Institute, the Council of Federations and Welfare Funds, the American Academy for Jewish Research and Dropsie College for Hebrew and Cognate Learning. Mention has already been made of the small funds allocated for purposes of research on questions of vital importance to American Jewish life.[20a] Yet, if all the funds devoted to research by the dozen or more of the largest, most influential and most prominent Jewish organizations in the United States were pooled in one national research organization— like the former Bureau of Jewish Social Research—and if this Bureau were staffed with the best personnel among the Jewish statisticians of the United States, the results would far surpass what is forthcoming today.

A word is in place on this former Bureau of Jewish Social Research. It was established as one of the functioning agencies of the New York City Kehilla. When the Kehilla went out of existence, the Bureau of Jewish

Social Research continued to operate and its functions covered the entire United States. From 1910 or 1915 through 1925, the Bureau made a vast number of Jewish community studies and helped lay the groundwork for the organization of the National Appeals Information Service and for the creation of the National Council of Jewish Federations and Welfare Funds. When the latter came into being it absorbed the Bureau. The present research activities of the Council of Federations and Welfare Funds represents a small part of the year-round research activity which used to be carried on by the Bureau of Jewish Social Research. No other national organization of its type has superseded it.

Although in other Jewish functional activities central bureaus have been established to clear program and policy, no such development has taken place in the field of Jewish social research. The Conference on Jewish Demography, called together in the winter of 1945, comes closest to such a development. But it is still too young to be of influence.

10. *Palestinian Organizations*

First to be mentioned, of course, is the Zionist Organization of America, which is the oldest and the largest of the centralized organizations concerned with Zionist theory, membership and national and international activities for Palestine. It is the American branch of the World Zionist Organization. Hadassah, originally organized by Henrietta Szold as an organization of American women to assist her in the medical and special services Palestine required, has since become the Women's Branch of the Zionist Organization of America. Junior members and young adults belong to such subsidiary organizations as Masada, Avukah, Junior Hadassah and Young Judea.

The Mizrachi Organization of America and its Women's Branch represent those American Zionists who are Orthodox in religion and who take the position that the Palestinian Jewish commonwealth must have a definitely religious and Orthodox orientation in addition to secular nationalist objectives.

A substantial number of Zionists have a labor orientation. These are represented by the Labor Zionist Organization of America (Poale-Zion) and the Zeire-Zion, both of which are combined in the United Zionist Labor Party. In a sense, the Pioneer Women's Organization constitutes the women's division of these groups, although labor Zionist organizations include both men and women in their memberships. Another organization with a labor philosophy is the League for Labor Palestine; its youth organization is Habonim.

Also among the labor Zionists is the National Labor Committee for Palestine which was organized to assist the Histadruth (Histadruth Ha-Obdim Ha-Kelalit be-Eretz Yisrael) in every possible way. The Histadruth is the general federation of Jewish labor in Palestine—a sort of

C.I.O. and A.F.L. combined. In addition to its trade union functions Histadruth is also involved in numerous cultural, industrial, commercial, housing, health and welfare activities. It should be noted that the letter-head of the League for Labor Palestine carries this phrase: "Dedicated to a Jewish labor commonwealth in Palestine through the Histadruth." In the spring of 1946, when the various labor Zionist groups were campaigning along with other Zionists for votes, the "labor Zionist and progressive bloc" was represented by the following organizations: the Labor Zionist Organization of America, the Jewish National Workers' Alliance, the Pioneer Women's Organization, League for Labor Palestine, Women's League for Palestine, Left Poale-Zion [which separated from Poale-Zion in 1922] and the Habonim Labor Zionist youth. In addition, there were shekel committees from trade unions, the Workmen's Circle and the *Landsmannschaften*.

There are organizations which combine both the Orthodox religious and the labor interests. These include the League for Religious Labor in Palestine and the Ha-Shomer Ha-Dati. To the members of Ha-Shomer Ha-Dati, Torah and labor in Palestine are indivisible.

Another important organization, operating in many countries, is Ha-Shomer Ha-Zair. This organization is interested in recruiting and training *Halutzim*, pioneer workers, for the *kibbutz* in Palestine. It is generally known by the name of the "He-Halutz movement." It has consistently opposed what is known as the "Biltmore Program" of the Z.O.A., and is opposed to a Jewish commonwealth in Palestine.

During World War II, while millions of European Jews were murdered and exiled, efforts were increased to open the gates of Palestine to immigration. It was then that a number of Zionist groups got together and organized the American Zionist Emergency Council. The Council worked zealously and effectively, and through political action helped many of the homeless Jews to reach Palestine.

The experiences of the Jewish population in Palestine during World War I subsequently led to increased dissatisfaction, and a militant group in Palestine, headed by Vladimir Jabotinsky, broke away from the World Zionist Organization and founded, in 1925, the World Union of Zionist Revisionists. This group favors the establishment of armed military units to defend and fight for the homeland, mass immigration into Palestine, is opposed to non-Zionist representation on the Jewish Agency with rights equal to those of Zionists, and is the strongest advocate for a "Jewish state" in Palestine. Representatives of the Revisionists in the United States established the New Zionist Organization of America in 1926. Those Revisionists who remained within the framework of the Zionist Organization organized themselves as a separate group and are known as the Jewish State Party.

Three organizations interested in the economic development of Palestine are the Palestine Economic Corporation, the American Economic Committee for Palestine and the American Eretz Israel Corporation (Ameic). Through their activities, indeed, they have increased the absorptive capacity of the land. The Palestine Economic Corporation was created in 1926; it is made up of stockholders who have invested their funds in shares paying dividends, and who underwrite various investments for the economic development of Palestine. The Corporation has been unusually successful; most of the investors reinvest their dividends in order to increase the capital of the Corporation and thus larger funds are available for the support of needed enterprises.

The American Economic Committee for Palestine, established in 1932, was organized to make available technical and business specialists to Palestinian industry, agriculture and commerce. The American Eretz Israel Corporation, established in 1944, attempts to stimulate trade and commerce between the United States and Palestine, thereby encouraging Palestinian industries and economic resources.

Two important associated activities of the Zionist Organization of America are the Jewish National Fund (Keren Kayemet) and the Palestine Foundation Fund (Keren Hayesod). The Jewish National Fund, organized in 1910, collects funds for land purchase in Palestine. This land can be distributed only on lease; it remains the permanent possession of the Jewish people of the world. A substantial portion of the land that has been converted for agricultural use has been made available through Jewish National Fund purchases.

The Palestine Foundation Fund came into being in 1920-1921, to raise funds from Jews throughout the world for the establishment of industry, commerce and agricultural enterprises in Palestine. The Palestine Foundation Fund differs from the Palestine Economic Corporation in this, that the funds of the former, like the land purchased by the Jewish National Fund, belong to the Jews of the world; there are no dividends to contributors. The Jewish Agency for Palestine determines the manner in which these funds shall be applied for Palestinian reconstruction.

Mention should be made of a Zionist fraternal order, the B'nai Zion, formerly known as the Order Sons of Zion, established in 1910, with a current membership of approximately five thousand. The Order's major interest is the rebuilding of Palestine.

Three organizations interested in the intellectual, professional and scientific developments in Palestine are the American Friends of the Hebrew University, the American Jewish Physicians Committee and the recently organized American Committee for the Weizmann Institute.

The American Friends of the Hebrew University was established in 1925 to raise funds for the support and development of the Hebrew

University on Mt. Scopus in Palestine. This program provides the Friends with the opportunity to teach American Jews the significance of this institution of higher learning, not only for the Jewish, Arab and other populations in or near Palestine, but also for the general advancement of scientific and humanistic studies throughout the world.

The American Jewish Physicians Committee was established in 1921 to enlist the co-operation of American medical men and organized American Jewish communities in making available advice, co-operation, funds, supplies of medical materials and books, for medical education and practice in the Orient.

Early in 1946, the cornerstone of the Weizmann Scientific Institute in Palestine was laid. The Institute was the result of a special campaign launched in the United States and in other countries for the construction and maintenance of a technical school to train scientists and carry on extensive experimentation on problems affecting Palestine and the sciences as a whole.

B'rith Trumpeldor of America, Inc., established in 1929, aims to train American Jewish youth in the principles of state Zionism and to prepare them as pioneers and future citizens of Palestine. In addition to the general program of education, there is an extensive program of physical education.

The American Red Mogen Dovid for Palestine was organized in 1941 to provide funds for the equivalent of an American Red Cross in Palestine.

The above list does not exhaust all the existing organizations in behalf of Palestine. However, the major organizations have been presented and their programs summarized. Perhaps someday all these groups will also learn to co-ordinate their activities and function in a more unified manner.

11. *Desiderata*

a. There is no graduate school for the training of Jewish social workers, although such a school was in existence from 1915 to 1929. Since then the need for it has become greater. Currently, its re-establishment has been under discussion by a number of the more important national Jewish organizations. A Training Bureau for Jewish Communal Workers was initiated in the fall of 1947 in New York City.

b. There is no national Jewish social research organization.

c. There is no national association of Jewish Community Councils. At present, the Council of Jewish Federations and Welfare Funds, which might be the organization interested in the development of this newer type of community organization, is primarily concerned with making the Federation the representative body for the entire Jewish community. In view of the traditions and practices of Federations in the past, it is questionable whether they can be democratized sufficiently to serve as a substitute for a genuine Jewish Community Council.

d. There is no central and co-ordinating Jewish body, although the American Jewish Conference (later the American Jewish Assembly) gave some promise in that direction. At present, the professional Jewish social workers in the different fields are not represented and have no voice in the programs and activities of the American Jewish Assembly.

These are not the only needs, but they are perhaps the outstanding ones.

2. THE TWO MAJOR DRIVES OF 1946

1. *The United Jewish Appeal*

As far back as 1919, the Jews of America have been appealed to for substantial funds for the rebuilding of Palestine. In addition to the Jewish National Fund, which had been in existence much earlier and which had relied upon the collections of charity boxes in Jewish homes and public places (restaurants, synagogues, recreation halls, community centers, Hebrew schools, etc.), the Palestine Foundation Fund launched its first extensive and country-wide drive in 1921 and brought Nachum Sokolow to this country especially for this purpose. As the work and number of the Palestinian agencies grew, the campaign was intensified in 1931 under the designation of the American Palestine Campaign. Shortly thereafter, this annual fund-raising effort of the American Zionists came to be known as the United Palestine Appeal and it is so designated at present.

When and how the American Jewish Joint Distribution Committee came into existence has been described already. It is worth noting that since its organization during World War I there has been so much suffering in various settlements of Jewry throughout the world that the Joint Distribution Committee has been compelled to run a fund-raising campaign for purposes of relief every year. Perhaps this may serve as a test: the world will have become civilized when the American Jewish Joint Distribution Committee will no longer be necessary.

The United Service for New Americans, formerly the National Refugee Service is a third beneficiary of the nation-wide campaign for the United Jewish Appeal. The National Refugee Service co-operated with the National Council of Jewish Women, the Hebrew Sheltering and Immigrant Aid Society (HIAS), the Joint Distribution Committee and a number of Christian and nonsectarian organizations interested in various aspects of the refugee problem. Although the National Refugee Service carried on an extensive correspondence and an advisory and consultation service for European refugees, all its funds are limited to expenditure in the United States. Under the circumstances, the major activity of the United Service for New Americans has been to receive the refugees as they enter United States ports and to help them get settled. Among its chief accomplishments was a resettlement program which effected the distribution of a large number of refugees among hundreds of Jewish communities throughout the United States. Some of the sad experiences of the earlier Industrial Removal Office did not recur because the earlier lessons were not forgotten and the type of immigrant involved was different. Another outstanding achievement was the placement of scholars and scientists in schools, research laboratories and industries where their education and talents could be utilized for the greatest benefit of America.

Up to 1934 the Joint Distribution Committee and the Zionist groups conducted separate campaigns. Three to four million dollars were raised and distributed, about equally, between the two national organizations. In 1934 and 1935 they joined forces in a united campaign, dividing the income on an even basis. As a result of suspicions, and differences in ideology and loyalties among contributors, separate campaigns were carried on in 1936 and 1937. In 1936 each group attempted to raise $3,500,000 for its own needs, but both were unsuccessful. Despite this failure, however, they decided again to conduct separate campaigns in 1937, for approximately $4,500,000 each.

The undesirable results of separate campaigns were so obvious that annually beginning with 1939, when the United Jewish Appeal was established a joint appeal has been conducted in which the National Refugee Service (United Service for New Americans) has also been included.

In Table 3 figures are presented covering the United Jewish Appeal for refugees, overseas needs and Palestine campaigns from 1939 through 1945.

One of the major causes of friction between the Zionists and those devoted to the cause of the Joint Distribution Committee has been the question of the division of funds raised from the Jews of America. The American Jewish Joint Distribution Committee has always been opposed to an even distribution of these funds. When the separate campaigns were conducted in 1937 with each of the organizations determined to raise approximately $4,500,000, there was established a 60:40 ratio for the guidance of local federations and welfare funds in allocating funds to the Joint Distribution Committee and to the United Palestine Appeal. In the 1941-1942 joint campaign it was agreed that the initial sum of $9,100,000 raised would be appropriated to the three organizations as follows: J.D.C., $4,525,000; U.P.A., $2,575,000; N.R.S., a guaranteed sum of $2,000,000. It was also agreed that additional sums raised over and above $9,100,000 would be divided between the J.D.C. and the U.P.A. by an allotment committee, and that the division would be along the lines of similar allocation committees in previous years. The table indicates how these procedures actually worked out in practice.

The 1946 campaign goal of $100,000,000 is one which not only proved staggering when first proposed but would have been unbelievable as late

TABLE 3

Cumulative Summary Report on U.J.A. Campaigns
1939 through 1945
(Figures as of Nov. 30, 1945)

Campaign	Gross Pledges as of Nov. 30, 1945*	Cash Received on account to Nov. 30, 1945†	Campaign, Administration, Collection and Allotment Committee Expenses
1939**	$16,096,547	$15,227,061	$441,188
1940	13,846,271	12,969,792	456,083
1941	14,154,787	13,219,046	552,498
1942	14,468,259	13,735,821	497,260
1943	18,184,032	18,158,607	503,061
1944, Estimated	27,000,000	26,697,344	597,386
Total 1939–1944	$103,749,896	$100,007,671	$3,047,476
1945, Estimated	35,000,000		
Estimated Total, 1939–1945	$138,749,896		

	Percentage of Expenses to		Allocations Paid through Nov. 30, 1945‡			
Campaign	Pledges	Cash as of Nov. 30, 1945	J.D.C.	U.P.A.	N.R.S.	Balance on hand for Distribution
1939**	2.7	2.9	$ 7,957,249	$ 3,978,624	$ 2,600,000	——
1940	3.3	3.5	6,092,446	2,921,263	3,500,000	——
1941	3.9	4.2	6,122,842	3,668,706	2,875,000	——
1942	3.4	3.6	7,090,908	4,147,653	2,000,000	——
1943	2.8	2.8	9,473,000	6,682,000	1,500,000	$ 546
1944 (est.)	2.2	2.2	14,372,558	10,627,442	1,051,954	48,004
Est. Total 1939–1945	2.9	3.0	$51,109,003	$32,025,688	$13,526,954	$48,550

* Funds raised in the U.J.A. campaign of any given calendar year are credited to the campaign of that year, regardless of when official notification of pledges or cash is received. As official notifications of additional allotments are received, the gross pledges will be increased.

† As the fiscal years of local campaigns vary and as in many cases local pledges are redeemable on an installment basis, it is understood between the U.J.A. and the individual local communities that allocations will be paid over a certain period of time, but credited to the calendar year of national campaign for which the pledges were made.

‡ Allocations are paid to the beneficiaries as the checks clear through the banks. Additional allocations are voted by the Allotment Committees. Allocations are based on pledges to the national campaign of a given calendar year and are distributed as cash on account of these pledges is received from the communities.

** In 1939 an allocation of $250,000 was also made for Christian refugees.

as five or ten years earlier. There is every indication, however, that this sum will be raised.[21] [Actually, in 1946 $102,000,000 was raised; in 1947, $125,000,000.]

Among all professional campaign workers the question is frequently raised, "How far are we from scratching the bottom of the barrel in reaching our campaign goal?" As far as is known, no one has ever been able to offer a satisfactory answer to that question. It is evident that the "bottom of the barrel" cannot be fathomed and a good many factors must be taken into consideration—the purposes for which the funds are solicited; the type of publicity and community education preceding the collection of funds; the techniques employed to make people willing to contribute.

The possible consequences of spending such huge sums inevitably raises the question of national budgeting.

2. *The Joint Defense Appeal*

The 1946 Joint Defense Appeal set a national goal of $5,000,000; $3,500,000 was raised for this purpose in 1945.

The Joint Defense Appeal is the fund-raising effort of two organizations, the American Jewish Committee and B'nai B'rith (Anti-Defamation League). Other organizations interested in civic-protective work, such as the American Jewish Congress, the Jewish Labor Committee, the Jewish War Veterans, are not included as beneficiaries in this Joint Defense Appeal.

The Joint Defense Appeal has been conducting campaigns since 1941. It has been successful in reducing unnecessary expenses due to the competition between two major civic-defense organizations and in co-ordinating efforts on program, although ideological differences remain.

3. *National Budgeting*

For the past ten years the question of devising some machinery to bring order out of the chaos of allocations has held an important place on the agenda of Jewish communities throughout the United States. No one can estimate the amount of money the Jews of America will be contributing to local, national and overseas philanthropic work. A total sum in the neighborhood of $150,000,000 (in 1946) is not an exaggeration. This means approximately a $30 contribution per capita for every Jewish man, woman and child—assuming that there really are 5,000,000 Jews in the United States (the figure is probably high). It is likely that in order to make such a sum available American Jews have been compelled seriously, for the first time, to make some material sacrifice.

All agencies, local, national, overseas, are constantly demanding tremendous sums. Jewish communities are anxious to do their share, but they are unable properly to estimate the nature of the respective needs. Some agencies—they are in an extreme minority—do not pad their budgets at all. Many do, however, in order to make sure that, after debate and discussion, they will receive their minimum requirements. Others, again, are altogether extravagant in their demands, but feel that certain local influences will make possible what they wish. Under such circumstances, then, some objective group must undertake to discriminate and determine appeals wisely.

The Council of Jewish Federations and Welfare Funds has been advancing the idea and a program for national budgeting—and more recently, to assure local freedom of action, a national *advisory budgeting* program.

At the general assembly of the Council of Jewish Federations and Welfare Funds (Detroit, 1946) this problem was discussed at length. Preceding the assembly, there had been considerable discussion on the pros and cons of national budgeting in the various Jewish communities represented in the Council. When the vote on a national advisory budgeting program was taken, representatives of 137 communities, including practically all the major cities, voted five to one to reject the proposal of the Board of Directors of the Council. Even before the delegates arrived in Detroit the majority, by the way, had been instructed by their communities how to vote.

There are several reasons for this. Leaders of certain national organizations feared that their interests would not be properly protected. Communities feared that a national advisory body would neglect to take particular local preferences into account. Perhaps basic to the whole outcome was the fear on the part of individuals and communities that the Council of Jewish Federations and Welfare Funds would be unable to give balanced consideration to Zionist matters, for it was assumed that a predominant element in the Council was non-Zionist.

Regardless of the present (1946) status of a national budgeting program, there can be no question as to its desirability, and many professional and lay leaders earnestly hope for a sound solution—for the present chaos is detrimental to all desirable purposes. With greater democracy in Jewish communal life, with courage and imagination, some budgeting program can be found to satisfy the local as well as the over-all scene. There may be some blundering at first; with experience, however, communities and the national board might get together to determine the proper local maxima and minima.

3. Some Current Problems in Jewish Community Organization

In discussing some of the current problems affecting the Jewish community in the United States, it should be kept in mind that, in some respects, these problems are common to all forms of group association. The difficulties in social relationships, to which attention will be called, are not necessarily unique among Jews. If a careful, objective analysis were made, perhaps we would find that despite all their weaknesses Jewish communities are the best organized communities in the United States. Even if true, however, this fact should not lead to complacency.

Jewish community life may be better organized for the following reasons: First, there is a traditional pattern for Jewish community behavior. Whether problems relate to religious life, Jewish education, Jewish philanthropy, the protection of civil rights, vocational guidance, or the satisfaction of cultural and other secular needs, the organization of Jews into satisfactorily operating units is essential.

Another reason for Jewish community organization is the threat from without—anti-Semitic discriminations of one type or another. Unity through organization makes for strength. And this strength must be utilized not only for the protection of those Jews, scattered all over the world, whose existence is threatened, but against the less virulent forms of antagonism manifested in America.

If there were no distinctive religious and cultural needs which Jews had to provide for themselves, and anti-Semitism were to disappear entirely, it is quite likely that Jewish community organization would soon vanish.

A third reason for the possibly better organization of Jewish community life is this: American Jews are aware of the fact that they represent a substantial and significant proportion of world Jewry, and hence carry a major responsibility for their brethren in other sections of the world.

There is much still to be done if the efficiency of the American Jewish community organization is to be increased and its functions improved. Some of the pressing needs have been discussed above under desiderata. It is clear that unless the Jews of America study their life with greater intelligence than has been the case to date, unless constructive measures are undertaken on a democratic and practical basis, there is no guarantee that Jewish life in America will not some day disappear. No sound social statistician will deny this possibility.

An analysis of Jewish communities in one city after another reveals strikingly that the chief preoccupation of almost every community is with fund raising. This has become virtually an end in itself. That this is no exaggeration is reflected by the fact that in the administrative structure the largest salaries are paid to the most expert fund-raisers.

It is also obvious that the level of Jewish communal work can be no higher than the competence level of its professionally trained workers. Eighty per cent of the Jews in the United States live in large communities. Occupational and professional activities have become highly specialized, and unless men and women are trained to become specialists in Jewish community life, there will be no such life worthy of the name.

Although it is evident that without adequate statistical information it is impossible to contemplate intelligent community organization, the fact remains that in Jewish life there is a vigorous and effective battle against all attempts to compile satisfactory data about Jews. The figures available at the present time (1946) are hardly to be taken seriously. Next to nothing is known about Jewish population figures, death and birth rates, occupational distribution, delinquency, religious affiliation and observance, conversions and a host of other important facts. All of which is of course incongruous, but this incongruity is responsible for the hit-and-miss character of so much Jewish communal planning and activity. Such escape from reality becomes serious when the American community is spending substantial sums on various local and national Jewish projects. Clearly, unless in the near future the Jews can substitute for the charts and numbers on which agencies today base their operations, the work of serious statisticians, Jewish community life can expect nothing but continued and progressive anemia.

To date there are still no adequate texts, studies and other resource material that could be used for an extensive program in community education. Moreover, the printed page is itself not sufficient for a complete education. What is required is a program, or series of programs, of participation in group life at various age levels.

Whether there is a vital Jewish community in the United States in the years to come will depend on how well prepared Jewish youth will be to take over leadership. It is well to remember that much of what the present older generation is doing in the Jewish world is the result of influences during youth.

Much could surely be gained from a national conference held once in three or five years at which representatives of organizations like the rabbinical assemblies, the Assembly of the Council of Jewish Federations and Welfare Funds, the National Conference of Jewish Social Welfare, B'nai B'rith, National Council of Jewish Women and others could meet together to discuss and plan for activities affecting all Jews, and not merely the membership of each of the respective individual organizations. The educational value of rabbis, social workers, labor leaders and lay leaders getting together and thinking together would be enormous. Certainly, the sooner each national organization or agency comes to realize that *kelal Yisrael* is greater than any of its particular societies, the sooner will Jews approach what might properly be called the American Jewish Community.

NOTES

[1a Cf. above Anita Libman Lebeson, "The American Jewish Chronicle," pp. 317 f. and Moshe Davis, "Jewish Religious Life and Institutions in America," pp. 355 f.]

2 Perhaps another Jewish community, which might be listed sixth in the order of establishment, was the one in Richmond, Va. Congregation Beth Sholem was already in existence in 1791. One is therefore justified in concluding that during the Revolutionary War there was already a Jewish community in that city. In fact, the evidence of the existence of the Richmond Jewish community is substantiated by the fact that a joint letter dated Dec. 13, 1790, was addressed to George Washington by the congregations of Charleston, New York, Philadelphia and Richmond, congratulating him upon his election to the presidency of the United States.

[3a Cf. Davis, op. cit., pp. 357 f.]

[4a Cf. ibid., passim.]

[5a Cf. above Israel S. Chipkin, "Judaism and Social Welfare," pp. 724 f.]

[6a Cf. also her chapter cited above.]

[7a Davis, op. cit., pp. 409 f.]

[7b Cf. above Jacob Lestschinsky, "Jewish Migrations, 1840-1946," passim, and Nathan Reich, "The Economic Structure of Modern Jewry," passim.]

[8a Cf. Reich, op. cit., pp. 1241 f.]

[9a Cf. Chipkin, op. cit., pp. 721 f.]

[10a Cf. ibid., pp. 718-721.]

[11a Cf. Lebeson, op. cit., pp. 337-338.]

[12a Cf. Davis, op. cit., section vii, beginning p. 414.]

[13a Cf. above Cecil Roth, "The Jews of Western Europe (from 1648)," pp. 264 f.]

[14a Cf. Chipkin, op. cit., pp. 716-718.]

[15a Cf. above Simon Greenberg, "Jewish Educational Institutions," pp. 943, 946.]

16 Since the above was written, a fourth session was held in Chicago in November, 1947, at which the name of the Conference was changed to the American Jewish Assembly.

17 On the Jewish Occupational Council, see above p. 1309.

[18a Cf. Reich, op. cit.]

[19a Cf. Greenberg, op. cit., pp. 943-946; also cf. Davis, op. cit., passim.]

[20a On the growth of American Jewish scholarship cf. Davis, op. cit., pp. 395-397.]

21 Over $102,000,000 was actually raised. In 1947 the goal was set at $175,000,000. Over $125,000,000 was collected by the end of that year. In 1948 the goal has been set for $250,000,000. Of this amount the U.P.A. is listed for a larger proportion of the collections than was the case in any previous U.J.A. campaign.

BIBLIOGRAPHY

American Jewish Yearbook Annuals, especially sections entitled "Review of the Year—United States." Philadelphia, 1899-1947. Vols. 1-48.

BARON, SALO W., *The Jewish Community; its history and structure to the American revolution.* Philadelphia, 1942.

BERNHEIMER, CHARLES S., *The Russian Jew in the United States.* Philadelphia, 1905.

BOGEN, BORIS D., *Jewish Philanthropy; an exposition of principles and methods of Jewish social service in the United States.* New York, 1917.

Council Jewish Federations and Welfare Funds, *Notes and News,* Reports of Annual Assemblies, Sundry Studies and Surveys.

DRACHMAN, BERNARD, "The Jewish Communal Organization of Tomorrow," *Israel of Tomorrow,* ed. Leo Jung. New York, 1946. Chap. 18, pp. 401-407.

DUKER, ABRAHAM G., *Jewish Survival in the World Today.* New York, 1941.

———, "Structure of the Jewish Community," *The American Jew; a composite portrait,* ed. Oscar Janowsky. New York and London, 1942. Chap. 6, pp. 134-161.

ELBOGEN, ISMAR, *A Century of Jewish Life.* Philadelphia, 1945.

FRIEDMAN, ELISHA M., "America and Israel of Tomorrow," *Israel of Tomorrow,* ed. Leo Jung. New York, 1946. Chap. 19, pp. 411-465.

FRIEDMAN, LEE M., *Jewish Pioneers and Patriots.* Philadelphia, 1945.

GRINSTEIN, HYMAN B., *The Rise of the Jewish Community of New York, 1654-1860.* Philadelphia, 1945.

JANOWSKY, OSCAR I., (ed.), *The American Jew; a composite portrait.* New York and London, 1942.

JUNG, LEO, *Israel of Tomorrow.* New York, 1946.

KAPLAN, MORDECAI M., *Judaism as a Civilization.* New York, 1934.

———, *Judaism in Transition.* New York, 1936.

KARPF, MAURICE J., *Jewish Community Organization in the United States.* New York, 1938.

LEBESON, ANITA LIBMAN, *Jewish Pioneers in America* (1492-1848). New York, 1938.

National Conference of Jewish Social Service, *Annual Proceedings.* New York, 1929-1941.

———, *Jewish Social Service Quarterly.*

National Jewish Welfare Board, *The Jewish Center,* Annual reports, Sundry Studies and Surveys. New York.

PILCH, JUDAH, *Jewish Life in Our Times.* New York, 1943.

STEINBERG, MILTON, *A Partisan Guide to the Jewish Problem.* New York, 1945.

WIERNIK, PETER, *History of the Jews in America.* New York. 1931.

IV

THE JEWISH RELIGION

CHAPTER 35

THE JEWISH RELIGION: ITS BELIEFS AND PRACTICES

By Louis Finkelstein

INTRODUCTION

Judaism is a way of life that endeavors to transform virtually every human action into a means of communion with God. Through this communion with God, the Jew is enabled to make his contribution to the establishment of the Kingdom of God and the brotherhood of men on earth. So far as its adherents are concerned, Judaism seeks to extend the concept of right and wrong to every aspect of their behavior. Jewish rules of conduct apply not merely to worship, ceremonial, and justice between man and man, but also to such matters as philanthropy, personal friendships and kindnesses, intellectual pursuits, artistic creation, courtesy, the preservation of health, and the care of diet.[1]

So rigorous is this discipline, as ideally conceived in Jewish writings, that it may be compared to those specified for members of religious orders in other faiths. A casual conversation or a thoughtless remark may, for instance, be considered a grave violation of Jewish Law. It is forbidden, as a matter not merely of good form but of religious law, to use obscene language, to rouse a person to anger, or to display unusual ability in the presence of the handicapped. The ceremonial observances are equally detailed. The ceremonial Law expects each Jew to pray thrice every day, if possible at the synagogue; to recite a blessing before and after each meal; to thank God for any special pleasure, such as a curious sight, the perfume of a flower, or the receipt of good news; to wear a fringed garment about his body; to recite certain passages from Scripture each day; and to don *tephillin* (cubical receptacles containing certain biblical passages) during the morning prayers.

Decisions regarding right and wrong under given conditions are not left for the moment, but are formulated with great care in the vast literature created by the Jewish religious teachers. At the heart of this literature are the Hebrew Scriptures, usually described as the Old Testament, consisting of the Five Books of Moses (usually called the *Torah*), the Prophets and the Hagiographa. These works, particularly the Five Books of Moses, contain the prescriptions for human conduct composed under

Divine inspiration. The ultimate purpose of Jewish religious study is the application of the principles enunciated in the Scriptures, to cases and circumstances the principles do not explicitly cover.

Because Judaism is a way of life, no confession of faith can by itself make one a Jew. Belief in the dogmas of Judaism must be expressed in the acceptance of its discipline rather than in the repetition of a verbal formula. But no failure either to accept the beliefs of Judaism or to follow its prescriptions is sufficient to exclude from the fold a member of the Jewish faith. According to Jewish tradition, the covenant between God and Moses on Mt. Sinai included all those who were present and also all their descendants. This covenant was reaffirmed in the days of Ezra and Nehemiah, when the people together with their leaders made "a sure covenant to walk in God's law, which was given to Moses the servant of God, and to observe and do all the commandments of the Lord our Lord, and His ordinances and His statutes" (Neh. 10:30). To apply the words used by Scripture in another connection, this covenant has thus been made binding upon the Jews, "and upon their seed, and upon all such as joined themselves unto them" (Esth. 9:27). There is therefore no need for any ceremony to admit a Jewish child into the faith of Judaism. Born in a Jewish household, he becomes at once "a child of the covenant." The fact that the child has Jewish parents involves the assumption of the obligations that God has placed on these parents and their descendants.

This concept of the inheritance of religious traditions does not imply any sense of racial differentiation. The concept derives simply from the belief that a person may assume binding obligations not only for himself, but also for his descendants. Thus anyone who is converted to Judaism assumes the obligation to observe its discipline, and makes this obligation binding on his descendants forever, precisely as if he had been an Israelite, standing with Moses, before Mt. Sinai on the day of the Revelation.

The ancestry of the proselyte, and therefore his "race," are quite irrelevant. Whether he be of Arabic background like Queen Helene, or Roman like Aquila, or Khazar like the members of the south Russian kingdom that became converted to Judaism in the eighth century of the Common Era, or Norman like Obadiah, the well-known Crusader who became a proselyte, or Polish like the famous Count Valentine Potocki of the eighteenth century, his descendants, from the point of view of Judaism, would all be bound by his obligation to follow the laws and customs of Judaism.

On the other hand, in view of the Jewish attitude toward other monotheistic faiths, it is considered improper for a Jew to urge a member of another faith to become a Jew. Indeed, a person who desires to adopt Judaism must be told of all the difficulties inherent in affiliation with the faith. Only a person who persists in his desire to become a Jew, and demonstrates that his desire is based on no mundane motive, may be accepted into the Jewish fold.

Because of the special place that the home occupies in Judaism as a center of religious life and worship, almost co-ordinate with the synagogue itself, Judaism holds it essential that both parties to a Jewish marriage be members of the Jewish faith. There is, of course, no objection to marriage with a sincere convert to Judaism. But it is not possible for the home to function in the manner prescribed by Jewish law unless both husband and wife are of the Jewish faith.

In the case of a mixed marriage, the status of the children is determined by the faith of the mother, as the greatest influence in their lives. The children of a Christian mother are considered Christians; the children of a Jewish mother are considered Jews. The Jewish partner in such a mixed marriage is considered living in continual transgression of Jewish law, but remains, like those who deviate from the Law in other respects, within the fold of Judaism, entirely subject to the duties and obligations placed on other Jews.

While no one outside of the Jewish faith is bound by the rules of Jewish ceremonial discipline, Judaism draws a distinction between the adherents of monotheistic faiths—including Christianity and Islam, which are recognized as each making a distinctive contribution to the realization of the Kingdom of God on earth—and nonmonotheistic faiths. The various regulations Judaism, like early Christianity, established to prevent reversion to paganism, obviously have no application to the relationship between Jews and their neighbors in Christian and Mohammedan countries. A Jew may not enter a building dedicated to idol-worship even to protect himself from inclement weather; and of course he cannot participate in any festivity dedicated to any form of idol-worship.

These ceremonial rules are intended to register a protest against paganism; they do not place the pagan in any inferior position with regard to Jewish law or ethic. According to Philo and Josephus, it is a violation of Jewish law for a Jew to speak with disrespect of the gods of any people, for the verse "Thou shalt not revile God" (Ex. 22:27) is interpreted as applying to all gods. While this interpretation is not accepted in the Rabbinic tradition, it does express the spirit with which Judaism approaches all systems of belief, regardless of the extent of their difference from itself.

This spirit is expressed in the principle that every rule of moral conduct a Jew must observe toward another Jew applies also to relations with persons of other faiths. The laws of justice, kindness, and charity, as well as the obligation to visit the sick, bury the dead, support the needy, must be assumed for all people.

Like other religions, Judaism can be, and indeed has been, practiced under various forms of civil government: monarchical, semimonarchical, feudal, democratic, and totalitarian. Adherents of the Jewish faith, like those of other religions, regard themselves as citizens or subjects of their respective states. In every synagogue prayers are offered for the safety of the government of the country of its location; and in the ancient Temple of Jerusalem daily sacrifices were offered on behalf of the imperial Roman government, as long as Palestine remained under its dominion. This patriotic loyalty to the state has often persisted in the face of cruel persecution. The principle followed has been that formulated by the ancient teacher, Rabbi Haninah: "Pray for the welfare of the government; for without fear of the government, men would have swallowed each other up alive."

Despite this ability to adjust itself to the exigencies of any form of temporal government, Judaism, like other faiths derived from the Prophets, has always upheld the principles of the Fatherhood of God and the dignity and worth of man as the child and creature of God; and its ideals are more consistent with those of democracy than any other system of government.

The most vigorous and consistent effort to formulate the discipline of Judaism in terms of daily life was that made in ancient Palestine and Babylonia. The Palestinian schools devoted to this purpose were founded in the second century before the Common Era, and flourished in their original form for six centuries and in a somewhat altered form until the Crusades. The Babylonian schools were founded in the third century of the Common Era and ended the first and most significant phase of their activity about three hundred years later.[2a]

The rules of conduct worked out in the discussion of these academies form the substance of Jewish Law. In arriving at these precepts, the ancient teachers were guided by their desire to know the Will of God. So far as possible they sought to discover His will through an intensive study of the Scriptures. Where Scripture offered no clear guidance, they tried to ascertain His will by applying its general principles of moral right. In addition, they had a number of oral traditions, going back to antiquity, which they regarded as supplementary to the written Law, and equal to it in authority and inspiration.

The high purpose of the discussions made them of monumental importance to Judaism. As a result, they were committed to memory by eager and faithful disciples, until the memorized material grew to such proportions that it had to be reduced to writing. The work in which the discussions were thus preserved is known as the Talmud. As there were two groups of academies, differing slightly from each other in their interpretation of the Law, and widely in their manner of approach to the subject, we have two Talmudim, that of Palestine and that of Babylonia. Both are considered authoritative guides for Jewish Law. Where they disagree, the Babylonian Talmud is, for historical reasons, considered the more authoritative.

THE PLACE OF STUDY IN JUDAISM

It is impossible to understand Judaism without an appreciation of the place it assigns to the study and practice of the talmudic Law. Doing the Will of God is the primary spiritual concern of the Jew. Therefore, to this day, he must devote considerable time not merely to the mastery of the content of the Talmud, but also to training in its method of reasoning. The study of the Bible and the Talmud is thus far more than a pleasing intellectual exercise, and is itself a means of communion with God. According to some teachers, this study is the highest form of such communion imaginable.[3]

Because the preservation of the Divine will regarding human conduct is basic to all civilization, none of the commandments is more important than that of studying and teaching the Law. The most sacred object in Judaism is the Scroll containing the Five Books of Moses. Every synagogue must contain at least one copy of it. The Scroll must be placed in a separate Ark, before which burns an eternal light. The position of this Ark in the synagogue is in the direction of Jerusalem; everyone turns toward the Ark in prayer. When the Scroll is taken from the Ark for the purpose of reading, all those present must rise. No irreverent or profane action may be performed in a room which contains a Scroll, nor may a Scroll be moved from place to place except for the performance of religious rites. From time to time the Scroll must be examined to ascertain that its writing is intact.

The preparation of the Scroll is a task requiring much care, erudition, and labor. It is usually done by a professional copyist called a *sofer* (scribe). The text is written on sheets of parchment, especially prepared for the purpose. Only skins of animals permitted for food, in accordance with Lev. 11:1-9 and Deut. 14:3-9, are used. The whole work is then attached at the beginning and at the end to wooden rods, so that it can be rolled in the form of a scroll.

The ink used in writing must be black, and should be indelible. Before beginning to copy the text, the scribe must say, "I am about to write this book as a sacred Scroll of the Law." He must repeat a similar formula every time he is about to copy the Divine Name, saying, "I am writing this word as the sacred Name."

Like other Semitic languages, Hebrew requires only a consonantal text for reading: the vowels are omitted in classical texts. Hence the Scroll of the Five Books of Moses contains only the consonantal text. This text is fixed by tradition, almost to the last detail. Even such matters as division into paragraphs and sections, and the special size of certain letters, which are particularly large or particularly small, is determined. The texts of all the extant Scrolls are thus virtually identical. Any significant deviation from the traditional text makes a Scroll unfit for use, and must be corrected as soon as it is discovered. No decorations or illuminations are permitted in the Scrolls intended for the public service. Tradition prescribes, however, that certain poetic portions are to be written in verse form and that certain letters shall have little coronets adorning them.

No less important than this homage paid to the Scroll as symbol of the Law, is that paid to the living Law itself. Fully three-fourths of the Hebrew literature produced within the first nineteen centuries of the Common Era, is devoted to the elucidation of the Law. Many of the best minds in Judaism have been devoted to its study. Every parent is required to teach his child its basic elements. Its study is considered vital not only for the guidance it offers in the practice of Judaism, but for liberation from the burden of secular ambition and anxieties. The study of the Law is believed to be a foretaste of the immortal life, for the Sages of the Talmud believed that Paradise itself could offer men no nearer communion with God than the opportunity of discovering His will in the study of the Law.

The Talmud derives its authority from the position held by the ancient academies. The teachers of those academies, both of Babylonia and of Palestine, were considered the rightful successors of the older *Sanhedrin*, or Supreme Court, which before the destruction of Jerusalem (in the year 70 of the Common Era) was the arbiter of Jewish Law and custom. The Sanhedrin derived its authority from the statement in Deut. 17:8-13, that whenever a question of interpretation of the Law arises, it is to be finally decided by the Sages and priests in Jerusalem.

At the present time, the Jewish people have no living central authority comparable in status to the ancient Sanhedrin or the later academies. Therefore any decision regarding the Jewish religion must be based on the Talmud, as the final résumé of the teachings of those authorities when they existed. The right of an individual to decide questions of religious Law depends entirely on his knowledge of the Bible, the Talmud, and the later manuals based on them, and upon his fidelity to their teachings. Those who have acquired this knowledge are called *rabbis*. There is no sharp distinction in religious status between the rabbi and the layman in Judaism. The rabbi is simply a layman especially learned in Scripture and Talmud. Nor is there any hierarchical organization or government among the rabbis of the world. Yet some rabbis, by virtue of their special distinction in learning, by common consent come to be regarded as superior authorities on questions of Jewish Law. Difficult and complicated issues are referred to them for clarification.

To be recognized as a rabbi, a talmudic student customarily is ordained.

A Scroll in its Case with a Crown of the Law

This Scroll was made in Spain in the 17th century. The silver case of repoussé, embossed, pressed and cast work was made in Paris about 1860 by Maurice Mayer, court silversmith to Napoleon III.

Traditionally, the authority to act as rabbi may be conferred by any other rabbi. It is usual, however, for students at various theological schools to receive this authority from their teachers. In America, there are several rabbinical schools, each of which ordains its graduates in the manner in which degrees are conferred on graduates of other institutions of learning. At present (1948) the best known of these schools are as follows:

Hebrew Theological College, Chicago
Hebrew Union College, Cincinnati[4]
Jewish Institute of Religion, New York City
Jewish Theological Seminary of America, New York City
Rabbi Isaac Elchanan Theological Seminary, New York City[5a]

There is considerable variation among the interpretations of Judaism taught at these seminaries, and consequently there is a considerable difference in emphasis on the subjects included in their respective curricula. This has resulted from the fact that during the second half of the nineteenth century various groups of rabbis, primarily in Germany and America, claimed authority not merely to interpret but also to amend talmudic, and even biblical Law. These rabbis are known as Reform rabbis, and their congregations as Reform congregations. Of the rabbis who adhere to traditional Judaism, some reject any significant innovations from customary practice; these rabbis are called Orthodox. Others maintain that Jewish law is a living tradition, subject to change, but they insist that such changes must be made in accordance with traditional canons for the interpretation and development of Rabbinic law. These rabbis are usually called Conservative.[6a]

The differences between the various groups of American rabbis have not led to any sectarian schism. Although the difference in practice between the traditional and Reform groups is considerable, each accepts the other as being within the fold of Judaism. It is possible for them to do so, because of the principle that even an unobservant or a heretical Jew does not cease to be a member of the covenant made between God and Israel at the time of the Revelation. Only actual rejection of Judaism, by affiliation with another faith, is recognized as separating one from the Jewish community.[7] So long as a follower of the Jewish faith has not by overt act or word and of his own free will declared himself a member of another religion, other Jews are bound to regard him as one of their own faith, and to seek his return to its practice and beliefs.

The Place of Ethics in Judaism

The ceremonial discipline is considered obligatory only for members of the Jewish faith, but the ethical element in Judaism is universal in scope.[8a] The commandment against murder is explicitly stated in Scripture to have been revealed to Noah (Gen. 9:5); and therefore applies to all human-kind. By analogy, the commandments against theft, cruelty to animals, sexual license, blasphemy, idol-worship, and the violation of civil justice are considered to be universal. Those who observe these fundamental laws are considered "the righteous of the peoples of the world," who will par-take in the resurrection and in immortality.

One further distinction is made between the ethical and the ceremonial content of Judaism. When faced with the danger of death, one may violate any of the commandments, save only those against murder, sexual license, and idolatry. This rule does not apply in the event of a religious persecution. When a government undertakes to suppress the observance of Judaism, it becomes the duty of the Jew to submit to martyrdom rather than deviate from his faith in even a slight matter.

The duty of accepting martyrdom, either for the ethical Law in the normal course of events or for the whole of the Law in times of persecu-tion, is called *Kiddush ha-Shem* (sanctification of the Name of God). Any violation of this duty is called profanation of the Name of God, *Hillul ha-Shem*. These terms may also be applied to situations that do not call for martyrdom, but where it is possible to increase or lessen respect for religious faith through action. Anyone who through sacrifice and saint-liness brings others to more profound recognition of God "sanctifies" the Name of God. But anyone whose actions bring religion generally and Judaism in particular into disrespect is guilty of *Hillul ha-Shem*. Because of this principle, religious leaders are expected to be particularly careful of their ethical conduct, for even the slightest deviation from propriety on their part naturally casts aspersion on the whole faith. Similarly, any impropriety on the part of a Jew in his relations with members of other faiths tends to decrease respect for Judaism as a faith, and is therefore a "profanation of the Name of God."

The application of the ethical teachings of Judaism to every aspect of daily life has necessarily involved the creation and development of a system of civil law. Like contemporary Christians, the Jews of the talmudic period believed it wrong to resort to the pagan courts of their time for adjudication of civil differences. Not only did the Jewish conception of justice frequently differ from that of the pagans, but the pagan courts were often corrupt, and almost always cruel. The tradition opposing the use of civil courts for adjudication of civil disputes persisted during the Middle Ages. For many centuries secular courts were few and inaccessible, and even in later periods their judgments were generally considered unfair. Only with the enlightenment of the eighteenth and nineteenth century, and the disappearance of the Ghettos, have Jews become ac-customed to apply to secular courts of justice for settlement of litigation. However, it is a fundamental principle of talmudic Law that the civil law of a country is binding there, and a Jewish court would necessarily have to take cognizance of the civil law on any disputed point.

The necessity of dealing with civil litigation compelled the talmudic Sages and their medieval successors to give much attention to this aspect of the Jewish Law. Hence, about one-fourth of the Babylonian Talmud, and a proportionate share of later Rabbinic literature, is devoted to questions of civil law. The latest compilation of this law is to be found in the *Hoshen Mishpat*, the fourth volume of Rabbi Joseph Caro's famous code, the *Shulhan Aruk*.

The Jewish civil law is frequently applied even today in the adjudication of disputes arising among religious functionaries, and is sometimes used as a basis for arbitration agreements.

But the Jewish conception of justice transcends the realm of civil law. Justice includes all ethical conduct, as well as philanthropy. Indeed, the word for charity in Rabbinic Hebrew is *zedakah*, or righteousness. Under certain circumstances, talmudic Law actually permits courts to compel a man to do his duty by the community or by individuals, beyond the letter of the law.

As a rule, a Jew is expected to give between one-tenth and one-fifth of his income to charitable purposes. To give less than one-tenth is to fail in duty to the community; to give more than a fifth may involve injustice to his own immediate family. Beyond provision of material assistance for the needy and suffering lies the duty of encouraging them with personal attention and kind words, of recognizing them as personal friends, and above all enabling them to help themselves. In his Code, Maimonides recognizes eight types of philanthropy, arranged according to their merit, as follows: (1) helping the needy to be independent by providing opportunity for work; (2) giving charity to the poor in such a way that neither the donor nor the recipient knows the other; (3) giving charity in such a way that the donor can identify the recipient but the recipient cannot identify the donor; (4) giving in such a way that the recipient can identify the donor but the donor cannot identify the recipient; (5) giving in such a way that the donor and recipient know each other, provided the gift is made before it is requested; (6) giving after a request is made, provided the amount is sufficient to meet the need; (7) giving less than is needed, but with a kindly countenance; (8) giving less than is needed, and without a kindly countenance.[9a]

Judaism lays great stress on the importance of personal ethical relations between friends. The last of the Ten Commandments is a prohibition against "coveting" the blessings of a neighbor. Other regulations warn against talebearing, gossip, envy, and dislike of a neighbor. Any form of vengeance also is prohibited. If a person says to another, "Lend me your hatchet," and the second replies, "I will not lend you my hatchet today, because yesterday you refused to lend me your sickle," the second transgresses the commandment, "Thou shalt not take vengeance" (Lev. 19:18). If the second replies, "I will lend you my hatchet, despite the fact that yesterday you refused to lend me your sickle," he transgresses the second half of the verse, "nor bear any grudge." The importance of these commandments in Judaism is such that one of the most distinguished Jewish scholars of the eleventh century, Bahya ibn Pakudah, devoted a whole book to their analysis, the *Book of the Duties of the Heart*.[10a] In our own generation, the famous Rabbi Israel Meir Kahan (better known by the title of his book, *Chofetz Chayyim*, first published anonymously) devoted his life to warning against the transgression of these laws of ethical conduct. During the nineteenth century, there developed under the influence of Rabbi Israel Salanter (1810-1883) a whole group of students who refrained from conversation over long periods, in order to discipline themselves against the sin of "evil speech."

In accordance with the precept of Lev. 19:17, Judaism considers every member of the faith responsible for the moral conduct of those neighbors over whom he is able to exert influence. To see injustice done without protesting against it is to participate in the injustice. To provoke a man to anger is to partake of the sin of unjust anger. To permit an opposing litigant to take a false oath is to share in the transgression of perjury; just as to listen to blasphemy, gossip, or talebearing is to be a party to them. The concept is summarized in the teaching of Rabbi Jacob that "a person, on whose account God has to inflict punishment on another, will not be admitted into the presence of God" (*Shabbat* 149b). The underlying principle of this teaching is the doctrine that a victim of injustice falls short of the ideal of Judaism to the extent that he fails to obtain Divine forgiveness for the person who acted unjustly toward him.

The public confession of sins prescribed for the Day of Atonement reflects this consciousness that every member of the community is to some extent responsible for the sins of every other member. The confession lists not only the sins the average man is liable to commit through oversight, but also such sins as theft, unchastity and rendering false judgment, of which the vast majority are usually innocent.

THE BASIC CONCEPTS OF JUDAISM

The central doctrine of Judaism is the belief in the One God, the Father of all mankind. The first Hebrew words a Jewish child learns are the confession of faith contained in the verse "Hear, O Israel, the Lord is our God, the Lord is One," and every believing Jew hopes that as he approaches his end in the fullness of time he will be sufficiently conscious to repeat this same confession. This monotheistic belief is subject to no qualification or compromise.

We owe this monotheism to some of the earliest teachers of Israel who, having discovered that the Lord is One and His name One, devoted their lives to the propagation of this teaching. But the prophets proceeded a step further. To whom shall you compare God, they exclaimed, and what manner of likeness shall you set up alongside Him? This served as a cue to sages and philosophers who pondered over the meaning of God. Through their insight the Jew learned that at most every description of God was a metaphor, due to the limited idiom of man. God is not to be compressed into physical form (He is incorporeal), He is not subject to the boundaries of time, of beginning and end (He is eternal), He cannot be confined by space (He is omnipresent). As one of the talmudic Sages put it, "In God is the universe fixed, not He in it."

True enough, not only the simple but the learned, not only the average but the saintly, have described God as wise, just, long-suffering, merciful; and, depending on the occasion, have appealed to Him because pre-eminently these attributes are His. When our motives are questioned we call upon Him for support, for in His wisdom He knows the deepest stirrings of our hearts. When we suffer, we invoke His justice. When in haste we sin, we plead for sufferance on His part. Where we have been exacting or rebellious, we cry for His mercy. What, however, does such language suggest? That man in his dependence and helplessness employs as best he may, to the stretching point if necessary, the sounds and vocabulary at his disposal. These terms, and others like them, are the finest human beings have developed. But even at their finest they will not do; they cannot be precise; they are a stammering to which we have simply grown accustomed. God, the nature of God, rises higher than our discourse. As He is the source of wisdom, we call Him wise; as He is the fullness of mercy, we call Him merciful. But the words fall short of His being.

Put thus, monotheism may strike us with the chill of an intellectual premise, necessary for an adequate interpretation of the universe but inaccessible to man, who is matter, transient and earth-bound. Indeed, these are the qualities that forever interfere with our ambition to understand the meaning of God in full. Fragments, approximations of this understanding, have been the privilege of the saintly in every age. Yet the more they beheld the more they saw that their ignorance was endless. It was as though one filled his cup once and again and once more and still again with water from the ocean; the sea was not diminished.

God's uniqueness and transcendence, however, have not discouraged the Jew from the effort to understand Him and cleave to His ways, for Judaism has also told him that the Lord is near unto them that call upon Him, to all that call upon Him in truth, God's proximity and majesty form a speculative paradox only if they are regarded as categories unrelated to man's own awareness of his shortcomings, to his perennial urge to supersede his *status quo* of deed and thought. To the self-satisfied, it is probably true, God is not nigh; otherwise, how could such a one be con tent? His charity is niggardly, his justice expedient, his patience mannered, when weighed against Him Whose qualities are a contradiction of the imperfect.

The very surpassing nature of God has taught the Jew that God is not only to be revered, but loved, that the Creator of the heavens and earth, and all that in them is, is also his Rock, his Father, his Shepherd, his Beloved. And in order to escape being remote from God he utilizes every phenomenon and occasion to remind him of the Creator and Father of all. This his prayers accomplish for him. A new morning begins; God has created this light, his morning liturgy reminds him. An evening arrives; and the prayers force upon him the realization that God's activity is once more manifest. For every occasion, experience, event, the Rabbis declared, man ought to pray. The sight of the rainbow, the new moon, a shooting star, the sea, a wise man; deliverance from peril; a visit to historic scenes, particularly those related to biblical history; good fortune, tragedy—each has its proper blessing, and these Rabbinic formulations are the Jew's memoranda. Nothing happens but that his thoughts are at once directed to God. Nothing is taken for granted, nothing is ordinary. Everything is alive with the reality of God, at once man's support and dwelling on high.

Man differs from all other creatures in that he is made "in the image of God." Because Judaism denies that God has any physical form, the image of God in this passage refers to man's mind, unduplicated self, individuality. Created in the image of God, all persons must be accorded the respect due to this dignity which the Divine grace has accorded them. There can, therefore, be no differentiation between various human personalities in their status before God. From the time when the prophet Amos declared, "Are ye not as the children of Ethiopians unto Me, O children of Israel" (9:7), until this day, Jewish religious teachers have continuously emphasized this doctrine. To Ben Azzai, the great teacher of the second century, the most inclusive principle of the whole Law is to be found in the verse "In the day that God created man, in the likeness of God created man, in the likeness of God made He him, male and female created He them" (Gen. 5:1-2). He considered this verse uniquely important because it expresses unequivocally the equality and dignity of all human beings, irrespective of nationality, sex, color, creed, or genealogical origin.

The discovery of self, of that element in each of us which is absolutely and unmitigatedly singular, is undated, never complete, and the most momentous experience of life. There are men who may recall that as children they never grasped or gave thought to phenomena of their individuality. Who can, however, recall the instant when that knowledge first pressed itself upon him? Dates, let us grant, are sometimes dispensable, and it may not be necessary to recall that exact instant. It is enough that the mature person recognizes the reality of that self. But even in maturity the recognition is only partial, not altogether clear. Though we find it impossible to picture ourselves disembodied, we know that our self is more than our body. That self is not merely our rational being, for this often may withdraw or fail—in sleep or in delirium—while the self, the "I," has not vanished. Yet awareness of our individuality, incomplete as that awareness may be, constitutes the final appeal and justification for our value. It cannot be exchanged.

Again, it is the prophets of Israel whom we must thank for the most vigorous emphasis on the supreme value of each soul *qua* its individuality. They, not alone but most clearly, saw that the classification of men according to color, the accident of ancestry or purely material condition was never more than secondary; and they, too, perceived that the relation of body to self was not definitive and exclusive.

To the prophets and later the Rabbis, the self therefore appeared so precious that they could not believe that it was coterminous with body. Man's body cannot be proxy for his personality; how then can the body determine life span? Even as self is something more than body, so its survival need not depend on body. Bearing in himself the image of God, man is also—Jewish doctrine insists—endowed with immortality. As conceived by most Jewish theologians, immortality implies the endless persistence of the human personality. This personality is believed to find its consummate expression in the ultimate reunion with God, and to lose all concern with the divisions, rivalries and antagonisms characteristic of physical life.

Attainment of this endless communion with God is the highest reward reserved for man, and its loss the greatest punishment he can suffer. The evil of wickedness consists, therefore, not merely in the harm it does a man in his mundane life, but in the fact that it deprives him of immortal existence. There are many Rabbinic authorities who believe, as do members of other faiths, that certain sinful people may attain immortal life, after having undergone temporary suffering after death. It is held in the Talmud that "the punishment of the wicked in Gehenna does not exceed twelve months." According to Maimonides, this punishment consists of the keen awareness by the soul of its failure to utilize its opportunities for the service of God, and is analogous to the shame sometimes felt by adults for unwise and unkind acts in their youth. We might almost say, the "righteous" is he who has refined and perfected his own self (and obviously other selves along with his own) so that there is an entity capable of reuniting with God; there is the "reward." The "wicked" is he who has neglected and demolished his self so that nothing survives the death of his body and there is an emptiness incapable of reunion with anything; God abhors a vacuum, and there is the "punishment." Be that as it may, a fundamental principle in Judaism, formulated as an ethical norm by Antigonus of Socho, one of the founders of Rabbinic Judaism, declares that men "should not be as servants, who serve their Master with the expectation of receiving reward, but rather as servants who serve their Master, without expectation of receiving reward." In other words, the belief in immortal life is accepted as a metaphysical and theological truth. But it is not to be considered a motive for proper conduct. Proper conduct should be based simply on love of God and the desire to see His will performed in the world.

That the principle of "reward and punishment" cannot be translated into commercial or nursery terms was already demonstrated by the superb author of Job. In what sense the principle is to be understood remains a mystery, and man repeatedly collides with righteous who suffer and wicked who prosper. Unlike Job, most of us are not even granted the dramatic rejoinder that silences without answering all protest. But in some measure we escape utter confusion if we perceive that "reward" and "punishment" are terms often equatable with *result*. Rebellion against the Will of God, contempt for moral law, perversion of personality, cannot have peace, friendship or love as a consequence. These are the harvest, if harvest there is to be, of submission to God's will, obedience to the demands of morality and integrity. The lines of the philosopher-poet Rab Saadia (882-942 c.e.) express this thought beautifully: "Not Thee, O Lord, have I injured, but myself. For if man sin, wherein doth that affect Thee? And if his transgressions be multiplied, how doth that harm Thee? But alas for the men who have sinned against Thee, and alas for their souls, for they have brought evil on themselves."

The mystery of reward and punishment remains a mystery; its truth is but too often vindicated; and for all that Judaism insists that conduct must be motivated by that love of God the fullest satisfaction of which is found when His will is done. Many Rabbinic Sages endured personal affliction without murmur, but suffered anguish at the frustration of God's Will in the world through human sin and waywardness.

Because of God's love for men, He has made it possible for them to escape some of the consequences of error and sinful conduct. Most errors can be rectified through earnest repentance. Indeed, repentance sometimes makes it possible for the experience of error itself to become a virtue. The fact that a person has not lived in accordance with the discipline of religion does not, therefore, condemn him to suffering. It merely places on him the obligation to repent of his error and return to God. In this return to God he obtains the same measure of happiness awarded to the "righteous." Repentance, however, cannot always be achieved. If a man injures his neighbor, he will not be able to repent completely or win peace of mind until he has won the forgiveness of his neighbor. Rulers who mislead their people, causing whole nations and races to indulge in wrongdoing, and to that extent deflecting the development of human civilization, cannot repent.

To be effective, repentance must be more than sorrow or remorse; it must include a determination never again to commit the transgression, and a rearrangement of one's way of life so as to avoid the temptation to fall into the transgression. Thus, for example, if a person has been guilty of theft, repentance requires not merely restitution of the stolen article and a determination never to steal again, but also a study of the motives that led to the theft, and an endeavor to prevent them from being effective in the future.

One of the most important stimulants to the good life is the companionship of well chosen friends. It is a duty to select friends with a view to their probable influence on character. But the greatest possible deterrent from evil deeds or evil thoughts, the greatest stimulant to good, is the study of the Torah. It removes from man the temptation to infringe on the rights of others or the commandments of God. "He who faces temptation should diligently study Torah."

It is through the Law, the prophets, and the Holy Writings that God's Will was revealed to man. Literary excellence and wisdom do not belong to Scripture alone and the riches, artistic or intellectual or scientific, available in the world's classics are not to be minimized without grave sacrifice to civilization. But there is an excellence to Scripture which these other works do not share, for in Scripture came the expression of those truths whose nature has and will admit further elucidations, finer expansion, and interpretation—but never displacement. "It hath been told thee, O man, what the Lord doth require of thee: but to do justly, love mercy, and walk humbly with thy God." Time and discipline may teach us profound meanings of these ideals, meanings perhaps unknown to our predecessors. Dynamically, we may discover implications to these commandments which are thus far unsuspected. But that justice, mercy, humility, and other ideals fixed for man's destiny by Scripture are makeshift standards or temporary hypotheses, Judaism has never been even tempted to accept. There is a finality to these ideals, which does not mean that we know everything there is to know; what it does mean is that these ideals do represent the ends of being and ideal grace and that their removal from life is nothing less than blasphemy. Man is eternally obliged to discover fresh possibilities inherent in these ideals, to extend their applicability, and to be their recurrent expositor.

That is why, though other writings may share with Scripture properties of merit in one thing or another, Scripture is unique in its holiness. And that is why works devoted to the analysis and interpretation of Scripture, to its greater fulfillment, that were developed in its spirit, share in a degree its sacredness. Through the insight of the Talmud—the discussions of Scripture in the Palestinian and Babylonian academies, the commentaries on the Talmud, the codes based on these, and all instruction clarifying Scripture—we see light.

This is what Jews mean when they say the Law is immutable. The statement is not intended as a denial of progressive knowledge or illumination, or to affirm that everything had been discovered in antiquity. Much indeed is new under the sun. But the ultimate imperatives of the Holy Scriptures are absolute. They are not prudential or conditional.

The people to whom this revelation was made was the people of Israel, of which only a remnant now survives, known as the Jewish people. The fact that the people of Israel received the Law and heard the prophets does not, according to Jewish teaching, endow them with any exclusive privileges. But it does place upon them special responsibilities. "You only have I known of all the families of the earth," the first literary prophet (Amos) exclaimed, "therefore I shall visit all your iniquities upon you." These responsibilities—to observe the Law, to study it, to explain it, and to be its unwavering exponents—are expressed in the term "The Chosen People." For similar reasons the Hebrew language, in which these permanent ideals were articulated and recorded, is the holy language; and Palestine, the country where the prophets lived and whence spring so many discoveries of these extraordinary men, is the Holy Land.

Virtually every prophet in Scripture has predicted that in the fullness of time man will gain a more complete understanding of God and a reign of justice and peace on earth will be inaugurated. According to the interpretation of this prophecy in the Talmud and later writers, this age of universal peace will be established by a great, but humble teacher of the lineage of David: the Messiah. Reform and many Conservative Jews expect that the Messianic age will come about through the gradual enlightenment of men and through the work of many thinkers and teachers. All agree that the age will be one of profound and universal faith in God, recognition of human brotherhood, and an unprecedented knowledge of the universe. There will be no discrimination between persons because of sex, origin, faith, occupation, nationality, or any other reason. The evils of human origin will have been overcome; those inherent in nature will be mitigated through further knowledge and increased piety. In this world of brotherly love there will be no room for pride in achievement, nor for memories of past bitterness and oppression.

The prophetic tradition, originating in the teachings of Moses, may be considered a continuous endeavor, looking to the fulfillment of this vision. Together with other faiths derived from Scripture, Judaism has a unique contribution to make to the enlightenment of the world. Its special gift consists, in part, in the preservation of the Hebrew language and the original form of the Hebrew Scriptures, as well as in the transmission unchanged of the ethical ceremonial and intellectual disciplines that were native to the prophets and the later Sages.

The increased hatreds and persecution of our day do not weaken the Jew's faith in God and in His prophets, or his conviction that ultimately the age of universal human brotherhood will be established on earth. In the most trying moments of his own and world history, the Jew repeats with assurance the ancient declaration: "Thou are faithful, O Lord our God, and Thy words are faithful. And not one word of Thine shall ultimately remain unfulfilled; for Thou art a great, holy, Divine King."

There is a wide variety of interpretation among Rabbinical scholars, both ancient and modern, with regard to the concepts of Judaism. In some instances, the differences of interpretation are so great that it is difficult to speak of a concept as being basically or universally Jewish or Rabbinic. There are thus a number of concepts, each having its own limited authority and following.

This applies also to a degree to the fundamental beliefs which have been brought together in the best known Jewish creed, that of Maimonides. According to this creed, there are thirteen basic dogmas in Judaism. They are as follows:

1. The belief in God's existence.
2. The belief in His unity.
3. The belief in His incorporeality.
4. The belief in His timelessness.
5. The belief that He is approachable through prayer.
6. The belief in prophecy.
7. The belief in the superiority of Moses to all other prophets.
8. The belief in the revelation of the Law, and that the Law as contained in the Pentateuch is that revealed to Moses.
9. The belief in the immutability of the Law.
10. The belief in Divine providence.
11. The belief in Divine justice.
12. The belief in the coming of the Messiah.
13. The belief in the resurrection and human immortality.

This creed has been incorporated in the Jewish liturgy, in the famous hymn *Yigdal*. Nevertheless, various distinguished authorities, including such teachers as Hasdai Crescas[11a] and Joseph Albo, rejected the classification of the doctrines, and even denied the basic character of some of the doctrines themselves. Because of this divergence of opinion among the most eminent authorities on the subject, traditional Judaism cannot be described as having a universally accepted creed or formulation of its dogmas. This has led to the assertion that "Judaism has no dogmas." The assertion is true only to the extent already indicated. On the other hand, as Rabbi Albo pointed out, the requirement that Jews observe the discipline of the Law implies the belief in God, in Revelation, and in Divine providence.

Orthodox and Conservative Jews have in general followed the example of the ancient and medieval teachers in avoiding any effort to formulate a generally adopted Jewish creed, beyond the informal consensus of opinion found in traditional writings. As a result, there is still wide latitude of interpretation of Judaism among both Orthodox and Conservative Jews.

Reform Jews have tried to formulate a definite platform outlining the principles on which they agree, and which they believe basic to Judaism. The most recent platform is that adopted at a meeting of the Central Conference of American Rabbis (the organization of American Reform rabbis) in 1937. In this platform no effort is made to indicate the way Reform Judaism deviates from the Orthodox or Conservative interpretation of Judaism. And, indeed, the platform does not contain much to which Orthodox and Conservative groups can take exception. It is rather in its implications than by its direct statements that it deviates from tradition.

Known as the Columbus Platform from the city in which the meeting was held, the statement reads as follows:

In view of the changes that have taken place in the modern world and the consequent need of stating anew the teachings of Reform Judaism, the Central Conference of American Rabbis makes the following declaration of principles. It presents them not as a fixed creed but as a guide for the progressive elements of Jewry.

I. Judaism and Its Foundations.

1. NATURE OF JUDAISM. Judaism is the historical religious experience of the Jewish people. Though growing out of Jewish life, its message is universal, aiming at the union and perfection of mankind under the sovereignty of God. Reform Judaism recognizes the principle of progressive development in religion and consciously applies this principle to spiritual as well as to cultural and social life.

Judaism welcomes all truth, whether written in the pages of Scripture or deciphered from the records of nature. The new discoveries of science, while replacing the older scientific views underlying our sacred literature, do not conflict with the essential spirit of religion as manifested in the consecration of man's will, heart and mind to the service of God and of humanity.

2. GOD. The heart of Judaism and its chief contribution to religion is the doctrine of the One, living God, Who rules the world through law and love. In Him all existence has its creative source and mankind its ideal of conduct. Though transcending time and space, He is the in-dwelling Presence of the world. We worship Him as the Lord of the universe and as our merciful Father.

3. MAN. Judaism affirms that man is created in the Divine image. His spirit is immortal. He is an active co-worker with God. As a child of God, he is endowed with moral freedom and is charged with the responsibility of overcoming evil and striving after ideal ends.

4. TORAH. God reveals Himself not only in the majesty, beauty and orderliness of nature, but also in the vision and moral striving of the human spirit. Revelation is a continuous process, confined to no one group and to no one age. Yet the people of Israel, through its prophets and sages, achieved unique insight in the realm of religious truth. The Torah, both written and oral, enshrines Israel's ever-growing consciousness of God and of the moral law. It preserves the historical precedents, sanctions and norms of Jewish life, and seeks to mold it in the patterns of goodness and of holiness. Being products of historical processes, certain of its laws have lost their binding force with the passing of the conditions that called them forth. But as a depository of permanent spiritual ideals, the Torah remains the dynamic source of the life of Israel. Each age has the obligation to adapt the teachings of the Torah to its basic needs in consonance with the genius of Judaism.

5. ISRAEL. Judaism is the soul of which Israel is the body. Living in all parts of the world, Israel has been held together by the ties of common history, and above all, by the heritage of faith. Though we recognize in the group loyalty of Jews who have become estranged from our religious tradition, a bond which still unites them with us, we maintain that it is by its religion and for its religion that the Jewish people has lived. The non-Jew who accepts our faith is welcomed as a full member of the Jewish community.

In all lands where our people live, they assume and seek to share loyally the full duties and responsibilities of citizenship and to create seats of Jewish knowledge and religion. In the rehabilitation of Palestine, the land hallowed by memories and hopes, we behold the promise of renewed life for many of our brethren. We affirm the obligation of all Jewry to aid in its upbuilding as a Jewish homeland by endeavoring to make it not only a haven of refuge for the oppressed but also a center of Jewish culture and spiritual life.

Throughout the ages it has been Israel's mission to witness to the Divine in the face of every form of paganism and materialism. We regard it as our historic task to co-operate with all men in the establishment of the kingdom of God, of universal brotherhood, justice, truth and peace on earth. This is our Messianic goal.

II. ETHICS.

6. ETHICS AND RELIGION. In Judaism religion and morality blend into an indissoluble unity. Seeking God means to strive after holiness, righteousness and goodness. The love of God is incomplete without the love of one's fellowmen. Judaism emphasizes the kinship of the human race, the sanctity and worth of human life and personality and the right of the individual to freedom and to the pursuit of his chosen vocation. Justice to all, irrespective of race, sect or class is the inalienable right and the inescapable obligation of all. The state and organized government exist in order to further these ends.

7. SOCIAL JUSTICE. Judaism seeks the attainment of a just society by the application of its teachings to the economic order, to industry and commerce, and to national and international affairs. It aims at the elimination of man-made misery and suffering, of poverty and degradation, of tyranny and slavery, of social inequality and prejudice, of ill-will and strife. It advocates the promotion of harmonious relations between warring classes on the basis of equity and justice, and the creation of conditions under which human personality may flourish. It pleads for the safeguarding of childhood against exploitation. It champions the cause of all who work and of their right to an adequate standard of living, as prior to the rights of property. Judaism emphasizes the duty of charity, and strives for a social order which will protect men against the material disabilities of old age, sickness and unemployment.

8. PEACE. Judaism, from the days of the prophets, has proclaimed to mankind the ideal of universal peace. The spiritual and physical disarmament of all nations has been one of its essential teachings. It abhors all violence and relies upon moral education, love and sympathy to secure human progress. It regards justice as the foundation of the well-being of nations and the condition of enduring peace. It urges organized international action for disarmament, collective security and world peace.

III. RELIGIOUS PRACTICE.

9. THE RELIGIOUS LIFE. Jewish life is marked by consecration to these ideals of Judaism. It calls for faithful participation in the life of the Jewish community as it finds expression in home, synagogue and school and in all other agencies that enrich Jewish life and promote its welfare.

The Home has been and must continue to be a stronghold of Jewish life, hallowed by the spirit of love and reverence, by moral discipline and religious observance and worship.

The Synagogue is the oldest and most democratic institution in Jewish life. It is the prime communal agency by which Judaism is fostered and preserved. It links the Jews of each community and unites them with all Israel.

The perpetuation of Judaism as a living force depends upon religious knowledge and upon the education of each new generation in our rich cultural and spiritual heritage.

Prayer is the voice of religion, the language of faith and aspiration. It directs man's heart and mind Godward, voices the needs and hopes of the community, and reaches out after goals which invest life with supreme value. To deepen the spiritual life of our people, we must cultivate the traditional habit of communion with God through prayer in both home and synagogue.

Judaism as a way of life requires in addition to its moral and spiritual demands, the preservation of the Sabbath, festivals and Holy Days, the retention and development of such customs, symbols and ceremonies as possess inspirational value, the cultivation of distinctive forms of religious art and music and the use of Hebrew, together with the vernacular, in our worship and instruction.

These timeless aims and ideals of our faith we present anew to a confused and troubled world. We call upon our fellow Jews to rededicate themselves to them, and, in harmony with all men, hopefully and courageously to continue Israel's eternal quest after God and His kingdom.

None of the basic doctrines of Judaism deals expressly with the teachings, principles or leading personalities of the younger religions derived from it. As Judaism antedates the origin of both Christianity and Mohammedanism, its views regarding both faiths are simply negative: it has not accepted their teachings. This attitude does not, however, prevent Judaism from endeavoring to appraise the significance and value of other faiths as spiritual and moral phenomena. Rabbi Jacob Emden (1697-1776), one of the foremost teachers in the history of Judaism, summarized the general Jewish view regarding Christianity in the following words:

It is, therefore, a customary observation with me that the man of Nazareth wrought a double kindness to the world: On the one hand he fully supported the Torah of Moses, as already shown, for not one of our Sages spoke more fervently about the eternal duty to fulfill the Law. On the other hand he brought much good to the Gentiles (if only they do not overturn his noble intention for them, as certain stupid people, who did not grasp the ultimate purpose of the New Testament have done; in fact, just recently I saw a book from the press whose author did not know himself what he had written; because, had he known what he had written, then his silence would have been more becoming than his speaking, and he would not have wasted his money nor spoiled the paper and the ink uselessly; just as among us are to be found stupid scholars who know not between their right hand and their left in the written, nor in the oral law, but deceive the world with a tongue that speaks arrogantly; but there are highly educated men of intelligence among the Christians, even as there are among the students of our Torah a few outstanding individuals, men of lofty erudition). For he (the man of Nazareth) forbade idol-worship and removed the image-deities, and he held the people responsible for the seven commandments, lest they be like the animals of the field; he sought to perfect them with ethical qualities that are much more rigorous even than those of the Law of Moses (as is well known), a policy that was surely just for its own sake, since that is the most direct way to acquire good traits . . .[12]

None of the articles of faith in the creed of Maimonides deals with the holiness of Jerusalem, as the Holy City, or Palestine; yet the concept that Jerusalem, as the Holy City, and Palestine, as the Holy Land, have a special relation to the Jews and its religion is fundamental to all Judaism. Every service contains a petition for the welfare of the Holy City and the Holy Land, and it is a basic principle in Judaism that to provide for the settlement of Palestine is to fulfill one of the biblical commandments. A Jew seeing a Palestinian city in ruins must recite the benediction of bereave-

ment, for every member of the Jewish faith is expected to regard the
desolation of the Holy Land as a personal loss.

In the course of the centuries since the destruction of the Jewish community of Palestine, many efforts have been made to resettle considerable
numbers of Jews there, to reclaim its arable land, and to restore some of
its ancient forests. Within recent decades, the increased persecution of the
Jews in certain countries made the resettlement of Palestine a matter of
practical importance, as well as religious significance. The difficulty encountered in observing certain aspects of Judaism in other countries has
also stimulated many to return to Palestine. As a result, there has developed in the Holy Land a community numbering about 750,000 Jews
at the present time (1948).

In this restored Palestinian community, Hebrew has once more become
a spoken language. Hebrew literature flourishes; there has been a rapid
development of Hebrew poetry and prose, a greatly stimulated interest
in the study of the Holy Scriptures, the Talmud, and later Jewish literature. A considerable portion of the new settlers has devoted itself to agricultural pursuits and lives in "colonies." Many of these are situated in
lands which have been reclaimed from the pestilential marshes that covered
them after the Arabic conquest, and perhaps for generations before.

In 1917 the British government issued its famous Balfour. Declaration,
stating that "His Majesty's Government view with favor the establishment
in Palestine of a national home for the Jewish people." This Declaration
was subsequently incorporated into the mandate for Palestine, given by the
League of Nations to Great Britain. Under the terms of this mandate, the
Jewish community in Palestine enjoyed a certain degree of autonomy,
enabling it to regulate in part its own educational system, as well as to
administer certain aspects of talmudic civil law. One of the results of the
development of the new settlement in Palestine was the creation of the
Hebrew University in Jerusalem in which the language of instruction is
Hebrew.

The sporadic efforts at a renascence of Hebrew as a living tongue, which
had been made in different parts of the world during the past century, have
received a great impetus from the developments in the Holy Land. At the
present time, Hebrew is taught as a spoken language in a considerable
number of Jewish communities in all parts of the world.

The group among the Jews who have been most active in the development of Palestinian life are called Zionists. Among the Zionists, those who
are especially interested in re-establishing Palestine as a center of Jewish
religious life are called the *Mizrachi* ("of the East"). Besides organized
Zionists, there are Jews who are convinced that the development of a
flourishing Jewish community in Palestine might become an important
contribution to the development of human life. These men point, for

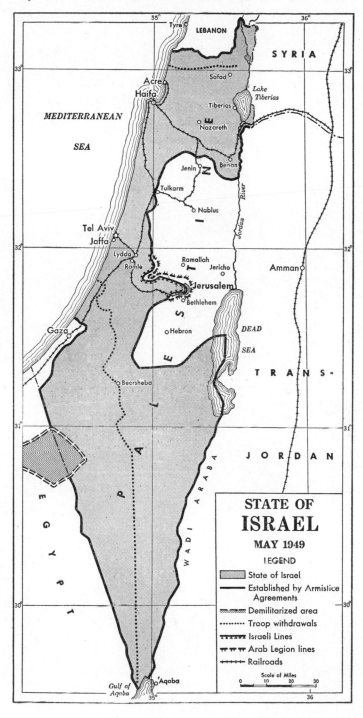

STATE OF
ISRAEL
MAY 1949

LEGEND

State of Israel

Established by Armistice
Agreements

Demilitarized area

Troop withdrawals

Israeli Lines

Arab Legion lines

Railroads

Scale of Miles

0   10   20   30

example, to the interesting manner in which men and women trained in European university life have returned to the simple life of agricultural settlements, finding full satisfaction in the sense of creation this return has given them. Some of the experiments in communal life now being conducted in Palestine may have significance for other parts of the world.

The complexity of modern life persuaded a considerable number of Zionists that the future of the Palestinian community and its full usefulness to the development of civilization would be impeded unless that community had self-government. Through a vote of the United Nations, November 29, 1947, it was agreed that Palestine should be partitioned in such a way as to create in the predominantly Jewish section an independent republic; leaving Jerusalem and its immediate environs as an international enclave, under the immediate rule of the United Nations itself, and the rest of Palestine as a predominantly Arabic, Moslem state. The Negeb, the desert region extending into the peninsula of Suez, was added to the Jewish section. At the termination of the British mandate over Palestine, on May 15, 1948, the leaders of the Jewish community there announced the establishment of the Republic of Israel in the territory assigned to it by the act of the United Nations of November 29, 1947. The United States, Russia and other governments granted the new republic recognition as a *de facto* government.

The problems of the new republic, political, economic and spiritual, are enormous. As an independent state, it claims the political allegiance only of its own nationals and inhabitants. Yet as the first state in almost two thousand years in which the majority of the population are members of the Jewish faith, in which the Jewish Sabbath is a national holiday, and the Hebrew language the official tongue, its establishment clearly opens a new chapter in the history of Judaism as well as that of the Jews. How the theoretical discussions of human relations in the Talmud and the medieval Jewish writings will be translated into concrete policies, to what extent the solution of the internal and external problems of the Republic of Israel will be affected by the tradition in which it has so many roots, whether the civilization fostered by the state of Israel will in any wise differ in emphasis from that of purely secular countries, how far the influence of the very soil of the Holy Land will determine the character of the community that is now to be self-governing upon it, are issues arousing today (June 8, 1948) violent differences of opinion.

ELEMENTS OF UNITY AND DISUNITY IN JUDAISM

From what has been said, it is clear that Judaism is not a unit in any organizational or institutionalized form. There is no person or group of persons to whom the Jewish people everywhere owe obedience, or whose views must be accepted by all Jews as authoritative and binding. The principle set down in Deut. 17, ff., making the Sanhedrin at the Temple in Jerusalem the final authority in the interpretation of Jewish Law, ceased to be effective when the Temple was destroyed by the Romans in the year 70. Every effort since that time to re-establish some center of authority has failed. At times local groups and even countrywide communities have agreed to recognize rabbinic or lay councils or individuals as their guides. During some periods, scholars and groups of scholars have been accepted over far wider areas. The views of the Geonim (the heads of the Babylonian academies from the seventh to the eleventh century c.e.) were considered binding on most Jewish communities of the Diaspora during that period. Ashkenazic Jews, in general, still follow the ordinances established by Rabbenu Gershom, the Light of the Exile, in the eleventh century, and by "the communities" of the Rhineland in succeeding centuries. Toward the end of the nineteenth century, Rabbi Isaac Elhanan Spektor, the Rabbi of Kowno, won recognition first as the leading guide in Jewish Law in his own country of Lithuania, and then throughout Russia and a large part of the Western world.

While there is thus no central Jewish religious organization, there have been various attempts to create worldwide organizations of Jews for special purposes. The most effective of these was the World Zionist Organization, which was expanded in 1929 through the addition of Jewish non-Zionists, and became the Jewish Agency for Palestine. But even the Jewish Agency did not include representatives of all Jewry, and claimed authority to act on behalf of the Jewish people only in connection with the establishment of a Jewish community and state in Palestine.

Organizations like the American Jewish Committee, the Order B'nai B'rith, the American Jewish Congress (part of the World Jewish Congress) and similar agencies in lands other than America, have arisen to make articulate special requests and wants of the Jewish community. The American Jewish Joint Distribution Committee has become a nationwide effort to provide assistance to Jews in distress abroad. The National Council of Federations and Welfare Funds represents virtually every large fund-raising committee in the cities of the United States outside New York and Chicago, and has been constituted by philanthropic agencies throughout the country for mutual discussion of joint problems.

But Judaism seems to resist organization as a denominational group, and preserves the independence of its many diverse elements, despite the common bond of tradition and history. It does not seem likely that in any foreseeable time, any organization will be established approaching the strength and comprehensiveness of Judaism in the times of the Temple. Yet the ties of history make for consciousness of a *Keneset Yisrael* (the congregation of Israel) which Solomon Schechter translated into "Catholic

Israel." This mystic, abstract entity existing without organization, power or authority, is the only bond that can be described as uniting the Jewish people.

The System of Blessings

The fundamental concept of the Jewish ceremonial system is that God continually reveals Himself in nature, in history, and in man's daily life. Each ceremony seeks to emphasize some aspect of this Divine revelation, and thus becomes a special means for communion between man and God. By stressing the common dependence of all men on God, ceremonies strengthen the sense of human kinship. By drawing attention to the phenomena of nature, they help develop man's sense of the aesthetic and increase his joy in the contemplation of beauty. By opening vistas of achievement and satisfaction, they help free him from subjection to material needs and desires, and enable him to fulfill his higher potentialities.

Jewish tradition has evolved the system of ritual blessings as an effective means for achieving continual realization of God's manifestation in the world. According to Rabbinic Law, a Jew is expected to recite a blessing whenever he enjoys any particular aspect of the world.

When he awakes, he thanks God for having created the day, for having granted him the power of sight, for the creation of the earth, for the gift of clothes, for the power to walk, and for the renewal of his strength in sleep. He also thanks God that he is not an idolator nor a slave. Mindful of the severity of woman's lot in the world, and her consequent inability to fulfill some of the rituals, the man recites a benediction that he is male, rather than female; while a woman thanks God that He "has created her according to His will." The observant Jew also recites some verses from Scripture and a passage from the Talmud. Before doing so, he thanks God for the revelation through the Law, and for the commandment to study the Law.

Before sitting down to his morning meal, he is expected to recite special prayers. At the meal itself, both before and after eating, he recites pre-scribed blessings. These blessings are repeated at every meal. The blessing at the beginning of the meal is the simple benediction, "Blessed art Thou, O Lord, our God, King of the Universe, Who dost bring bread out of the ground." The blessing after the meal consists of four paragraphs. The first is devoted to thanks to God for supplying all men and indeed all living things with their daily needs. The second is an expression of gratitude for His having caused ancient Israel to inherit the Holy Land. The third is a prayer for the restoration of Jerusalem. The fourth paragraph is a blessing of God for His continued goodness to all men.

When three people eat together, the blessing after the meal is recited in unison. Such a group is popularly called *mezuman* (prepared), because before he begins the person reciting the grace asks whether all are prepared for it. If there is a guest at the table, the recital of the grace is assigned to him. If there are several guests, the most learned is expected to recite it. At the end of the grace, the person reciting it invokes a blessing on his host and hostess: "May the All-merciful bless the master and mistress of this house, them, and their house, and their children, and all that is theirs; us, and all that is ours, as our ancestors, Abraham, Isaac, and Jacob were · blessed."

At every meal attended by three or more persons "words of the Torah" should be spoken. If this is done, the meal becomes sanctified, and "it is as though they have partaken of the table of the Lord," *i.e.*, of a sacrificial meal. In order to fulfill this requirement, it is customary to recite a psalm at every meal. Psalm 137 is recited on weekdays, and Psalm 126 on Sabbaths, festivals, and half-holidays. On festival occasions, and other occasions when it is possible, the recital of these psalms is supplemented by discussions of questions related to religious or spiritual life. To emphasize the sacred character of the meal, one's hands should be washed both before and after it, just as was done at sacrificial meals in the Temple.

In addition to these blessings which are recited virtually every day, there are special blessings to be repeated, such as those for the sight of the trees in the spring, a view of the ocean, a meeting with a friend after a long absence, the appearance of meteors, lightning, the rainbow, the new moon, the sight of strange creatures, the acquisition of new clothes[13] or new possessions, and the reception of good news. On hearing bad news, a special benediction must be recited, accepting the Divine judgment. This benediction, "Blessed art Thou, O Lord our God, King of the Universe, the true Judge," is also recited on the occasion of any bereavement. Finally, there are prayers prescribed for the afternoon and the evening and a concluding prayer at bedtime.

THE SYNAGOGUE AND THE PRAYERS

In ancient times, the center of Jewish worship was the Temple in Jerusalem, where sacrifices were offered in accordance with the prescriptions of the Law. But there were prophets in Israel even in the days of priests, and the prophets frequently organized prayer meetings at which people assembled for devotion and religious exhortation. From these meetings eventually the synagogue was to develop; and subsequently the church and the mosque. As the chief element in the Temple service was sacrifice, so that of the synagogue was prayer. The precedent for prayer was, of course, ancient. Abraham interceded with God on behalf of the people of Sodom. Fearing attack, Jacob uttered the beautiful prayer that contains the memorable words, "I am not worthy of all the mercies, and of all the truth, which Thou hast shown Thy servant; for with my staff I passed this Jordan, and now I am become two camps" (Gen. 32:11). Hannah came to the Temple to petition and praise the Lord. Indeed, Solomon in his dedication service referred to the Temple essentially as a house of prayer in which men would supplicate the Lord.

Even before the Exile, gatherings for prayer were to be found among the people. The Babylonian Exile and the return to Palestine,[14a] however, were especially instrumental in strengthening the synagogue. The institution offered an opportunity not only for pious devotion but for study as well, for it was at these assemblies that Scripture was read and explained. The assembly for worship, which proved of such importance in Palestine while the Temple at Jerusalem still endured, became indispensable when the Temple was destroyed. Since that time, the synagogue has been the sole sanctuary of the Jewish people.

The architecture of the synagogue varies according to country and age. The essential elements of the institution are the Ark containing the Scroll of the Law, a stand for the reader of the service who faces the Ark, and in most traditional synagogues a second stand in the middle of the gathering for the reading of the Law. In a large number of American synagogues, no provision is made for this second stand.

In accordance with the tradition derived from the Temple in Jerusalem, the "court of women" is separated from that of the men in traditional synagogues. It is either marked off by a partition or is situated in a gallery. Again, a considerable number of American synagogues, including most of the Conservative synagogues and all the Reform synagogues, have deviated from tradition in this respect, and permit men and women to sit together.

No human figures may be used in the decoration of the synagogue. However, it is permitted, and has even become customary, to depict on the Ark and elsewhere in the building a lion or an eagle, suggesting the latter half of the Rabbinical injunction: "Be bold as the leopard, fleet as the deer, light as the eagle, and strong as the lion, to do the will of thy Father Who is in Heaven." In many synagogues, the passage is inscribed over the reader's stand. It is also usual to place over the Ark a symbolic representation of the two tablets containing the Ten Commandments. Generally, only the first words of each of the commandments is inscribed on the tablets. The so-called Shield (or Star) of David found in many synagogue buildings, and otherwise in Jewish symbolism, is of unknown origin. But its use can be traced back to Rabbinic times.

In many synagogues, there is to be found over the reader's desk a candelabrum, or two candelabra, symbolic of that which stood in the Temple of Jerusalem. But because it is forbidden to set up in a synagogue an exact replica of the utensils used in the ancient Temple, such candelabra usually have, instead of seven, eight or nine, sometimes fourteen branches.[15a]

In further deference to the unique sanctity of the Temple, kneeling or prostrating oneself in the synagogue worship is forbidden, except on certain occasions in the services of the New Year's Day and the Day of Atonement. Prayers are said either standing or sitting. It is customary to bow one's head on entering the synagogue and while reciting certain portions of the prayers. In Orthodox and Conservative synagogues, men pray with covered heads. It is considered a violation of custom to perform any act of worship, including study of the Scripture or the Talmud, with uncovered head. This custom derives from that prescribed for the priests of the Temple in Ex. 28:40-42. The custom has been abandoned in most American Reform synagogues.

It has become customary to speak of Reform synagogues and Conservative synagogues, as temples. This change of name does not imply any difference other than those already indicated.

The essential element in the synagogue is, of course, not the building, but the community. Public worship may be conducted in a building or out of doors. But it can be held only in the presence of a congregation, which theoretically consists of a minimum of ten heads of households. For the purpose of prayer, and because of the difficulty in finding ten heads of households in very small communities, ten males (over thirteen years of age) are considered heads of households. The assembly of ten such people is called a *minyan* (quorum) sufficient for public service.

The group that habitually prays together each day develops an astonishing community of interest and personal friendship. It is the experience of many who attend synagogue services regularly that the ties of association between the members of a *minyan* is a source of especial delight. Because the daily attendance at prayer is usually small, each person counts; the failure of anyone to come, because of illness or for any other reason, may disrupt the services. Perhaps in no other relationship of life is the personal worth of the individual—no matter how humble his status—so unmistakable as in this religious worship, which requires ten adult Jews and cannot be performed with a lesser number, no matter how learned, how pious, or how distinguished.

Any adult male Jew may lead the congregation in public prayers. The rabbi participates simply as a member of the congregation. It has become usual in large congregations to appoint a special official to read the prayers, especially those of the Sabbaths and festivals. Such a reader is called a *hazzan*. In some congregations the *hazzan* has a choir to assist him. In Orthodox congregations, this choir consists only of men; in some Conservative and in all Reform congregations, women are also admitted to the choir. A number of passages in the service are traditionally sung by the whole congregation in unison. The tendency of modern Orthodox and Conservative synagogues is to extend this practice to include a much larger part of the service.

In addition to the *hazzan*, the congregation may require the services of a special reader for the Scriptures. He must be able not only to read the consonantal text of the Scroll without the aid of vowels, but must be expert in the traditional system of cantillation of the Scriptures. This system of chanting is of great historical interest, because at least certain parts of it, particularly that prescribed for use on the High Holy Days, are of great antiquity.

The duty of looking after the arrangements for the service, that is, seeing that the Scrolls are prepared for reading, that the prayer books are available for the worshipers, and that the members having special duties during the service know their assignments, devolves generally on a functionary called the *shammash* (sexton).

In addition to these officials, who generally are remunerated for their duties, American Jewish congregations usually have lay officers, a president, one or more vice-presidents, a secretary, a treasurer, and board of directors, upon whom devolves the responsibility for the material well-being of the congregation.

As already indicated, tradition expects every member of the Jewish faith to pray at least three times a day: in the morning, *shaharit;* in the afternoon, *minhah;* and in the evening, *maarib.* On Sabbaths and festivals, an additional prayer is assigned for morning service, called *musaf* (addition), to commemorate the special sacrifices offered on such days at the Temple in Jerusalem. On the Day of Atonement, a fifth prayer is recited at sunset. This prayer, in some respects the most solemn of the year, is called *neilah* (closing), and commemorates the service held at the Temple when its gates were closed at the end of the sacred day.

All these prayers should, so far as possible, be recited at a public service. But if it is difficult to arrange to participate in a public service, they can be recited in private (with omissions of certain portions which belong only to the public service). Most observant Jews attend synagogue services at least on the Sabbaths and holidays; every Orthodox and Conservative synagogue endeavors to arrange for public services also on weekdays.

The essential element in all these services is the prayer called *amidah* (literally, standing, so called because one must rise to recite it). The weekday version of this prayer consists of nineteen paragraphs. But in the original Palestinian form, given it by Rabban Gamaliel II eighteen centuries ago, it contained only eighteen paragraphs; and the prayer is therefore frequently called *shemoneh esreh* (eighteen).

At all services, except the evening service, this prayer is recited twice.

It is first recited in an undertone by each individual in the congregation; and then aloud by the reader, on behalf of the congregation. The first and last three paragraphs of the *amidah* are identical for all the services. The first paragraphs consist of confessions of faith in God as the God of the Patriarchs, Abraham, Isaac, and Jacob; as the One Who gives strength to the living and new life to the dead; and as the Holy One, Who has no equal. The final paragraphs include a prayer for the return of God's presence to Jerusalem; an expression of gratitude for all the goodness God has shown; and a prayer for peace.

On the festivals, it is the rule in all Orthodox and in many Conservative synagogues, that the descendants of the ancient Aaronid priests bless the people before the final paragraphs of the public reading of the *musaf amidah*. The formula used in this blessing is that prescribed in Num. 6:22-27, "May the Lord bless thee and keep thee; may the Lord cause His countenance to shine upon thee and be gracious unto thee; may the Lord lift His countenance upon thee and give thee peace."

Before reciting this blessing, the descendants of Aaron who are in the synagogue remove their shoes (as was the custom in the Temple in Jerusalem). The Levites who are present in the synagogue then wash the hands of the Aaronids, who thereupon step forward, face the congregation, and recite the ancient blessing.

The middle paragraphs of the daily *amidah* contain petitions for the fulfillment of various needs for the granting of wisdom, repentance, and forgiveness, for the redemption of Israel, for the healing of the sick, for prosperous years, for the gathering of the dispersed, for the restoration of the Sanhedrin, for the suppression of tyranny, for the protection of the righteous, for the rebuilding of Jerusalem, for the coming of the Messiah, and for the acceptance of prayer.

All the prayers are for the good of the whole community. Petitions for private needs may be inserted in their appropriate place. For example, the prayer for a sick person may be included in the general prayer for the sick of the world.

On Sabbaths and festivals, these petitions for the satisfaction of material wants are omitted; for it is forbidden to consider material needs on such days. On these occasions there is a single prayer for a complete rest on the Sabbath, and for happiness on the festival.

At every service the silent reading of the *amidah* ends with the prayer which begins: "O my God! Guard my tongue from evil, and my lips from speaking guile. To such as curse me, let me be dumb. Let me, indeed, be as dust unto all. . . . If any design evil against me, speedily make their counsel of no effect, and frustrate their intentions."

At the morning and evening services the *amidah* is preceded by the recital of the *Shema* and the various benedictions with it. The *Shema* begins with the verse, "Hear, O Israel, the Lord is our God, the Lord is One" (Deut. 6:4), and includes Deut. 6:5-9, 11:13-21, and Num. 15:37-41. In all services the recital of the *Shema* is preceded by a blessing of God for His revelation in the Law, and is followed by a blessing for His redemption of Israel from Egypt. In the morning, there is also a blessing for the light, in the evening a blessing for the darkness.

Each of the services begins and ends with the recital of the *Kaddish*, an Aramaic prayer for the coming of the Kingdom of God. It is, in effect, a prayer on behalf of the congregation by the reader before he enters on his service and after he ends it. Its essential element is its first section, reading: "May the great Name of God be exalted and sanctified in the world which He created according to His will, and may He cause His Kingdom to come, in your lives and in your days, and in the lives of all the House of Israel; speedily, and in a short time. Amen."

In the course of time, it has become customary to recite this prayer at other parts of the service. Since the Middle Ages, it has been usual also for the observant Jew to recite it at services during the year of a bereavement, and on the anniversary of the death of his parents.

In the morning services held on Mondays and Thursdays (the market days of ancient Palestine, when a larger congregation would be available than on other weekdays), as well as on Sabbaths, festivals, new moons, and fast days, portions of the Five Books of Moses are read from the sacred Scrolls. The readings are so arranged that the whole of the Pentateuch is covered within a year. On Sabbath and festival mornings, as well as at the afternoon services on fast days, selections from the Books of the Prophets are read in addition to those from the Torah. Such a portion is called the *haftarah*, and the person reading it is called the *maftir*.

As stated above, the reading from the Torah is now assigned to a special functionary. In ancient times, the members of the congregation would each in turn perform this duty. In deference to this tradition, it is still customary to call various individuals to read special portions of the Torah, though they merely repeat the words *sotto voce*, while the reading aloud is the duty of the professional reader. There are seven such participants in the Sabbath morning reading of the Torah; six in that of the Day of Atonement, five in those of the festivals; four in those of new moons and the festival weeks; and three at all other services when the Torah is read. Whenever the Torah is read, the first person to be called must be a descendant of Aaron, if there is any in the synagogue. The second to be called must be a Levite, and the others are chosen from the remainder of the congregation. When the prophetic portions are read at the morning services of the Sabbaths and festivals, an additional person is called for that purpose. He may be either an Aaronid, a Levite, or any other Israelite.

There are certain occasions when it is considered an especial obligation to participate in the public reading of the Torah. The most important of these are the Sabbath succeeding a boy's thirteenth birthday; the Sabbath preceding one's marriage; the anniversaries of the death of one's parents; and the Sabbath following one's recovery from illness or escape from danger. It is usual for persons who are thus required to participate in the reading of the Scriptures to be assigned to the *haftarah*. A person who reads the Torah after recovering from illness or escape from danger recites a special blessing on the occasion, saying: "Blessed be Thou, O Lord, our God, King of the Universe, Who dost grant kindness to the undeserving, and Who has granted me every good." The congregation, hearing the blessing, responds, "He Who has granted thee kindness, may He ever continue to grant thee kindness."

The language of the prayers of the traditional service is for the most part Hebrew. However, a number of prayers are in Aramaic, the vernacular of the Jews in the first centuries of the Common Era in Palestine and Babylonia. At the present time the proportion of Hebrew to some other language (in America, for example, English) will vary with the individual congregation. But everywhere some portions of the public service are read in Hebrew.

According to Rabbinic tradition, it is customary for men to wear a prayer shawl called the *tallit* (garment) during the morning prayers. This prayer shawl is a square or oblong woolen cloth, with fringe at each of its four corners. It is a very ancient garment, probably worn in antiquity as a cloak. The purpose of the fringe (*sisit*) at the four corners is explained in the Bible: "That ye may look upon it and remember all the commandments of the Lord and do them . . . and be holy unto the Lord your God" (Num. 15:39-40). In addition, it is customary for men to don the *tephillin* (phylacteries) during the morning services on weekdays. These *tephillin* consist of two boxes of parchment to which are attached long leather straps. In the boxes are deposited little strips of parchment with the contents of Ex. 11:16, 13:1-10; Deut. 6:4-9, 11:13-21. The Bible also gives the meaning of this symbol: "And it shall be for a sign unto thee upon thy hand, and for a memorial between thine eyes, that the Law of the Lord may be in thy mouth; for with a strong hand hath the Lord brought thee out of Egypt" (Ex. 13:9). To the ancient Rabbis the *tephillin* on the head, and on the left arm close to the heart, represented the concentration of the intellect and the emotion on the Divine. As Maimonides subsequently expressed it: "As long as the *tephillin* are on the head and on the arm of a man, he is modest and God-fearing; he will not be attracted by hilarity or idle talk, and will have no evil thoughts, but will devote all his thoughts to truth and righteousness."

Two of these biblical sections, namely, Deut. 6:4-9 and 11:13-21, are also inscribed on pieces of parchment which are placed in receptacles, attached by the observant Jew to the doorposts of every room. Such receptacles are called *mezuzot* (literally, doorposts). These inscriptions are intended to remind man, as he enters home or leaves it, of the unity of God and of the duty of loving Him.

THE SABBATH AND THE FESTIVALS

While according to the Jewish faith God's presence can be felt at any time and place, there are times, just as there are places, which through their associations have come to lead especially to communion with God. Of these the most important are the Holy Days and the fast days. The Holy Days, according to the Jewish ritual, are the *Shabbat* or Sabbath, celebrated on the seventh day of each week, *Pesach* (Passover), *Shabuot* (Pentecost), *Rosh Ha-Shanah* (the Jewish religious New Year's Day), *Yom Kippur* (Day of Atonement), and *Sukkot* (Tabernacles).

In order that these days may be devoted as completely as possible to the spiritual life, work is forbidden on them. This prohibition includes not only all gainful occupation, but also household tasks.

As a result of these various prohibitions, the Sabbath and festivals become virtually periods of cessation of all labor on the part of observant Jews. Because of the difficulties involved in maintaining this rigid discipline in an industrial society, many Jews otherwise very observant do not refrain from all labor on the Sabbath. Nevertheless, even among these a large number set aside the free hours of the day for spiritual contemplation and for prayer, and mark the Sabbath with the ceremonials devoted to it.

Theoretically, observant Jews should not benefit from the willingness of members of other faiths to perform tasks for them on the Sabbath day. But because of the severity of the winters in northern and central Europe, and the consequent danger of disease, it became customary in the Middle Ages to permit people who were not Jews to kindle the fire for the Jews on the Sabbath. As a result, in time Christian and Moslem boys came to look after the heating of Jewish homes on the Sabbath. In recent centuries, people of other faiths also extinguish lights for Jews on the Sabbath, on the theory that rest is as imperative for health as warmth.

In the Jewish religious calendar, the observance of festivals begins a little before sunset on the preceding day. Because no fire is kindled on the Sabbath, it has been customary from time immemorial for Jewish housewives to conclude all their household arrangements for the day of rest by preparing the lights, which have therefore become known as the "Sabbath lights." The great antiquity of this usage, and the significance that came to be attached to it, have sanctified it, and consequently in modern Jewish homes the Sabbath candles are lit, even though other means of illumination are available and are in use. Many a Jew has tender memories of his mother lighting the Sabbath candles. As their light is not to be enjoyed by her before the blessing, the Jewish mother with her hands over her eyes recites, "Blessed art Thou, O Lord our God, King of the Universe, Who has sanctified us with Thy commandments, and commanded us to kindle the Sabbath lights."

In the absence of the mother of the household, the lights are kindled by someone acting for her. If by chance the lights have not been kindled on a Sabbath, it is customary for her to kindle an additional light before every Sabbath afterward throughout her life.

The beauty and impressiveness of the custom of the Sabbath lights has caused it to be extended, so that similar lights are now kindled also on festivals for which the use of fire is permitted, and when therefore there is no special reason for lighting candles before dark. In kindling the lights on the seasonal festivals the mother recites the special prayer of thanks for life called *sheheheyanu* (Who has kept us alive), "Blessed art Thou, O Lord our God, King of the Universe, Who hast caused us to live, and attain this day."

Evening services are held in the synagogue on the eve of festivals and Sabbaths at dusk. After the services, the members of the family return home for the Sabbath meal. On the table are placed a flask of wine and two loaves of bread. The Sabbath loaf of bread is called by its Hebrew name, *hallah* (plural, *hallot*, or as popularly pronounced, *hallos*). The two loaves of bread are said to symbolize the double share of manna God granted the Israelites in the wilderness on Fridays to provide for the Sabbath (Ex. 16:5). It is customary in many localities to prepare these loaves in an especially attractive form, made of twisted strands of dough. On festivals, the bread is further enriched by a plentiful supply of raisins. (On Passover the bread is replaced by unleavened cakes.) Recalling the ancient Rabbinic custom of setting the table only after the Sabbath or festival has been ushered in, the loaves of bread are covered with a napkin, and remain concealed, while the head of the household takes a cup of wine, and recites over it the blessing called the *kiddush*, or sanctification of the day. This blessing consists of a prayer of thanks to God for the gift of the wine, and then for the gift of the special festival. The head of the household drinks some of the wine, and distributes the rest among the others present. On seasonal festivals, the *kiddush* also includes the blessing *sheheheyanu*, mentioned above. Then follows the ritual washing of the hands, the blessing for the bread, the breaking of the bread, the meal itself, the special hymns of the Sabbath or festival meal, and the blessing after the meal.

In many Conservative and Reform congregations, special services on Sabbath eve are held after the Sabbath meal. These services are intended to enable those men and women who because of modern industrial conditions do not attend the traditional service at dusk to commune with God during the course of the holy day. The ritual used at these services varies considerably. In some congregations it is the usual Sabbath eve service. In others it consists of the hymns sung at the Sabbath evening meal. In virtually all congregations where such services are held it is customary to include a sermon by the rabbi.

The Sabbath and festival morning service are longer than those of the weekdays, and occupy most of the morning hours. As it is considered improper to eat before prayers, traditional Jewish homes do not provide for any breakfast on Sabbaths or festivals. The ritual of the noon meal is similar to that of the evening. It includes a blessing over the cup of wine, the blessing for the bread, the breaking and distribution of the bread, the meal itself, and the blessing after the meal.

In observant homes it is customary to arrange for another meal to be served in the late afternoon of the Sabbath day, so as to complete three Sabbath meals. This third meal is called *seudah shelishit* (third meal) or, more popularly and less correctly, *shalosh seudot* (three meals). No wine need be drunk before the third meal, but the blessing for the bread is recited as usual.

In Palestine it has become customary within the past generation, as a result of the influence of the famous Hebrew poet, Chayyim Nahman Bialik,[16a] to substitute for the third meal a public gathering, preferably one at which refreshments are served, called *oneg shabbat* (the delight of the Sabbath). The practice of holding such gatherings has become an institution in other parts of the world, and is rapidly being adopted by congregations in the United States. It is an effort to bring people together on the Sabbath afternoon for a discussion of religious, literary, or ethical problems, while participating in a symbolic Sabbath meal.

The Sabbath is concluded about half an hour after sunset with a blessing called *habdalah* (division, that is, marking the division between the Sabbath and the weekdays). A flask of wine and a box of incense are set on the table, and a light is struck. It seems appropriate that the workaday week should begin with the taste of the wine, the odor of the incense, and the appearance of the light, which, satisfying three different senses, increase man's awareness of his dependence on God for all his needs. The blessing consists, therefore, of thanks to God for the gift of the wine, of the incense, and of the light; and ends with further thanks for the division between the Sabbath and the weekdays. It is customary to let the cup of wine for *habdalah* overflow, as a symbol that the happiness of the week may likewise overflow. It is also customary to use a candle with three or four wicks (resembling an ancient torch) for the light of the *habdalah*.

The same ritual of *habdalah* is recited in the synagogue, in order to provide for those who cannot observe it in their homes. It also concludes the Day of Atonement and, with the exception of the blessing for the incense and the light, all the other festivals.

The rigid prohibition of work on the Sabbath does not, as is frequently believed, make it a day of gloom for the observant Jew. On the contrary, the complete release from all mundane concern, the concentration on the study of the Torah, and the joy in the sense of communion with God, make it a day of great, though perhaps indescribable, delight. To participate in the observance of the Sabbath gives such happiness that one of the prayers added to the blessing after the meal on the day asks that Paradise may be one long Sabbath. As twilight descends on Sabbath afternoon, some feel an ineffable sense of yearning and loneliness, which the mystics among the Jews have characterized as the loss of part of one's soul.

Aside from the Sabbath, the major Jewish festivals are Passover, Pentecost, New Year's Day, the Day of Atonement, and the Feast of the Tabernacles. Each of these is, according to tradition, a day of judgment for all mankind. "On Passover the world is judged regarding its grain; on Pentecost regarding the fruits of the tree; on New Year's Day (and also on the Day of Atonement) all creatures pass before God in review; and on Tabernacles they are judged concerning the rain."

While this consciousness of judgment gives an air of solemnity to all the festivals, the three festivals of the ancient pilgrimages, Passover, Pentecost, and Tabernacles, are primarily periods of joy. The manner in which the joy of the festival is combined with the sense of solemnity and judgment before God is difficult to explain to the uninitiate. The festival prayers, as well as the special melodies which in certain rituals accompany them, reflect a feeling of awe, arising from the sense of communion with God as Judge and Ruler of the universe; yet united with this feeling and permeating it is a sense of confidence that His judgment will be one of mercy rather than severity, as that of a father upon his child. The joy of the festival is thus prevented from becoming one of physical pleasure or self-indulgence. Ideally conceived, it is a joy arising largely from participation in synagogue and home rituals, that bring about a closer communion with God.

The significance of each festival is enhanced through the natural and historical interpretations associated with it. All are intended to increase man's faith in God by reference to His revelation in the natural order and also in the succession of human events. Their symbols are particularly significant in an industrial and commercial civilization, where man tends to be separated from nature; and their reflection of the Divine purpose in history gives one strength in times of international crisis, and fills one with humility in moments of peace and prosperity. The purpose of the festivals may thus be said to place human life in both its cosmic and historical perspectives. They enable man to see himself both as part of nature and as distinguished through the providence of God. Passover, occurring on the full moon of the first month of spring (toward the end of March or the beginning of April), is the great festival of the rebirth of nature, and also commemorates historically the Exodus from Egypt. The concentration of Jews in the cities during past centuries has tended to minimize the agricultural aspect of the Passover. Nevertheless, certain ancient customs emphasizing the seasonal character of the festival are still observed. The first month of spring in Palestine marks the end of the rainy season and the beginning of the dry season. In this dry season the crops are saved from destruction by a heavy dew each night. Hence Passover became a festival of prayer for the dew, and the *musaf* (additional) prayer of the first day of Passover is dedicated to petition for copious dew on the earth. The second night of Passover was celebrated in ancient Palestine as the beginning of the barley harvest. In accordance with Lev. 23:14, no part of the new crop might be eaten before that night, when the first sheaf (the *omer*) was harvested and prepared as a sacrifice to God. While the observance of the sacrifice is impossible today, it is still customary for men of great piety in European communities to avoid eating new grain before the second night of Passover. All traditional Jewish communities mark the second night of Passover as the beginning of the barley harvest in ancient Palestine; and, following a literal interpretation of Lev. 23:15-16, include in the daily evening service an enumeration of the forty-nine days from that night until Pentecost, the festival of the wheat harvest.

But the historical significance of Passover as commemorating the Exodus and the promulgation of the idea of freedom in the world has far overshadowed the agricultural phase of the festival. The ceremonies prescribed for the festival in Scripture and the additional rules established by the Rabbis have as their purpose emphasis on the idea of human liberty and equality. The most obvious characteristic of the festival is the use of the unleavened bread (called *massah*, pronounced *matzah*), the bread of affliction (Deut. 16:3), recalling to each Jew the bondage of his ancestry in Egypt, and emphasizing by inference his equality with the humblest and most oppressed of men. The significance of the custom has become such that it is observed with greater precision than almost any other law in Scripture. Observant Jews abstain on the festival from eating not only any leavened bread but even any food which might conceivably have a taste or trace of leaven. The grain used for *massah* is carefully examined to see whether any of it has become leaven. The examination is usually performed by a rabbi, who takes a sampling. If he finds that none in his sample has become leaven, the contents of that granary may be used for Passover. After the examination, the grain must be carefully guarded against moistening that might cause it to leaven. The mills in which it is ground are carefully scoured and purified from all leaven. The flour is then again guarded from moisture, until it is brought to the bakery. In the bakery, expert mechanics and especially devised machines make it possible to prepare the dough and bake it with such speed that no leavening can take place. No salt and of course no yeast or any material other than flour and water enter into the making of the *massah*. After the *massah* has been baked, it may be ground again into flour (*matzah meal*), which can then be used for making pastries and other dishes for consumption on the Passover.

Traditional observance of the Passover requires that no prepared food such as dried fruits or vegetables shall be used, unless it has been made certain that not a speck of flour attaches to them. For this reason, raisins, prunes, coffee, pepper, and similar foods are used by observant Jews during the Passover only if they are prepared under the supervision of a rabbi. Dried peas or beans may not be eaten under any circumstances. Ashkenazic Jews do not eat rice on Passover, though following the tradition of their ancestors, Jews of Sephardic descent consider it permitted.

Special cooking utensils and dishes are set aside for the Passover week, so that no utensils or dishes which have contained leaven will come in contact with the Passover food. Families which cannot afford a complete set of special dishes may cleanse their metal utensils and certain types of glassware for use during the Passover week. Such cleansing must follow the ritual prescriptions, and should be done only after consultation with a rabbi.

To purify the home from all leaven before the Passover, it is customary on the night before the festival eve to "search the house" for any bread or leaven. In earlier ages, this searching had the practical purpose of discovering such leaven, for in the simple one-room homes of the ancient East it was possible to delay the removal of leaven until the night before the festival. In modern homes, this cleaning naturally occupies several days or even weeks, and the ritual searching for the leaven has become almost a formal custom. Nevertheless, it is observed in most Orthodox and Conservative homes. The head of the household searches for the leaven, removes all he finds, and puts it aside until the next morning, when it must be burned during the first quarter of the day, that is, around 9:00 A.M. After that hour it is forbidden to eat or to own leavened food. As it is usually difficult to destroy all the leavened food in a home and quite impossible to dispose of all the dishes used for leavened food, many groups of observant Jews transfer the title of their leavened food to the rabbi of the community during the Passover week. The rabbi in turn technically transfers the title to a member of another faith.

On the first and second nights of Passover there is celebrated a unique home service called the *seder* (order), because the whole meal follows a prescribed ritual order. In addition to a festive gathering of the whole family in each household, strangers separated from their families are invited as guests. In communities where the number of strangers is considerable, provision is frequently made for a group *seder* at a public institution.

The poignant beauty of the *seder* service leaves an indelible impression on every Jewish child who participates in it. It is in effect a pageant in which ancient Palestinian life is re-created in as detailed and precise a form as possible. The head of the household (or, at a public celebration, the leader of the service) is provided with a divan on which after the fashion of the ancients he may recline during the meal and the celebration. According to some rituals, he is expected to don a *kittel*, a white linen garment worn in ancient Jerusalem on festive days.

The service followed at the *seder* is described in a special prayer book, the *Passover Haggada*. This book contains directions for arranging the Passover dish to be placed before the master of the house, and detailed instructions for the procedure during the service.

One of the most significant elements in the *seder* is its highly developed pedagogical technique. In order to impress the child, he is urged to observe the various ceremonies and to ask for their explanation. As the service is recited it thus becomes fundamentally a reply to these questions. The child is informed that the celebration is in memory of the Exodus from Egypt; he is told the story of the Israelite bondage; of the redemption of the people through the mercy of God; and is taught to respect the liberty he has inherited through this redemption.

At the end of the Passover meal, which is eaten in the course of the *seder*, the door is opened as a symbol of the entry of Elijah the Prophet. A cup of wine, "the cup of Elijah," is filled, the whole company rise, and cry, "Blessed is he who has come!" The concept that Elijah, the immortal prophet, visits every Jewish home on the Passover eve emphasizes the significance of the festival as a symbol of eternal freedom, as well as memorial of a past emancipation; for Elijah is the prophet who, according to the words of Malachi, will be the precursor of God's establishing His Kingdom on earth, at the end of days.

The *seder* ends with the recital of various psalms, the tasting of a fourth and final cup of wine, the singing of various hymns, and finally with popular songs dating from medieval times. In many communities the head of the household concludes the whole service by reading Canticles (The Song of Songs). The joyful spirit of youth, which permeates that portion of the Bible, seems appropriate for the spring festival; and its allegorical meaning as an epic of God's relation to Israel is particularly fitting for recollection on the festival of the Exodus.

The period between Passover and Pentecost is now observed in many Jewish communities as one of partial mourning, because it is traditionally described as the time when the disciples of Rabbi Akiba, one of the foremost teachers of the Talmud,[17a] died. Except for certain special days within the period, no weddings are celebrated by observant Jews; and they also abstain from listening to music, attending the theater, or other pleasures.

The thirty-third day of this period, called *Lag Ba'Omer* (literally, the thirty-third day of the *Omer*), is a half-holiday, devoted to the celebration of weddings and other festivities. It is sometimes said to be the anniversary of the death of Rabbi Simeon ben Yohai, the foremost disciple of Rabbi Akiba, which is marked in this way as the occasion of his translation to the Heavenly Academy. To this time it is therefore customary in Palestine to mark the day with a festive pilgrimage to the supposed grave of Rabbi Simeon in Meron, a village of Galilee.

Pentecost, or *Shabuot* (occurring toward the end of May or the beginning of June), is described in Scripture primarily as the festival of the wheat harvest (Ex. 23:16). But it also commemorates the Revelation on Mt. Sinai, and is therefore the festival of the Ten Commandments. The reading of the Law assigned to it covers the chapter telling the story of the Revelation (Ex. 19:20); the liturgy of the day is also dedicated in part to commemorating this incident. In many Orthodox congregations, the evening of the first night of Pentecost is spent in reading Scriptural passages. Among some especially pious Jews, it is customary to remain awake all night, reading the Bible and the Talmud. In many modern congregations, the first day of Pentecost is celebrated by the confirmation of boys and girls.

The third of the great joyous festivals is that of Tabernacles, or *Sukkot*, marking the coming of the autumn and the late harvests (some time in October), and also commemorating God's protection during the period when Israel dwelt in the wilderness (Lev. 23:43).

Both the seasonal and the historical aspects of the festival are symbolized in the *sukkah*, the booth in which observant Jews eat their meals during the holiday week. This booth is essentially a rustic cabin, with improvised walls, and a covering of leafy branches and twigs instead of a solid roof or ceiling. Both the covering and the walls are usually adorned with vegetables and fruits, in order to emphasize the harvest rusticity of the surroundings.

The festival is celebrated further by the ceremonial of the *lulab*, a cluster of a palm branch, three myrtle twigs, and two willow sprigs. During the recital of the *hallel* (*i.e.*, Ps. 113-118) in the morning service of the festival, the *lulab*, together with a citron, is taken in hand, and at certain portions of the prayer, they are moved to and fro, eastward, southward, westward, northward, upward, and downward, to indicate that God, Who is being thanked for His gifts, is to be found everywhere. At the end of the service, a Scroll is taken out of the Ark, and each of those having a *lulab* marches about the Scroll in a festive procession, commemorating the similar procession about the altar in Jerusalem in the days of the Temple. On the seventh day of *Sukkot* (*Hoshanna Rabba*) there is a special service of prayer for abundant rains. After the usual service of the day, the palm branches are put down, and the willow (symbolic of abundance of rain, because it grows by the river) taken up. With these willow sprigs in hand, the congregation recites various hymns having the refrain *hoshanna* (or, as it was frequently pronounced in ancient times, *hosanna*), meaning "Help, we pray Thee." At the end of these hymns, the willows are beaten against the floor of the synagogue.

Following *Hoshanna Rabba* is the "eighth day of solemn assembly" or, as it is called in Hebrew, *Shemini Azeret*. This festival is intended as a climax for the joyful season, which begins with *Sukkot*. The festival is marked especially by the prayer for rain in the additional (*musaf*) service, which is therefore called *tephillat geshem* (the prayer for rain).

The final, or ninth, day of the autumn celebration (properly the second day of the *Shemini Azeret* festival) is popularly called *Simhat Torah* (the day of rejoicing in the Law). On this day, the last section of the Five Books of Moses, *viz.*, Deuteronomy 34, and the first section of Genesis are read. In celebration of the annual completion and fresh beginning of the reading of the Pentateuch, all the Scrolls of the Law are taken from the Ark and carried about the synagogue in a procession. To enable every member of the congregation to participate in this ceremonial, the procession moves about the synagogue hall at least seven times in the evening, and then seven times more at the morning service. It is also customary in certain rituals for each member of the congregation to participate in the public reading of the Pentateuch on *Simhat Torah*. Immediately before the reading of the last section of the Pentateuch, it is customary in most congregations to call to read from the Torah one of the distinguished members of the congregation together "with all the children" (Hebrew, *kol ha-nearim*), so that even minors may participate in the reading on this occasion.

The person called to complete the reading of the Pentateuch on *Simhat Torah* is called *hatan ha-torah* (bridegroom of the Law, popularly pronounced, *hoson torah*). The person called to read the first chapter in Genesis on that day is called *hatan bereshit* (the bridegroom of the beginning, popularly pronounced, *hoson bereshis*). These offices are usually bestowed on men of especial piety or learning, and are among the highest honors that can be given in the synagogue service.

While on these festivals communion with God is sought through joy, on *Rosh Ha-Shanah* and *Yom Kippur* it is sought through solemnity. They are described as Days of Judgment when all living things pass before God, to stand in judgment for their deeds during the past year. During the month before *Rosh Ha-Shanah* (which usually occurs during the last three weeks of September or the beginning of October) preparation is made for the festival by sounding a ram's horn, or *shofar*, at the synagogue service each morning, and reciting Psalm 27 each morning and evening. Beginning with the Sunday preceding *Rosh Ha-Shanah* (if *Rosh Ha-Shanah* occurs on Monday or Tuesday, beginning with the Sunday of the preceding week), special prayers (called *selihot*) are recited at dawn of each day, beseeching Divine forgiveness for man's transgressions. While only the most pious assemble at the synagogue to recite these prayers each day, many recite them on the first day, and on the day before *Rosh Ha-Shanah*. In some congregations, these prayers are recited at midnight rather than at dawn, to make possible a larger attendance.

The festival of *Rosh Ha-Shanah* itself is particularly devoted to prayers for peace and prosperity for all mankind, and for life and happiness for individual human beings. It also emphasizes the recognition of God as King of the universe. This phase of the festival is reflected not only in the prayers of the day, but in several of the ceremonials. The *shofar* is sounded before, during, and after the additional morning prayer. The notes sounded by the *shofar* tend to arouse the people to repentance, reminding them that the Kingdom of God can be realized in our hearts and in our personal lives, even in the world in which we live. In the afternoon of the first day of the festival it is customary in many communities to walk to a river bank, as was sometimes done in ancient times at the anointing of a king. This custom is called *tashlik* (throwing), because of the popular belief that it is intended to cast off one's sins into the river.

On the evening of the first day of *Rosh Ha-Shanah* it is customary to eat apples and other fruits, dipped in honey, saying, "May it be Thy will that this year shall be happy and sweet for us." In many localities bread is dipped in honey at all the meals eaten on *Rosh Ha-Shanah*, and during the days following it until the Day of Atonement. On the second evening of *Rosh Ha-Shanah* it is customary to eat new fruit, over which the blessing *sheheheyanu* (Who has kept us alive) is recited.

The ten days beginning with the first days of *Rosh Ha-Shanah* and ending with *Yom Kippur*, are called the "Ten Days of Penitence." It is expected that everyone will observe particularly high standards of ethical and ceremonial conduct during these days. There are special prayers assigned for the period, beseeching continuance of life and peace, and the *selihot* are recited on them as on the days preceding *Rosh Ha-Shanah*.

On the day preceding *Yom Kippur* (the ninth of Tishri) tradition prescribes festive meals. The final meal of the day, eaten before the sundown that ushers in *Yom Kippur*, thus is marked by a peculiar combination of joy and solemnity. Before eating this meal, an oral confession of sins is recited by each person as part of the afternoon prayer. It is also customary during the day to distribute money for charitable purposes. After the meal the head of the household kindles a lamp or candle to burn for twenty-four hours, that is, until the end of the day. The mother kindles the usual festival lights, and the family proceeds to the synagogue.

The Day of Atonement is a season not only for repentance for trespasses against the ceremonial law but more especially for trespasses committed against ethical conduct in relations between men. Forgiveness for these trespasses can be obtained only when the man who suffered wrong pardons the injustice. It is therefore customary for anyone who is conscious of having injured a neighbor to obtain forgiveness before the Day of Atonement.

Men and women may unwittingly injure even those dear to them, including members of their families. Such thoughtlessness may raise a barrier to friendship and love. The eve of the Day of Atonement is considered an appropriate time to remove these barriers; relatives and friends call upon each other or write, offering good wishes for the coming year and either directly or indirectly asking forgiveness for any misunderstanding. Parents and grandparents bless their children and grandchildren. The moving prayer which is recited just before the evening service closes with the words: "I completely forgive anyone who has committed a trespass against me, whether against my person or against my property. . . . May no man suffer punishment because of me. And may it be Thy will, that just as I offer my forgiveness to all my fellows, that I may find grace in their eyes, so that they, too, will forgive my trespasses against them."

The Day of Atonement thus becomes a day for the renewal of bonds of affection and friendship.

The evening service in the synagogue, which must be recited before dark, is called *kol nidre* from its first words (meaning all vows), and is a service of absolution for ceremonial vows. This ceremony is made necessary by the rule of Jewish Law requiring fulfillment of every vow, even at great sacrifice. The vows that the ceremony of *kol nidre* releases are of course only those relating to ritual and custom. Without the consent of his neighbor, no ceremony can release anyone from a vow or promise made to his neighbor.

Because the *kol nidre* opens the service of the Day of Atonement, it is a particularly solemn ceremony. Its melody is probably the best known of all those associated with synagogue services.

The Day of Atonement is the major fast in the Jewish calendar, a day on which all principal sensual pleasures are interdicted. Men of piety also avoid wearing shoes made of leather on this day, particularly in the home or in the synagogue.[18]

The prayers of *Yom Kippur* are so arranged that they continue uninterruptedly from their beginning in the morning until their end in the *neilah* service after sunset. At each service, there is a confession of sin and a prayer for forgiveness. During the additional prayer of the morning (*musaf*) there is a re-enactment of part of the ancient service at the Temple. In its course, the members or at least the elders of the congregation prostrate themselves four times, just as the community gathered in the ancient Temple prostrated itself whenever the Divine Name was pronounced in the service.

The melodies of each of the *Yom Kippur* services follow definite traditions, and are reflective of the mood in which the service is expected to be pronounced. In the course of these services (as well as in those of *Rosh Ha-Shanah*) the Ark is frequently opened for the recital of especially impressive hymns and poems. The service of the Day of Atonement ends with the sounding of the ram's horn, and the joint cry by all of the congregation, "Hear, O Israel, the Lord is our God, the Lord is One."

There is a curious difference between Palestine and other countries with regard to the observance of the Jewish festivals. In Palestine Passover is observed for seven days, in accordance with the rule set down in Ex. 12:15; outside Palestine it is observed for eight days. Similarly Pentecost and *Shemini Azeret* are each observed for one day in Palestine, but for two days elsewhere. Moreover, in Palestine work is forbidden only on the first and seventh days of Passover, and on the first day of *Sukkot;* outside Palestine it is forbidden also on the second and on the eighth day of Passover, and on the second day of *Sukkot.*

The reason for this variation of custom is historical. In ancient times the beginning of the Jewish month was fixed when the authorities of the Temple in Jerusalem observed the new moon. As the lunar month had been accurately measured in antiquity, it was comparatively easy to foretell when the moon ought to appear in Jerusalem. But the first crescent of the new moon was frequently so thin and set so soon after the sun, that it was impossible to be certain that it had actually been observed. Therefore, those away from Jerusalem always had some doubt as to whether the Temple authorities had proclaimed one day or the next as the beginning of the calendar month.

To meet this difficulty, Temple authorities would send out messengers informing distant communities of the precise day they had fixed as that of the new moon. These messengers were able to reach all parts of Palestine in a comparatively short time, but they could not reach the distant communities of Babylonia. Hence the Babylonian Jews were always in doubt as to whether the month had begun on the precise day of the new moon, or the day following. This put them in doubt regarding the exact day of all the festivals. Therefore, in order to avoid any possible violation of a holy day, they observed all the customs relating to each festival for an additional day. In the fifth century of the Common Era, the Jewish

A HANUKKAH LAMP

This lamp from the home of Mr. and Mrs. Jacob H. Schiff, was a gift from Mrs. Felix M. Warburg. It is silver with enamel medallions on the base depicting biblical scenes, and was made at Frankfort in the early 18th century by Johan Adam Boller.

ILLUMINATED MEGILLAH OR SCROLL OF ESTHER (1.19-3.6)

Italian, 18th century

The figures are Vashti, Mordecai, and Esther. The medallions above are of three courtiers.

calendar was reduced to a fixed computative system, and thereafter no one could be in doubt with regard to the time of a festival. Nevertheless, the Jews outside Palestine continued to observe their ancient custom. In Palestine, uncertainty regarding the precise period of the festival could occur only with regard to *Rosh Ha-Shanah*, which occurs on the first day of the month. Hence, *Rosh Ha-Shanah* is observed for two days in Palestine as well as in other countries. It is not customary to observe the Day of Atonement for two days because it is considered impossible to impose the severity of two successive days of fasting on the whole community. Reform Jews have, in general, abandoned the observance of the second day of the holidays.

In addition to these major festivals, whose celebration is commanded in the Law of Moses, there are two lesser festivals in Judaism, which are occasions of great religious joy and sense of communion with God: *Purim*, the Feast of Esther, and *Hanukkah*, the feast commemorating the rededication of the Temple during the time of the Maccabees.

In accordance with the prescription of the Book of Esther, *Purim* (occurring in the first half of March) is celebrated as a day of rejoicing and thanksgiving, with the exchange of gifts between friends, and charity to the poor. The Book of Esther is read publicly both at the evening and at the morning service. In the late afternoon, a family festival, second in importance only to that of the *seder* service, is usually held. This festive dinner is called the *seudat purim* (*Purim* meal).

Hanukkah (the midwinter festival that occurs in the month of December) is celebrated in commemoration of the purification of the Temple by the Maccabees, after it had been defiled by the Syrian king, Antiochus IV, in the year 168 before the Common Era. Led by Judas the Maccabee, the Jews won amazing victories over outnumbering Syrian armies, and finally reconquered Jerusalem, drove the pagans out of the Temple, and re-established it as a place for the worship of God. The day of the rededication of the Temple was the third anniversary of its first defilement, the twenty-fifth of Kislev, and that day, together with seven succeeding days, is observed as *Hanukkah* (the feast of dedication).

On the first night of *Hanukkah* a candle is lit, and on each succeeding night of the eight-day festival an additional candle is lit, in celebration of the holiday. It is also customary to mark the festival with family meals, games, and the exchange of gifts, particularly within the family.

Besides *Yom Kippur*, there are several lesser fasts in the Jewish calendar. Of these the most important is *Tisha B'ab* (popularly pronounced *Tishoh B'ov*), the ninth day of the month of Ab, the anniversary of the burning of the first and also of the second Temple. In memory of these catastrophes, it is the rule to fast from sunset on the evening before this day until the sunset of the day itself. The Book of Lamentations is recited in the evening, and in the morning a number of dirges record ancient and medieval sufferings of the Jewish people. To increase a sense of bereavement it is customary in many communities to spend the afternoon of *Tisha B'ab* visiting the graves of relatives.

There are several other fasts, less commonly observed, during which food is forbidden only during the day. These are the fast of *Gedaliah* (on the day following *Rosh Ha-Shanah*); the tenth day of the month of Tebet; and the seventeenth day of the month of Tammuz. All these fasts are mentioned in Zech. 8:19. The fast of *Gedaliah* commemorates the murder of the last governor of Judah in the year 586 before the Common Era (Jer. 41:2). The fast of Tebet commemorates the beginning of the siege of Jerusalem by the Babylonians (Ez. 24:1-2). The seventeenth day of Tammuz is the anniversary of the breach in the wall of Jerusalem by the Romans in the year 70.

Partial mourning is still observed during the three weeks between the seventeenth day of Tammuz and the ninth of Ab, the period when Jerusalem was pillaged by the victorious Roman soldiery. No weddings are performed; other festivities and the wearing of new clothes are considered inappropriate. During the last nine days of this period it is customary for many Jews to abstain from meat and wine (except on the Sabbath day).

The Jewish religious calendar begins in the autumn with *Rosh Ha-shanah*, the festival of the New Year. The names of the months were adopted from the Babylonian calendar and are as follows: Tishri, Marchesvan (frequently called Heshvan), Kislev, Tebet, Shebat, Adar, Nisan, Iyyar, Sivan, Tammuz, Ab, Elul.

The length of the month is fixed by the lunar cycle of twenty-nine and a half days and therefore is alternately twenty-nine and thirty days. The length of the year of twelve months is thus 354 days, though under special circumstances it may be 353 or 355 days. To make up the difference between this period and that of the solar year of 365¼ days, an additional month is added to the year, seven times in a cycle of nineteen years. This additional month is added immediately before Nisan (the month of the Passover) and is called the Second Adar. The additional month is added on the third, sixth, eighth, eleventh, fourteenth, seventeenth, and nineteenth years of the cycle.

Because of the character of the Jewish calendar, the beginning of each month coincides with the new moon, and the first days of the festivals of Passover and *Sukkot* (falling on the fifteenth day of their respective months) occur at the full moon.

Rabbi José ben Halafta, a great scholar who lived in Palestine in the first half of the second century c.e., compiled a history of the Jews, which, following the example of Scripture, opened with the Creation. This book is called *Seder Olam* (The History of the World). Utilizing the chronology of Scripture for its time, and reconstructing postbiblical history as well as he could, Rabbi José arrived at the conclusion that the world was created in the year 3828 before the destruction of the Temple at the hands of the Romans. As by Rabbinic tradition the date of the destruction was placed in the year 67-68 c.e., the Creation according to his calculation occurred in the year 3761-3760 b.c.e., or to be more exact, in September or October, 3761 b.c.e.

The most significant confusion in Rabbi José's calculation was that reducing the whole period from the rebuilding of the Temple by Zerubabel in 516 b.c.e. to the conquest of Persia by Alexander (which he dates 318 b.c.e.) to no more than thirty-four years. Like other Rabbinic scholars he believed that Zerubabel (sixth century b.c.e.), Malachi, Ezra Nehemiah (all fifth century b.c.e.) and Simeon the Righteous (third century b.c.e.) were all contemporaries.

For many centuries this calculation by Rabbi José was of interest only to talmudic students, who also tried to satisfy a curiosity for historical reconstruction. The usual calculation adopted by Jews in Rabbinic and even post-talmudic times, was that of the Seleucid monarchy, that assumed rule over Syria and Palestine in the year 312 b.c.e. This era is in Jewish literature usually referred to as that of "legal documents," for it was in dating such documents that it generally occurred.

Only when the center of Jewish life was moved from Babylonia to Europe, and the era calculation based on the rule of the Seleucids seemed anachronistic and became meaningless, was it replaced by that based on the calculations of Rabbi José ben Halafta. Though this calculation (making 5709 the equivalent of 1948-1949) is now in universal use among Jews, it has no dogmatic sanction and is in effect simply an arbitrary figure used for convenience and uniformity.[19]

Special Occasions in the Course of Life

The occasions of special joy or sadness in human life are, in Judaism, surrounded with ceremonials intended to make them means for closer communion with God. These ceremonials aid the Jew to temper joy with solemnity and sorrow with resignation. When he is happy, the Jew is instructed to think with gratitude of God, Who is the source of happiness; and when he is in grief, he is likewise instructed to look to God, as the source of consolation. Birth, marriage, and death are thus more than incidents in temporal and sensual existence. They are the occasions for thinking more deeply than usual about the meaning of existence, and the relation of man to God.

Every person born of Jewish parents is considered bound to observe the covenant of Sinai, and therefore subject to the observance of Jewish ceremonial. Although mixed marriages are prohibited, the child of a Jewish mother is regarded as a Jew and need undergo no ceremony of conversion to be admitted to the Jewish faith. A member of another faith who desires to be converted to Judaism must (according to traditional ritual) appear before a rabbi and state his desire to be converted. The rabbi will then provide for his instruction in the elements of Jewish law, belief, and practice. Before admitting him to the Jewish fold, the rabbi must warn him of the severe discipline of Judaism and the difficulties involved in adherence to the Jewish faith. If the applicant persists in his desire to enter the Jewish faith, the rabbi will arrange for the ceremony of proselytization. A male applicant must be circumcised. According to the traditional ritual followed by Orthodox and Conservative Jews, both male and female applicants become proselytes by immersion in a pool of running water, declaring that they are performing the ceremony in order to be admitted into the Jewish faith, and reciting as they emerge from the water the benediction, "Blessed art Thou, O Lord, our God, King of the Universe, Who didst sanctify us with Thy commandments, and hast commanded us regarding the ceremonial immersion of the proselyte." Reform rabbis do not include this ritual immersion in their ceremony of proselytization.

In accordance with the prescriptions of Gen. 17:9-14, the son of Jewish parents is circumcised on the eighth day of his life. (The ceremony may be postponed for reasons of health.) Because the ritual of circumcision involves at once a knowledge of surgery and of traditional customs, it is performed by a man especially trained for the purpose, called a *mohel* (one who circumcises). At the circumcision, the father recites the benediction, "Blessed art Thou, O Lord, our God, King of the Universe, Who didst consecrate us with Thy commandments, and hast commanded us to bring this child into the covenant of our ancestor, Abraham." All those present respond, "Just as he has entered the covenant of Abraham, may he also enter into the study of the Law, into marriage, and into good deeds!" The *mohel* or some other person present, then prays for the child's future piety and welfare and that of his mother, and announces his name.

A girl is named at the service in the synagogue on the Sabbath (or any other day when the Torah is read) following her birth, when the father is called to participate in the reading of the Torah. One of those present then prays for the health of the mother of the child, and for the health of the child, and announces its name.

Boys under thirteen and girls under twelve years of age are theoretically not obligated to observe the discipline of the ritual Law. In order to be trained in the Law, they are expected to observe such parts of it as they can without impairing their health. As soon as a child can speak, he is taught to recite simple evening and morning prayers, consisting primarily of the first verse of the *Shema*. When the child reaches school age, he is taught the Hebrew language, the Bible and, as he grows older, advanced Jewish studies. The instruction is given the child by his parents, by a private teacher, or in a religious school. The traditional school devoted to this purpose is called a *Talmud Torah* (the place of the study of the Law). In America, these institutions usually provide instruction for children for either three or five (in some instances, seven or ten) hours per week, after the regular secular school hours on weekdays, and on Sunday mornings. There are also Jewish day schools established in some communities, providing both secular and religious education. These are sometimes called *yeshibot* (singular, *yeshiba* or *yeshiva*, academy). The name *yeshiba* or *yeshiva* is also used for traditional schools of advanced talmudic study in Europe and for similar institutions in America[20a]

A month before a boy has reached his thirteenth birthday he is expected to begin to don the *tephillin* each morning. On the Sabbath following his thirteenth birthday, he is called to participate in the formal reading of the Torah at the usual synagogue service. The ceremony of which this is part is popularly called *bar mitzva* (son of the commandment, in reference to his obligation to perform the commandments thereafter). Parents frequently arrange a celebration in honor of this occasion.

In many American synagogues similar note is taken when a girl attains the age of twelve, and therefore becomes subject to the commandments. The ceremony which is called *bat mitzva* (daughter of the commandment, popularly pronounced *bas mitzva*) is variously observed in different communities. In some, the girl is permitted to read the prophetic portion in the vernacular. In others, there is simply a family festivity.

Many Conservative and Reform congregations have established, either in lieu of these *bar mitzva* and *bat mitzva* ceremonies or in addition to them, that of confirmation. This ritual is usually observed on Pentecost. Boys and girls from fourteen to sixteen are taught the elements of Jewish faith and history in preconfirmation classes, and are then called to announce their devotion to the faith at a public synagogue ceremonial.

In the traditional marriage service, the ceremony takes place under a canopy (*huppah*), which symbolizes the home established through the marriage.

Judaism regards complete mutual understanding and trust between the bride and the bridegroom as a basic requirement for a valid marriage. A number of ceremonies have been established to give expression to this conception, and there are even several legal forms which emphasize it.

Before the wedding, the rabbi or other person in charge of the ceremony asks the bridegroom whether he undertakes to fulfill all the traditional obligations of a Jewish husband to his wife. These include various provisions for the maintenance of the wife, both during married life and, if the occasion should arise, during her widowhood. As these are civil obligations, a formal agreement must be made to provide for them. On the bridegroom's assenting, the ceremony of *kinyan* (agreement) is performed. This consists of the rabbi's handing the bridegroom an object of value, usually a handkerchief, as a symbolic consideration, to make the bridegroom's acceptance of the conditions of the marriage valid. The rabbi then draws up a document called a *ketubah* (writ, popularly pronounced *kesubah*) detailing these obligations as well as those of the wife. This *ketubah* is witnessed by two observant Jews, neither of whom may be related to the bride or bridegroom. The officiating rabbi, if not a relation, may act as one of these witnesses.

The language of the *ketubah* is Aramaic, the vernacular of the Jews of Palestine during the period when the present text was composed. The document is sometimes artistically decorated; and a number of the *ketubot* preserved in various museums of Jewish antiquities are of great interest to the student of art.

The wedding ceremony itself consists of a series of benedictions, having for their purpose the expression of thanks to God for the institution of marriage and the family, for having implanted His image on the human race, and for the joy of the wedding, and including prayers for the happiness of the bride and bridegroom and for the restoration of Jerusalem. After the first of these benedictions, the bridegroom hands the bride a ring, and says to her in Hebrew, "Thou art sanctified unto me, with this ring, in accordance with the Law of Moses and of Israel." At the end of the ceremony a glass is broken to commemorate the destruction of Jerusalem.

There is a considerable difference between the marriage customs of traditional and Reform Jews. In the marriage service of the Reform group, the canopy and the *ketubah* are generally omitted. The wedding is usually celebrated in the synagogue. The special prayer for the restoration of Jerusalem is omitted. On the other hand, several prayers in English on behalf of the bride and the bridegroom are added. The service ends with the recitation of the priestly blessing (Num. 6:24-26) by the rabbi.[21]

Jewish Law forbids husband and wife to cohabit or to come into physical contact during the period of menstruation or for seven days afterward. At the end of the period the wife is required to take a ritual bath in a pool of running water, or one especially built for the purpose (*mikveh*). A bride also bathes in such a *mikveh* before her wedding. The value of these regulations in preserving Jewish family life and in the prevention of certain diseases has been recognized by various Christian and Jewish writers on genetics.[22]

In Jewish Law marriage can be terminated by a religious divorce (called *get*). In practice such a divorce is granted by a rabbi only if both parties consent, and have already been divorced in the civil courts. The ritual of divorce is extremely complicated, and is performed only by specially trained scholars. Reform rabbis generally recognize a civil divorce as terminating a Jewish marriage from a religious as well as from the secular point of view, and therefore do not insist on a religious divorce as prerequisite for remarriage of either husband or wife.

There is one instance in traditional Jewish Law in which the death of the husband does not completely break the marriage bond; that is the case of a childless widow, described in Deut. 25:5-10. Biblical Law, as stated in Deuteronomy, requires such a childless widow to marry her husband's brother, so that her first-born son, by the second marriage, may "succeed in the name of the brother which is dead, that his name be not put out of Israel." Later Rabbinic ordinances forbade the performance of such a Levirate marriage, but nevertheless insisted that the widow may not remarry without performing the ceremony of *halitzah*, ordained in Deuteronomy, as alternative to such a marriage.

When a Jew feels that the end of his life is approaching he should confess his sins in accordance with the fixed ritual, making special mention, however, of any sin which he is conscious of having committed, and which is not mentioned in the traditional formula. In his last conscious moments he recites the traditional confession of faith, "Hear, O Israel, the Lord is our God, the Lord is One." Those about him may help him recite the formula by repeating it with him.

According to Rabbinic tradition, the body should be washed after death and dressed in linen shrouds. The universal use of linen shrouds dates back to the beginning of the second century of the Common Era. Rabban Gamaliel II, the head of the Academy of Jabneh and one of the most distinguished scholars and communal leaders of his time,[23a] specifically requested that no elaborate provision such as was then customary be made for his burial, but that he be interred in a shroud like those used for the poor. The custom has been universally adopted by observant Jews to stress further the equality of all men.

The body must be interred in the ground, as soon after death as possible. Cremation is forbidden, as being an implicit denial of the resurrection.

The funeral service is usually recited in the home of the deceased, though in the case of a person of special piety it may be recited in the synagogue. Because of the conditions of modern urban life, funeral services are sometimes held in rooms especially devoted to that purpose, so-called funeral chapels. The purpose of the service and the ceremonies associated with it is to give expression to the natural grief of the bereaved, and at the same time to inculcate in the bereaved resignation to the Will of God.

The service consists of the recital of one or more psalms and selections of appropriate verses from other psalms. Usually Psalm 16, 23, 90, or 91 is recited. The reading of the psalm may be followed by an address;

and the service closes with a prayer for the peace of the soul of the deceased. This prayer is repeated at the grave, and a second psalm is recited, after which the bereaved recite the *kaddish*. Either during the funeral services or immediately before the burial, the person officiating at the ceremonies asks the near relatives of the deceased (husband, wife, son, daughter, father, mother, brother, or sister) each to cut one of his garments. This ceremony is called *keriah* (tearing the garment) and is reminiscent of the ancient Jewish usage of tearing one's clothes in bereavement (see II Sam. 1:11). After tearing the garment, each of the bereaved recites the blessing of resignation to the justice of God: "Blessed art Thou, O Lord, our God, King of the Universe, the true Judge."

During the week after the burial of a relative, near relatives, including husband, wife, children, brothers, sisters, and parents, remain at home. They must not engage in any gainful occupation, unless the income is vital to their subsistence, or unless they will otherwise forfeit their employment. It is customary for friends to visit the mourners to console them, and to arrange community prayers in the house of the deceased. During the whole week of mourning (called *shiva*, seven, *i.e.*, the seven days of mourning) a lamp is kept burning in the house of the deceased. None of the mourners wears any jewels, and mirrors, considered a luxury, are covered. The mourners sit on low stools instead of chairs; they do not study the Law or the Scriptures, save such solemn works as the Books of Job and Lamentations, the dire prophecies in Jeremiah, and the laws of mourning in the Talmud and Codes; and they are forbidden to wear shoes made of leather.

After the completion of the *shiva*, the relatives observe partial mourning for the remainder of the month. They do not don new clothes, and avoid taking part in festivities, or listening to music. On the death of a parent, this partial mourning is observed for a whole year. In order to make grief itself a means for closer communion with God, the bereaved children are expected, during this year of mourning, to be particularly mindful of religious observances, to attend synagogue service regularly, and to recite the *kaddish* at each prayer. Whenever possible, a bereaved son serves as reader of the public prayers on weekdays during this year of mourning. These customs are also observed on the anniversary of the death of one's parents. Such an anniversary is called *yahrzeit* (a German name, because the custom assumed its present form among the German Jews). It is customary, also, to have a light burning at home during the day marking the anniversary of the death of a near relative. This light symbolizes the belief in human immortality, in accordance with the Rabbinic interpretation of the verse (Pr. 20:27), "The spirit of man is the lamp of God, searching all the inward parts." About a year after the death of a relative, the mourners set up a monument marking the place of the grave. At the unveiling of this monument, called *massebah* (pillar, popularly pronounced *matzevah*), psalms are read, prayers are recited for the peace of the soul of the deceased, and the *kaddish* is repeated.

THE JEWISH HOME AND THE DIETARY LAWS

Like every other authentic experience, piety cannot stop short of the home. If religion were to be merely ecclesiastical, it would soon cease to be that too. The Psalmist who was told "Let us go up to the house of the Lord" rejoiced because in his own house the reality of God was never forgotten. Throughout Jewish history the attempt to reproduce in the home the order and mood of the place of worship has never been relaxed.

The interrelationship of sanctuary and home has been responsible for at least two significant results. On the one hand, the Jew did not remain a stranger to the ceremonial and purpose of his sacred institutions. On the other hand, his home and home life were transfigured. His residence became a habitation of God.

This sanctification of the home was achieved by a religious discipline whose purpose was constantly to prompt a remembrance of God. The Jew who visited the ancient Temple, for example, readily understood that the elaborate rites, precautions, exactitudes and purifications were the appropriate expressions of the beauty of holiness. "If you were to serve a king of flesh and blood," the saintly Hillel once reminded a guest, "would you not have to learn how to make your entrances and exits and obeisances? How much more so in the service of the King of kings!"

That such fastidiousness was therefore required in God's House the Jew accepted unquestioningly. The forms reminded him of God. And because they did, and because Israel's teachers tried to prevent the Jew from forgetting God even when he was away from the Sanctuary, corresponding rituals and attitudes were introduced into the Jewish home. Thus the Jewish home became a sanctuary in miniature, its table an altar, its furnishings instruments for sanctity.

In a sense, every detail of home life is an expression of the pattern of sanctity. Jewish homes, for example, are generally expected to contain basic religious texts such as the Bible, usually accompanied at least by the commentary of Rashi, the Talmud, perhaps an abbreviated code (the short *Shulhan Aruk*), some of the magnificent moralistic works, and of course the prayer book—actually one of the most extraordinary anthologies of Jewish classical literature. It is not uncommon to find in a Jewish home an excellent library with volumes handed down from father to son, volumes which reveal constant use.

Similarly, the various family festival celebrations with their rituals constitute activities that bring the Divine message very close to the Jew.

It is an insensitive Jewish child who forgets the beauty of the *seder* at Passover, or the kindling of the lights during *Hanukkah,* or the sight of his mother kindling the Sabbath lamps at dusk. These and like activities collaborate to make holiness a familiar emphasis and delight.

Part of the daily pattern of sanctity is formed by the so-called dietary laws. As is well known, Jewish law prohibits the eating of certain foods. These prohibitions are enumerated essentially in Lev. 11, and again in Deut. 14. No vegetable growths are prohibited; but of animal life the Law permits fish having scales and fins, certain types of fowl, and only those quadrupeds that chew their cud and have cloven hoofs. Among the domestic quadrupeds this includes only oxen, sheep, and goats.

According to traditional Judaism, warm-blooded animals may be eaten only if they are ritually slaughtered, *i.e.,* if they are slaughtered in the manner used in the Temple for sacrificial purposes. The knife used in slaughtering must be sharp, and must be examined both before and after slaughtering to be certain that its edge contains no notch, which by tearing the animal's throat might give it unnecessary pain. The animal must not, however, be stunned before slaughtering, for stunning prevents the free flow of the blood, and the absorption of the blood in the meat makes the food prohibited. To ensure the animal's speedy death, the person who slays it must be trained for the work. He must know enough of the diseases of animals to be able to examine the body and to make certain that it was suffering from no serious disease. A person so trained is called a *shohet* (slaughterer). In order to be allowed to perform his duties, he must receive authorization from a rabbi.

After an animal is slaughtered, its lungs are examined to guard against symptoms of various communicable diseases, mainly tuberculosis. The Talmud, its commentaries, and the later codes, contain an impressive amount of veterinary information regarding the symptoms of disease in animals, so that an examination based on this information is a valuable means of detecting disease.

If an animal has been found to be free from serious disease, its meat is declared *kasher* (fit, popularly pronounced *kosher*).

The meat must not, however, remain unwashed for three days. If it does, the surface blood is believed to be absorbed in the tissues, and the food becomes prohibited. After the meat is cut, the various parts are placed in a container of water for half an hour to be cleansed of surface blood. Thereafter the meat is covered with salt, to draw out the blood further, and remains in the salt for at least an hour. The salt is then washed off, and the meat may be boiled. Meat which is to be roasted on a spit need not be soaked in water or salted. Meat from the udder or the liver may be prepared only by roasting.

In addition to the various laws prohibiting certain types of food, there is a rule mentioned thrice in Scripture against seething a kid in its mother's milk (Ex. 23:19 and 34:26; Deut. 14:21). This rule was originally intended, according to Maimonides, to extirpate an idolatrous practice. It is interpreted as prohibiting the cooking or eating the meat of any warm-blooded animal with milk, or a derivative of milk. Hence to serve meat and milk or butter or cheese at the same meal is prohibited. In order to avoid any possibility of a mixture of meat and milk, observant Jews provide themselves with two types of dishes, one of which is used only for meat foods, the other only for milk foods. Further, it is customary in many countries not to eat milk dishes for six hours after a meat meal.

THE STATUS OF WOMAN IN JEWISH LAW AND RITUAL

From its beginnings, Judaism has consistently endeavored to proclaim and effectuate the equality of the sexes before God and in society. The first chapter of Genesis describes Adam as created "male and female" (v. 27), and continues to narrate how "God blessed them, and God said unto them, Be fruitful and multiply and replenish the earth and subdue it. And have dominion over the fish of the sea, and over the fowl of the air, and over every living thing that creepeth upon the earth." This description emphasizing the equality of woman and man, is repeated at the beginning of the fifth chapter of the Book.

Though in the general pattern of Mediterranean society, in which Judaism originated, the status of women was definitely inferior to that of men, Jewish law in its biblical and particularly in its postbiblical stages endeavored to overcome this differentiation between the rights of the sexes. Among the most significant reforms introduced by the talmudic Sages was that providing for the inheritance by orphan daughters, even when they had brothers.

Plural marriage had become virtually obsolete in Rabbinic times. It was formally interdicted by Rabbenu Gershom who lived in Germany in the eleventh century. As the foremost Rabbinic scholar in the Europe of his day, he issued a decree of excommunication against any Jew who would practice plural marriage (except under a dispensation to be granted by one hundred Rabbis, in cases other systems of law would regard as justifying divorce or annulment of marriage). He also declared an excommunication against anyone who would divorce his wife against her will. With these measures, and those of older times that permitted a wife to apply to a Jewish court for a writ of divorcement under certain circumstances, the status of husband and wife was practically equalized in regard to marriage law.

While formal education in Rabbinics was generally limited to men, provision was often made also for the education of women. During Rabbinic times, and even more frequently in the Middle Ages, some women achieved high distinction in scholarship. In later ages, books were written in Yiddish for the edification and instruction of women; and many achieved an astonishing degree of erudition simply through listening to the learned disquisitions of rabbis on the Sabbaths.

While the service at the synagogue, like that of the priests in the Temple, is conducted by men, what might be called worship at home is largely the prerogative of the wife and mother. Kindling of the Sabbath lights, supervision of the child's education, maintenance of the food laws, and preparation for the festivals are considered especially part of woman's share in Divine worship.

In the latter part of the nineteenth and in the twentieth century Reform Jews and many Conservative Jews abolished the separation of the sexes in the synagogue. In all groups, there is in modern days far greater participation of women in synagogue work and administration, growing provision for the education of girls, and increasing opportunities for women to serve as teachers and school executives. In many congregations, Orthodox as well as Conservative and Reform, women serve on the lay boards of the synagogues and of synagogue organizations. They serve as members of faculties of teachers institutes, and have been known to be admitted as students in rabbinical schools.

PROHIBITIONS OR NEGATIVE COMMANDMENTS

Most of the laws so far described are affirmative commandments. They tell the Jew what he is expected to do on particular occasions. But according to Rabbinical calculation, the greater part of the biblical Law consists of negative regulations or prohibitions. In fact, a Palestinian scholar of the third century maintained that Scripture contains no less than three hundred and sixty-five prohibitions but only two hundred and forty-eight positive injunctions. Since his time these have been variously enumerated; the most important codification being that of Maimonides, in his Book of the Commandments and in the introduction to his Code.

The system of negative commandments is as vital to Judaism as are its positive ceremonials. Some of the prohibitions have been discussed in preceding sections, and are associated with the ceremonial observances themselves. Thus the observance of Passover includes not only eating *matzah*, but also abstention from leaven. Worship of God involves rejection of all idolatry, including rituals which were part of ancient pagan faiths no longer in existence.

Whatever may be the significance of a particular rule—whether personal hygiene, the extirpation of idolatry, the inculcation of gentleness—the whole system of prohibitions has a common goal. It is to make the awareness of God a continuous, uninterrupted experience. Affirmative actions and gestures are, by their nature, limited to stated occasions. Negations are timeless. The positive ceremonial is intended to arouse man's spirit to particular heights; the prohibition prevents him from forgetting God at any time. There is never a time or place when, to quote the Rabbinic phrase, "a person is naked of the commandments." He is always on the alert against possible violation of the Law. He has more prohibitions to guard against on the Day of Atonement than on the Sabbath; and on the Sabbath than on weekdays. But he is never without the possibility of falling into error, and therefore never free from the responsibility of avoiding sin.

It is in his relations with fellow men that a person becomes especially aware of the presence of God; love for them inevitably develops into love for Him. Jews are therefore warned in their Law to beware any infringement of the rights and privileges of others. "What is distasteful to thee, do not to thy neighbor" was the summary of the Law made by the great talmudic teacher Hillel. To develop such sensitivity to others' feelings as to avoid what may give them pain, and to concentrate on what will cause pleasure, is a discipline demanded by Judaism not simply as courtesy and politeness but as the Law of God. It was the apparent purpose of the Lawgiver and his disciples to create a group for whom the service of God would be the principal vocation of life, and all earthly interests an avocation; for whom the presence of God would be so manifest that the trivialities and temptations of mundane existence would appear unimportant.

The very incongruity between the traditional Jewish system of life and one which lays great stress on efficiency, productivity and abundance is a basic, implicit idea of the faith. The first premise of the Torah is that "man doth not live by bread alone," and that there are joys in the sense of communion with God, in the awareness of His being and His kingdom, of His love and of love for Him, so deep and all-pervading as to make all other experiences of life insignificant. As neither man as a whole nor Jews as a group have reached this stage of sensitivity to the Deity, the hastening of the process leading to it is a primary obligation. Life in accordance with Torah is a preparation for the detachment from material affairs, a means to attain absorption in spiritual ones. Without such absorption, man may seek compensation for his unhappiness and frustration in domination of his fellows; and his very search for earthly goods may become his undoing. Judaism assumes that there are many ways that man can learn to love God, so as to rise above interest in the physical world. But for its adherents, traditional Judaism prescribes the austerity of a system of conduct, involving not only ethics but ceremonial, which it regards as especially inconsistent with material ambition and especially conducive to spirituality.

LOVE FOR GOD

Love for God is thus both the beginning and the end of the Jewish way of life. Awareness of God's Being, the essence of this love, fosters the observance and study of the rituals and commandments, and is itself stimulated by them. The Torah draws Israel nearer to God; and God draws Israel nearer to the Torah. The greater man's love for God the easier his escape from the futilities of earthly temptation and ambition; the more complete his transcendence of his irrational and perverted hungers for immediate and transient goods the easier for him to attain preoccupation with God.

Absorption in God is man's perfection. As man tears himself free from the chains binding him to animal and less than animal existence, he finds himself contemplating the Eternal and the Spiritual; and conversely, as he, by an act of will, focuses his intellect on the transcendent, his reason allies itself with his good propensities to make him more nearly divine.

This interrelation of love for God and perfection of man is a basic postulate of Judaism. "And thou shalt love the Lord thy God with all thy heart and with all thy soul and with all thy might" is alpha, as well as omega of Judaism. That man is capable of loving God gives promise of his future; the future will be fulfilled as man attains increasing love for God and immersion in Him.

This doctrine teaches man humility, but denies his insignificance. He can escape frustration, and perhaps self-destruction, through the discovery that he is a mere incident in the Divine process of creation.

The recognition of that elemental relationship between him and God and the achievement of the humility indispensable to the service of God give him a unique role in the process of creation. "If I labor not to perfect myself, who will perfect me? Yet if I labor only for myself, what am I?" asked Hillel.

The triviality of man, both in his physical being and in his temporal aspirations, is in sharp contrast to the vastness about him. It is tempting to seek escape from responsibility as an instrument of Divine purpose through the illusion that the immensity of the universe and his own physical insignificance are a measure of relative value. Yet in view of the proverbial prodigality of nature no consideration could be more preposterous. Flowers produce millions of pollen grains, so that one may find its way to an ovule; trees bear fruit without number, so that the species may survive through a few. That galaxies and supergalaxies, numbering many millions and containing millions of suns, should derive meaning from the evolution on a minor planet in one of the less important systems of a sentient creature, knowing good and evil, is far from inconsistent with the usual procedures of Creation. If it be true that of all the conglomerations of atoms, man alone has the power to be like God, in his ability to choose his path, fulfilling or resisting the Will of his Maker, he is indeed the ultimate triumph of Creation. The universe as a whole proceeds according to its inexorable laws; in man God has created a being which can obey, because it can also defy; which can attain perfection, not through a process beyond its control, but through one which it itself directs.

Aware of the possibility that he has this unique role in existence, man will find its rejection for the sake of trifling advantages of power and luxury difficult indeed. To know God metaphysically may be consistent with rebellion against Him; but to know Him religiously is not. Men habituated to serve God, out of love for Him, will develop the calm detached resignation of the Stoic, and yet combine with it a passionate desire to see His will done. They will not hate, but pity, those who have no share in this enterprise, or who, through ignorance or malice, impede it. They will not resent the painful and heart-rending tarriance; nor will they count the cost for themselves or for their fellows. Yet transcendence of life's vicissitudes will not harden their hearts and freeze their emotions. They will have faith in the ultimate fulfillment of the Divine purpose, and in man's proving himself worthy of his Maker. But they will wish to hasten the progress, and they will wish to share in it. They will want the Master to be pleased with their participation, though it is inconceivable that the effort as a whole should fail even without them.

In a world in which mankind as a whole achieved love of God, to live in accordance with Jewish ritual and morals and for the goals Judaism has set will not seem curious and awkward, but natural and rational. Such a world, still finite, still imperfect, still mortal, will yet be a Kingdom of God, because it will be comparatively free from the ills produced through the confusion of men. Those who bring it nearer may be said to accept the Kingdom of God, though its realization be in the distant future. The faith of Israel teaches that this Kingdom will come, in part through the observances and teachings of Judaism itself. Whatever else a Jew may be able to offer to the world, whether in science, art, philosophy, letters, or industry, his supreme contribution is, therefore, that which he can make through the fulfillment of his religious duties, his perfection as a human being, and his development of all-embracing love for God.

NOTES

[1] Without desiring to ascribe to them any responsibility for this statement, the author records with deep gratitude the assistance in its preparation given by colleagues from different schools of Jewish thought. These include Rabbis Max Arzt, Ben Zion Bokser, Samuel S. Cohon, Judah Goldin, Israel M. Goldman, Simon Greenberg, David de Sola Pool, Samuel Schulman, and Aaron J. Tofield.

[2a Cf. above Judah Goldin, "The Period of the Talmud," *passim*.]

[3] Cf. the essay on "Study as a Mode of Worship," by Professor Nathan Isaacs, in *The Jewish Library,* edited by Rabbi Leo Jung, 1928, pp. 51-70.

[4] On June 16, 1948, the Hebrew Union College and the Jewish Institute of Religion announced their merger.

[5a Cf. above Moshe Davis, "Jewish Religious Life and Institutions in America," pp. 390 f., 406 f. and Simon Greenberg, "Jewish Educational Institutions," pp. 943-946.]

[6a For a survey of the Orthodox, Conservative and Reform movements in the United States, cf. above Moshe Davis, *op. cit.*]

[7] The extent to which even conversion to another faith affects the status of an individual within Judaism is a subject of considerable discussion in Rabbinical literature. Many authorities consider such a person a Jew, despite his conversion. The prevailing opinion, however, recognizes as effective the voluntary separation of a person from Judaism.

[8a Cf. above Mordecai M. Kaplan, "The Contribution of Judaism to World Ethics."]

[9a Cf. above Israel S. Chipkin, "Judaism and Social Welfare," pp. 736-738.]

[10a Cf. above Alexander Altmann, "Judaism and World Philosophy," p. 641.]

[11a Cf. *ibid.,* pp. 645-646.]

[12] From Jacob Emden's Letter in his edition of *Seder Olam Rabba we-Sutta u-Megillath Taanit* (Hamburg, 1757). A translation of the whole text is given by Oscar Z. Fasman in "An Epistle on Tolerance by a 'Rabbinic Zealot'," in *Judaism in a Changing World,* ed. Rabbi Leo Jung (New York, 1939), pp. 121-136.

[13] This blessing is not recited when wearing leather garments because it is not considered fitting to thank God for life when using material produced at the cost of life.

[14a Cf. above William Foxwell Albright, "The Biblical Period," pp. 45-50, and Elias J. Bickerman, "The Historical Foundations of Postbiblical Judaism," pp. 70 f.]

[15a For further details on the decoration of synagogues throughout the ages, cf. above Rachel Wischnitzer, "Judaism and Art," *passim*.]

[16a Cf. above Hillel Bavli, "The Modern Renaissance of Hebrew Literature," pp. 581-583.]

[17a Cf. Goldin, *op. cit.,* pp. 156-158.]

[18] Shoes or sandals were considered an object of luxury in the ancient Orient. It was therefore considered improper to wear them on days of fasting or mourning.

[19] For further discussion of the chronology of R. José, cf. Professor Alexander Marx in the introduction to his edition of *Seder Olam* (Berlin, 1903), pp. viii ff. and the references there given.

[[20a] Cf. Greenberg, *op. cit.*, pp. 931-933, and 941-943.]

[21] Rabbi's Manual, edited and published by the Central Conference of American Rabbis (Cincinnati, 1928), pp. 39 ff.

[22] For a further discussion and bibliography, see Mrs. R. L. Jung, in *The Jewish Library*, edited by Rabbi Leo Jung, Third Series, pp. 355-365.

[[23a] Cf. Goldin, *op. cit.*, pp. 149-151.]

BIBLIOGRAPHY

EPSTEIN, I., *Judaism*. London, 1939.

FRIEDLAENDER, GERALD, *Laws and Customs*. London, 1921.

FRIEDLAENDER, MICHAEL, *The Jewish Religion*. New York, 1923.

GREENSTONE, JULIUS, *The Jewish Religion*. Philadelphia, 1920.

JOSEPH, MORRIS, *Judaism and Creed and Life*. London, 1903.

KAPLAN, M. M., *The Meaning of Modern Jewish Religion*. New York, 1937.

PHILIPSON, DAVID, *Reform Movement in Judaism*. New York, 1931.

STEINBERG, MILTON, *Basic Judaism*. New York, 1947.

APPENDIX

"What questions should be answered in
the book on Judaism and the Jews?"

Following are the questions raised most frequently in 209 replies to a questionnaire sent scholars and educators throughout the United States in 1946-1947. Material in answer may be found in this book, as indicated.

1. What is a Jew?
   Anthropological and biological discussion
   Melville J. Herskovits, Chapter XXX.
   Archaeological definition and discussion
   William Foxwell Albright, Chapter I, esp. pp. 3-6.
   Considered in relation to "New Christians"
   Cecil Roth, Chapter IV, esp. pp. 236-239.
   Anita Libman Lebeson, Chapter VII, esp. pp. 315-316.
   Charles Singer, Chapter XXVI, esp. pp. 1074 ff.
   Nazi definition
   Cecil Roth, Chapter V, p. 280.
   Theological and religious discussion
   Louis Finkelstein, Chapter XXXV, esp. pp. 1327 f., 1333, 1375 ff.

2. What is the Jewish creed?
   Moshe Davis, Chapter VIII, passim.
   Louis Finkelstein, Chapter XXXV, esp. pp. 1336 f., 1343 f.
   Is there a distinction between the ceremonial and the ethical in Judaism?
   Mordecai M. Kaplan, Chapter XV.
   Louis Finkelstein, Chapter XXXV, esp. pp. 1333 f.
   What was the origin of the synagogue and its development?
   Simon Greenberg, Chapter XXII, esp. pp. 919 f.
   Rachel Wischnitzer, Chapter XXIV, esp. pp. 994 f.
   Louis Finkelstein, Chapter XXXV, esp. pp. 1354 f.
   Is there a systematic Jewish theology?
   Louis Finkelstein, Chapter XXXV.
   Can Jewish theology be modified in the light of changing conditions?
   Louis Finkelstein, Chapter XXXV, esp. p. 1341.

3. What is the Jewish attitude to marriage with members of other faiths?

Statistics
> Uriah Zevi Engelman, Chapter XXXI, esp. pp. 1190 ff.

Theological and religious
> Louis Finkelstein, Chapter XXXV, esp. pp. 1375 f.

4. Does Judaism seek or accept converts?

Historical
> Elias J. Bickerman, Chapter II, esp. p. 77.

Theological and religious
> Louis Finkelstein, Chapter XXXV, esp. pp. 1328 f., 1375.

5. What is the Jewish attitude toward members of other religions?

Historical and general
> Elias J. Bickerman, Chapter II, esp. p. 77.
> Milton R. Konvitz, Chapter XXVII.

Sense of obligation to non-Jews
> Israel S. Chipkin, Chapter XVI, esp. p. 738.

Theological and religious
> Louis Finkelstein, Chapter XXXV, esp. pp. 1328 f., 1375.

6. What is the concept of the Chosen People?

> Milton R. Konvitz, Chapter XXVII, esp. pp. 1094 ff.
> Louis Finkelstein, Chapter XXXV, esp. pp. 1341 f.

7. What is the attitude of Judaism to Jesus?

Historical discussion
> Judah Goldin, Chapter III, esp. pp. 137 ff.

Concept of love
> Mordecai M. Kaplan, Chapter XV, esp. pp. 707 f.

Theological and religious
> Louis Finkelstein, Chapter XXXV, esp. pp. 1328 f., 1347 f.

8. What is the Jewish doctrine of immortality?

> Louis Finkelstein, Chapter XXXV, esp. pp. 1339 f.

9. What is the Jewish concept of a Messiah?

Historical discussion
> Judah Goldin, Chapter III, esp. pp. 137 ff., 190 f.
> Cecil Roth, Chapter V, esp. pp. 250, 259 ff.

In literature
> Walter J. Fischel, Chapter XIX, esp. pp. 839 f.
> Yudel Mark, Chapter XX, esp. pp. 865 f.

Theological and religious
> Louis Finkelstein, Chapter XXXV, esp. p. 1342.

10. What are the ceremonials and rituals of Judaism?
   General
      Louis Finkelstein, Chapter XXXV.
   Circumcision
      Moshe Davis, Chapter VIII, esp. pp. 408-409.
      Arturo Castiglioni, Chapter XXV, esp. p. 1017.
      Louis Finkelstein, Chapter XXXV, esp. p. 1376.
   Confirmation
      Louis Finkelstein, Chapter XXXV, esp. pp. 1376 f.
   Dietary laws
      Moshe Davis, Chapter VIII, esp. pp. 408-409.
      Louis Finkelstein, Chapter XXXV, esp. pp. 1381 ff.
   Position of women
      Judah Goldin, Chapter III, esp. p. 176.
      Jacob J. Rabinowitz, Chapter X, esp. pp. 511 f.
      Louis Finkelstein, Chapter XXXV, esp. p. 1383.
   Sabbaths and holidays
      Moshe Davis, Chapter VIII, esp. pp. 408-409.
      Louis Finkelstein, Chapter XXXV, esp. pp. 1372 f.
   Wearing of head covering
      Louis Finkelstein, Chapter XXXV, esp. pp. 1356 f.

11. What is the Jewish attitude to marriage and the family?
      Jacob J. Rabinowitz, Chapter X, esp. pp. 511 f.
      Simon Greenberg, Chapter XXII, esp. pp. 917 f.
      Louis Finkelstein, Chapter XXXV, esp. pp. 1328 f., 1346, 1359, 1375,
         1377-1378.

12. Is there a Jewish "unity"?
      Louis Finkelstein, Chapter XXXV, esp. pp. 1351-1353.

13. What are the divisions in modern Judaism?
   Anthropological and biological
      Melville J. Herskovits, Chapter XXX.
      Jacob Lestschinsky, Chapter XXXII.
   Historical discussion
      Anita Libman Lebeson, Chapter VII, esp. pp. 331 ff.
      Moshe Davis, Chapter VIII, esp. pp. 364 ff., and Section iv beginning
         p. 378.
   Organizational and communal
      Samuel C. Kohs, Chapter XXXIV, esp. pp. 1280 ff., 1310 ff.
   Theological and religious
      Louis Finkelstein, Chapter XXXV, esp. pp. 1342 f.

14. What is the Jewish attitude to the Bible?
      Judah Goldin, Chapter III, esp. pp. 151 ff.
      Robert Gordis, Chapter IX, esp. pp. 457 ff.
      Jacob J. Rabinowitz, Chapter X.

Shalom Spiegel, Chapter XI.
Abraham J. Heschel, Chapter XIII.
Mordecai M. Kaplan, Chapter XV, esp. pp. 690 ff.
Israel S. Chipkin, Chapter XVI, esp. pp. 730 f., 738 f.
Ralph Marcus, Chapter XVII.
Abraham S. Halkin, Chapter XVIII.
Walter J. Fischel, Chapter XIX, esp. pp. 826 f.
Yudel Mark, Chapter XX, esp. pp. 861 ff.
Julius B. Maller, Chapter XXI, esp. pp. 897 ff.
Simon Greenberg, Chapter XXII.
Rachel Wischnitzer, Chapter XXIV.
Arturo Castiglioni, Chapter XXV.
Charles Singer, Chapter XXVI, esp. p. 1040.
Milton R. Konvitz, Chapter XXVII.
David Daiches, Chapter XXVIII.
Frederick Lehner, Chapter XXIX.
Louis Finkelstein, Chapter XXXV, esp. pp. 1327 ff., 1330, f., 1341, f.,
    1360 f.

15. What is the Jewish attitude to Revelation?

Cf. the references re the Bible.

16. What is the Jewish attitude to the Talmud?

Judah Goldin, Chapter III.
Abraham J. Heschel, Chapter XIII.
Israel S. Chipkin, Chapter XVI, esp. pp. 734 f., 738 f.
Abraham S. Halkin, Chapter XVIII, esp. pp. 799 f.
Julius B. Maller, Chapter XXI, esp. pp. 900 f.
Simon Greenberg, Chapter XXII.
Rachel Wischnitzer, Chapter XXIV, esp. pp. 993 f.
Arturo Castiglioni, Chapter XXV.
Milton R. Konvitz, Chapter XXVII.
Louis Finkelstein, Chapter XXXV, esp. pp. 1330, 1331 f., 1332 f., 1339
    f., 1384.

17. What is the Jewish attitude to rabbinical literature?

Abraham J. Heschel, Chapter XIII.
Charles Singer, Chapter XXVI.
Milton R. Konvitz, Chapter XXVII.
Louis Finkelstein, Chapter XXXV.

18. What is the Jewish attitude to Philo?

Alexander Altmann, Chapter XIV.
Ralph Marcus, Chapter XVII.
Charles Singer, Chapter XXVI, esp. p. 1044.
Louis Finkelstein, Chapter XXXV, esp. p. 1329.

19. What is the Jewish attitude to Maimonides?
Alexander Altmann, Chapter XIV.

Abraham S. Halkin, Chapter XVIII, esp. pp. 802 f.
Arturo Castiglioni, Chapter XXV, esp. pp. 1022 f.
Louis Finkelstein, Chapter XXXV, esp. pp. 1343 f., 1347, 1360 f., 1382.

20. What is authority in Judaism?

Judah Goldin, Chapter III, esp. pp. 152 ff.
Moshe Davis, Chapter VIII, esp. p. 363.
Abraham J. Heschel, Chapter XIII, esp. pp. 612 f.
Mordecai M. Kaplan, Chapter XV, esp. pp. 695 f.
Louis Finkelstein, Chapter XXXV, esp. pp. 1332 f.

21. What is the position of the rabbi in modern Judaism?

Moshe Davis, Chapter VIII, esp. pp. 373 f.
Louis Finkelstein, Chapter XXXV, esp. pp. 1332 f.

22. What is the place of study in Judaism?

Moshe Davis, Chapter VIII, esp. pp. 395 f., Section 6, beginning p. 397.
Julius B. Maller, Chapter XXI.
Simon Greenberg, Chapter XXII.
Samuel C. Kohs, Chapter XXXIV, esp. pp. 1294, 1296 ff.
Louis Finkelstein, Chapter XXXV, esp. pp. 1331 ff.

23. What are the contributions of Jews to the cultural development of civilization?

Robert Gordis, Chapter IX.
Jacob J. Rabinowitz, Chapter X.
Shalom Spiegel, Chapter XI.
Hillel Bavli, Chapter XII.
Abraham J. Heschel, Chapter XIII.
Alexander Altmann, Chapter XIV.
Mordecai M. Kaplan, Chapter XV.
Israel S. Chipkin, Chapter XVI.
Ralph Marcus, Chapter XVII.
Abraham S. Halkin, Chapter XVIII.
Walter J. Fischel, Chapter XIX.
Yudel Mark, Chapter XX.
Julius B. Maller, Chapter XXI.
Simon Greenberg, Chapter XXII.
Eric Werner, Chapter XXIII.
Rachel Wischnitzer, Chapter XXIV.
Arturo Castiglioni, Chapter XXV.
Charles Singer, Chapter XXVI.
Milton R. Konvitz, Chapter XXVII.
David Daiches, Chapter XXVIII.
Frederick Lehner, Chapter XXIX.
Louis Finkelstein, Chapter XXXV.

24. What is the present extent of synagogue affiliation?

> Anita Libman Lebeson, Chapter VII, esp. pp. 342 f.
> Moshe Davis, Chapter VIII, esp. Section 7.
> Samuel C. Kohs, Chapter XXXIV, esp. pp. 1282 f., 1322 f.

25. What is the proportion of Jews in agriculture as compared with urban pursuits?

> Judah Goldin, Chapter III, *passim* and p. 176.
> Cecil Roth, Chapters IV and V.
> Anita Libman Lebeson, Chapter VII, esp. pp. 327 ff., 341 f.
> Uriah Zevi Engelman, Chapter XXXI, esp. p. 1193.
> Jacob Lestschinsky, Chapter XXXII, *passim* and esp. pp. 1228 ff.
> Nathan Reich, Chapter XXXIII.
> Samuel C. Kohs, Chapter XXXIV, esp. pp. 1276, 1308 ff.

26. What is contemporary Jewish institutional organization—congregational and secular?

> Anita Libman Lebeson, Chapter VII, esp. pp. 345 ff.
> Moshe Davis, Chapter VIII, esp. pp. 354-436.
> Israel S. Chipkin, Chapter XVI.
> Samuel C. Kohs, Chapter XXXIV.
> Louis Finkelstein, Chapter XXXV, esp. pp. 1356 ff.

27. How many Jews are there? In the world? In the U.S.A.? In the U.S.S.R.? What is the postwar distribution?

> Arieh Tartakower, Chapter VI, esp. pp. 290 f.
> Anita Libman Lebeson, Chapter VII, esp. pp. 342 f.
> Melville J. Herskovits, Chapter XXX.
> Uriah Zevi Engelman, Chapter XXXI.
> Jacob Lestschinsky, Chapter XXXII.
> Nathan Reich, Chapter XXXIII.
> Samuel C. Kohs, Chapter XXXIV.

28. What was the Jewish participation in the wars fought by the U.S.A.?

> The Revolution
>   Anita Libman Lebeson, Chapter VII, esp. pp. 322 f.
> The War between the States
>   Anita Libman Lebeson, Chapter VII, esp. p. 324.
>   Moshe Davis, Chapter VIII, esp. p. 413.
> World War I
>   Anita Libman Lebeson, Chapter VII, esp. p. 324.
>   Moshe Davis, Chapter VIII, esp. p. 413.
> World War II
>   Anita Libman Lebeson, Chapter VII, esp. p. 324.
>   Moshe Davis, Chapter VIII, esp. pp. 438 ff.

29. What is the relation of the Jews throughout the world to Palestine and the state of Israel?

> William Foxwell Albright, Chapter I, esp. p. 53.
> Arieh Tartakower, Chapter VI, esp. pp. 301 f.
> Anita Libman Lebeson, Chapter VII, esp. pp. 339 f.
> Moshe Davis, Chapter VIII, esp. pp. 354-355.
>   392, 399, 403, 426, 442.
> Hillel Bavli, Chapter XII, esp. pp. 578 f., 593 f.
> Israel S. Chipkin, Chapter XVI, esp. p. 715.
> Walter J. Fischel, Chapter XIX, esp. pp. 854 f.
> Simon Greenberg, Chapter XXII, esp, pp. 947 f.
> Eric Werner, Chapter XXIII, esp. p. 982.
> Rachel Wischnitzer, Chapter XXIV, esp. p. 1003.
> Jacob Lestschinsky, Chapter XXXII, esp. pp. 1203 f., 1233 f.
> Nathan Reich, Chapter XXXIII, esp. pp. 1251 f.
> Samuel C. Kohs, Chapter XXXIV, esp. pp. 1312 f.
> Louis Finkelstein, Chapter XXXV, esp. pp. 1347 f.

LIST OF ABBREVIATIONS

Ameic
   American Eretz Israel Corporation
Am. Jour. Sem. Lang.
   American Journal of Semitic Languages
Annual Am. Sch. Or. Res.
   Annual American Schools of Oriental Research
Antt.
   Antiquities, Josephus
Archiv f. Orientf.
   Archiv fuer Orientforschung
ARN
   Abot of Rabbi Nathan
AZA
   Ahavah Zedakah Ahdut (B'nai B'rith Youth Organization)
b.
   ben (son of)
B.
   Babylonian Talmud
B. B.
   Baba Batra
B. C. E.
   Before the Common Era
Beih. Zeits. Alttest. Wiss.
   Beihefte zur Zeitschrift fuer die Alttestamentliche Wissenschaft
Bell. Jud.
   De Bello Judaico, Josephus
Ber. Saechs. Akad. Wiss.
   Berichte ueber die Verhandlungen der saechsischen Akademie der Wissenschaften
Bull. Am. Sch. Or. Res.
   Bulletin American Schools of Oriental Research
Bull. de l'inst. Français d'Archéol. Orient.
   Bulletin de l'institut Français d'Archéologie Orientale
Bull. Jew. Pal. Explor. Soc.
   Bulletin of the Jewish Palestine Exploration Society
C. Ap.
   Contra Apionem, Josephus

C. E.
  Common Era
CCAR
  Central Conference of American Rabbis
CJFWF
  Council Jewish Federations and Welfare Funds
cod.
  codex
Comp. Rend. Acad. des Inscr.
  Comptes-Rendus de l'Académie des Inscriptions
De Abr.
  De Abrahamo, Philo
De Ant. Jud.
  Antiquitates Judaicae, Josephus
De Cher.
  De Cherubim, Philo
De Conf.
  De Confusione Linguarum, Philo
De Congr.
  De Congressu Eruditionis Gratia, Philo
De Dec.
  De Decalogo, Philo
De Ebr.
  De Ebrietate, Philo
De Fuga
  De Fuga et Inventione, Philo
De Gig.
  De Gigantibus, Philo
De Mig. or De Migr.
  De Migratione Abrahami, Philo
De Mut.
  De Mutatione Nominum, Philo
De Op.
  De Opificio Mundi, Philo
De Plant.
  De Plantatione, Philo
De Post.
  De Posteritate Caini, Philo
De Praem.
  De Praemiis et Poenis, Philo
De Sacr.
  De Sacrificiis Abelis et Caini, Philo
De Somn.
  De Somniis, Philo
De Vita Contempl.
  De Vita Contemplativa, Philo

Dion. Halic., *De. Thuc.*
  Dionysius of Halicarnassus, *On Thucydides*
Ec. Hist.
  Ecclesiastical History, Eusebius
Enn.
  Ennead, Plotinus
Ep.
  Epistulae Morales ad Lucilium, Seneca
Epist.
  Epistles, Horace
Eur.
  Euripides
Gen. R.
  Genesis Rabbah
Harv. Theo. Rev.
  Harvard Theological Review
Heracl.
  Heracles, Euripides
HIAS
  Hebrew Sheltering and Immigrant Aid Society
HICEM
  • Combination of HIAS—Hebrew Sheltering and Immigrant Aid Society
  ICA—Jewish Colonization Association, Emigdirect
HUCA
  Hebrew Union College Annual
ICA
  Jewish Colonization Association
ICOR
  Gesellschaft tsu Helfen der Yiddisher Kolonizatzie in Sovetn—Verband
  (Association for Jewish Colonization in the Soviet Union)
JBL or *Jour. Bib. Lit.*
  Journal of Biblical Literature
J. D. C.
  American Jewish Joint Distribution Committee
JE
  Jewish Encyclopedia
JQR or *Jew. Quar. Rev.*
  Jewish Quarterly Review
JQR N.S. *Jewish Quar. Rev.* N.S.
  Jewish Quarterly Review New Series
J. W. B.
  Jewish Welfare Board
Jour. Near East. Stud.
  Journal of Near Eastern Studies
Jour. Pal. Or. Soc.
  Journal Palestine Oriental Society

Jour. of the Warburg Inst.
  Journal of the Warburg Institute
Ket.
  Ketubot
KOMZET
  Komitet po Zemelnonne Ustroistvu, Trudyachchikhsya Yevreyev (Committee for the Settlement of Toiling Jews on the Land)
Lam. R.
  Lamentations Rabbah
Leg. All.
  Legum Allegoria, Philo
Lev. R.
  Leviticus Rabbah
Mas. Soferim
  Masseket Soferim
MGWJ
  Monatsschrift fuer Geschichte und Wissenschaft des Judenthums
n.d.
  no date
N.F.
  Neue Folge (new series)
N.S.
  New Series
n.s.D.
  new series, D.
NAIS
  National Appeals Information Service
ORT
  Organization for Rehabilitation and Training
OSE
  World Union for the Protection of the Health of the Jews
PAJHS
  Publication of the American Jewish Historical Society
Pal. Explor. Quar.
  Palestinian Exploration Fund Quarterly
Pal. Explor. Fund Quar. State.
  Palestinian Exploration Fund Quarterly Statement
Parm.
  Parmenides, Philo
Quis Rer.
  Quis Rerum Divinarum Heres, Philo
Quod Deus
  Quod Deus Sit Immutabilis, Philo
Quod Omn.
  Quod Omnis Probus Liber Sit, Philo
R.
  Rab or Rabbi

Rev. études juiv.
    Revue des Études Juives
R.S.P.C.A.
    Royal Society for the Prevention of Cruelty to Animals
s.a.
    sociedad anonima (corporation)
Shab.
    Shabbat
SI
    Studies of the Research Institute for Hebrew Poetry (Hebrew)
Sifre Deut.
    Sifre on Deuteronomy
Sifre Num.
    Sifre on Numbers
Sitz. Heidelberger Akad. Wissen.
    Sitzungsberichte der Heidelberger Akademie der Wissenschaften
Sitz. Preuss. Akad. Wissen.
    Sitzungsberichte der Preussischen Akademie der Wissenschaften
TOZ
    Towarzystwo Ochrony Zdrowia (Polish), Society for the Protection of Health
U.J.A.
    United Jewish Appeal
U.P.A.
    United Palestine Appeal
Yer.
    Yerushalmi
Zeit. Alttest. Wiss.
    Zeitschrift fuer die Alttestamentliche Wissenschaft
Zeit. Deutsch. Pal. Ver.
    Zeitschrift des Deutschen Palaestina Vereins
Zeits. Deutsch. Morg. Ges.
    Zeitschrift der Deutschen Morgenlaendlichen Gesellschaft
Zeits. Neutest. Wissen.
    Zeitschrift fuer die Neutestamentliche Wissenschaft
Z.O.A.
    Zionist Organization of America

INDEX

Persons, places, and subjects omitted from the index due to limitations of space may be located by reference to the main subject, *e.g.*, to locate a chemist, look under *Science*; an author, look under *Literature*.

Publications are in general not indexed by title but by author.

Names containing *bar, ben, ibn, ha-*, etc., are indexed by the first word of the compound.

Persons and publications cited in Notes or Bibliographies have not been indexed.

Before May, 1948, references are to *Palestine*; after that date to *Israel, State of*.